D0955571

The Gay and Lesbian Self-Esteem Book

A GUIDE TO LOVING OURSELVES

Kimeron N. Hardin, Ph.D.

New Harbinger Publications, Inc.

Publisher's Note

This publication is designed to provide accurate and authoritative information in regard to the subject matter covered. It is sold with the understanding that the publisher is not engaged in rendering psychological, financial, legal, or other professional services. If expert assistance or counseling is needed, the services of a competent professional should be sought.

Distributed in the U.S.A. by Publishers Group West; in Canada by Raincoast Books; in Great Britain by Airlift Book Company, Ltd.; in South Africa by Real Books, Ltd.; in Australia by Boobook; and in New Zealand by Tandem Press.

New Harbinger Publications, Inc.
5674 Shattuck Avenue
Oakland, CA 94609

Cover design by Blue Design.
Front cover photographs by Robert Giard.
Text design by Michele Waters.

Library of Congress Catalog Card Number: 98-68746
ISBN 1-57224-131-4 Paperback

New Harbinger Publications' Website address: www.newharbinger.com

01   00   99

10   9   8   7   6   5   4   3   2

Contents

Part II
Choices:
Self-Esteem and Your Daily Life

Part III
Healing:
Ways of Improving Self-Esteem

Acknowledgments

I would like to thank the following people for their assistance in producing this book: Robert Allen, M.D., Katherine Bowman, Ph.D., Chad LeJeune, Ph.D., Jack Huntington, Jim Raines, Gary Grossman, Ph.D., and Rev. Mel White. I am also grateful for the support I received from the folks at New Harbinger, including Kristin Beck, Farrin Jacobs, Lauren Dockett, Matthew McKay, Kirk Johnson, and the rest of the crew.

Special thanks to the people in my life who have helped me grow along the way: Vera D. Hardin, Virginia Taylor, Tina Dawkins, Martha Vinson, Ph.D., my family and James E. Seegars, Jr., Ph.D., the psychologist who told me at age seventeen that I was "okay."

Most importantly, I would like to thank my life partner, William Watson, for his constant love, strength, support, and faith.

Introduction

*I'm good enough, I'm smart enough, and doggone it . . .
people like me!*

—Stuart Smalley

You may recognize Stuart Smalley's words from the opening of Al
Franken's hilarious *Saturday Night Live* parody of someone in "recovery" from childhood abuse, alcoholism in the family, and even overeating. Stuart, having found a method of boosting his very low
self-esteem, faces a mirror, looks lovingly into his own eyes, and
repeats these words, presumably with results so successful that he
now has his own TV show.

We can laugh because we know that Stuart Smalley is fictional.
If you have struggled to overcome problems with self-doubt or a difficult childhood or chemical dependency you may also feel an extra
"chuckle" because you have heard of or met people in real life like
Stuart who believe they have found simple answers to life's difficult
problems. In reality, you know that life is not simple. You understand
that it is in fact complicated by events in your past and present, and
even by your expectations for the future.

Recent studies have supported the notion that growing up gay
or lesbian, or even living as an "out" adult, can be both difficult and
dangerous in this society. For example, it has been found that gays
and lesbians are at greater risk for attempting or committing suicide
and are more likely to abuse alcohol or other drugs than their heterosexual counterparts (Saghir and Robins 1973; Rich et al. 1986; Proctor
and Groze 1994). Lesbian and gay youth are also at significantly
higher risk than heterosexuals for suicide attempts, substance abuse,
school problems, running away from home, and prostitution (Savin-
Williams 1994). In 1989, a study by the U.S. Department of Health
and Human Services (Gibson 1989) found that gay and lesbian youths

are two to three times more likely than other youths to kill themselves. Since much of the available evidence suggests that being lesbian or gay in itself does not lead to these behaviors, such self-destructiveness is more likely the result of verbal and physical harassment or social rejection. Other risk factors for developing these behaviors include social isolation, depression, negative family interactions and social attitudes, and most relevant to this book, low self-esteem (Remafedi et al. 1991; Sears 1991; Schneider, Farberow, and Kruks 1989; Savin-Williams 1989a, b).

Society is full of mixed messages for gays and lesbians. Stigmatizing and hostile messages exist in the form of anti-gay rights initiatives, brutal hate crimes committed against lesbians and gays, and right-wing political strategists promising "cures for homosexuality" through religion or behavior modification. On a less hostile level, but equally as damaging in some ways, gay and lesbian couples are currently not allowed to marry, thereby eliminating the social reinforcers of marriage such as tax breaks, wedding showers, and automatic joint custody of children; but at the same time they are often condemned for "living in sin" or having sex outside of marriage. Confusing, isn't it?

I've written *The Gay and Lesbian Self-Esteem Book: A Guide to Loving Ourselves* to help gays and lesbians of many different backgrounds, upbringings, and levels of professional or personal success with the ongoing process of healing from the past, coping with the present, and planning for the future. Regardless of where you are in your life, or how you came to read this book, you will find something here that relates to your own personal journey—where you have been, where you are now, and where you might be going.

Why a Book Just for Gays and Lesbians?

Self-esteem is something that anyone, regardless of sexual orientation, might have issues with. Why then do we need a special book for gays and lesbians? First, and foremost, I've always hated reading a book about self-healing or growth and having to translate the exercises or examples from a heterocentrist viewpoint. For example, books that say things to male readers like, "Think of your first special relationship with a woman," or writers who assume that all women want a male counterpart. It's challenging enough to try to understand the principles of change without having to take the extra step of mentally shifting the examples toward something that fits your own situation. In some cases, trying to play the translation game may leave you feeling even more confused and frustrated than before you started reading.

The other reason for writing this book specifically for gays and lesbians is that there are clear differences between heterosexuals and homosexuals. For example, understanding the factors affecting a committed relationship between two women or two men is vastly different than understanding the various forces in a relationship between a woman and a man. This book will address many of the unique issues faced by gays and lesbians. I will discuss the messages about homosexuality that you likely received as a child, but even more importantly, the messages that you continue to face every day. How many other communities continue to be openly derided, abused, and condemned in our society today? Racism and sexism continue to exist in our country, but I would argue that often the strongest public language is still reserved for lesbians and gays. Hate crimes against us are finally being tracked, but this acknowledgment is a double-edged sword because it increases our awareness of how much fear and disgust there is for us. The evening news still sends us messages that we are not completely accepted or "normal."

Although lesbians and gays have made tremendous political gains in recent years, I believe our next frontier is within ourselves. We can finally organize, demonstrate, and flex our political muscle; the next step, however, is to move beyond self-hating ("I am disgusting"), beyond the community identification only ("I am a lesbian"), to a place of true self-respect, self-nurturing and internal peace ("I am worthwhile").

How to Get the Most out of This Book

The process of loving yourself means not only learning to accept who you are, but also to change self-destructive behaviors and habits that are the opposite of self-respect. I don't want you to stare blindly into a mirror like Stuart Smalley and repeat silly phrases until you somehow start to believe them. My hope is that this book will guide you from the distortions of old, through the challenges of today, and into the peace and joy of tomorrow.

This book was not designed like a good novel to be read as quickly as possible, but as a paced, self-help guide. Learning to recognize the old distorted messages and the current negative messages society feeds you is covered in parts 1 and 2. Part 3 teaches you to stop the influence of these messages. Yet blocking the negative is only a part of building self-esteem. To begin your healing process, you must learn how to explore the real you, your true self—the perfect and the not-so-perfect, the excellent and the average parts—from a more objective viewpoint. The last chapter of part 3 will teach you ways to expand the way you view yourself, both alone and with help from others you trust. Each chapter will provide you with many questions to ask yourself so that you can explore emotionally. In some chapters, I will even give you specific exercises to do to help you understand the concepts and apply them to your own experience. It's important for you to take your time when doing the exercises to get the most from this book. If you prefer, you can read through the book from beginning to end initially and then come back for a second, more in-depth read that includes doing the exercises. The key is to be patient with yourself since, after all, it took many years to come to the place you are at now. You may need to re-read some chapters, even after attempting all the exercises, as you reach deeper layers of self-awareness.

My goal is not only to help you stop the constant battering (from outside and inside), but also to help you see the beautiful, wonderful parts of you that existed all along. All babies are born "good" and innocent. It takes a lot of years of distorted and harmful information to make that baby believe that she or he is imperfect, less than, or bad. As an adult, you have the opportunity that you didn't have as a child to make more rational judgments about the information that bombards your inner self. You can decide what is objective, realistic information and what are negative and even warped messages that should be discarded. You now have the opportunity to provide the nurturing, loving environment for yourself that you may not have had as a child.

If you are currently in psychotherapy you may find this book to be a helpful adjunct to your therapy. You may even decide to work through the exercises with help from your therapist. If you are working through this book alone and find that it brings up intense feelings for you that make you uncomfortable or uneasy, read chapter 13, which addresses how to find an effective psychotherapist to deal with these issues. This book is not a substitute for therapy, especially if you find that problems exist or arise that are causing you immediate harm or distress, such as depression that interferes with your everyday functioning, feelings of hopelessness, suicidal thoughts, or significant alcohol or other drug use.

I hope that when you've finished this book, you will have found a sense of peace, better self-esteem, and a greater appreciation for the authentic and wonderful person that you are. As you now embark on this process, let me congratulate you for taking the first steps toward learning to love yourself!

Part I

Origins: Influences on Your Self-Esteem

1

What Exactly Is Self-Esteem and Can You Really Change It?

All that we are is the result of what we have thought. The mind is everything. What we think we become.

—The Buddha

Most people have a general idea about what the term *self-esteem* refers to, but when you really think about it, what exactly is the self? Many philosophers have suggested that humans differ from animals because we are aware of something called the self. This self, or *identity*, is really a way of thinking about who you are that is shaped by your life experiences, both positive and negative. For example, if the majority of your life experiences have been positive and the only kind of feedback that you've ever received about yourself has been favorable, then you will generally think highly of yourself. On the contrary, if your life experiences have been primarily negative, then your identity is based on feeling worthless, incapable, or in some cases, even evil.

Early Life Experiences and Self-Esteem

When you were born, you had no concept of self. Imagine how you must have floated in the nice warm amniotic bath, with only muted sounds in darkness—and then were suddenly thrust into bright lights, strange and loud sounds, and an intense sensation of cool air on your skin. Your biggest concern was probably finding warmth again, getting away from the lights and noises, and snuggling into any comfortable spot. You had no sense of who, or even what, you were, and your only needs involved food, warmth, comfort, and elimination. If your parents provided these basic necessities, you most likely had the freedom to explore your world and yourself, both physically and emotionally. You probably learned first about your physical self by discovering your hands and feet, maybe by sucking your thumb or toes. After a while, you figured out what those tiny hands could do and then what sounds you could make with your mouth. Soon, you became a child who learned to communicate, first through crying then babbling and finally talking. Your brain grew rapidly and expanded during this time, enabling you to put together the meanings of events that happened to and around you.

Once you began to understand and use language, you learned not only the meanings of words, but most likely the meanings of certain facial expressions and tones of voice. You probably knew what "No!" meant even before you knew how to talk. You learned to comprehend both verbal and nonverbal forms of communication. The information that you used to develop your understanding of the world came from your immediate surroundings, and as an infant, most of your time was spent with parents or other caregivers. When you imagine that time of your life (or reconstruct it from family stories), were your basic needs taken care of quickly? Or did you have to wait to have your hunger satisfied or your skin dry and warm? How you answer questions like these most likely provides some insight into how you view yourself and your worth even today. The way your parents treated you, and the messages they intentionally or unintentionally gave you, helped form your identity, both then and now.

As you got older, and you ventured out into the world, you received messages about life, living, and your value from other sources like school, your community, your place of worship, and even the media. A child's mind is hungry for new information and experiences that will help it be able to interpret the sights and sounds and meanings of the world.

Some child psychologists believe that your earliest years are the most important in shaping your later view of the world and yourself. Unfortunately, a child is not born with the ability to screen out inaccurate or distorted information and forms opinions about him- or herself based on the information reflected back from the environment. Generally, if the messages you received about yourself when you were very young were mostly positive, loving, or nurturing, you are likely to have a more positive view of yourself today. If the majority of those messages about yourself were negative, you were just as likely to believe them and then begin incorporating them into your overall view of yourself. Not only was your general view of yourself shaped by these messages, but you may tend to continually *repeat* these early messages about yourself, often leading to regular feelings of insecurity, fear, and inadequacy.

So back to the question, *What exactly is self-esteem?* Your level of *esteem* (or high regard) for yourself depends a great deal on how you formed your identity of self through your background and your growing-up experiences. My primary goal for this book, however, is not to rehash old material that you'd just as soon forget, but to help you improve the quality of your life now.

Self-Esteem and Self-Confidence

Your self-esteem has an impact on every aspect of your current life—romantically, professionally, spiritually, and recreationally. It affects how you see your face or body in the mirror, your ability to socialize at a party, your dating options, and your job promotions. Your self-confidence will either be undermined or enhanced by the overall view you have of yourself. Every decision you make will be influenced to some degree by your level of confidence in your presentation and abilities. In short, how effective you feel you'll be in any situation is highly influenced by whether you view yourself as powerful or weak, attractive or plain, intelligent or average.

If you are aware of who you are and are satisfied with yourself, you are able to navigate through life fairly effectively—taking challenges as they come and feeling self-confident in your ability to overcome or handle them. You may even take some reasonable risks because you know that even if your plans fail, you have the resources to rebound and move on. You like yourself enough to forgive mistakes that you might make and move on without needing to punish yourself with negative thoughts like "That was stupid!" or "You are such a loser!" Without a pervasive sense that you are basically good enough, self-doubt may linger and affect your ability to take the kinds of risks that could propel you toward satisfying relationships and careers. You may feel as though you are an observer of life instead of someone who lives it, like a "wallflower" waiting for someone to ask you to dance. Good self-esteem leads to higher self-confidence, which then allows you to take chances and make choices without fear of the inevitable mistakes. Everyone makes mistakes sometimes, but people with good self-esteem seem to rebound faster, shake off the disappointment, and get back into the saddle!

Changing Your Self-Esteem with Cognitive Behavioral Therapy

Over the last twenty or so years, a powerful new form of treatment has emerged that focuses on the identification and modification of negative styles of thinking. This treatment, referred to as *cognitive behavioral therapy (CBT)*, has been successfully applied to many problem behaviors including low self-esteem. It involves learning how to recognize and replace negative messages you give to yourself with healthier alternatives.

The early founders of the current forms of cognitive behavioral therapy, Dr. Aaron Beck and Dr. Albert Ellis (who called his form *rational-emotive therapy*), began their careers as psychoanalysts, adhering to the predominant psychological theory of the first half of the 1900s. They both became unhappy with the traditional form of psychoanalytic therapy, which suggested that a client's problems were a result of unconscious conflicts between various biological drives such as aggression and sex. Ellis particularly found the traditional process of interpreting a client's problems over many months or years until they gained insight into the origins too slow and the length of time in therapy too long.

Within months of each other, both Dr. Beck and Dr. Ellis presented new forms of treatment that they developed independently but which shared common characteristics. They both observed that clients who shared similar symptoms, such as depression or anxiety, tended to have certain similar patterns of thinking. Beck (1991), for example, found that depressed clients tended to focus more on the negative than positive aspects of a troubling situation they were discussing. And not only did these clients tend to focus more on the negative in bad situations, but when they were depressed, they also tended to actually distort the meanings of events that were relatively benign or neutral. Ellis (1975), whose emphasis in this new theory was on *irrational beliefs*, observed that not only did his clients who were troubled tend to interpret neutral events negatively, but they also tended to hold beliefs about themselves that were long-standing and were completely unreasonable or illogical.

They both then took these clinical observations and applied them therapeutically to try to help their clients recover and feel less troubled. They did this by training the clients to refute overly negative, irrational, or distorted *cognitions* (beliefs, thoughts, and attitudes) as they occurred, which immediately led to relief from the unpleasant emotions.

Over the years, cognitive behavioral therapy has gained in popularity and has gone through many refinements. It continues to be one of the fastest growing forms of psychotherapy in the country, and its effectiveness has been demonstrated with many different types of problems from depression and anxiety to obsessive-compulsive disorders and major psychoses. Because the techniques involved with CBT are relatively straightforward, they have been effectively communicated through self-help formats, like this book, to treat a full range of problems, including low self-esteem.

As I mentioned in the introduction, however, none of these books has been written specifically for gay and lesbian people. In most cases, it can be a smoother process for heterosexuals to identify distorted cognitions and change them because they are often no longer bombarded with illogical or negative messages as adults. Their experiences as adults help them to disconfirm old childhood messages more easily. Gay men and lesbians however, must not only identify cognitions fueled by old negative messages, but they must also learn to resist the pervasive negative messages that are present in our everyday culture.

The Cognitive Behavioral Model

My goal for this chapter is to help you understand the basic concepts of cognitive behavioral therapy and how to apply them to yourself. Once my patients understand these concepts, and learn to apply them to themselves, the benefits seem to generalize across many areas of their lives. They describe the process as enlightening, especially regarding the constant inner dialogue that they were always dimly aware of, but did not know how or where to begin to interrupt and change. They find that old negative images or messages, that previously went unchallenged, are much easier to recognize, challenge, and change.

The basic premise of cognitive behavioral therapy is simple. Negative thoughts lead to uncomfortable emotions that lead to ineffective or self-destructive behaviors. In order to improve your effectiveness in the world or to reduce feelings of insecurity, fear, worry or helplessness, you must learn to identify a negative thought, evaluate its validity, and if necessary replace it with a more realistic or healthy thought. To learn this process adequately, you must have an understanding of the CBT model in greater detail. According to the model, there are three layers to the thoughts: automatic thoughts, conditional beliefs, and core beliefs.

Automatic Thoughts

When an event such as a perceived rejection or failure occurs, you tend to have *automatic thoughts*. Automatic thoughts are triggered by situations that carry emotional significance. Such situations are often both personally relevant (related to specific traumatic or negative experiences in your life) and culturally relevant (related to stigma based on larger cultural beliefs rather than on personal experience). These thoughts are just below the surface of your usual awareness and they send and confirm messages about yourself. If you have low self-esteem, chances are that most of your automatic thoughts are negative, so you immediately blame yourself in most negative situations and you also tend to interpret even ambiguous situations negatively. Because these negative messages, also known as *negative self-talk*, are automatic, replacing them with positive messages takes some commitment. But doing so is an essential part of increasing your self-esteem.

Here's an example of a situation provoking automatic negative thoughts: Let's say that Christina has started dating someone new and after a few weeks of bliss, she promises to call Christina after work at 5:30 P.M. Then 5:30 comes and goes and no call. So Christina waits and waits, going through the various possibilities in her head about why there has been no call. She feels glimpses of shame, rejection, and anger and finds herself saying, "I knew this could never work out" and "She is already tired of me."

Obviously, the person was not able to keep her promise, which is an issue that must be discussed with her. What is problematic, however, is the automatic interpretation of not calling. In this example, an ambiguous event (one in which there are many unknowns) is seen through a cognitive lens, one that distorts the meaning into a negative, self-doubting thought process leading to hurt feelings and potentially an angry confrontation. A more rational, healthy approach in this case might be for Christina to recognize her concern about the "not calling" but quickly remind herself that there are many reasons that someone may not call, such as a personal emergency or no access to a phone. Even if memory failure is the cause, it would be helpful for Christina to understand that there are many reasons people fail to remember something other than lack of interest.

Making an emotional judgment about the friend who didn't call, and her intentions, *before* she has adequate information is emotionally inefficient and potentially inhibiting in making sensible decisions. By stepping back from the automatic thoughts and examining them more objectively, Christina will find that the feelings she experienced initially begin to change, to become less intense and perhaps even soothing.

Conditional and Core Beliefs

Conditional beliefs are the assumptions and rules that you live your life by. These beliefs function to help you survive and, like most other types of beliefs, are formed early in childhood. The rules you had to learn and follow as a child were not always written or spoken clearly and you may have had to develop rules that were unique to surviving in your own household. For example, in your parent's home, there may have been clear rules about when and where sexuality was discussed, if ever. There may also have been rules about what sexual behavior was acceptable, such as only having sexual relations after heterosexual marriage, and which types were not acceptable, such as same-sex attraction. As a gay or lesbian child, you most likely learned to avoid discussing your budding sexuality, particularly areas that were considered deviant or abnormal. A conditional belief that became established for you therefore may have been something like, "Never share your true intimate feelings with anyone or they'll reject you." You can see how such a rule might inhibit your ability to form close relationships as an adult. You'll read more about the development of conditional beliefs in chapter 2, Hand-Me-Down Messages.

Core beliefs are your true views of yourself—the relationship you have with yourself at your deepest levels. They may be so deep that you've never articulated them, even to yourself; yet they are often experienced as absolute truths. Some theorists believe that core beliefs are activated particularly when a person is depressed. The depressed person then tends to focus almost exclusively on information that confirms the negative core belief and she or he filters out any positive evidence to the contrary. Others feel that core beliefs are active continuously and affect every decision you make, either by making choices that support the belief or choices that are a reaction against them. The beliefs act as a lens through which you see the world—if they are distorted, the lens will provide a distorted picture of each person or situation you view. The saying "seeing the world through rose-colored glasses" is based on this concept; a person who does this tends to see everything from a positive frame of reference. According to the cognitive model, your lens (or beliefs) can range from very positive and optimistic to very negative and pessimistic.

The idea of an information lens helps explain why you maintain the old distorted beliefs even though you know them logically to be untrue. Core beliefs tend to be rigid and can influence the conditional beliefs that you live by, which in turn influence your automatic thoughts. For example, if one of your core beliefs is, "Being gay means you're not good enough," one of your conditional beliefs might be, "I must work twice as hard as straight people to prove I'm just as competent." If you don't live up to your expectations in a given situation, you're automatic thoughts will confirm to you that you're not good enough. You can see how this might be emotionally and physically exhausting for you over the years as you struggle to prove yourself. Figure 1 is a graphic representation of these constructs and their relationships to each other.

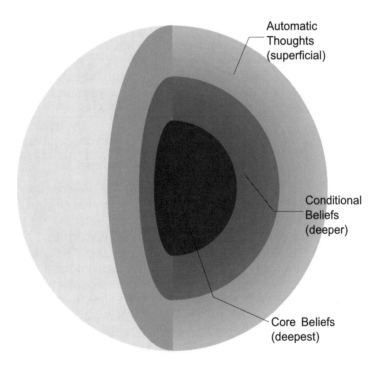

Automatic
Thoughts
(superficial)

Conditional
Beliefs
(deeper)

Core Beliefs
(deepest)

Figure 1. Structure of Cognitions and Depth of Awareness

You will read about exploring the kinds of messages you received as a child, and how they affect your life today, in more detail later in the book. In fact, I will not only invite you to explore your early family life to uncover and challenge the foundations for your negative self-talk, but will also encourage you to examine other important influences on your self-esteem such as your community culture, religion, and the politics of the day. Once you learn to identify the origins of your self-esteem, you can begin to retrain yourself and challenge your negative beliefs.

Recognizing Negative Patterns

Before you can begin challenging and changing those long-standing, negative ways of thinking, you must first train yourself to recognize the patterns and catch them when they occur. Reading about such patterns on the page is one thing; identifying your own patterns is another. Here's an example that may help you recognize some ways you think negatively and then talk negatively to yourself: Let's say that you have an assignment at work with a deadline that according to your supervisor must be met or you and the organization will suffer. Also imagine that you have a limited amount of time to complete the task and while it's difficult to get started, you work very hard on it and complete it just before the deadline. The project must be at the copy store before it closes at 5:00 P.M. so that it will be ready the next morning for a big meeting. You glance at your watch and see that it is 4:30 P.M. now and it takes fifteen minutes to get there. You jump in your car, head off to the copy store, and on the way you hear on the radio that there's a huge accident creating a traffic jam for miles. At this point, you may already begin feeling a little irritated and anxious to get to the store. The jam breaks at 4:50 P.M. and you are on your way, perhaps at an unsafe speed. You finally arrive at the store parking lot at 5:02 and are horrified to see the shades closed and the "Closed" sign on the door. Your first reaction is one of numbness, but then you slowly become aware of a heavy feeling and you take a little gasp for air. Then the self-talk begins. Can you imagine what you might be saying to yourself in this situation? Can you feel the feelings you might be having, the physical reaction to the event?

For some people, the voice that follows such an event will be harsh and punitive with phrases such as, "You can't do anything right!" or "You are incompetent" or "You failed again." You may be particularly hard on yourself if you were raised to have unrealistic expectations of yourself, or if making mistakes or having an accident when you were a child was followed by humiliation or other punishments. The emotions you might expect to feel following such harsh self-talk would likely include intense panic, fear, despair, or a desire to run and hide. You might feel like dropping the project out of frustration and a sense of failure.

For others, the voice may be less harsh, but it still serves to promote a self-image of incompetence, or at least an inability to succeed. This voice may sound something like, "I did my best, but it's just not good enough . . . I'm not as smart as most people." While you may not be overtly punishing yourself at this level, you may experience a de-motivating effect or a sense of failure.

Then there are those who might blame the traffic jam or the copy place for closing on time and get incredibly angry and agitated. The voice is harsh, but it is directed at someone (or something) else. You may be so agitated that your sleep that night is disrupted or you are short with family and friends. If you explored a little deeper, you would likely find that the anger is directly proportional to the amount of underlying anxiety you have about how your boss will react the next day or about how horrible you expect to feel when you have to admit that the work is not ready. Regardless of whether you blame yourself and feel anxious or depressed or you blame the traffic and get upset and angry, the net effect is disruptive emotional upset.

Another, perhaps healthier, way to respond to this unfortunate occurrence might be to have a more balanced, more accurate appraisal of the situation that tends to focus less on punishing yourself for missing a deadline and more on encouraging yourself to deal with the situation effectively. Recognizing your inner voice, evaluating it for accuracy and utility, and then actively making changes if necessary is the basis for enhancing your self-esteem. Learning some basic techniques to help you recognize and evaluate your self-talk will help you confront situations throughout the day that may threaten your confidence and initiate feelings of anger, depression, or sadness.

You may have found that in the preceding example, you did not respond with negative self-talk, but managed to focus on solutions to the problems immediately. There are two reasons that this may be the case: First, we all develop areas in our lives that we feel better or more confident about than other areas. Professional competence may be that area for you, so your professional self-esteem is relatively healthy. However, you may find that events related to situations outside of work trigger the negative self-talk and uncomfortable feelings.

The second reason is that you may not recognize your own negative self-talk because of the relative depth of your negative beliefs. You may be so used to burying the negative self-talk that it takes time for you to learn to hear the messages more directly. It may take a little extra work on your part to recognize your negative self-talk, but having better self-esteem is well worth the effort.

Automatic thoughts are typically the easiest to recognize and begin to address. In fact, most cognitive behavioral therapists begin treatment by having the client keep track of automatic thoughts as they happen and then teaching the client to analyze the thoughts carefully and objectively. Examining the patterns of your automatic thoughts will help you determine the rules you live by, which can be assessed for effectiveness. Then, the core beliefs that underlie all beliefs and rules will begin to emerge and can be assessed for accuracy and usefulness.

As a child, you didn't have the power to assess the accuracy of these beliefs as they were forming. One of the nice things about being an adult is you now have the ability to make more objective and healthy choices about how you view yourself. You have the power to change a self-image that is not healthy. So make a decision to begin the process today. For the next week, keep a record of your daily thoughts and how they affect your mood. Use the Daily Thought Record on the following page to help you keep track.

When you have become aware of your self-talk, you should then attempt to recognize patterns that will give you insight into your core beliefs about yourself. Once you recognize some of these patterns, and the emotional costs they have for you, you can then begin the process of challenging them, replacing them with more effective self-statements, and feeling the positive changes in your self-esteem. Recognizing your negative self-talk is an effective beginning; but it's often not enough to lead to significant change. The next step, and the most important one, is to help yourself engage in a rational debate with these old messages, evaluating their effectiveness, usefulness, and distortion.

It can be difficult to effectively recognize and challenge old ways of thinking. This battle is made more challenging when you continue to hear distorted and negative messages on a regular basis. Every time you hear a story about gay-bashing, listen to a homophobic joke, or watch a heterocentrist advertisement, you receive direct and indirect messages that suggest you are inferior, damaged, evil, or worthless. Your special challenge is to overcome the negative distortions from your childhood as well as to actively challenge current negative messages. You must become especially skilled at recognizing distortions or biases that are held as universal truths.

Before you begin your self-exploration, make sure that you understand the following central concepts of cognitive behavioral therapy:

- Like all human beings, you are constantly talking to yourself; you may or may not be fully aware of the things that you say to yourself.

- You are constantly interpreting events that occur in your life by using old information about yourself and your ability to handle the situation.

- Most events trigger automatic thoughts, or self-talk, that help you interpret the situation. These automatic thoughts can be negative and can trigger unpleasant emotions such as anxiety, sadness, and anger or a sense of failure. Automatic thoughts are usually situation specific.

- The pattern of responding is maintained by deeper beliefs called conditional beliefs, which are the rules you live your life by. These rules are usually established early in life and may have been directly taught by your parents or other caregivers. The rules may work well in childhood, but often, they don't apply as well to adulthood.

- At the deepest level of your personality are your core beliefs—the absolute value you place upon your worth.

Although your family is one of the main influences on your early self-concept and your self-esteem, there are multiple other factors that shape the way you view yourself and the world. In the next few chapters, I will help you examine the origins of the core and conditional beliefs that underlie your automatic thinking. You will begin by examining family factors that shape your self-view and will go on to explore other important influences such as your religious background, your school experiences, and memorable media images. By understanding these influences more thoroughly, it will be easier for you to evaluate your self-talk more accurately and dispute it more effectively.

Daily Thought Record

For the next week, when you find yourself feeling down, anxious or angry, keep track of what was going through your mind at the time. Write the time, day, and date in the first column, the particular event or situation that triggered the reaction in the second column, the automatic thought or thoughts that went through your head in column three, and the feeling you experienced in the last column.

Time/Day/ Date	Event	Automatic Thoughts	Feelings
5:02 P.M., *Monday, 7/15*	*Copy store* *closed.*	*"What if I get* *fired?"*	*Fear, anxious.*
		"I'm so *incompetent."*	*Despair, sad.*

2

Hand-Me-Down Messages: What You Learned from Your Family of Origin

We are born innocent, believe me Adia, we are still innocent . . .

—Sarah McLachlan and Pierre Marchand, "Adia"

The adults you rely upon as an infant, child, and adolescent for basic survival needs also provide the basic information you need as you grow to interpret the meaning of the world around you and your place in that world. The messages your family gave you, and in some cases may still give you, shape the core beliefs you have about your value, your effectiveness, and your lovability. Think of these messages as being recorded onto a blank compact disc you are born with and which plays, continually over and over. These messages teach you to see the world as your parents or other caregivers do, distortions and all. In fact, the deepest beliefs that you have about yourself usually come from very early childhood and are reinforced over time until you inevitably reach a stage of rebellion and rejection of parental or other family values, usually in adolescence. In some particularly rigid or hostile families, however, you may never reach a safe place to reject family values for fear of physical or mental harm; either the rebellion doesn't take place at all or it happens after you've been able to leave this family environment. Several aspects of your family of origin affect your self-esteem, namely parenting styles, expectations, your role in the family, and methods of communication.

Parenting Styles

The parenting style you were brought up with can have a major impact on the development of your core beliefs and consequently your self-esteem. There are three basic styles of parenting that have been identified by social psychologists: *authoritarian, permissive,* and *authoritative* (Baumkind 1968). Each style sets the tone for the family communications, rules, and expectations, which you'll read about in more detail later in this chapter.

Because your inner, cognitive messages are informed by how you were raised, you may find that your core beliefs were shaped by a parenting style that is similar to one of these three. It's certainly possible, however, that your parents may not fit neatly into one of these categories. They may have qualities of one, two, or all three types of parenting styles. They may also have changed their style over time or following a major family disruption such as divorce or separation. Parenting style may change after the birth or addition of a new sibling, with more attention paid to the baby and less to the older children. Just as your family might not have been all one style or another, your cognitions may at times be fairly reasonable and at others harsh and punitive. How often you are hard on yourself may depend on the situation and your previous levels of success or failure in a similar situation.

Authoritarian

In *authoritarian* families, rules of authority are a defining feature in this hierarchical family organization. This style is most often associated with the lowest self-esteem in later adulthood. The central figures in this type of family include a *dictator* (or dictators) at the top, with children clearly in subservient, submissive roles. Dictators often have little regard for the needs of the children, physically or emotionally. The children are told directly, through words, and indirectly, by not allowing the children to grapple with tough decisions for themselves, that they are incompetent. The emotional needs of the dictator, usually the parent or parents, are the primary driving force of the family, and children may never be allowed to express feelings directly, especially when those feelings are in conflict with the dictator's needs. Dictators often will attempt to invalidate the children's feelings to avoid any challenge to their own rigid, but amazingly fragile and easily threatened, belief systems. They often rely on harsh and forceful physical disciplinary techniques such as spanking and slapping, as well as verbal abuse, to force compliance with their view of the world. Respect for authority and work, order and tradition, and conformity are highly valued. This type of rigidity, when mixed with excessive physical punishment, often leads to the development of maladaptive personality structures for the children including extreme dependence, submissiveness, and a strong desire to conform. It also tends to make children less confident in their own abilities, less self-reliant, emotionally immature (which means they have difficulty developing mature emotional attachments to others), and perhaps over-aggressive.

A few years ago, a national TV commercial powerfully illustrated the words of an authoritarian parent. The commercial begins by showing the beautiful face of a young girl with large, dark eyes standing in front of a black, empty background. Out of the blackness come the harsh and angry words, "You're so stupid . . . I wish you were never born." The child's expression subtly changes to reflect the lonely darkness. Silently, tears roll down her face to show that she is internalizing these words and adding them to her self-concept. The commercial goes on to remind us that children are listening to everything adults say, even when the adults say things they may not really mean.

Psychologists have done extensive studies on people with authoritarian personalities. It has been hypothesized that authoritarians are generally anxious about their own self-worth and feel they must rely on harsh disciplinary methods to force their children to give them respect and be obedient. They cannot tolerate open defiance or hostility from their children and therefore make it unacceptable for the children to express such feelings, or even healthy questioning, openly (Adorno et al. 1950).

Some psychologists believe that the roots of prejudice toward other races or socioeconomic classes lie in the repression of these early angry feelings. In order to justify a hierarchical organization of a family, its members must believe that there are people who hold more correct views than others. A typical paternalistic, authoritarian family, for example, would believe that men are the head of the household, women are lesser than men, and children are lesser still (although male children would rank higher than female children). This is not to say that women cannot be authoritarian, and in some cases they may certainly become the dictatorial force in the home, even if the actual discipline is carried out by the father figure.

Typically in an authoritarian household, the dictator must see him- or herself as more powerful than those outside the family in order to feel important. The more unlike the authoritarian figure a person is, the more negatively that person will be viewed because he or she represents a challenge or threat to the dictator's way of thinking. People of a different race/ethnicity or a lower socioeconomic status, or people with more education, different religious beliefs or social values, and different sexualities may all pose threats to the authoritarian personality. Dictators tend to be overtly judgmental about differing opinions, often not only devaluing the opinions or traditions of those who are different, but belittling, actively shunning, discriminating against, or perhaps even being aggressive toward people who are different and threaten their authority.

Children of authoritarians often learn to continue this devaluing process, toward themselves as well as others. They learn that they have a certain place in the world and that there is no room for questioning the authoritarian parent or making decisions about even their most intimate likes and dislikes on their own. The official word from the dictator is "you are whatever I say you are." By not allowing free thinking, the parent is saying "you are incapable of making these decisions," leading to uncertainty or difficulty making decisions later in life.

Of course, not all control in an authoritarian household is exerted directly. Aggressiveness or threats may be implied or may be expressed passively. Passive aggression can be particularly difficult for a child to see clearly, since the parent's displeasure may not be as obvious as a slap or immediate verbal put-down would be but comes more indirectly, for example through the "silent treatment" or exhibiting feelings of emotional detachment or rejection. Passive-aggressive parental behaviors may not immediately follow the "transgression" of the child but may come later when the child least expects it, say as an embarrassing comment by the parent at a party or in front of the child's friends. It's difficult to link these angry behaviors to the event that prompted them because the passive-aggressive person cannot handle his or her own anger effectively and directly, thereby thwarting healthy communication. Passive-aggressive parents may use shaming and guilt rather than direct aggression as methods of control. They know exactly when and how to emotionally "blackmail" a child into conforming to their wishes. Implicit threats of rejection, literally or emotionally, may be all it takes to extinguish the child's initiative, questioning, or exploration. Whether the control is direct or indirect, the same message underlies it: "You must live according to my rules or risk the consequences." We will discuss styles of family communication and their effect on self-esteem again later in this chapter.

An authoritarian does not believe in accidents and punishes the child for her or his mistakes. Spilling the milk is attributed to stupidity or irresponsibility rather than simply to normal human imperfection. This leads children to develop self-talk like, "I must be perfect" or "When I make mistakes, I am a failure."

Permissive

On the other side of the spectrum of parenting are *permissive* parents. These parents may offer emotional support or caring but few limits or boundaries. They tend to allow the children to do as they please, make all decisions for themselves, and have everything they want. Certainly, the parents may make this choice intentionally, believing that children learn to be independent by making their own decisions early in life and facing the natural consequences. They assume that if a child makes a decision that results in discomfort, the child will learn not to make this choice again. Parents might be considered permissive for other reasons such as the need to work long hours with little support, or self-absorption in their own lives and problems. Or perhaps they had inadequate models of good parenting from their own parents.

Children of permissive parents can, like children from authoritarian families, have problems with self-esteem. Some studies have suggested that these children behave selfishly when interacting with others and may be insecure and emotionally immature (Baumkind 1968). Most importantly, however, they often interpret their parents' lack of control as emotional neglect, even if the parents feel great love and caring toward them. The messages children hear from being unacknowledged and then incorporate into their self-talk may include such statements as "I am unimportant," "I do not exist," or "Nothing I do matters."

At times, children may consciously or unconsciously seek to test their parents' limits, looking for any response that signals an emotional connection. At times when children "act out," or break a rule, what they really may be looking for is acknowledgment by the parents that they exist in their parents' world. All children have a need as part of the natural development process to be recognized as independent and powerful. Having parents acknowledge children by attending to their wishes, thoughts, and feelings allows the children to gauge their effectiveness in the world by observing the parents' reaction. For example, sometimes behaving badly may be the behavioral equivalent of saying "look at me, look at me."

Narcissism, a deep-seated form of insecurity, often manifests in adulthood as selfishness, self-centeredness, and self-aggrandizement. It may be that children who are unattended to emotionally and physically go on to become narcissistically oriented adults, constantly looking for the attention and recognition they did not receive at home. This core, yet unfulfilled, need may have an impact on one's ability to develop mutually gratifying, adult relationships.

Authoritative

The *authoritative* parenting style appears to be associated with higher levels of self-esteem later in life. Although authoritative parents are still the ultimate source of authority in the family, like authoritarians, one major difference is that authoritative parents are more democratic and allow children to have a role in family decision making. Children are allowed to question the authority figure, and reasons for rules are explained at a level they can understand in most cases. When the parents and children reach an impasse, and the parents exert their ultimate authority, they allow the children to have feelings about the decision without condemnation. Children are taught that their feelings are valid, but that some behaviors are socially unacceptable. The children learn invaluable methods of dealing with adult situations by being allowed to question and reason.

Authoritative parents attempt to establish an atmosphere of respect, trust, and open communication within the family. They establish clear and firm rules and usually spell out the consequences for breaking them. The consequences are applied uniformly across the household and in a nonhostile and nonabusive way (as opposed to what you might expect from an authoritarian parent). The goals are to allow children to learn mastery of their environment by providing clear guidelines for living, which ultimately increases children's sense of personal power and positive self-image.

Beyond the effective limit-setting, authoritative parents provide consistent emotional support and love during stressful events. Children learn that they don't have to feel alone, but can reach out for comfort when they feel frightened or needy. Reason is valued and encouraged as well as the need to respect oneself and others. The messages you may learn and incorporate into your self-talk from authoritative parents may sound like, "Your feelings are valid, but we all have to live together" or "You exist and have value in this family."

Striking a Balance

One of my goals in this book is for you to learn to recognize when you may be perpetuating the negative parenting you may have received as a child. It will be essential for you to become more balanced in your cognitive dealings with yourself, more like an authoritative parent who controls with love and respect than an authoritarian who controls with fear, or an emotionally neglectful permissive parent. You can learn to tend to yourself, to respect and nurture yourself when you have feelings, to validate rather than invalidate, and to allow yourself to make mistakes. I will ask you to explore more about your family's primary methods of parenting at the end of this chapter to help you examine your own *inner parenting* style.

Family Systems

In addition to having overt rules, families may have a variety of unspoken expectations for what is considered acceptable and unacceptable behavior. How these expectations are conveyed is unique to each family. All families have their own sets of rules, roles, and methods of communication and we can only understand them in the context of how the family functions as a system.

When you're looking at the family as a system, it's important to understand that systems attempt to remain static, even if the system is dysfunctional. In other words, static systems resist change. When one member of a family upsets the stasis by breaking the unspoken rules, challenging the way the system functions, or otherwise behaving in a way that is not sanctioned by the family, the system will often attempt to force the disruptive member to return to old patterns.

Many family systems encourage forms of communication they deem acceptable over other unacceptable forms of communication. For example, one family rule may be that children do not question a parent's decisions and when this happens, the child is chided or forced into complying by the parents, siblings, or even the extended family (grandparents, aunts, uncles). Perhaps your family encouraged or discouraged expressing physical affection or openly talking about problems.

Rules and Boundaries

Boundaries are limits that we attempt to place between ourselves and others, and rules are made to enforce boundaries. Knocking before entering someone's room is an example of a healthy boundary that indicates respect for privacy. When someone does not respect your rights, physically or emotionally, that person has violated a boundary. Good boundaries are necessary for healthy development of the self. As children grow from completely dependent infants to healthy independent adults, they must learn to construct barriers between themselves and the world around them in order to protect themselves from harm. They must learn to say "no" when something does not feel safe. They must develop private thoughts, ways of coping with the world, and decision-making skills. The parents' role in this process is to model and teach effective and healthy ways of being in the world.

Of course boundaries can be healthy or unhealthy in a family. Too many boundaries might be considered rigid and lead to feelings of isolation and alienation. You may be able to protect yourself with the walls you construct, but then you cannot open any doors to intimacy or affection. Too few boundaries or weak boundaries allows others to take advantage of you through disrespect or abuse. Parents with unhealthy boundaries themselves will often raise their children with few or no boundaries. These children may not have the tools to protect themselves as adults and allow others to push them around. Their self-talk sends messages like, "I deserved that" or "I'm useless anyway," which leads them to be passive when treated unfairly.

Babies cannot initially establish healthy boundaries when they are born. Only through exploration of their bodies and their environment do they learn that they are separate from the world. They also learn about their ability to affect change, protect themselves, and reach out for what they need through their experiences as they grow. The adult caregivers shape the experiences that infants and children have, thereby shaping the beliefs that they have about their effectiveness, or their self-efficacy. When parents provide everything or nothing, children may learn distorted messages about their own ability to cope with the world. Parents who continually violate the boundaries of growing children teach the children that they cannot or do not have the right to say "no" or to fend for themselves. Children also learn by watching their parents interact with others. So a parent's relationship with other adults also demonstrates boundaries for a child.

A family that has unclear or too few boundaries is referred to as *enmeshed*. As we discussed earlier, children with parents who do not allow them to be a part of decision making do not develop strong identities as independent decision makers. At some point in children's development, they must be given opportunities to make decisions for and about themselves so that they will be able to apply this skill later in life. Parents who will not allow children to think independently because of their own insecurities are effectively crossing the children's healthy boundaries. Other, more overt, forms of boundary violations in families include incest and emotional abuse.

When attempts to establish effective and clear boundaries in the family are met with resistance, sometimes the child, adolescent, or young adult may try to establish an ultimate barrier by leaving the family system altogether. Running away from home may actually be a form of separating from dysfunctional family systems and can be viewed at times as healthy individuation (development of a healthy and independent identity). The pressures in some family systems may be so intense that children see only two options—escape or conform.

Gay and lesbian children are much more likely to run away from home and even attempt suicide than their heterosexual peers, probably as a form of escape from a dysfunctional family system that resists the notion of a child with a nonconforming identity. Sometimes, a family chooses to send the child who does not conform, or who otherwise disrupts the family system, away to boarding school or military school with the temporary goal of re-establishing family rules and with the long-term wish that the child be "transformed" into a conformist. Often healthy lesbian or gay children or adolescents learn to compartmentalize their lives, placing the secret parts of themselves (namely their sexuality) deep inside. They develop a conformist exterior self that follows the rules of the family system and allows them to function in relative safety until they are able to arrange to move to an environment that is more healthy or accepting.

Family Roles

You may have learned about your value by the role you were asked to play in your family. Often, each member of a family is assigned a task or role to play in the family. In most cases this is an unspoken act, with family members taking on certain roles because of the behavior of other family members. Common dysfunctional family roles include the scapegoat (the one who always gets the blame), the caretaker or rescuer (of siblings, mother, father), the black sheep (similar to the scapegoat but more overtly rejected), and the hero (the one who must succeed). John Bradshaw, author of several books dealing with families and their effect on individuals, is an ardent supporter of the notion that the family role you were expected to play as a child has an influence on your adult self-esteem.

As an adult, you may find that you continue to play the role that was assigned to you as a child. You may have chosen your career because it fits the early role you assumed. For example, people attracted to helping professions, such as psychotherapy and nursing, may have grown up tending to the needs of their parents and siblings, sometimes continuing to place their own needs lower on their list of priorities. Gay and lesbian children often take on the caretaker role in the family, both to focus attention away from their own unmet needs and to gain recognition and attention for their caregiving behaviors. They may learn from this that their value to the family comes from attending to the others' needs, rather than feeling they have intrinsic value in and of themselves. Common messages that result from rigid role playing include, "I must take care of others even at my own expense," "Taking care of my own needs or listening to my own feelings is selfish," or "I won't fit in if I act the way I truly feel."

Forms of Family Communication

Much of the language in the messages you give yourself comes from the forms of communication you learned in your early family life. You may in fact hear those messages in the voice of the person who said them the most when you were young. It's important to recognize the various forms of communication your family used to help you see how you may be continuing to communicate in an unhealthy way with yourself and others even today.

Nonverbal Messages

While some messages are conveyed verbally, many of the messages you receive and observe are unspoken. In fact, research suggests that up to 90 percent of all communication between human beings is nonverbal (Mehrabian 1972). Nonverbal communication includes behaviors like making facial expressions that suggest strong approval or disapproval (smiles or frowns). Many families develop their own system of nonverbal codes that they can use at home and in public; these codes are so unique to that family that others may not recognize their meanings or importance. Other nonverbal forms of communication include body language, such as whether someone hugs you or "stiffens" as you approach; eye contact, such as whether someone looks at you directly or indirectly; or even the amount of silence at the dinner table.

Sometimes, your negative internal messages are in fact visual images, rather than auditory, drawn from the stern looks or negative events that occurred in response to your behaviors as a child. For example, you may have always gotten looks of disgust or disapproval whenever you tried to discuss issues of sexuality or intense emotion, sending you the message that there is something wrong about discussing that particular issue or something wrong with you for wanting to discuss the issue.

Tone of voice can also suggest that you or something you wish to express is unacceptable, even if the words the other person uses suggest that he or she is willing to listen. This is called *double-bind* communication, since a parent may say one thing, but the tone of voice says something else. This type of communication is confusing and may teach children to mistrust what they are told. Body language may also contradict words, sending a confused message. For example, a parent may say, "I need a hug" but will stiffen when the child approaches to do so. Sometimes what people say they want and what they really want are two different things. You may in fact have developed this indirect style of communicating with others without realizing it until this moment. Pay attention to your own tone and body language for the next few days to see if your body and words are in sync.

Expressing Anger

You may treat yourself in a passive-aggressive way if your family was not comfortable with the direct expression of anger. Rather than saying harsh things to yourself such as "You are foolish and unworthy" (a directly aggressive self-statement), you may unconsciously (and indirectly) sabotage your own success at times. It may be difficult for you to recognize the messages your family's passive-aggressiveness taught you if the messages were never spoken out loud, but always inferred. It may be easier for an experienced psychotherapist to help you sort out these kinds of messages when nonverbal communication and passive-aggressiveness were the primary forms of communication in your family.

Dawn's mother, Doris, would always give Dawn a look of shock whenever Dawn tried to speak up for herself. Although Doris never verbally chastised Dawn, from her facial expressions, Dawn felt she was saying, "You are disappointing to me. I may withdraw my love from you if you continue on this path." If Dawn persisted in her argument, her mother would become cold and distant, sometimes for days on end. Without words, Dawn learned from those experiences that, according to her mother, there are correct and incorrect ways of expressing herself. Although she had always maintained that her parents had never been abusive and were always willing to talk about issues with her, it was not until she was an adult with difficulties in her own relationship that Dawn realized how much of her mother's communication style she had brought to her own relationship with her partner. Dawn found that she was passive-aggressive with herself at times. Instead of allowing herself to feel disappointed when things didn't work out the way she wanted, she realized that she was more likely to turn down invitations to socialize with friends or to reject support from her partner because she felt she didn't deserve it.

Rewarding and Acceptance

What the family recognizes and rewards may be characteristics that they value like compliance, conformity, academic achievement, beauty, etc. You may or may not be able to live up to these standards. When you are able to meet the family's standards and the family rewards you with praise or acceptance, you will likely continue to try to meet those standards again in the future. Academic achievement for example is an area where many children excel and are then rewarded for their success at home. We will discuss the impact of school on self-esteem in greater detail later in the book.

The Secret Self

Many gay and lesbian adults remember feeling either a directly communicated or unspoken disdain for same-sex attraction. Even while your family may not have discussed the issue of your homosexuality or even sexuality in general, you probably knew the family's attitudes toward these issues and learned to hide those feelings.

A child's early recognition of same-sex attraction in a family or culture that does not have tolerant attitudes toward this orientation can lead the child to develop a split self—one that is public and one that is private, or secret. The public self behaves in a way that is most likely to please the parents, friends, and society. This self follows all the rules and behaves in ways that are expected, even when the deeper feelings or experiences do not match those of friends or family.

Heterosexuals may have secret selves as well, regarding other issues. For example, girls with a heterosexual orientation may actually prefer activities that are more traditionally masculine, but they learn early on that they will be ridiculed or punished for pursuing these interests so they accommodate by accepting more traditionally feminine roles assigned to them. This usually leads to chronic feelings of boredom or even depression. Lesbian or gay children often are invalidated not only in their sexuality, but also in their other nontraditional inclinations. Some gay men can identify with the familiar story of being forced into participating in sports rather than learning about music or art, to avoid Dad's humiliation. Many lesbians share similar war stories of being told to wear a dress or makeup or being scolded for "unladylike" behavior until they complied.

Not all gay men or lesbians feel this type of gender discomfort. Certainly there are lesbians with more traditionally feminine interests and gay men who enjoy traditionally masculine pursuits. What most gay or lesbian people have in common in this country, however, is the constant invalidation of their sexual interests. The overwhelming messages a child learns from living a split life are "I must live to please others rather than listen to my own feelings or needs," "My true feelings are invalid or unacceptable and I must always hide them," or the more deeply held belief, "My secret self is shameful, unworthy, or evil."

Abuse and Neglect

While I have yet to find a completely nondysfunctional family over my ten-plus years as a therapist, there are certainly family characteristics that seem more harmful than others and can affect your overall level of self-esteem. No one would dispute the fact that abuse is harmful in many ways—physically, emotionally and spiritually. Abuse can be divided into different types, such as physical abuse, sexual abuse, and emotional abuse. These types of abuse are also most commonly associated with the authoritarian style of parenting.

Common types of *physical abuse* include beating, slapping, restraining, or otherwise causing physical discomfort or pain. This abuse may or may not be a punishment in response to a child's behavior. Sometimes physical abuse stems from the parent's mood or need to release anger or anxiety. In this case, the message being conveyed is a confusing one, since the child will often attempt to correlate his or her own behavior with the parental outburst. If there is no logical correlation, sometimes arbitrary behaviors, like wearing blue, can become associated with negative outbursts in the mind of the child. The pressure of attempting to predict the parent's outbursts and avoid provoking them can lead to chronic feelings of anxiety. Physical punishment has the power to shape a child's self-esteem for many years with only a few such violent incidents. A child is often a convenient target for a psychologically immature parent with poor emotional coping skills because the child is powerless to resist and can be intimidated into silence. The messages are loud and clear: "You do not have the power to defend yourself" and "Great harm will befall you if you make the wrong step."

Sexual abuse includes behaviors from outright rape (forcing a child to accept sexual behavior that he or she finds unacceptable/frightening/painful) to seduction (convincing the child that inappropriate sexual behavior is acceptable and consensual). Specific behaviors include all forms of intercourse, fellatio, cunniligus, and other touching of private parts, as well as less obvious but also sexualized forms of behavior like voyeurism, exhibitionism, flirtations, and making embarrassing sexual comments. Sexual abuse can occur inside the family (incest) as well as outside the family by someone of the same or opposite sex. Victims of sexual abuse can often have unresolved or mixed feelings about the abuse itself, particularly if they experienced any pleasure from the act sexually or emotionally. They may often feel guilty and responsible for the abuse, especially if the abuser framed the abuse as consensual or mutually pleasurable. They often also feel guilty and ashamed as adults if they did not speak out about the abuse.

Sometimes, gay or lesbian people have been convinced that sexual abuse when they were young was responsible for their later-emerging sexual identity. This argument is often made as an explanation for the origin of homosexuality, suggesting that something abnormal has occurred in order for a gay or lesbian identity to develop. One problem with this reasoning, however, is that it's self-validating. One could argue that a woman became a lesbian both because she was sexually abused by a woman (and liked it) or because she was sexually abused by a man (and didn't like it). Conducting research to validate these types of theories is almost impossible since it would involve measuring sexual orientation before childhood sexual abuse and then again after the abuse. As you can see, this type of research would be difficult to conduct ethically and practically. Although more and more evidence is surfacing suggesting that sexual orientation begins to take shape very early in life, we still are relatively ineffective at determining which children might grow up to be gay or lesbian. In fact, the most current scientific data suggests that sexual orientation is shaped by many factors including nonenvironmental factors like genetics or biology.

Emotional abuse may be overt or covert and therefore not everyone agrees on what exactly constitutes emotional abuse. It doesn't necessarily involve physical or sexual abuse, but each of these most certainly involves emotional abuse. Clear examples of overt emotional abuse include subjecting a child to frequent yelling, insulting or degrading comments, and both verbal and nonverbal threats of physical, sexual, or emotional harm. Less clear examples include implied threats, rejection, avoidant behaviors, smirks, passive-aggressive behaviors, and sarcasm. Emotional abusers share many of the same general characteristics of physical and sexual abusers, if not the specific behaviors. For example, they often respond to children in an abusive way because of their own needs or inability to control impulses, rather than in direct response to the behaviors of the child. The sting of emotional abuse carries the same effect on self-esteem as physical or sexual abuse. Emotional abuse may be particularly damaging to a child's self-esteem because the parent may be able to abuse in this way more often with less challenge from other family members or outsiders. Emotional abuse may not be exhibited in distinct events as is often the case with physical or sexual abuse, but may exist constantly in the form of insults, intimidation, and verbal or nonverbal threats. A child who grows up in an environment with a constant barrage of negative evaluation will most likely have low self-esteem. The more negative the messages, the lower the self-esteem.

Often, if parents indulge in one form of abuse, they may also indulge in others. A common thread for all forms of abuse is the concept of *boundary violation*. Boundaries are healthy in many ways and are particularly relevant to people who were raised in abusive families. Parents who do not encourage the formation of healthy boundaries in their children or do not respect these boundaries when they are formed are in effect teaching their children to be victims. They teach their children that their thoughts, feelings, and desires are invalid and that the needs of others are more important. They also teach them that even if these desires are valid, the children are not powerful enough to reach for these desires or wishes. Repeated violation of physical, sexual, or emotional boundaries teaches the child that they are unworthy of respect, love, or happiness. The cognitive messages that abused children develop sound like this: "You are not worth respect from others," "You don't deserve to be loved," and "You are meant to be abused by others."

Certainly there are many reasons that parents abuse their children beyond a conscious intent to inflict short-term and long-term damage. Many of the parents grew up in homes that were violent and abusive themselves and learned their parenting styles from their own parents. Many also have problems that are overwhelming, such as poverty, loss of a job, or marital difficulties, and they have few effective means for coping with these pressures. They may also have psychological problems or conditions, including alcohol or other substance abuse or dependency. It's important to keep in mind that the abuser may not realize that their choices are inappropriate and harmful. In many cases, they may be intending to do the right thing, but their own backgrounds prevent them from making the right decisions in parenting.

Another potentially harmful type of parental behavior, neglect, is less likely to raise the public ire, except in extreme cases. Such extremes include leaving a child alone for long periods of time or not attending to life-threatening health or safety needs of a child. Less extreme forms may simply be the emotional or physical unavailability of a parent, lack of attention to longer term health issues like proper nutrition or exercise, or ignoring signs of potential problems for a child in school or in relationships. Certainly, parents can be both loving and neglectful, selecting issues that are appropriate in their minds for discussion and ignoring the child's other needs. These children learn to believe that they are unimportant, "not good enough to be attended to," or "incapable of making a difference."

Children who grow up with parents who have significant psychological illness or drug or alcohol abuse or dependency often take a backseat to the needs of the parents or other family members exhibiting the most serious problems. The children may learn from this that in order to be attended to, they must be sick or otherwise disruptive. These families tend to form an unhealthy system around the individual's (or individuals') sickness and disruptive behavior; emotional health or striving for independence is discouraged. Parents who have an untreated mental illness or substance abuse/dependency problem may exhibit physically, sexually, or emotionally abusive behaviors toward their children due to difficulty with impulse control or intense self-absorption. Children who grow up in this type of environment learn that the world is an unpredictable and frightening place and they must attend to the needs of others rather than their own needs. Inconsistent messages of support or nurturing may indeed make it more difficult for the children to form clear expectations of the world and themselves.

Evaluate the Messages

The goal of this chapter is to help you understand the messages—both direct and indirect—you heard repeatedly in your family of origin about yourself. By exploring these messages, as an adult, you have an advantage over when you were a child: *You can evaluate the messages more objectively and choose to reject the ones that are not accurate.*

Many times, my lesbian or gay clients have not been aware of how they perpetuate feelings of inadequacy, doubt, anxiety, or depression by continuing to play the old family "compact disk" through their self-talk. The first step to changing these feelings, from a cognitive perspective, is recognizing the messages in your self-talk. While your family is certainly a major source of negative self-statements, there are often other major sources of negative messages about being gay that shape our self-beliefs such as our larger culture and the media, our schools, and some organized religions. We will explore these other major sources of negative and distorted information in the next few chapters to help you continue identifying the sources of your self-talk before we turn to the real work of change, challenging, refuting and altering the "CD" self-talk.

It's important for you to recognize the beliefs that you carry with you from your childhood. Answering the following questions will help you clarify family beliefs, values, and messages that you received when you were growing and forming your self-concept. It will then be important for you to consider the validity of these beliefs and their usefulness to you now as an adult. Just because your family believed something about you does not make it true. Just because they taught you what they knew does not mean what they taught you is helpful for you. In fact in many cases, what they learned as heterosexuals about gays or lesbians, or about sexuality in general, may be quite unhealthy and unhelpful for you.

Questions for Reflection

Take some time to ask yourself the following questions derived from this chapter's concepts. You do not have to write down your answers, but you may choose to begin keeping a journal of memories, thoughts, and feelings for later review.

- Which style of parenting—authoritarian, permissive, or authoritative—was most evident in your family when you were growing up?

- If you were raised in an *authoritarian* family:

  Who was the "dictator" (or "dictators")? How did this person use discipline? Was he or she physical with you or did he or she use psychological or emotional strategies to control you? How was punishment, or the threat of punishment, used when you thought or felt something that the dictator did not value? Were you scolded or punished for accidents or mistakes? How do you feel today when you make mistakes? In what other ways do you recognize your upbringing affecting your life today?

- If you were raised in a *permissive* family:

  How often did you feel totally accepted? Were there times as a child when you felt alone, neglected, or unattended to? Were there times you secretly wished for an argument in order to feel some emotional connection with a family member? Could you "get away" with things you did wrong? What happened when you brought home a good grade or received some other recognition for good work? As an adult, do you ever feel the need to have an argument with a friend or significant other just to "break the silence"? Do you sometimes feel like you have to be the life of the party at social gatherings? In what other ways do you recognize your upbringing affecting your life today?

- If you were raised in an *authoritative* family:

  How often did you feel totally accepted? Was there a time when your parents changed their parenting style? Was there an event that had a significant impact on your family, such as a divorce, death, or change in financial status? How often were you included in major family decisions? In what other ways do you recognize your upbringing affecting your life today?

- Did your family exhibit characteristics of two or all three family styles? In what ways? How do you perpetuate the same kind of parenting you were raised with?

- Can you identify which style you use with yourself now? To motivate yourself? To deal with mistakes? Do you say things to yourself or others that are aggressive or do things that are passive-aggressive?

- What were the family rules about privacy? Were you allowed to have time and space alone? Were your thoughts, feelings, and possessions respected?

- Did your parents have healthy boundaries with you?

- Were you aware of a secret self that you felt you had to hide?

- Were you physically, sexually, or emotionally abused?

- Did you have a parent (or parents) with mental illness, substance abuse problems, and so on? How did you compensate for their problems?

- What unresolved emotional issues do you have from your childhood?

- What patterns do you perpetuate with yourself now?

3

Inescapable Messages: The Media, Culture, and Politics

How do you document real life when real life's getting more like fiction each day?

—Jonathan Larson, *Rent*

Much of what you learned about yourself and your value as a lesbian or a gay man was absorbed from the cultural markers around you. We are all a product of our society and the times; we may conform to it, rebel against it, or both. The family system that you explored in chapter 2 is a part of the larger society that contains it. If your family members conform to the neighbors' expectations and attitudes, then they will likely expect you to conform. People conform both to feel accepted and to avoid the pain of rejection and isolation.

How Attitudes Are Formed

Before we move on to examine specific views that our culture holds and communicates regarding homosexuality and the history of those views, let's spend a little time discussing how people form attitudes about other individuals or groups. My goal is to help you understand the origins of the fear, the hate, and discrimination that affect us all.

Attitudes are like filters that influence the way people perceive and evaluate things, events, and other people. They provide a way to organize and simplify a complex world. People learn attitudes from family, peers, educators, the media, and other cultural sources of information. The desire for acceptance leads people sometimes to shape their attitudes and beliefs to match those of the majority. There are several factors involved in how attitudes are formed, including social influence (other people's attitudes), cognitive influence (a person's own reasoning or thinking style and the messages he or she learned as a child), and behavior.

It's clear that attitudes can influence behavior, like when a wealthy child who was taught that poor people are stupid talks down to a homeless person on the street. But in fact, the opposite is also true in that people may form attitudes to justify their behaviors. When people do not have an obvious justification for behaviors they exhibit, they tend to adopt an attitude that is consistent with their actions. For example, a man who takes part in gay bashing because he feels a need to control something in his world might adopt the attitude "Gays must be inferior to me" to explain to himself why he must lash out.

Many psychologists are interested in how to change attitudes in order to try to solve a number of long-standing problems in our society. For example, racial discrimination is essentially rooted in racist attitudes. For discrimination to end, people's attitudes must change.

Attributions

Attribution is the process of explaining why people behave as they do. When people make an attribution, they are in effect trying to decide what causes a behavior. Essentially, this process involves deciding whether someone's behavior is caused by something in the person (an internal attribution) or by something in the situation or environment (external attribution).

Social scientists have observed that an individual tends to exhibit characteristic patterns of attribution. A well-known concept in social psychology referred to as the *fundamental attribution error* observes that people tend to underestimate the role of causes for behavior that are outside of the individual and to overestimate the role of internal causes. For example, you might conclude that a young girl who does poorly in school is not very smart (an internal attribution), when her bad grades are really due to problems at home (an external cause). Or you might assume that you've been rejected by an organization because you are homosexual (internal attribution), when in fact you were rejected because the organization decided weeks before you applied that they would take no more new members this year (external cause).

You may lean toward always attributing behavior to something within yourself or another person, rather than looking for external explanations, or vice versa. Or you may always give others the benefit of the doubt, but always blame yourself when things go wrong without ever considering an external explanation.

Many cultural messages are phrased in ways that are blaming of individuals or identifiable groups of people. For example, the president is often blamed or praised for how the economy is doing by political groups and the media. However, in reality, it's clear that many factors are responsible for the ups and downs of the economy, such as market activity and the economic health of other countries with which we trade. If the president was a high internalizer and therefore accepted complete blame for a failing economy, he would likely become so distraught that he would be distracted from the other aspects of his job.

Lesbians and gays often are blamed or scapegoated by members of our culture for certain social problems. For example, some religious groups suggest that gays and lesbians are responsible for the breakdown of "traditional family values." If you tend to feel guilt or shame when you hear such messages, you may be a high internalizer. People with low self-esteem tend to internalize responsibility more often than they externalize it. If you are a high internalizer, part of your strategy to raise your self-esteem will be to begin evaluating external reasons for problematic behavior, rather than always accepting full responsibility and blaming yourself. In the example, then, nuclear family "breakdown" might be viewed as a result of economic factors rather than moral ones.

Prejudice, Stereotypes, and Discrimination

People's attitudes and attributions affect how they evaluate and treat other people. Positive attitudes/attributions will lead them to treat those people favorably. Negative attitudes can quickly lead to prejudicial behavior toward, and stereotyping of, the person or people toward whom they hold those negative beliefs. For clarity's sake, a *prejudice* is a negative attitude toward a person solely due to her or his membership in a group. A *stereotype* is a set of beliefs about the characteristics of people in a specific group that is then expanded to all members of that group. *Discrimination*, in simple terms, is the behavioral expression of prejudice and involves actions that harm members of the targeted group. Although certainly most gay or lesbian people can quickly name instances of discrimination they have encountered, both directly and indirectly, many do not recognize the ways that they may internally stereotype, hold self-prejudicial attitudes, or even self-discriminate.

As products of a generally gay-intolerant culture, you cannot help but internalize the negative attitudes that may be held by your family, friends, or larger culture. This can create an ongoing internal battle between your desires and your behaviors. This tension, sometimes referred to as *internalized homophobia*, may result in behaviors of self-punishment through negative thinking, self-censorship, decreased assertiveness, and self-fulfilling prophecy.

For example, Miriam was worried that being a lesbian would cause her to lose out on a high level job she really wanted. Before she even went in for her interview she had convinced herself that being a lesbian was a liability since she was "out" to everyone she knew and she believed that her company was much too conservative to tolerate someone at upper management levels who was openly lesbian. Her thoughts just before the interview ran the gamut from "My sexual orientation will be a handicap to me in this job" to "I should just be happy with what I already have," increasing her anxiety about the interview to the point of having sweaty palms and a racing heart. Although she knew that questions about her sexual orientation would likely not come up during the interview, she didn't perform nearly as well as she knew she could have. As she had predicted, she did not get the job, which she took as a confirmation that being an out lesbian was not compatible with this level of management. Unfortunately, Miriam could not see that being a lesbian in itself likely had less to do with not getting the job than did her anxiety. Her lowered self-expectations actually interfered with her ability to present herself as the competent and capable employee that she was.

Society's Messages

Although society's rules for conforming often are made explicit through laws and ethics codes of formal organizations (such as the government and religious institutions), many of society's rules are communicated more subtly and informally. Just as parents can communicate messages overtly by yelling, name-calling, or beating—or subtly through facial expressions, silence, and other covert forms of rejection—society's messages about homosexuality can also be obvious or hidden. Society's overt homophobia can be found in anti-gay employment policies, sodomy laws, and hate crimes. The indirect negativity toward homosexuals is more difficult to see, just as the nonverbal cues within a family may be more difficult to recognize as inappropriate. Examples of covert or less formalized homophobia include such societal behaviors as the stereotyping of homosexuals in the media and public conversations, voting against pro-gay issues or HIV funding initiatives (which may be easier for some homophobes with a conscience because they feel uncomfortable with voting directly *for* an anti-gay initiative), and teaching children distorted information about lesbian and gay sexual behavior.

Some segments of society often have a need to stereotype groups of people in order to exert some form of control over them. Stereotyping allows for the marginalization of minorities or subgroups and thereby allows the majority to disseminate inaccurate information that keeps the oppressive attitudes alive. Depicting the "lesbian" character in a TV show or movie as the murderer or crazy, condoning or not speaking out against the telling of "fag" jokes by heterosexuals, or making assumptions about gay family or friends based on general expectations for "those people" are forms of covert homophobia—no direct intent to harm may be obvious in these examples.

Historical and Cultural Contexts of Society's Messages

In order to evaluate the negative messages you perceive in your world today, it's helpful to understand where these messages may have come from. It's clear from the history books that various world cultures have had different attitudes regarding sexual relations between people of the same sex. And while cultures themselves may have held different attitudes, positive or negative, toward same-sex attractions during the same period of time, each culture may have changed its views of this behavior across different time periods. In other words, many of societies' attitudes toward same-sex attraction are dynamic, constantly changing as the society evolves and changes. Nowhere is this more obvious than in one well-known historical record we know as the Bible. Certainly part of the larger value of this book is its documentation of the attitudes, laws, and customs of Judeo-Christian peoples thousands of years ago. Most people observe the change in customs and values that have occurred since the original writings due to cultural advances in areas such as science, medicine, and technology. We also know from this record that at times certain standards of behavior within the Bible changed over time; for example, polygamy was a common practice during the time of Abraham, but went out of fashion when Paul suggested "Christian" monogamy. Certainly, other major religious historical texts outside the Judeo-Christian perspective, including Eastern, Native American, and African perspectives, also document changing cultural practices across hundreds or thousands of years.

Neil Miller's book *Out of the Past: Gay and Lesbian History from 1869 to the Present* includes much information about American (and other cultural) views of gays and lesbians. Miller points out an inherent difficulty in the study of lesbian and gay history: the term *homosexual* did not even exist prior to the nineteenth century. Most likely, even the concept of homosexual identity was not understood the way we understand it today. He effectively argues that same-sex attraction or behavior has occurred throughout history, but that the behaviors themselves were either tolerated or prohibited without identifying people who exhibited the behaviors as having a separate identity. He goes on to argue that only as industrialization allowed for more economic independence from extended families did people develop unique lifestyles that suited their primary sexualities. Thus it's only over the past 150 or so years that gay and lesbian people have been identified as separate subpopulations within the dominant culture and therefore have been subject to the development of the larger society's prejudicial and discriminatory attitudes. Even today, there are widely varying opinions about homosexuality both within this country and in other countries. For a deeper perspective on society's attitudes toward homosexuality, see two other excellent books by Neil Miller entitled *Out in the World: Gay and Lesbian Life from Buenos Aires to Bangkok* and his significant *In Search of Gay America*, an American Library Association prizewinner and Lambda Literary Award winner.

All of this suggests ultimately that there are no cultural absolutes. Just because the regional/geographical or chronological attitudes are gay and lesbian intolerant, it does not mean that these attitudes are correct and should be readily accepted by you without careful reflection and assessment. Luckily, you are not a sponge that soaks up the liquid around it without a filter. You have the ability to evaluate the values that the culture around you puts forth as absolutes and apply the same objective reasoning process that you are beginning to learn from this book. You can assess whether specific cultural prohibitions or negative attitudes are healthy, helpful, or beneficial and rationally make your own decision about their value to you.

Certainly this is not to say that cultural norms are never helpful. There are standards of behavior that are rational, healthy, and beneficial for the greater good. Some examples of these include sanctions against murder, rape, and other behaviors that directly or indirectly harm others. But it takes some extensive twisting of logic and history by people in positions of authority to justify the persecution of two consenting adults who wish to enter into an affectionate, mutually satisfying, integrity-filled relationship! Such arguments often include vague warnings of "the decay of the moral fiber of America" if homosexual relationships are accepted and honored and are usually fear and ignorance based rather than based on facts. Let's look at a few examples of the types of attitudes and beliefs Americans have held about homosexuals and homosexual behavior in recent times and the messages these attitudes and beliefs send.

Since the concept of homosexual identity did not begin to form until the mid–nineteenth century, specific sexual behaviors were more likely to be judged as wrong rather than the people themselves being deemed entirely evil. Before that time, there was no concept that an individual's sexual behavior determined who the entire person was. Societal standards for what was considered appropriate and inappropriate changed with the times.

With greater industrialization, and subsequent economic independence, people were freer to move away from the traditional family setting and into urban areas with larger populations. People with attractions to the same sex would eventually find one another and establish their own social networks and customs. But with the self-identification of men and women as homosexual came the greater society's reaction to a fledgling and minority community.

Nineteenth-century society attempted to understand the phenomenon of two people who chose to reject traditional roles assigned to them and live according to their own standards. By rejecting traditional roles of husband and wife, several problems were created. First, the society as a whole may have felt frightened by people who would not conform, and therefore attempted to pathologize or demonize this behavior. Second, once lesbians and gay men rejected the norms for behavior, with no prior role models, they themselves had to determine what they felt were appropriate forms of behavior.

Early attempts to explain why people were homosexual included the concept that since the "correct" way to relate sexually for males was to females and females to males, then people who related sexually to other people of the same sex must be a separate, or third, sex.

Heterosexism and Heterocentrism

Society indirectly communicates negative messages to you about your worth through heterosexism or heterocentrism. These two terms are similar but have subtle distinctions. *Heterosexism* refers to the economic exploitation and social domination of homosexuals by heterosexuals. For example, there are groups of people who assume that gay or lesbian employees do not deserve domestic partner benefits because in their view we cannot marry, do not maintain long-term relationships, or are simply not deserving of what they feel are special privileges. Certainly heterosexists can and often do base their voting decisions and beliefs on their "heterosexual is superior" attitude.

The term *heterocentrism* is based on the term *egocentrism*, which refers to the world view that everything in a person's life should and does revolve around that person. Egocentrists tend to focus on their own needs before they focus on the needs of others. At times, they may not even acknowledge the needs of others or understand that by focusing only on themselves, they deprive or harm others. *Heterocentrism* therefore refers to the view that heterosexuality is all that exists. People who think from a heterocentrist perspective assume that single men they meet must be looking for a woman to date or that two middle-aged women who live together must be "very good friends" or "old maids" just waiting for the right man. Heterocentrists may not intend to be harmful, they just cannot see beyond their own values and experiences. Heterocentrists may be equally as discriminatory as heterosexists in the lack of recognition and acknowledgment of the needs of the lesbian or gay community, but likely it is out of self-absorption rather than an overt need to dominate.

Javier's family had always voiced support for him as he was coming out and assured him that his sexual orientation had no effect on their love for him. He felt accepted at family gatherings and was always included in important family discussions. When he compared himself to his gay friends who had not been so lucky and had been rejected or abused by their families because of their sexuality, he felt he should consider himself lucky.

So, it came as a surprise to Javier when his partner of six years, Rusty, expressed to him that he felt as though he was an outsider at Javier's family gatherings, never becoming more to them than "Javi's friend." Javier began to realize that, although they were always nice to Rusty, his family had often extended invitations to family events to him that did not include Rusty. He remembered that his sister's husband was instantly considered a part of the family after they married four years ago and that most family discussions always included his brother-in-law.

As he paid more attention to the differences in how his family responded to him as a part of a couple and how they responded to his sister and her husband, he could clearly see the subtle signs of heterocentrism, without an obvious intent to harm.

The messages of these attitudes, both formal and informal, are clear: "Homosexuals are inferior to heterosexuals and thereby deserve less privilege." Sometimes the message is stronger: "Homosexuals deserve to be jailed, abused, or killed." Many people receive complicated messages like, "If you act like a heterosexual and never speak of your true nature, then you can have some of the privileges of society." Lesbians may receive these messages about homosexuality in addition to negative societal messages toward women such as, "Women are inferior to men" or "Powerful women are freaks." People of color have a whole other contingent of negative societal messages. Lesbians of color have been referred to as having "a triple strike" against them in this culture for their sex, their race, and their sexuality.

Sexual Stereotypes: Male and Female Characteristics

One of the most pervasive stereotypes about gay men and lesbians is that gay men are effeminate and lesbians are masculine. Some theories have suggested similarities in brain tissues, hormones, or other brain chemistry between gay men and straight women and lesbians and straight men. Early reasoning assumed that males who were attracted to males must actually have female characteristics. Since physically they still looked like "regular" males, then they must be internally (or psychologically) more like females. The argument is reversed for lesbians (i.e., they must be internally more like men). In fact, an early term for lesbians and gay men was *inverts*, a shortened form of the term, *inversion*. This early logic has continued in some form even until today, despite scientific advances in the study of homosexuality and sex role development. It would not be unexpected for gay people themselves to buy into this explanation and understanding of themselves and having done so, begin to adopt other features of the sex role to which they have now been assigned. If you accept, for example, that you, as a biological male, are in fact internally like a female, then you may readily accept (and even cultivate) other traditionally feminine characteristics. You might adopt stereotypical behaviors of the opposite sex for many reasons, but it may simply be to reduce conflicting self-expectations that produce anxiety. For a woman who loves women, the only largely available role model for loving women is men. The women might therefore feel as though she must act like a man if she loves women.

Another theory is that if people who are attracted to the same sex reject the larger society's view of what constitutes normal sexuality, then they may also feel more free to reject other social roles that do not fit. This leaves them more free to express characteristics that fall outside of the acceptable norm. For example, women may choose to be more athletic, assertive, or independent, all of which are stereotypically assumed to be masculine characteristics, and men may choose to express characteristics such as nurturance and emotional expression, which are stereotypically seen as feminine.

The stereotype that gay men are effeminate and lesbians are masculine is so commonplace that this view of homosexuals is often the first information that children get about same-sex attraction. Whether or not your parents held this view, many adult gay and lesbian people were exposed to this idea as they were growing up through the larger culture (movies, TV, books, and so on).

One of the earliest gay male icons, Oscar Wilde, became a household name following a long and scandalous trial during which his private life was held up for public scrutiny in the 1890s. Many of Wilde's personal attributes—wit, flamboyance, and hedonism—were quickly assumed to be characteristic of all men with homosexual inclinations, leading to further embellishment of the stereotype. It was commonplace after this trial for men suspected of being gay to be referred to as "the Oscar Wilde sort," as in the E. M. Forster novel, *Maurice*. A similar figure for lesbians in twentieth-century history is Radclyffe Hall, author of the influential lesbian novel, *The Well of Loneliness*, who faced a similar courtroom scandal in 1920 with major media coverage. Hall's novel became widely distributed (sometimes through the lesbian underground) and her conceptualization of the lesbian characters as "femme" and "butch" likely influenced later social views of lesbian roles.

The messages that a large segment of our society continues to send to children include "gay men are effeminate sissies" and "lesbians are masculine." Not only does straight society send this message, but the gay and lesbian community often perpetuates these myths unknowingly.

We now realize that gay men and lesbians manifest the same range of masculine and feminine characteristics as the heterosexual community. Some theories suggest that the dichotomy between heterosexuality and homosexuality is an artificial one, with human sexual variations falling on a continuum between the two extremes (Kinsey 1948; 1953). Several theorists have suggested that most people are in fact bisexual (or capable of attraction to both sexes), with very few people attracted exclusively to the opposite or same sex. Exclusive heterosexuality might for example suggest that an exclusively heterosexual woman could not judge the attractiveness of another woman because she did not feel a desire to have sexual relations with her. Many "heterosexual" males claim to be unable to determine whether another male is handsome or not, yet through social science research, we find that most males and females rate an attractive male higher than an unattractive male on scales of personal attributes such as strength, intelligence, and friendliness. Human sexuality is complex, involving both behavior and attraction, the former of which can be altered and the latter of which can not be altered.

In reality, all minority groups defy the general stereotypes associated with them. While some members of the group may indeed seem like the view held by the larger culture, there will very likely be those whose belong to the group that do not fit the stereotype. There are indeed effeminate gay men and butch lesbians, but I also know gay men and lesbians who would not fit that description.

Other prominent stereotypes for gay men include being unathletic, weaker than straight men, passive, dependent, sensitive, into the arts, "bitchy," and fastidious. For lesbians, often-repeated stereotypes include being "butch," loud, aggressive, insensitive, nonmaternal, athletic, clumsy, and co-dependent. Many other stereotypes exist both outside and within the gay community. Many comedians use community-based stereotypes as a basis for humor. Of course, even the humor itself can be harmful if it clearly perpetuates attitudes that may lead to harmful behavior. Gay and lesbian comedians may be able to get away with this type of humor because ultimately the humor mocks the stereotyping, rather than using the humor to mock the individuals themselves.

Socioeconomic Messages

Your socioeconomic status while growing up (and as an adult) can have a significant effect on your self-esteem. While it is beyond the scope of this book to discuss the many ways that low socioeconomic status can affect a child's development, it is certainly a powerful influence on physical, emotional, and cognitive growth. Clearly, our culture maintains many negative stereotypes about the poor, stigmatizing this group as "lazy," "stupid," or of "low character." Unfortunately, it often seems that the poor in the United States are used as pawns in the political struggle between political groups. Describing with contempt the "welfare mother" and the "liberal agenda" to develop large programs for the "unmotivated lower class" are subtle and not-so-subtle themes discussed by middle-class and wealthy voters. Contempt for the poor is encouraged by arguments that maintain that most poor people are intentionally "bilking the system." The messages that filter through are meant to shame and vilify: "You are poor because you are lazy" and "You cannot escape because you are worthless." If you are gay and poor, you are doubly stigmatized.

Purveyors of Society's Messages

How do you learn the messages from society? You learn about them from many sources but some major ones include the media and the government. Two other obvious and primary sources include religious institutions and schools, both of which teach you directly about appropriate ways to believe, think, and act from their own perspectives. These last two sources of information are important since they often serve to reinforce the attitudes of parents and family, be it positive or negative, toward you and your self-concept. This will be discussed in chapters 4 and 5.

The Media

One of the most powerful ways you learn about social expectations is through the images and messages of the media—books, movies, magazines, newspapers, and television. Many people believe that these forms of communication are actually reflections of what is happening in the society as a whole. Others point out, however, that the effect may be bi-directional: what the media says may in turn have an effect on society. Nowhere is this debate more clear than in the debates about the effect of TV sex and violence on children, the rating of movies and now television shows, and more crudely, the banning of books or boycotting of films.

How gay or lesbian characters are portrayed in literature and film may have the effect of establishing, perpetuating, or contradicting social stereotypes. We also know that while the media is to a degree reflective of our larger culture, the content of the images is subject to the control of publishers, studios, the large corporations who own the studios, government regulators and pressure from special interest groups of all types. For example, the portrayal of homosexual characters in the movies in a negative way is largely ignored by anti-gay religious groups. It is okay in their opinion for the gay character to fit unflattering stereotypes or to be portrayed as the bad guy or to ultimately suffer and die. However, when a gay or lesbian character is portrayed in a healthy, positive light, these same forces mobilize to protest, boycott, and condemn the movie's makers and sponsors. It is not the portrayal of a homosexual character that is condemned, it only becomes a problem when the characters are portrayed in ways that are contradictory to a certain group's own purposes or values. Vito Russo (1987) provides a wonderful and detailed history of homosexuality in the movies in his book *The Celluloid Closet* (as well as in the film inspired by the book).

Think about the portrayal of lesbian or gay characters in the literature or media of your childhood and adolescence. Do you remember any positive portrayals of gays or lesbians? If the character was not evil, was she or he stereotypically flamboyant or butch in an exaggerated way for humor? Did the character ultimately change his or her sexual orientation (that is, "choose" to be heterosexual), go to prison, or die? Obviously, there were and are subtle messages about being gay or lesbian that you learned from these portrayals. Even the absence of positive portrayals of gay characters subtly communicates that healthy gay people don't exist in our culture.

Steps have been taken in recent years in an attempt to remedy the inaccurate messages from the past in literature and the media. Movies are beginning to allow gay and lesbian characters to live, to be "normal," and even to reflect higher values of integrity, loyalty, and honor. Television took a big step in 1997 by allowing lesbian comedian Ellen DeGeneres to continue with her hit sit-com, even after she publicly acknowledged her sexual orientation. For the first time in history, the main character of a TV series was an out lesbian. DeGeneres has taken her place in history as she attempted to move public opinion by portraying the "real life" experiences, feelings, and dreams of hundreds of thousands, if not millions, of gay and lesbian people in this country. I was especially impressed with her attempts to avoid using old gay male and lesbian stereotypes for humor.

A special organization in the gay and lesbian community has been developed recently to monitor the portrayal of lesbians and gays in the media: Gays and Lesbians Against Anti-Gay Defamation (GLAAD). One of this group's main goals is to attempt to exert some pressure on writers and the show business industry to portray our community more accurately and sensitively, rather than resorting to inaccurate stereotypes.

Even how stories about gays are shaped in the evening news serves to perpetuate or disconfirm gay stereotypes. Ethical journalists attempt to present a story in a balanced manner. This means that if conflict exists about an issue, both sides should be allowed to represent their opinion so that viewers can make their own decisions. However, some people suggest that ethics in journalism is waning with the rise of entertainment-owned networks focused on ratings and advertising dollars. This translates into the "trash talk show" version of news stories where the most extreme sides of an issue are invited to participate in the debate with the hope of overt conflict and increased viewers. Many times, I've watched what appeared to be a serious, issue-oriented news story about gay legal rights take a dive when the journalist interviews a radical right-winger espousing a distorted and irrational perspective that is shared by only a tiny fundamentalist organization. To say that this is a balanced perspective is a serious underestimation of the intelligence of the viewer and removes the debate from the rational, fact-based arena. By granting "moral" extremists the opposing perspective in an issue-oriented debate, the media in fact legitimizes at some level the extremists non-mainstream and often emotion-based propaganda. For a more in-depth discussion of the influence of dualism in the American culture, see Deborah Tannen's 1998 book, *The Argument Culture.*

The Government and Politicians

Our country's government is largely shaped by our culture's moral values, which are in turn shaped by predominant religious institutions in the country. The government in itself can be a cause of discrimination and distress in the way that it encourages or discourages intolerance or acceptance of its people. The government, which for these purposes includes all levels—local, state, and federal—both directly and indirectly shapes public attitudes through the laws that it makes and enforces. As the keeper of legal authority, the government has the power to define as criminals those the church defines as immoral. Although sexuality between consenting adults would not technically constitute a crime (that is, no one is harmed by injury, theft, or death), most states in the early part of this century made certain sexual acts—homosexual and heterosexual—a crime. You're certainly aware of the direct penalties suffered by those convicted of a crime. Yet even people who are known to have "broken the law" but are not arrested or convicted are stigmatized by the culture at large. The threat of being arrested in itself has been used throughout the years to control gay men and lesbians through intimidation.

Sometimes, the laws do not threaten to punish us directly, but simply do not allow us to fully participate in the cultural traditions that the heterosexual majority enjoys. We are not allowed to marry, but are looked down upon for "promiscuous" sex or sex outside of marriage. We also cannot file our taxes jointly with our partners and enjoy the tax benefits afforded to a married couple. When our sexuality is made known at our jobs, we can be fired and the employer suffers little penalty. When we want to join the country club, move into an exclusive apartment building, or join the military, we can be turned away. When we want to visit our partners in the hospital or adopt a child, we must rely on the kindness of strangers rather than the protection of our Constitution.

When you were a child, these direct and indirect messages contributed to your negative self-perceptions. Children reason that if the government does not protect them from ignorance and intolerance, then surely they are worth nothing. As an adult who is continually bombarded with these messages in your own life and in the news, you may find it hard to maintain the sense of well-being you are entitled to and the motivation to keep working for change. The messages from the government sound like this: "You are second class," "You are not worthy of the rights granted all other Americans," and "You are part of a gullible voting block to be courted and then discarded."

Theoretically, our government is meant to serve the needs of the people of this country. However, the good of the people generally seems to take a backseat to the needs of the political process and the politicians themselves. Lesbians and gays are often a convenient subgroup within this country for attacking, scapegoating, and fundraising. It's not unusual for politicians to blame minority groups for economic problems and/or moral decay. Over the years these scapegoat groups have included people of color, non-Christians, the poor, and immigrants.

Recently, it has become unacceptable to directly attack many minority groups for the sake of getting votes, especially on the basis of race or religion. Much of this may be due to the rising political clout these groups have enjoyed as they have organized politically themselves. Gays and lesbians, however, remain a convenient target for doom-crying politicians (and some religious leaders) since we've only begun the process of organizing our political muscle.

Evaluate the Messages

It's important for you to recognize that the larger society sends messages just as your family of origin did. Although our culture seems to be slowly moving away from condemnation of lesbians and gays, negative messages still exist. In order to effectively protect your self, you must become more aware of these negatives messages and evaluate them as you evaluated the negative family messages you may still carry with you. These messages can be disputed, challenged, and changed. Keep in mind that society's views are not absolutes but change over time. When the larger culture appears to reject you or condemn you, remember that it is their values and beliefs that are the problem, not you!

Questions for Reflection

- What were the social values concerning homosexuality where you were raised? Was it accepted and tolerated? Were lesbians or gay men mocked, repudiated, or condemned?

- What was the first book, TV show, or movie you remember that mentioned lesbians or gay men? What was the tone of the book, show, or movie? Was the gay or lesbian character portrayed as a positive figure or role model? Did the character suffer or die? Were the characters stereotypical? What were those stereotypes for lesbians? For gay men?

- What have been your personal experiences with discrimination or harassment for being gay or lesbian? A woman? A person of color? Do you know anyone personally who has been the victim of discrimination, heterocentrism, or heterosexism? How did these experiences affect your self-concept and behaviors?

- In what ways have you internalized the homophobia of the culture in which you live? How do you perpetuate society's negative stereotypes within yourself? Toward others?

- How does it make you feel to hear an anti-gay politician use lesbian and gay rights as a way to mobilize voters? Refer to basic civil rights as "special rights"? Do you hold onto these feelings or can you let go of them quickly and easily?

- When something goes wrong, to whom or what do you tend to attribute the blame? Are you an internalizer (you blame yourself) or externalizer (you blame others)? How does this affect your self-esteem?

4

Messages of Faith: Religious Authorities

What is morality in any given time or place? It is what the majority then and there happen to like, and immorality is what they dislike.

—Alfred North Whitehead

Religion plays an important role in the moral development of both the individual and the larger culture. Even if you were not raised by a "religious" family, you still were affected by those around you who subscribed to religious values and teachings. While the framers of the Constitution were explicit in the separation of church and state, the United States' legal system nonetheless is highly influenced by larger cultural and religious attitudes. In fact, the entire U.S. society is heavily influenced by the Judeo-Christian values of its founders.

Certainly the culture itself is a product of both direct and indirect influence by religious ideology. Our country in fact was borne out of reaction to religious intolerance in Europe and the desire for freedom from religious and governmental oppression. In some current world cultures, the government itself is headed by spiritual/religious leaders. Even today in the United States, religious organizations and figures have had more or less direct influence on our government's policies and laws.

While many religious organizations themselves function to maintain some social controls, governmental laws are made also in an attempt to control the larger society. The larger and more diverse our society becomes, it would appear the more laws we need. Laws are meant to protect us and to preserve order. Some laws are fairly universally accepted such as prohibitions against murder or harming someone else through physical threat or theft. How far to go with legislation is often unclear and hotly debated, however. A lot of people believe that while some behaviors do not directly harm another individual, they have the potential to cause harm through gradual social decay ("If you give them an inch, they'll take a mile" or "We'll be going down the slippery slope . . ."). These thinkers would prohibit certain behaviors that while not harmful now, appear to them to lead to greater problems with social control later on.

Morality

It is important to keep in mind that, although religion heavily influences our culture's moral debate, morality in itself is something quite different. According to psychologist Betty Berzon (1996), in our culture, there are two interpretations of what morality is: one based on intrinsic, personal experience and one based on religious dogma. The ability to know right from wrong and to behave in a way that is consistent with what you know to be right (particularly with regards to how you treat others) is consistent with the first type of morality. Conforming to what a particular religion says is the right way to act and live without question is often mistaken for morality. People who believe in this interpretation are considered immoral if they do not conform and moral if they do conform to the religious teachings.

Many people believe that morality is determinable and is the same for everyone. Certain laws that exist today attempt to legislate moral issues that ultimately may not have a clear "right" or "wrong" position. Unfortunately, determining these absolutes has not been easy. Abortion laws, for example, attempt to set a specific moment at which life occurs, which is a point that has many different perspectives associated with it. Moral values can be relatively dynamic. Even the mainstream religions that have existed for thousands of years have seen changes in policies and teachings. Yet fundamentalists of almost every religion believe that absolute morality exists.

Christian fundamentalists propose that we take the Bible, the "word of God," literally for our legal and moral guidelines. This position is flawed for several reasons, however. For example, not every situation that needs guidance is addressed in the Bible, leaving modern "interpreters" (that is, preachers) to extrapolate God's intent from the words. Now we not only have introduced a fallible human element to the Biblical "absolutes," but we have to consider which translation of the Bible that the interpreter might be working from, which in itself might be a flawed interpretation.

There are also contradictions within the Bible itself that cannot be explained if you take a literal approach to the interpretation as is beautifully explained in the book *Rescuing the Bible from Fundamentalism* by Episcopal bishop John Shelby Spong. Even literalists are making interpretations, since language itself is often imprecise and single words can have multiple meanings.

What seems clear is that while there are certain moral values that are more or less universally accepted by the world's major religions, there are many issues upon which they do not agree and in fact may have completely opposite teachings. It appears that many of these "lesser" values, such as those dealings with appropriate styles of dress or ways to prepare food, are incorporated for culture-specific reasons at the time of the founding of the religion. This makes them appropriate at that time and place, but perhaps less appropriate in a modern world or a with a different culture. Many experts feel that even if you take a literalist's interpretation of, for example, the Biblical passages typically used to justify anti-gay rhetoric (e.g., Leviticus 18:22—"You shall not lie with a man as one lies with a woman"), you must realize these passages had specific cultural relevance for the times in which the passages were written and have little to no relevancy now. Others argue that since the concept of homosexuality as we know it did not even exist then, those same passages are best interpreted as metaphors for deeper messages and values, such as respecting the rights and dignity of others, honoring a commitment to a spouse, and being truthful.

Many religious organizations have adopted a position that other world religions, or even different sects within the same religion, are incorrect or "evil." This type of attitude (that other belief systems are wrong) serves not only to reinforce their own beliefs as the "correct" views, but also serves many times to coerce followers to accept all or none of the beliefs and thereby commit their spiritual and financial resources to one organization.

Religious Systems

Religious organizations can function very much like other systems we have discussed, such as families or the government. Just like families, they can exhibit varying degrees of dysfunction. Communication within the system can be direct or indirect. The religious organization itself usually has a structure and often this structure is hierarchically organized with one ultimate human authority figure (such as the Pope for Catholics) or governing body and then successive levels of authority down to the local congregation leader. Each level of organization has its own designated leader or leader committee. Even the lowest or local level of organization (for example, church, synagogue, mosque, and so on) functions as a system. Just like city governments must cooperate with county, state, and federal levels of authority, so do most local religious institutions.

Also, just like family systems, these successive systems may be organized in a relatively authoritarian, authoritative, or permissive way. Ultimate authority over questions of morality are relegated to the holy texts in some organizations (as interpreted by the local leaders). Sometimes, the final judgment about moral questions rests with the titular head of the religious organization or sometimes with the local leader him- or herself. As with the parenting styles, some religious organizational styles are more associated with investing the individual with feelings of autonomy and self-worth than others. These styles promote messages like, "You are born good and loved by God (or the Universe, etc.)." However, an authoritarian organization may, for example, diminish the value of a person in this "earthly form" so as to promote the focus on the next life (the "otherworldly" form). These teachings may in fact encourage the acceptance of suffering and the basic premise that all human beings are born evil with "original sin," and only through practicing certain religious tenets can they hope to find peace. Redemption from evil is always precarious and may be lost at any particular time should thoughts, feelings, or behaviors become less than holy. The self-messages this type of religious organization promotes may include thoughts like, "I am unworthy of respect or love without penance or suffering" or "If I can only reach perfection, then I may become worthy of peace and forgiveness." Authoritarian religions often use psychological, if not overtly physical, threats to keep followers under control, much in the way authoritarian parents try to control their children. Interestingly, it appears that people who tend to be more rigid or authoritarian personally, choose religious organizations that reflect their own personalities.

Mark's family of origin belonged to a fundamentalist church that taught that all thoughts, feelings, and behaviors were reflective of one's degree of moral purity. Thinking anything deemed impure was the same as acting on it and must therefore be confessed and punished. Mark's feelings of attraction to other males began at a very early age, but he knew without ever having had a conversation with anyone about these feelings that they were unacceptable to his church and his family. He tried to deal with these feelings the best way that he could by developing a secret self that he was ashamed of, that he could try to either eliminate or control. His attempts to eliminate his secret self included prayers to God to "take it away" and to make him "normal," sometimes viciously condemning himself whenever he had feelings of attraction to another male. Eventually, Mark realized he could not control his feelings and after much mental preparation, spoke to his minister. Almost immediately, Mark's fears were confirmed. His minister told him that these feelings were in fact evil and that Mark could only be saved from hell through intense spiritual cleansing. Mark's family was immediately notified about Mark's conversation, and Mark spent many months being watched and prayed over. He was sent to a counselor within the religious system's control who tried even more intense and painful forms of conditioning and behavior modification.

For a while, Mark believed that he had successfully eliminated these attractions to men, and was convinced that he could establish a successful relationship with a woman. Eventually, though, the old feelings returned despite his earnest religious practices and sincere desire to change. This time, he chose to seek help outside of his religious institution. He read a number of books and articles and after a thorough search, he found a psychotherapist who helped him learn to accept himself as he was and realize that he could live a happy and satisfied life as a gay man. Mark continues to work on reducing and eliminating the strong negative messages he received from his church and his family and feels much more hopeful about himself and his life.

Some religious organizations are less hostile to lesbians and gays, and less rigid overall, than Mark's religion. Some are more like the authoritative forms of parenting, with firm rules but an overall respect for the follower's dignity and inherent worth. A few may be more like the permissive parents, focused on validating the individual's belief system or understanding of how the world is organized, rather than supporting the overall organization's doctrine.

Many lesbians and gays have felt that they needed to leave the religious organization of their upbringing for many of the same reasons they have left their families—to find complete acceptance as individuals and to diminish the constant barrage of negative messages. Some choose to avoid religion altogether and have many unpleasant memories about the rejection or degradation they felt at the hands of religious organizations in their early lives. Others find more contentment with religions that are either more accepting of gays and lesbians in general or are at least less overtly condemning. A few continue to try to find ways to work within the religion of their upbringing because they have positive memories of their religious experiences. They find specific local congregations that are more tolerant, continue living with a secret self, or work within the organization for change.

Faith and Acceptance

Both the beauty and the irony of a religious belief system is that you accept things based on faith, not logic. If something doesn't make sense, and you question it, you may be told, "Just believe." When believers are taught something that intuitively or logically doesn't make sense and they begin to ask questions, they are often met with reactions suggesting that they need to comply and accept the messages anyway. Not only might there be no attempt made to answer the question itself, but even the process of questioning is discouraged. Depending on how threatening the questions are, the response from religious leaders can vary from loving words meant to encourage unquestioning faith to threats of expulsion from the organization or even threats of spiritual condemnation. You may be encouraged to accept absolute definitions of morality unquestioningly.

Religious Indoctrination

Many religious institutions have ways of educating children about the larger values of the organization. In Christian churches, education begins in Sunday school, where children learn about what the beliefs and values of the larger organization are. They often use stories based on Bible passages that have been interpreted through the lens of Christian educators, usually at a central location within the larger institution. The stories can range from happy, cartoonlike representations of a loving, accepting God to a raging and judgmental God who sends "bad" children to eternal torment (hell).

If you were raised to be religious, your view of God and yourself may be shaped by these early lessons, with reinforcement from parents, and sometimes school (particularly if you attended a private, religious school). If all of these sources of information were strongly anti-gay, then you likely continue to perpetuate strong anti-gay messages within yourself.

Kathy was raised by religious parents who attended services regularly, at least several times per week. She also was sent to a private school associated with the church that included the teachings of her parent's church in the daily activities. Because Kathy's worldview did not extend much beyond those of her parents and her church, she developed core beliefs about herself that reflected what she had been taught about lesbians and gays. Because she had only heard strongly anti-gay information all of her life, Kathy felt a deep sense of shame and guilt about her attraction toward other women. The anti-gay rhetoric all around her led her to develop strong messages about her own self-worth and value. Because she had never been exposed to other ideas and ways of thinking about things, it was initially much more difficult for Kathy to change the negative self-talk about her sexuality. However, with much practice and support, eventually she was able to find new, more positive ways of seeing herself and her sexuality.

Religious Harm

There are many ways that a religion can be directly and indirectly harmful to gays and lesbians, both as growing children and active adults. The public positions that religious organizations hold about our sexuality can themselves be harmful. While the Pope may be a good and moral man in his own frame of reference, his position that gays and lesbians are morally corrupt is in reality harmful to lesbians and gays. When he teaches that homosexuality is a moral "choice" that is wrong, he in many ways gives license to people who look for justification to act out their own frustrations by harming lesbians and gays all over the world. This harm may certainly be through direct and violent means, but extends more covertly into their homophobic attitudes. At some level, people who are homophobic or heterocentrist can feel validated in their views by their religious institution when they hear religious anti-gay rhetoric. Even though he may try to counteract behaviors such as discrimination, stigmatizing and physical harm by teaching his followers to "love the sinner and hate the sin," the Pope's practice of describing homosexuality as a "moral choice" ignores many other forms of information that suggest otherwise. Homosexuality is not a choice, but self-acceptance is.

Sometimes the negative messages you heard as a child are indirectly related to negative feelings about being attracted to someone of the same sex. For example, some institutions teach that sexuality in general is bad, except as a means for procreation. The specific messages behind this follow the reasoning that sexual activity of any kind, even between a man and a woman who are married to each other, is sinful unless the sole purpose is to create a pregnancy. Thus, according to these institutions, sex using birth control, sex to express emotional intimacy alone, or sexual practices that could never lead to pregnancy, such as masturbation and oral or anal sex, are all wrong and should never be practiced. It logically follows from this stance that since homosexual sex cannot lead to pregnancy, it must also be wrong. You did not have to hear the words "Gay and lesbian sex is wrong" to glean from this message that you would be a sinner if you engaged in sex for enjoyment's sake.

Often the messages children hear within anti-gay religious institutions are more direct about the prohibition of homosexual sex as well as homosexuals themselves. Some institutions teach directly that homosexual sexual activity, as well as homosexual thoughts or feelings, are forbidden and lead to condemnation. Some adult gay men and lesbians who were raised in this type of environment can recall the specific language that was used to chastise them and may incorporate this language into the messages they replay to themselves as adults. Extreme and repeated forms of condemnation such as "You are unworthy of social acceptance" easily become part of the core belief system in a child with a developing self-identity. Challenging these messages will become a part of your strategy to increase your self-esteem as you work through this book.

Many religious institutions tend to ignore scientific research if it threatens to undermine established traditions within the organization. In some cases, giving up control to science threatens to demystify the beliefs that served to enhance the religion's power in the society. If all traditional beliefs were debunked, many people would lose faith and stop supporting the religious institution, and, from the perspective of the religious institutions, chaos in society would erupt. It's impossible to ignore the fear that religious leaders must feel when they realize that a long-cherished ritual is challenged—their very professional existence is threatened. But they also must be seen for who they are—upholders of tradition, teachers of belief, and encouragers of faith, as well as humans who have their own needs, internal conflicts, and feelings.

Religions change over time, slowly and subtly. Yet many religions are not ready for confident, healthy lesbians and gays. We must push them to accept us as we are by first accepting ourselves as inherently valid and worthy of respect.

Spirituality versus Religion

Religion is different from spirituality. Religion usually has some central organization and is generally more formal than spirituality, with rules, doctrine, and guidelines that function to maintain social control. Spirituality on the other hand is much more personal. It is the idiosyncratic way that you answer the larger questions of life—for example, "Why am I here?" "What is the meaning of life?" "What is my purpose?" "Where is my place in the universe?" Sometimes people are chronically unhappy, anxious, or unfulfilled when they cannot understand the answers to these types of existential questions. Organized religions attempt to answer these questions for the individual. For example, reincarnation is a concept that helps explain why we may have tragedy or success in our lives today. It suggests that these events are linked to a larger purposeful progression through many lives that increase our experience and understanding of the world and lead to our ultimate enlightenment.

Often, however, a gay person's experience is different from what he or she is told by a religious institution. For example, while some anti-gay religions clearly condemn same-sex relationships as *choices* that are sinful, many lesbians and gays do not ever remember choosing to make themselves attracted to certain individuals (as if this was possible for heterosexuals or homosexuals). This difference between an individual's experience and what the doctrine of the religion says you should feel often blunts or confuses the individual's experience of spirituality.

The underlying philosophical systems within a particular religion may vary from a more positively focused, nurturing or soothing emphasis to a more negative, fear-based emphasis. For example, some religious institutions attempt to limit themselves to a creation-centered spirituality, focusing on the life-affirming side of religion (the basic idea that all humans are valued unconditionally by the universe or a God-figure) while others are centered around the fear-of-God theme (the idea that if you don't follow the rules, you will suffer). In addition to the basic philosophical differences, some fear-based religions attempt to answer all questions in a polarized way, that is, that there are only two ways of thinking about the world— "good and evil" or "right or wrong." This type of thinking can be effective by reducing anxiety when questions appear to have simple answers. Yet when complex questions, with no obvious right or wrong answers, need equally complex answers, dichotomous thinking can actually increase anxiety.

Religions that are based on dichotomous concepts tend to rely upon the conditional love of a higher power. If you don't accept all conditions totally, then you will be rejected and condemned. Some religions attempt to label morally acceptable behaviors without condemning the individual, although it is inherently impossible to say that you love a person unconditionally, if you don't accept certain thoughts, feelings, or behaviors. People who subscribe to this "love the sinner and hate the sin" idea may be attempting to resolve conflicts between their personal experiences and their rigid belief system. They may also be looking to justify personal self-righteousness. Stepping outside of a religious belief system by loving someone who does not follow all the rules threatens to undermine a religious person's own belief systems in general. Because people are attracted to a particular religion with a particular style of thinking that they are comfortable or familiar with, threats to that system may represent a personal threat to that individual.

While a religion itself may not promote anti-gay beliefs, it is likely that followers who have these values may inappropriately (and illogically) rationalize that their beliefs are correct, through their distorted interpretation of their religion's actual teachings. Often they feel more empowered in their hostility and judgments if they believe that there is a holy precedent or justification for their personal feelings of fear, disgust, or self-righteousness. It may be difficult to feel compassion for people who use their religion in this way to lash out at others. However, in many cases these angry people may be completely unaware that they are perpetuating intolerance, because they are following the models that were available to them as they grew up.

How You Can Reap the Benefits of Religion

There are many advantages to formal worship. Weekly meetings serve to strengthen social connections and support within a community, reinforce positive values for the common good, and provide opportunities to perform good works for the community at large. Not all religions, or local congregations within a larger religion, perpetuate negative views of lesbians and gays. Even within larger organizations that have explicitly expressed anti-gay views, you can find individuals and leaders who do not support these views.

Gays and lesbians now have options if they desire to remain affiliated with such institutions and adjust to anti-gay rhetoric. First, you can challenge the interpretation of anti-gay Biblical or other sacred writings based on cultural relevancy theory or on inaccurate linguistic interpretation. In this case, you would either reject the translation as flawed or not applicable to modern times or argue that the original writer was homophobic or otherwise personally deficient. Fundamentalists, of course, would strongly reject both of these challenges as inaccurate since they believe that God wrote the original words (and presumably all subsequent translations of the text) by using a human being as a writing implement. Second, you can accept most tenets of your religion and ignore those that are condemning or rejecting.

Others choose to reject religion altogether. By choosing this method, aside from giving up the potentially positive sides of being a part of a larger social support system, they also tend to ignore the spiritual sides of themselves also. Too often spirituality has been equated with religiosity, and anything that remotely resembles religion has negative associated memories. Particularly if you have been damaged, harmed, or rejected by the people and beliefs of your religious background, the hurt and anger may prevent you from finding inner spiritual peace and self-acceptance.

Many people who have rejected religious teaching incorrectly assume that you must be involved with a formal religious institution in order to develop your spiritual side. Religious institutions do represent a formalized attempt to help the masses cultivate spirituality in most cases. For me, spirituality includes the individual's search for his or her personal answers to questions about existence, God or other Higher Power, or the Universe. How you answer these questions can help you resolve long-standing inaccurate core beliefs. Even if you find no specific answers to the larger questions, attending to the process of asking after years of neglect can be emotionally healing.

Many mainstream religions now have subgroups just for gays and lesbians and their supporters, although these groups may not be officially recognized or sanctioned by the larger organization. For example, the Catholic Church has a group called "Dignity," the Episcopal Church has "Integrity," and the Church of Jesus Christ of Latter Day Saints has groups called "Mormons Concerned." In San Francisco and other progressive urban areas with large gay communities, many other types of religious institutions, such as the synagogue Sha'ar Zahav and the Gay Buddhist's Group, include the needs of gays and lesbians in their meetings and services. All of these groups attempt to resolve the conflict for gays and lesbians within the larger organization by allowing them to participate in their chosen faith in a more directly relevant and consistent way.

Lesbians and gays now have other alternatives as well. In 1967, Rev. Troy Perry founded the Metropolitan Community Church, a Christianity-based church specifically for lesbians and gays. Other smaller religious organizations, like the Unitarian-Universalists and Quakers (Friends), have accepted homosexuals on equal footing with heterosexuals for years.

Note: My discussion of religion tends to center around Judeo-Christian traditions and perspectives since I am influenced by my own experiences with having been raised in a fundamentalist Christian home and community. I believe that the majority of the U.S. culture has also been shaped by this particular form of thought, including our concepts of freedom, self-sufficiency, and struggle. I would highly recommend, however, that for a more well-rounded discussion of other world religions, you read Arlene Swidler's book, *Homosexuality and World Religions*.

Evaluate the Messages

Religion, like family and culture, is a powerful force in shaping the cognitions of many individuals—and our society as a whole. However, even as dogmatic as many religions are, they still rely heavily on interpretations that are open to distortion and irrationality.

As an adult, you have the opportunity to evaluate and challenge the religious messages you received as a child. You can make conscious choices about which messages are useful and which are harmful. If you received messages as a child that being lesbian or gay was unacceptable or lessened your sense of value as a human being, then you must begin to find other alternative messages that contradict these teachings.

If every religion believes that every other religion's followers are incorrect, then it appears that everyone is viewed by someone as incorrect. In other words, ultimately there is no proof that one religion is any more correct than any other religion. When you ask religious people how they know their beliefs are true or correct, they will often say that they "just know" or that they "feel it" or that "the Bible says so." If you therefore cannot determine the superiority of one religion, then either none or all must be true.

People who have learned not to think in a dichotomous way can see other alternatives, specifically that some tenets of each religion may be true, and that for certain people, each may work well as a path to spirituality. However, if a particular religion does not fit you, then you owe it to yourself to search for a path to healthy, human spirituality that does fit you. Find something that is healing rather than harmful. Chapter 12 will help you explore and develop your own spirituality more directly and completely.

Questions for Reflection

- If you were raised in a family that practiced a particular religion, what was that religion's view on homosexuality? Do you remember specific religious teachings that were anti-gay/lesbian? What was the religion's perspective on sex in general?

- How was guilt used as a form of control over you?

- How were you threatened with negative spiritual consequences (e.g., going to hell) for ways of behaving? Thinking? Feeling?

- How were your questions about the religious teachings handled? Was the general process of questioning encouraged or discouraged?

- What was the intensity or firmness of your family's religious belief system?

- What were the role expectations for women, men, and children within the religious teachings? Were you taught that certain people or acts were evil and others good or righteous?

- How did your family tolerate the beliefs of others within other religious systems?

- Was your religious upbringing from a creation-centered perspective or a fear-based (i.e., "hell and damnation") perspective?

- How might the religious views of your parents serve them psychologically? Did they experience reduced anxiety by having clear answers to difficult or complex questions? Was it easier for them to ignore the "gray areas" of life?

- What are the messages from your childhood about religion that surface in your self-talk today?

- How do you practice spirituality today?

5

Schools, Peers, and Other Influences

Stand firm in your refusal to remain conscious during algebra. In real life, I assure you there is no such thing as algebra.

—Fran Lebowitz

In the three previous chapters you explored your early family life, the larger culture, and your religious upbringing to find some of the origins of your self-talk. Yet the sources of self-reflective messages do not end there. Other powerful influences may exist as well that can contribute to both the positive and negative opinions you have about yourself. Two worth mentioning here include the experiences you had as a child in school and the peer groups you've associated with during your life.

School

Education is so valued in the United States that the government requires that all children receive formal schooling from age six until age sixteen. A typical school day lasts about six and one-half hours, and until recently the academic year ran for nine of the twelve months in a year. That means that you probably spent a significant amount of your early life in an academic setting, learning basic math and science, history, the rules of language, and other skills. You are also probably well aware that aside from formal learning in school, you learned some of your most powerful social and psychological lessons in school informally. You learned to interact with peers outside of your family or your religious institution and you may have gotten very different feedback about yourself through these experiences than what you heard about yourself at home.

School may have been the first place where you received formal education on the "rules" of the world such as how to read, write, multiply, and divide, as well as how to control your behavior, work with others, and interact with authority figures. General school experiences can vary widely depending on the setting (private or public), the size (large, medium, or small), the region (rural, suburban, or urban), the affiliations (religious or secular), and the educational philosophy (progressive or conservative). Your individual experiences may also have been shaped by your interactions with individual teachers, whose values and beliefs informed the way that they taught and the forms of communication they used.

The school setting, the teachers, and your peers may have reinforced messages that you learned about yourself at home. This is a good thing if those messages were healthy, but is not so great if the messages were unhealthy. It's possible that school was a source of healthy messages when the ones you received at home were negative. In this case, school might have become an "escape" from turmoil, rejection, neglect, or abuse.

Many lesbian and gay adults who as youths were good at school-related activities found a way to meet some emotional needs for attention, positive strokes, and acceptance through achievement. They may have been recognized by a respected or cherished teacher and given reassurance as to their worth and potential. A healthy, nonjudgmental mentoring relationship with a teacher may actually have ameliorated some of the effects of negative messages from home.

While school successes were healthy and provided needed acceptance and empowering experiences, these same experiences may have created patterns and self-expectations that led to a lack of balance in your current life. You may have certain areas of your life that are satisfying and successful, and perhaps a source of self-esteem, while other areas may be underdeveloped from neglect or fear of negative consequences if those areas were explored. For example, Charlotte came from a quiet, middle-class home that was almost always serene and pleasant. She was the youngest of three children. Her parents were gentle people, but were always somewhat distant and generally avoided displays of affection. They were never abusive or even discouraging to her and in fact they often praised her for her athletic and academic accomplishments. Charlotte, however, often felt a subtle sense of loneliness and was never truly able to discuss with her family her innermost feelings about herself and her budding sexuality. She felt as if other members of her family didn't experience the depth of feelings she had and couldn't understand her desire to talk about these feelings.

At school, Charlotte excelled at all levels—in grades, sports, and social situations. She won many awards and received a lot of school recognition for her gifts and was often allowed special privileges by teachers who encouraged her to strive for her eventual goal of law school. Charlotte felt very comfortable in this academic environment and achieved most of her ultimate professional goal by the time she was thirty years old—a professorship at a prestigious university law school.

Once her life as a student was over, Charlotte started noticing that the old feelings of emptiness and loneliness were resurfacing. She was becoming exhausted from the time she devoted to her career and had nothing in her personal life that was satisfying. She began to realize that perhaps her attention to her academic success, which gave her wonderful feelings of accomplishment throughout the years, had been at the expense of exploring the emotional side of her life. Although she had quite high regard for herself professionally, personally she felt unfulfilled and undeveloped. She had never connected on an intimate level with anyone; she'd only had a few, almost superficial, friendships over the years. While she had recognized an attraction to women, she never acted on these feelings in any way. So at the age of thirty, Charlotte began searching for ways to correct the imbalance, to explore ways to find herself emotionally.

Charlotte never had models of how to deal with emotional or sexual feelings in a healthy way. She would not consider her parents abusive, but they were emotionally distant and were uncomfortable with intimacy. Because she was rewarded for achievement both at home and at school, she took this path all the way to its logical conclusion for her, which included law school and a professorship. This was the only way she could feel accepted and capable. This left her, unfortunately, with mixed feelings of self-esteem. She knew she was intelligent and professionally competent, but she felt emotionally immature.

Most schools are set up to reward academic achievement as their highest value. Occasionally, through interaction with a warm and positive institutional representative such as a teacher, principal, or counselor, a student may learn about his or her worth as a person in addition to his or her value as an academic achiever. But school has the potential to be a powerful agent for building positive self-esteem for lesbian and gay youth by providing accurate portrayals of gays and lesbians in the classroom and in the more general encouragement of respect for alternative ways of thinking, feeling, and believing. While several progressive school systems in this country are beginning to actively encourage programs that foster gay-positive curricula and positive self-esteem skills, most schools don't have such programs.

Many schools, teachers, and counselors remain ignorant or are homophobic, and encourage the same negative and stereotypical views of homosexuality held by the larger society. A school often reflects the values of the larger community, and in many cases parents have chosen where they live based on values in the community similar to their own. In other words, authoritarian, conservative parents often either choose conservative communities to live in with similarly focused public schools or they send their children to private or religious schools that will teach values similar to their own. In recent years, many religious fundamentalist groups have targeted school board elections as a focus of their activities in an attempt to assure that their perspective becomes more pervasive in school systems across the United States—a frightening prospect for the lesbian and gay youth of America.

Like families, our culture, and our religious institutions, schools are subject to the same systemic forces. The types of communication practiced, the value of the individual's needs versus those of the larger group, and respect for authority are all systems and beliefs that can harm or heal. If home life was abusive and degrading, your school life may have provided a haven, with contradictory and positive information about yourself and your worth. On the other hand, home life may have been wonderful and supportive, and your school experiences could have been negative. A learning disability requiring special services, for example, may have made it difficult to feel successful in school and therefore left you with self-messages such as "I'm not smart enough" or "I'm not like everyone else." Negative messages from a teacher ("You're a troublemaker") or rejection by peers ("You're a sissy") can add to the core beliefs you have about yourself just as potently as can the messages you hear at home.

It's worth examining the messages you received from your experiences with school as you examine your automatic thoughts and conditional and core beliefs. The questions at the end of the chapter will help you think about your general experience of school and your feelings about achievement as well as help you remember specific events from school that helped shape your identity as a gay man or lesbian.

Peer Groups

People often identify with a group of peers in order to feel that they fit in. The groups people choose to identify with can be based on any number of factors such as race, gender, socioeconomic status, acceptance or rejection of societal norms, mutual need for protection in a hostile environment, religious upbringing, age, or education. To some degree, your behaviors are shaped by your relative acceptance or rejection by your peer group. Adolescents and young children certainly may succumb to pressure from the group to act in ways that would not necessarily feel satisfying unless they were receiving some type of recognition, praise, or acceptance from their peers. At times, peers can take the place of the family in supplying safety needs and a sense of belonging when family members are overtly or covertly rejecting of a child or adolescent.

Some lesbian and gay youth grow up experiencing the benefits of membership in peer groups such as sports teams, school clubs, neighborhood cliques, and religious youth groups. Most, however, tend to feel only a limited acceptance and may never discuss their sexual identity for fear of expulsion from the group. They continue to hide their secret self and show other qualities that they learn are acceptable. The message they learn is, "You may belong to this group only if you act, or pretend you are, heterosexual." So, while belonging to a group may have some important positive qualities such as allowing for emotional support, social skill development, and increased independence from family values, it also can be a source of negative self-statements and other distorted beliefs.

Some groups are by nature exclusive. Their members tend to view outsiders as inferior and encourage the development of stereotypes, racist or homophobic stances, and other separatist attitudes. In order to avoid rejection from a peer group, children may succumb to overt or covert pressure to behave in ways the group deems acceptable, which in fact may be harmful in the long run. Many urban youths who join gangs for protection and the positive sense of belonging also feel they have no choice but to follow the leaders' direction to fight, use or sell drugs, or otherwise prove their worthiness of the group membership.

David and his mother had moved from a small town in Ohio to Cleveland when he was ten. It had been difficult for David to leave his friends and cousins, and he had a hard time making new friends in the city. His mother worked such long hours that he ended up spending a lot of time alone.

When David entered high school, it was clear that many of the other boys belonged to "clubs," which he soon realized were actually gangs. His mother had warned him about these groups and he generally avoided them, but after he was threatened a few times, he decided that he needed to join one for his own protection. At first, he found it somewhat satisfying to finally feel like he belonged and he did his best to stay out of trouble. It became clear, however, that he was expected to conform to the wishes of the leaders of his group. Although he considered leaving, he was repeatedly told that he could not protect himself if he didn't belong and he understood that if he left, his own group would turn against him. Not only could he not leave, but the leaders instructed him in virtually every detail of his behavior, from the types and colors of clothes he wore to the way he wore his hair. They even told him who he could and could not date.

Although David liked women, he found himself having feelings for other guys, which disturbed him. He was well aware that he couldn't discuss these feelings with anyone in the gang. In fact, "fags" were occasional targets of gang violence "just for fun." What started out as a means of self-protection and belonging had ended up as a trap for David. He found himself doing and saying things that he found unacceptable because of the incredible pressure he felt to conform.

When he turned eighteen, David moved to New York and started a new life for himself. He was able to see a counselor, who helped him deal with his past and learn to be true to himself.

Peer groups may be highly organized and hierarchical, with either clear rules for membership, or rules that may be unspoken but clearly understood by all who belong. Within such a structure, there is always the potential threat of rejection. Being accepted by and remaining a member of the group may be extremely important to someone who has not developed a strong sense of self with positive self-esteem. It may be that people with higher self-esteem, especially those who value their own unique ways of thinking and feeling, can more easily withstand peer pressure to conform. That's why encouraging children to feel good about themselves for standing up to peer pressure is a frequently used theme in anti-drug and anti-smoking campaigns. Having the courage to stand on your own requires both self-confidence and self-esteem, qualities that are often lacking in lesbian and gay children and adolescents.

Lesbian and Gay Peer Groups

Sometimes even gay and lesbian peer groups perpetuate the larger society's stereotypes as well. During the early years of movie making in Hollywood, African-Americans were limited to playing small parts in films—often the role of slave, servant, or other cultural stereotypes. The actors who were fortunate enough to get parts in this white-dominated industry had their own acting organizations that supported and encouraged African-Americans in the film industry. However, when the young and multi-talented Lena Horne began demanding larger roles outside of the traditionally accepted "Negro" domain of roles, she was not only rejected by the white establishment (or relegated to walk-on singing roles only), but she was astonished to find herself rejected by her own peers, African-American actors whose own stereotyped self-images may have been threatened by her success.

Often, individual gays and lesbians are attracted to the larger gay and lesbian community after they come out to themselves or their family members. They may feel a wonderful sense of belonging and acceptance for who they really are, sometimes for the first time in their lives. Due to the lack of obvious role models in our culture (until recently), often the first lesbian or gay group you socialize with becomes an important source of information about what is "socially acceptable" within the community. You may have wanted to fit in with this group almost immediately, or you may have found yourself slowly becoming more like the people with whom you associate. Gay peer groups often become the source for your tastes in clothes, hair, attitudes, and behaviors. Unfortunately, as with other types of peer groups, you may also feel some pressure to conform to the styles and attitudes of the "fashionable" and visible lesbian and gay leaders. This may lead you back to self-disparaging messages when you find that you don't fit the socially acceptable norms. For example, aging for some gay men becomes a source of distress when the group they most closely associate with places a high value on youth and beauty. Because the peers with whom they have associated most frequently sometimes seem as if they are the whole of the community rather than a small segment of it, many men do not realize that there are other aging gay men for whom youth is not an important value.

You may fall victim to your own stereotypes at times. You are a part of the larger American society and thereby are influenced by its general stereotypes of gay people. Some lesbian and gay writers, such as Andrew Sullivan (1995), have discussed the role of the gay community in perpetuating its own stereotypes. For example, many personal ads written by gay males have been criticized for listing such desired qualities for future mates as "straight-acting" or "no fats or fems," suggesting that men who act "gay" or are not "gym-fit" are not desirable. A similar phenomenon was observed in the African-American community by director Spike Lee in his film *School Daze* in which he explores the cultural divide between light-skinned and dark-skinned African-Americans.

The gay community obviously provides a lot of benefits, such as support, education, and general acceptance of sexual orientation to name a few. But, like families and religious institutions, which also have many good features, the gay community with which you interact can also contribute to the reservoir of negative messages you may send to yourself. That's why you also need to examine the messages you give yourself that are based on your relationships with your peers both for accuracy and utility. As with the other influences on self-statements, you do not have to reject your peer group in order to dispute the negative and inaccurate messages; you can accept the components that are healthy and supportive and reject the ones that are harmful.

Other Influences

We have now covered most of the major influences on daily self-talk: your family of origin, culture, religion, school, and peers. However, you may have received feedback from other sources in your childhood that may have contributed to your negative self-talk.

Special Authority Figures

When you think back to your childhood and adolescence, you might easily remember specific authority figures, usually adults, who had some significant impact on how you felt about yourself. We've already discussed some of the obvious figures that likely have had either a positive or negative influence on you—these certainly can include one or both parents or other family members such as a grandparent, aunt, or uncle. There may have been other important figures outside your family who served both as a role model for you and as a source of information about yourself as you were developing. These figures may have been your teachers, ministers or other religious leader, physicians, coaches, tutors, or neighbors. The information that they reflected back to you may have closely resembled that which your family provided. Their messages to you may have been as positive or as negative as those supplied to you by your family.

Because these people may not have been a part of the system in which you grew up, they may have provided you with a different perspective about your identity, your value to the world and to them, and your special talents or gifts. Their insights may have provided a safe haven for you, allowing you a respite from the negativity of other sources. The positive images these figures provided for you may have helped you survive your early years with some sense of self-satisfaction, even if this was for one particular quality or skill that you possessed. The positive strokes you received from a coach you admired may have helped you feel good about your athletic abilities and gain feelings of self-acceptance in this area of your life. If you were fortunate, you had a positive figure whose influence extended beyond one limited area of your life and they provided a place where you could be unconditionally accepted and nurtured. This figure might have been able to help you recognize that some of the negativity you were exposed to in other aspects of your life was inappropriate. If you were very lucky, you had a figure who taught you that being gay or lesbian was not something awful, sinful, or sick, but a natural part of who you are. Think about some of the positive influences you may have enjoyed as you grew up who may have helped salvage your self-esteem from total devastation and distortion.

Sports and Other Extra-Curricular Activities

Our culture certainly values competition in sporting events and in other areas. Our school systems often incorporate athletics into the curriculum at a high level. Most children are required to have some form of physical education and many participate in some type of after-school sport.

Certainly, there are a number of ways that sports can be quite beneficial. Aside from reaping the general health benefits, if you were a particularly gifted athlete, you may have received much recognition and praise for your accomplishments. This may have been one of the most important factors in how your self-perception was formed. You may have found a great deal of value in your athletic ability and you possibly learned to highly value and enjoy competition as a way of demonstrating your self-worth. But this positive association of competition with self-worth may later have generalized to your professional and personal life and your typical style of thinking may sound like this: "If I don't win, then I'm a failure" or "I am worthless if I don't finish first."

If you were not gifted in sports, this may also have presented information that was important in how you defined yourself. Being rejected for a team or chosen last is a lasting memory for many children. You can imagine the messages you might have developed about yourself if you were consistently not chosen or if you faced the wrath of the rest of the team for errors or clumsiness. You may still carry messages about yourself from these experiences such as "I am awkward and a nerd" or "I cannot become a team player because I may let the team down."

Being especially talented in sports may have had its own challenges as well. Teams are a powerful form of peer groups. While being a contributing member of a sports team can be a powerful positive influence in many ways, it may also be difficult since you may have felt that you could not risk expressing your sexuality openly with these very close peers for fear of rejection. You may have chosen to develop a secret self in order to remain on the team. The sometimes difficult but recently improving life stories of lesbian and gay professional athletes have been well-described in the books *Jocks: True Stories of America's Gay Male Athletes* by Dan Woog and *Lesbians and Gays and Sports* by Perry Young and Martin Duberman.

Disability

Certainly having a healthy self-esteem is important for everyone, but it is even more significant to feel good about your strengths if you have a disabling condition. Disability exists in many forms, for example, paraplegia, deformity, or a congenital or chronic disease that may impair mobility or the ability to perform functional activities of daily living. It also may exist in the form of a mental illness such as schizophrenia, bipolar disorder (formerly called manic-depressive), or even endogenous depression (depression with biological causes). For some, the disability is in the form of difficulty with learning in academic-type activities, for example, difficulty with reading, writing, and arithmetic or requiring special tutoring or alternative forms of education.

When children are viewed as different by peers because of a disability, they may become the object of ridicule or may be rejected from participation in peer group activities. Sometimes if children with disabilities are placed in special schools or classrooms for children with similar problems, they may not face as much rejection. However, some disability specialists have advocated for mainstreaming, or the integration of children with disabilities into regular classrooms with non-disabled students. The supporters of this approach believe that it is important for disabled children to learn to get along in the larger society and that it helps non-disabled children better understand those who are disabled. Unfortunately, in both situations, children with disabilities must cope with the directly and indirectly stigmatizing messages our larger culture has about disability. These messages are often harsh and belittling such as, "You are not normal, therefore you are inferior," or "You are to be pitied and are in need of help." Lesbians or gay men who also have a disability need to pay particular attention to building solid self-esteem and positive self-talk. They must work extra hard refuting old, distorted messages about their value and worth in this society.

Attitudes about AIDS

The impact of AIDS on the gay community has been immense. As with other large health and social issues, the full impact of AIDS on our society, the world, and the individual cannot be fully discussed here. It is, however, worth mentioning as an important influence on self-talk and self-esteem.

When AIDS first started appearing, it created a good deal of hysteria in those who became aware of its existence, first within the gay male community, who seemed to be its only victims, and only later in those outside of the gay community. Because it seemed to specifically target gay males, many people were quick to draw conclusions about the connection between gay male behavior and the development of this disease. The hysteria around AIDS became a prime medium for judgmental propagandizing from the media, society, and the pulpit. Fundamentalist religious leaders drew embarrassingly naive conclusions about AIDS as some sort of retribution from God against gay men for so-called immoral behavior.

Jeff, who came from this type of religious background and never learned to challenge these harmful messages, struggled with the negative and incorrect assumptions made by these misinformed factions. He began to doubt at some level his own sexual legitimacy. Deep down, he even wondered if there was some credence to the fundamentalists' claims. His family had never been supportive of him, so he'd always experienced a certain level of shame. Only through talking about these claims with his friends was Jeff able to begin refuting them. People not only suffered from the tons of misinformation that was rampant about AIDS and the stigma it now brought to homosexuality, but the threat of the disease and death was a significant source of distress for many gay men at the time. How could you explore your sexual identity if it possibly meant that you would die? Many felt that they must either choose sex and risk death or choose abstinence and lead an incomplete life.

Fortunately, many gay men and lesbians kept their cool during this early period and began insisting on rational debate and scientific study regarding AIDS rather than allowing fear and moral opportunism to reign supreme. Some lesbian and gay historians, in fact, feel that AIDS brought the larger gay community together in a way that it had never before been organized (Herek and Greene 1995; Miller 1995). They had common enemies to fight against: ignorance, disease, and bigotry. While the lesbian community appeared to be less affected directly by this disease, it certainly suffered from the incredible anti-gay hysteria that was quickly becoming widespread. At some level, this was and is a lesbian and gay issue, rather than just a gay male one.

Gay men and lesbians who were growing up during this time were likely dramatically affected by the cultural hysteria. In some ways, our community was just beginning to enjoy more societal visibility and was beginning to flex some political muscle that had been gained with the symbolic "victory" at the Stonewall riot in 1969 and continued through the liberating 1970s. Initially, AIDS seemed to threaten the gains made during the prior years, setting back the gay rights movement and having a negative effect on the newly positive self-images within the gay and lesbian community. Because many gays and lesbians began organizing and educating themselves, the government, and the health care system, we have seen the facts emerge above the hysteria and health education take priority over irrational beliefs. AIDS is still a concern for us all, but we now understand it for what it is—a disease, not a verdict.

Evaluate the Messages

In this and the previous chapters, I have briefly begun to explore some of the factors that have shaped the messages you give yourself about how to view yourself, the world, and others. If you have taken the time to answer the questions posed to you at the end of each chapter, you may be starting to recognize the specific influences that shaped your life and the messages you continue to give yourself, both positive and negative.

Yet, the sources of messages do not stop with these influences. There may be other people, places, or experiences you can remember that added to your self-perception that I did not discuss here—for example, living through a once-in-a-lifetime trauma of some kind like a flood or war, moving frequently as a child, or living through one or multiple divorces. Only you can begin to hear the residual voices from your past and learn to take control of them. Remember that these voices may have been sending distorted messages and that you are capable of changing those messages.

Questions for Reflection

- What kinds of positive experiences did you encounter in school as you were growing up? What kinds of negative experiences?

- What kinds of messages did you receive about yourself from teachers? Peers?

- What messages about homosexuality in general do you remember from your school experiences? From your teachers and peers?

- How did your general experiences with school affect your current professional identity or the development of your self-confidence?

- How were your achievements (or lack there of) in school received at home? How were your negative experiences in school handled at home?

- Were there any people you thought were lesbian or gay in your school, including teachers, staff, or peers? What images of gays or lesbians do you continue to carry based on these people? Were they stereotypical? Overt? Closeted?

- What memories do you have about interacting with peers as a child? Were you accepted? Rejected? Social? A loner or outsider?

- What attitudes did your peer group hold about homosexuals?

- Do you remember pretending to be heterosexual to fit in or avoid rejection?

- Were there specific authority figures in your life who provided a source of unconditional acceptance?

- How did participation or nonparticipation in sports shape your self-identity?

- How has AIDS changed your behaviors and self-concepts?

- What kinds of pressure to conform do you experience from your current peers?

Part II

Choices:
Self-Esteem and Your
Daily Life

6

Your Career

By working faithfully eight hours per day, you may eventually get to be a boss and work twelve hours per day . . .

—Robert Frost

Now that you've explored some of the origins of self-talk, you're ready to look at some ways this self-talk may be affecting your life today. One area that self-esteem affects is your daily job performance and overall career successes.

Some of the ideas you have about yourself as an employee or professional may relate directly to ideas that you have about yourself in general. For example, if you feel unworthy of praise or attention in your personal life, you also likely feel this way in your professional life. Feeling uncomfortable with praise, or unentitled to it, may prevent you from performing in ways that would bring special attention or recognition your way.

It's important to examine your professional life and any self-esteem obstacles that may be hindering you from excelling at your career in order to determine whether the way you view yourself generally has any negative impact on your work life. In this chapter you'll examine how self-esteem can affect career choices, job performance, and on-the-job relationships. You can also use this information to explore whether your career may be having negative impact on your self-esteem.

Fitting In at Work

Some people find themselves in quite a double-bind at work since they desire the raises and promotions that doing work worthy of recognition can bring, but at the same time, they resist doing anything that would cause them to feel uncomfortable or put them in the spotlight.

If you learned as a gay or lesbian child that calling attention to yourself often invited public speculation about your sexuality, you may have a tendency to try to "fit in" by remaining mediocre. By avoiding the extra look from your employer, you may be telling yourself that you are protecting yourself from your sexuality being discovered. Certainly job discrimination does exist in this country, due to one's gender, race, religion, disability, or sexual orientation; and people have been fired for reasons that are not related to the job and in no way affect their performance. Unfortunately, because we are not offered protection against discrimination in many settings, the fear of exposure and job loss may be realistic. Thus, your career can have both positive and negative consequences on self-esteem and vice versa. Finding a comfortable balance between personal and job needs will be important in your overall life satisfaction.

How Self-Esteem Can Affect Career Choice

People choose a particular career for many reasons aside from love of the work, including potential earnings, economic necessity, availability of options, and family pressure. There are certainly also many ways that self-esteem may ultimately affect career choice as well. You may remember the time in your life when you were considering your first career path and ruling out certain options based on lack of interest or confidence, or self-doubt. Perhaps you had people in your life who strongly encouraged you to follow one path versus another, such as a coach, parent, or high school guidance counselor. They may have selectively invalidated some of your choices as "unrealistic" or "beyond your abilities" while encouraging you to follow paths that they approved of or had followed themselves. They also could have seized upon a strength of yours and pushed you to follow it professionally, even if you would have preferred to pursue a path you were more passionate about. You likely heard many messages during this decision-making period that began to shape your professional path and identity. If the people in your life invalidated your feelings and thoughts in general, they may have attempted to shape your career choice using the same methods of invalidation. Adults who have become dissatisfied with their jobs question their original choice of career and regret decisions they made early on in their working lives.

Many lesbians and gay men not only had these types of external pressures to follow a certain career path, but were also faced with internal conflicts. Given the negative stereotypes our society has about homosexuality, many gay men and lesbians may choose certain careers and avoid others based on the appearance or level of social acceptability of the career. Some gay men, for example, may have avoided taking creative/artistic career paths because of the level of discomfort they anticipate feeling from homophobic people in their community, even though they may have felt drawn to this type of work. Others may in fact choose a specific career because of their sexual orientation, gender, race, or other oppressed minority status, feeling as if they would not be accepted in other careers. In the absence of personal validation by society, many lesbians and gay men choose a career path that will provide levels of prestige and self-validation otherwise not received. For example, if you found success and validation through academic achievement, it is likely that you chose a profession that values academic achievement. Either way, career choices are often made for reasons other than personal satisfaction or a match between strengths and the job requirements themselves.

Brad, a forty-five-year-old physician, came to my office complaining of job burnout and had many signs of what most people would call a midlife crisis. In many ways his career had been stellar—early academic success in high school led him to a remarkable undergraduate effort at a major university where he majored in biochemistry and pharmacology. His hard work paid off when he was admitted to medical school and later obtained prestigious residency and fellowship training. Upon completion of his fellowship, he was offered a plum position at one of the top medical schools in the country where he quickly made a name for himself as a talented clinician, administrator, and colleague.

Six years later, however, Brad found himself dissatisfied with both his work and his personal life. He readily admitted that his personal growth and difficulties with maintaining relationships were likely related to the disproportionate amount of time that he spent on his career versus the rest of his life. While he still enjoyed many parts of his job, such as the respect afforded him by the medical community, his patients' recovery and gratitude, and the comfortable salary, he found himself longing to get off of the "achievement treadmill" and put more energy into the rest of his life. Although he was good at what he did for a living, and it provided him with many positive advantages, Brad was not completely satisfied with the day-to-day aspects of his job. He had grown tired of his position of authority but felt trapped because he had little confidence that he could do anything besides medicine. He also worried about the family repercussions if he were to leave medicine altogether since his parents and friends were so proud of his accomplishments as a doctor. Self-doubt and fear kept him from exploring other career options.

Brad and I began to explore how he came to choose his career path and discovered that his sexuality was one of several important factors that influenced his choices. He remembered that he chose to become a physician at some level to prove to himself and his family that he was worthy of the respect that he feared they would not give him because of his sexual orientation. Physicians were highly respected by Brad's parents and family and were held in quite high esteem by American culture at the time he was making his career decisions.

While he had developed a healthy and positive professional self-concept (he saw himself as good at what he did and had external indicators of success), this high professional self-esteem didn't seem to extend to relationships and other endeavors. He still felt unworthy of being loved by others, especially if they really knew who he was or understood the less successful parts of him.

Brad's experience is not uncommon in people whose self-esteem is based on their career successes. Building core self-esteem beyond a career is one way to begin to ease the feelings of being trapped or feeling like an impostor. For Brad, this meant changing careers altogether and choosing something that he felt would make him more satisfied regardless of the impressions of others. For others, it may mean learning to change how they behave in the career itself by standing up for themselves, making choices that may lead to success and recognition, and living more openly and authentically.

While self-esteem may have had an impact on your job choice, your job may also have an impact on your self-esteem. Your job may in fact be a source of self-esteem (and positive self-messages) in a larger life system that is rewarding and satisfying.

There may, however, be aspects of your job that are not fulfilling. Perhaps you are not moving along as quickly as you desire, or certain work-related situations keep your job from being as satisfying as it could be. For example, you may feel uncomfortable talking about your personal life at work for fear of homophobic reactions of others, or you may actually have heard co-workers make heterocentrist assumptions or inappropriate jokes or remarks. You may also feel frustrated as you watch others get promotions and recognition that you feel you deserve but don't get because you are afraid to confront the company. Sometimes those promotions may be based on the sociability (that is, ability to interact with others comfortably) of the employee, and you suspect that keeping your personal life private may have actually worked against you.

The Secret Self on the Job

Many lesbians and gay men feel as if they must keep their personal lives exceedingly private to succeed in the workplace. Yet most heterosexuals do not compartmentalize in this way, often sharing many details of their family life including how it may affect their daily moods and productivity. Compartmentalization may actually diminish the full range of creativity of an employee and leave him or her feeling alienated from others at the office. Feeling limited in this way often leads to feelings of frustration and job burnout. Working in an environment where you feel you cannot be yourself may lead to a lowered sense of self-esteem as you begin to justify why you cannot be as open as co-workers: "I must keep this secret self hidden and I should be grateful for the opportunity to hold this position."

It is not always easy to find a balance in such a situation since homophobia and discrimination do exist. Some people who have taken the risk to be more open about themselves on the job have suffered from discrimination while others have found the environment accepting and actually began to excel afterwards. If you feel that you cannot make the choice to reveal your true self on your present job, you may eventually choose to leave and search for a position where you would feel comfortable about living more openly. This is not a book about coming out, and these are choices that you must make for yourself. Regardless of the choices you make, it is important for you to recognize the messages you're sending yourself about the workplace. While you may not choose to change your workplace or your "out" status, you certainly can change the negative self-talk that may be interfering in your day-to-day functioning.

On-the-Job Relationships

One of the most potentially rewarding or frustrating aspects of a job is the relationship you have with your co-workers—the people who supervise you, your colleagues at the same level, and the people you supervise.

People Who Supervise You

Dealing with a boss or supervisor can be tricky because this person has the power to help or harm your career by praising or criticizing your work, giving you good or bad performance evaluations, promoting or firing you, and affecting future letters of recommendation. If your supervisor is in any way homophobic this may certainly affect your working relationship. It can also be difficult to stand up for yourself or to avoid self-blame when you encounter prejudice and discrimination from a supervisor unless you have a strong sense of self-esteem.

Your relationship to people in authority may be affected by your past experiences. Were the people who oversaw your duties as a child patient and nurturing, or were they demanding and rigid? If you had an authoritarian family structure that left little room for you to make independent decisions, you may be indecisive as an adult. Your experiences may have led you to always wonder, "Am I capable of making this decision?" If you were abused as a child by an authoritarian parent, you may have difficulty working with authoritarian-type leaders now. You may have negative expectations of your current supervisor simply because he or she reminds you of an abusive adult from your past. This adult may not have been a parent, but could have been a teacher, coach, or caretaker who was particularly belittling and oppressive.

Even if past experiences with authority figures have been primarily positive, it is possible that your overall expectations for your boss and yourself are lower than necessary because of the heightened alertness you developed to protect yourself from homophobia. If your view of society is that lesbians and gay men are seen as being of lesser value than heterosexuals, then you may expect less for yourself in general on the job—less recognition, less value to the company (or perhaps you even see yourself as a liability), and less entitled to the perks, such as health benefits for your partner. If you have lowered expectations for appropriate treatment (which can be viewed as a form of lowered self-esteem), then you will likely behave in ways with your boss that do not cue her or him to give you what you deserve. These behaviors include both direct communication, such as saying, "I deserve a raise," and indirect communication, such as saying nothing when your boss makes an effort to ask about your needs.

Workplace Anger

Expecting that you will not be offered equal status at your job can lead not only to negative self-talk but also to emotional frustration. Dealing with your frustration and anger in an appropriate manner is very important, particularly on the job. Inappropriate ways of dealing with this anger might include passive-aggressive behaviors such as showing up late for meetings, "forgetting" deadlines, and ignoring potential problems that are not part of your responsibilities so that the workplace will suffer consequences. More direct expressions of inappropriate anger include forms of aggression like losing your temper and raising your voice, making threats (about harming someone or quitting your job), and sabotaging a project or other hostile employee.

An appropriate way of managing anger involves behaving assertively when you have unmet needs or when your rights have been violated. If your self-esteem is low, you may have difficulty standing up for yourself and behaving assertively at work. This may lead you to say things to yourself like, "Don't say anything about that nasty comment, just be grateful you have a job" or "I really wanted that promotion, but they wouldn't have taken me seriously if I had said something about it." Learning to change the way you see yourself, interpret the meaning of a supervisor's behaviors, and stand up for yourself when necessary are appropriate ways of managing anger in your job.

Boundaries

Appropriate boundaries are important for the person with good self-esteem. The better your self-esteem, the less likely you are to tolerate boundary violations like being exploited, devalued, or passed over on the job. Working on maintaining healthy boundaries in your career life means giving yourself permission to ask your boss for what you want or need to perform your job well, expressing your opinions about a project or decision, saying "no" when you feel overloaded, and setting limits on personal intrusiveness by co-workers or other company personnel. Healthy boundaries, however, are not so rigid that they require excess energy to maintain them. For example, as mentioned previously, most heterosexual employees do not worry about keeping their private lives a complete secret, even while they may not feel that this information is particularly relevant to share at work. If you find that you spend a significant amount of time concerned about managing your personal image ("I don't want anyone to know I'm a lesbian or I will lose the respect of my peers"), then you may be depleting your creative energy by consciously maintaining this personal/professional separation. Of course, this does not mean that you should come out to your boss and co-workers, especially if sexual orientation is not a protected status in your company or city. There are certainly still many jobs in which self-identifying as a gay man or lesbian can lead to discrimination, as in the U.S. military for example. As some people build their self-confidence, they feel a strong need to come out in the workplace no matter what the consequences. Coming out to others is a highly personal decision and should be made only when you are ready to handle the reactions (both positive and negative) of the people around you.

Your Co-workers

While your co-workers may not have the authority to fire you, they are important sources of support and cooperation in the workplace. They can make the difference for you in terms of overall job satisfaction and a day-to-day sense of security or ease. Co-workers who see your work and your style can be helpful in shaping the impression that your boss or company has of you.

As with your boss, you may spend significant time and energy diverting the topics of conversation with co-workers away from your personal life or simply pretending as if you have no personal life. Although you may not be aware of it, years of living in a self-protective way may have led you to settle for less than total acceptance ("I cannot expect the same emotional support as my heterosexual coworkers"). These types of long-standing beliefs may inhibit you from building relationships that could be supportive of and even nurturing of your professional talents. Many people develop friendships outside of the job with co-workers. While sometimes a friendship can be difficult to keep separate from the working relationships, particularly if the relationship is with a superior, it also can be quite empowering professionally. It is important for building self-esteem for you to examine your long-standing beliefs regarding what you will and will not allow yourself to have at work in terms of support.

The People You Supervise

While most positions of responsibility require self-confidence, it is particularly so for positions that call for you to supervise others. Supervising others requires above all patience, tact, poise, and a sense of fairness. Think about some of the supervisors you've worked with. Perhaps you worked under supervisors who seemed personally threatened by your job performance because they were evaluated in terms of the success or failures of their employees by their own bosses. Supervisors with particularly low self-esteem are more likely to take your performance mistakes personally and respond in a personal, rather than professional, manner. The less self-confidence they have in their own abilities as supervisors, the more threatened they may be by your successes. While your success reflects positively on them in most cases, your achievements may threaten those who are insecure about their own merits as supervisors.

In order to become an effective supervisor, you must work on building professional self-esteem, not only in a general way, but specifically in a position of authority over others. In order to use and believe healthy self-statements, such as, "I am competent to supervise someone who is a talented employee," you must make sure that you have adequate support and training in this position. Managing employees requires that you have specific knowledge about communication, an understanding of company systems and expectations, and adequate support and modeling from your own supervisor. As with any position, make sure you have at least the minimum skills required for the job before launching into it. If you have these basic skills, then your challenge is to avoid negative self-talk that may sabotage your performance or lead you to feel insecure, frustrated, or overwhelmed.

A position of authority within a company can bring with it a subordinate or co-worker who is threatened by your success regardless of your sexuality. As a lesbian or gay man, being a supervisor may lead to special concerns. Often employees who have lower self-esteem themselves may take personally decisions you make and may react with anger directed at you personally. You may feel particularly vulnerable to threats because of your sexual orientation (that is, you may fear being outed, humiliated, and so on). For this reason, it is not uncommon for gay male or lesbian supervisors to feel as if they need to walk a fine line between being authentic and protective regarding their personal lives. There isn't one correct way to resolve this conflict, but regardless of the way you decide to perform your job, you can be in control of any self-talk that leads you to feel insecure and indecisive. The questions at the end of this chapter will help you to evaluate your self-talk regarding how you see yourself in a position of authority.

Is Your Self-Esteem Too Dependent on Your Job?

It's possible to feel strong, secure, and empowered at times and still have self-esteem issues. You may be wondering, "How can people have self-esteem at times and not at others?" Because self-esteem is a multi-layered concept that is affected by many things in your past, present, and future, you're likely to have areas in your life where you feel self-confident and accomplished—and other areas where you don't. It's possible to find a single source of external reinforcement, like work success, upon which to base your self-esteem or against which to measure your sense of worth. For example, many people find helping others beneficial in raising their sense of self-esteem. For many people, work becomes one source of self-esteem, if not *the* source.

While these ways of building a good sense of self-esteem are important for developing positive self-talk, it's possible to place so much emphasis on the external reinforcers in your life that you risk neglecting the internal structure that is important to building good self-esteem overall. Basing your self-esteem solely on something that is dependent on your performance, like a job, puts you at risk for lowering your self-esteem if you can no longer perform that job. The key to building lasting and pervasive self-esteem is to work at learning to love yourself at your core. This means truly learning to accept yourself as you are, being kind to yourself with the choices you make and with the self-talk you carry with you.

Questions for Reflection

- How has your professional life affected your view of yourself? How has your view of yourself affected your job?

- Are you happy with your current job? Why or why not?

- How did you make the decision to follow the career path you have followed? What factors did you weigh in choosing a career? How much of your career choice was based on what others expected of you versus what you wanted to do?

- How did consideration of cultural stereotypes for lesbians and gay men affect your decisions?

- Does concern about negative consequences at your current job keep you from sharing your personal life or going for advancement?

- What are your current supervisor's attitudes toward gay men and lesbians? Upon what information is this based?

- How has homophobia in the workplace affected your day-to-day comfort level?

- What is your level of confidence as a supervisor?

- What messages from the past or about your sexual orientation affect your self-talk on the job?

7

Relationships

To have healthy relationships with others, we must first be at home with ourselves.

—Susan L. Taylor, *Lessons in Living*

Your core beliefs affect the development, quality, and ultimate success of your personal relationships. The value you place on your self-worth, how safe you feel with others, how much independence you need, whether or not you feel you deserve love, and how you expect to be treated by others are all determined by your core beliefs. If your core beliefs cause you to have low self-esteem, you may feel powerless to avoid manipulation or outright abuse by others. You may feel less than adequate in relationships or as if you don't deserve to be in a relationship with someone who is healthy and reciprocative.

Having low self-esteem not only affects romantic relationships, but also affects your ability to make close friends or feel connected to your family. Establishing trust, the building block of deepening in relationships, means learning to express vulnerability while simultaneously protecting yourself from potential harm. Learning when to allow yourself to depend on someone else and when to remain independent can be confusing and can act as a barrier to satisfaction in your relationship to others. What you learned about depending on others, trusting them with your vulnerable sides, and what type of person makes a good mate was affected by the models of relationships you had when you were growing up and by the messages you were given about your value to others.

It's also helpful to consider that self-esteem is a kind of relationship with yourself. How you talk to yourself, what you say, and the rules you make yourself follow may be quite different from how you are with others. Often, people who are hard on themselves would never consider treating someone else so severely. The demands that they make on themselves are sometimes so unrealistic that they can almost never successfully meet them, leading to more punitive self-statements and feelings of inadequacy. If you have an adversarial relationship with yourself, one that relies on self-criticism for motivation for example, you may be affecting your ability to relate to others. You may be preventing yourself from experiencing pleasure or others from enjoying you completely. In part 3, you'll read about addressing the relationship you have with yourself and ways to improve this important relationship.

Intimacy

Intimacy, a necessary component in close relationships, may be difficult to achieve if you undervalue yourself and the potential contributions you could make to another person. While sometimes the word *intimacy* is used as a euphemism for sexual activity, in this chapter I will use the word in a broader context, meaning the sharing of the most private or personal feelings and thoughts you have with another person. Certainly your past experiences with emotional intimacy (if any at all) may be affecting your ability to achieve true intimacy with a partner or close friend. If you learned as a child that certain feelings and thoughts were not to be shared, you may still have difficulty sharing your true feelings with someone with whom you would like to be close. Many gay and lesbian people who have had the experience as children of having a secret self have a difficult time as adults sharing their true feelings for fear of rejection or abandonment. The messages they received as a child about being honest and open may have sounded like this: "Some feelings are bad or evil and must never be talked about" or "If you tell me something I don't want to hear, I will punish or leave you." Some people may have had direct experience with coming out to someone they care about and then having the person desert the relationship.

One advantage to not sharing your innermost thoughts and feelings is that it acts as a form of protection, keeping people from using this information to hurt you or leave you. One disadvantage, however, is that maintaining a barrier between you and others can become too rigid, preventing you from experiencing the joy of a mutually intimate and trusting relationship. Without good modeling for how to set strong but flexible boundaries, you can either leave yourself open for abuse or you can shut everyone out. By teaching yourself to change negative self-talk and by learning to value and protect yourself, you will simultaneously raise your self-esteem and change the way you relate to others.

Sexual Development

Heterosexuals typically learn about their sexual selves around the onset of puberty and early adolescence. They learn about physical changes in their bodies and then begin to feel the effects of the physical and hormonal changes emotionally. They begin to pay attention to their physical attractiveness and how the opposite sex views them. Most heterosexuals go through adolescence and sexual experimentation at around the same age. In other words, they learn to form relationships, sexual and romantic, with the opposite sex through a recognizable process. First, adolescents typically socialize with the opposite sex in small groups (i.e., going to the movies, the mall, or a dance as a group rather than one-on-one dating). As they gain confidence, they begin to date as couples. Expectations for sexual exploration are usually clearly spelled out by concerned parents—no touching, petting, or kissing until a specific age or status. It is commonly understood and desired that parents educate their children about sexuality and sexual behavior, often referred to as "the facts of life" or "the birds and the bees." Interestingly, these terms reflect the level of discomfort that our culture seems to have about discussing sexual issues, and some studies have suggested that most adolescents learn about sex from sources other than their immediate family.

Heterosexuals have the benefit of society's general approval for experimentation in relating to the opposite sex during adolescence. Lesbians and gays, however, generally do not have the approval of society to learn about dating and sex with members of the same sex, so they are faced with several uncomfortable alternatives. One alternative is to avoid dealing with emotional attractions and sexual feelings altogether ("I must not allow myself to feel these things" or "My feelings are invalid or inappropriate"). If they are aware of these feelings, they may opt to actively hide them. Many lesbian and gay youths may not recognize or be able to label these feelings because they are unconsciously holding this information away from their awareness. They may then focus on other activities for diversion of this energy. A positive diversion might be schoolwork, jobs, or other productive or benign hobbies and interests. Unfortunately, a negative diversion might include rebelliousness against parents, drug abuse or dependency, or other self-destructive behaviors.

Another way of handling these feelings might be to acknowledge them openly, but then risk the rejection of family and friends. Rejection leads to its own consequences: loneliness, isolation, and depression. In some extreme circumstances, open acknowledgment of same-sex attractions can lead not just to rejections, but also open hostility and physical harm. Developing a secret self seems to be another alternative chosen by many. Maintaining the separate identities may be exhausting and confusing for the developing youth, leading to feelings of anger, depression, and emotional fatigue.

There are many ways that avoidance or suppression of normal feelings may be harmful to a developing youth. First, these youth are not allowed the same support and guidance through their sexual development that heterosexual adolescents are universally granted. Many lesbians and gays must be their own guides as to appropriate attraction, dating, and sexual behaviors and are able to successfully find their own rules and expectations. Others, however, do not comfortably experience the development of the sexual components of themselves until some time later in adulthood when they are more comfortable with these feelings.

In essence, heterosexuals have an advantage of going through sexual development at relatively the same age, while lesbians and gay men may have a much larger range of ages when these sexual identity processes occur. This may make it especially difficult for gay and lesbian adults to find compatible partners since chronological age may be less related to the person's stage of sexual identity development. In other words, it may be that a forty-five-year-old man who has come to realize that he is gay may in some ways be at a similar place to a twenty-five-year-old man who has the same realization. With fewer markers of who the developmentally similar partners are, the dating and intimacy process may be more complicated for gays and lesbians. Perhaps with greater social acceptance of lesbian and gay youth and support for age-appropriate sexuality education, the gay community will begin to enter self-discovery and exploration phases in sync as do many heterosexuals.

Self-Esteem and Stages of a Relationship

Building successful and satisfying relationships is not accomplished overnight. Although you might meet people you find exciting and attractive almost immediately, it usually takes times to develop trust and emotional intimacy. Building a relationship usually happens in phases—meeting others, following through, deepening the relationship, and maintaining the connection—and each phase can be affected by your self-talk. Improving your self-esteem then will help you strengthen your relationships every step of the way.

Meeting Others

One of the first problems you may have with relationships is knowing where and how to meet people. There are many venues through which you can meet others ranging from the local supermarket to social networks designed specifically to bring singles interested in dating together. Most people who feel isolated can think of places or groups through which they would be interested in socializing, but they cannot see themselves fitting in or cannot find the motivation to get there. Often, these blocks are related to inhibiting self-messages like, "I'm not very experienced with hiking so I probably would look like a klutz if I went to a hiking club meeting." These messages lead them to expect disappointment and then to convince themselves to avoid even trying.

Feeling Like You Don't Fit In?

Many lesbians and gay men feel as though their alternatives for meeting people are limited because they don't think they fit their image of the lesbian/gay community's standards. A common complaint I hear from urban gay (mostly white) men is that they perceive themselves as "too average," overweight, or not "buffed" enough to fit into the local and most visible gay male scene.

Many of my clients assume that because they don't use alcohol or they tend to have more conservative views of sexual behavior than what they believe are the norm, they will not be accepted in social circles. Sandra, who has had only a couple of short-term relationships, is opting out of the search for a relationship altogether, dooming herself to a life alone. She has a close circle of friends but has given up on finding a potential partner. She tends to focus on what she can't offer someone in a relationship rather than what she can. Her low self-esteem is perpetuated by the messages she sends herself: "I'm too fat, boring, or poor to be of interest to anyone else."

Learning to value yourself and your positive qualities can help you overcome such negative thinking and can help you find the motivation to seek out friends and partners who share your values. You must also remember that lesbians and gays represent a full range of physical, emotional, intellectual, and professional types, including your own. Those people that you see in the bars, the social clubs, or the political groups that seem trendy or ideal are all subgroups that are part of a larger, diverse gay and lesbian population.

Social Skills

You may find that you have access to potential friends, but you tend to feel awkward in social settings, often stifled by anxiety. If you did not develop effective ways of initiating or carrying on a conversation early on in your life, your feelings of anxiety now about socializing may be justified until you gain experience and practice with these skills. Recognizing that you may have to work on your social skills is the first step in opening yourself up to learning how to access other relationships. In order to increase your range of communication strategies and tools, practice these skills on friends or family before you attempt to reach out for new relationships. This can increase your confidence in new social situations and help you reduce the negative self-talk. Two excellent books about developing communication skills are *Messages* (McKay, Davis, and Fanning 1995) and *Couple Skills* (McKay, Fanning, and Paleg 1994). If you feel particularly lost in this process, consulting a psychologist who specializes in building relationships may be helpful. He or she can provide you with ways to help you feel more comfortable in new social situations through such techniques as role playing or visualization (to practice using social skills) and assertiveness training (to help you understand how to speak up more effectively).

When you are getting ready to meet new people, it's important to examine carefully the messages you are giving yourself about how you will be perceived by others in a new situation ("They will see me as a geek"), who you feel you are able to approach ("Someone like her would never talk to someone like me"), and your likelihood of making a positive connection ("Even if I can get up the nerve to say something, he would never be interested in going out with me"). The negative self-statements associated with these messages serve to reduce your motivation to even attempt social behaviors and can leave you feeling depressed, awkward, and intimidated. They also set you up sometimes to choose people you may feel are safe or approachable, but are not necessarily who you would prefer to meet in that setting. The questions at the end of the chapter will help you analyze the inhibiting self-statements that you may be making to yourself.

Following Through

Once you've met someone that you like, you have to follow through with developing a relationship. This, like the initial phase, is also a place where your self-talk can be either inhibiting or enhancing. "To call or not to call" is a dilemma that can make or break the connection that you established upon your first meeting. People with low self-esteem often assume that while the initial contact went well, it may have been a fluke. They say things to themselves like, "If he only knew the real me, he wouldn't want to get together again." These kinds of messages may then lead to behaviors that discourage further development of the relationships like not taking the next step of calling for another meeting, staying too distant by revealing minimal personal information during subsequent contacts, or even actively turning down future invitations, all out of a fear of being rejected.

Learning to value yourself as an interesting, worthwhile friend or potential partner will involve recognizing the automatic negative self-talk and replacing it with supportive self-talk. Replacing statements like, "If she really liked me, she would call me first" with "Things seemed to go well the first time we met. I'd like to see her again and I find out if the feeling is mutual. Even if she is not interested in meeting again, it doesn't mean that it's because of any perceived shortcoming on my part." Learning to talk to yourself in a more rational and self-respecting way like this takes practice but can be mastered.

Deepening the Relationship

When you move beyond the initial meeting and following through phases and realize that you are forming a new relationship, you are faced with deciding how quickly or completely to trust the new person in your life. The real work of developing an honest, sincere relationship begins with this phase. Many gay men and lesbians were raised feeling that they had to keep their inner selves a secret from those around them. This included not only their sexuality but honest feelings, reactions, and thoughts. Living as though you are someone you are not, however, can lead to feeling chronically like an impostor or fraud. Developing relationships with others from this perspective is confusing and complex because you can never be sure if what they care about in the relationship is the image you portray or the real you.

You may have learned that you deepen a relationship by making yourself indispensable to the other person or by doing things that please the other person even if it means sacrificing your own needs. People with low self-esteem often value the needs of others over their own needs and desires, then later can feel the frustration of not being attended to by those whom they have cared for. It's almost as if they have shown that their feelings are invalid, especially since they do not appear to value the feelings themselves. The thing that they want, being cared about for who they really are, doesn't happen because they don't allow anyone to access the vulnerable but real opinions and needs inside. The messages they have learned include "I must hide my real feelings or desires or else the person will then know how to hurt me through rejection or harm." Messages like this are often deeply embedded, so it's important to examine your core thoughts and emotions about relationships to be able to develop honest and satisfying relationships.

Even if you feel that you can be honest with your thoughts and feelings, it is important during this phase to maintain some sense of self-protection as you move into deeper trust in a relationship. Particularly if you have no experience in trusting, honest relationships or have been hurt in the past by someone whom you trusted, it will be important for you to take your time as you become more honest with your friend or partner, progressing slowly as you become more comfortable.

Healthy boundaries are important in this phase. They will protect you from being taken advantage of while at the same time allow you to open the gate to other people who have proven themselves trustworthy. This means that you maintain control over personal information about yourself (particularly information that can make you feel vulnerable, like your feelings, thoughts, desires, and wishes) until you have enough evidence that the person to whom you are relating can respect and value that information. Evidence for moving forward can be gathered by observing how that person treats or values other people with whom they have relationships or by providing the person with bits of information about yourself that are personal but not too personal.

These strategies may seem a bit calculating to some but they are not intended as a guide for everyone. These steps are primarily designed for people who recognize in themselves a difficulty with trusting others and developing deeper relationships. The idea is not to create tests for the people in your life that they must pass in order to gain your trust, but to make appropriate and well-informed choices about the people in your life with whom you can take emotional risks.

Maintaining the Connection

After you have built substantial relationships in your life, it takes work to keep them satisfying and honest. People with good self-esteem can use significant relationships to experience intimacy at its deepest levels. Feeling close to someone, allowing yourself to ask for what you need, and then allowing yourself to accept affection are experiences that most people look for to make their lives feel complete. If you have low self-esteem, however, you may feel unworthy of such experiences. Movies, literature, and popular culture are full of images of ideal love and friendships and perhaps sometimes portray intimacy unrealistically. Lovers who *never* argue or disagree, friends who are *always* faithful, and people who make *no* mistakes are inappropriate models in most cases and can lead you to feel hurt or disappointed prematurely. Learning to have reasonable expectations for yourself and others in a relationship that is well-established is an important part of maintaining a connection and growing together. Examining unrealistic expectations, such as expecting your partner or friend to be able to know what you're thinking, and learning to be flexible and realistic is a part of expressing mutual respect and support.

Healthy self-esteem grows as you negotiate between your own needs and the needs of your partner, without diminishing the value of either person's experience, feelings, or way of thinking. Intimacy continues to grow as you realize that two people do not need to feel the same way about an issue to be able to accept the other's perspective. In a healthy relationship, you learn to respect yourself and your partner, each maintaining your own individuality.

Learning to accept your own responsibility during a conflict with someone you care about is equally important. While some people with low self-esteem assume *all* responsibility for mistakes in a relationship, it is important to stand up for yourself when you feel that your rights have been violated or your feelings not considered. This is not always easy, particularly if you tend to send distorted messages to yourself.

People with low self-esteem are often afraid to admit mistakes, feeling as if making mistakes proves that they are worthless. They avoid accepting responsibility for their part in disputes, which in time can lead to further problems. Elizabeth and Sharon began to have problems in their relationship because Elizabeth never admitted when she was wrong. Their arguments always ended with Sharon apologizing and shouldering the responsibility for their problems.

After a while, Sharon began to resent Elizabeth for this and would pick fights just to get a reaction from her. In this case, it is likely that both partners suffer from self-esteem problems since no one always is correct or always to blame in every single conflict during a relationship. The best strategy is to have open, honest discussions about feelings, perceptions, and assumptions and to accept your part in the argument or misunderstanding. Learning to understand and forgive a partner who has made a mistake is important for both people as you grow as a couple or close friends.

Successful Relationships

Negative self-talk can hamper your ability to have a successful relationship at every level. Just as you may be talking yourself out of putting your best foot forward on the job, you may also be inhibiting or sabotaging yourself in relationships with rigid, self-negating messages that rule you out before you are even in. Once a relationship is formed, learning to accept yourself more completely and present yourself more genuinely (warts and all) to the other person can help you experience greater satisfaction in your relationships. Answering the following questions can help you examine your own negative self-talk and determine where you need to begin making changes.

Questions for Reflection

- What lessons did you learn as you were growing up about depending on others?

- What did you learn about being vulnerable in relationships?

- What kind of model did your parents provide you about adult, romantic relationships?

- What kind of models did you have for adult lesbian or gay male relationships? What were the stereotypes for these relationships?

- At what age did you begin to experiment with sexual behavior? dating? committed relationships? Did these ages correspond to the ages that your heterosexual friends began their experimentation? At what chronological age did you go through your "adolescent" phase of development in terms of sexual exploration?

- How do your past experiences with intimacy affect your current relationships or attitudes about having a relationship?

- Does your self-talk create a barrier to developing satisfying relationships? How does it adversely affect you in meeting others? In following through? In deepening the relationship? In maintaining relationships?

- Do you question your ability to have a relationship? In what ways?

- Do you try to diminish anxiety or reduce the potential of rejection and subsequent pain by talking yourself out of a relationship? How do you do this?

- How might you keep sexual activity apart from intimacy? How does sexual activity get in the way of intimacy?

8

Lifestyle

What an absurd amount of energy I have been wasting
all my life trying to figure out how things "really are,"
when all the time they weren't.

—Hugh Prather, *Notes to Myself*

This chapter is meant to explore ways that self-esteem affects daily
choices and self-identification. Your lifestyle depends on the choices
you make—whether or not you use alcohol and other drugs, interact
with the bar scene, or protect yourself from AIDS. The type of social
community you choose to associate with and the effects of such self-
identification also play a part in your lifestyle.

Alcohol and Other Drug Use

People take drugs for many different reasons—to enhance their
mood, to reduce pain, to encourage healing, to contact the spirit
world, to escape from reality to name a few. The decision to use a
chemical for legal or illegal reasons is often influenced by social messages such as "When you are sick, take some medicine" and "Alcohol
will make you more relaxed if you are nervous." If you tend to
devalue your own experiences, thoughts, and feelings, you may be
more susceptible to the influence of others around you. You may
drink or take drugs in an attempt to fit in, reduce your uncomfortable
feelings (such as anxiety, anger, or grief) that arise from negative
self-talk, or prove your worthiness or hipness.

It's important to become aware of the messages you give yourself about when, how, and if you should use alcohol and other drugs.
Many of these messages may be distorted, irrational or not helpful. If
you have progressed in your substance use to the point of excessive

use and dependency, it is likely that negative self-talk perpetuates your use of these substances. While traditional twelve-step programs are a part of a successful chemical dependency treatment program for many people, an alternative based on the work of Dr. Albert Ellis was developed. Originally called Rational Recovery, the program is now called SMART (Self-Management and Recovery Training), (Trimpey 1996). This program asserts that cognitive distortions and irrational ideas keep people using chemicals in a harmful way. It includes a step-by-step guide to overcoming negative self-talk.

Much research supports the link between low self-esteem and substance abuse. Children and teenagers with low self-esteem more often tend to experiment with alcohol and other drugs when compared to the same aged children and teens with higher self-esteem. While researchers don't know the exact link, it's safe to assume that these youths are perhaps more vulnerable to peer pressure, tend to take more risks, or like many adults, use drugs or alcohol to escape from their own negative self-talk and volatile self-perceptions.

If you use alcohol or other drugs, at some level you may be telling yourself it's okay to use chemicals to make things better or that chemicals are better than your own coping skills. If you have less confidence in your own abilities, you might believe that alcohol or drugs are acceptable to use as a performance enhancer. If you've been told that you are worthless, you may feel that you can't cope without alcohol or drugs, then verbally beat yourself up and drink or use to reduce the emotional pain.

Short-Term versus Long-Term Hedonism

People who seek pleasure in the short-term, through the excessive use of alcohol, other drugs, or cigarettes, often tell themselves that the long-term effects of these activities do not matter because "we all die anyway." Chemical dependency is a complex phenomenon with multiple causal factors. Sometimes, however, actively continuing to use substances excessively may be an indication of deeper problems with self-esteem. Dr. Albert Ellis was a proponent of a concept he called *long-term hedonism*. He suggested that we can make our choices today with an eye on our future. He believed that if we truly valued ourselves, we would choose not to engage in behaviors that lead to short-term pleasure but may ultimately shorten or reduce the quality of our lives. He closely tied the idea of taking care of ourselves (an aspect of self-esteem) with the choices that we make and the irrational beliefs that we hold today. Examples of these beliefs that may be tied to excessive substance use include "My life is so bad that it doesn't matter if I have an accident and die," "I can't take another rejection; it'll help if I take a drink," or "I really can't control myself." His method was to challenge these irrational beliefs and replace them with more realistic ones.

Interacting with the Bar Scene

A common problem for gay men and women is the fact that many urban social activities are centered around gay or lesbian bars. While there is nothing inherently wrong with attending these centers of socializing, they can be problematic for those who have problems with alcohol and other drug use or who do not feel that they "fit the norm" for the bar crowd. You may feel like options are limited for meeting people, and feel depressed if you are passed over or not approached by others. For some, the bar scene can feel like a meat market, where looks are valued over deeper qualities. You may tend to compare yourself to others and feel inferior, particularly if your self-esteem is low. You may find that you avoid going out at all because of extreme self-messages about not fitting in, such as, "No one would want me looking like this."

When Justin was younger, he frequented some of the local gay clubs on a regular basis. He had no trouble making friends or meeting people when he was in his twenties and thirties, but now that he was approaching fifty, he found that men his age made up a smaller proportion of the crowd. He also felt less attractive as his waist began to spread and his hair began to thin. Justin had always felt that he would be in a comfortable relationship by the time he was fifty and he felt uneasy about his chances at a long-term relationship at this age. Now when he went out to bars, it was rare that anyone would ask him to dance or even speak to him if he didn't initiate the conversation. Because of these experiences, Justin began to feel old and unattractive. He began to avoid going out to clubs, feeling that they were too youth oriented. Since bars and dance clubs had been his primary places for socialization, he found himself becoming more isolated socially and more depressed. He told himself that he would probably die "alone, old, and bitter."

Fortunately, Justin heard about a social group for gay men over forty that met at a local Unitarian Church. With some encouragement from his friends, he went to a few meetings and found other men like himself who were single, attractive, and energetic. He realized that gay men could age gracefully and that not all gay men were attracted to youth and external beauty. He began to change how he viewed himself and the self-talk that he used when he was alone. His depression began to lift and he felt able to make new, more comfortable choices for socializing.

AIDS and Self-Esteem

AIDS is a major issue within the gay and lesbian community not only for those who have contracted it, but also for the non-infected. In a recent study of 301 gay men between the ages of eighteen and twenty-seven who were determined to be least accepting of their gay identity (Waldo, Kegeles, and Hays 1998), 46 percent of the men reported having had unsafe sex compared to only 30 percent of those who reported higher levels of self-acceptance. According to an article by *Bay Area Reporter* journalist Timothy Rodrigues (1998), other researchers, such as Rafael Diaz at the San Francisco AIDS Foundation, are also finding a significant relationship between low self-esteem and the transmission of HIV in men, particularly as they look for experiences that make them feel, even temporarily, better about themselves. According to Rodrigues, Hazel Betsy of the Women's AIDS Network finds that self-esteem is also an issue for women with HIV but feels that the cause may be different in that they may simply not know how to say "no."

Although the great losses caused by AIDS are overwhelming, some people feel that AIDS may have affected the community in some beneficial ways. The world's attention became focused upon gay and lesbian issues in ways that made those issues more difficult to ignore or deny. In some ways this is good because the more exposure the general population has to the gay and lesbian community, the more likely it is that they will begin to change stereotypical views. AIDS has also served to bring the community together to fight the disease and the stigma. People have joined forces to create AIDS service delivery organizations across the globe, challenge the political and economically motivated systems that ignore or abuse gay and lesbian rights, and, by virtue of AIDS education, increased the visibility of larger gay and lesbian issues. Because many employers had to deal with the issues of HIV in the workplace, for example, they had to deal with gays and lesbians in terms of policy as well. While many took the opportunity to discriminate and harass people with AIDS and lesbians and gays in general, a few noble businesspeople took the opportunity to do the right thing by expanding benefits and family policies to include lesbians and gays in a supportive way.

Lesbians' and gay men's initial response to the AIDS epidemic was also positive in that it helped the community organize around the common goal of survival. Many AIDS organizations developed all over the country, providing models for health education and support services that had never been accomplished before on such a scale. AIDS activism helped challenge old, antiquated drug approval systems and helped forge new policies that affected not only people with AIDS but also people with other diseases who were waiting for new drugs to enter the market.

The down side is that the AIDS epidemic gave homophobes and other ignorant people the opportunity to make inappropriate and hurtful links between sexual behavior and retribution. They claimed it justified their positions that homosexuality is wrong, evil, or sick. As author Susan Sontag (1990) suggests, AIDS became known as a metaphor for sexual perversion and death. Many AIDS sufferers were led to feel guilty and ashamed of contracting the disease early on, leading some to self-destructive or suicidal behavior. Gay men who became infected in the early '80s were often terrified of this mysterious and virulent illness as they watched larger and larger numbers of their friends and family die with little medical attention. The President of the United States at the time, Ronald Reagan, completely ignored the issue in terms of discussion, action, or funding, some say largely because the first victims were gay men. Urban areas, such as San Francisco and New York, with large lesbian and gay communities, saw rapid and devastating changes as the hospitals and health clinics filled up with patients who would die sometimes frightening and painful deaths.

The effect on gays and lesbians as a group was powerful. Many who tested positive but were asymptomatic and those who were not infected often suffered multiple losses of people they loved and cared for. The work of author/activist Larry Kramer portrays both the deep grief and intense rage experienced by many gay men and lesbians during this time. Many who have survived through the early years of AIDS feel as though they are veterans back from a war, emotionally burned out with too many faces to mourn.

The effect on self-esteem in someone who has survived such loss, fear, and turbulence has to be significant. Facing your mortality is difficult for anyone. Most Americans live in some form of denial about our eventual deaths in order to keep functioning. If you thought about your death every second of every day, you would likely not be able to make appropriate choices, perform your daily tasks, or keep your attention focused on your job. People who are HIV-positive, even if they are asymptomatic, often struggle to regain some sense of normality in their lives as they try to psychologically adjust to a diagnosis that remains without a cure at this writing and with seemingly infinite variations of opportunistic infections. It is not the inevitability of death that can be so devastating since this is true for every human being. It appears that the constant daily reminders of mortality—every benign physical symptom, every medication dose, every evening news story about AIDS—seem to prevent people with HIV from settling back into a comfortable, moderate level of denial of death. Too much denial can lead you to avoid proper medical treatment, too little overwhelms you emotionally.

Many lesbians and gay men carry messages in their daily self-talk that relate directly or indirectly to AIDS. For example, even though Margaret did not have HIV, and she did not know anyone personally who had HIV or died from it, she had friends who did have these experiences and had been deeply affected by them. Although the rate of transmission of the disease in the lesbian population was low compared to other affected groups, Margaret had found her own sexual behavior altered by her awareness of AIDS. She was aware that there were women who identified themselves as bisexual and that some of them had contracted HIV by sleeping with men. She also had heard about needle-sharing by lesbians who used IV drugs. She tried to practice safe sex with her partners, but occasionally found herself wondering if she might become infected. She began to wonder whether she should even have sex at all or whether she should just be comfortable with a nonsexual companion. She found herself even wondering whether it was possible to contract some type of new and equally horrible disease that affected lesbians as AIDS had affected gay men in the beginning of the epidemic. The messages she heard herself saying as she began to try to form new relationships were things like, "She looks nice enough but she may have a history that she hasn't told me about. I think I'll pass on that dinner invitation."

Margaret's self-talk regarding the potential of contracting a disease seemed to become more extreme over time. In fact, her fear actually dovetailed into her negative self-talk about herself with such statements as "I won't go out with her because she wouldn't really understand my need for safety," leading her to continue to avoid relationships. For Margaret, her fear of contracting a disease, stimulated by the larger gay and lesbian population's emphasis on disease prevention, actually provided her with a comfortable way to avoid relationships altogether.

Aside from providing an excuse to avoid intimacy, AIDS has other effects on self-esteem. Sometimes, it is difficult to resist the negative messages promulgated by the media and public figures. During a recent interview, U.S. Senate majority leader Trent Lott (R-Miss.) answered the interviewer's question, "Is homosexuality a sin?" by saying "yes" and then went on to say that homosexuals should be treated as if they were people with problems like "kleptomania . . . alcoholics . . . sex addicts." In one statement, he condemned gay men and lesbians as immoral, but then made a comparison with "other illnesses." Most religious leaders would agree that an illness is not a sin and a sin is not an illness. The rhetoric espoused by the Senator is either incredibly ignorant or blatantly political, attempting to placate voters who believe either one model or the other.

Attaching the stigma of having AIDS, which is contracted through sexual contact and other exchanges of bodily fluids that are often condemned as immoral, with the stereotype of hypersexuality and promiscuity allows other people like Lott to make just such inaccurate and distorted statements. It can be difficult to resist the constant messages in the media about who you are, particularly when the messages are sent by politically powerful figures in our country. Even if you have no problem dismissing such ignorance directly, the ripple effect of such talk likely encourages, and in a way even endorses, people who feel discrimination and overt harm to gays and lesbians is acceptable.

People who live with HIV must not only deal with the negative messages about being lesbian or gay, but the residual fears about AIDS left over from the time when not much was known about the epidemic. They may find that once a stranger whom they have just met finds out that they are HIV-positive, the attitude and behavior of that person changes dramatically—perhaps to negative and avoidant or sympathetic to the point of discomfort. People who are HIV-positive may feel as though they are now treated as a disease instead of as a person or as if they are dying instead of living.

If you are HIV-positive, it's important to maintain positive self-esteem. You must challenge negative thinking about the future ("Why bother planning for the future since I won't be around for it"), self-blame about the past ("I was so stupid to have contracted this disease"), and distorted messages in the present ("It's not worth trying for a relationship because no one will want to be with a sick person"). Maintaining a healthy self-image may be difficult with constant reminders of HIV such as reports of fluctuating viral load and T-cell counts, opportunistic infections, and medication side effects. Low self-esteem that existed prior to the contraction of HIV, or as a result of repeated losses or health scares, can decrease your motivation to take care of yourself properly. It may be more difficult when you are tired and sick to challenge the inaccurate messages from the media and from your internal critic. Getting enough emotional support is both important and effective, as is learning to view yourself with compassion and self-nurturing.

For some individuals with HIV or AIDS, there can be personal gains. While certainly no one wants the disease itself, some of my patients have found that being HIV-positive forced them to examine themselves at deeper levels and to re-examine the priorities in their lives. Some have found themselves connected or re-connected to their family and friends in ways that didn't seem possible in the past. Others have explored their spiritual or religious lives and found new meaning and value. Facing your mortality, often a frightening experience, can help you learn to listen to what's important and to make your choices more thoughtfully and with self-compassion—a goal for us all.

Everyday Choices

Even your common daily choices can be affected by your self-esteem level. For example, Cliff, a twenty-eight-year-old African-American gay man, was raised in a predominantly white, midwestern small town and was often the only person of color in his class during his elementary and high school years. His main contact with other African Americans came when his family visited his relatives in Chicago, once or twice each year. Cliff loved his family dearly, particularly his cousins, but he had never revealed his sexual orientation to them for fear of their reaction. He often didn't feel as though he fit in at school because of his skin color, leaving him feeling like an outsider most of the time.

Cliff was conscious of trying to fit in as best he could. He generally tried to look and act like his friends at school, but also became quite adept at adopting the language and patterns of his family in Chicago. He became quite good at matching the style of almost anyone he interacted with, which provided him with both acceptance and protection from being rejected or ostracized. Unfortunately, although Cliff could always make himself fit in no matter where he was, he never felt satisfied. He rarely took risks to explore his own likes and dislikes for fear of standing out or being subject to ridicule, rejection, or potential harm. He developed a secret self regarding his sexuality and personal likes and dislikes. As an adult, he often worked quietly and effectively at his job, but didn't interact much with his co-workers or do anything to draw attention to himself. His self-talk often revolved around messages like "Don't rock the boat. Just do what you have to do and leave. You don't fit in here anyway."

Never having learned to explore his African roots or his sexuality, Cliff was unhappy with his life on many levels. He finally sought out a counselor to help him understand his chronic feelings of emptiness and dissatisfaction. She helped him to recognize the negative self-talk and to understand how his family and society affected his self-esteem. He began to understand that he developed his approach to life as a way of surviving as a man of color in a white community and a gay man in a heterosexual world. His counselor began to help him explore his true feelings about the choices in his life instead of *always* making the choice that was least obtrusive or most conservative.

Cliff learned to quiet the stifling self-talk and to listen to his true likes and dislikes, which led him to make some significant changes in his lifestyle and ultimately to feel more satisfied. He began to take more risks in the way he dressed, the music he listened to, and even in the food he ate, often finding that there were many more choices available to him than he had imagined. Occasionally, Cliff found that his friends, co-workers, and family disapproved of some of his choices, but he learned to trust his own judgments and recognize that it was not his responsibility to deal with other people's distress about conformity. As he began to trust his own choices, feelings, and opinions, Cliff found the chronic emptiness subsiding and a growing sense of well-being and self-confidence.

Social Communities

Some social and psychological theorists (Cass 1984, 1990) have proposed that the development of a healthy lesbian or gay identity involves identification with a larger community. Although social/political organizations for lesbians and gay men existed earlier, many historians point to the riots at the Stonewall Inn, a Greenwich Village gay bar, as the single pre-AIDS event that sparked social and political activism. Tired of being humiliated and harassed by New York City police, the gay and lesbian patrons turned on the police that night, yelling and throwing bottles, uprooting parking meters, and loudly protesting the years of abuse with chants of "Gay power!" Newspaper headlines the next day proclaimed to the world the beginnings of a new, historic movement in which lesbians and gays would no longer passively accept identification as second class citizens.

For many gay and lesbian people, coming out involves finding and bonding with others who are similar. Many remember fondly the first time they attended a gay or lesbian social or political event. They felt frightened as they made the choice to attend, often taking weeks or months to work up the courage to venture into a gay or lesbian bar, a Metropolitan Community Church service, or a lesbian or gay AA meeting, potluck, or community center. They may have felt disoriented initially, but found that this feeling gave way to excitement and later a sense of belonging. That feeling of acceptance and understanding provided a powerful bond between the strangers with a common identity. For many, such meetings became a safe haven and place to share the secret self before returning to the heterocentric worlds in which they lived.

As more and more people became aware of their sexual orientation and had such experiences, organized opportunities for socializing and living grew. And as with any large group, subgroups began to form within the larger organizations. These lesbian and gay subgroups included the original "Castro clones," gay men in the Castro district of San Francisco, California who adopted ways of dressing and grooming that included short hair, mustaches, flannel shirts and jeans. Over the years, as the full diversity of the larger gay and lesbian culture became apparent, other groups within groups developed emphasizing similarities and common interests, such as lesbians with children, people who enjoy drag (impersonation of the opposite sex personally or as an observer for entertainment) or dressing in leather, women living in communities without men, circuit or gym "boys" (men who value being tanned and buff), and "lipstick lesbians" (those who wear makeup and traditionally feminine clothing). The list goes on and on with subgroups within subgroups within subgroups.

Belonging to a group can provide many positive and life enhancing experiences. The members become your peer group and provide a place for bonding and sharing, a place to "fit in" especially after years of real or feared rejection or condemnation. As with most peer groups, however, over time these groups can become limiting and the same processes that led to the development of such a specialized group can lead to pressure to conform within the group itself. Socializing only with people from your group may in itself become confining, leaving you feeling as if you cannot express opinions that deviate from the group's norms or expectations. As you get older, move into different life stages, or change your views, you may find yourself feeling rejected, even if there have been no overt behaviors from group members to exclude you. You may find that you say things to yourself like, "My friends will laugh if I go out with someone his age" or "Even though I have a different view of that person running for office, I'd better keep it to myself at the party." The pressure to keep up with your peers can be immense and if your self-esteem is low, you may find it difficult to be yourself and have your own opinions, thoughts, and feelings.

It's easy to forget that there are other ways to connect socially, emotionally, or intellectually if your range of experiences is too narrow. Just as people who subscribe to heterocentrist or homophobic thinking tend to stay within groups that hold the same beliefs they do, so can any other exclusive peer group, with both groups potentially losing many opportunities for growth. Finding a balance between having a group with which you can identify, yet feeling free to follow your own path, takes time and effort but is an achievable and worthwhile goal. Learning to tolerate others with different opinions and finding peer groups with the capacity to tolerate individual differences can be satisfying.

You may have learned to devalue, ignore, or repress your natural intuition and feelings based on the values of your family of origin, the community, and the larger culture around you but that doesn't mean your lifestyle has to suffer for it. Building self-esteem holds the promise of greater self-acceptance and it includes learning to value your own natural responses to people and events in your life. You must learn to make decisions based on how you feel, rather than what others expect from you and what your negative self-talk has led you to believe. The last section of this book will teach you to change negative self-talk, attitudes, and beliefs that are distorted or that keep you from feeling healthy, happy, and secure.

Questions for Reflection

- What were the early messages you learned as a child about using alcohol or other drugs? What were your family models for the use of alcohol and other drugs?

- If you drink or use today, under what conditions do you drink? Are you usually in a social setting or alone?

- Do you drink or use to reduce anxiety or relax? To help you with performance?

- What messages do you give yourself today about when, how, and whether to drink or use?

- Do you take a short-term or long-term approach to your future quality of life? If you take a short-term approach, what negative or distorted messages do you give yourself that keep you feeling pessimistic about the future?

- What messages are activated when you go to a lesbian or gay bar or other social gathering?

- How has AIDS affected your life? How has the stigma of AIDS had an impact on you directly or indirectly? How have your thoughts, feelings, and behaviors been altered because of AIDS?

- How does your sexual orientation, your ethnicity, and your gender interact to affect your self-esteem?

- How would you describe your personal circle of friends? Are they diverse in gender, sexual orientation, race, socioeconomic status? If not, how does the lack of diversity affect your freedom to make choices?

- Do your friends share common interests, activities, and goals? How easy is it for your to choose to change the way you dress or look in terms of how your friends might respond?

- How much do you consider what your friends will think when you are making decisions about clothes, hair, who you will date, etc.?

- What advantages are there to having the friends you have? What are the disadvantages?

Part III

Healing: Ways of Improving Self-Esteem

9

Feeling the Feelings

Those who don't know how to weep with their whole heart don't know how to laugh either.

—Golda Meir

If you've read through parts 1 and 2, then you've begun to identify the specific thoughts, conditional beliefs, and core beliefs that affect your feelings and behaviors. If you have answered the questions at the end of each chapter (and if you haven't, you still have time later when you're ready), you may even recognize some common themes that still surface for you.

As discussed in chapter 1, a basic tenet of cognitive behavioral therapy is that *thoughts lead to feelings*. An event occurs in your life that in itself has no meaning. Then almost immediately you have a thought about the event that leads to feelings. Sometimes, you might actually feel the emotion before you recognize the thought and believe that the thoughts come afterwards. But most often, you actually did have a thought or interpretation of the event, however brief and unnoticed, that led you to feel the emotion. It's your self-talk, in fact, your running inner dialogue with yourself, that helps you interpret the world and your relationship to it.

Sometimes you are aware of this constant chatter and sometimes you don't even realize it's there. Many people react to even minor failures in their daily lives with the retort "That was so stupid of me!" either in their head or out loud. We are like sports commentators with ourselves, commenting on every move, every decision, and every event in our lives.

If you are less aware of this self-talk, then you may only feel the emotional consequences of it. It's like seeing the aftermath of a tornado without having actually witnessed the tornado itself—you still feel the devastation and the fear of something powerful having been there. Unfortunately, if you're not aware of this talk, or if you're aware of it but have no tools for challenging or altering it, you've left yourself at the mercy of the distortions, irrationality, and maliciousness of your past.

Cognitive behavioral therapy is focused on becoming aware of your self-talk so that you can evaluate it in a more rational and objective fashion. The negative self-talk will begin to lose its power to cause feelings of sadness, anger, doom, or despair. You can challenge the negative voices that may put you down and cause you to feel or anticipate rejection. Chapter 10 provides some techniques that are commonly used to challenge automatic thoughts as they occur.

Uncovering your automatic thoughts is the first step in raising your self-esteem, and you may have already felt some positive feelings of relief by reading the preceding chapters and recognizing the flaws in some of the influences in your life. Initially, however, you may have experienced an increase in negative feelings while reading the chapters. This would not be unexpected given the depth and breadth of issues that were covered—early neglect, abuse, rejection, and abandonment. These events, and what they meant and still mean to you, are likely painful or uncomfortable at best to think about. Your family's rules about having and expressing feelings are important to think about. What were your family's rules about emotions? Which emotions were okay and not okay to express? How did your own family handle their feelings? Did your parents model using alcohol when they were tense or screaming when they were angry?

Certainly our culture values some feelings over others. There are even gender differences for which feelings are "appropriate" to feel and which ones aren't. For example, men are encouraged to feel anger and to act aggressively at times, while women are often trained to respond passively. And in a patriarchal society, male characteristics are often seen as signs of strength and female characteristics are devalued as signs of weakness.

As you begin to recognize and deal with negative self-talk, you will likely begin to feel some of the emotions you would have felt as a child had you been able to think like an adult. You may feel anger toward the systems that taught you that you were powerless, inferior, or worthless. You may also find that you are angry at yourself for perpetuating this negative and distorted self-talk or angry at others as you remember yourself as an innocent and optimistic child who was methodically taught to view yourself as weak, ignorant, and ineffective. Many adults are afraid to allow themselves to feel feelings because they never learned how to process feelings in a healthy way or they were taught that having feelings meant you were weak or immature. In fact, if you did not have good role models for how to process feelings appropriately, the problem is one of a skill deficit. Luckily, something you did not learn as a child is learnable as an adult.

It will be important for you to give yourself time to feel these feelings as they come up and allow them to resolve more naturally, without cutting yourself off from them or putting yourself down for having them. It will also be important for you to have adequate support in your life while you are resolving intense feelings. You can get this support from close friends, family, or other loved ones who can provide a caring and listening ear, can allow you the freedom to feel your feelings without having to make suggestions, and can listen nonjudgmentally. Sometimes, the people you love may not be able to provide this type of support for you because of their own discomfort with being around someone having intense feelings. In this case, it might be important for you to find a trained professional who can allow you to express your feelings in a nonjudgmental environment (one in which you feel you can safely and honestly express yourself).

Others have found that peer support groups are valuable in this regard, particularly if the group has clear rules for how the group can respond to a member's emotional expression. The goal is not for someone to fix you by helping you suppress feelings or to distract you from them, but to support you in your natural ability to process an emotion. With experience, some guidance and nonjudgmental support, you can build your skills in handling feelings of different types and intensities. The important thing to remember is not to invalidate or minimize your natural feeling processes.

Jane came from a family that did not allow direct expression of emotion. She was taught early on about the family's strict rules about not allowing others to see your feelings. By age ten, she clearly understood that "big girls don't cry" and that if you did, you were seen as "weak" and "different" from the rest of the family. She learned to suppress her feelings about many things—anger, loneliness, even unbridled joy or passion. Emotional control was valued and honored in her family. Her father seemed proud that he did not weep at his mother's funeral when Jane was fifteen and he saw not missing a day of work around her death as an accomplishment of which to be proud.

Jane learned these family rules quite well and others saw her as quite unflappable, often relying on her strength and calm during crises. She was the "strong, silent type" in her relationship with her partner of fourteen years, Marga. They had managed to do quite well for themselves over the years, building a network of friends, developing independent and successful careers, and living in a home they built themselves.

When Marga died suddenly after a brief bout with breast cancer, Jane's world seemed to come crashing in. She immediately felt an overwhelming grief that was paralyzing in many ways. She had never experienced an emotion this intense and unrelenting. She did her best to choke back the tears and go on with her life as quickly as possible, much like her father did when his mother died. At first, she found some solace in her work. She found that the more involved she became with her job, the less she thought about Marga. When being at home alone became too difficult, she took work home with her and made sure that she had very little quiet time to herself. She kept going at this pace for almost two years, getting special recognition and advancement at work for her extra effort and she found that she thought very little about Marga and their past together. Eventually, she began to find herself feeling worn down, exhausted, and unhappy. She started having trouble sleeping and she felt lonely but could not bring herself to go out on dates or to social events with her couple friends.

Jane's story is a classic example of unresolved bereavement. Jane did not have the family modeling or emotional tools necessary to allow her to process her grief regarding her overwhelming loss of the love of her life. She took the only path she knew: suppress the emotion and distract from the thoughts as long as possible. I often see patients in my practice who have not allowed themselves permission to fully feel the genuine emotions that have arisen in their lives.

Grief was a healthy emotional response to this loss. Not all painful emotion is a result of distorted thinking. Getting angry when someone abuses you or violates your rights is an appropriate emotional response. But many people have trouble dealing in a healthy way with these honest emotions. Anger, as an emotion, is as valid as any other feeling—it has no more nor less value in your repertoire of feelings. What you *do* with your anger or grief behaviorally is very important, however. Unhealthy ways of dealing with emotions include suppression (on a permanent rather than short-term basis), acting on the feelings impulsively through activities with short- or long-term negative consequences (such as fighting or drinking excessive alcohol), and getting stuck in self-deprecating cycles of setting up situations that validate your intense emotional experience (giving yourself a reason to continue to feel sad or angry). The last behavior is often referred to as a *self-fulfilling prophecy*, where you cause your worst fears to happen simply because you are so focused on them. It's like learning to ride a bike and you are so worried about hitting a pothole and falling off that you can't pay enough attention to actually riding the bike. You ultimately hit a pothole and crash to the ground!

If in recognizing your negative self-talk, you find yourself feeling moments of sadness about the pain you suffered as a child who was not fully accepted or grief over the loss of the image of the perfect childhood, allow yourself time to feel and process these natural emotions. Some people use this opportunity to begin keeping a journal of their feelings. A journal can be simply a notebook in which you can document your feelings, explore them safely, and keep track of them for further discussion with a therapist or close friend. I often encourage my clients to keep track of their feelings at the same time that they are keeping track of their thinking. The whole process of self-discovery may be tracked in this way for your later review. It's nice to look back at times and see how far you've come from where you were when you first began the journey to better self-esteem.

Giving yourself permission to feel emotions that come bubbling up may be easier said than done. Often people who do not have much experience with processing emotions feel awkward and uncomfortable attending to their feelings. They may even feel frightened of "taking the lid off" of intense emotions and imagine that if they do begin to open up, the feelings will never end. Often, my patients tell me that they sense when there are feelings that are bottled up inside but they fear losing control of them if they begin to process them. I often introduce them to the idea of *controlled release* of feelings, in which they designate a specific time and place that they feel safe opening the door and letting the feelings come out. For example, you tell yourself that you will attend to the feelings when the time is appropriate, like after dinner at home in your study. It is important to keep this contract with yourself. Using this technique without following up is like promising a child that you will take them to the movie and then canceling later with no explanation.

While feelings themselves are not to be feared, certainly the behaviors that they lead to can be dangerous or harmful. People who are not practiced at allowing themselves to feel great sadness, fear, or anger may have developed powerful ways to distract themselves from the overwhelming depth of the emotions. These include alcohol or other drug use, destruction (of self, others, or things), and even recklessness. If you have a history of acting in potentially destructive or impulsive ways when feelings become overwhelming or if you have a fear of this happening, *do not attempt to process these feelings alone.* Feelings that seem overpowering should be processed in a setting that will be safe, where you will be protected from harming yourself or someone else. A qualified psychotherapist's office is the best setting to learn to deal with powerful feelings more effectively. Chapter 13 deals with how to find an appropriate psychotherapist.

In the course of this book, you are learning to have a better relationship with yourself and that includes both listening to and validating your emotional self. As an adult, you have the capacity to change the voice in your head from a harsh, punitive, and authoritarian one to a more reasonable, validating, and nurturing one. This means not ignoring, punishing, or avoiding the emotional side of yourself. Healthy parents do not punish children for the feelings they have. Healthy parents help the children understand their feelings by validating them and teaching them that feelings should be listened to and responded to in an appropriate way.

By learning to listen to your feelings and not be afraid of them, you can more carefully determine the source of those feelings. The sources may be events that would provoke these feelings in almost anyone, like feeling grief after a loss or anger after an insult. Sometimes, however, the feelings are in response to your interpretation of an event and this interpretation is distorted. The value of the work you are doing in this book is in its ability to help you learn to evaluate your automatic thoughts and interpretations for their rationality. Thinking that is distorted by inaccurate information from your past or the present can be modified with practice.

Sometimes, you may find that an interpretation is accurate and does lead to the corresponding emotion. For example, you may find that you frequently feel a sense of insecurity when you have thoughts like, "Most of the people in my office are homophobic." This thought may be accurate, but it certainly may not always be useful. Having this thought regularly may interfere with your work by keeping you hesitant to make tough decisions or say what you think in a meeting. Recognizing when you are saying things to yourself that are either distorted or are interfering with your ability to function effectively is an important skill that you are learning.

Modifying Self-Talk

> We want to make ourselves clear: our first job is to free
> ourselves; that means clearing our heads of the garbage
> that's been poured into them . . .

> —Carl Wittman, "A Gay Manifesto"

Recognizing your self-talk is only the first step in raising your self-esteem. Actually changing it involves learning to evaluate and respond to both the content of what you are saying and the type of distorted thinking you commonly use. You'll need to take your time reading through this chapter and may want to repeat sections as necessary.

Problematic Thoughts

At this point in the book, you have a better understanding of the self-talk and automatic thoughts that are stylistic for you. If you have been keeping track of your thinking with the Daily Thought Record from chapter 1, you may be able to clearly recognize patterns of what you say to yourself and how you treat yourself. Most people find that when they are beginning to try to pay attention to their thinking, it's easier to analyze an event that led to a thought and then the feeling after the fact. Learning to catch yourself at or near the exact moment you are saying negative things to yourself feels awkward or unnatural when you first try it. Over time and with practice, however, it becomes easier and easier to catch yourself making negative or even punitive self-statements that in turn lead to unpleasant emotions. The key is not to give up. Try not to say things to yourself about the process like, "I'll never learn this technique . . . it just confirms my worthlessness!"

Automatic Thoughts: A Review

Once you become more comfortable with recognizing your automatic thoughts, you will be ready to implement the second step in building your self-esteem: evaluating the accuracy and usefulness of the thinking. But before you begin learning how to change them, it may be helpful at this point to examine some key points about automatic thoughts.

1. They are usually experienced as *brief self-statements*, sometimes in the form of just a few words like "Stupid!" or "I can't handle it!" or for some people they are experienced as quick, negative images, perhaps from the past or of an anticipated negative consequence. Both the automatic words and images are usually experienced as having popped up spontaneously and can be so fleeting that you don't notice them unless you're trying to.

2. You experience most automatic thoughts or images as if they were true since they arise out of childhood, a time of your life when you did not have the capacity or freedom to question them. You also experience them like reflexes, happening so quickly when a trigger event occurs that you feel as though you have no power over them or as if they can never be changed.

3. Many times these automatic thoughts are phrased in the extreme and include rigid rules hidden in the words *should*, *must*, or *have to* such as, "I must always be perfect (happy, young, clean, responsible)." Many of the rules that you had to live by as a child helped you survive and can be viewed as adaptive back then. However as an adult, many of these rules no longer apply or are unnecessary since you now have the power to make your own choices. Many "should" statements set up unreachable standards for you that leave you chronically feeling like a failure when you fail to live up to them.

4. Because these thoughts pop up so quickly and spontaneously, you often do not challenge them and may forget about information that contradicts them. They happen so naturally that you may forget that the automatic thinking is learned and not something you were born with.

5. While automatic thoughts are usually specific to the situation you are in, there are deeper levels of beliefs that represent common themes. After you begin to recognize the many spe-

cific types of automatic thoughts that you have, it will then be important to start to recognize themes or patterns of underlying beliefs. You will have fewer underlying beliefs than specific automatic thoughts. Your core beliefs, at the deepest level, will actually be quite few in number.

Styles of Thinking

Now that we've reviewed some key concepts about automatic thoughts, it's important for you to understand that not only do you have automatic thoughts and underlying beliefs about yourself, but that you also likely use some characteristic styles of thinking. While there are many problematic styles of thinking, the following are most prevalent.

Many of these patterns share common characteristics. You'll find that you do not fit just one of these patterns, but may have aspects of several different kinds of thinking at different times and places. All of the patterns, however, tend to take a distorted view, either overemphasizing the negative aspects of a situation or person or de-emphasizing the positive. They all are missing balance in perspective and tend to stir up intense and negative feelings. All ways of thinking also share another common feature in that they are learned.

Polarized or Black-or-White Thinking

This is one of the most common types of thinking. People limit their options or way of seeing a situation to two alternatives: yes or no, good or bad, right or wrong. They often cannot see the gray areas of life. People who use a lot of *musts*, *shoulds*, and *have-tos* fall into this category and can become quite self-punitive when they do not perform perfectly.

Example: "If I make a mistake on this project, I'll be fired."

Filtering, Discounting the Positive, or Tunnel Vision

These people tend to see life through a filter or lens that distorts their perspective. A form of filtering Dr. Aaron Beck called *selective abstraction* refers to a process of selectively attending to certain, usually negative, cues in your environment rather than seeing a situation more realistically and completely, including the positives. This type of thinking can lead you to feel overwhelmed in a situation because it leads you to have an exaggerated emotional response, based on the fact that you are attending only to the negative. Often, filtering self-talk includes words like *horrible*, *awful*, *unbearable*, and *overwhelming*. Such words suggest that the situation has no solution and that you have no control over it. Someone with low self-esteem might for example interpret going out to a social gathering and not meeting anyone as a sign of being "completely alone and unlovable," forgetting the fact that he or she has family or friends and dismissing the past relationships in which he or she felt loved.

Example: "Since my lover left me, I have nothing left."

Catastrophizing or Fortune Telling

People who catastrophize predict or expect the worst possible scenario for the future regardless of how likely this outcome really is. Although the worst-case scenario may be highly unlikely, a catastrophizer will focus on negative future outcomes, keeping him- or herself in a perpetual state of anxiety and worry.

Example: "Because I failed this first test, I'll probably fail the whole course."

Overgeneralizing, Magnifying, and Labeling

This is when you take a single event in your life and make larger conclusions about your life based on it. Often people who have this style of thinking believe that they cannot make mistakes or that they have to be perfect. When they do make a mistake, they feel like a failure or as though they are destined to repeat the same mistake in the future. Words that are often reflective of overgeneralizing include extremes like *all* or *none*, *everybody* or *nobody*, *never* or *always*. People who overgeneralize tend to make global, labeling statements that are inflated and overreaching for themselves, or other people, places, and things in their lives, often based on a single encounter. A Senate majority leader's ignorant remarks about lesbians and gays leads you to think, "All Republicans are ignorant," or when you make an error during a complicated calculation, you think, "I'm so stupid," as if one mistake reflects a person's entire worth.

Magnifying happens when you elevate the importance of an event beyond its actual importance, such as forgetting something on your grocery list and then putting yourself down as a homemaker. You can also minimize the positive in a situation, downplaying the good outcomes and overemphasizing the bad with self-statements like, "Even though the boss liked my work today, it doesn't mean that I am a strong employee."

Example: "Because I was hurt in my last relationship, I'll never be able to trust anyone again."

Musts and *Shoulds*

These are absolute rules for living that you routinely apply to yourself and others. When you or others do not follow these rules, by mistake or intentionally, you become irritated, angry, and judgmental. Often, the expectations you have in the form of rules are irrational, yet because you likely learned them as a child, you accept them without question. Also, since you are not always aware of these should statements, you respond emotionally to them automatically and do not have the opportunity to challenge them. Having unrealistic expectations for yourself or others leads to mistakes or times when you cannot reach the unreasonable standards, which can leave you constantly feeling like a failure or irritated at the people around you.

Example: "I must always control myself emotionally."

Personalizing

This style refers to how you view yourself in relation to others. One way you can personalize a situation is by always comparing yourself to others, usually unfavorably, with such self-statements as "She's so much more intelligent than I am" or "My body is hideous compared to his." You tend to make value judgements about yourself on a continuous basis, ultimately devaluing yourself if your self-esteem is low. Another way you can personalize is by always assuming that you are the source of other people's problems or the cause of a negative event. For example, you may blame yourself for the failure of a team project even though the outcome was most likely related to a number of problems throughout the process.

Example: "That cashier is scowling because he doesn't like me."

Other Styles

Other types of errors in thinking include *emotional reasoning*, or making decisions based solely on your feelings rather than rational consideration of all information; *mind reading*, where you are highly sensitive to what you believe others are thinking about you or a situation and you fail to consider other alternatives; *blaming*, which involves finding fault in any situation and making yourself or someone else responsible even when their is no one clear source of responsibility; *entitlement fallacies*, which involve the irrational belief that you should always win, get what you want, and have a positive outcome from every endeavor, and lead to extreme disappointment and negative self-talk or blame when the outcome is not in your favor; and *control fallacies,* where you expect yourself to have control over a situation that is uncontrollable, like the weather or illness.

Many people start to change negative patterns of thinking simply by increasing their awareness of when and how they happen. Some of my patients feel some initial excitement as they begin to become aware of negative self-talk and then go on to recognize patterns of distorted thinking. I hope you have begun to feel a greater sense of self-awareness at this point in the book and even a greater sense of control as you begin to understand why you sometimes think or feel as you do.

Problematic Nondistorted Thinking

Sometimes, you may recognize an automatic thought that does not appear distorted or irrational that leads to negative or immobilizing emotions. For example, by all standards, Jeff was considered overweight at close to four hundred pounds. As Jeff's weight increased over the years, he found himself becoming more and more depressed and socially isolated. He recognized that he clearly had developed distorted ways of thinking about himself that sabotaged his plans. For example, about three years ago he decided to try to change his life by following a professionally developed and sensible weight loss program that included moderate exercise, a change of eating habits, and emotional support. He began the program with considerable enthusiasm and followed the plan exactly for the first five days. On day six, however, Jeff woke up to a phone call from his mother about his father's recent hospitalization with chest pain and shortness of breath. Worried about his father and living too far away to get there quickly, Jeff spent the day catastrophizing about the outcome of the doctor's tests, imagining that his father was dying and even that he himself was likely going to die from obesity.

Jeff completely abandoned his careful weight loss plan that day, finding himself eating more than normal as he struggled to deal with the anxiety of his father's symptoms. His thoughts not only turned to *catastrophizing* about himself and his father's future, but he also then began to *blame* himself for ruining his weight loss plan, *overgeneralizing* that one day of emotional intensity meant that he could never lose the weight and on and on.

What really seemed to bother him the most, however, was when he looked into the mirror. All he saw was fat. He couldn't ignore the scale that registered 389 pounds, just two pounds down from where he started five days ago. He found that all he could think at times was, "I am fat. I am not a normal size and I am slow." Then he would immediately feel sad and lonely. Jeff had learned how to recognize his distorted or unreasonable thoughts and had relatively good success at challenging and replacing them with healthier thinking. But he always seemed to stumble when he looked in the mirror and began the repetitive self-statements about his size. In fact, he felt as though he deserved to be depressed when he tried to find the distortions in the mirror statements and couldn't disagree with the content. He felt that it was true that he was fat, his weight was outside of the "norm" for males his size, and he did take longer to climb stairs or walk down the hall than most people. He didn't know what to do about these powerful thoughts that elicited strong depressing and demotivating feelings.

There certainly are times when the thoughts you recognize that create negative feelings such as depression or insecurity are triggered by thoughts that are true. One could argue that for gay men and lesbians, some of the frightening cultural messages we receive like, "If you are gay, you are at risk for harm," are also true since we live in a relatively homophobic society. The key then is not whether the thoughts are distorted or not, but whether they are useful or helpful. Repetitive thoughts that may be true, but serve to undermine your confidence, enrage you for hours, and depress your mood are also problematic and can be challenged.

Changing the Self-Talk

Several techniques have been found useful and powerful in learning to change negative self-talk. Evaluating your thoughts, the ABCD model, and thought stopping are the most effective.

Evaluating Your Thoughts

At this point, you are thoroughly acquainted with the idea of identifying and evaluating automatic thoughts and distorted thought patterns. Review some of your Daily Thought Records (from chapter 1) so you can identify your thought patterns. For each event that triggered a feeling, you should have identified an automatic thought. Not only is it important to evaluate the content of the thoughts, but you must also pay attention to the tone and images associated with the thoughts. I'm sure you will recognize that at times, what people say with words and what they mean can be very different. For example, someone can say the words, "Don't you look nice today!" but just a slight alteration in the delivery, with a scowl or smirk, radically changes this from a compliment to sarcasm. Therefore it's important to not only determine the words that you say to yourself, but also to consider the tone with which you say them. I've had some patients tell me that they actually "hear" the words or phrases they heard from parents during childhood with the same tone of voice that their parents used. If you find that the actual content seems reasonable but you still feel put down or insecure, try digging a little deeper for the sarcasm or implicit threat that you may still be using on yourself.

The next step is to identify the distorted thinking pattern. Is it an example of filtering, polarized thinking, or personalization? Or is it nondistorted but problematic as in the example about Jeff?

Once you've identified the pattern, the next step is to come up with a healthier alternative to the negative thoughts, making a conscious effort to think about the event in a more reasonable way. The following list of thinking distortions and ways to refute them may be helpful:

Style of Thinking	Suggestions for Counteracting
Polarized Thinking (thinking in extremes)	Think about options along a continuum rather than as "black or white" and appreciate the complexity of life
Example: *If I make a mistake on this project, I'll be fired.*	Example: *I may make a mistake on this, but I'm only human and sometimes there are things beyond my control. My boss may be disappointed but probably won't fire me.*
Filtering, Discounting the Positive, or Tunnel Vision (attending to only the negative aspects of a situation)	Consider the positives, the good things you have to be grateful for.
Example: *Since my lover left me, I have nothing left.*	Example: *It hurts that she left me, but I do have some wonderful and supportive friends who still love me.*

Catastrophizing or Fortune Telling (always predicting the worst-case scenario)	Remind yourself of the realistic likelihood of your prediction occurring.
Example: *Because I failed this first test, I'll probably fail the whole course.*	Example: *Failing the first test doesn't mean that I can't learn this material. I'll just have to study a different way.*
Overgeneralizing (making general conclusions from a specific event)	Put the specific into the larger context.
Example: *Because I was hurt in my last relationship, I'll never be able to trust anyone again.*	Example: *It will take time to heal from that last relationship, but I'll learn from this and eventually find someone I can trust.*
Musts and *Shoulds* (inflexible, absolute rules)	Allow mistakes to happen, be more reasonable and flexible with yourself.
Example: *I can't believe I didn't see that problem coming. I should always anticipate every potential problem.*	Example: *I'm upset about that problem, but I can't expect myself to anticipate every potential problem.*
Personalizing (assuming everything relates to you)	Don't make unproven assumptions without checking them out in real life. Recognize that all humans have positive and negative qualities.
Example: *That cashier is scowling because he doesn't like me.*	Example: *That cashier must be having a bad day.*

For these and the other styles of negative thinking mentioned but not covered here, the key is to recognize that each has some systematic way of distorting the accurate perception of yourself, a situation, or other people. Counteracting your negative thoughts may take some practice and you may need to use the Daily Thought Record regularly at first to get the hang of it.

When counteracting a distorted thought, it is sometimes helpful to imagine responding to the distorted self-talk as if you were responding to a close friend in a gentle, compassionate voice. One strategy that has been helpful to some of my patients is to imagine that your counteracting voice is that of an ideal parent, one who is totally accepting, unconditionally loving, and nurturing. Some have even found it helpful to imagine how they might speak to a child who was feeling shamed, inadequate, frightened or alone, since it is easier in the beginning to feel compassion for someone else (an innocent child for example) rather than themselves. They then gradually learn to immediately recognize the negative self-talk as soon as they begin to feel uncomfortable feelings and how to quickly counteract it with a new, self-nurturing voice. I will expand on the use of these techniques later in the self-nurturing chapter.

The ABCD Model

Another more structured method for understanding your self-talk is called *the ABCD model* and is commonly used in cognitive behavioral therapy. Each letter stands for a step in recognizing and disputing negative self-talk.

A stands for the *activating event* that triggers the negative self-talk. An example might be reading the newspaper and seeing a story about a hate crime toward a lesbian or gay person.

B stands for the *belief* (or negative thoughts) that are triggered. After seeing the story about the hate crime, you may think, "The world is a dangerous place for me" or "I will probably be attacked soon."

C is for the *consequences* of having that thought—the feelings you have, such as anxiety, insecurity, or rage, and the behaviors that these feelings lead to, such as avoiding going out, dating, or trusting someone you care about.

D stands for the *disputing* self-talk that you use to counteract the negative distortions. In this case, you might say something like, "I'm generalizing a specific event (someone who was attacked) to myself ('The world is a dangerous place . . .'), which is a form of *personalizing*, and I'm expecting the worst ('I will probably be attacked soon.') which is *catastrophizing*." Even if it is true that violence against lesbians and gays happens, it is not helpful to ruminate about it. Your disputing thoughts could be, "It makes me angry/frightened/sad to read about violence against gays, but all I can do is learn to protect myself and to remind myself of the fact that the vast majority of gays and lesbians are not victims of violent attacks."

It might be helpful to write this model down. Practice going through it regularly until you reach a point of quickly identifying and disputing distorted thinking. With practice, most people can learn to do this without writing each step down and find that they feel a sense of emotional relief almost immediately when they dispute the negative thinking.

Thought Stopping

One of the most basic and most effective techniques for dealing with distorted or harmful thinking is called *thought stopping*. As I mentioned before, self-talk occurs quickly when you are in a triggering event or situation. The moment you interpret the event, even if it is objectively vague or ambiguous, and begin the self-talk, you will immediately feel an emotion in reaction to the self-talk. The more negative the talk about your value, your abilities, or your potential, the lower you will find your self-esteem and the more insecure you will be about making choices. This self-talk can set up a self-perpetuating cycle that leads to more negative feelings and more negative self-talk. The first step in interrupting this cycle is learning to recognize the negative self-talk immediately. This process involves first concentrating on the negative or unwanted thought for a short time, then quickly stopping it and clearing your mind.

Before you attempt this technique, you must first prepare yourself to respond with healthy self-talk when you do recognize and stop the negative self-talk. Make up a list of healthy responses that are counter to the typical thought processes you have observed in yourself while reading this book. Some general, but positive self-statements that you can use might include the following:

- "I am not worthless, stupid, or evil. I am worthy, intelligent, and good."
- "I do not have to be perfect. All human beings make mistakes."
- "Relax and breathe. I can cope with this situation."
- "It is not helpful to think like this. I do not deserve to treat myself like this. This self-talk is just an old habit."
- "Even if she rejected me, I know that I am lovable."
- "I have value regardless of what anyone else says."

- "It's okay to have feelings about this situation, but I will not let the feelings trigger the old habitual self-punitive thinking."

Some of these statements may be difficult to say to yourself initially and they may feel forced or unnatural. The next chapter, Self-Nurturing and Forgiveness, will address some of the core beliefs you hold that may make saying anything positive to yourself feel artificial or faked. You may need to construct your own list of positive self-statements that feel more comfortable to you. Don't say things to yourself that are blatantly untrue such as, "I am a math genius," if you have trouble balancing your checkbook. Try to make the list balanced, realistic, and believable to you. The specific words are less important than the attitude of self-acceptance and encouragment. Write your own list of pleasant, encouraging, or positive thoughts in your journal or on a blank piece of paper.

Occasionally, I find that some people have difficulty saying more positive and encouraging things to themselves because they say at a deeper level they can't or don't believe the statements. Essentially, I believe that they have spent so many years repeating the same negative self-statements until they believe them at their core. If this is the case for you, it is to be expected that you might have trouble changing some of these core beliefs overnight. Changing the thoughts is just the beginning of building your core sense of self-esteem. The final chapters of this book delve into other ways that you can begin to change core beliefs and, essentially, your relationship with yourself. For now, practice stopping the negative thinking and developing a new habit of thinking something encouraging or more positive.

Saying to yourself in a forceful way, "Stop it!" can interrupt this spiraling negative process and allow you to begin the process of challenging and replacing your initial and distorted thinking with healthier thoughts. One particularly well-know behavioral treatment for stopping smoking uses a variation on this technique in which the smoker interrupts the craving for a cigarette by wearing a rubber band around his or her wrist and snapping it when necessary. This technique has been used in many other behaviorally oriented therapies from dieting programs to the treatment of phobias.

It is not necessary to use such techniques if you find that you can successfully talk your way into stopping the negative talk. Some people find that simply saying to themselves "Stop!" is sufficient to interrupt the automatic thinking spiral. Others have found that at times, the thinking pattern feels so strong that they have to say it out loud, yell it, or even clap their hands or snap their fingers. I recommend that you practice thought stopping when you are alone until you can reliably interrupt the process either by thinking it to yourself or using some silent reminder like clenching your fist or tapping your forehead (something less likely to draw attention to yourself in public).

If you find that your frustration builds with repeated unpleasant thoughts and images, you can make some type of angry statement as a form of fighting back against the negative self-talk. For example,

- "Stop the blaming and catastrophizing!"
- "This negative garbage is not helping!"
- "These old messages are wrong and unfair!"
- "Enough is enough!"

Come up with your own angry rebuttal statements. You can be as colorful with your language as necessary. Just remember that you are rebutting the old, negative messages, *not* speaking to yourself in a self-punitive way. Write these down in your journal or on a blank piece of paper (and keep it with your other lists).

After you have interrupted your undesired thoughts, you're ready to insert the more positive self-talk. You also can substitute pleasant scenes at this point, including your favorite and most relaxing images. The more vivid you can make your image, recalling the sights, sounds, smells, and tastes, the better able you will be to break the negative thinking spiral. If the negative thoughts come back within thirty seconds, keep saying "Stop!" to yourself, counteracting the negative thinking and substituting the same or another pleasant scene. You will want to practice some pleasant imagery at other times so that you can be more prepared for using it quickly to interrupt negative thinking.

Take a moment and describe a scene now for yourself that makes you feel relaxed and comfortable. Make sure you include the location and all the sensory aspects of the place such as the sights, smells, feel, and sounds. Beaches are common relaxing scenes for many people. If this is the case for you, you would want to imagine the feel of the warm sand, the sounds of the tide, the smell of the ocean air, and maybe even the taste of salt as you swim or float in the water. In your journal or on a piece of paper, write down your own relaxing scene. Be sure to include the location, sights, sounds, smells, and tastes.

We will discuss the use of imagery and visualization for building self-esteem in more detail later in the book. For more information about thought stopping and other cognitive-behavioral techniques, I highly recommend the book *Thoughts & Feelings: Taking Control of Your Moods and Your Life* by McKay, Davis, and Fanning (1997).

At this point, it might also be helpful for you to revisit the Daily Thought Record from chapter 1 and add two new columns on the right side of the form. After the "Automatic Thoughts" column, make a column with the heading "Counteracting Arguments." This column will be where you record an adaptive, alternate way of thinking that will help reduce the negative feelings. To help with this column, ask yourself the following questions adapted from the book *Cognitive Therapy: Basics and Beyond* by Judith Beck (1995):

1. What evidence do I have that this thought is true or will happen?

2. Are there other ways to think about this situation or explain it?

3. What is the worst (and best) thing that could happen in this situation? Will I live through it? What is the most likely, realistic outcome?

4. How could changing my thinking effect this situation or my reaction?

5. What should I do about about the situation that will help me cope?

6. If my friend was in this situation and had this thought, what advice would I give him or her?

After you have come up with a counteracting argument to the irrational or maladaptive thought, make another heading beside it to the right and call it the "Results" column. Here, you will record the effect of changing your thinking on your feelings and behavior. See the revised Daily Thought Record for an example.

Revised Daily Thought Record

Time/ Day/ Date	Event	Automatic Thoughts	Feelings	Counteracting Thoughts	Results
5:02 pm. Monday 7/15	Copy store closed.	1) "What if I get fired?"	Fear, anxious.	This is a mistake that anyone could make. I'll find a store that's open later or go	Less anxiety.

first thing in the morning.

2) *"I'm so incompetent."* *Despair, sad.* *This has nothing to do with my competence. I could not control the traffic.* *Less sad, more reasonable thinking.*

Responding to External Messages

If you find yourself responding emotionally to public statements made by people in the media such as politicians, religious figures, and others, take a few moments to do the following:

Consider the source. Does this person represent a radical constituency? If he or she is speaking as a representative of a larger organization, is this person speaking from his or her own personal biases rather than as a true representative of the views of the entire membership of his or her total organization?

Consider what the person's motivation for making such a statement might be. What does the speaker have to gain, personally or politically, from making the statement? If the person is speaking from a personal standpoint, did he or she have a negative interaction with a lesbian or gay person in the past? Is he or she struggling with his or her own sexual identity issues and therefore threatened by gay men or lesbians who are out? Is he or she responding to social stereotypes and misinformation? Does this person get paid to make false and inflammatory statements by the media or his or her organization? If the person does represent the views of a larger organization, is this a way to divide or unite political constituencies? Is this a calculated "hot button" statement meant to stimulate fund-raising based on fear-mongering?

Ask yourself if the statements they make are distorted. Do statements by such an individual make the content of what he or she says true just because he or she said it? Could the person be using unscientific or unproven data? Is he or she manipulating or misinterpreting the results of a legitimate study? Is he or she egocentric and noncontextual in his or her approach to interpretation of the Bible, Torah, Koran, or other religious materials?

Decide whether the media has omitted the position of people with similar levels of authority who have different or more mainstream or more healthy views of gay men and lesbians. Did the producers of the show seek out a public figure who would make inflammatory remarks to boost ratings? Did they set the tone of the discussion up to be conflictual between two opposite viewpoints instead of having a range of perspectives? Are you allowing yourself to be manipulated by the media for their own gain?

These are questions that may be helpful in getting yourself to de-escalate, or reduce the intensity of your feelings. Hopefully, you will see that the opinions or statements of the person who is speaking negatively about gays and lesbians are distorted in the way that your thinking may be at times. You may find that simply hearing the negative statements that you have learned to say to yourself spoken out loud is enough to trigger the negative and punitive spiraling of thoughts. It would then be appropriate for you to begin the process of stopping the negative thoughts you are having and begin substituting healthier ones.

However, I also believe that on a larger level, sometimes building self-esteem internally means taking action externally. Social activism can take many different forms including staging a "kiss in" protest with ACT UP; writing letters to your congressperson, the editor of your local paper, or the producers of a show with unbalanced perspectives; or even refusing to do business with companies that discriminate against lesbians or gay men. Other forms of social action include helping friends and family understand gay and lesbian issues more completely, marching in a pride parade, calling your cable company to complain about programming that is offensive to you, and doing business with lesbian/gay-owned or -friendly companies. There are many levels of action with which most people can be comfortable no matter how bold or timid they feel. Everyone can turn off the television or change the channel when a zealot or intolerant viewpoint is given air time and everyone can learn to turn off the residual effects of hearing such talk.

You can't change the world overnight, but you can teach yourself to feel less powerless in a complex and sometimes overwhelming world. As you change the way you think and take action to change the world when you can, you will find a growing sense of personal power and greater self-esteem.

11

Self-Nurturing and Forgiveness

"There, there Lucille," said Lucille here. I tried remembering what words my mother used when I was sick. I needed me a nice soothing nickname to goo-goo at myself. Who else would?

—Alan Gurganus, *Oldest Living Confederate Widow Tells All*

While changing your negative self-talk is crucial to improving your self-esteem, it's only the beginning of the process of improving your view of yourself. It is even more important to work on changing the core beliefs you have about yourself—those beliefs that are so deeply held it's difficult for you to even recognize them as distorted.

Changing your core beliefs requires a change of attitude in your relationship to yourself. You can no longer afford to continue to treat yourself with less respect than you would treat a stranger. You will be required to take an honest look at who you really are, rather than who other people wish you were or want you to be. Taking an honest look may be uncomfortable at times, especially if you feel emotions that you would rather not feel. You may find that you don't have feelings you expected to have, which can also be uncomfortable.

The key to treating yourself with respect is understanding who you really are and feeling some sense of compassion, affection, and eventually unconditional love for yourself. This means getting to know what you really feel and what you honestly think about things, rather than trying to feel and think about things the way others expect. It also means finding out what you like and what you don't like without being judged.

This process can be a long one. Learning to overcome years of training to suppress and repress your true feelings about sexuality and the larger desires in life will take time and patience. You may never completely erase all traces of core beliefs that you learned as a child. The best you may be able to do is spend less time suppressing feelings and harshly judging your thoughts and behaviors and more time feeling compassion toward yourself as you would toward most other human beings. That is a worthy goal in itself for living. If you spend more time being gentle toward yourself and self-nurturing, you will likely feel less angry and judgmental toward others—a benefit for the world as a whole.

Some important keys to self-nurturing include learning to revise old negative core beliefs, learning to listen to and validate your feelings, reconstructing a more balanced picture of yourself with both positives and negatives instead of just the negatives, protecting yourself from harm or abuse by constructing healthy boundaries, and appropriately asking for what you want and need.

Changing Your Core and Conditional Beliefs

As I mentioned in chapter 1, building your self-esteem goes deeper than just changing maladaptive or distorted thinking habits. Beneath the automatic thoughts that you have learned to recognize, evaluate, and change are the conditional beliefs (or the rules you live by) and underlying those at the deepest levels are the core beliefs—the ones that feel absolute and perhaps unchangeable. To get at these deeper, gut-level feelings of self-worth, you can apply similar techniques to those mentioned in the previous chapter.

For example, with experience you will start to hear the common themes underneath the automatic, situation-specific thoughts. For example, one common core belief for lesbian and gay people with low self-esteem is that "Gay and lesbian people are morally inferior to straight people." This belief is reinforced in many ways, through some religions, the culture, and families, as we explored in the first section of the book. And not only will you have specific beliefs about being gay or lesbian and about sexual behavior in general, but you will also have core beliefs about your value as a human being aside from the negatives society holds about homosexuality. Some of these core beliefs may make you feel like "you are bad, evil, unworthy of love, or will always be rejected."

Notice that I said that these beliefs may make you *feel like* you are evil or unworthy. Intellectually you may be able to dismiss this belief as irrational, but the feelings are more difficult to dismiss. It may be helpful first to recognize and articulate your deepest held core beliefs and conditional beliefs and then revise them into more objective and realistic beliefs.

The following example and exercise can help you be prepared cognitively to deal with your thoughts and feelings when you recognize a core belief directing your thoughts or behaviors.

Old Core Belief	Revised Core Belief
I am inferior to others because I am gay.	Gay people are humans and thus equal to all others.
I must always be perfect to be accepted.	No one is perfect.
I am evil/sinful/bad because I am lesbian.	Sexual orientation is not a moral issue. Mutually consensual sexual and emotional relationships between adults are my right and choice.
I am unworthy of love/joy/peace.	All human beings have worth, even if we don't understand the specifics (i.e., how you fit in).
I am stupid.	I have been smart enough to survive, learn, and change.
I am helpless.	I am not helpless. I am an adult with a brain, supportive friends, etc.

In your journal or on a piece of paper, try writing down some of your own core beliefs and then some revised, healthier ones. The same strategy will also be helpful for changing the conditional beliefs, or rules that you live by, that may be extreme, irrational, or maladaptive.

In your journal or on a piece or paper, try listing some of your rules that you make yourself live by and rewriting them to make them less extreme. Make a column on the left side that you call "Old Rules" and a column on the right that you call "New Rules." For each old rule on the left, write a new, more reasonable rule on the right.

Old Rule	New Rule
I must always be slim/buffed/on a strict diet.	I will try to stay healthy and in shape, but gaining a few pounds here and there is normal.
If people make a mistake with me in a relationship, they are to be avoided.	Making mistakes is completely human. I will communicate how I feel and work through the conflict.

Again, changing the self-talk and evaluating and revising core beliefs and your rules to live by are important first steps to take in making change in your overall self-esteem. However, I occasionally find that even when my patients do the exercises faithfully, and they feel significant reduction in anxiety, insecurity, anger, and despair, it does not always mean that they experience an increase in happiness, peace, joy, and satisfaction with their lives. Beyond challenging the dysfunctional thinking you must develop emotional connectedness with yourself and work toward a more nurturing relationship with yourself.

Ideally, you would have been raised to believe you were valuable from the moment you were born, simply because you existed. That may not have been the case, however. Your parents may not have taught you that the moment you entered the world, you changed it in ways that could not be reversed. Your presence changed all decisions and choices that your parents and other caregivers made. It's important for you to remember this. Great spiritual and religious belief systems have developed out of a need that we have as humans to understand our place in the universe, to understand our meaning and purpose. The next chapter is designed to help you access internal and external resources to help you with finding your own answers to these questions. Each person's search and each person's answers are unique. Understanding that you have a place in this world and that your very existence is evidence of some greater value and purpose is the key to developing a more nurturing relationship with yourself.

Self-Nurturing: Beyond the Cognitive

Imagine that dealing with your self-talk is like living in a barracks with a loudspeaker blaring personal insults throughout the day whenever you make a mistake—"You're stupid!" "You'll never succeed!" "You're worthless!" "You must accomplish more to make up for your deficiencies!" And so on. Imagine the anxiety, irritability, and ultimately despair you would feel if you never heard a word of encouragement. You would eventually learn to expect nothing from yourself and see yourself as worthless and inferior. You would also likely begin to feel as though you could not make important decisions without guidance. You might become passive, trying to avoid making mistakes that would lead to more verbal abuse.

Consider the overall quality of your self-talk and your typical emotional responses to it. Is the self-talk something you would say to another person? In most cases where the self-talk is predominantly negative, people would almost never want to say to someone else what they say to themselves. For example, you might say to yourself, "You deserve to be punished because you are so lazy," in an attempt to motivate yourself to do something you are not looking forward to. However, most people would be quite hesitant to say those words to a stranger, out of a sense of respect and propriety. You would choose to motivate someone in a different way and might say, "I know you must be tired of doing this work, but there's only an hour left and I know you can get through it."

The second statement is obviously less punitive and more encouraging. Imagine now that you live in a barracks where there is a loudspeaker that shouts words of encouragement when you make a mistake or you are tired—"That's okay, everyone makes mistakes! You'll get it eventually." "Keep trying. I know you can figure it out." This voice might also comment on things you have done well—"That was great! Keep up the good work!" "You're a model employee!"

Obviously, it is not a simple task to move from a negative, de-motivating basic stance to an encouraging, nurturing one. You have to ask yourself the following question at some point: "Do I *deserve* compassion?" The correct answer is "Yes." Everyone deserves compassion. No matter who you are, the color of your skin, the amount of money you have, the religion you follow, your past behaviors, or the gender of the person you love. Only through compassion can people trust enough to make changes. Blaming an addict, condemning a criminal, judging another person's value, all fall into the punitive camp. Some of you might say things like, "How can I feel compassion toward a murderer or child molester? Don't they deserve to be punished? Aren't they evil?" All good questions with a simple answer: All people have value and deserve compassion; it is their behavior that is unacceptable.

This is an important distinction. All people have some value, even a murderer or rapist. In the movie *Dead Man Walking* (based on the real life experiences of Sister Helen Prejean), Susan Sarandon plays a nun who goes to visit a man on death row who was convicted of committing a horrific murder. She is convinced that the man, played by Sean Penn, is deserving of forgiveness and spiritual redemption, even though the families of the murder victims are hurting and angry, wishing him dead quickly and painfully. The families don't feel that he deserves forgiveness from God or anyone else and want the nun to punish the prisoner, even if in a spiritual way. The nun is able to draw a distinction between the value of a human, which she feels is inherent, and the behaviors that he has committed, which can be forgiven and changed.

Some prominent leaders think they are being compassionate when they draw a similar distinction between being lesbian or gay and the act of having sex with another person. You've probably heard the saying, "Love the sinner and hate the sin," used by some right-wing religious leaders in this country. This distinction is a deception, implying that somehow adult consensual sexual activity is equal to murder or rape. A newer twist made by some political extremists tones down that rhetoric a bit into "Love the sinner, but their acts are an illness (or addiction) that must be treated."

It's important for you to understand that parallels between adult, consensual sex and harming another person or having a problem are totally inappropriate. As we discussed earlier, many religious and political figures continue to view gay and lesbian people from completely disproven and outdated models such as the illness model and the moral model. You must say to yourself clearly, "I am not evil because I am gay. I have value." These words will be the foundation of developing self-compassion, self-encouragement, and self-esteem. They will help you fight the negative messages that are all around you in the media, the workplace, and sometimes in your family. It should be your choice to love whom you choose to love, not the decision of someone who is not gay or lesbian or has their own ideas of what is right and wrong. Sometimes, this means confronting the lawmakers about their attempts to deprive you of your civil liberties. On a deeper level, it's important to understand your right to love, acceptance, and freedom. The following is a list of core principles to use as a guide for developing your own beliefs:

- **You are not responsible for your family's ignorance or mistakes.** They bear at least some responsibility for their ignorance and misjudgments even if they did not intend harm.

- **Society is the problem, not your sexuality**.

- **There are many spiritual paths and religious systems, only some of which are anti-gay and homophobic.** There are plenty of other belief systems that are gay-affirmative and no one has a monopoly on God or spirituality.

- **You deserve (and are worthy of) love, acceptance, and respect exactly as you are**. Your feelings and opinions are valid and deserve a chance to be considered regardless of what others want.

- **You are perfect in your imperfection**. No one is perfect and therefore when you make mistakes, you are enjoying a common bond with all other humans.

- **You have inherent worth simply because you were born**. Your value does not come from what you accomplish or who you please. You hold a place in the world for a reason, even if you haven't figured out exactly what that reason is.

- **You can give yourself permission to let go of the past**. You have the capacity to adhere to higher values such as forgiving others even when they do not seek it. Forgiving yourself for mistakes you have made is essential to your future growth.

Forgiving and Moving On

A few of my patients bring up the fact that they have done things that they are ashamed of or feel guilty about in the past. They have a difficult time forgetting about behaviors like lying to family or friends, overusing alcohol and other drugs, lashing out, and so on. In our culture, when someone does make a choice to act in a way that does harm others, it is common to expect negative consequences imposed by the law enforcers or by the courts. There are also natural consequences for behaviors that create harm. For example, people who overuse alcohol for extended periods of time can end up with serious medical problems. Other natural consequences include the guilt people feel.

If you have a lot of guilt and remorse for past behaviors, it's time to feel the regret and then forgive yourself. You have likely paid your debt for behaviors that you regret and it is now time to begin a new relationship with yourself, a more compassionate one. If you do not feel your debt is paid, consider constructive ways to give back to your community or the people you may have hurt along the way. You may try to repair old relationships if those people are willing. It is not absolutely necessary to apologize to people with whom you have interacted negatively for several reasons. First, these people may be unable or unwilling to accept your apology. Second, if they are particularly uninterested in repairing the relationship, they may take the opportunity to harm you further. Third, if you feel you cannot control yourself should they take the opportunity to mock you or "push your buttons," it is better to forego such an interaction. If you cannot heal the old wounds in a relationship in person because of the other person's unwillingness or instability or your fear of your own reactions, you can do so figuratively. Here are some suggestions for ways to do this:

Letter Writing Ritual

Write a letter to the person or persons who have hurt you or you have hurt. Write the letter with the expectation that you will *not* send it so that you can express yourself more freely. Explain how you perceive that you hurt them and how they may have hurt you. Ask this person to forgive the hurtful behaviors and say that you will do the same. Express why the person is important to you and why you would like to have the connection repaired. Let yourself feel the feelings that come up, whether they be anger, grief, or fear, and put all of this down in the letter. When you have finished, put the letter aside for a day or two to let your feelings subside. Then choose a time and place to destroy the letter and let go of the issues and feelings you've written about. Tear it up, burn it in a fireplace, or find another creative way of disposing of it. As you see it disappear, allow yourself to put the unsettled issue to rest.

Empty Chair Technique

Another common way to heal old wounds is to use the *empty chair technique*. This is a simple but powerful way for you to have a conversation between you and someone (or even some*thing*) when the other participant in the discussion is not physically present. Essentially, to have such a conversation, some people find it easier to actually sit across from an empty chair and imagine that the person or entity that they would like to have a dialogue with is sitting in the empty chair. The advantage of this method is that you can imagine the person under your complete control, forced to listen to you and to let you finish your thoughts.

In this scenario, you might explain to the person in everyday language what you feel the problems were between the two of you, how you felt hurt by the person, and what led to your lashing out. To help yourself progress with the dialogue, you might then switch to the other chair and become the person to whom you are speaking. What might this person say in response? Remember that you have the power in this exercise to have the person respond appropriately, rather than defensively or with hurtful rage. This is your opportunity to have the kind of dialogue you have always wanted to have with the person who has hurt you, or whom you have hurt. If you are trying to let go of your own hurtful behavior, it is your opportunity to apologize and ask for forgiveness. If you were hurt by the person, it is your chance to take the high road and make peace.

If you find that you cannot forgive someone else, particularly when that person is not actually in dialogue with you, you may need more time to heal. It is especially important then that you learn how to self-nurture now so that you can provide an environment for yourself that encourages healing.

The empty chair technique has been used in many other ways that can be helpful in your daily life. For example, you can practice conversations you might have with someone in your life now. You also can use this technique to begin a dialogue with parts of yourself that seem anxious, afraid, or confused. I will discuss this type of internal dialogue a little later in this chapter.

If you do choose to attempt peacemaking with family or friends, and you feel psychologically ready to do so, here are a few pointers:

- **Make sure that you will be safe from the other person's feelings as well as your own.** Choose a public place or take someone with you if you have a real fear of the other person's response. Your safety is paramount.

- **Don't apologize for being lesbian or gay.** Only apologize for your behaviors that were unnecessarily hurtful.

- **Don't expect them to apologize to you.** Sometimes those same people may have been hurtful to you but are not ready to admit their own responsibility.

- **Be prepared to leave if old tensions start to brew.** You must be in control of yourself and be prepared to protect yourself by leaving.

- **Understand that by making the first move, you have made restitution regardless of the outcome.**

If you find that you need more time with the issue of forgiving yourself, I recommend that you read *The Self-Forgiveness Handbook* by Thom Rutledge (1997).

What Self-Nurturing Is and Is Not

Now that you are ready to make real changes in how you treat yourself, let's take a moment to reflect on what exactly self-nurturing is and what it is not. Some people believe that they are great "self-nurturers" because they treat themselves to dessert occasionally or they get a massage once a month. While those behaviors can be a part of learning to self-nurture, just doing things that are pleasurable does not constitute a complete self-nurturing attitude. To nurture something means to feed or provide nourishment, to foster an organism's growth by providing for its needs. *Self-nurturing* means to provide yourself with a nourishing environment, an environment that encourages your health and growth physically, emotionally, cognitively, and spiritually. Getting an extra dessert now and then is physically rewarding, especially in terms of the taste, smell, and sight of something like a hot fudge sundae or strawberry tart. Unfortunately, having an extra dessert regularly as a form of self-reward can actually be damaging in the long run as you gain weight, watch your cholesterol rise, and even learn to substitute sugar for emotional intimacy.

Self-nurturing therefore is not just rewarding yourself for a job well done or task accomplished on time. It is also not just rewarding yourself with immediate gratification as with desserts, alcohol, drugs, or other quick fixes. Self-nurturing is about doing the right thing for yourself in the big picture, also referred to as *long-term hedonism* by Dr. Albert Ellis, a founder of cognitive behavioral therapy. A short-term hedonist is someone who lives for the moment, grabbing every ounce of pleasure she or he can. However, as Dr. Ellis points out, too much immediate gratification can lead to problems down the road that can make life more miserable. He believes that it is much more rational, and self-nurturing, to consider the long-term consequences of immediate gratification and to attempt to care for your body, mind, and spirit in ways that will keep you feeling good over time. Think about the attitude you might adopt if you were caring for a child. Would you feed the child candy every day? Or would you teach the child to have a balanced diet and make healthy choices?

Think about your priorities. What would you say is the most important thing in your life? Take a look at the following list and rank the items by placing a number from 1 to 10 (with 1 being the most important and 10 being the least important) by each. I've added two "Other" categories for any issues I may have omitted that are important to you. Then take a minute and roughly estimate what percentage of time you spend per week on each of these (your total should equal 100 percent).

Priority	Rank	% of Time
Job/Career/Money (time spent working, thinking about work, paying bills, etc.)	_____	_____
Home (cleaning, decorating, remodeling, gardening, etc.)	_____	_____
Taking care of others	_____	_____
Spirituality (meditation, prayer, religion)	_____	_____
Health (exercise, medical, dental)	_____	_____
Sex	_____	_____
Education/Growth (not job related)	_____	_____
Building relationships (partner, friends, family)	_____	_____
Entertainment (TV, movies, recreation)	_____	_____
Other _____	_____	_____
Other _____	_____	_____

When you look at this list, are there any discrepancies between the amount of time you spend doing something and where it falls on your list of priorities? Many people find that what they would *like to be emphasizing* in their lives and what they *actually are doing* are disproportionate to one another. If you have low self-esteem, you often place the needs of others before your own, feeling as though you don't deserve special attention or somehow have to make yourself indispensable to others in order to have value.

Building good self-esteem will involve attempting to redistribute your energy in ways that place your personal needs higher on the list of priorities. Ultimately, you are in the best position to listen to what you need emotionally, physically, and spiritually and then become your own best caretaker. Imagine how much more enjoyable life would be if you felt attended to, acknowledged and nurtured. I encourage you to begin placing yourself higher on your list of priorities and to spend more time in self-care activities. If necessary, add another column and re-do your rankings or percentages to reflect your long-term goals.

Learning to Nourish the Self

Let's now get even more specific about how to live day to day in a more self-nurturing way. You are beginning to develop an attitude toward yourself that is encouraging rather than discouraging, forgiving rather than condemning, and respectful instead of belittling. You have learned strategies for changing your attitude and monitoring your thoughts and feelings. What about putting these strategies into day-to-day practice?

In this section, I will make some specific suggestions about living a more self-nurturing life from three perspectives: cognitively, emotionally, and behaviorally.

Cognitive Guidelines for Every Day

Once you have mastered the techniques in chapter 10 and can more easily recognize negative, distorted, or harmful thinking, your cognitive daily living goals are simple.

- When you find yourself feeling insecure, sad, angry, or confused, search your thoughts for self-talk that is discouraging, frightening, or otherwise irrational.

- Evaluate the self-talk for accuracy or usefulness and begin using thoughts that dispute this type of thinking. For example, "Where's the proof that this thought will actually happen?"

- If you find that negative thoughts are repeating and creating a negative spiral, use thought stopping techniques followed by pleasant imagery.

- Think about what core beliefs are being activated by the situation and if the belief is negative, try to respond with a revised, more accurate core belief. For example, "I am a responsible adult" in response to "I am an irresponsible child." (You can do this one later when you have time for a break if you are trying to finish a task.)

• When you are disputing a negative thought, remind yourself that you are your own best guardian or the parent you always wanted. Your new voice (or self-talk) is respectful of you, is wise and understanding, has endless patience, and believes in your absolute value to the world.

Emotional Nourishment

Many lesbian and gay people have had years of being told what they can and cannot feel and how to disregard feelings that are deemed unacceptable. Men are taught that they cannot be emotionally sensitive and be truly masculine while women are taught that showing too much emotion makes them weak and fragile. Years upon years of these types of messages tend to make a very simple process seem quite complicated. It no longer surprises me when patients come to see me who are confused by their feelings, alienated from themselves emotionally, and convinced that they cannot deal with their feelings.

To give yourself emotional nourishment, you must learn to work your way through all of these negative and distorted messages about emotions. Feelings are a natural part of every human being. You have them for a reason—to guide you in your everyday life. They are like reflexes in response to your brain's interpretation of an event. Feelings happen automatically in reaction to a perception and are not within your power to select. For example, you do not need to tell yourself to feel frightened when you hear a strange noise late at night that awakens you from sleep. Your brain picked up a sensation from your ears and then took the available data (darkness, the fact that you are supposed to be alone in the house), and your emotions immediately responded appropriately with fear. The fear then motivated you to get up quickly (and quietly) and check your surroundings. It would've been strange to have been awakened, perceived danger, and then felt sad. When your perception of an event is distorted, you will have the response that is appropriate for the perception, but it is based on inaccurate data. When you learn to correct your self-perception or interpretation of an event, the emotion that follows will more accurately reflect the situation you are in.

More than half of what I do with patients is to teach them how to objectively evaluate their perceptions and then to trust the feelings that follow. As a lesbian or gay child, you were told from many sources that your feelings and attractions were inappropriate or just plain wrong. You then grew up not always knowing when to trust certain feelings. This self-doubt translates into insecurity and thereby affects self-esteem.

Learning to trust your feelings takes time. Every feeling is a signal or a form of communication to the thinking part of yourself. Fear, based on an accurate perception, instructs you to be alert and to protect yourself. Anger is a signal that you perceive some type of injury, slight, or disregard and suggests that you must seek to clarify what you have perceived and to make right what was wrong. Grief, which follows some type of loss, allows you to try to understand that things will be different and that you must adjust.

Chances are, if you learned not to trust yourself emotionally, you also will have a difficult time allowing yourself to feel more positive feelings like happiness, joy, excitement, and calm. If you do have fleeting moments of happiness, you may find that you talk yourself out of feeling good, as if you were waiting for the other shoe to drop. Self-nurturing involves not only doing things for yourself that make you feel good feelings, but it also means making room for you to have *all* of your feelings.

There are several ways to begin allowing yourself to have feelings more directly. First, if you are particularly concerned about how to begin the process or you fear your feelings, you may want to consider getting into counseling. A good psychotherapist can help you learn to process feelings in a healthy way. You may need some instruction in how to process feelings such as anger and grief if your family did not handle these feelings well. Chapter 13 is all about how to find a good psychotherapist.

Next, if you are ready to attend to your feelings, I highly recommend keeping a daily journal of your feelings. The goal of the journal is not necessarily to track specific events of the day but to keep track of what you felt at various points during the day and what you feel as you write. Allow yourself the freedom to go off on tangents, keep track of dreams (and the feelings in them), and observe unusual feelings that seemed to pop up out of nowhere. Try not to judge yourself for the feelings, but accept them as is. Later you can go back and evaluate whether the feelings were in reaction to distorted thinking or a misinterpretation on your part. There are structured forms of journals available that may provide you with more direction, but if you have no trouble writing down your feelings, a plain spiral notebook will do. One patient of mine who had spent years suppressing her feelings began journaling about three years ago and is now up to over a dozen volumes!

Another excellent way of learning about feelings is to try to talk to someone you trust with whom you can share your feelings. A partner might be a good choice. A supportive family member or friend might also be willing to listen and give you some validation. It's important that his person be nonjudgmental and supportive of your feelings. The person can give feedback about your perceptions that led to the feelings when you are ready, but he or she is not allowed to make judgments about the feelings themselves (which you can clarify up front).

Again, the goal of getting to know your feelings is so that you can begin to use them as a guide, a form of intuition. You can think of your feelings as tools that you have been hesitant to use in the past and were actually warned away from. You are an adult now and can train yourself to use your feelings confidently and proudly. You can start today by not judging yourself when you have feelings, but by listening to them, honoring them, and using them to help you decide what to do in any given situation.

Giving Yourself Permission

Allowing yourself to feel affection for yourself when you need it might sound like a strange concept for some people, especially if they feel at some deeper level that they do not deserve affection. The empty chair technique, which I described earlier in the chapter, could be of some value here. If you are having a difficult time feeling self-compassion or self-nurturing but you know you need it, imagine that a child about six or seven years old, is sitting in the empty chair, feeling the way you are currently feeling—perhaps alone, scared, and confused. What are your natural impulses? Would you sit there and let the child cry? Would you tell her or him to shut up? Hopefully, you would be able to find some compassion for the child and would try to say something soothing like, "You'll be okay" or "I'll protect you."

Some people actually practice a form of visualization in which they imagine taking the child onto their laps and hugging or soothing them. In the beginning, you may need to imagine the child as a neighbor or even stranger, but eventually, as you become more self-compassionate, you can imagine the child as the emotional part of yourself or the child who needed hugging and unconditional love when you were growing up.

As you begin to self-nurture, it's important for you to get to know and appreciate your good qualities, strengths, and efforts. Make a list of things that you feel are your best qualities. Add to that list any qualities you have received recognition for by family members, peers, friends, employers, or teachers. The list can include anything from intelligence to personality characteristics (such as kindness, calming, trustworthiness, caring, and so on) to special abilities and talents (for example, musical or artistic skill, an ability to put people at ease or to listen attentively). Allow yourself to enjoy any compliments or praise you've received recently or in the past and dispute any negative thinking or self-talk that won't allow you to hear the positive feedback. If you've had difficulty seeing yourself as having any positive attributes in the past, try to construct an image of yourself now that is more balanced. You might want to include the things you like and the qualities about yourself you hope to change. Put this list in your journal or on a piece of paper. Here are the categories you should include: Things I Am Good At, Personal Characteristics I Have Been Complimented For, Abilities or Talents I Have, Accomplishments I'm Proud Of, and Evidence That I'm Liked or Valued.

Easy Self-Nurturing Activities

Aside from the emotional work of self-nurturing, there are behavioral ways to nurture yourself. Finding activities that bring you pleasure and reward you when you have worked hard or withstood something difficult to bear are a part of what it means to take care of you. I've certainly indulged in a gift to myself here or there, like saving up for a professional massage occasionally when I feel tired, or treating myself to a good meal when I've had a busy week of quick, but not so nutritious, meals. Treat yourself as you would a friend who deserved or needed cheering up.

The important thing to remember is to find a range of things that you can use to treat yourself for a job well done, or even when you wake up feeling irritable or lonely. Behavioral rewards can include treats like special meals, desserts, professional massages, and vacations. But they can also include things that don't cost money like a slow walk through the park, intimate time with a partner or close friend, playing with a pet, taking a hot bath, meditating or praying, scheduling time to relax and NOT work on a project or job task, or even listening to your favorite music or reading a great book. Try not to rely too much on rewards that may have other long-term negative consequences, like too many fattening pieces of pie or an excessive amount of alcohol. If you can only think of a few ways to reward yourself, you may need to do some investigating to find new ways to treat yourself. One particularly creative person I know took herself to the largest music store in San Francisco to try to discover more about her music preferences. She, in fact, spent the afternoon there at each of the store's numerous listening stations until she found new music that she enjoyed. This is the kind of homework assignment we could all use!

Protecting the Self

Anyone who nurtures also protects. Learning to protect yourself from harm is also a type of self-nurturing. Setting firm limits in relationships is an important skill that you may or may not have learned as a child. If your self-esteem is low, your rights were likely not always respected when you were growing up. In some cases, parents who have low self-esteem themselves often don't have a concept of what constitutes a healthy boundary as I described in chapter 2. As an adult, it's important that you learn to construct healthy boundaries to keep yourself from being hurt needlessly. Consider the figure on the next page, which represents a person with healthy boundaries.

The inner circle of the diagram represents you where you are most vulnerable. This is the place where you can most easily share intimacy. Around this circle is a strong fence with only one door, one way in. A person with strong boundaries knows how to keep the door closed as a form of protection against intruders, only allowing the most trustworthy partner or family member in. The entrance standards to the innermost circle are high. Anyone allowed to enter into this level must have shown you enough evidence that they will not use information you share against you. A second, larger fence around the first one has a few more doors. The entrance standards are less stringent, but people who get to enter here have shown you that they have an interest in being close to you and that they do not intend to hurt or manipulate you. Finally, the largest circle represents the outermost boundary, with many gates. People you meet whom you find interesting but have little history with or friends you only socialize with in groups usually enter here. Outside the largest fence are the strangers, acquaintances that make you a little nervous, and people who you know have the potential to hurt you. If you build your boundaries effectively, you have some control over who enters at each of the outer levels and complete control over who you choose to be emotionally intimate with or vulnerable to at the innermost level. As you grow to understand and appreciate yourself more, you will find that it becomes easier to keep your boundaries strong without locking all the doors to the healthy people in your life who can increase your sense of love and belonging.

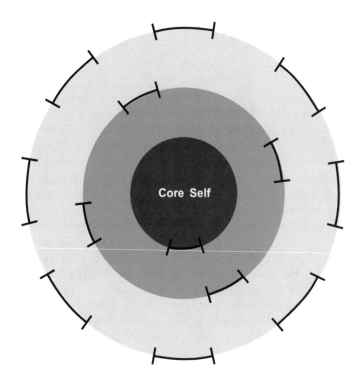

Figure 2. The Core Self and Healthy Boundries

Becoming Assertive

One way of protecting your boundaries is by learning to speak up for yourself when you feel someone is taking advantage of you. Sometimes in families with dysfunctional systems, self-protection takes the form of acting aggressively or passive-aggressively. Assertiveness, an appropriate alternative to any forms of aggression, can be learned just like other skills you may not have been exposed to before. The keys to learning assertive behavior include learning how to stand up for yourself and getting what you want without feeling guilty, acting and communicating with reason instead of emotion, and avoiding feeling resentment that turns into disparaging self-talk when your rights are violated. If you'd like to read about becoming more assertive, I recommend the classic book *Your Perfect Right: A Guide to Assertive Living* by Robert Alberti and Michael Emmons (1995).

You have the power to choose whether you will continue the negative self-talk you likely learned when you were a child or whether you will begin to transform your relationship with you to one of self-compassion and affection. It is my hope that through this book, you will see the choices more clearly and choose the latter.

12

Spirituality

. . . love thy neighbor as thyself . . .
—Leviticus 19:18

Given the huge amount of damage that some parts of organized religion have done to lesbians and gays over the years, it is not surprising that many have severed their ties to religion and developed an attitude of suspiciousness toward people who are a part of a larger religious institution. Those who have felt condemned, ostracized, or even abused in the name of God and religion may remain skeptical about religious groups who purport to be gay-friendly, gay-tolerant, or even gay-centered. Even if you were not raised in a religious family, you probably were familiar with the major religious institutions' positions on sex and sexuality from your exposure to the larger culture through peers, school, the media, and other public activities. Because of the painful association you may have had with organized religion, you may have actively avoided spirituality.

You may ask, "Why is it important to have a spiritual life? I've done just fine without one!" A few of my patients have expressed their beliefs that there is no God or that they are agnostic (someone who believes that the human mind cannot know whether there is a God or not) at most. For these people, even the word *spirituality* has meanings or images associated with it that are distasteful to them. Some feel that when I use the word *spirituality*, I must obviously be referring to spirits or other divine entities that shape our world, such as angels, wood nymphs, fairies (no pun intended), or the Holy Spirit. When I use the term *spirituality*, I use it inclusively to include both the external conceptualizations of God and the internal resources of the human spirit. Based on my personal and clinical experience, it seems to me that all humans have a need to understand the larger questions of living. These questions include, "Where do I fit in?" "What is my part in the world or universe?" and "Where do I find meaning in living?" Regardless of whether you believe in a God that is larger than, or exists outside of you, or if you believe there is no larger force than what resources you have within, I use the term *spiritual* to describe the search for answers to the questions.

Many people have a highly personal, yet organized system for attending to their spiritual needs. Some people find that organized religion provides the best answers to these questions of why they exist and what their role is on this planet. They find comfort and a significant reduction in general anxiety (or angst) by relying on their faith in their concept of God or in their religious organization's teachings. By practicing the rituals of the organization (such as daily prayer or meditation, religious ceremonies, reading religious materials or texts) they find peace and satisfaction, a closer relationship with their concept of God, and some answers to everyday problems.

Others find that the explanations provided by religious doctrine or dogma do not feel comfortable. They find that using their own reason or logic, rather than faith in a religious institution, fits them better and provides just as much peace. They feel an added boost to their self-confidence when they solve a problem on their own. Some have developed a heightened sense of intuition as a guide to navigating daily hassles and dilemmas. I find that most people who consider themselves atheists have a well-developed sense of how the world is organized and a spiritual sense of their own power to affect change in their environment and in themselves.

I have found that many gays and lesbians actively avoid acknowledging their spiritual side or assume that spirituality must be connected to organized religion. Who can blame them when many religions have been at best silent on the spiritual concerns of lesbians and gays and at worst condemning and rejecting. Being rejected by a religious institution is particularly painful for those who were raised to believe that a specific religious organization speaks for God. If the institution rejects them, they feel they have been rejected by God. Even if many of you were not directly rejected or harmed by a religious institution or person, the fear or anticipation of rejection may have led you to reject religion and anything remotely associated with it, including your spiritual search. But a healthy, well-constructed, and active spiritual life (in the larger sense) can be a great source of peace, strength, and growth when confronting life's struggles. Your views on spirituality may be central to core beliefs about your place in the world and your ultimate sense of self-esteem.

A purpose of this chapter is to provide some suggestions for how to improve or develop your own personal spirituality.

Spirituality may be defined in many ways. It is not the same for any two individuals any more than any two fingerprints are alike. My intent therefore is not to tell you exactly how to be spiritual but to help you learn to make more of a place for the consideration of it in your life. Spirituality does not mean that you must believe in a God or gods, or in spirits that roam the earth. Spirituality in this chapter may or may not include a concept of a God or a higher power, but includes developing a system of beliefs that helps you feel like you belong, deserve to be included, and have an important role to play on the planet. An obvious advantage to beginning a spiritual search is that as you grow, you will feel more relaxed, more secure, and more prepared for stressors in daily living.

Making Time to Be Spiritual

One of the most important aspects of developing your spiritual side is making the time for it in your life, just as you make time to brush your teeth, groom, and dress before work or take time to work out, run, or nap. Think of it as building a healthy and balanced life for yourself that includes attending to all of your basic needs. The following diagram shows areas of healthy living that need your regular attention. If you ignore any one or more of these areas, your life may become out of balance.

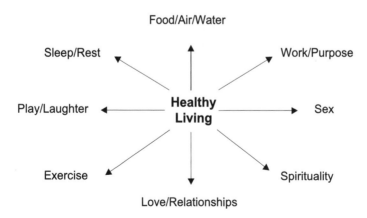

Figure 3. Aspects of a Balanced Life

As you make time for developing your spiritual life, you will find that it becomes more and more important and helpful in your life. Keep in mind that, usually, developing the spiritual side of yourself is a lifelong process and one that may wax and wane over time. If you find that it is difficult for you to maintain consistency in your practices, don't be hard on yourself or give up! Give yourself a break and start again where you left off.

If you came from a place where you were hurt by religious people or teachings, the spiritual side of you may be absent or scarred. By realizing that religion and spirituality are two different things that sometimes overlap but not always, you may be able to allow yourself to tend to this very human need without fear and without reactivating the trauma that you may have experienced at the hands of religious people in the past. The key is for you to remain in control of the process and not allow yourself to be guided by other spiritual or religious people who have an agenda to make you conform to their beliefs. If you had a particularly traumatic experience with religion in the past, I recommend that initially you avoid placing yourself in a religious context until you feel spiritually stronger and can resist people who would have you conform to ideas that don't feel right to you.

Some of the best spiritual advice that I received came from an Episcopal priest following a long discussion about common spiritual values and those issues upon which we differed in opinion. After the civil and mutually considerate talk, he commended me on my sincerity and perspective and encouraged me to add rituals to my spiritual practice. I asked him what he meant by rituals, imagining that he was speaking of attending his church, partaking of communion, and so on. He told me he felt that to maintain consistency and growth on a spiritual path, one must practice some form of regular engagement with the spiritual side of one's self. He believed that for religious people, the habit of attending weekly meetings, participating in standard ceremonies, and regularly attending to spiritual matters as a group were helpful in maintaining a perspective about daily living that helped them get through the hassles of the week. He encouraged me to find my own rituals to do regularly, such as sitting quietly, taking a walk through a garden, or practicing deep breathing, where I could attend to the larger questions of how I fit into the universe at large.

His advice was remarkable for two reasons. First, he accepted my individual belief system as valid even though in some ways it differed from his own. I found later that applying a regular spiritual routine was helpful in remaining centered. In fact, the weeks following the discussion were exciting as I explored the possibilities for my routines. I continue to practice some of these original personal rituals today and find that even when I get absorbed in my various projects or work for a period of time, I can return to my routines pretty easily.

Here are some suggestions for developing your own rituals:

1. Set aside a regular time every day to allow yourself to attend to your belief system. Taking some quiet time for reflection first thing in the morning can sometimes help set a positive and relaxed tone for the rest of the day. Five or ten minutes to calm yourself at the end of the day before going to bed, to step back and take a larger perspective on your life, can help you let go of minor daily worries and get a better night's sleep. The important thing is not whether you take five minutes or an hour initially, but to practice self-reflection on a regular basis. If you can manage to practice at the same time every day, you will find yourself beginning to relax as that time approaches in anticipation of your quiet time.

2. Pick a comfortable place to practice your daily ritual. Find a spot that feels quiet, private, and free from distraction. Inside the house, you could pick a favorite chair, room, or window with a view. Outside the house, you could pick a spot in the yard, in the garden, or by a favorite tree. You can sit quietly while you practice your ritual or practice as you are taking a walk, running, or cycling. One of my patients practices her spiritual ritual as she walks on the treadmill in the morning. She finds the repetitiveness of the activity soothing and quieting.

3. Experiment with various ways of enhancing feelings of self-acceptance and self-nurturance. Some people use a ritual that was effective for them from the religious tradition in which they were raised, like prayer. Some find the repetition of a formal prayer relaxing and empowering while others prefer to pray as if they were having a conversation with a nurturing God, higher power, or themselves. Meditation is helpful for becoming more centered and mindful of the values that are most important to you. Imagery or visualization can be a powerful form of ritual, using only visual or auditory images of healing, self-nurturing, or growth. Actively visualizing yourself performing a dreaded task, handling a difficult situation successfully, or modeling yourself after a respected spiritual leader can enhance your performance in real life.

4. If you do believe in the existence of God or a higher power, you may initially need to work on changing your image of

God, perhaps from angry and condemning to unconditionally loving, forgiving, and accepting. Some of my gay and lesbian clients have come from such emotionally abusive backgrounds that they were constantly told, "God despises you," or that they were "sentenced to hell" for having an attraction to someone of the same sex. These messages became a deep-seated scar for many of them, making them feel that they did not deserve spiritual nurturing or to even feel any joy at all. The *empty chair technique*, as described in the previous chapter, may be a useful exercise if you've been exposed to these types of messages. You might first imagine that God is in the chair across from you. How do you feel? Are you afraid? Ashamed? Angry? These feelings are keys to understanding how your thoughts were shaped about your role in the spiritual world.

Next, you might try imagining the God-image becoming more approachable, willing to listen to your feelings and answer your questions. Give your image the qualities of an unconditionally loving, ideal parent or grandparent. Express any old feelings that you may have left over from years of rejection, such as grief, confusion, or even anger. The entity you imagine is wise enough to accept your feelings without judgment. Ask the image to begin a new relationship with you, leaving behind the old messages you were taught. Continue with this image as long as you like, taking it in a positive and inclusive direction.

If you do not believe in a God entity or higher power, you can substitute a conversation with yourself for the times when you feel alone, using your revised core beliefs from chapter 11 as guides for words that might feel soothing. You can imagine the "child" part of you that is feeling emotional or alone sitting in the empty chair and the "adult" you taking the child into your arms for a hug and comfort.

Some of my patients have taken this exercise further in their daily spiritual practice by calling upon the image that they developed whenever they feel alone or vulnerable to hold them, nurture them, or support them. Others visualize a real adult figure from their childhood who was unconditionally accepting of them and nurturing.

5. Don't be afraid to try other creative forms of spiritual reflection like giving yourself a special self-nurturing or restorative retreat now and then. Some find that planning a professional massage or a trip to the mountains, beach, or river helps

them let go of extraneous worries and focus on what's important—the positive things or people in their lives and the things they have to be grateful for. Some people have built altars in their homes that included items such as pictures of loved ones, candles, incense, and flowers so that they would have a special place to open up to inner reflection and spiritual practice. Some find that they can augment their experience by listening to music or by doing something artistically creative like playing an instrument, drawing, painting, or doing crafts.

6. If you find that you need more guidance in your spiritual search (as I found I did along the way), it may be helpful for you to speak with a religious or spiritual figure about some of your questions. It's important to find someone who will discuss with you your beliefs, but will not attempt to force you to conform to his or hers. I recommend that you try to find someone who comes from a tradition that is known to be gay/lesbian affirmative or at least is known to respect the traditions of other religions as well as his or her own. You may need to do some homework about the reputation and position of the person before you actually meet the person. If you need assistance with finding such a person, you may want to try the following:

   - Call a local lesbian or gay switchboard (if one is available) to ask for lesbian/gay spiritual resources in your area.

   - Ask your lesbian or gay friends if they have had positive experiences with a local religious leader.

   - Look for an interfaith agency or chaplaincy program in your area since these agencies would be more likely to respect a wide range of religious views.

   - Attempt to locate a school of theology or divinity school at a larger state or private university where a diversity of views are represented.

   - Contact national offices of organizations like Dignity (for Catholics), Integrity (for Episcopalians), and the Metropolitan Community Church for names of local groups that may have suggestions.

Pastoral counselors also exist as an independent profession in many parts of the country, but do not automatically assume that they do not have a particular religious agenda to promote with clients. I will discuss the concept of pastoral counselors and religion-based psychologists in the next chapter, Choosing Psychotherapy.

These suggestions are meant to be general and do not even begin to explore the many ways you could foster or improve your own unique spirituality. You may already have well-developed spiritual practices and find these suggestions too elementary. In that case, you might want to continue your growth by reading about other spiritual practices or by finding a group of people with similar spiritual interests to practice with. All of the people in the group need not have the exact same beliefs as long as everyone respects the rights of others to believe as they choose. Some find that by trying to understand and respect the beliefs of others, they gain new insights into their own belief system that expand and enhance it.

Interacting with Established Religions

While developing your spirituality does not require association with a particular religion, the advantages of doing so, such as the social support it provides to members and the charitable activities it may perform, may outweigh the disadvantages for you. Some religious organizations, in fact, are attempting to resolve some of the contradictions within their own teachings regarding gays and lesbians. For example, while the Presbyterian church recently voted not to extend leadership positions to gays or single heterosexuals who are not celibate, the fact that the issue was debated within the church for several years, and that there are a significant number of people within the church who supported the ordination of lesbian or gay people, signals that further change may be ahead. Officials in the United Methodist Church acquitted Rev. Jimmy Creech of charges that he disobeyed church rules by performing a unity ceremony for a lesbian couple in September of 1997, although he was later fired by his bishop for "other reasons." Many Reform and Reconstructionist Jewish groups also tend to view homosexuality as a state of being into which some people are born and is therefore not in the category of being moral or immoral (Kertzer and Hoffman 1993).

If you have a strong connection to a particular religion, and wish to continue practicing the basic traditions and teachings of the religion, look into whether a gay or lesbian subgroup within your organization exists and contact them for support and assistance with maintaining religious ties with a gay- or lesbian-affirmative focus. Despite the stance of the national organizations, it is possible to find individual congregations within the larger religious organization that do not accept the anti-gay rhetoric of their governing bodies. Many lesbians and gays find comfortable homes within such local groups and are able to pursue their spiritual needs with dignity, respect, and acceptance. The more accepting of yourself you are, and thus the higher your self-esteem, the more easily you will be able to maintain connections with mainstreams religions, recognizing them as complex systems that have both healthy and unhealthy qualities.

Many gay and lesbian people have moved away from Western-based belief systems to more Eastern-based ones, such as Buddhism. Buddhism is fairly neutral on the issue of sexual orientation, thus making it an attractive alternative for spiritual exploration by gays and lesbians. While individual practitioners of Buddhism may exhibit culturally prevalent homophobic attitudes, the institution itself does not discriminate with regard to sexual orientation, allowing openly gay and lesbian practitioners the opportunity to become ordained.

The key is to trust your feelings and your ability to use reason. Use the same type of strategy to evaluate the appropriateness of the words of the religious leaders as you do your own thinking: dispute the irrational, distorted, and hypocritical.

Finding Your Own Path

Regardless of the path you choose for exploring your spirituality, whether it be totally or partially within established religious practices or outside of organized religion altogether, the key is to recognize that the spiritual side of yourself is a part of who you are as a whole human being. Starting your own path does not have to be difficult. If you can do nothing more than take time to reflect on day-to-day experiences and allow yourself to place them in a larger perspective, you have begun the process of spiritual self-soothing. Allowing your-self to feel your feelings—both the negative and the positive—is another part of the spiritual experience. Learning to listen to negative feelings like anger, sadness, and frustration provides you with an opportunity to expand your view of a situation and perhaps teach yourself to take a different stance next time in a similar situation. It also gives you the chance to practice some of the cognitive skills you have learned in the book, including evaluating negative thinking and disputing irrational or distorted self-talk.

Having a sense of spirituality will help you feel connected to the world as you sense that life is an ongoing process and that you have value because you exist. If you can give yourself permission to enjoy the positive feelings, your spirituality becomes a part of the self-nurturing process you read about in the previous chapter.

It is important for you to remember that you can't develop spirituality overnight. It is an ongoing process that will continue for the rest of your life. No one is perfect, and life is certainly not predictable. How you take care of yourself—emotionally, cognitively, physically, and spiritually—will affect how you will experience life. If you begin to understand that you are entitled to joy and peace, and you learn how to love and respect yourself completely, the journey will seem more than worth it.

13

Choosing Psychotherapy

If one does not understand a person, one tends to regard him as a fool.

—Carl Jung

Making a change by reading a book can be difficult. Staying focused, avoiding distractions, and handling the feelings that arise when trying to explore yourself at deeper levels may require support or at least a more intensively structured program. You may already have an ongoing relationship with a psychotherapist and may choose to work through this book with your therapist. Or you may have never seen a psychotherapist before and have no idea how to go about determining whether you need one or how to find one. This chapter will help you determine if psychotherapy would be beneficial to you and, if you believe it would be, how to go about finding the right person. You have choices in every step of the process, and this chapter will help you make these choices more effectively as it examines important psychotherapist characteristics as well as what to expect in terms of duration of therapy, frequency of visits, and payment issues. I will also provide you with information about finding lesbian, gay, or L/G affirmative therapists, what types of therapies to avoid, and other issues that are important for you to know about before you begin the process.

There are several ways that psychotherapy can be helpful. In the short term, it can provide you with an extra, albeit temporary, support in your life. A psychotherapist will be a nonjudgmental listener who'll help you organize your thoughts and put them in a larger perspective, get through a crisis when you may be overwhelmed emotionally, and find the motivation to make significant change in your life. Psychotherapy can also be highly focused to work on specific issues like changing an unhealthy eating pattern or addiction, negotiating the start or breakup of a relationship, and changing negative or dysfunctional thought patterns or feelings. In the longer term, psychotherapy can help you examine habits that have been difficult to change or personality characteristics that you feel are self-defeating.

Some people choose to enter therapy for an opportunity to grow, gain insight or greater self-awareness, and even just to try to understand why they do things even if they don't particularly want to change. Usually, however, people go to therapy because they are unhappy with themselves or a situation and want assistance with change. Many gay men and lesbians go to therapy because they were raised in an environment that was homophobic and heterocentric. Without support and without role models, they now experience pain and self-doubt that they want to overcome.

Psychotherapist Characteristics

A *psychotherapist* is anyone who treats mental disorders or applies behavioral or psychological techniques to patients in order to help them change. There are many different types of psychotherapists (often referred to simply as *therapists*). The most common are psychiatrists, psychologists, and counselors. There are significant differences between these types of mental health professional that are worth knowing about before making your selection.

Psychiatrists

Psychiatrists are physicians who have attended medical school and have an M.D. (doctor of medicine) degree. As physicians, psychiatrists are the only mental health professionals who can prescribe medications. For many years, psychiatrists provided what most people think of as "talking" therapy where they met with their patients for forty-five minutes to an hour and explored many of the same kinds of issues you have read about in this book. With the advent of drug therapy for treating mental health problems in the 1950s, psychiatry as a field became more biologically focused in its approach, with practice increasingly limited to evaluation and diagnosis of mental health problems and treatment primarily with medication.

Today psychiatrists who ascribe to this approach will often see the patient for a lengthy initial evaluation, prescribe a medication and then see the patient monthly for a brief medication monitoring and support session. It is likely that today's health insurance environment, where quality care is often sacrificed for cost savings, has contributed to this change in approach. Since psychiatrists are typically paid more than other health care professionals, many insurance companies attempt to limit the psychiatrist's role as much as possible by paying only for essential prescription services only they can provide.

While some psychiatrists continue to provide traditional "talking" therapy in addition to prescribing medication, many tend to limit their role to symptom management and monitoring of psychiatric medications such as antidepressants, anti-anxiety medications, and medications for other serious psychiatric symptoms. Often they will work in conjunction with another mental health care professional, who continues to use primarily talking and behavioral therapies for change.

The majority of psychiatrists are represented nationally by an organization called the American Psychiatric Association (APA), which oversees the training, ethical standards, and professional practice guidelines for psychiatrists in the United States. This organization provides the most frequently used diagnostic guide in the country called the *DSM-IV* (*Diagnostic and Statistical Manual of Mental Disorders*), which most psychotherapists use or refer to in order to help them make or understand a formal psychological diagnosis. In 1973, after reviewing available research data on homosexuality, the APA board of trustees decided that homosexuality in itself did not constitute a mental disorder and the larger membership of this organization went on to vote to back the board's decision. In 1986, all references to homosexuality were finally removed from the DSM. In 1998, APA's board voted to condemn therapy aimed at turning lesbians and gays into heterosexuals.

Psychologists

Psychologists are also doctors, though they are not medically trained. The field of psychology developed in the academic side of educational institutions rather than through medical schools. A psychologist has attended graduate school beyond college and received a doctorate in psychology which can be a Ph.D. (doctor of philosophy), a Psy.D. (doctor of psychology), or an Ed.D. (doctor of education) with an emphasis in psychology.

There are many areas of treatment in which psychiatrists and psychologists overlap. They both are equipped to make psychological diagnoses and to provide some form of behavioral and psychological treatment. They also both have doctoral degrees and can provide talking psychotherapy. Since psychologists do not attend medical school, they typically cannot prescribe medications as a part of their therapy. But as mentioned previously, they may work in conjunction with a psychiatrist who will prescribe and monitor the medication if it is deemed necessary and appropriate by both providers. Psychologists are usually uniquely qualified to perform certain types of psychological assessments, including intelligence and learning disability testing, personality testing, and neuropsychological testing. The hourly fees for psychologists generally tend to be less than for psychiatrists (although there are exceptions), but tend to be higher than that for the average counselor.

Most psychologists are represented by the American Psychological Association, also known as APA. This organization also supports the view that homosexuality in itself is not a disease.

Counselors

This term applies to a wide range of mental health practitioners with an equally wide range of degrees and training. This category represents the largest number of practitioners. Most mental health counselors have a master's degree in some form of social science. These practitioners are also typically trained in an academic setting, like a university or college, and the most common degrees include an M.S. (master of science) or M.A. (master of arts) in psychology or counseling, an M.Ed. (master of education) in psychology or counseling, or an M.S.W. (master of social work) with an emphasis in counseling.

To avoid some confusion, it is important for you to understand that the term *counselor* is sometimes applied to other types of helping professionals including alcohol and drug counselors, crisis counselors, peer counselors, school or camp counselors, financial counselors, vocational counselors, nutritional counselors, and spiritual counselors. These types of professionals do not necessarily have a master's or higher degree or have any specific training in psychotherapy. Alcohol and drug counselors typically have some form of training to work with people in treatment for addiction, but the training varies widely from center to center and state to state and they typically are not trained in general psychotherapy practice (although a psychotherapist may also be an addiction counselor or specialist).

Because the term *counselor* is usually not limited as to who can use it, most states allow anyone to take the title of counselor and hang a sign on their door. It is particularly important that you use the information regarding assessing credentials that I will suggest later in the chapter when choosing an appropriate psychotherapist.

In some states, master's level counselors can perform most, if not all, of the services offered by a psychologist while in others, they may be restricted from performing certain duties that the state feels only a psychologist can provide, like certain types of psychological testing. Counselors also are not allowed to prescribe medications since they did not attend medical school.

The national organization for most counselors is called the American Counseling Association. Like the two APAs, this organization supports viewing homosexuality as a healthy alternative to other sexualities.

Licensure or Credentialing

In every state, there are laws governing the practice of counseling, psychology, and psychiatry and regardless of the level of training, people who call themselves psychotherapists must meet the standards set by the state. As a consumer of mental health services, you are protected by state regulation through either licensing or other credentialing like certification or registration. Although licensing laws and procedures vary from state to state, most states have a central body that controls the licensing and credentialing of mental health professionals. In most states, there is a board that sets minimum standards that professionals must meet for their particular specialty and they review the qualifications of a professional applying for a license. This board is usually appointed by the governor or elected by a state professional association or a combination of both. This board's primary responsibility is to insure the safety of the public by not allowing people who are incompetent or otherwise not qualified to practice. They handle complaints against licensed psychotherapists and may take disciplinary action in the form of license suspension or revocation in the case of therapist misconduct.

Therapeutic Orientation

Psychotherapists usually have a primary theoretical perspective (or psychological theory from which they base their practice). If you've never been in therapy before, you may not have a sense of what type of approach makes sense for you. In some cases, the actual theory to which a therapist ascribes may be less important than your level of comfort in relating to the therapist. In many cases, a therapist will have a flexible range of therapeutic approaches that can be tailored to meet the specific needs of an individual patient. If you're interested in reading about different forms of therapy, *A Guide to Psychotherapy* by Gerald Amada (1995) is a great source for such information.

Many studies have attempted to decipher what makes psychotherapy most effective. Interestingly, what researchers found was that it is not necessarily the theoretical approach that is most related to successful outcomes, but some key characteristics shared by most experienced therapists. These key elements appear to be the motivation of the person who is seeking help, the training and experience of the therapist (and how much the therapist believes in his or her skill and approach to therapy) and, most importantly, the level of trust between the client and the therapist. These findings suggest that the best fit for you may be as simple as finding a therapist you feel comfortable with, who takes an approach to therapy that makes the best sense to you.

Duration of Psychotherapy

Many people are afraid to enter into psychotherapy for fear that they will never get out. There are many preconceived ideas about how therapy works and how long it takes, which are usually portrayed in the most unflattering way in the movies and on TV. Woody Allen's neurotic views of life and relationships have created many moments of humor for millions of his fans, as has his fascination with and portrayals of extended psychotherapy. Keep in mind though that many of the ideas you may have about what to expect in psychotherapy may be inaccurate if they are based on one or two friends' experiences or the media's portrayal of psychotherapy. The amount of time that you can expect to spend in therapy will depend on many factors including the issues on which you choose to work, the goals you have for change, the type of therapist you select, and even your financial status (number of sessions covered by insurance, and so on).

Some therapists work from a long-term change model (meaning their method requires months, maybe years of participation) while others work from a short-term perspective (weeks to months). Also significant to the duration is whether you want to change a specific behavior or core aspects of your personality and whether you are in crisis or looking for growth opportunities. Sometimes, it's difficult at first for you and your therapist to determine exactly how long it will take you to reach your goals, but you may get a better idea as you get to know one another after a few sessions. Usually, most therapists work with their patients to determine when it is time to end therapy.

Psychotherapist Specialties

Therapists may advertise themselves as having a specialty or particular area of expertise. These specialties are sometimes in working with people with particular diagnoses or emotional problems like depression, anxiety, chemical dependency, or stress. Some even subspecialize within larger diagnostic categories like postpartum depression, fear of flying, cocaine abuse, or post-traumatic stress disorder (which develops following a major trauma). Others specialize in growth- or insight-oriented therapies meant to help people who are not necessarily having emotional problems or a mental illness. These therapists may work with issues like building self-esteem, coming out to yourself or to others, or learning to become more assertive.

There are few rules that govern when psychotherapists can call themselves a "specialist," but some have actually had formal training in their specialty or subspecialty, while others simply feel that they have sufficient experience in working with patients with particular problems to call themselves a specialist.

Therapists also may advertise qualities about themselves that they feel might be attractive to various groups, such as acknowledging that they are themselves lesbian or gay (or lesbian/gay friendly), Asian American, Jewish, disabled, Russian-speaking, and so on.

Other Practical Issues

Some therapists work primarily with individuals, others work with couples, families, or groups of people who bring the same types of issues to therapy. Most see patients on a weekly basis, while others may see you less often or taper down from once a week to once every two weeks, then once a month as therapy progresses. Some particular types of therapies require frequent visits, from two to four times per week.

Fees that are charged vary and depend on the level of training and experience of the therapist. Psychiatrists generally charge the highest amount per hour with psychologists charging the next highest and counselors charging the lowest. Actual prices can range from a high of over $150 per hour down to $75 per hour. There are exceptions to every rule and a highly specialized counselor may charge as much as or more than a psychiatrist in some locations. Prices also vary according to the local markets. University-associated therapists typically are on the higher end of the scale, but are also usually involved in highly specialized training or research programs.

Some therapists (and clinics, particularly training ones) offer some or all of their practice slots to patients who pay out of their own pocket on a *sliding scale*, where the client is charged a fee per session based on income. This fee can be very low ($5 to $40 per session, for example) if you do not have a large income. Many insurance companies also offer mental health benefits. These benefits can mean that you pay a low copayment for each visit directly to the psychotherapist with the insurance company paying the rest or that the insurance company pays the fees in full. Most HMOs offer mental health coverage on a controlled basis, meaning that they will only pay for a limited number of sessions per year. They may also have a lifetime limit of money that they will pay for mental health services. Some may only cover inpatient psychiatric treatment or crisis situations. Most require that you see a provider on their panel or list of approved providers. These therapists can be made up of a wide variety of practitioners from M.D.s to M.A.s and they have agreed to work within the guidelines of the company that contracts with them to provide services. The company typically has a mechanism in place to approve or deny the provision of mental health services, based on assessment of your need for these services. They may ask your mental health provider to provide them with information about the therapy and about your diagnosis before they will agree to extend authorization for more services. The general guideline for an HMO or managed care company is "less is more"—the less therapy they provide, the more money they save.

Finding the Right Therapist

Finding a therapist who'll fit you and your budget might seem somewhat daunting at this point. If you live in a large metropolitan area, your choices may be overwhelming. In Los Angeles County, for example, a recent compilation revealed that there are over twelve thousand licensed psychotherapists in the county, not including psychiatrists! On the other hand, if you live in a rural area, your choices may be quite underwhelming. This problem became evident at one point in my life when I became aware that I was one of only two openly gay psychologists in a relatively conservative Southeastern city with a population of over 400,000. But now that I live in San Francisco, I am an "ordinary" psychologist who is one of many openly lesbian and gay psychotherapists.

While finding the right therapist may take some time and several false starts, here are a few recommendations for where to begin.

1. Check with local or state professional associations for psychiatrists, psychologists, or counselors. Most will have a referral directory with the therapist's specialties listed including "gay/lesbian" issues, self-esteem, and so on. If you can't find a local or state association, check with the national organizations for information about the nearest resource to you. The contact information for some of these organizations is included at the end of the chapter.

2. Ask your primary care doctor. Most physicians have referred many of their patients to psychotherapists for various life crises, emotional difficulties, and so on and usually they hear back from the patient at a future visit about whether the interaction was positive or negative. The physician then typically begins to send referrals to the psychotherapists that patients report back on most favorably.

3. Contact local gay or lesbian organizations. Often, they have listings of gay or lesbian professionals for making referrals, and if they do not have a formal listing, they may be able to provide you with a helpful lead. If you live in a rural area, try calling the nearest urban area for lesbian or gay resources since they often will list resources that extend beyond the urban area itself. You also might call a general crisis line or local community mental health center for leads on lesbian and gay (or L/G affirmative) counselors.

4. Look in lesbian, gay, or other "alternative" newspapers for advertisements by psychotherapists.

5. Go to the Yellow Pages in your phone book and look under Psychotherapists, Psychologists, or Physicians (with a psychiatric specialty). Often, you will find listings that are large enough to include at least some information about the therapists, their specialties, and their approach. While some will actually mention "lesbian and gay" issues in their listing, others may use language that suggests that they may be open to working with gays and lesbians like "specializes in women's issues," "sexual identity work," "alternative lifestyles," or "HIV support." Also in the Yellow Pages under Psychologist, Psychotherapist, or Psychiatrist, there are often ads for psychotherapy referral services. These organizations are usually made up of a large network of local psychotherapists who financially support the referral service phone number, advertisement, and so on and who benefit from it by directing call-

ers to therapists within the service. They typically also list their specialties and theoretical approaches for callers with specific requests. Keep in mind that each referral service does not usually have a complete listing of psychotherapists in your area. You may need to try another (or several) referral services before you find one that meets yours needs.

6. Ask your close friends or family members, if you are comfortable doing so. Sometimes you can get great leads from people who are or have been in therapy themselves or know someone who has been. It is not necessary to disclose why you might be thinking about therapy nor is it necessary for them to know that the referral is for you personally. If you feel that a person you ask may be manipulative with the knowledge that you asked, don't ask that person! You have a right to your privacy about this issue.

Limits to Confidentiality

Most psychotherapists strive to keep the therapy environment safe and the information discussed secure and confidential. In order to make it easier for you to talk about painful emotional issues, they realize that you must be able to trust that they will not use the information against you or otherwise harm you. Most therapists will attempt to protect your right to privacy, and most professional mental health organizations consider it unethical to violate a patient's right to confidentiality unnecessarily. Most will also only provide information to other people outside of the therapy situation with your written permission.

There are exceptions to every rule, including confidentiality. In certain very limited situations, confidentiality can be breached by the therapist. These situations basically include those in which the therapist has a legitimate reason to believe that you are going to harm yourself or someone else. Specifically, a therapist may break confidence if you

- Say you're going to kill yourself
- Say you're going to kill or hurt someone else or damage their property
- Are unable to take care of yourself due to a mental or medical illness (like being unable to feed yourself or get clothing or shelter because of confusion, hallucinations, etc.)
- Are abusing a child or dependent adult

In most states, not only are psychotherapists ethically allowed to break a confidence in order to either get help or warn a potential victim, but they are mandated by law to report certain activities. Most often, psychotherapists are required to report suspected abuse of a child (regardless of whether you are the abuser or you have knowledge of someone else abusing a child) to the state's Child Protective Services and could lose their licenses or face other legal penalties if they do not make this report.

An important exception to confidentiality involves the right of insurance companies to receive information about your treatment when they are paying the therapist's fee. In most cases these days, insurance companies and especially managed care companies feel that they have the right to review the notes your therapist may keep or to discuss your case with your therapist. They feel they are making sure that you receive effective therapy by ensuring that you are progressing and that the therapist is managing your care appropriately. Most psychotherapists feel that this attempt to monitor care is an intrusion into their patients' right to privacy, but are basically placed in the position of not being paid if they do not cooperate. Most will also make you aware that they may have to share information with your insurance company and will have you sign a release of information statement acknowledging that you have been made aware of this fact. The only sure way to avoid this intrusion is to find a way to pay for your services yourself, through a reduced or sliding scale fee arranged with the therapist.

If you cannot afford to pay out of pocket, here are a few suggestions:

1. Talk to the therapist about how much information he or she provides to insurance companies and how often. Sometimes, the therapist only has to provide an indication that you are benefiting from therapy without going into specifics. Ask the therapist to provide as little information as possible to meet the minimum requirements of the company.

2. When selecting an insurance company, ask about their mental health benefits and what their policy is regarding obtaining psychotherapy notes or records or talking directly to therapists. Also ask them if you must see only a provider within their network or if you can use your benefits with any psychotherapist. You may need to look at other insurance options if you feel that the company is too controlling. You and your psychotherapist are most likely the best judges of the progress of your treatment.

3. Ask your therapist to keep your best interests in mind when keeping notes, documenting visits, or communicating with insurance company case managers. Most psychotherapists are already ethically bound to keep your best interests at heart, but a reminder will not hurt.

Is It Important to Have a Lesbian or Gay Therapist?

Although this seems like a relatively straightforward question, the answer is actually quite complex. If you live in a rural or more conservative area, access to openly gay or lesbian psychotherapists may be limited. Even if they do exist in your area, they may not advertise their sexual orientation for several reasons.

Some therapists generally feel that it is not appropriate for them to disclose personal information in the therapy context while others feel that a limited amount of disclosure may be effective in normalizing the experience of the patient and building trust. Therapists may also feel a need to protect themselves professionally and personally particularly in conservative or homophobic communities and therefore may choose not to advertise their sexual orientation. In some small areas, there may actually be no lesbian or gay psychotherapists.

There may be advantages to having a psychotherapist who is lesbian or gay. If you are going to psychotherapy for the first time, it might reduce your initial anxiety to know that the therapist is at least comfortable enough to acknowledge his or her sexual orientation in public. Chances are, if the therapist advertises being lesbian or gay, he or she will have personal experience or at least awareness of some of the issues that you need to discuss and can relate to or empathize with you. The therapist also is likely to have had other clients who are gay or lesbian, which suggests that he or she may be experienced professionally in this area as well. Aside from personal experiences and previous work with lesbian or gay clients, the therapist may also have studied the psychotherapeutic theories and research regarding healthy gay and lesbian development.

The disadvantages include actually increasing your anxiety, especially if you are in the initial questioning phase of discovering your sexuality and you are afraid that the therapist might direct you to commit to one sexual orientation or another. However, keep in mind that in most cases, it is the typical therapist's position to not lobby a patient to follow one path or the other, but to find what works best for the patient, regardless of the sexual orientation of the psychotherapist. It is also important to recognize that the sexual orientation of the psychotherapist alone does not automatically insure the quality or credentials of the psychotherapist. Whatever choice you make, it is important to check professional credentials.

There are many heterosexual or bisexual psychotherapists who consider themselves "lesbian/gay affirmative." This term generally means that the therapist believes that being gay or lesbian is normal and that many problems for these clients revolve around society's nonacceptance and homophobia. They recognize that the problem is not with being lesbian or gay in itself, but with the negative social messages, lack of role models, and other social failures that lead to low self-esteem, relationship difficulties, and negative emotional consequences. While it's true that a heterosexual psychotherapist cannot ever know completely the experiences of being lesbian or gay, often he or she does have similar (though not exact) personal experiences to draw upon to help provide you with support. If appropriately trained and credentialed, the therapist also will likely understand and utilize strategies for self-acceptance, problem-solving, and attitude change that will help you become more comfortable with yourself and help you grow, regardless of whether he or she has personally had your exact experience or not.

Whether it is essential for your psychotherapist to share similar personal or cultural characteristics to you for therapy to be effective is a debatable question. Some might argue that therapy may be more successful if a woman sees a woman therapist and an African-American sees an African-American therapist. Others feel that it is more important that the patient feel comfortable with the relationship, confident in the therapist's knowledge and experience, and aware of the therapist's nonjudgmental attitude and respect. I've often heard the old joke that goes "If you have appendicitis, who would you like to remove it—a trained and competent surgeon or someone who has had appendicitis before?" The joke of course is that most of us wouldn't really care if the surgeon had personally gone through an appendectomy, only that the surgeon knew what to do. Fortunately, there are usually a range of options from which you can choose in your search for a competent and credentialed psychotherapist including both gay/lesbian therapists and lesbian/gay affirmative therapists. Ultimately, the decision is yours.

What About "Religious" or "Spiritually Based" Psychotherapists?

Some psychotherapists either bill themselves as practicing from a particular religious perspective, such as someone who calls him- or herself a Christian psychologist, pastoral counselor, or Mormon psychotherapist, or indicate that they practice from a spiritual perspective. Those who identify with a particular religious system claim to provide psychotherapy that is consistent with the particular brand of religious belief system to which they ascribe.

Psychotherapy within a set religious value system, or one that is determined by an external source like a religious leader or organized religious body, can be problematic, because psychotherapy itself should strive to be nonjudgmental. A therapist should not attempt to change a person's religious beliefs. The last thing you need when you go to therapy is to be provided more "shoulds" or standards to which you must conform.

I have met some psychotherapists who place in their advertisements information about their personal religious affiliation. They insist, however, that they do not express their personal religious values within the context of psychotherapy. These therapists feel that advertising as a religious psychotherapist is a way for their patients to feel more comfortable initially, much like therapists who advertise as bilingual or gay or lesbian.

Some approaches to psychotherapy (in contrast to approaches that focus on feelings, thoughts, or behaviors) believe that the spiritual side of human beings is an important area to address. These approaches do not generally provide specific values or beliefs themselves, but encourage patients to nurture and validate individual experiences of spirituality and healing. Keep in mind that a trained and licensed psychotherapist who addresses spirituality as a part of a broader approach to therapy is very different from someone with no legitimate credentials who calls him- or herself a spiritual counselor, guide, or healer. Use great caution when approaching any untrained or uncredentialed professional.

"Ex-Gay" Ministries and "Reparative Therapies"

The most dangerous group of religious psychotherapists are those who purport to change sexual orientation from gay or lesbian to heterosexual (or gay/lesbian and "celibate"). These types of *orientation change* therapies are promoted primarily from a religious perspective and are often called *ex-gay* ministries. They include such fringe groups as Exodus International and Transformation Christian Ministries and they are supported by the right-wing Christian Coalition. The basic premise is that being gay or lesbian is a sin and that through prayer and religious counseling, patients can either change their sexual orientation to heterosexuality or at least stop having same-sex relations. The approaches assume that their value system is correct and all others are incorrect. Anyone who disagrees is labeled "evil" or a "sinner."

Many lesbian and gay people who go through these programs end up either dropping out or experiencing significant emotional distress. Most have low self-esteem prior to entering these programs and are therefore vulnerable to misinformation and extreme forms of emotional abuse that many of these programs use in their training. These programs attempt to condition participants to ignore their natural attractions and to superficially behave as if they felt attracted to the opposite sex. They often focus on changing behaviors like the way one walks, talks, sits, and dresses so that the participants know how to "act like a heterosexual."

There are many problems with this approach, not the least of which is that being gay or lesbian is not a moral issue. It is not a choice. Most scientists and scholars agree that human sexuality is a complex phenomenon influenced by a combination of biological, genetic, psychological, and environmental factors. Most who have legitimately studied the development of sexuality agree that it is determined very early in childhood and that who you are attracted to sexually is not the result of making a choice. Most also agree that sexuality is not bipolar, where a person is either homosexual or heterosexual, but that it lies on a continuum with many variations between people who are exclusively attracted to the same sex and those who are exclusively attracted to the opposite sex.

An extremely small minority of psychotherapists continue to believe that homosexuality is a result of abnormal development and believe that they can change sexual orientation through *reparative therapy*. These professionals are not sanctioned by any legitimate professional organization and some have even been ousted due to reports of unethical or harmful forms of treatment. Although some claim to have successfully transformed gays and lesbians into heterosexuals, none have collected credible evidence that the change lasts over time.

An extensive and recent review of sexuality research (Haldeman 1994) found that almost all gays and lesbians go through some period of wanting to change their sexuality since the society is so rejecting. Dr. Haldeman, who works with many patients who have attempted to go through reparative and ex-gay treatments, finds that these people are often frightened, have low self-esteem, and are even suicidal, feeling as though they have "failed." He then works to help them become more self-accepting and see society as the problem and not themselves. Recently, in fact, the American Academy of Pediatrics, the American Psychiatric Association, and the American Psychological Association have issued statements suggesting that conversion therapies for gays and lesbians may not only not result in change in sexual orientation, but can actually provoke psychological harm. For more on this topic, author Andrew Sullivan (1998) examines in detail the arguments of the reparative therapists in his book *Love Undetectable: Notes on Friendship, Sex and Survival.* My recommendation is to avoid ex-gay ministries and reparative therapies altogether. Being gay/lesbian is not a sin or an illness.

How to Interview a Potential Psychotherapist

Many psychotherapists will want to discuss information about who you are as a potential patient before they decide to work with you, so it's only fair that you be able to ask about their background and approach. Some will agree to provide this information by phone while others prefer an initial face-to-face interview. Here are a few suggestions for what to ask potential therapists:

1. *Are you gay/lesbian or gay/lesbian affirmative?* If they are not gay/lesbian themselves, or refuse to answer the question about their own sexuality because of their theoretical orientation, ask if they are gay affirmative.

2. *What experience do you have in working with gay issues and/or my specific problem?* For example, you may want to know if they have worked with gay/lesbian people who are attempting to raise their self-esteem.

3. *What is your therapeutic approach or theoretical orientation?* Do they believe that homosexuality represents an abnormal developmental process or do they believe that homosexuality is one of many normal developmental paths for sexuality?

4. *What training have you had and what are your credentials?* Are they psychiatrists, psychologists, counselors, or something else? Are they licensed or credentialed through the state? It also may be helpful to know if they belong to any professional organizations since these, along with the licensing boards, provide some avenue for complaints if you were to feel that a therapist was inappropriate or unethical. You can also call state licensing boards before seeing a therapist for information on past complaints filed about that therapist.

5. *How long do you expect therapy to take and how often do you expect us to meet?* While most therapists cannot give an exact estimate, they can give you an average number of sessions, based on their past or current experiences with patients. You can also ask if they generally provide short-term (weeks to months) or more long-term (months to years) therapy.

6. *What other expectations do you have for your patients?* It will be helpful later to know their appointment cancellation policies, scheduling systems, and payment methods (cash, check, billing, etc.).

7. *How much do you charge per session?* This may be a good opportunity to discuss whether they accept your insurance or whether they are on the "approved provider" panel for your managed care company. They may also provide a sliding scale to some, if not all, of their patients based on income and ability to pay.

8. *How do you feel about using medications as an adjunct to treatment?* Some therapists do not believe in the use of medications as an adjunct to psychotherapy and others frequently support the use of them. Most psychotherapists believe that there are occasions where medications can be beneficial when they are combined with talking therapy. Although you may not have an opinion about this issue, it may be helpful to know the potential therapist's view about it and, if they do not prescribe, to whom they refer their patients for such prescriptions.

When interviewing potential therapists, observe how they respond to your discussion of your sexuality. Look for nonverbal cues that they are affirmative/nonaffirmative or uncomfortable with certain topics. Are they supportive, unconditional, empathic, easy to talk to? Are you aware of an immediate physical attraction or an immediate negative response that might inhibit you or interfere with developing a trusting, professional relationship?

What If Your Therapist Says or Does Something Inappropriate or Unprofessional?

As I have mentioned previously in the chapter, if you are seeing a psychotherapist who is licensed or certified by your state, he or she is bound to follow both ethical and legal mandates. If you feel that you've been violated or harmed in some way, there are actions you can take. If it seems to be a relatively minor disagreement or misunderstanding, you may feel comfortable confronting the therapist directly about the behavior. You may be able to resolve the issue to your satisfaction through discussion and then feel you can continue therapy together. You may also decide that you cannot work together and it would then be appropriate for your therapist to refer you to someone else. You might also get an opinion from another mental health professional about the situation and your options.

If you feel that the situation is serious, you then have several options. You can file a formal grievance against the psychotherapist to the state licensure board. Most boards have a specific process for filing complaints against a licensed psychotherapist. You can also file a complaint with the therapist's professional organization, such as the American Psychiatric Association, the American Psychological Association, or the American Counseling Association. You can also file legal charges against the psychotherapist if he or she has broken the law. Some behaviors are considered unethical, like disclosing personal information outside of therapy without your consent (and when it is not one of the exceptions to confidentiality that I mentioned earlier), but are not illegal. Other behaviors, like coercing a patient to have sex, is in some states both unethical and illegal.

The following is a basic summary of the Ethical Principles of Psychologists (APA 1993):

- Psychologists do not exploit the trust of their patients (including making sexual contact).

- Psychologists avoid situations that might be construed as a conflict of interest and would impair their professional judgment.

- Psychologists should acknowledge the limits of their experience and knowledge, and seek supervision or consultation from other experienced psychologists when necessary.

- Psychologists respect the diversity of their patients' backgrounds including race, gender, ethnicity, and socioeconomic status and get training to provide adequate services to various groups.

- Psychologists provide some services or work in which they receive little or no financial compensation.

- Psychologists maintain an awareness of their own personal problems and try not to let them interfere with their ability to provide services to patients. If they cannot control these personal problems, they refrain from providing services until these problems have been resolved.

- Psychologists protect the confidentiality of their patients as much as possible, except in the case of a danger to self or others or with the patient's written consent.

- Psychologists are encouraged to end therapy when it becomes obvious that the patient is no longer benefiting from it and refer the patient to another psychotherapist if necessary.

The most important thing in finding a therapist is to look for one who shows concern for your well-being and in whom you feel some sense of trust. In many cases, you can enter the process in a very controlled way, by taking the time to look for good referral leads, asking essential questions, and avoiding those who may not have your best interests at heart.

National Mental Health Practitioner Organizations

Each of the following organizations has subcommittees on gay/lesbian issues and may be able to help you locate a professional in your area. They can also provide information on professional ethics and grievance procedures.

American Association of Sex Educators, Counselors and Therapists
P.O. Box 238
Mt. Vernon, IA 52314
www.aasect.org

American Counseling Association
5999 Stevenson Avenue
Alexandria, VA 22304-3300
www.counseling.org
(800) 347-6647

American Psychiatric Association
1400 K Street, N.W.
Washington, DC 20005
www.thebody.com/apa/apapage.html
(202) 682-6325

American Psychological Association
750 First Street, NE
Washington, DC 20002
www.apa.org
(202) 336-5500

National Association of Alcoholism & Drug Abuse
Counselors
1911 N. Fort Myer Dr., Suite 900
Arlington, VA 22209
www.naadac.org
(703) 741-7686 or (800) 548-0497

National Association of Social Workers
750 First Street NE, Suite 700
Washington, DC 20002-4241
www.naswdc.org
(202) 408-8600

14

Growth and Change

Although this book is not specifically about how to improve your relationships, your career, your sex life, your health, or your diet, as you begin to see your self-esteem improve you will find that all of these areas begin to improve as well. In every area, you will place your best interests first, taking a long-term hedonist perspective versus a short-term, impulse-driven perspective. You will find yourself wanting to overcome self-destructive habits like smoking, using alcohol and other drugs, procrastination, and avoiding exercise. You will come to care more for yourself and want to be more loving and self-nurturing, which in turn will change the quality of your relationships with others. Healthy people attract other healthy people. And when unhealthy people or other crises come into your life, you will learn to appropriately deal with them and waste little emotional energy obsessing over things beyond your control. You will treat yourself more like a best friend and when you do slip up and say or do unhealthy things, you will take note and move on, promising yourself you will work on having that happen less often without beating it into the ground.

Having good self-esteem will not make you selfish or demanding. It will not make you narcissistic, taking advantage of or dismissing others for your own gain. Selfish behavior and attention-seeking are in fact outward manifestations of inner insecurity and low self-esteem. It will make you feel things more authentically and help you use your feelings as guides to appropriate behavior. It involves developing a whole new perspective on living from one of feeling flawed, anxious, and unentitled to one of feeling okay with human imperfection, feeling more peaceful and deserving of respect and affection.

I have encouraged you to feel your feelings at times in this book. You may have felt sadness for a loss you suffered, like the loss of an ideal childhood. Or, you may have felt anger, perhaps at people who feel entitled to judge you, your experiences, your feelings, and your behaviors, assuming that their way is correct and appropriate for you and everyone else.

As you become more familiar with your emotional life, it will be like getting to know a new friend—you will discover your true likes and dislikes, your preferences, your positive and negative qualities. Building your self-esteem can be exciting and incredibly freeing. It can also be frightening and frustrating, requiring deeper work on your own or with a professional. You will most likely have moments like both of these. Hopefully, you will become more adept at navigating the ups and downs, accepting yourself as a human, and understanding that all humans are imperfect. It is normal to have ups and downs! No one has all ups! It is okay to make mistakes, to relapse, to hear yourself say the very things over and over that you recognized as irrational because building self-esteem is a lifelong process. Think again of the long-term, of having peaks and valleys from time to time, but the larger curve moving upward, with you moving along it being less self-punitive and more self-loving.

As your self-esteem grows, you will find yourself becoming less tolerant of people around you stepping over appropriate boundaries. The goal for you will be to learn to set firm limits to protect yourself, but at the same time not shut everyone out. You are one important part of something big and beautiful. You must protect yourself but you must also open yourself up when it's appropriate.

In some ways, when your self-esteem grows, you will feel more empowered to take risks, some small—like showing your talents unabashedly at work—some big—like coming out to family or co-workers. This is not to say that everyone reading this book should take these same risks. You must gauge for yourself what is reasonable, what is in your own best self-interests, and what will maintain your livelihood.

One of the greatest missing pieces for people with low self-esteem is a well-developed spiritual life. People with low self-esteem often lack a part of themselves that helps them feel connected to the world and universe, that they can rely on to help them through crises, emotional fatigue, and stagnation. Gays and lesbians too often have been told that they are not a part of the world spiritually, that there is no room for them in religion (unless they change). Take back your right to a healthy spiritual life, however you choose to define it—a belief in God or a higher power, or just an understanding of the valuable role you play in the organization of the world as a whole. You are a complex organism, capable of thinking about issues on multiple levels, not just right or wrong, yes or no. Push the limits of your thinking, weigh issues from several perspectives, find options and choices beyond the two most obvious. Live for the moments of joy you can find every day.

I find comfort sometimes in envisioning myself as a part of a thin cotton fiber, twisted into a thread, braided into yarn, and woven into a huge tapestry that is the universe. I know that although my fiber may have tiny flaws or imperfections, it still provides some of the strength and color of the thread that holds together the yarn that colors and shapes the much larger tapestry. Someone looking at the tapestry from a distance sees only the great beauty, the completeness, the masterful design and genius behind it, not the tiny imperfections in each fiber underneath. In fact, it may just be the case that the imperfections are what give the piece texture and depth. This image is powerful to me because it reminds me to step back and take a new perspective, to see where I fit even if others cannot.

I hope this book has provided you with the beginnings of seeing yourself from this perspective and that as you grow, you will remember that you are a part of the world, you have a right to exist, and you are worthy of love. If you have read the book without doing the work, start the process now, today. Do the exercises, find a therapist, start a spiritual journey—do whatever you feel is necessary to just start loving yourself.

References and Resources

Introduction

Gibson, P. 1989. Gay male and lesbian youth suicide. In M. Feinleib, ed. *Prevention and Intervention in Youth Suicide* (Report to the Secretary's Task Force on Youth Suicide, 3:110–142). Washington, D.C. U.S. Department of Health and Human Services.

Proctor, C. D., and V. K. Groze. 1994. Risk factors for suicide among gay, lesbian and bisexual youths. *Social Work* 39:505–513.

Remafedi, G., J. A. Farrow, and R. W. Deisher. 1991. Risk Factors for attempted suicide in gay and bisexual youth. *Pediatrics* 87:869–875.

Rich, C. L., R. C. Fowler, D. Young, and M. Blenkush. 1986. San Diego suicide study: Comparison of gay to straight males. *Suicide and Life-Threatening Behavior* 16:448–457.

Saghir, M. T., and E. Robins. 1973. *Male and Female Homosexuality: A Comprehensive Investigation.* Baltimore: Williams & Wilkins.

Savin-Williams, R. C. 1994. Verbal and physical abuse as stressors in the lives of lesbian, gay male and bisexual youths: Associations with school problems, running away, substance abuse, prostitution and suicide. *Journal of Consulting and Clinical Psychology* 62(2):251–269.

———. 1989a. Parental influences on the self-esteem of gay and lesbian youths: A reflected appraisals model. *Journal of Homosexuality* 17:93–109

———. 1989b. Coming out to parents and self-esteem of gay and lesbian youths. *Journal of Homosexuality* 18:1–35.

Scheider, S. G., N. L. Farberow, and G. N. Kruks. 1989. Suicidal behavior in adolescents and young adult gay men. *Suicide and Life-Threatening Behavior* 19:381–394.

Sears, J. T. 1991. *Growing Up Gay in the South: Race, Gender, and Journeys of the Spirit.* New York: Harrington Press.

Chapter 1

Beck, Aaron. 1991. Cognitive therapy: A 30-year retrospective. *American Psychologist* 46:368–375.

Ellis, Albert. 1975. *Guide to Rational Living*. New York: Wilshire Book Company.

Chapter 2

Adorno, T.W., E. Frenkel-Brunswick, D.J. Levinson, and R.N. Sanford. 1950. *The Authoritarian Personality*. New York: Harper.

Baumkind, D. 1968. Authoritarian vs. authoritative parental control. *Adolescence*. 3:255–272.

Bradshaw, John. 1988. Healing the Shame That Binds You. Deerfield Beach, Fla.: Health Communications, Inc.

Forward, Susan. 1989. *Toxic Parents: Overcoming Their Hurtful Legacy and Reclaiming Your Life*. New York: Bantam Books.

Isensee, Rik. 1991. *Growing Up Gay in a Dysfunctional Family: A Guide for Gay Men Reclaiming Their Lives*. New York: Prentice Hall.

Mehrabian, A. 1972. *Nonverbal Communication*. Chicago: Aldine-Atherton.

Chapter 3

Kinsey, Alfred C. et al. 1953. *Sexual Behavior in the Human Female*. Philadelphia: Saunders.

———. 1948. *Sexual Behavior in the Human Male*. Philadelphia: Saunders.

Miller, Neil. 1995. *Out of the Past: Gay and Lesbian History from 1869 to the Present*. New York: Vintage Books (Random House).

———. 1992. *Out in the World: Gay and Lesbian Life from Buenos Aires to Bangkok*. New York: Random House.

———. 1989. *In Search of Gay America*. New York: Atlantic Monthly Press.

Russo, Vito. 1987. *The Celluloid Closet: Homosexuality in the Movies (Revised Edition)*. New York: Harper and Row.

Sullivan, Andrew. 1995. *Virtually Normal: An Argument about Homosexuality*. New York: Alfred A. Knopf.

Tannen, Deborah. 1998. *The Argument Culture: Moving from Dialogue to Debate*. New York: Random House.

Chapter 4

Berzon, Betty. 1996. *Setting Them Straight: You Can Do Something About Bigotry and Homophobia in Your Life*. New York: Plume.

Fox, Matthew. 1983. *Original Blessing*. Santa Fe, N.M.: Bear & Company Publishing.

Helminiak, Daniel. 1994. *What the Bible Really Says About Homosexuality*. San Francisco: Alamo Square Press.

Kertzer, Rabbi Morris, and Rabbi Lawrence Hoffman. 1993. *What Is a Jew?: A Guide to the Beliefs, Traditions, and Practices of Judaism That Answers Questions for Both Jew and non-Jew*. New York: Simon and Schuster.

Leyland, Winston, ed. 1998. *Queer Dharma: Voices of Gay Buddhists*. San Francisco: Gay Sunshine Press.

Murray, Stephen, Will Roscoe, Eric Allyn, and Louis Crompton. 1997. *Islamic Homosexualities: Culture, History and Literature*. New York: New York University Press.

Spong, John Shelby. 1991. *Rescuing the Bible from Fundamentalism*. New York: HarperCollins.

———. 1988. *Living in Sin: A Bishop Rethinks Human Sexuality*. New York: HarperCollins.

Swidler, Arlene, ed. 1993. *Homosexuality and World Religions*. Valley Forge, Penn.: Trinity Press International.

Online Resources for Lesbian and Gay or Affirmative Religious Organizations

Affirmation (Latter Day Saints)
http://ng.netgate.net/~jfirth/affirmation/

Association of Welcoming and Affirming Baptist Churches
http://members.aol.com/wabaptists/index.html

Brethren/Mennonite Council for Lesbian and Gay Concerns
http://www.webcom.com/bmc/welcome.html

Cathedral of Hope
http://www.cathedralofhope.com

Christian Science Lesbian Connection
http://www.geocities.com/WestHollywood/1892/lesbian.html

Dharma-dykes
http://www.cpsc.suu.edu/users/henderso/lzg.htm

Dignity/USA (Catholic)
http://www.dignityusa.org

Evangelical Network
http://www.xroads.com/~ten_net/home.html

Friends for Lesbian and Gay Concerns (Quaker)
http://tps.stdorg.wisc.edu/MGLRC/Groups/

Gay Buddhist Fellowship
http://www.vidaviz.com/~geewhiz/adpages/gbf/gbf.html

Integrity (Episcopal)
http://members.aol.com/natlinteg/index.html

The Interfaith Working Group
http://www.libertynet.org/~iwg

Jewish Activist Gays and Lesbians
http://www.actwin.com/stonewall/handouts/JAGL.html

Lutherans Concerned
http://lcna.org/

National Gay Pentecostal Alliance
http://www.cris.com/~Ngpa/

Presbyterian Lesbian and Gay Concerns
http://www.epp.cmu.edu/~riley/PLGC.html

Queer-Friendly Religious Links
http://world.std.com/~rice/q-light/links.html

Rainbow Spirituality Ring
http://www.geocities.com/WestHollywood/3528/rainbow.html

Rainbow Wind Home Page (Pagan)
http://users.aol.com/RainbowWind/rbwintr.htm

Seventh Day Adventist Kinship International
http://www.qrd.org/qrd/www/orgs/sdakinship/

Twice Blessed- Jewish GLBT Archives
http://www.magic.ca/~faygelah/index.html

Universal Fellowship of the Metropolitan Community Churches (MCC)
http://www.ufmcc.com/

What the Bible Says About Homosexuality
http://web.canlink.com/ocrt/hom_bibl.htm

World Congress of Gay and Lesbian Jewish Organizations
Http://www.wcgljo.org/wcgljo/

Chapter 5

Herek, G.M., and B. Greene. 1995. *AIDS, Identify, and Community: The HIV Epidemic and Lesbians and Gay Men*. Thousand Oaks, Calif.: Sage.

Jennings, Kevin. 1998. *Telling Tales Out of School*. Los Angeles: Alyson Publications.

Kominars, Sheppard, and Kathryn Kominars. 1996. *Accepting Ourselves: A Journey into Recovery from Addictive & Compulsive Behaviors for Gays, Lesbians & Bisexuals*. Center City, Minn.: Hazelden Publications.

Miller, Neil. 1995. *Out of the Past: Gay and Lesbian History from 1869 to the Present*. New York: Vintage Books.

Shilts, Randy. 1988. *And the Band Played On: Politics, People and the AIDS Epidemic*. New York: Viking Pen.

Sullivan, Andrew. 1995. *Virtually Normal: An Argument about Homosexuality*. New York: Knopf.

Thompson, Rosemarie. 1996. *Extraordinary Bodies: Figuring Physical Disability in American Literature and Culture*. New York: Columbia University Press.

Woog, Dan. 1998. *Jocks: True Stories of America's Gay Male Athletes*. Los Angeles: Alyson Publications.

———. 1995. *School's Out: The Impact of Gay and Lesbian Issues on America's Schools*. Los Angeles: Alyson Publications.

Young, Perry, and Martin Duberman. 1996. *Lesbians and Gays and Sports: Issues in Lesbian and Gay Life*. New York: Chelsea House.

Chapter 6

O'Hara, Valerie. 1995. *Wellness at Work: Building Resilience to Job Stress*. Oakland, Calif.: New Harbinger Publications.

Rusi, Richard, and Lourdes Rodrigues-Nordes. 1995. *Out in the Workplace: The Pleasures and Perils of Coming Out on the Job*. Los Angeles: Alyson Publications.

Chapter 7

Berzon, Betty. 1997. *The Intimacy Dance: A Guide to Long-Term Success in Gay and Lesbian Relationships*. New York: Plume.

———. 1990. *Permanent Partners: Building Gay and Lesbian Relationships That Last*. New York: Plume.

Black, Jan, and Greg Enns. 1997. *Better Boundaries: Owning and Treasuring Your Life*. Oakland, Calif.: New Harbinger Publications.

McKay, Matthew, Martha Davis, and Patrick Fanning. 1995. *Messages: The Communication Skills Workbook. second edition.* Oakland, Calif.: New Harbinger Publications.

McKay, Matthew, Patrick Fanning, and Kim Paleg. 1994. *Couple Skills: Making Your Relationship Work.* Oakland, Calif.: New Harbinger Publications.

Chapter 8

Cass, Vivienne C. 1984. Homosexual identity formation: testing a theoretical model. *Journal of Sex Research* 20(2):143–167.

————. 1990. The implications of homosexual identity formation for the Kinsey model and scale of sexual preference. In *Homosexuality/Heterosexuality: Concepts of Sexual Orientation.* The Kinsey Institute Series, Vol. 2, edited by David P. McWhirter, Stephanie A. Sanders, and June M. Reinisch. New York: Oxford University Press.

Herek, Greg, and Beverly Greene. 1995. *AIDS, Identity, and Community: The HIV Epidemic and Lesbians and Gay Men.* Thousand Oaks, CA: Sage Publications.

Rodrigues, Timothy. 1998. UCSF study shows HIV risk tied to self-esteem issues. *Bay Area Reporter.* July 2, 33.

Sontag, Susan. 1990. *Illness As a Metaphor and AIDS and Its Metaphors.* New York: Anchor.

Trimpey, Jack. 1996. *Rational Recovery: The New Cure for Substance Addiction.* New York: Pocket Books.

Waldo, C., S. Kegeles, and R. Hays. 1998. Paper presented at the June 29th, 1998, 12th International Conference of AIDS.

Chapter 9

Bourne, Edmund. 1995. *The Anxiety and Phobia Workbook. second edition.* Oakland, Calif.: New Harbinger Publications.

Caplan, Sandi, and Gordon Lang. 1995. *Grief's Courageous Journey: A Workbook.* Oakland, Calif.: New Harbinger Publications.

Copeland, Mary Ellen. 1992. *The Depression Workbook: A Guide for Living with Depression.* Oakland, Calif.: New Harbinger Publications.

Cornell, Ann. 1996. *The Power of Focusing: A Practical Guide to Emotional Self-Healing.* Oakland, Calif.: New Harbinger Publications.

Markway, Barbara, Cheryl Carmin, Alec Pollard, and Teresa Flynn. 1992. *Dying of Embarassment: Help for Social Anxiety and Social Phobia.* Oakland, Calif.: New Harbinger Publications.

Potter-Efron, Ron, and Pat Potter-Efron. 1995. *Letting Go of Anger: The Ten Most Common Anger Styles and What to Do About Them.* Oakland, Calif.: New Harbinger Publications.

Chapter 10

Beck, Judith. 1995. *Cognitive Therapy: Basics and Beyond.* New York: The Guilford Press.

McKay, Matthew, Martha Davis, and Patrick Fanning. 1997. *Thoughts & Feelings: Taking Control of Your Moods and Your Life.* Oakland, Calif.: New Harbinger Publications.

McKay, Matthew, and Patrick Fanning. 1992. *Self-Esteem.* second edition. Oakland, Calif.: New Harbinger Publications.

Greenberger, Dennis, and Christine Padesky. 1995. *Mind Over Mood: A Cognitive Therapy Treatment Manual for Clients.* New York: The Guilford Press.

Chapter 11

Alberti, Robert, and Michael Emmons. 1995. *Your Perfect Right: A Guide to Assertive Living.* New York: Impact Publications.

Cash, Thomas. 1997. *The Body Image Workbook: An 8-Step Program for Learning to Like Your Looks.* Oakland, Calif.: New Harbinger Publications.

Finney, Lynne. 1997. *Clear Your Past, Change Your Future: Proven Techniques for Inner Exploration and Healing.* Oakland, Calif.: New Harbinger Publications.

McKay, Matthew, and Patrick Fanning. 1992. *Self-Esteem: A Proven Program of Cognitive Techniques for Assessing, Improving, and Maintaining Your Self-Esteem.* Oakland, Calif.: New Harbinger Publications.

———. 1991. *Prisoners of Belief: Exposing and Changing Beliefs That Control Your Life.* Oakland, Calif.: New Harbinger Publications.

Rutledge, Thom. 1997. *The Self-Forgiveness Handbook: A Practical and Empowering Guide.* Oakland, Calif.: New Harbinger Publications.

Chapter 12

Fabry, Joseph. 1988. *Guideposts to Meaning: Discovering What Really Matters.* Oakland, Calif.: New Harbinger Publications.

Fox, Matthew. 1991. *Creation Spirituality: Liberating Gifts for the Peoples of the Earth.* San Francisco: HarperCollins.

Hanh, Thich Nhat. 1991. *Peace Is Every Step: The Path of Mindfulness in Everyday Life.* New York: Bantam Books.

Kabat-Zinn, Jon. 1994. *Wherever You Go, There You Are: Mindfulness Meditation in Everyday Life.* New York: Hyperion.

———. 1990. *Full Catastrophe Living: Using the Wisdom of Your Body and Mind to Face Stress, Pain, and Illness.* New York: Bantam.

Kertzer, Rabbi Morris, and Rabbi Lawrence Hoffman. 1993. *What Is a Jew?: A Guide to the Beliefs, Traditions, and Practices of Judaism That Answers Questions for Both Jew and Non-Jew.* New York: Simon and Schuster.

Martin, Michael. 1992. *Atheism: A Philosophical Justification.* Philadelphia: Temple University Press.

O'Neill, Craig, and Kathleen Ritter. 1992. *Coming Out Within: Stages of Spiritual Awakening for Lesbians and Gay Men.* San Francisco: HarperCollins.

Taylor, Susan. 1995. *Lessons in Living.* New York: Doubleday.

Winell, Marlene. 1994. *Leaving the Fold: A Guide for Former Fundamentalists and Others Leaving Their Religion.* Oakland, Calif.: New Harbinger Publications.

Chapter 13

Amada, Gerald. 1995. *A Guide to Psychotherapy: An Accessible Guide That Demystifies Psychotherapy.* New York: Ballantine.

American Psychology Association. 1993. Ethical principles of psychologists and code of conduct. *American Psychologist.* 47:1597–1611.

Haldeman, Douglas C. 1994. The practice and ethics of sexual orientation conversion therapy. special section: Mental health of lesbians and gay men. *Journal of Consulting and Clinical Psychology* 62(2): 221–27.

———. 1991. Sexual orientation conversion therapy for gay men and lesbians: A scientific examination. In *Homosexuality: Research Implications for Public Policy,* edited by John C. Gonsiorek and James D. Weinrich. Newbury Park, Calif.: Sage Publications, Inc.

Sullivan, Andrew. 1998. *Love Undetectable: Notes on Friendship, Sex and Survival,* New York: A. A. Knopf.

More New Harbinger Titles

COMING OUT EVERY DAY
Challenging exercises and personal inventories provide a structured approach to the often intimidating process of self-examination that gay or bisexual men face when they disclose their sexual orientation to others.
Item OUT Paperback $13.95

SEX SMART
Demonstrates how childhood family dynamics shape and influence our sexual selves and suggests strategies for counteracting troublesome emotional patterns.
Item SESM Paperback $14.95

A WOMAN'S GUIDE TO OVERCOMING SEXUAL FEAR AND PAIN
This workbook provides a series of exercises designed to help women map the *terra incognita* of their own bodies and begin to overcome the fear or pain that blocks their sexuality.
Item WGOS Paperback $14.95

CLEAR YOUR PAST, CHANGE YOUR FUTURE
Your step-by-step guide to a process that will let you heal old psychological wounds and permanently change the core patterns of belief and behavior that limit who you are and who you can become.
Item PAST Paperback $13.95

DON'T TAKE IT PERSONALLY!
Reveals the power of negative childhood messages and shows readers how to depersonalize their responses, establish boundaries, and develop a new sense of self-acceptance and self-confidence.
Item DOTA Paperback $12.95

Call **toll-free 1-800-748-6273** to order. Have your Visa or Mastercard number ready. Or send a check for the titles you want to New Harbinger Publications, 5674 Shattuck Avenue, Oakland, CA 94609. Include $3.80 for the first book and 75¢ for each additional book to cover shipping and handling. (California residents please include appropriate sales tax.) Allow four to six weeks for delivery.

Prices subject to change without notice.

Some Other New Harbinger Self-Help Titles

Claiming Your Creative Self: True Stories from the Everyday Lives of Women, $15.95

Six Keys to Creating the Life You Desire, $19.95

Taking Control of TMJ, $13.95

What You Need to Know About Alzheimer's, $15.95

Winning Against Relapse: A Workbook of Action Plans for Recurring Health and Emotional Problems, $14.95

Facing 30: Women Talk About Constructing a Real Life and Other Scary Rites of Passage, $12.95

The Worry Control Workbook, $15.95

Wanting What You Have: A Self-Discovery Workbook, $18.95

When Perfect Isn't Good Enough: Strategies for Coping with Perfectionism, $13.95

The Endometriosis Survival Guide, $13.95

Earning Your Own Respect: A Handbook of Personal Responsibility, $12.95

High on Stress: A Woman's Guide to Optimizing the Stress in Her Life, $13.95

Infidelity: A Survival Guide, $13.95

Stop Walking on Eggshells, $14.95

Consumer's Guide to Psychiatric Drugs, $16.95

The Fibromyalgia Advocate: Getting the Support You Need to Cope with Fibromyalgia and Myofascial Pain, $18.95

Healing Fear: New Approaches to Overcoming Anxiety, $16.95

Working Anger: Preventing and Resolving Conflict on the Job, $12.95

Sex Smart: How Your Childhood Shaped Your Sexual Life and What to Do About It, $14.95

You Can Free Yourself From Alcohol & Drugs, $13.95

Amongst Ourselves: A Self-Help Guide to Living with Dissociative Identity Disorder, $14.95

Healthy Living with Diabetes, $13.95

Dr. Carl Robinson's Basic Baby Care, $10.95

Better Boundries: Owning and Treasuring Your Life, $13.95

Goodbye Good Girl, $12.95

Being, Belonging, Doing, $10.95

Thoughts & Feelings, Second Edition, $18.95

Depression: How It Happens, How It's Healed, $14.95

Trust After Trauma, $15.95

The Chemotherapy & Radiation Survival Guide, Second Edition, $14.95

Surviving Childhood Cancer, $12.95

The Headache & Neck Pain Workbook, $14.95

Perimenopause, $16.95

The Self-Forgiveness Handbook, $12.95

A Woman's Guide to Overcoming Sexual Fear and Pain, $14.95

Don't Take It Personally, $12.95

Becoming a Wise Parent For Your Grown Child, $12.95

Clear Your Past, Change Your Future, $13.95

Preparing for Surgery, $17.95

The Power of Two, $15.95

It's Not OK Anymore, $13.95

The Daily Relaxer, $12.95

The Body Image Workbook, $17.95

Living with ADD, $17.95

When Anger Hurts Your Kids, $12.95

The Chronic Pain Control Workbook, Second Edition, $17.95

Fibromyalgia & Chronic Myofascial Pain Syndrome, $19.95

Kid Cooperation: How to Stop Yelling, Nagging & Pleading and Get Kids to Cooperate, $13.95

The Stop Smoking Workbook: Your Guide to Healthy Quitting, $17.95

Conquering Carpal Tunnel Syndrome and Other Repetitive Strain Injuries, $17.95

An End to Panic: Breakthrough Techniques for Overcoming Panic Disorder, Second Edition, $18.95

Letting Go of Anger: The 10 Most Common Anger Styles and What to Do About Them, $12.95

Messages: The Communication Skills Workbook, Second Edition, $15.95

Coping With Chronic Fatigue Syndrome: Nine Things You Can Do, $13.95

The Anxiety & Phobia Workbook, Second Edition, $18.95

The Relaxation & Stress Reduction Workbook, Fourth Edition, $17.95

Living Without Depression & Manic Depression: A Workbook for Maintaining Mood Stability, $18.95

Coping With Schizophrenia: A Guide For Families, $15.95

Visualization for Change, Second Edition, $15.95

Angry All the Time: An Emergency Guide to Anger Control, $12.95

Couple Skills: Making Your Relationship Work, $14.95

Self-Esteem, Second Edition, $13.95

I Can't Get Over It, A Handbook for Trauma Survivors, Second Edition, $16.95

Dying of Embarrassment: Help for Social Anxiety and Social Phobia, $13.95

The Depression Workbook: Living With Depression and Manic Depression, $17.95

Men & Grief: A Guide for Men Surviving the Death of a Loved One, $14.95

When Once Is Not Enough: Help for Obsessive Compulsives, $14.95

Beyond Grief: A Guide for Recovering from the Death of a Loved One, $14.95

Hypnosis for Change: A Manual of Proven Techniques, Third Edition, $15.95

When Anger Hurts, $13.95

Call **toll free, 1-800-748-6273**, to order. Have your Visa or Mastercard number ready. Or send a check for the titles you want to New Harbinger Publications, Inc., 5674 Shattuck Ave., Oakland, CA 94609. Include $3.80 for the first book and 75¢ for each additional book, to cover shipping and handling. (California residents please include appropriate sales tax.) Allow two to five weeks for delivery.

Prices subject to

Advance praise for

THE POWER OF 5

by HAROLD H. BLOOMFIELD, M.D., and ROBERT K. COOPER, Ph.D.

"The ultimate one-stop source for effective 5-second to 5-minute techniques to revitalize your health, weight control, relationships and longevity. Brilliant, powerful! The first self-help book that improves all of your life without wasting any of your time."

DEEPAK CHOPRA, M.D.
best-selling author of
Ageless Body, Timeless Mind

"A masterpiece. *The Power of 5* will instantly change your life. Read it!"

JOHN GRAY, Ph.D.
best-selling author of
Men Are from Mars, Women Are from Venus

"A goldmine of practical, proven advice on health, longevity and relationships."

ART ULENE, M.D.

"Groundbreaking! *The Power of 5* is a treasure trove of valuable insights and immensely practical action steps for invigorating your health, relationships and creative energy. Brilliant!"

STEPHEN R. COVEY, Ph.D.
founder and chairman of the Covey Leadership Center and best-selling author of *First Things First* and *The Seven Habits of Highly Effective People*

"*The Power of 5* goes beyond self-help to total self-transformation. To lead the maximum life, with minimum strife, you need a new game plan and superb, cutting-edge 'coaching.' These are the coaches. This is the plan. Now is your time to choose success, over stress, with *The Power of 5*."

DENIS WAITLEY, Ph.D.
best-selling author of
The Psychology of Winning

"Packed full of all the information and common sense one may need in a lifetime—a long lifetime."

NORMAN LEAR
producer, *All in the Family*

"This is a breakthrough book to improve your health and success and make the rest of your life the best of your life."

KEN BLANCHARD, Ph.D.
best-selling coauthor of
The One-Minute Manager

"*The Power of 5* is the one book that helps you heal all areas of your life. I know it will be your personal health bible."

LOUISE L. HAY
best-selling author of
The Power within You and *Self-Healing*

"*The Power of 5* contains an abundance of fast, wonderful tools for keeping you and your loved ones healthy—in body, mind and spirit. This is a *must* for your family bookshelf, to be referred to over and over again."

> SUSAN JEFFERS, Ph.D.
> best-selling author of
> *Feel the Fear and Do It Anyway*
> and *Dare to Connect*

"*The Power of 5* is one of the best guides to come along in years. It is packed not with opinion and hype but with actual evidence on how to make your life healthier—physically, psychologically and spiritually. This book could change your life."

> LARRY DOSSEY, M.D.
> best-selling author of
> *Healing Words* and *Meaning & Medicine*

"*The Power of 5* is a wonderful collection of bite-sized insights and highly practical tools for wellness, productivity and fulfillment."

> TOM FERGUSON, M.D.
> founder and editor-in-chief of *Medical Self Care*,
> coauthor of *The Peoples' Book of Medical Tests* and
> author of *Health Online*

"*The Power of 5* is an exciting new book for all those in pursuit of wellness. It's filled with hundreds of specific ways to improve your life. It's easy to read and based on up-to-date scientific references. *The Power of 5* should be included in the health promotion library of every hospital, clinic and corporate wellness program nation-wide. On a personal level, I've already found a number of suggestions that are valuable to me. Great job!"

> BILL HETTLER, M.D.
> co-founder of the National Wellness Institute
> and National Wellness Association and director
> of health services at the University of Wisconsin
> (Stevens Point)

THE POWER OF 5

THE POWER OF 5

Hundreds of 5-Second to 5-Minute
Scientific Shortcuts to Ignite Your
Energy, Burn Fat, Stop Aging
and Revitalize Your Love Life

BY HAROLD H. BLOOMFIELD, M.D.,
AND ROBERT K. COOPER, Ph.D.

Endorsed by the Editors of **PREVENTION** Magazine Health Books

Rodale Press, Emmaus, Pennsylvania

Copyright © 1995 by Harold H. Bloomfield, M.D., and Robert K. Cooper, Ph.D.

Illustrations copyright © 1995 by Narda Lebo

Printed in the United States of America on acid-free ∞, recycled paper containing a minimum of 20% post-consumer waste ♻

Art Director: Stan Green
Cover Designer: Larry Freedman
Interior Designers: Larry Freedman, Stan Green
Interior Layout: Sandy Freeman, David Q. Pryor
Cover Photographer: Ron Krisel
Illustrator: Narda Lebo

Library of Congress Cataloging-in-Publication Data

Bloomfield, Harold H., 1944-
    The power of 5 : hundreds of 5-second to 5-minute scientific shortcuts to ignite your energy, burn fat, stop aging and revitalize your love life / by Harold H. Bloomfield and Robert K. Cooper.
        p. cm.
    "Endorsed by the editors of Prevention Magazine Health Books."
    Includes bibliographical references and index.
    ISBN 0–87596–201–7 hardcover
    1. Health. 2. Mental Health. 3. Self-help techniques. 4. Time management. 5. Stress management. 6. Conduct of life. I. Cooper, Robert K. II. Title. III. Title: Power of five.
    RA776.5.B564   1994
    613—dc20   94–33084
                                                            CIP

Distributed in the book trade by St. Martin's Press

2   4   6   8   10   9   7   5   3   1   hardcover

_____ OUR MISSION _____

We publish books that empower people's lives.

RODALE 🍃 BOOKS

Deep within man dwell these slumbering powers; powers that would astonish him, that he never dreamed of possessing; forces that would revolutionize his life if aroused and put into action.
—Orison Swett Marden

Contents

PART III: PERMANENT WEIGHT CONTROL AND DO-IT-ANYWHERE FITNESS

ACKNOWLEDGMENTS

If I have seen farther than most men, it's because I have stood on the shoulders of giants.
—**Sir Isaac Newton**, English mathematician and physicist

Dr. Harold Bloomfield

This book is the result of a creative collaboration by myself and Robert Cooper. Robert is a brilliant researcher and a superb writer. He is a remarkable human being who walks his talk. My heartfelt thanks to his beloved wife, Leslie, and their three children for being so understanding and supportive of the demands on Robert's time.

My love and appreciation to my beloved wife, Sirah Vettese, for her special devotion, wisdom and contributions to this book. Much love and appreciation to my daughter, Shazara, and my stepsons, Michael and Damien, for their support. My love and gratitude to my dear mother, Fridl, departed father, Max, Nora and Gus.

My heartfelt appreciation to Deepak and Rita Chopra, Mike and Donna Fletcher, Susie Gomez (my devoted personal assistant), John and Bonnie Gray, Arnold Lazarus, Norman and Lyn Lear, Peter McWilliams, Marly Meadows (my wonderful office manager), Jack Pursel, Vince and Laura Regalbuto, Ayman and Rowan Sawaf and Ted and Diana Wentworth. Special gratitude to Lazaris and Maharishi Mahesh Yogi.

Dr. Robert Cooper

I wish to acknowledge Harold's heartfelt presence in the creative collaboration that produced this book. He is one of my best friends and a true pioneer in the worldwide self-help movement. I feel honored to share so many of his professional and personal values. My warmest thanks to his wife, Sirah Vettese, for her strong support of Harold's efforts as well as my own, and to their family.

My deepest appreciation to my wife, Leslie, for her radiant, enduring love and unwavering personal support. Much love and gratitude to our son, Chris, and daughters, Chelsea and Shanna. Love and appreciation to my father, Hugh, my mother, Margaret, my sister, Mary, my brother-in-law, Pedro, my brother, David, and my sister-in-law, Nan. Special thanks to Lisa Schoppmann, my research assistant at the University of Michigan Medical Library.

We gratefully acknowledge Bill Gottlieb, senior vice president and editor in chief of Rodale Books, for his masterful and detailed editing and for his friendship and commitment to this project from its inception. We also wish to acknowledge the exceptional efforts given on behalf of this project by other key people at Rodale Books, including Pat Corpora, Lynn Gavett, Linda Johns, Lois Hazel, Larry Freedman, Stan Green, Jane Sherman and Anita Small. And for his initial guidance and continued support we wish to thank Jonathon Lazear.

We are deeply grateful to the following professionals who have influenced our thinking and inspired our efforts over the years: Linda Perlin Alperstein, Ph.D., Liz Applegate, Ph.D., James A. Autry, Neil Barnard, M.D., Aaron T. Beck, M.D., Robert O. Becker, M.D., George L. Blackburn, M.D., Ph.D., Steven N. Blair, P.E.D., Jeffrey Blumberg, Ph.D., William M. Bortz II, M.D., Kelly D. Brownell, Ph.D., Robert N. Butler, M.D., Rene Cailliet, M.D., C. Wayne Callaway, M.D., Thomas F. Cash, Ph.D., Michael Castleman, Michael D. Chafetz, Ph.D., Deepak Chopra, M.D., Kenneth H. Cooper, M.D., Stephen R. Covey, Ph.D., Kathryn D. Cramer, Ph.D., Susan E. Crohan, Ph.D., Winnifred D. Cutler, Ph.D., Ellington Darden, Ph.D., Edward deBono, M.D., Dean C. Delis, Ph.D., Marian Cleeves Diamond, Ph.D., Carlo C. DiClemente, Ph.D., Norman Epstein, Ph.D., Joan M. Erikson, Erick H. Erickson, Clarissa Pinkola Estes, Ph.D., William Evans, Ph.D., Tom Ferguson, M.D., Frederic Flach, M.D., Martha E. Francis, Ph.D., Howard S. Friedman, Ph.D., Robert Fritz, William F. Frey, Jr., M.D., Daniel Goleman, Ph.D., John Gottman, Ph.D., Etienne Grandjean, M.D., John Gray, Ph.D., Thich Nhat Hanh, John D. Hatfield, M.D., Peter Hauri, Ph.D., Gay Hendricks, Ph.D., Kathryn Hendricks, Ph.D., Sheldon Saul Hendler, M.D., Ph.D., Douglas J. Hermann, Ph.D., William Hettler, M.D.,

Robert Hirschfield, M.D., James A. Horne, Ph.D., Jean Houston, Ph.D., Richard C. Huseman, Ph.D., Evan Imber-Black, Ph.D., Michael F. Jacobson, Ph.D., Ruthellen Josselson, Ph.D., Jon Kabat-Zinn, Ph.D., Peter Koestenbaum, Ph.D., Lawrence E. Lamb, M.D., Ellen J. Langer, Ph.D., Arnold J. Lazarus, Ph.D., Monique le Poncin, Ph.D., Harriet Goldhor Lerner, Ph.D., James J. Lynch, Ph.D., Allan Luks, Barbara Mackoff, Ph.D., Vernon H. Mark, M.D., Howard J. Markman, Ph.D., Robert Masters, Ph.D., Emmett E. Miller, M.D., Wayne C. Miller, Ph.D., Thomas Moore, Ph.D., Martin Moore-Ede, M.D., Ph.D., David G. Myers, Ph.D., William Nagler, M.D., Joyce D. Nash, Ph.D., John C. Norcross, Ph.D., Clifford Notarius, Ph.D., Esther M. Orioli, Dean Ornish, M.D., Robert Ornstein, Ph.D., James W. Pennebaker, Ph.D., Christopher Peterson, Ph.D., James Perl, Ph.D., Ronald M. Podell, M.D., John Potter, M.D., Karl H. Pribram, M.D., James O. Prochaska, Ph.D., Richard Restak, M.D., Janine Roberts, Ph.D., Judith Rodin, Ph.D., Irwin H. Rosenberg, M.D., Saul H. Rosenthal, M.D., Ernest Lawrence Rossi, Ph.D., Martin L. Rossman, M.D., Virginia Satir, James Scala, Ph.D., Sandra Scantling, Ph.D., Roger C. Schank, Ph.D., Julius Segal, Ph.D., Martin E. P. Seligman, Ph.D., Anees A. Sheikh, Ph.D., Katharina S. Sheikh, Porter Shimer, Sidney B. Simon, Ph.D., David G. Simons, M.D., David Sobel, M.D., Robert C. Solomon, Ph.D., Bryant A. Stamford, Ph.D., Robert L. Swezey, M.D., Deborah Tannen, Ph.D., Robert E. Thayer, Ph.D., Janet G. Travell, M.D., Art Ulene, M.D., Peter D. Vash, M.D., Daniel M. Wegner, Ph.D., Wayne L. Westcott, Ph.D., Redford Williams, M.D., Virginia Williams, Ph.D., Arthur Winter, M.D., Janet Wolfe, Ph.D., Judith J. Wurtman, Ph.D. and Bernie Zilbergeld, Ph.D.

Finally, we want to thank the many other dedicated researchers, educators and clinicians throughout the world who regularly bring forth vital revelations that give hope to our collective future and wings to our personal dreams.

PART I

THE POWER OF 5:
HOW TO MAKE IT
YOUR POWER

Doing Less, Accomplishing More

Making New Choices: 5 Seconds
to 5 Minutes at a Time

You know: You're giving everything you've got to stay ahead.

You feel: You're working longer and harder to be successful, healthy and fit—but more often than ever you're tense and tired, stretched to the limit and scrambling for time.

You need: Practical, on-the-spot, real-life ways to ignite your energy, stop aging, shed excess body fat, expand your mind, bring more enjoyment into your days and revitalize your love life and family relationships.

You deserve: To accomplish and enjoy more of whatever matters most in your life.

All across America we're getting trapped. Trapped in a maze of well-intentioned but often unsuccessful "self-help" programs. Hit from all sides with fragmented advice: diet-only, relationship-only, fitness-only, mind-only programs. Encouraged to strive for expectations that are unrealistic. Exhausted by the effort. Confused by quick-fix fad books that promise the moon but don't deliver. Left feeling guilty about complicated health and fitness advice that just isn't practical for our hectic lives.

But what's the alternative? Where do you turn for immediately useful advice?

The Power of 5.

POWER

A highly personal—and deeply universal—source of energy, intelligence and commitment; the ability to enjoy a high level of health and fitness, think creatively under pressure, nurture your love life and family relationships and effectively accomplish your goals and dreams.

The deepest reality you are aware of *is the one from which you draw your power.*

—Deepak Chopra, M.D.,
*Ageless Body,
Timeless Mind*

We invite you on an exciting journey. In the pages ahead, you'll discover some of the best tools to make your life *easier* and *more enjoyable*, instead of more complicated. *The Power of 5* is the first program that invites you, the reader, to *start anywhere*, with *any* 5-second to 5-minute strategy, *anytime during your day*, and immediately feel an increase in Personal Power. You'll boost your energy and ability to think creatively and act effectively in *accomplishing more of whatever matters most to you* in your life and work, at the same time you're making simple yet significant improvements in your health, work and relationships.

Changing habits becomes difficult, if not impossible, when you have to spend hours at a time *trying* to do it; you feel more like a *human doing* than a *human being.* Research suggests that what works best are *ultra-specific, highly practical* choices that you can use on the spot, wherever you are.[1] In *The Power of 5*, for example, we offer choices that you can use to:

• Increase your energy and alertness.
• Become more at ease and revitalize your mind and body in the midst of your hectic schedule.
• Sleep more deeply, night after night.
• Stay on track to your goals and dreams—to *accomplish more* of whatever matters most to you and *do less* of whatever doesn't.
• Rev up your metabolism to automatically "burn off" excess body fat 24 hours a day.
• Maintain lifelong health and greater fitness *without the hassles.*
• Boost your spirit to bring out more of your best during difficult times.
• Become more compassionate and loving in your relationships with others.
• Create more genuine inner peace and happiness.
• Balance the competing demands of work and home life.
• Discover greater intimacy and lifelong sexual pleasure.

WHY *THE POWER OF 5*?

The truth is, to a great extent we are a product of our *choices*, not our *circumstances*. We're constantly making choices—or unconsciously letting the choices be made *for* us—and we're living with the consequences of those choices. And many of us don't like the consequences. When your days are packed and you rush through life and work on "autopilot" most of the time, reacting to whatever urgent demands appear, it feels as if you're a victim of circumstance, that bad things "just happen" to you. Chances are, though, what's *really* happening is that you're stuck, limited by reacting unconsciously and, all too often, counterproductively. *The Power of 5* is designed to offer you a collection of highly effective new ways to get *un*stuck and accomplish more of whatever you want in life.

Why 5? First and foremost because the range of 5 seconds to 5 minutes is an ideal time-frame in which to respond effectively to rising pressures, to head off fatigue or upset and to learn—and *apply*—new information to change health, work and relationship habits.

Five seconds is all it takes to:
• Jump to a higher vantage point.
• Take a deep breath and reduce tension.
• Turn on one of your biological "switches" of alertness.[2]
• Fire up your powers of imagination.
• Interrupt cycles of anger or argument.
• Take a deep breath and remain more open-minded.
• Notice someone in need—and say a kind word or give a gesture of support.
• Acknowledge what you *really* feel and want.
• Straighten out negative thoughts and clear up misperceptions.
• Spark creative thinking with a quick dose of humor.
• Refocus your attention on what's ahead—and access your Personal Power.

With *The Power of 5* you have many new options for responding more *consciously* and *effectively* to life's daily *turning points*, or *moments of truth*.[3]

But, you may be wondering, am *I* actually capable of responding this rapidly with *The Power of 5*? Absolutely. Brain messages travel along the pathways in your nervous system at up to 200 miles an hour and produce complex interactions in perception, attention, neuromuscular activation and responsiveness.[4] The power of this phenomenon is

APPLY THE 5 "Ws"

To make each *Power of 5* choice match *your* needs and goals:

WHO?

Does this choice make sense, or feel right, *to me*?

WHAT?

What, *exactly*, am I going to envision or do?

WHY?

Why am I doing this? Does this choice support my intentions?

WHEN?

Is it *practical* for me to do? What's the best *timing*?

WHERE?

At home? At work? In what setting is this *appropriate*?

> All advances in life come through the power of choice.
>
> —**Eric Allenbaugh, Ph.D.,**
> *Wake-Up Calls*

exemplified by the fact that the brain can simultaneously compare at least 10,000 separate factors or choices[5] and can recognize the meaning of more than 100,000 words or images in less than 1 second.[6] Furthermore, it takes only one one-hundredth of a second for the eye to blink completely, and at least 600 individual muscular actions can occur in a single second; researchers say the number may be much higher.[7]

Five minutes is a useful time-frame for presenting new information "bites" and providing practical tools and techniques. According to some authorities on adult learning, 5 minutes is a realistic *maximal focus span* for many time-pressed men and women.[8] "Recent brain/mind research has shown that the mind's attention span is extremely short—between 5 and 7 minutes depending upon subject matter and level of interest," explains creative problem-solving consultant Joyce Wycoff. "The mind works best in these short bursts of activity."[9]

"LEVERAGE POINTS": WHEN LESS *IS* MORE

In *The Power of 5*, we're not going to add more to your "to-do" list. Rather, our objective is to assist you in actually doing *less* yet accomplishing *more* of whatever matters most to you. To *let go of* unrealistic, guilt-loaded, time-gobbling attempts to improve your health, work and relationships and substitute simple, more powerful choices. It's much more a matter of *what*, specifically, you do, and *why* and *when* you do it, than how fast you can get it done.

The Power of 5 presents what researchers in "systems thinking" call Leverage Points—the small, well-focused actions that can, when used at the right time and in the right place, *produce significant, lasting benefits* exponentially *beyond the effort required to take the action step itself.*[10] Often these Leverage Points follow the principle known as *economy of means*—where the best results come not from large-scale efforts but from simple, highly specific actions. In sailing, this is referred to as trimtabbing—making a quick, precise and minor adjustment in the sails to accelerate far more efficiently, using the focused force of the prevailing winds. *The Power of 5* is about making the *key personal choices* that can lighten your load, raise your vantage point and renew your body, mind and spirit—not just *figuratively* but *literally, physiologically.*

> Anything less than a conscious commitment to the important is an unconscious commitment to the unimportant.
>
> —**Stephen Covey, Ph.D.,**
> *First Things First*

There are 100 trillion cells in your body. About 6 trillion reactions take place in these cells *every second*. The rate at which you age, for example, is extremely fluid and changeable—your thoughts, feelings and behaviors can influence every one of these cells; your aging processes can speed up, slow down or even reverse themselves.

Surprised? There's more. Your metabolism—a highly responsive, intelligent process whereby your cells make energy and "burn off" fat—is powerfully influenced by what you think and do *every minute of the day*, not just three times a week during formal exercise sessions!

Here's another fact: Your mind/body reaction to small hassles and other stressful events *starts instantly, again and again*, and mobilizes millions of messenger chemicals and potentially harmful glucocorticoid hormones. Every belief you hold, every thought you generate, every choice you make, every emotion elicited within you, activates messenger molecules in your brain and is transformed into physiological impulses that instantly *change your biology*.

FIRST THINGS FIRST: THE POWER OF *TIME*

"I don't have time." "Time flies." "Time's running out." "Timeline." "Time pressures." Numerous opinion polls in the United States and Europe show that people complain more about a lack of time than a lack of money or freedom.[11] There are 1,440 minutes in a day. That means 86,400 seconds—the same length of time that has filled each day for millennia on earth. Yet in recent years, our collective sense of life's quickening pace—the feeling that time is growing shorter, more scarce—has become exaggerated, not alleviated. We're hurrying. We're falling behind. We're straining to catch up. We're frustrated about time. We're resentful about time. We feel helpless about time. And nationwide surveys indicate that this pervasive time-crunch seems to be prompting more of us each year to say "forget it" to their efforts toward a healthy diet, regular exercise and stress management.[12]

After a Concorde landing in New York, an on-board electrical malfunction prevented the exit doors from opening. Even though maintenance workers were busy repairing the problem, after 5 minutes the passengers were angrily deciding what they were going to demand from Air France in compensation for lost time. After 15 minutes, they were on the verge of rioting.[13]

"Time is the psychological enemy of man," wrote the famous spiritual teacher J. Krishnamurti, referring to the observation that most of us see time as an absolute over which we have little or no control. However, contrary to conventional thinking, the opposite is true—and this book is about taking back the *power of time*. It's about *choosing* to turn

YOUR 5 LEVELS

OF PERSONAL POWER

The Power of 5

is designed to strengthen

each level and draw them

into greater balance.

1. Your *spiritual* power

2. Your *intellectual* power

3. Your *emotional* power

4. Your *physical* power

5. Your *social* power

time into your ally instead of your enemy. This subject has never been more crucial. Here are several more of the reasons why.

It's no accident that the word *deadline* contains the word *dead*: the human body is not well-suited to time-struggle. Research strongly suggests that people who suffer from "hurry sickness"—the chronic feeling that there's never enough time—may be at increased risk for developing or aggravating health problems such as high blood pressure, heart disease and certain forms of cancer.[14] A *struggle with time* is also linked to chronic anger and hostility, depression, bitterness, resentment and sudden cardiac death (an unexpected fatal heart attack).[15] On the other hand, researchers suggest that *time competency*—using your time effectively and freeing yourself from anxious watch-watching and a nagging sense of impatience—is a prerequisite to success in improving your health, fitness and relationships.[16]

As you read this book, we encourage you to pause frequently and listen to your own mind and heart. What new choices seem on-target to make desired changes in your life and work? Which action steps might best serve as Leverage Points in saving you time and effort?

By using *The Power of 5*, your perspectives will be changed. More than that, *you'll* be changed. You'll see the world differently. You'll relate to time differently. You'll experience relationships differently. You'll make new choices. And you'll be able to close the gap between how you spend your time and what's deeply important to you.

YOU DESERVE . . .

Throughout this book we emphasize "You deserve . . ." It's not something you have to earn or wait for—it's your natural birthright, your Personal Power. Its essence is the feeling that you are whole and worthy. In *The Power of 5* you'll learn to take a few moments or several minutes at key points throughout the day to immediately experience more vigor, creativity, inner joy and purposeful focus.

When you learn to consciously respond to life's problems and challenges with *The Power of 5*—5 seconds to 5 minutes at a time—the results can be truly amazing. That's the feedback we've already gotten from the tens of thousands of people who have attended our seminars—people from all walks of life, backgrounds and countries around the world. We welcome you to the discoveries on the pages ahead. We have written this book for you.

THE NEW SCIENCE OF SELF-HELP

Bringing Lasting Benefits to Your Health and Life

Science is the systematic means of gaining reliable knowledge.
—**John Dewey**, American philosopher and educator

The Power of 5 breaks new ground in what we call the science of
self-help. It's well known that, for better *and* worse, the self-help book
market exerts considerable influence in Western society. A surprising
number of self-help books sell hundreds of thousands—sometimes millions—of copies, and in some cases, have a profound effect on the perspectives and habits of the general public.[1]

One survey, conducted by a professor of medical psychology at the
Oregon Health Sciences University, reports that the public overwhelmingly (83.3 percent in this survey) endorses a "rather positive" to
"very positive" evaluation of self-help books.[2]

But what about all the misinformation contained in many of these
books? The tangents and contradictions? The lack of scientific studies?
Well, despite these shortcomings, the public is buying the books anyway, hungry for self-help knowledge. Unfortunately, most scientists
and qualified professionals who complain so often and loudly about the
second-rate quality of information in many self-help books have been
trained to write in a style that is colorless, wordy and impersonal—like
lifeless prose from a machine. The public is turned off by this writing.
Fad-book authors, on the other hand, may lack substance, but they've
learned to craft compelling, snappy pages that draw in the reader. These
authors make the information *fun* to read, whether or not it is accurate,
practical or effective.

> Properly, we should read for power. Man reading should be man intensely alive. The book should be a ball of light in one's hand.
>
> **—Ezra Pound,**
> American poet

> No one could make a greater mistake than he who did nothing because he could do only a little.
>
> **—Edmund Burke,**
> British statesman and orator

The challenge is clear: To meet, and exceed, the public's rightful demand for entertaining reading, but to do it in a responsible way, based on science. "We are at the beginning of *the age of public participation in science*," says Maurice Goldsmith, director of the International Science Policy Foundation in London. "This has occurred as it has become clearer that science is not a private game, but is for everybody; that it has a function in society; and that if used in a planned way could improve our condition immeasurably."[3]

In writing *The Power of 5*, we've drawn upon computer database searches of the world's scientific and medical literature, as well as interviews with leading research scientists, physicians, psychologists, physiologists and educators in North America and throughout the world. Yet this book offers you more than a bundle of techniques based on narrow, rational analysis. Instead, we've chosen insights and ideas, tools and strategies, that we believe may be extraordinarily useful for a busy person like you. Using our interdisciplinary backgrounds in the health sciences, medicine and psychology, and with support from a network of specialists in many different fields, we've worked hard to untangle contradictory advice, dispel popular fads and misconceptions and pinpoint priorities.

DISCOVER YOUR OWN ACCELERATIVE LEARNING STYLE

You'll notice that, in a number of ways, The *Power of 5* is different from other self-help books. Our goal is to welcome and allow readers to follow whatever "learning style" appeals to them as individuals. We've incorporated a host of unique and useful features for *accelerative learning*—to help you more quickly understand and benefit from *The Power of 5*.

Variety: We've broken up the text with sidebars, highlights, section dividers and Power Actions.

Easy-access chapter sequences: You can either:
• Go directly to what you need.
• Scan and browse.
• Read straight through.

5-second and 5-minute choices: We've highlighted the fastest *on-the-spot techniques* for you to try, and there are also instant reminders for heightened awareness or a mental lift anytime, anywhere.

"Power Action: First Option" and "Power Action: More Options:" In each chapter we've presented our most practical recommendations in two parts—the "Power Action: First Option" is one of our own favorites or a popular choice with our patients, clients and audiences; "Power Action: More Options" offers alternatives and added ways to increase the benefits and bring everything into balance.

Power Quotes: We've gathered some of our favorite timeless quotes to inspire you, prompt reflection, motivate and guide you.

Resources: These are our recommendations for the best sources of information—books, articles, audiotapes and organizations—that you can use to learn more about the subjects in each chapter.

Personal Power Notes: This single page at the end of each chapter takes less than 5 minutes to read; it offers an at-a-glance review of the chapter's Power Actions.

References: If you've already scanned ahead in *The Power of 5*, you may be wondering about the small numbers that appear frequently throughout the text. These numbers correspond to the numbered reference notes listed at the end of each part. Why did we include reference notes, a feature that's usually found in scientific and academic books, in *The Power of 5*? We did it so that you can easily find a reference—a scientific or medical study, for example, or a professional publication—that substantiates our recommendations. The information in these sources can help you work more closely with your health professional or follow up on a specific study or expert's advice.

Another reason we've included references in *The Power of 5* is to promote an important change in self-help books—giving *you, the reader, greater access to the science of effective self-help.* One of the problems with many popular self-help books is that the authors' statements such as "a recent study shows . . ." or "researchers have discovered . . ." or "experts say . . ." aren't referenced—and, in an alarming number of cases, may actually be inaccurate or untrue. We believe that reference notes can help solve this problem by giving you or your health professional easy access to *what* study or *which* researchers or specialists we're citing. This is one of the many valuable and uncommon ways in which *The Power of 5* puts more *information power* directly in your hands.

> The most valuable work you do may be done in as little as 5 seconds to 5 minutes. A higher vantage point, a brilliant idea, a key change in habit, a break from pressure, a boost in metabolism or a pivotal decision can produce significant, lasting benefits.
>
> **—P. M. Senge,**
> *The Fifth Discipline*

> All of our life is but a mass of small habits—practical, emotional, intellectual and spiritual—that bear us irresistibly toward our destiny.
>
> **—William James, M.D.,** founder of modern psychology

So where's the best place to start? That's up to you. "But," you may be wondering, "do I need to do *everything* in this book to get results?" Absolutely not. You can begin anywhere, with whatever first interests you. And you can browse in any direction.

On the pages that follow, you'll find a path to living at your full potential, not a rigid set of rules. It's vital not to confuse the map with the territory, and in that light this book sets out a journey for you to take, and we invite you to explore the possibilities with us. We see ourselves as friendly travelers and teachers, not as autocratic authorities.

In personal changes, as in most aspects of life, your success depends on timing. According to three of America's leading psychological researchers on change—James O. Prochaska, Ph.D., John C. Norcross, Ph.D., and Carlo C. DiClemente, Ph.D.— "at certain moments . . . there are individuals whose minds are prepared to recognize the importance of things that unprepared minds ignore or throw away." In *The Power of 5*, you'll gain access to hundreds of specific, practical ways to move forward in your life and work and support yourself and others in making small, significant changes that last.[4]

With each insight and strategy from *The Power of 5*, listen to the inner wisdom of your body, which expresses itself through signs of comfort or discomfort, alertness or fatigue. When making choices, ask yourself, "How do I *feel* about this?" And pay attention to the answers you get. Make the choices that seem right for *you*—simple, comfortable, unforced, effective, revitalizing. And watch the results. Our goal is to help you achieve a higher state of personal well-being and power with *less* struggle and strain, not *more*. And remember that small decisions can sometimes pay the largest dividends.

References

CHAPTER 1

1. Senge, P. M. The Fifth Discipline (New York: Doubleday, 1990); Sternberg, R. J. The Triarchic Mind (New York: Penguin, 1988); Mitroff, I. I., and Linstone, H. A. The Unbounded Mind (New York: Oxford University Press, 1993); Stroebel, C. F. The Quieting Reflex (New York: Berkley, 1982); M. R. Ford et al. "Quieting Response Training: Predictors of Long-Term Outcome." Biofeedback and Self-Regulation 8 (3)(1983): 393–408; M. R. Ford et al. "Quieting Response Training: Long-Term Evaluation of a Clinical Biofeedback Practice." Biofeedback and Self-Regulation 8 (2)(1983): 265–278; Stroebel, C. F., Ford, M. R., Strong, P., and Szarek, B. L. "Quieting Response Training: Five-Year Evaluation of a Clinical Biofeedback Practice." (Hartford, Conn.: Institute for Living, 1981); Stroebel, C. F., Luce, G., and Glueck, B. C. "Optimizing Compliance with Behavioral Medicine Therapies." Current Psychiatric Therapies (1983/1984).
2. Moore-Ede, M. The 24-Hour Society (Reading, Mass.: Addison-Wesley, 1992).
3. A management concept articulated by Jan Carlzon and discussed in his book Moments of Truth (New York: Ballinger, 1987).
4. The Behavioral and Brain Sciences 8 (1986): 529–566; "Brain Shows Activation before Conscious Choice." Brain/Mind Bulletin (May 5, 1986): 1; Cattell, R. B. Abilities: Their Structure, Growth and Action (Boston: Houghton Mifflin, 1971); Pribram, K. H. Brain and Perception (Hillsdale, N.J.: Erlbaum, 1991).
5. Wenger, W. Beyond Teaching and Learning (Gaithersburg, Md.: Project Renaissance, 1992).
6. Winter, A., and Winter, R. Build Your Brain Power (New York: St. Martin's Press, 1986): 90.
7. Jaret, P. "Mind: Why Practice Makes Perfect." Hippocrates (Nov./Dec. 1987): 90–91; Salthouse, T. Scientific American (Feb. 1984).
8. Wycoff, J. Mindmapping (New York: Berkley, 1991); Steibach, R. The Adult Learner: Enhancing Learning Skills (Crisp Publications, 1993); Merriam, S. B., and Caffarella, R. S. Learning in Adulthood: A Comprehensive Guide (San Francisco: Josey-Bass, 1991); Candy, P. C. Self-Direction for Lifelong Learning (San Francisco: Josey-Bass, 1991); Mezirow, J. Transformative Dimensions of Adult Learning (San Francisco: Josey-Bass, 1991); Brookfield, S. D. Understanding and Facilitating Adult Learning (San Francisco: Josey-Bass, 1991).
9. Wycoff. Mindmapping: 40.
10. Senge. The Fifth Discipline: 63–64; 114–116.
11. Servan-Schreiber, J. L. The Art of Time (Reading, Mass.: Addison-Wesley, 1988).
12. Stein, J. "From Fitness Fan to Sure Sloth." Los Angeles Times (Mar. 6, 1994).
13. Servan-Schreiber. The Art of Time: 28.
14. Dossey, L. Meaning and Medicine (New York: Bantam, 1992); Eliot, R. S. From Stress to Strength (New York: Bantam, 1993); Williams, R., and Williams, V. Anger Kills (New York: Times Books, 1993); Chopra, D. Ageless Body, Timeless Mind (New York: Crown, 1993).
15. Chopra. Ageless Body: 284.
16. Everly, G. S. "Time Management: A Behavioral Strategy for Disease Prevention and Health Enhancement," in Behavioral Health: A Handbook of Health Enhancement and Disease Prevention, eds. J. D. Matarazzo et al. (New York: Wiley, 1984): 363–369;

Everly, G. S. "Time Urgency and Health-Related Coping Behavior" (research report, Loyola College, 1982).

CHAPTER 2

1. Green, L. W. "Three Ways Research Influences Policy and Practice: The Public's Right to Know and the Scientist's Responsibility to Educate." Health Education 18 (4)(Aug./Sept. 1987): 44–49.
2. Starker, S. Oracle at the Supermarket: Exploring the American Obsession with Self-Help Books (Far Hills, N.J.: New Horizon Press, 1988).
3. Goldsmith, M. The Science Critic (New York: Methuen, 1986): 12.
4. Prochaska, J. O., Norcross, J. C., and DiClemente, C. C. Changing for Good (New York: Morrow, 1994): 59.

THE POWER OF 5

PART II

GAINING ENERGY, ERASING TENSION

Staying Calm under Pressure

On-the-Spot Ways to Release Tension

Men are disturbed not by things, but by the view which they take of them.

—**Epictetus**, Greek philosopher

In today's stressed-out world, your best health and performance, and your Personal Power, depend on remaining *calm* under pressure, alert yet relaxed. *Stress* originates from the French word *estrece*, meaning narrowness, a constriction or limiting of your power.

The most debilitating type of stress—*negative stress*—generally occurs when you view change and pressure as burdens and perceive rising demands as threats. You feel a sense of alienation or frustration or helplessness. You perceive yourself as the victim of circumstances, to a great extent powerless to influence the events in your life. Repeated or prolonged negative stress can trigger complex physiological reactions that may involve more than 1,500 different chemical changes in the brain and body—and may lead to an exhaustion of mental and physical energies and increased susceptibility to disease.

When you're hit with stressful events, and in those first moments, you react negatively to the stress, brain messenger chemicals from the hypothalamus and hormones from your pituitary gland signal your adrenal glands to produce cortisol. Nerve impulses stimulate the adrenals to produce noradrenaline and adrenaline, which surge into the bloodstream and alert the body by stimulating millions of special nerve fibers. Both adrenaline and cortisol raise blood pressure during stress. Adrenaline increases the "stickiness" of blood platelets (blood-clotting elements), and cortisol can increase their number, which can cause platelets to adhere to artery walls, narrowing them. Over time, "excess adrenaline and cortisol may bombard the artery walls," explains cardiologist Robert S. Eliot, M.D., "damaging them and leaving places for the blood fats and other elements to lodge. . . . Excess adrenaline can also overcontract and rupture heart muscle fibers, making the heart vulnerable to an electrical short-circuit and weakening it. Excess cortisol can also raise cholesterol, contributing to hardening of the arteries."[1]

In a landmark Harvard study, people who coped poorly with stress became ill four times more often than those with good coping styles.[2] Mismanaged "negative stress" affects the immune system, heart function, hormone levels, the nervous system, memory and thinking, physical coordination and metabolic rate; it raises blood cholesterol, blood pressure and uric acid levels; and it increases the risk of many diseases, including heart disease, cancer, immunodeficiency diseases and even the common cold.[3] As explained in chapter 12, new research has linked mismanaged stress to gaining abdominal body fat. In addition, negative stress kills brain cells and appears to prematurely age the adult brain.[4] A continuous bombardment of stress hormones on the brain seems to destroy cerebral hormone receptors and weaken the brain areas that control emotions.[5] Then adrenal stress hormones—glucocorticoids—can block the entry of glucose into brain cells, killing them.[6]

What's the worst kind of stress? The answer is highly personal. What's chronically upsetting to you may not irritate your spouse or next-door neighbor at all. However, you may be surprised to learn that, for many of us, the ability to stay calm and healthy amidst life's constant pressures comes down to the "small things." How, precisely, we respond to the irritations of everyday life—such as anger, rejection, interruptions, broken appointments, the inescapable telephone, financial anxieties, bad weather, traffic jams and deadlines—is often a more powerful predictor of psychological and physical health than is our reaction to major life crises.[7] *Your own reactions—and overreactions—are the key.*[8] Managing stress really means managing the tension, anger and anxiety you feel in stressful situations so that you can respond creatively and healthfully. This doesn't mean you won't suffer sometimes. What it does mean is that you can learn ways to break the ongoing grip of harmful pressure.

Few of us realize that *relaxation does not mean depleted energy or dulled senses.* By developing your ability to quickly enter a state of profound, revitalizing relaxation—restful alertness—you can distance yourself from life's noise and distractions and promote greater clear-mindedness and awareness. Once you notice the everyday signs of ris-

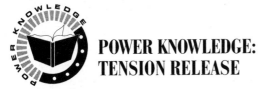

POWER KNOWLEDGE: TENSION RELEASE

MYTH: Even though my life is stressed-out, I'm filled with energy. That must mean I'm handling things just fine.

POWER KNOWLEDGE: Not necessarily. According to a pioneering researcher on the subject, Robert E. Thayer, Ph.D., professor of biological psychology at California State University,[13] there are two primary energy states—the one where most of us are trapped is called *tense-energy* and the other, which most of us have lost touch with, is called *calm-energy*.

Tense-energy (high tension and high energy) is a stress-driven mood characterized by an almost pleasant sense of excitement and power. Your physical energy feels high, even though you may face a high level of stresses and strains from long hours on a hectic work schedule. In a tense-energy state, you tend to impatiently push yourself toward one objective after another, rarely pausing to rest or reflect. Your efforts are infused with a moderate to severe level of physical tension which, after a while, may be imperceptible to you. Without realizing it, by allowing this tense-energy state to persist, you can suddenly wake up to find yourself at the edge of burnout and exhaustion.

Calm-energy (low tension and high energy) is a mood state that few of us experience often enough. Calm-energy feels remarkably serene and under control. It replaces tense-energy with an alert, more optimistic presence of mind, peaceful and pleasurable body feelings and a deep sense of physical stamina and well-being.[14] Your mental and physical reserves are high, and when you are in calm-energy, you have the best combination of healthy vitality and increased creative intelligence.[15]

"When an individual feels highly energetic, and at the same time is relatively calm," explains Dr. Thayer, "his or her perception of both self and the world are distinctly different from when that person is tired and at the same time tense. Not only are memories of past successes and failures likely to be different, but perceived likelihoods of future successes and failures are also different."[16]

19

ing stress at home and work, you can use the one of the on-the-spot techniques in this chapter. With practice, you'll be able to quickly dissolve excess tension and head off the damaging effects of distress— much like a champion tennis player "resting between volleys" during an important match.

POWER ACTION: FIRST OPTION
One-Touch Relaxation

Here's one of the simplest, fastest ways to relax, anywhere, anytime. One-Touch Relaxation is elicited through key muscles that, with gentle fingertip pressure, can trigger a "cascade" effect that quickly dissolves tension throughout the body. This concept has been explored by Massachusetts General Hospital neurosurgeon Vernon H. Mark, M.D., and others.[9] Here's one example: Place your fingertips on your jaw joints just in front of your ears. As you inhale, tense your jaw muscles—bringing the upper and lower jaw together, which will feel like you're clenching your teeth—for 5 seconds. Then, as you exhale, let the jaw muscles go totally loose, releasing all tension, letting the lower jaw drop and relaxing your tongue. What does this feel like? Focus on the contrast between tension and relaxation sensations. Then repeat the exercise, but use only half the tightness in your jaw muscles. Hold for 5 seconds, then release. Repeat with one-fourth the original tension, and then one-eighth—where it is much harder to discern differences in tension. What you're doing is using touch to set a sensory cue for relaxation. In this case, you're linking the sensation of your fingertips pressing on the jaw muscles, followed by the highly desirable sensation of releasing tension. The process is triggered by a combination of your touch and the accompanying mental command to relax.

Now take a deep breath as you press and—using one touch with your fingertips against the jaw—relax the muscles there on the exhalation (you should feel the jaw slackening), while saying "Ah-h-h-h" (either silently or aloud) and letting your tongue relax and settle down into the base of your mouth, with its tip lightly touching your lower front teeth. Imagine yourself breathing out tightness and putting aside your "shoulds," duties and emotional burdens.

You can elicit a similar response by shrugging your shoulders, lifting them up toward your ears and then totally relaxing all of the muscles from your neck down your shoulders and across your chest and upper back, saying "Ah-h-h-h" as you breathe away stiffness and release inner pressures. Once you're comfortable using either of these examples, you can pick whatever other muscle areas of your body tend to stiffen up whenever stress mounts—such as the lower back or abdomen—and develop a similar "quick release" technique for each of them.

With some practice you'll be able to simply reach up and use *a single touch* on your tense jaw or shoulders—or to reach up and place your hands on a loved one's shoulders—to trigger an immediate "wave" of relaxation through that area, as if you're standing under a waterfall that washes away all the tension and strain. You get such an instantaneous payoff because you elicit *a powerful quieting response from the brain.*[10]

We strongly encourage you to experience various methods of releasing tension in order to deepen your effectiveness with One-Touch Relaxation. As the jaw muscles relax more deeply, for example, the lightening of tension can quickly extend, spreading relief to the neck and back areas, too. Once you've had a chance to try the following long-proven techniques, retest your skill at One-Touch Relaxation. Does fingertip pressure on a key muscle area—such as on both sides of the jaw or above your shoulder blades or with your thumbs pressing on the lower back area—and the mental command "Relax" trigger a greater release of tension than before? Chances are, it will.

Here are two focused 5-minute approaches to deeper relaxation. They focus the mind strictly on dissipating tension.

5 Minutes of Deep Relaxation

1. Select a quiet place and a comfortable position. Take a moment to loosen all constricting clothing.

2. Give yourself full permission to relax. Missing this simple step is one reason many relaxation plans don't succeed. Choose some object in the distance to look at and keep your eyes fixed upon it as you repeat silently to yourself, "There's no place I have to go right now, nothing I have to do and no problem I have to solve. . . . I give myself permission to relax."[11] Repeat several times.

3. Focus on your breathing as you begin to release tension. After repeating the words above several times, and really hearing their meaning, let your eyelids close and take a deep breath in, filling your abdomen, your middle chest and your upper chest. Hold this breath for a moment without closing off your throat, then let it go, imagining that as you breathe out, you're breathing all unnecessary tension out of your body. As you breathe out, repeat to yourself the words, "Letting go . . . and relaxing." Repeat several times.

4. Have a strategy for dealing with unnecessary thoughts. You may discover that as your body relaxes and your emotions calm, unnecessary thoughts continue to parade through your mind. It's important not to fight or resist those thoughts—that only makes their distraction more powerful. "Imagine," suggests Emmett E. Miller, M.D., a specialist in stress reduction, "that your nostrils are like two tiny exhaust pipes that go up into your mind and that with each breath out you are breathing out unnecessary thoughts. Imagine that with each breath in, fresh, clean air is being breathed in through your nostrils and is cleansing your mind of unnecessary thoughts."[12]

5. Relax by letting go. You can't force yourself to relax—it doesn't work. Relaxation is basically a "letting go" process, and there's simply no need to try to become relaxed. Just let it happen.

6. Select a specific relaxation technique—either the progressive relaxation method or the autogenic approach, which we will describe in the next few paragraphs. Try both techniques to find which works best for you. Once you've chosen your favorite, you may want to record your own relaxation audiotape, using these six-step instructions followed by either the progressive relaxation or autogenic relaxation instructions for the following areas, one at a time.

1. Right leg, foot and toes
2. Left leg, foot and toes
3. Hips and buttocks
4. Abdomen
5. Chest
6. Back
7. Shoulders
8. Right arm, hand and fingers
9. Left arm, hand and fingers
10. Neck
11. Jaw
12. Tongue
13. Eyelids
14. Face and scalp

Progressive relaxation. This technique was developed by Edmund Jacobson, M.D., whose research on stress and relaxation began in 1908 at Harvard University. Also known as the tense-relax method, progressive relaxation systematically tightens and releases every major muscle group of the body. Dr. Jacobson discovered that people can relax a muscle to a much greater degree after first tensing it.

Progressive relaxation employs the body-tension scan principle (discussed in chapter 4) and boosts your ability to detect—and eliminate—unnecessary tension.

Instructions: For each body area in sequence from 1 through 14 as listed on the previous page, repeat, "I am becoming fully aware of my _____ and any sensations I feel there. Now I am tightening *all* the muscles in that area, taking several seconds to become completely aware of holding tension there. What does it feel like? Now, after taking a smooth, deep breath and holding it for a moment, I'm exhaling as I tell those muscles to *relax and let go*, fully releasing all tension and feeling a wave of deep relaxation spreading into that area."

Autogenic ("self-regulation") relaxation. Dr. Johannes H. Schultz and Dr. Wolfgang Luthe of Germany developed this method. More than 50 years of medical documentation verify its effectiveness. Autogenic relaxation uses mental imagery and verbal cues to regulate breathing, heart rate, blood pressure and muscle tension. The autogenic method emphasizes calm, rhythmic breathing, a slow heartbeat and muscular sensations of heaviness (relaxation) and warmth (increased circulation).

Instructions: For each body area in sequence from 1 through 14 as listed, repeat: "Warmth and heaviness are flowing into my _____. Warmth and heaviness fill my _____ and it feels relaxed, comfortable, heavy and warm. I feel my whole body relaxing ever more deeply as the heaviness and warmth fill my _____. I am letting go of all my tensions and worries. I feel peaceful and calm."

Once you have completed either the progressive or autogenic relaxation sequence, take a few extra moments to remain quiet and relaxed, enjoying the calmness. Then return slowly to the active world; count from 1 to 10, completing a breath cycle with each number and becoming ever more alert while maintaining your sense of peacefulness. Now slowly move and stretch your body before returning to your activities.

POWER ACTION: MORE OPTIONS
Recognize Early Warning Signs of Hurry-Up Stress and Strain

When you're tense and tired, there's a natural tendency for the problems in your work and life to appear magnified.[17] Disappointments loom up as disasters, helpful advice stings like criticism, daily hassles feel like a personal curse from the Almighty, and there's a greater chance you'll get upset over trivialities,[18] as illustrated in "The Shoelace," a poem by Charles Bukowski:

> *It's not the large things that*
> *send a man to the madhouse . . .*
> *not the death of his love*
> *but a shoelace that snaps*
> *with no time left . . .*

Yet, as Robert E. Thayer, Ph.D., professor of biological psychology at California State University in Long Beach, points out, these very same events and problems seem dramatically more manageable when you're feeling relaxed, strong and vigorous.

One troublesome symptom of excessive mental stress and tension is a distortion of your sense of time. Larry Dossey, M.D., an internist and author of *Meaning and Medicine,* has treated many superstressed executives, diagnosing mental stress—what is sometimes called hurry sickness—by asking the patient to rest quietly in a chair and say when he or she thinks a minute is up. The record belongs to a manager who said "Now" after only 9 seconds.[19] Try this exercise yourself from time to time, trying to guess when a minute is up.

The truth is, many of us waste enormous amounts of energy reacting automatically and unconsciously to even the most minor delays.[20] We have thoughts such as, "There's never enough time" and "What else can go wrong today?" If you notice feelings of time frustration day after day, it may be an early warning sign that your burden of stress and tension has entered an intense and potentially harmful level. It is time to do something right now—time to think about making a change. Yes, hurry . . . hurry when you must, but do it while recognizing *why* you're doing it, and do it with less tension. Begin to make this change by sharpening your senses: Wherever you are, notice—precisely—*where* you are. Clearly observe your environment, what's happening inside and around your space right now, how it feels. The lighting, sounds, movement, your posture, other people. Now, within that sharpened scene, pay closer attention to exactly *what* you are thinking, feeling, saying, seeing or hearing and exactly *how* you are doing it. Studies indicate that, simply by increasing your awareness in this manner, you'll be more efficient, more directed in your actions, less prone to tension and common, mindless errors.[21] If you find that as you rush ahead, your mind is making lists and compelling you to get every last thing done, remind yourself that some of it can probably wait. Move forward on the most essential points. If you notice yourself getting anxious or hurrying so much that you're snapping at others or getting really close to the edge, stop completely and ask yourself, "Is this really *that* important?"

Contrary to popular thinking, stress itself is not an affliction or a disease. It's simply a *force*—a powerful pressure that can be recognized and channeled productively or overlooked and allowed to undermine your efforts and hurt your health. In our harried world it's easier than ever to get overloaded with "got-to's" and "shoulds"—and fall victim to *hurry-up stress and strain*. Because of this, it has become very important to sharpen your skill in recognizing certain mind/body signals that alert you it's time to pull back and use a *Power of 5* exercise.[22] These signals of distress may include the following:

Time urgency: Trying to do more and more in less and less time but falling behind; chronically glancing at your watch, becoming angry when other people seem too slow; feeling locked in a struggle with the clock.

Tension: Noticing your muscles tightening or your posture slumping—or sensing the need to stretch, move or change your routine.

Tiredness: Feeling increasingly fatigued in mind, emotions or body.

Mistakes: Noticing a drop in your performance—such as making careless errors or noticing diminished coordination in your speech, writing or movement.

Irritability: Feeling a rise in frustration, pessimism, impatience or hostility, or wanting to distance yourself from other people or events.

Distractions: Finding your mind wandering, having difficulty concentrating, experiencing some forgetfulness or procrastination.

Hunger or thirst: Sensing the first deep pangs of hunger or thirst.

Feeling blue: An emotional downturn—feeling empty, despairing or pessimistic or having a heightened sense of vulnerability.

Aggression or hostility: Feeling a surge of anger at other people, accompanied by an urge to harm them or by a wish that they be harmed or "taught a lesson."

De-stress with a High-Power, High-Carb Snack

In recent years, one of the surprise findings in nutritional research has been the discovery that, in many cases, eating carbohydrate-rich snacks can actually help reduce feelings of impatience or distress. First of all, as we'll explain in detail in chapter 9, it's important to recognize that healthy snacks provide a variety of vitality and work benefits. There's considerable evidence indicating that light between-meal snacks—at midmorning and midafternoon, for example—promote better health and aid in losing excess body fat and gaining work effectiveness.[23] Research published in the *New England Journal of Medicine* suggests that this eating pattern may help lower blood cholesterol levels and boost your energy.[24]

The best between-meal snacks are, to put it plainly, those that *taste great to you*—and those that also happen to be high in complex carbohydrates and fiber and low in fat (which matters for two reasons: high-fat foods promote body fat gain and cause fatigue[25]). Furthermore, what you choose to eat may also influence the production of brain messenger chemicals called neurotransmitters, which affect your mental alertness, concentration, attitude, mood and performance.

According to some leading nutritional scientists, there's compelling evidence of the power of food over mind and mood.[26] Just a few bites of healthy, *high-protein* food may contribute to increased energy, greater attention to detail and alertness lasting for up to three hours. Options include a sandwich with chicken breast, turkey breast or fish; a cup of bean or lentil soup; or a small serving of nonfat yogurt, cottage cheese, cream cheese or skim milk—with fruit. When you're "on the run," try a small handful of almonds, raisins or figs or a whole-grain cracker with a very small portion of lox or a thin slice of low-fat, low-salt cheese.

On the other hand, one of the simplest ways to reduce mental distress and tension can be to avoid overstimulating yourself with caffeine (in coffee, tea and soft drinks) and to eat something that is low in fat, low in protein and *high in carbohydrates*—because this kind of snack influences the production of neurotransmitters and may help produce a calm, focused state of mind and relaxed emotions—a state that can last up to three hours. Options include low-fat cookies or a low-fat muffin, bagel or English muffin; cooked whole grains (rice, wheat, oatmeal, corn, buckwheat, barley, etc.) eaten with fruit or a sweetener but without milk; low-fat pasta salad with fruit or vegetables; or some whole-grain bread, low-fat (baked) chips or rye crackers topped with your favorite all-fruit preserves.

Take a Different Look at Things

Many of us fail to realize that tension and headaches are often brought on or worsened by eyestrain.[27] To help dissolve visual tension, here's the simplest do-it-anywhere technique we've found: If you've been doing close work, take 5 seconds or more to blink your eyes and look at more distant objects; if you've been scanning faraway scenery, switch to focusing on something nearby. Whenever you can, take another half-minute or so to brighten or dim the lighting (discussed in chapter 24), move your seat closer to or away from a window, or step outside for some fresh air and a fresh viewpoint. These kinds of simple "visual shifts" draw new blood to the eyes, relax tired ocular muscles and reduce brain fatigue.

You might also combine your eye relaxation with a positive mental distraction by putting up some enlarged photographs or colorful posters of your favorite scenery or vacation spot and then sinking into one of these sights, into whatever depths of awe and wonder and enjoyment and memory the scene brings you, as you relax your eyes and draw your mind fully *away* from the task at hand.[28] There is evidence suggesting that this brief, vivid "escape" will help keep you feeling younger.[29] Even more startling, "the chemistry of billions of cells throughout your body—especially in your central nervous system—will immediately change in response to what you vividly visualize," says psychologist James E. Loehr, Ed.D.[30]

> Creativity can solve almost any problem. The creative act, the defeat of habit by originality, overcomes everything.
>
> **—George Lois,** American advertising executive

Resources

A Little Relaxation by Saul Miller, Ph.D. (Hartley & Marks, 1990). A brief, enjoyable, how-to-relax-more book.

Managing Your Mind and Mood through Food by Judith J. Wurtman, Ph.D. (HarperCollins, 1987). A nutritional researcher's compelling discoveries on how foods may influence brain neurotransmitters, emotions and alertness.

Source Cassette Learning Systems (Emmett E. Miller, M.D., P.O. Box W, Stanford, CA 94309; 800-52-TAPES or 415-328-4412). One of the most popular and comprehensive collections of relaxation and mental imagery audiocassette tapes available.

From Stress to Strength: How to Lighten Your Load and Save Your Life by Robert S. Eliot, M.D. (Bantam, 1994). A cardiologist's plan for reducing heart-threatening stress.

PERSONAL POWER NOTES
A Quick-List of This Chapter's Power-Action Options

One-Touch Relaxation.
- *Five minutes of deep relaxation.*
- *Progressive Relaxation.*
- *Autogenic ("self-regulation") relaxation.*

Recognize early warning signs of hurry-up stress and strain.
- *Time urgency.*
- *Tension.*
- *Tiredness.*
- *Mistakes.*
- *Irritability.*
- *Distractions.*
- *Hunger or thirst.*
- *Feeling blue.*
- *Aggression or hostility.*

De-stress with a high-power, high-carb snack.

Take a different look at things.

PERSONAL NOTES

_____

_____

_____

_____

_____

_____

_____

_____

_____

BE BOLD—
IMMEDIATE ENERGY
ACTIVATORS

Fast, Simple New Ways to Revitalize Your Mind
and Body—Anytime, Anywhere

Whatever you can do, or dream you can do, begin it. Boldness has
genius, power, and magic.
—**Johann von Goethe**, German poet and dramatist

Most Americans no longer know what it feels like to be fully
alert," observed a Stanford University researcher recently in a *Time*
magazine article.[1] Just think about it for a moment. How many times
this week have you said (or wanted to say) to someone who asked you
to do something, "Sorry, I just don't have the time or *energy*."

You are not alone in being frustrated by this feeling of powerless-
ness. More and more of us have the same complaint. And have you noticed that whenever you start feeling increased pressure—too many
demands, new or repeated hassles and problems—your mind has a maddening tendency to get distracted, shut down or become worry-filled?
It's time to be *bold*—to claim our Personal Power and take action to
break out of fatigue.

POWER ACTION: FIRST OPTION
One-Breath Meditation

"It is the inner breathing of the [100 trillion] cells in your body that enables you to produce biological energy," writes Sheldon Saul Hendler, M.D., Ph.D., biochemist, internal medicine specialist and professor at the University of California at San Diego School of Medicine. "Out of this comes what I call the basic currency of life, adenosine triphosphate or ATP. . . . Without ATP there is no energy, no life. It is ATP that we utilize to act, feel, think. . . . The body and brain are ex-

POWER KNOWLEDGE: ENERGY

MYTH #1: It's natural to feel tired and "stressed out"—that's life!
POWER KNOWLEDGE: That isn't life—it's a rut. Just because it's gotten *common* to feel fatigued and overloaded doesn't mean it's *normal* or *natural*.

MYTH #2: Mental and physical fatigue are an unavoidable part of growing older.
POWER KNOWLEDGE: That's not true. Worldwide studies confirm that, in most cases, your mental and physical alertness, energy and stamina can actually keep *increasing*—at 40, 50, 60 and beyond.

MYTH #3: When you're healthy you can keep going nonstop. There's no need to waste time slowing down or taking breaks.
POWER KNOWLEDGE: Dozens of scientific studies indicate the opposite is true.[11] According to Dr. Entienne Grandjean, an expert on work productivity at the Swiss Federal Institute of Technology, introducing short breaks actually *speeds up* work, yielding greater total accomplishments per day, with less distress and fatigue.[12] You need to

tremely sensitive to even very small reductions in ATP production. This sensitivity is expressed in terms of aches and pains, confusion, intermittent fatigue and greater susceptibility to infection. . . . *Breathing is unquestionably the most important thing you do in your life.* And breathing *well* is unquestionably the most important thing you can do to *improve* your life [emphasis added]."[2]

Deeper breathing during exercise plays a key role in expanding your capillary network and producing increased feelings of alertness and well-being. And research also indicates that deep breathing *anytime* is one of the simplest, most powerful ways to activate your energy and alertness, enabling you to experience life more fully and vigorously.[3]

One-Breath Meditation is a remarkably effective, on-the-spot technique that's based on a combination of modern and ancient re-

know when and how to take scientifically designed pauses, because every day you experience natural, powerful "waves" of biological energy that strongly influence your thoughts, feelings and actions—biologically lifting you up and pushing you down, unavoidably, *every hour of every day.*[13] When you fail to respond appropriately to these downturns, your mental "fade-outs" and other fall-offs in energy and performance get deeper and more costly as the day—and your life—wears on. The only reason you might not notice it is that it's *so* common that almost everyone around you is also fatigued.

MYTH #4: It's not the small stuff that makes you exhausted and uptight, it's the big, real-life problems—putting the kids through college, paying taxes, coping with losses.

POWER KNOWLEDGE: The way you respond to daily hassles is often a more powerful predictor of psychological and physical health than is your reaction to major life crises.[14] Research at Bowman-Gray School of Medicine in Winston-Salem, North Carolina, indicates that mishandling these chronic, unavoidable irritations and pressures hurts health and performance,[15] and a growing number of scientists are warning that "it's the little things that can make or break your relief of stress."[16]

search into the energy-giving power of deep breathing. This simple meditation—straightening the back, drawing in a fresh breath, completely clearing your mind for a moment—can be effectively used to break the grip of tension and tiredness and provide a refreshing island in the rush and roar of everyday life.[4] Within moments you can capture some of the well-documented benefits of longer periods of meditation (discussed later in this chapter). With practice, you can use One-Breath Meditation whenever you start to feel fatigued or jolted off-balance by life's demands.

Right now, take in a deep breath of air. Don't force it; be *aware* of your breath coming in, *feel* the sensation—does the breath feel warm or cool? On the inhalation, relax your shoulders, straighten your back and let the air "open" your chest as you take a moment to be silent and to vividly imagine yourself drawing in vitality and strength from the oxygen-rich air.[5] Draw the breath into every fiber of your being, into every cell of your body, and imagine new light filling every corner of your mind. Hold the breath for an extra few moments, feeling it lift your spirit, and then, as you exhale, release every bit of darkness and tension from your thoughts and muscles, letting your attention sink into the center of your chest.

Some people like to add a word or sound to help the mind focus as the breath goes in and out. Some individuals use *one* or *God* or *aum* (*om*). *Hu* is an ancient sound for Power. One of the first names humans ever gave to a supreme being was *hu*.[6] Some good words begin with *hu*: human, humor, hum, hub (the center), hug, huge, hue, humus ("the good earth"), humble and, of course, hula. *Hu* is pronounced "hugh." You can say it silently as you breathe in and again as you breathe out. Or you can pronounce the letter *H* on the inhalation and the letter *U* on the exhalation.

In order to make One-Breath Meditation highly effective, we encourage you to link it to a specific and consistent hand position—perhaps pressing your thumb lightly against the side of your index finger—as a "memory cue." After a while, the touch alone can help elicit and deepen the immediate effects of One-Breath Meditation.

You may also wish to use One-Breath Meditation as a reminder to yourself to accentuate or deepen certain values or qualities in your life, such as assertiveness, inner calmness, expanded creativity, compassion or forgiveness or planning ahead. You can also use it as a cue to help you counter the pressures so many of us feel to judge, and find shortcomings in, ourselves and others. Here's how: As you breathe in, visualize filling yourself with increased compassion—toward yourself, the people around you or humanity as a whole. As you breathe out, see yourself forgiving yourself and others.

One-Breath Meditation certainly *is* a simple technique, but it works. Many people feel the effects right away, and it can be used again and again throughout the day—particularly as an easy way to stay calmer when things around you are especially hectic or tempers are short. (A recent study reports that people who practiced daily breathing exercises were able to cut their levels of tiredness and tension in half![7]) Do One-Breath Meditation before picking up the phone or greeting loved ones or the people you work with.

We also strongly suggest that you experience a variety of ways to deepen your breathing and gain greater benefits from brief, on-the-spot meditations. Here are two examples.

5-Minute Body Scan

Many of us live out of touch with our senses. We're so busy, so tense, that we have drifted away from the landscape of sights, sounds, smells, tastes and touch around us and the subtle yet important sensory "signals" that arise from the body within us. Without heightened awareness, we make it easy for stress to win; we fail to catch—and neutralize—negative pressures.

One easy way to begin sharpening your awareness is by learning to detect tight muscles. A body-tension scan technique can help you become alert to your muscles and relax them more easily. Scanning uses your *inner* awareness, rather than your eyes, to check for tight muscles. With practice, this technique can be used quickly—even instantly—to help you find and release tension.

To learn scanning, choose an environment that's free from distractions. Set aside about 5 minutes. Sit comfortably in a chair or lie on your back on a padded surface such as a carpeted floor or a sofa or bed. Spread your legs slightly and relax your body. Close your eyes and begin taking smooth, deep breaths.

After 30 seconds or so, mentally scan a muscle area as you inhale. As you breathe out, imagine the tension releasing as that muscle becomes more comfortably relaxed. After several breaths, shift your attention to another area. Systematically search your entire body: begin at the scalp and work down through the face, eyes, ears, jaw, tongue, neck, shoulders, upper arms, forearms, wrists, hands, fingers, chest, upper back, abdomen, lower back, pelvis, thighs, lower legs, ankles, feet and toes.

Scan for tight areas on each inhalation and then visualize the tension melting away—like an ice cube being heated by the sun, for example, and turning into a pool of water—as you exhale. Don't be alarmed if your mind wanders. Just bring your attention back and continue scanning.

Once you've finished, remain completely relaxed for half a minute more. Notice the warm sense of ease in your body, especially in those places—perhaps the face, neck, jaw, shoulders, abdomen or back—where you tend to hold tension.

There are many other ways to increase your sensory awareness. Can you feel your breath as it comes in and goes out? The slightest breeze on your cheeks or hands? The surface beneath your feet, legs or back? Which arm or leg is more relaxed right now? The more senses you involve—sight, touch, sound, smell and taste—the greater your gains in awareness.

5-Minute Power Meditation

What can meditation do for you? Through the regular practice of meditation, you may learn to access a profound inner silence and tranquility. Research indicates that this inner silence—free from pressure, concern, tension and anxiety—can nourish the body, mind and spirit.[8] During meditation, you may experience a state of very deep rest, marked by decreases in heart rate, breathing rate, oxygen consumption, muscle tension, blood pressure and levels of stress hormones. You may also achieve heightened mental clarity and emotional ease, possibly as a result of increased coherence of brain-wave activity.

Studies suggest that regular meditation may increase energy, heighten the body's immune response, improve learning, provide a buffer against stress, reduce high blood pressure, promote deeper sleep, reduce anxiety and nervousness, heighten self-esteem, boost creativity and even slow the aging process.[9] According to researchers at Harvard Medical School, evidence is growing that meditation can be an effective way to open the door to all kinds of self-improvement for a renewed mind and a changed life.[10]

> True silence is the rest of the mind; it is to the spirit what sleep is to the body, nourishment and refreshment.
>
> **—William Penn,** founder of Pennsylvania

Here is a *Power of 5* Meditation:

1. Select a quiet place where you will not be disturbed. Initially, it would be beneficial to schedule at least 5 minutes. Take the phone off the hook or put a "Do Not Disturb" sign on the door. Once you've learned to meditate easily and effortlessly, environmental distractions will be less bothersome.

2. Sit in a comfortable position, in a chair or on a couch, with your feet on the floor. Ever so gently, close your eyes.

3. Relax your muscles, letting go of tension with each breath out.

4. Become aware of your breathing in an easy, effortless way, without forcing it.

5. Silently—as a faint idea—repeat the word or sound "hu" with each breathing cycle. You might imagine or pronounce the letter *H* on the breath in and *U* on the breath out. With each inhalation, fresh, clean air is being brought in, and with it come sensations of peace, serenity, letting go, regaining balance; with each exhalation, you are breathing out all unnecessary thoughts and anxious feelings.

6. Don't judge your experience. If you begin to wonder how you are doing or why your mind keeps dancing off on other thoughts, don't worry about it. Don't be concerned about your performance or try to stop your mind from wandering. Just gently bring your focus back—regaining your sense of inner balance in an easy and effortless fashion.

Continue for 5 minutes. You may open one eye to check the time, but do not use an alarm clock. When you finish, sit quietly for another half-minute or so, at first with your eyes closed and then with your eyes open. Do not worry about whether you are successful in achieving a deep level of meditation. Maintain a passive attitude and permit your relaxation to deepen and expand at its own pace. With practice, this *Power of 5* Meditation technique will become more and more effortless.

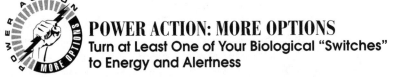

POWER ACTION: MORE OPTIONS
Turn at Least One of Your Biological "Switches" to Energy and Alertness

As explained by Martin Moore-Ede, M.D., Ph.D., associate professor of physiology at Harvard Medical School and director of the medical school's Institute for Circadian Physiology, "Because so many people are fatigued, there are countless minor errors—and they produce an enormous negative effect both on and off the job. A person's alertness is triggered by key internal and external factors that can be considered switches on the control panel of the mind. Understanding these key switches and how to manipulate them is the secret of gaining power over one of the most important attributes of the human brain."[17] There are many biological "switches" of alertness. Here are several practical examples.

Alertness Switch #1:
Gain Energy from Your "Power Place"

New research suggests that you'll be able to sustain greater energy and alertness whenever you take the opportunity to be in the right place at the right time.[18] By this we mean spending at least a few minutes whenever you can in one of your favorite rooms in your home or workplace, or stepping outside into a nearby garden or deck or park where you feel most comfortable and "at home." If you can't go there *physically*, you may still get some of the energizing benefits by simply *imagining* you are there.[19] As Winnifred Gallagher, psychology editor of *American Health* magazine, explains in her book *The Power of Place*, "the basic principle is simple: A good or bad environment promotes good or bad memories, which inspire a good or bad mood, which inclines us toward good or bad behavior. We needn't even be consciously aware of a pleasant or unpleasant environmental stimulus for it to influence us."[20]

"There is mounting evidence," write David Sobel, M.D., and Robert Ornstein, Ph.D., in *Mental Medicine Update*, "that even brief exposures to a natural scene can be an excellent antidote to *mental fatigue*. In studies of workers with desk jobs, [access to a view of] natural scenes nearly doubled satisfaction ratings.[21] Workers with a view of nature felt less frustrated and more patient, found their job more challenging and interesting, expressed greater enthusiasm for their work and reported greater overall life satisfaction and health."[22]

Alertness Switch #2:
Enjoy a Burst of Light

More than half of your body's sense receptors are clustered in your eyes.[23] Studies show that the eyes need regular doses of novel images, beauty and brightness and act as *light harvesters*—firing neurological impulses in a direct stream to the pineal gland and the higher centers of your brain.[24] This process powerfully influences your biological sleep/wake cycles and can produce invigorating, antidepressant effects.[25]

For an energy lift, experiment with turning up the lights. Many people report a sense of calmness followed by a surge of energy when exposed to bright sunlight or some extra indoor light (even at the intensity level of normal room lamps[26]). Try to do some of your daily work close to a source of sunlight (such as near a window) or turn on several extra lights, such as inexpensive incandescent "task" lights—each with a full-spectrum "daylight" bulb. Spend a few minutes outdoors during daylight hours by taking a 5-minute "mini-walk" (see chapter 11) during your lunch hour or on other breaks during the day.[27]

Alertness Switch #3:
Perk Up with a Few Minutes of Muscular Activity

Nearly any type of muscular activity—such as walking up a flight of stairs or down a nearby hallway, can immediately increase your energy and alertness. This is one of the many scientific reasons why *The Power of 5* program suggests doing about 5 minutes of exercise here and there throughout the day (see chapter 10) rather than relying solely on the usual health-club schedule of a long, formal fitness session a few days a week. According to Dr. Moore-Ede, "You do not have to be running a mile or lifting weights—taking a walk, stretching or even chewing gum can stimulate your level of alertness."[28]

Alertness Switch #4:
Stimulate Your Senses with a Cool, Fresh Breeze

Few of us realize that something as simple as a cool, fresh breeze or some cold water splashed on the face and neck can be quick, effective ways to get an invigorating rush of circulation that promotes alertness.[29]

Alertness Switch #5: Inhale an Energizing Scent

Researchers at Harvard Medical School's Institute for Circadian Physiology report growing evidence that the power of smell can, at least in some cases, strongly influence mental alertness.[30] The human nose, with practice, may be able to discern more than 7,500 different fragrances. And the sense of smell is so powerfully connected to the brain that some scents elicit pronounced changes in energy, emotions and memory. Your sense of smell contains "all the great mysteries," says physician and essayist Lewis Thomas, M.D.[31] Every breath you take passes currents of air molecules over the olfactory sites in your nose—and odors flood the nerve receptors in your nasal cavities, where five million cells fire impulses directly to the brain's cerebral cortex and limbic system—the mysterious, ancient, intensely emotional area of the brain where you experience feelings, desires and wellsprings of creative energy. Certain scents seem to activate specific chemical messengers, or neurotransmitters, in the brain.[32]

Teams of researchers in the United States, Europe and Japan have published dozens of new studies on the behavioral influence of smell.[33]

> To learn, to raise new questions, explore new possibilities, to regard old problems from new angles, requires creative imagination with all of the senses.
>
> **—Albert Einstein,**
> American physicist

Tests at the University of Cincinnati indicate that fragrances added to the atmosphere of a room can help keep people more alert and improve performance of routine tasks.[34] Controlled brain-wave studies by professors at Toho University in Japan have produced surprising indications about which scents tend to stimulate and which ones relax, as well as which promote significantly fewer errors on the job.[35] Research at Rensselaer Polytechnic Institute in Troy, New York, shows that people who work in pleasantly scented areas perform an average of 25 percent better than those who do not,[36] and also carry out their tasks more confidently, more efficiently and with greater willingness to resolve conflicts.[37]

To date, the top scent for *raising* energy and attention seems to be peppermint. Another option to consider is lemon. Test the effect of these two scents by sipping some peppermint or lemon tea or opening a small bottle of peppermint or lemon extract or perhaps even by chewing a piece of peppermint-flavored gum.

Alertness Switch #6:
Jump-Start Your Speed-Learning Power

For many of us, it's common to feel overwhelmed by information—yet we cannot stop reading and still be effective in today's society. Here's a way to find more enjoyment on the "information highway"—and benefit more from the actual reading along the way.

Beginning with the next book or article you read, the following techniques may actually help to *double* your "learning power" (including reading speed and comprehension)[38].

Use "Active Creative Observation":[39] This is an innovative expansion of one of Albert Einstein's little-known avenues to expanded, accelerated learning[40]—using *more* of your senses. Here are some examples:

• Scan each new book or article before reading it paragraph by paragraph. What is the context? The format? What is the sequence or outline? Are there references? Is this philosophical or practical—or both? In what way might it be meaningful or important to me or my family?

• Link hand/eye movements, moving your fingertips across the page under the lines as you read (this anchors your eyes to the page and frees you from the needless, slow-down habit of "subvocal linear reading," silently repeating every word you read).

• Increase the lighting brightness in your work area.

• Choose a comfortable reading position. Loosen and "open" your chest and neck position so that it's easier to maintain a smooth, rhythmic breathing pattern—and draw in more oxygen to your brain and senses.[41]

• Use "mind play" to ask reflective questions as you learn. While reading, ask yourself questions such as:

What could *this* idea mean in my life? Can I apply it right now?

Where is the author heading? Does it make sense?

Questions like these help free your mind to connect the meanings and applications *behind* and *beyond* the written and spoken words.

• Read vertically: Once you can pick up your reading speed by moving your fingertips from left to right more quickly under each line, try tracing your fingertips under every other line, then every third line. The human brain can readily learn to accept words and phrases *out of the usual, expected order*—that is, with practice, in many types of reading your mind can make instant sense out of sentences and entire paragraphs rather than being dependent on reading every individual word in sequence.

• Get some "deep mental rest" after intensive learning. It pays to take rest pauses and hourly breaks during concentrated bouts of learning. In addition, neuropsychologists have found that in order for your brain to effectively "file away" and recall what it has learned, it's vital to get at least *several minutes of mental rest*[42]—which can be accomplished with such simple choices as a quick catnap or some radical change-of-mind such as thinking about something humorous or doing a crossword puzzle—after each concentrated learning experience.

Alertness Switch #7: Laugh!

There are strong scientific reasons to suspect that he or she who laughs, lasts.[43] Very few things so instantly form a bond between people as laughter. People who know how to have fun are generally healthier and better able to bounce back from stressful situations.

Humor has very little to do with telling jokes. It's about perceiving and chuckling at the absurdities of everyday life—from hassles to heartaches to hard times—and taking yourself more lightly even when you're doing serious work. And it's about laughing—harder and more often than most of us usually do. In *Taking Laughter Seriously*, philosopher John Morreall explains: "The person who has a sense of humor is not just more relaxed in the face of potentially stressful situ-

> Laughter is the shortest distance between two people.
>
> **—Victor Borge,**
> Danish composer and entertainer

ations, but is more flexible in his approach. Even when there is not a lot going on in his environment, his imagination and innovativeness will help keep him out of a mental rut, will allow him to enjoy himself, and will prevent boredom and depression."[44]

Humorous thoughts, and in particular "mirthful laughter," work their wonders by initially arousing and distracting the mind, and then leaving us feeling more relaxed.[45] Scientists theorize that laughter stimulates the production of brain cate-cholamines and endorphins, which affect hormonal levels in the body, some related to feelings of joy, an easing of pain and strengthened immune response.[46]

> Laughter is inner jogging.
>
> —Norman Cousins,
> American editor and essayist

"Humor," says Edward deBono, M.D., a leading authority on the physiology of creativity, *"is by far the most significant behavior of the human mind."*[47] A quick infusion of light-heartedness can not only boost your energy but may help make you more helpful toward others and improve cognitive processes such as judgment, problem solving and decision making.[48] Here are several ideas for lightening up.

Cultivate cosmic humor. Above all, spontaneous mirth is something you *allow* to happen naturally—through a sense of relaxation and fun. Start looking for more of the ridiculous, incongruous events that go on around you all the time. Point them out to others. Make up short stories about the funniest things you see or hear and use them to spice up family discussions at the end of the day.

Laugh more. William F. Fry, Jr., M.D., emeritus associate clinical professor in the Department of Psychiatry at Stanford University School of Medicine, suggests that laughing 100 times a day is a good, healthful goal.[49] And Dr. Fry even thinks that you don't always need humor to benefit from laughter.[50] When you're stuck in traffic, for example, just start laughing. Apparently the shift in facial muscles and changes in blood flow may trigger some of the benefits of genuine laughter.[51] Above all, look for more of the positive humor embedded in your life experiences and seek out other people you can laugh with.

> To change one's life:
>
> • Start immediately.
>
> • Do it flamboyantly.
>
> • No exceptions.
>
> —William James, M.D.,
> founder of modern psychology

Start a humor library. What makes you laugh? Whether it's cartoons, letters from friends, posters, old or new comedy movies, joke encyclopedias or humorous stories (in books or on audiotapes for listening while you work or drive), expand your collection. Pay attention to whatever tickles your funny bone—and make it a point to surround yourself with more of it. But avoid telling jokes based on ridicule; they inflict pain—and as a form of cynicism, they can backfire and may even increase your own risk of heart attack.[52] And skip hurtful sarcasm. A good pun that gives a twist of the unexpected can be wonderful. And cosmic humor—an appreciation of life's paradoxes and absurdities—can be the most fun of all.

Resources

American Association for Therapeutic Humor (1163 Shermer Rd., Northbrook, IL 60062; 708-291-0211). Sponsors seminars, workshops and conferences. Publishes *Laugh It Up* newsletter.

The Humor Project (110 Spring St., Saratoga Springs, NY 12866; 518-587-8770). Sponsors humor and creativity conferences, workshops and seminars. Publishes *Laughing Matters* magazine.

Laughter Therapy (P.O. Box 827, Monterey, CA 93942). Lends one-hour humor tapes free for a month to people suffering from serious health problems.

Levenger: Tools for Serious Readers (975 South Congress Ave., Delray Beach, FL 33445; 800-544-0880). A source of innovative products for increased effectiveness in reading and learning.

The New Three-Minute Meditator by David Harp (New Harbinger, 1990). A quick, creative method of meditation.

The Power of Place by Winnifred Gallagher (Poseidon Press, 1993). An insightful look at ways that our surroundings shape our thoughts, emotions and actions.

Remember Everything You Read by Stanley D. Frank, Ed.D. (Times Books, 1990). One of the best-proven methods of speed reading.

Super Reading Secrets: How to Read One Page in Three Seconds by Howard Stephen Berg (Warner, 1992). A collection of skills devised by the man recorded in the *Guinness Book of World Records* as the world's fastest reader.

Transcendental Meditation (TM). At the time of this writing, TM is the most well researched meditation technique,[53] and it is available as a standardized course of instruction in most major cities (check the telephone directory for a local TM center).

The 24-Hour Society by Martin Moore-Ede, M.D., Ph.D. (Addison-Wesley, 1993). An excellent resource on the biological "switches" of alertness, written by the director of the Institute for Circadian Physiology at Harvard Medical School.

PERSONAL POWER NOTES

A Quick-List of This Chapter's Power-Action Options

One-Breath Meditation.
- 5-minute Body Scan.
- 5-minute Power Meditation.

Turn at least one of your biological "switches" to energy and alertness.
- Gain energy from your "power place."
- Enjoy a burst of light.
- Perk up with a few minutes of muscular activity.
- Stimulate your senses with a cool, fresh breeze.
- Inhale an energizing scent.
- Jump-start your speed-learning power.
- Laugh!

PERSONAL NOTES

_____

_____

_____

_____

_____

_____

_____

_____

_____

_____

_____

_____

"LIMING"

Doing Nothing, Guilt-Free

All action begins in rest. . . . This is the ultimate truth.
—**Lao Tzu**, Chinese philosopher

Liming is the Caribbean art of "doing nothing, guilt-free," and it's a revitalizing habit that's virtually unheard-of in America. It's an ideal time—taking as little as 5 minutes—for personal pursuits instead of ordered recreation, for private reverie instead of public expectations. If you play a sport, for example, you would play it for the pure love of playing, not for winning or even doing well.

Liming can free you from the entanglements of convention and disengage the drive toward constant busyness. At its essence, all it takes is choosing one of your favorite healthy pleasures—such as telling jokes or flipping through an album of side-splitting cartoons, unplugging the office phone, humming a heart-warming song, reading an upbeat aphorism or poem, putting on your sunglasses and listening to "escape" music while sipping iced tea, leaning back in your chair and looking out the window with your feet propped up on the desk, remembering your favorite vacation or funniest stories about childhood or work or parenting.

Liming, at its purest, is a kind of moving meditation to break away from the stress of time, of clock watching. Surprisingly, this kind of daytime *mental rest* is also vital to your memory power, since it gives the brain a much-needed opportunity to sort out the load of information that has reached your mind during the past several hours.[1] The truth is, as little as 5 or 10 minutes of mental "playtime" during a work break can really pay off—and your options here can even include such things as doing a crossword puzzle, reading the paper, taking a "mental vacation" (visualizing a favorite getaway place, such as a quiet beach or a summer meadow), or anything else that stops the normal flow of pressure and lets your brain redirect. In some cases, *not choosing* is the best choice here—because it feels comforting and rejuvenating. Instead of speeding up and losing sight, you can slow down and take a good look, accomplishing what Ellen J. Langer, Ph.D., professor of psychology at Harvard University, calls "shaking free of the mindset of exhaustion."[2]

Time *off* is not the same thing as time *out*. The basic idea with liming is to shift yourself—as completely and deeply as you can—out of the rat race for at least 5 minutes, allowing your body to release tension at the same time your mind, senses and emotions savor the moment and

POWER KNOWLEDGE: LIGHTENING UP

MYTH #1: "Breathing space" is for lazy people. When you've got lots to do in life, you can't afford to waste time sitting back or playing around.

POWER KNOWLEDGE: It's the other way around—when we *don't* take the time to sit back and play around, we pay a hidden, and often huge, price. "Creative breathing space" includes those times when you choose to deliberately turn away from the work at hand and, for a few key minutes, enjoy a new thought-stream—to invigorate and expand your memory powers, open yourself to uncommon sources of inspiration and safeguard your health. When you fail to get enough of this creative breathing space, the brain becomes increasingly fatigued and your memory may falter, and neuroscientists report that your attention and mental focusing ability will tend to suffer.[3]

MYTH #2: Even if other people need "breathing space," I don't— I'm doing just fine without it.

POWER KNOWLEDGE: When you fail to get enough breathing space, you may be tricked into not noticing how much your performance fades at midmorning and midafternoon simply because everyone else is fading, too—so it just seems "normal." It isn't. When forgive other people for real and imagined transgressions. Immerse yourself in enjoying whatever experiences are close at hand. The ancient Chinese philosopher Lao Tzu advised taking time each day for precisely this kind of habit when he said: "Practice not-doing, and everything will fall into place."

POWER ACTION: FIRST OPTION
A Quick Escape to Your Own "Island of Peace"

The word *escape* comes from the Latin and Old Northern French and originally meant to "take off one's cloak." Today, as never before,

you ignore or override your natural, biological need for breaks, stress hormones—including adrenaline—are dumped into your bloodstream. Within minutes after deciding to skip a break ("Come *on*, I've got so much to do I can't *afford* to stop!"), you may feel what appears to be a "second wind" (which can trick you into thinking, "See, I really *didn't* need to take a break after all!").

In truth, however, it's only an illusion, and you're pushing yourself deeper and deeper into a tense, overtired state. Beneath the surface, problems are brewing as your mounting fatigue gets masked by stress hormone opiates, such as beta-endorphin, that give you a transient sense of feeling good even when you're increasingly worn down.[4] Throughout your brain and body, the microscopic cellular storage compartments for messenger molecules are becoming depleted; signal hormones that coordinate memory, perception and performance may be all but gone.

Before long it affects your work: You begin making dumb mistakes, judgment errors or physical gaffes, large and small. You can fight it by sheer willpower alone—but not for long. By the end of the day—tired out physically and worn down mentally from nonstop effort—there's an increased chance of getting impatient or irritable with family members. This negative spillover, as researchers call it, is becoming extremely common.[5] We may have all the right intentions but little remaining energy or ability to relate warmly and openly to loved ones and friends.

we each need to be able to take off the cloak of work at the end of the day and on weekends. For most of us, what's vanished from sight is any semblance of downshifting from work activities to nonwork activities.

In this strategy you're going to imagine your own "island of peace," a place where you can go to rejuvenate your mind and spirit, to escape—for 5 minutes at a time—from life's barrage of information, noise and demands. One of the simplest ways to create your own island of peace is to begin with breathing.

Sit comfortably in an upright chair. Slowly, gently and very smoothly, arch your lower back and then flatten it against the back of the chair. Practice this rocking motion for 10 to 30 seconds. Now breathe in, fully expanding your lower ribs as the air comes in and you arch your lower back. Breathe out smoothly and completely, releasing all muscle tension as you flatten your lower back against the chair. With each exhalation, imagine your worries and struggles floating out of your mind and body. Keep the rhythm slow and steady. After half a minute or so, allow your mind to drift off to your island of peace. Begin by using the following description of a *secluded beach*. Then, if you wish, write out your own description of some other beautiful, revitalizing scene—a *country garden* or a *mountain meadow* or whatever appeals most strongly to your senses. Whatever scene you choose, construct it in your mind's eye so vividly that it seems as if you're truly there.

> One doesn't discover new lands without consenting to lose sight of the shore.
>
> **—André Gide,** French novelist

"Escape to a secluded beach." For this sensory voyage, you're walking along a white-sand beach on a delightfully warm, sunny day. The afternoon sun is well past midday but has not yet begun its descent to dusk. The rhythmic waves are gently splashing not far from your bare feet, and the water reflects the indigo blue sky and the golden glimmer of the sun's rays. Feel the hot light against your cheeks and shoulders and the hot, dry, soft sand beneath your feet. Take a step into the surf and feel the cool, wet sand between your toes. Feel the breeze picking up and then dying off. Notice how it makes your skin feel: cooler, then hot again in the pulsing sun glare.

You walk down the beach with a loose, carefree stride, deeply relaxed, drawing in deep breaths of fresh air, looking far down the shoreline to the distant horizon, where the white sand disappears into the glittering silver shapes in the blue water and a few small white clouds are poised in the blue sky. Farther down the beach you come to a secluded inlet with a grassy bluff covered with white, pink and purple wildflowers—and your nostrils are seized by the mingling scents of fragrant lilies and orchids. You stretch out on your back on the grassy shoulder of the mound and stare up at the luminous sky and the sun's pure, white-hot light as it penetrates the cool breeze that turns the flower petals and pushes the scents skyward.

You fix your eyes on the gold-white light of the sun as it reflects off the shimmering blue water. You stare into that light as a hint of orange encircles the gold. Then red, fuschia and purple hues cross the sparkling waves as the sun begins to set, sinking into the water at the far western horizon, ever so slowly, and you feel the last of your tensions vanishing as a pink-purple twilight settles in and the first scattered silver stars shine forth in the night sky above the gentle waves. You feel the soft, steady breeze and smell the mingling scents of pure water and fragrant flowers. You feel yourself staring off into the purple immensity of the bright night, off into the heart of the universe, centering in your Personal Power, feeling all your struggles and sufferings falling away, lifted from your heart and shoulders . . .

POWER ACTION: MORE OPTIONS
Now and Then, Escape the Telephone

For many stressed men and women, the telephone—despite its obvious value—is the number-one irritant in their busy lives.[6] The crux of the problem appears to be sensory overload, the *invasion stress* of having no control over unexpected phone calls *during nonworking hours*—in the midst of your vital private and personal times, especially when those calls interrupt reading, thinking, relaxing and family time. When it comes to the telephone, the challenge is to control it rather than letting it control you. The truth is, all of us need stress breaks—and somewhere in the middle of our hectic daily lives and on weekends, we each need opportunities to get away from pressures and to "lime."

> All you have to do is pause to rest. Nature herself, when we let her, will take care of everything else. It's our impatience that spoils things.
>
> **—Jean Moliere,**
> French dramatist

But, you may be wondering, what if your job requires you to answer business calls 24 hours a day? Even in this case, it's essential to have some dependable way to rejuvenate your energies by leaving the battlefield—with an answering service, for example, or with the phone ringer turned off and the answering machine on during brief periods of creative thinking, study, unwinding and "liming."

As cardiologist Robert S. Eliot, M.D., writes in his

book *From Stress to Strength: How to Lighten Your Load and Save Your Life*, all of us can "think of other ways the telephone can be better managed and less stressful: What about the revolutionary idea of *not* having a phone in every room? Or *not* carrying a portable phone with you when you walk out into your backyard? Or something even more drastic—*not allowing* the phone to interrupt? If you are involved in work, study or contemplation, and the ringing phone is causing you undue stress, get yourself an answering machine, turn off the phone bell and simply answer your messages when you are ready. It gives you some space and time."[7]

Discover—or Rediscover—Simple, Healthy Daily Pleasures

One of the best ways to deepen and expand your experience of liming—and, at the same time, to gain a variety of well-documented health benefits—is to reclaim some of the *small daily pleasures* that have probably fallen by the wayside in your busy life. A recent Japanese study comparing working men and women in Tokyo, New York and Los Angeles found that though the typical time for relaxation at home after work varied from an average of 5 hours (New York) to 4 hours (Los Angeles) to 3 hours (Tokyo), residents of all three cities filled this time with one primary, voracious activity: watching television.[8] Three hours a day means 21 hours a week—an unprecedented chunk of time devoted to one pastime: staring at a glowing cathode-ray tube in a way that requires little energy and virtually no imagination. Adding to the life-sapping effect of this pervasive habit is new evidence suggesting that you may burn about 10 or 15 percent *fewer* calories watching television than you do when sitting still with the television off.[9]

In his research on "stress-resistant people," Raymond B. Flannery, Jr., Ph.D., a professor of psychology at Harvard Medical School, discovered that the healthiest people—those who had the lowest levels of distress and lowest rates of illness—were those who enjoyed some daily forms of "active relaxation" that each lasted at least 15 minutes.[10] In Dr. Flannery's research, this "escape time" ranged from more formal pursuits, such as meditation or relaxation exercises, to such informal activities as knitting or playing solitaire. When asked about relaxation, the people who were more vulnerable to stress were likely to reply, "I don't have time to relax."

As you ease away from television, it's the small, simple pleasures

> Every now and then go away, even briefly, have a little relaxation, for when you come back to your work your judgment will be surer; since to remain constantly at work will cause you to lose power . . .
>
> —**Leonardo da Vinci,**
> Italian painter and architect

that usually pay the greatest dividends.[11] As with any other change of habit, gradual is best. You might start by cutting out one television show on a certain week night and substituting some other enjoyable activity. Here's a list of some possibilities.

• Listen to your favorite music.
• Study the stars against the night sky.
• Watch a sunset or sunrise from beginning to end.
• Play a musical instrument (even badly).
• Write poetry, paint a landscape or relish a novel.
• Play cards or tackle a crossword puzzle.
• Sip tea, reflecting on life or snuggling with your romantic partner.
• Play hide and seek with your children or grandchildren.
• Garden, walk, go dancing, swing in a hammock, take a nature hike, bicycle, canoe, skate, fish, play catch, throw a Frisbee or shoot some baskets.
• Watch home movies, look through family photo albums or tell your favorite stories.
• Sit down with your parents or elderly neighbors and learn more about their journey through life.
• Arrange flowers, bake a loaf of your favorite bread and make small talk in the kitchen.
• Write down your innermost thoughts and dreams in a private journal.
• Play a rousing, laughter-filled board game.

> **REMINDER**
>
> Work hard when it truly matters; unplug and let go when it doesn't. Become an expert at knowing the difference.

As we see it, the only requirement is that the activity must give your heart and spirit a boost. When that happens, you'll not only feel more rejuvenated but will have given yourself and your loved ones a chance to more deeply engage in life.

Resources

Healthy Pleasures by David Sobel, M.D., and Robert Ornstein, Ph.D. (Addison-Wesley, 1989). An entertaining, informative account of "the pleasure factor" in health and longevity.

The Pursuit of Happiness: Who Is Happy—and Why by David G. Myers, Ph.D. (Morrow, 1992). A carefully reasoned, scientifically based book on increasing your happiness and improving your health.

From Stress to Strength: How to Lighten Your Load and Save Your Life by Robert S. Eliot, M.D. (Bantam, 1994). A cardiologist's excellent, medically founded plan to reduce the risks of stress-related heart attacks and put more enjoyment into your life.

PERSONAL POWER NOTES
A Quick-List of This Chapter's Power-Action Options

A quick escape to your own "island of peace."
 • *Escape to a secluded beach.*

Now and then, escape the telephone.

Discover—or rediscover—simple, healthy daily pleasures.

PERSONAL NOTES

_____

_____

_____

_____

_____

_____

_____

_____

_____

_____

_____

_____

_____

_____

_____

_____

DEEP, REFRESHING SLEEP

Creating a Timeless Bedroom

Sleep is interwoven with every facet of daily life. It affects our health and well-being, our moods and behavior, our energy and emotions, our marriages and jobs, our very sanity and happiness.
—**Peter Hauri, Ph.D.**, director of the Mayo Clinic Insomnia Program, and Shirley Linde, Ph.D., *No More Sleepless Nights*

Until recently, sleep has been the dark one-third of our lives, like the far side of the moon, a persistent mystery entangled with misconceptions and wonder. Sometimes you eagerly fall asleep. Other times you resist going to bed. And sometimes sleep eludes you, no matter how hard you chase it: You lie awake, tossing and turning, frustrated, muscles tight, mind racing; perhaps you finally get an hour or two of fitful, troubled rest, but upon awakening you feel robbed.

One thing's for certain, whether or not we understand the reasons: We all covet great sleep. It's a natural, deep, refreshing experience—a way of revitalizing your Personal Power—that depends, first and foremost, on knowing how to let go of each day. But it seems far too few of us have that know-how. There's growing evidence that the majority of adults are getting grouchier and more error-prone because we're suffering from chronic "partial sleep deprivation"[1]—we don't get enough sleep or, more often, we sleep poorly night after night. It's time for a change.

POWER ACTION: FIRST OPTION
Make Your Bedroom Time-Free

"For most people the bedroom should be a time-free environment," says Peter Hauri, Ph.D., director of the Mayo Clinic Insomnia Program in Rochester, Minnesota. "Set the alarm if you must, but—especially for insomniacs—put the clock where it can be heard but not seen. Then you won't wake up during the night and keep looking at the clock. People sleep better without time pressure."[2] Just as important, arrange for a gentle awakening. Leaping up to shut off an alarm clock is a jolt to your entire being, triggering a racing heartbeat, muscle tension, stressful "emergency" symptoms and a raw emotional tone that can last all morning.[3] Test some alternatives. Positive music—set with a timer and with the volume just loud enough so you'll notice it and awaken—is one example of a choice that's better than a traditional alarm.

> Man must not allow the clock and the calendar to blind him to the fact that each moment of his life is a miracle and a mystery.
>
> **—H. G. Wells,**
> British novelist and historian

If possible, wake up at least a minute or two earlier than usual so you can lie in bed, blink your eyes, move your arms and legs and allow your body to gradually adjust to being wide awake. How you spend these waking minutes can have a significant—and sometimes profound—influence on your energy and performance all day long.

POWER ACTION: MORE OPTIONS
Warm Up, Tune Out and Relax

Here are several more of the most practical, little-known tips and techniques to head off insomnia and renew your Personal Power by getting deeper, more revitalizing sleep.

Raise Your Temperature 3 to 5 Hours before Going to Bed

Sleep researchers have recently come up with some fascinating new information: A brief period of *moderate exercise*—lasting at least 5 minutes—within 3 to 5 hours of bedtime, or a *hot bath or shower* within 3 hours of slumber, can *measurably deepen your sleep.* Here's why: Physical inactivity ranks among the prime causes of insomnia, and studies link physical fitness with improved sleep quality.[11] But it's not just the exercise that's beneficial—*it's the increase in body temperature.*[12] "If you can increase your body temperature [with exercise, for example] about 3 to 6 hours before going to bed," explain Dr. Hauri and Shirley Linde, Ph.D., authors of *No More Sleepless Nights,* "the temperature then will drop most as you are ready to go to sleep. The biological 'trough' deepens, and sleep becomes deeper, with fewer awakenings."[13] And James A. Horne, Ph.D., a sleep scientist at Loughborough University in Great Britain, has discovered a similar beneficial effect when a hot bath or shower is taken within 3 hours of bedtime.[14]

Keep Problems Out of the Bedroom

Work and sleep just don't mix. Neither do family problems and sleep. So if you want the best possible rest, and especially if you suffer from insomnia, make it a family rule that your bedroom is reserved as a comfortable, relaxing haven and as the place for a warm, positive sexual relationship. Nothing else. Keep heated discussions, intense brainstorming, snacking, computer work, your briefcase and monthly budgets out of your bedroom—since they accustom your body to a learned association with sleeplessness,[15] and prime you for being awake and agitated in bed.

Enjoy a Pleasant, Mind-Calming Bedroom Scent

As we explained in chapter 4, scientists have long known that pleasing fragrances prompt us to take slower, deeper breaths and become more relaxed and refreshed.[16] Every breath you take passes currents of air molecules over the olfactory sites in your nose. Odors flood the nerve receptors in your nasal cavities, where five million cells fire impulses directly through the olfactory area of the brain to the cerebral cortex and limbic system—the mysterious, ancient, intensely emotional area of the brain where you experience feelings, desires and wellsprings of creative energy. Certain scents seem to activate specific chemical messengers, or neurotransmitters, in the brain.[17]

Researchers have identified two scents—vanilla almond[18] and apple spice[19]—that, in a number of cases, seem to help promote deeper, more restful sleep. You might set a small container of naturally scented potpourri (the effects of artificial scents are unknown and may even be detrimental to sleep) with either of these scents on your nightstand and see if it makes a difference in the quality of your rest.

POWER KNOWLEDGE: DEEP SLEEP

MYTH #1: As long as you can fall asleep, you'll get good rest.

POWER KNOWLEDGE: According to Robert E. Thayer, Ph.D., professor of biological psychology at California State University in Long Beach, there are two primary tiredness states.[4] The one in which most of us find ourselves at bedtime *and* during sleep is called tense-tiredness. The other, which we sorely need but rarely experience, is known as calm-tiredness.

Tense-tiredness (high tension and low energy) is characterized by general head-to-toe fatigue and high levels of tension. According to researchers, this pattern has become so common that many of us just accept it as normal or natural (which it isn't).[5] With tense-tiredness, you may have a "sinking feeling," or a sense of great weariness, pessimism, anxiety or self-doubt. Tense-tiredness is related to headaches, back-aches, impatience, arguments and anger—and is sometimes simply labeled "a bad mood."

In this deenergized but uptight state, you have a weakened capacity to cope with stressful events, and problems seem far more daunting. There's also a greater tendency for self-defeating thoughts and behaviors[6]—such as blindly pursuing a goal long into the evening, after it would have been better to quit or shift focus, ingratiation (using ploys in an attempt to win approval or affection), inadvertently creating your own obstacles and making excuses to protect yourself against taking risks.

Calm-tiredness (low tension and low energy) is a deeply pleasant feeling of restfulness, of releasing stress and winding down gently and naturally from the pressures and demands of the day. It might be simply identified as a relaxed, good mood that leads to relaxed, good sleep. Unfortunately, many—and perhaps most—adults now live day after day with tense-tiredness instead of calm-tiredness (which you may only experience during extended vacations). Whereas tense-tiredness is linked to insomnia, calm-tiredness promotes deep and untroubled sleep.

MYTH #2: Sleep problems are overblown in the media.

POWER KNOWLEDGE: "Our society does not yet appreciate that many Americans are dangerously sleepy during the day . . . ," warns a 1993 report by the National Commission on Sleep Disorders Research. "Forty million Americans have a chronic sleep disorder, including insomnia . . . 20 million to 30 million have intermittent sleep-related problems caused by rotating shift work or last-minute preparations for meetings . . . On any given day 25 percent of people with no [clinical] sleep problems did not get enough sleep the night before and are not alert."[7]

"One thing is absolutely certain in America: The quality and quantity of sleep obtained is substantially less than what is needed," says William Dement, M.D., chairman of the Sleep Disorders Clinic at the Stanford University School of Medicine. "A substantial number of Americans, perhaps the majority, are functionally handicapped by sleep deprivation on any given day."[8]

MYTH #3: Our mind slows down during sleep. The important things that happen in the brain happen when we're awake.

POWER KNOWLEDGE: Until recently scientists thought of sleep as a period of rest that the brain and other organs needed to recover from the wear and tear of daily life. But we now know that the brain does not rest during sleep—at least not all areas of the brain. Instead, electrical activity, oxygen consumption and energy expenditure in certain regions actually *increase* during sleep. Apparently, one purpose of this extra brain activity is "to reinforce memories"[9] and to renew and fortify your mental effectiveness for the day ahead.[10]

Eat for Deeper Slumber

The link between what you eat and the quality of your nightly rest has grown much clearer in the past decade. Beyond a healthy, energy-promoting diet—which we'll review in chapters 9 and 15—there are several nutritional suggestions that warrant some attention here. First, for obvious reasons, it's generally a good idea to avoid coffee, tea and other caffeinated beverages within 4 or 5 hours of bedtime. Second, don't go to bed hungry—because if you eat an early supper and then skip a mid-evening snack, you can end up with a drop in blood sugar in the middle of the night that will interfere with your sleep.

What are some good nighttime snacks? Several low-fat cookies, some air-popped or very-low-fat microwave popcorn, a serving of fresh fruit or fruit sorbet, a few low-fat tea cakes or some other high-carbohydrate, low-protein favorite—since, for the reasons given in chapter 5, foods such as these may help deepen your sleep by increasing those messenger chemicals in the brain that promote a calm state of mind and relaxed emotions.[20] And finally, if you choose to drink some alcohol in the evening, do it early—generally not less than 3 to 4 hours prior to bedtime. The reason is that although alcohol makes some people drowsy, it actually distorts the normal brain-wave pattern of sleep and prompts more frequent awakenings, sometimes causing difficulty in getting back to sleep.

Use One-Touch Relaxation before Falling Asleep

It's ironic that those of us who fall asleep quickly and easily are often the ones who unknowingly hold onto excessive muscle tension all night long. As a result, we end up feeling more tired in the morning than we should be. Here's a half-minute remedy for winding down before you drift off to sleep: First take several deep, pleasant breaths and then concentrate on tightening and then relaxing the muscles in your face, jaw, neck and tongue. Then, one body area at a time, extend this tense-and-release process across your chest and shoulders, down your back and abdomen and out to your fingertips and toes. With practice, the response will be so rapid that you can use the One-Touch Relaxation techniques introduced in chapter 4. As an alternative, you might try some soothing music, a hot bath or shower, bedtime prayers or positive affirmations—whatever you find helpful for putting the day to rest.

To deepen your pleasant drift into slumber—especially if you happen to find yourself feeling anxious about sleep during the day—take a few minutes to breathe deeply and to recall your fondest memories of soothing, wonderful sleep, perhaps from your childhood years. Then, whenever you feel a twinge of worry about falling asleep, notice your discomfort and bypass the worry by recalling the bright, pleasant image—the thoughts and feelings—of your best sleep, using it as a powerful "anchor" to ease the grip of insomnia.

Arise at Approximately the Same Time Every Morning

One widely celebrated American habit is "sleeping in" on weekends. Unfortunately, it actually confuses your body's biological clock—creating a disruption pattern known as free-running[21]—and tends to *lower* your energy rather than raise it. In addition to feeling "worn out" and less alert after too much sleep, you may also have more difficulty falling asleep the next night.[22] "The worst thing in the world you can do [for your energy and rest] is sleep in on Sunday morning," says Charles Winget, Ph.D., a National Aeronautics and Space Administration scientist who is an authority on sleep cycles. "Essentially, you're becoming jet-lagged. You might as well fly from California to New York."[23] Even if your night's sleep has been poor or cut shorter than usual, it makes sense to get up at about the same time you usually do, since this helps synchronize your body's biological rhythms.[24] When you do choose to sleep in, it's a good idea to limit your extra time in bed to not more than an hour or so, open the curtains to expose yourself to daylight as soon as you awaken and then take a walk in sunlight or sit near a bright window—since these actions help stabilize your sleep/wake rhythm.[25]

> A well-spent day
> brings happy sleep.
> —**Leonardo da Vinci,**
> Italian painter and
> architect

Resources

For medical information on sleep treatments and the addresses and telephone numbers of accredited sleep disorders centers, contact the **American Sleep Disorders Association** (604 2nd St. S.W., Rochester, MN 55902; 507-287-6006).

Easing into Sleep, an audiocassette program by Emmett E. Miller, M.D. (Source Cassette Learning Systems, P.O. Box W, Stanford, CA 94309; 415-328-7171), features two excellent listening options: "Put the Day to Rest" and "Escape from Insomnia."

No More Sleepless Nights by Peter Hauri, Ph.D., and Shirley Linde, Ph.D. (Wiley, 1990). An informative book by the director of the Mayo Clinic Insomnia Program and the co-director of the Sleep Disorders Center at the Mayo Clinic.

Sleep Right in Five Nights by James Perl, Ph.D. (Addison-Wesley, 1993). A clear-cut set of guidelines for deeper rest.

PERSONAL POWER NOTES
A Quick-List of This Chapter's Power-Action Options

Make your bedroom time-free.

Raise your body temperature 3 to 5 hours before going to bed.

Keep problems out of the bedroom.

Enjoy a pleasant, mind-calming bedroom scent.

Eat for deeper slumber.

Use One-Touch Relaxation before falling asleep.

Arise at approximately the same time every morning.

PERSONAL NOTES

Home Sweet Home

New Ideas on the Make-or-Break
Transition from Work to Home

Husbands, wives, children are not getting enough family life. Nobody is. People are hurting.
—Arlie Hochschild, "The Second Shift," in *Newsweek*

It's easy to feel lost in the thorny underbrush and swamplands of
daily existence. Sometimes life can seem like little more than a blur of
busy work, delays, interruptions, changes and conflicts. By the time we
walk in the door at home or finish the housework for the day, many of us
are still firmly seized by the mindset of work. You know the feeling.
Loose ends. Dangling objectives. Knotted muscles. Nagging mistakes.
Lost energy. Unexpected bills. Financial headaches. A vanishing sense of
job security. Recurring worries about your children and their future. Today's headlines about world and local problems. And then, compounding
all of this, there are the never-ending lists of things that have to be done—
yardwork, errands, transporting the kids, balancing the household budgets, cleaning, home repairs, laundry. It's *always* something.

The truth is, more and more of us are feeling the least "at home"
when we're at home. The mind buys into this sticky perception that work
never really ends and, obligingly, won't give it up.

Home sweet home has all but disappeared from the American scene,
and we're paying for it—more than most of us imagine. Recent Gallup
surveys report that "Americans feel fractured, scattered, torn in pieces
by the competing demands of work and home."[1] According to some re-

searchers, nearly half of all the adults who now have nightly "head-aches"—and are too tired for sex—are men![2] There is compelling new evidence that those of us who become most immersed in our jobs and have the greatest trouble letting go during time off are much more likely to suffer from burnout—mental or physical exhaustion and stress-related health problems—than those who clearly draw the line between work and home.[3] Yet research also indicates that *winning at work shouldn't have to mean losing at life.*[4]

POWER ACTION: FIRST OPTION
Use Mental Cues to Feel More "at Home"

The first strategy for greater life balance and heading off collisions between work and family comes from finding innovative new ways to ease away from your job and leave work behind. Because, no matter what your job, the rhythm of your work is considerably different and probably more intense than that found at home.[5]

It makes sense to arrange for some kind of brief *transition time* or *decompression period*—a personal plan for devoting the final minutes of your working day to your least-pressured tasks—which might include such things as returning selected phone calls (by this we mean picking through your messages and dialing only those numbers where the person on the other end is likely to be supportive and positive), cleaning up, finalizing tomorrow's schedule or organizing upcoming projects. This—and the ride home—may be ideal times to turn on some of your favorite music. Make a list: Which of your daily assignments do you find the least taxing? Which of them could you schedule during your final 5 to 15 minutes of work?

Then *jump the tracks with your thoughts*, perhaps by taking a half-minute—as you leave the office or prepare to greet your family at the door—to imagine your most pleasing image of "home sweet home," the sights, sounds, hugs and smiles that bring you your fondest memories of what nonwork time has been and can be. Thoughts and feelings of caring. Affection. Winding down. Laughing. Playing. Noticing the trees and clouds. Feeling the breeze and sunshine. Smelling the flowers. Simple pleasures. Leaving your worries behind. This mental release can be so powerful that in moments it can help put the day to rest and draw your mind and mood toward the slower rhythms of home, helping make the journey feel less rushed, the arrival less hurried.[6]

When you happen to find your thoughts ablaze with uncompleted

POWER KNOWLEDGE: BALANCE

MYTH: What's the big deal? The family will just have to adjust to my workaholic attitude—things are going to be rough until the economy gets better or my next promotion comes through.

POWER KNOWLEDGE: Millions of us are realizing that grueling hours and ever-greater demands are not just a bad patch to get through until the next economic recovery kicks in. The pressure is real, it's here to stay, and according to a growing number of business analysts, it's going to keep stress levels at a record-breaking high.[7]

The clash between job and home has never been more pronounced: Nationwide surveys report that 72 percent of men and 83 percent of women experience "significant conflict between work and family."[8] It's a spiral that's hard to break—mishandled stress at home interferes with work performance, and mismanaged on-the-job pressures create or magnify problems at home.[9] And there's considerable evidence that the quality of personal relationships strongly influences job productivity, disease resistance and longevity.[10] Workaholism is just as damaging: People who value power over family and friendships appear to have a harder time fighting off disease.[11] Plus, what if divorce eats up all your hard-earned assets? Workaholism leaves everyone feeling bitter.[12]

Day after day we walk in the door at home, hoping to unwind and relax, and instead we get knocked off balance or thrown for a loop in various collisions—of tempo and focus—between work and family. For example, as you're greeted by loved ones at the door perhaps everyone starts talking at once: This happened, that broke, he got sick, her feelings got hurt, blankety-blank called, and you-know-who forgot to pick up you-know-what on the way home. Even the best relationships can get rattled. So appropriate questions are "Where do I begin to change things? How can I leave work problems at work? How do I stop the stress of home from infiltrating the office? How can I balance these two phases of my life so that each is positive—and neither are in conflict?" On the most practical level, researchers suggest beginning with some minor adjustments in daily routine—taking small, well-focused actions to alter several of the common, counterproductive habits that influence work/family balance far more than most of us realize.[13]

business, put pen to paper. Otherwise, if you tell yourself something like, "I won't forget—I'll just keep it in mind for tomorrow," chances are your subconscious will do just that—and keep you distracted well into the evening. And if you're planning to tackle some after-hours work, ask yourself, "What's the best use of my time tonight—for myself *and* my loved ones? Can this task be postponed or delegated? Can I realistically complete it or will I be distracted and frustrated because I can't finish it all?" By making a clear separation in your mind between your *work* and your *life*—*before* you reconnect with loved ones—you're already taking greater control of work/family balance.

Most important of all is the need to feel, really *feel* you're "at home." In fact, being "at home" is one of the unifying principles of *The Power of 5*. In your heart and mind and spirit, in the very center of the whirl of life around you, *there is a place you can come home to.* But you cannot find it by going outward, by looking for a new house or waiting to fix up your present one. Being "at home" is a journey inward. It is a perception of a clear, nurturing space within you. And it's also a special, valued space in loved ones, co-workers and friends that each of us can learn to support and appreciate.

As the workday ends, you have a perfect time to use a vivid, multi-sensory mental image to more quickly reconnect with the feeling of being deeply, pleasurably "at home." Envision the best images of home. Roll out your favorite memories from the past. What does the most revitalizing image of "being home" look like, feel like, smell like, sound like and taste like? Focus until the image shines, until your chest glows and a smile comes across your face. Let your whole self hold onto this image for a few moments. Then let it go, but keep it always within reach.

Reflect: *Home sweet home. Home is where the heart is. Feeling safe and secure, caring and cared for, loving and loved.* Use this image as a cue to feel more "at home" during breaks on the job or when traveling. And call upon this vivid, nurturing, welcoming mind-picture to find your way back home each day.

POWER ACTION: MORE OPTIONS
"Take 5" for Rejuvenation after Coming Home

Like our families, yours may be in the habit of meeting at day's end with some mutual rendition of "here's what happened today." Little do we realize that this is a *danger zone* for relationships, a prime time for dumping complaints on each other and triggering fatigue-driven arguments.[14] Consider an alternative: Negotiate in advance with family members a different kind of greeting whereby you each express your pleasure at seeing the others in a warm, caring way, *but limit your first comment to about 25 words or less*, such as: "What a hectic day! It's great to be home" or "Things were *crazy* at work, but I'm really glad to see you!" And then, without ignoring your partner or other family members, *delay talking about your day* (or hearing about your partner's day or what the children argued about, which household appliances broke, who needs more money and so on).

These transitional, "buffer zone" minutes offer a precious chance to maintain a higher vantage point and take better care of yourself and your relationships and to anchor more of the warmth and pleasure you always look forward to feeling when you arrive home. You might use this brief interlude to go exercise, take a shower or hot bath, change clothes or partake of a relaxing "tea time" tradition and enjoy a small premeal snack (which happens to be a particularly good choice in light of recent evidence that simple hunger-related tensions trigger many needless arguments[15]).

For some families, this is one of the best times to employ a babysitter so you and your partner can go for a walk, sit for a while out on the balcony or deck, putter in the garden, give each other a back rub, enjoy some relaxing music and sip your favorite late-day cup of natural, flavored tea or a glass of wine. Often we act as though it is legitimate to take time for ourselves—even just a few minutes—only when we have satisfied all the demands of others. In other words, never. There's no surer way to lose sight of your path in life. To realize your dreams, sometimes you have to stop looking at your schedule.

Like most families, yours probably has a set of unwritten goals about household time. In looking back over the years and remembering when you were growing up, how much have you been relying on that list of things you promised *always* to remember when you became a parent or grandparent? How often do these ideals get obscured or forgotten in the rush of everyday living? What about the things you promised yourself *never* to do? When we overschedule family time or keep asking loved ones to defer the simple, shared pleasures of daily living until we make it in the work world—to hang on because things will get better—it assumes that the rewards of our work will justify the neglect of self and family. This is pure fantasy.

And remember what we've mentioned several times before: Lightheartedness pays off. In one study of 50 married couples, psychologists

> Happiness is having a large, loving, caring, close-knit family in another city.
>
> **—George Burns,**
> American actor and entertainer

found that *humor accounted for 70 percent of the difference in happiness between couples.*[16] In particular, the researchers found that happiness is often tied to having an amusing, responsive partner who finds simple ways, day after day, to make you laugh.

Use Daily or Weekly Rituals to Sweeten Your "Home Space"

Daily rituals surround us—and research indicates they shape family relationships and have a significant effect on our health and mental outlook.[17] The way we share meals, say hello and good-bye and bring the day to a close before bedtime reveals a lot about how, precisely, we honor the wondrous possibilities of family life. At their best, daily rituals give us a chance to have fun, strengthen our relationships and discover the meaning in our lives.

"Daily rituals give us a sense of the rhythm of our lives, help us in making the transition from one part of the day to another, and express who we are as a family," say family therapists Evan Imber-Black, Ph.D., and Janine Roberts, Ph.D. "They are not just routines. They are meaningful actions, often including symbols that can express far more than words. . . . Every time we participate in a ritual we are expressing our beliefs, either verbally or more implicitly. Families who sit down to dinner together every night are saying without words that they believe in the need for families to have shared time together. . . . Nightly bedtime rituals offer parents and children an opportunity to tell each other what they believe about all kinds of matters. The sheer act of doing the bedtime ritual expresses a certain kind of parent/child relationship where warmth and affection and safety are available."[18]

Take a few minutes right now to review a typical day in your life and your family's life. What are the special times you share? These may include leaving and returning home, after-school snacks, meals, evening talks, gathering to watch a favorite weekly television show, bedtime and special activities on weekends. These daily rituals confirm—over and over again—how we relate to each other and what we value. Daily rituals are also important for single adults, who have a special need to take symbolic daily actions and create a quiet space for themselves in their home.

Unfortunately, research indicates that many common arguments between partners often arise because of unspoken differences about rituals—especially about how to reenter the "home space" at the end of the day.[19] It's important to get the subject of daily rituals out in the open in order to find better ways for each family member to reconnect with others in a personally revitalizing way. Take 5 minutes tonight to talk about your daily rituals. Are you satisfied with them? Are the others in your household satisfied with them? How, specifically, could the rituals be made more meaningful and strengthen the bond of family or friendship? If it's not possible for the household to share evening meals during the week, how about a Friday night candlelight dinner or a Sunday brunch or a night without television?

Expand the "Pleasure Factor" in Your Evenings

Beyond the usual connotations of cooperation and intimacy, what does "being together" mean in your relationships? It likely includes discussing daily problems, but how often do these dialogues turn into arguments or drag on far into evening—at the expense of other types of togetherness, such as shared relaxation time?

"Decide whether you actually want to relive your experiences all over again," suggests psychologist Barbara Mackoff, Ph.D. "The question, 'How was your day?' is a lot like the question 'How are you?' . . . Your initial response should be succinct. Pick a sentence or two that summarizes your basic feelings and states your intentions."[20]

Here are some ways to shorten your stories and lengthen your evenings.

• Set aside a prearranged time to sit down with your partner to discuss the day's events—and be ready to change that time when tensions seem extra high or when it's been an unusually rough day.

• Begin with your conclusions, or the main points, rather than leading up to them with dozens of tiny details (which some people love but others find distracting or irritating).

• Whenever you can, keep it light: "The funniest thing that happened to me today was . . ."

• Avoid absolutes such as *never* and *always*—which tend to make things sound worse than they really are and may cause needless worry or stress for your listener.

• If you want advice, ask for it (and if you're not asked for it, don't give it).

• Agree to an average daily time allotment of perhaps 5 to 15 minutes per person for your shared, work-related dialogues.[21]

Take a few minutes right now to glance through chapters 26, 27 and 28. There you'll find a host of quick and proven ways to get closer to each other—and gain new intimate pleasures in your relationship.

Welcome Variety—It's the Spice of Family Life

Sometimes we forget that releasing tension and unraveling stress knots is a very personal concern and that everyone in the household deserves his or her own chance for relaxation and quiet, private time. By modeling the fact that certain healthy activities help you unwind and that you need specific interludes to be alone or with your partner, you promote the idea of a *healthy transition* from work to home for the entire family, and you confirm that it's all right for each individual household member to have a different preference in how to achieve relaxation and rejuvenation. It's also important to make it clear to one and all that your time spent alone is not a punishment for them; it is a special and essential break for you. To emphasize this point, you might, for example, get in the habit of closing your door after 9:30 or 10:00 and allowing for sweet time with your partner. Explain warmly, "Mom and Dad need time to talk and to feel close to each other."

Resources

The Art of Self-Renewal by Barbara Mackoff, Ph.D. (Lowell House, 1992). A clear, practical book about creating greater work/family balance.

Life and Work by James Autry (Morrow, 1994). A thought-provoking collection of one manager's insights on life balance in a complex and hectic world.

Rituals for Our Times by Evan Imber-Black, Ph.D. and Janine Roberts, Ph.D. (HarperCollins, 1992). A scholarly yet practical look at the value of rituals in every family's journey through life.

Staying Put: Making a Home in a Restless World by Scott Russell Sanders (Beacon, 1993). An engaging story of one man's practical and spiritual search for creating his own home.

PERSONAL POWER NOTES
A Quick-List of This Chapter's Power-Action Options

Use mental cues to feel more "at home."

"Take 5" for rejuvenation after coming home.

Use daily or weekly rituals to sweeten your "home space."

Expand the "pleasure factor" in your evenings.

Welcome variety—it's the spice of family life.

PERSONAL NOTES

_____

_____

_____

_____

_____

_____

_____

_____

_____

_____

_____

_____

_____

_____

References

CHAPTER 3

1. Eliot, R. S., and Breo, D. L. *Is It Worth Dying For?* (New York: Bantam, rev. ed., 1989): 31–33.
2. Vaillant, G. E. *Adaptation to Life* (Boston: Little, Brown, 1977).
3. Bjorntorp, P. *Obesity Research* 1(3)(1993): 206–222; A. Rozanski et al. "Mental Stress and the Induction of Silent Myocardial Ischemia in Patients with Coronary Artery Disease." *New England Journal of Medicine* 318 (16)(Apr. 21, 1988): 1005–1012; Boston University School of Medicine study. *Internal Medicine News* (June 15–30, 1987); G. B. H. Baker et al. "Stress, Cortisol, Interferon and Stress Diseases." *Lancet* 1 (8376)(1984): 574; D. C. McClelland et al. "Stressed Power Motivation, Sympathetic Activation, Immune Function, and Illness." *Journal of Human Stress* 6 (2)(1985): 11–19; Pelletier, K. R., and Herzing, D. "Psychoneuroimmunology: Toward a Mindbody Model—A Critical Review." *Advances: Journal of the Institute for the Advancement of Health* 5 (1)(1988): 26–56; "Cholesterol Level Is Affected by Stress: Duke University Research." *Environmental Nutrition* 11 (7)(July 1988): 5.
4. Sapolsky, R. "Glucocorticoids and Hippocampal Damage." *Trends in Neurosciences* 10 (1987); U. S. Department of Health and Human Services *Special Report on Aging* NIH No. 80–2135 (Aug. 1980); Troell, S. J. "Cerebral Atrophy in Young Torture Victims." *New England Journal of Medicine* 307 (21)(Nov. 18, 1982): 1341.
5. Winter, A., and Winter, R. *Build Your Brain Power* (New York: St. Martin's Press, 1986): 153.
6. "Research on Stress Hormones: Powerful Agents in Health and Disease." *Salk Institute Newsletter* (Summer 1986): 2–3.
7. Lazarus, R. S. *American Psychologist* 30 (1975): 553–561; A. DeLongis et al. "Relationship of Daily Hassles, Uplifts, and Major Life Events to Health Status." *Health Psychology* 1 (1982): 119–136; A. D. Kanner et al. "Comparison of Two Modes of Stress Measurement: Daily Hassles and Uplifts versus Major Life Events." *Journal of Behavioral Medicine* 4 (1981): 1–39.
8. Williams, R., and Williams, V. *Anger Kills* (New York: Times Books, 1993); Eliot, R. S. *From Stress to Strength* (New York: Bantam, 1994).
9. Mark, V. H. *Reversing Memory Loss* (Boston: Houghton Mifflin, 1992): 216–217; Mark, V. H. *Brain Power* (Boston: Houghton Mifflin, 1989): 186–187; H. Benson et al. *The Wellness Book* (New York: Birch Lane Press, 1992); Nathan, R. G., Staats, T. E., and Rosch, P. J. *The Doctors' Guide to Instant Stress Relief* (New York: Ballantine, 1987).
10. Sedlacek, K. *The Sedlacek Technique: Finding the Calm within You* (New York: McGraw-Hill, 1989): 14.
11. Miller, E. E. *Self-Imagery: Creating Your Own Good Health* (Berkeley, Calif.: Celestial Arts, 1978/1986): 75–76.
12. Ibid.
13. Thayer, R. E. *The Biopsychology of Mood and Arousal* (New York: Oxford University Press, 1989); Lazarus, R. S. *Emotion and Adaptation* (New York: Oxford University Press, 1991); Vincent, J. D. *The Biology of Emotions* (Cambridge, Mass.: Basil Blackwell, 1990); Gray, J. A., ed. *Psychobiological Aspects of Relationships between Emotions and Cognition* (Hillsdale, N.J.: Erlbaum, 1990).
14. Thayer, R. E. "Factor Analytic and Reliability Studies on the Activation-Deactivation Adjective Check List." *Psychological Reports* 42 (1978): 747–756.
15. Thayer, R. E., Takahashi, P. J., and Pauli, J. A. "Multidimensional Arousal States, Diur-

nal Rhythms, Cognitive and Social Processes, and Extraversion." *Personality and Individual Differences* 9 (1988): 15–24; Thayer. *The Biopsychology of Mood and Arousal*: 54, 149–151.

16. Thayer. *The Biopsychology of Mood and Arousal*: 9.

17. Ibid.: 73.

18. Lazarus, R. S., quoted in Executive Health Examiners. *Coping with Executive Stress* (New York: McGraw-Hill, 1983): 169.

19. Dossey, L., quoted in Fisher, A. B. "Welcome to the Age of Overwork." *Fortune* (Nov. 30, 1992): 71.

20. Kabat-Zinn, J., quoted in Ruben, D. "Pioneer Stress Reduction Clinic." *American Health* (Apr. 1991): 42–46.

21. Langer, E.J. *Mindfulness* (Reading, Mass.: Addison-Wesley, 1989); Kabat-Zinn, J. *Full-Catastrophe Living* (New York: Delacorte Press, 1990).

22. Rossi, E. L. "The Eternal Quest: Hidden Rhythms of Stress and Healing in Everyday Life." *Psychological Perspectives* 22 (1990): 6–23; Rossi, E. L. *The 20-Minute Break* (Los Angeles: J. P. Tarcher, 1991): 48–49; Lloyd, D., and Rossi, E. L., eds. *High Frequency Biological Rhythms: Functions of the Ultradians* (New York: Springer-Verlag, 1992).

23. Jones, P. J., Leitch, C. A., and Pederson, R. A. "Meal-Frequency Effects on Plasma Hormone Concentrations and Cholesterol Synthesis in Humans." *American Journal of Clinical Nutrition* 57 (6)(1993): 868–874; Grandjean, E. *Fitting the Task to the Man*, 3rd ed. (New York: Taylor, 1991): 213.

24. D. A. Jenkins et al. "Nibbling versus Gorging: Metabolic Advantages of Increased Meal Frequency." *New England Journal of Medicine* 321 (4)(Oct. 5, 1989): 929–934.

25. Wurtman, J. J. *Managing Your Mind and Mood through Food* (New York: Harper-Collins, 1987); Drewnowski, A. Report to the American Heart Association Scientific Sessions (Nov. 1989). *USA Today* (Nov. 11, 1989).

26. Wurtman. *Managing Your Mind and Mood*; B. Spring et al. "Carbohydrates, Tryptophan, and Behavior: A Methodological Review." *Psychological Bulletin* 102 (1987): 234–256; Benton. *Biological Psychiatry* 24 (1988): 95–100; H. R. Lieberman et al. "Aging, Nutrient Choice, Activity, and Behavioral Responses to Nutrients." *Annals of the New York Academy of Science* 561 (1989): 196–208; Wurtman, R. J., and Wurtman, J. J. "Do Carbohydrates Affect Food Intake via Neurotransmitter Activity?" *Appetite* 11 (Supp. 1) (1988): 42–47; Wurtman, J. J. "Recent Evidence from Human Studies Linking Central Serotoninergic Function with Carbohydrate Intake." *Appetite* 8 (3)(1987): 211–213; Wurtman, R. J. "Dietary Treatments That Affect Brain Neurotransmitters." *Annals of the New York Academy of Science* 499(1987): 179–190; Leathwood, P. "Food-Composition, Changes in Brain Serotonin Synthesis and Appetite for Protein and Carbohydrate." *Appetite* 8 (3)(1987): 202–205; B. Spring et al. "Psychobiological Effects of Carbohydrates." *Journal of Clinical Psychiatry* 50 (Supp.)(May 1989): 27–34; Wurtman, J. J. "Carbohydrate Craving, Mood Changes, and Obesity." *Journal of Clinical Psychiatry* 49 (Supp.)(Aug. 1989): 37–39; Okuyama, H. "Does Food Affect Brain Function?" *Tanpakushitsu Kakusan Koso* 35 (3)(Mar. 1990): 275–279; Wurtman, R. J., and Wurtman, J. J. "Carbohydrates and Depression." *Scientific American* 260 (1)(Jan. 1989): 68–75.

27. Stellman, J., and Henifin, M. S. *Office Work Can Be Hazardous to Your Health*, rev. ed. (New York: Fawcett, 1989): 28.

28. Hanley, G. L., and Chinn, D. "Stress Management: An Integration of Multidimensional Arousal and Imagery Theories with Case Study." *Journal of Mental Imagery* (1990); Kelly, J. R., and McGrath, E. "Effects of Time Limits of Task Types on Task Performance and Interaction of Four-Person Groups." *Journal of Personality and Social Psychology* 49 (1985): 395–407.

29. Montagu, A. *Growing Younger* (New York: McGraw-Hill, 1983).
30. Loehr, J. E., and McLaughlin, P. *Mental Toughness Training* (Chicago: Nightingale-Conant, 1990): 18.

CHAPTER 4

1. Dement, W., quoted in "Drowsy America." *Time*.
2. Hendler, S. S. *The Oxygen Breakthrough* (New York: Simon & Schuster, 1989): 7,8,94.
3. Fried, R. *The Breath Connection: How to Reduce Psychosomatic and Stress-Related Disorders* (New York: Plenum, 1990); Hendler. *The Oxygen Breakthrough*.
4. Snyder, G. "Just One Breath." *Tricycle Review* (Fall 1991): 55–61; Nathan, R. G., Staats, T. E., and Rosch, P. J. *The Doctors' Guide to Instant Stress Relief* (New York: Ballantine, 1987): 6; Loehr, J. E., and McLaughlin, P. J. *Mentally Tough* (New York: Evans, 1986); Eliot, R. S., and Breo, D. L. *Is It Worth Dying For?*, rev. ed. (New York: Bantam, 1989); Harp, D. *The New Three-Minute Meditator* (Oakland, Calif.: New Harbinger, 1990); Fried. *The Breath Connection*; Kabat-Zinn, J. *Full-Catastrophe Living* (New York: Delacorte Press, 1990).
5. Goleman, D., and Gurin, J. *Mind-Body Medicine: How to Use Your Mind for Better Health* (Yonkers, N.Y.: Consumer Reports Books, 1993).
6. Rogers, J., and McWilliams, P. *Wealth 101* (Los Angeles: Prelude Press, 1992): 237.
7. Hendricks, G., and Hendricks, K., "Effects of Daily Breathing on Tiredness and Tension." *At the Speed of Life*: 195–196.
8. Kabat-Zinn, J. *Wherever You Go, There You Are* (New York: Hyperion, 1994).
9. Ibid.; Benson, H., and Stuart, E. M. *The Wellness Book* (New York: Birch Lane Press, 1993); Kerman, A. D. *The H. A. R. T. Program* (New York: HarperCollins, 1992); Epply, K. *Journal of Clinical Psychology* 45 (1990): 957–974; C. Alexander et al. *Journal of Personality and Social Psychology* 57 (1990): 950–964; Kabat-Zinn. *Full Catastrophe Living*; J. W. Hoffman et al. "Reduced Sympathetic Nervous System Responsivity Associated with the Relaxation Response." *Science* 215 (1982): 190–192; I. Kutz et al. "Meditation and Psychotherapy." *American Journal of Psychiatry* 142 (1985): 1–8; Bloomfield, H. *The Holistic Way to Health and Happiness* (New York: Fireside, 1980).
10. Benson, H., and Proctor, W. *Your Maximum Mind* (New York: Times Books, 1987).
11. R. E. Janaro et al. "A Technical Note on Increasing Productivity through Effective Rest Break Scheduling." *Industrial Management* 30 (1)(Jan./Feb. 1988): 29–33; Penc, J. "Motivational Stimulation and System of Work Improvement." *Studia-Socjologiczne* 3 (102)(1986): 179–197; Foegen, J. H. "Super-Breaktime." *Supervision* 49 (Oct. 1988): 9–10; Bechtold, S. E., and Sumners, D. L. "Optimal Work-Rest Scheduling with Exponential Work-Rate Decay." *Management Science* 34 (Apr. 1988): 547–552; Krueger, G. P. "Human Performance in Continuous/Sustained Operations and the Demands of Extended Work/Rest Schedules: An Annotated Bibliography." *Psychological Documents* 15 (2)(Dec. 1985): 27–28; Boothe, R. S. "Optimization of Rest Breaks: A Productivity Enhancement." *Dissertation Abstracts International* 45 (9–A)(Mar. 1985): 2927; Gustafson, H. W. "Efficiency of Output in Self-Paced Work, Machine-Paced Work." *Human Factors* 24 (4)(Aug. 1982): 395–410; Janaro, R. E., and Bechtold, S. E. "A Study of the Reduction of Fatigue Impact on Productivity through Optimal Rest/ Break Scheduling." *Human Factors* 27 (4)(Aug. 1985): 459–466; Okogbaa, O. G. "An Empirical Model for Mental Work Output and Fatigue." *Dissertation Abstracts International* 15 (2)(Dec. 1985): 27–28; Thatcher, R. E. *Journal of Personality and Social Psychology* 52 (1987): 119–125; G. M. Zarakovski et al. "Psychophysiological Analysis of Periodic Fluctuations in the Quality of Activity within the Work Cycle." *Human Physiology* 8 (3)(May 1983):

208–220; S. E. Bechtold et al. "Maximization of Labor Productivity through Optimal Rest/Break Schedules." *Management Science* 30 (12)(Dec. 1984): 1442–1448.

12. Grandjean, E., *Fitting the Task to the Man*, 3rd ed. (New York: Taylor, 1991).

13. Thayer, R. E. *The Biopsychology of Mood and Arousal* (New York: Oxford University Press, 1989); G. G. Globus et al. "Ultradian Rhythms in Human Performance." *Perceptual and Motor Skills* 33 (1971): 1171–1174; Kleitman, N. *Sleep and Wakefulness*, rev. ed. (Chicago: University of Chicago Press, 1963); Kripe, D. F. "An Ultradian Rhythm Associated with Perceptual Deprivation and REM Sleep." *Psychosomatic Medicine* 34 (1972): 221–234; Lavie, P., and Scherson, A. "Evidence of Ultradian Rhythmicity in 'Sleep Ability.'" *Electroencephalography and Clinical Neurophysiology* 52 (1981): 163–174; Gertz, J., and Lavie, P. "Biological Rhythms in Arousal Indices." *Psychophysiology* 20 (1983): 690–695; W. Orr et al. "Ultradian Rhythms in Extended Performance." *Aerospace Medicine* 45 (1974): 995–1000.

14. Lazarus, R. S. *American Psychologist*, 30 (1975): 553–561; A. DeLongis et al. "Relationship of Daily Hassles, Uplifts, and Major Life Events to Health Status." *Health Psychology* 1 (1982): 119–136; A. D. Kanner et al. "Comparison of Two Modes of Stress Measurement: Daily Hassles and Uplifts versus Major Life Events." *Journal of Behavioral Medicine* 4 (1981): 1–39; Pelletier, K. R. *Healthy People*: 42–44; Sheehan, D. W. *Science News* 11 (2)(Aug. 1981): 119; London, P., and Spielberger, C. "Job Stress, Hassles, and Medical Risk." *American Health* (Mar./Apr. 1983): 58–63.

15. A. Brodish et al. *Brain Research* 426 (1987): 37–46.

16. Nathan, Staats, and Rosch. *The Doctors' Guide*: 6.

17. Moore-Ede, M. *The 24-Hour Society* (Reading, Mass.: Addison-Wesley, 1993): 53 and 69.

18. Gallagher, W. *The Power of Place: How Our Surroundings Shape Our Thoughts, Emotions, and Actions* (New York: Poseidon Press, 1993).

19. Finke, R. *Creative Imagery: Discoveries in Visualization* (Hillsdale, N.J.: Erlbaum, 1990); Sedlacek, K. *The Sedlacek Technique* (New York: McGraw-Hill, 1989): 144.

20. Gallagher. *Power of Place*: 132.

21. Kaplan, R. "The Role of Nature in the Context of the Workplace." *Landscape and Urban Planning* 26 (1993).

22. *Mental Medicine Update* 2 (2)(Fall, 1993).

23. Hyman, J. W. *The Light Book* (Los Angeles: J. P. Tarcher, 1990); Ackerman, D. *A Natural History of the Senses* (New York: Random House, 1990).

24. Sobel, D., and Ornstein, R. *Healthy Pleasures* (Reading, Mass.: Addison-Wesley, 1989).

25. Zajonc, A. *Catching the Light* (New York: Bantam, 1993); Moore-Ede. *The 24-Hour Society*: 60.

26. I. McIntyre et al. *Life Sciences* 45 (1990): 327–332. ; *Brain/Mind Bulletin* (Jan. 1990): 7.

27. "Battling the Indoor Blues." *American Health* (Jan./Feb. 1991): 42.

28. Moore-Ede. *The 24-Hour Society*: 55.

29. Ibid.: 60.

30. Ibid.: 61–62.

31. Thomas, L., quoted in *Vis-a-Vis* (Apr. 1988): 28.

32. Kallan, C. "Probing the Power of Common Scents." *Prevention* (Oct. 1991): 39–43.

33. Van Toller, S., and Dodd, G. H. *Perfumery: The Psychology and Biology of Fragrance* (London: Chapman and Hall, 1991); Kallan, C. "Probing the Power of Common Scents." *Los Angeles Times* (May 13, 1991); "24th Japanese Symposium on Taste and Smell: 64 Scientific Studies." *Chemical Senses* 16 (2)(1991): 181–208; "Renaissance of Fragrance." *Age of Tomorrow* 113 (Japan: Hitachi, Dec. 1989).

34. Dember, W., and Warm, J. (studies reported at the annual meeting of the American Association for the Advancement of Science, Washington, D. C., Jan. 1991).

35. Torii, S. *The Futurist* (Sept./Oct. 1990): 50.

36. Baron, R. Research paper presented at the annual meeting of the American Psychological Association, in *USA Today* (August 14, 1992).

37. Baron, R. Research cited in *The Futurist* (Sept./Oct. 1990): 50.

38. Dryden, G., and Vos, J. *The Learning Revolution* (Torrance, Calif.: Jalmar Press, 1994); Wenger, W. *Beyond Teaching and Learning* (Gaithersburg, Md.: Project Renaissance, 1992); Gross, R. *Peak Learning* (Los Angeles: J. P. Tarcher, 1991); Berg, H. S. *Super Reading Secrets* (New York: Warner, 1992); Siler, T. *Breaking the Mind Barrier* (New York: Simon & Schuster, 1990); Herrmann, D. J. *Super Memory* (Emmaus, Pa.: Rodale Press, 1990); Frank, S. D. *Remember Everything You Read* (New York: Random House, 1990); Rose, C. *Accelerated Learning* (New York: Dell, 1985).

39. Moore-Ede. *The 24-Hour Society:* 54-55.

40. Holton, G., ed. "Albert Einstein Autobiographical Notes," in *Albert Einstein: Philosopher-Scientist*, ed. and trans. by P. A. Schilpp (Evanston, Ill.: Library of Living Philosophers, 1949); Erikson, J. M. *Wisdom and the Senses* (New York: Norton, 1988): 30–33.

41. Cailliet, R., and Gross, L. *The Rejuvenation Strategy* (New York: Doubleday, 1987): 52; Hendler, S. S. *The Oxygen Breakthrough* (New York: Pocket, 1989).

42. Chafetz, M. D. *Smart for Life* (New York: Penguin, 1992): 63–65.

43. Ljungdahl, L. "Laugh If This Is a Joke." *New England Journal of Medicine* 261 (1989): 558; K. M. Dillon et al. "Positive Emotional States and Enhancement of the Immune System." *International Journal of Psychiatry in Medicine* 15 (1)(1985–1986): 13–18; P. Eckman et al. "Autonomic Nervous System Activity Distinguishes Among Emotions." *Science* 221 (1983): 1208–1210; A. L. S. Berk et al. *Clinical Research* 36 (1988): 121 and 435A; A. L. S. Berk et al. *The Federation of American Societies for Experimental Biology (FASEB) Journal* 2 (1988): A1570.

44. Morreall, J. *Taking Laughter Seriously* (Albany: State University of New York, 1983): 108.

45. Lefcourt, H. M., and Martin, R. A. *Humor and Life Stress* (New York: Springer-Verlag, 1986); A. M. Nezu et al. "Sense of Humor as a Moderator of the Relation Between Stressful Events and Psychological Distress: A Prospective Analysis." *Journal of Personality and Social Psychology* 54 (1988): 520–525.

46. Chapman, A., and Foot, H. *Handbook of Humor and Laughter: Theory, Research and Applications* (New York: John Wiley and Sons, 1982); K. M. Dillon et al. "Positive Emotional States and Enhancement of the Immune System." *International Journal of Psychiatry in Medicine* 15 (1)(1985–1986): 13–18; "Laughing toward Longevity." *University of California at Berkeley Wellness Letter* (June 1985): 1; "The Mind Fights Back." *Washington Post*; Brody. "Laughter." *New York Times*.

47. deBono, E. *I Am Right, You Are Wrong* (New York: Viking, 1991): 1.

48. Isen, A. M. "Toward Understanding the Influence of Positive Affect on Social Behavior, Decision Making, and Problem Solving: The Role of Cognitive Organization." (paper presented at the annual meeting of the American Association for the Advancement of Science, Boston, Mass., Feb. 11–15, 1988); A. M. Isen et al. "The Influence of Positive Affect on the Unusualness of Word Associations." *Journal of Personality and Social Psychology* 48 (1985): 1413–1426; A. M. Isen et al. "Positive Affect Facilitates Creative Problem Solving." *Journal of Personality and Social Psychology* 52 (1987): 1122–1131; and Isen, A. M. "Positive Affect, Cognitive Processes, and Social Behavior." *Advances in Experimental Social Psychology* 20 (1987): 203–253.

49. Fry, W. F., quoted in "Laughter: Just What the Doctor Ordered." *University of Texas Health Science Center Lifetime Health Letter* 2 (11)(Nov. 1990); Fry, W. F. "What Are the Physiological Effects of Laughter?" *Mind-Body Digest* (Institute for the Advancement of Health) 4 (1)(1990): 6.

50. Fry, W. F., quoted in Stone, J. *In Health* (Dec./Jan. 1992): 51–55.

51. Zajonc, R. B. "Emotion and Facial Efference: A Theory Reclaimed." *Science* 228 (4695)(Apr. 5, 1985): 15–21; S. E. Duclose et al. "Emotion-Specific Effects of Facial Expressions and Postures on Emotional Experience." *Journal of Personality and Social Psychology* 57 (1)(1989): 100–108.

52. Williams, R. *The Trusting Heart* (New York: Times Books, 1989).

53. Epply, K. *Journal of Clinical Psychology* 45 (1990): 957–974; C. Alexander et al. *Journal of Personality and Social Psychology* 57 (1990): 950–964.

CHAPTER 5

1. Chafetz, M. D. *Smart for Life* (New York: Penguin, 1992): 64–65.

2. Langer, E. J. *Mindfulness* (Reading, Mass.: Addison-Wesley, 1989): 137.

3. Chafetz. *Smart for Life*; Thayer, R. E. *The Biopsychology of Mood and Arousal* (New York: Oxford University Press, 1989); Rossi, E. L. *The 20-Minute Break* (Los Angeles: J. P. Tarcher, 1991); Moore-Ede, M. *The 24–Hour Society* (Reading, Mass.: Addison-Wesley, 1993).

4. Rossi. *The 20-Minute Break*: 93.

5. Bartolome, F., and Evans, P. *Must Success Cost So Much?* (New York: Basic Books, 1988); O'Reilly, B. "Why Grade 'A' Executives Get an 'F' as Parents." *Fortune* (Jan. 1, 1990): 36–46; O'Reilly, B. "Is Your Company Asking Too Much?" *Fortune* (Mar. 12, 1990): 38–46.

6. Eliot, R. S. *From Stress to Strength: How to Lighten Your Load and Save Your Life* (New York: Bantam, 1994): 122

7. Ibid.: 123

8. "Tokyoites More Tired, Stressed, Than Residents of N.Y. or L. A." *Montreal Gazette* (July 31, 1989).

9. Klesges, R. C. Report to the Society of Behavioral Medicine. Cited in *Environmental Nutrition* 15 (6)(June 1992): 1.

10. Flannery, R. B., Jr. "The Stress-Resistant Person." *Harvard Medical School Health Letter* (Feb. 1989): 5–7.

11. Diener, E., quoted in *Psychology Today* (July/Aug. 1989): 39; Ornstein, R., and Sobel, D. *Healthy Pleasures* (Reading, Mass.: Addison-Wesley, 1989).

CHAPTER 6

1. Dement, W. Series of *USA Today* articles—1992 and 1993; Dotto, L. *Losing Sleep* (New York: Morrow, 1991): 179.

2. Lamberg, L. "The Boy Who Ate His Bed . . . And Other Mysteries of Sleep." *American Health* (Nov. 1990): 56.

3. Williams, G., III. "Early Morning Dangers: Why Your Body Hates to Wake Up." *American Health* (Dec. 1986): 56–59; Arnot, R. B. *CBS News* (Jan. 13, 1987).

4. Thayer, R. E. *The Biopsychology of Mood and Arousal* (New York: Oxford University Press, 1989); Lazarus, R. S. *Emotion and Adaptation* (New York: Oxford University Press, 1991); Vincent, J. D. *The Biology of Emotions* (Cambridge, Mass.: Basil Blackwell, 1990); Gray, J. A., ed. *Psychobiological Aspects of Relationships between Emotions and*

Cognition (Hillsdale, N.J.: Erlbaum, 1990).

5. Thayer. *The Biopsychology of Mood and Arousal*: 53.

6. Baumeister, R. F., and Scher, S. J. "Self-Defeating Behavior Patterns among Normal Individuals: Review and Analysis of Common Self-Destructive Tendencies." *Psychological Bulletin* 104 (1988): 3–22.

7. Friend, T. "No Rest for the Weary." *USA Today* (Jan. 3, 1993), citing *Wake Up America: A National Sleep Alert*, report by the National Commission on Sleep Disorders Research (Jan. 5, 1993).

8. Dement, W., quoted in "No Rest." *USA Today* (Jan. 3, 1993).

9. Davis, B. *Perspectives in Biology and Medicine* 28 (1985): 457–464.

10. Chafetz, M. D. *Smart for Life* (New York: Penguin, 1992): 64.

11. C. M. Shapiro et al. "Fitness Facilitates Sleep." *European Journal of Applied Physiology* 53 (1984): 1–4; Baekland, F., Downstate Medical Center, N.Y., 1966 study; Shapiro, C., and Zloty, R. B. University of Manitoba studies. Reported in Mirkin, G., *Dr. Gabe Mirkin's Fitness Clinic* (Chicago: Contemporary Books, 1986).

12. Sewitch, D. "Slow Wave Sleep Deficiency Insomnia: A Problem in Thermo-Down Regulation at Sleep Onset." *Psychophysiology* 24 (1987): 200–215; Perl, J. *Sleep Right in Five Nights* (New York: Morrow, 1993): 232–233.

13. Hauri, P., and Linde, S. *No More Sleepless Nights* (New York: Wiley, 1990): 130–131.

14. J. A. Horne et al. *Sleep* 10 (1987): 383–392; Willensky, D. "Hints for Sound Sleep." *American Health* (May 1992): 50.

15. Perl. *Sleep Right*: 213.

16. Van Toller, S., and Dodd, G. H., eds. *Perfumery: The Psychology and Biology of Fragrance* (London: Chapman and Hall, 1991); Krier, B. A. "Scents of Health." *Los Angeles Times* (Mar. 27, 1991): E1; O'Neill, M. "Taming the Frontier of the Senses." *New York Times* (Nov. 27, 1991): B1.

17. Kallan, C. "Probing the Power of Common Scents." *Prevention* (Oct. 1991): 39–43.

18. Redd, W., and Badia, P. Studies cited in Kallan. "Probing the Power of Common Scents."

19. Schwart, G. Studies cited in Kallan. "Probing the Power of Common Scents."

20. Wurtman, J. J. *Managing Your Mind and Mood through Food* (New York: Harper & Row, 1987); Chafetz, M. D., ed. *Nutrition and Neurotransmitters: The Nutrient Bases of Behavior* (New York: Prentice-Hall, 1990).

21. Perl. *Sleep Right*: 205.

22. Broughton, R. "Performance and Evoked Potential Measures of Various States of Daytime Sleepiness." *Sleep* 5 (Supp. 2)(1982); Dott: *Asleep in the Fast Lane*: 138; Hauri, P. "Behavioral Treatment of Insomnia." *Medical Times* 107 (6)(1986): 36–47; Regestein, Q. R. "Practical Ways to Manage Insomnia." *Medical Times* 107 (6)(1986): 19–23.

23. Winget, C., quoted in Dolnick, E. "Snap Out of It." *Health* (Feb./Mar. 1992): 87; Perl. *Sleep Right*: 206.

24. Hauri. "Behavioral Treatment of Insomnia:" 36–47; Regestein. "Practical Ways to Manage Insomnia:" 19–23.

25. Perl. *Sleep Right*: 195, 209.

CHAPTER 7

1. Gallup Survey, reported in Peterson, K. S. *USA Today* (Dec. 21, 1992).

2. Wolfe, J. *What to Do When He Has a Headache* (New York: Hyperion, 1992).

3. Schor, J. B. *The Overworked American* (New York: Basic Books, 1991); Garden, A. M. *Journal of Occupational Psychology* 62 (1989): 223–224.

4. Crosby, F. J. *Juggling* (New York: Free Press, 1991); Schor. *The Overworked American* ; Eckenrode, J., and Gore, S., eds. *Stress between Work and Family* (New York: Plenum, 1990).

5. Mackoff, B. *The Art of Self-Renewal* (Los Angeles: Lowell House, 1992).

6. Miller, E. E. *Software for the Mind* (Berkeley, Calif.: Celestial Arts, 1988); Sheikh, A. A., ed. *Imagery: Current Theory, Research, and Application* (New York: Wiley Interscience, 1984); Marks, D. F., ed. *Theories of Image Formation* (New York: Brandon House, 1986); Suinn, R. M. *Seven Steps to Peak Performance* (Lewiston, N.Y.: Hans Huber Publishers, 1986).

7. Ehrbar, A. "Price of Progress: 'Re-Engineering' Gives Firms New Efficiency, Workers the Pink Slip." *Wall Street Journal* (Mar. 16, 1993): 1; Fisher, A. B. "Welcome to the Age of Overwork." *Fortune* (Nov. 30, 1992): 64–71; Huey, J. "Managing in the Midst of Chaos." *Fortune* (Apr. 5, 1993): 38–48.

8. Work/Family Directions, Inc. research, cited in *Achieving Balance* (Portland, Ore.: Great Performance, Inc., 1990).

9. N. Bolger et al. "The Contagion of Stress across Multiple Roles." *Journal of Marriage and the Family* 51 (Feb. 1989): 175–183; "Marital Problems Affect Job." American Psychological Study, reported in *USA Today* (Nov. 8, 1989).

10. Myers, D. G. *The Pursuit of Happiness* (New York: Morrow, 1992); J. S. House et al. "Association of Social Relationships and Activities with Mortality: Prospective Evidence from the Tecumseh Community Health Study." *American Journal of Epidemiology* 116 (1)(1982): 123–140; Berkman, L. F., and Syme, L. O. "Social Networks, Host Resistance, and Mortality: A Nine-Year Follow-Up of Alameda County Residents." *American Journal of Epidemiology* 102 (2)(1979): 186–204; Eisenberg, L. "A Friend, Not an Apple, A Day Will Keep the Doctor Away." *Journal of the American Medical Association* 66 (1979): 551–553; Cohen, S., and Wils, T. "Stress, Social Support, and Buffering Hypothesis." *Psychological Bulletin* 98 (1985): 310–257; Caplan, G. "Mastery of Stress: Psychological Aspects." *American Journal of Psychiatry* 138 (1981): 413–420; Lynch, J. J. *The Broken Heart: Medical Consequences of Loneliness* (New York: Basic Books, 1977); Jaffe, D. T., and Scott, C. D. *Take This Job and Love It* (New York: Simon & Schuster, 1988): 185.

11. Research by Princeton University psychologist John B. Jemmott III, cited in Elias, M. "Friends May Help Keep Disease Away." *USA Today* (Oct. 11, 1989); Fassel, D. *Working Ourselves to Death* (New York: HarperCollins, 1990).

12. Fassel, D. *Working Ourselves to Death* (San Francisco: HarperCollins, 1990).

13. Imber-Black, E., and Roberts, J. *Rituals for Our Times* (New York: HarperCollins, 1992); O'Neil, J. R. *The Paradox of Success* (New York: Tarcher/Putnam, 1993).

14. Mackoff. *The Art of Self-Renewal*.

15. Nagler, W. *The Dirty Half Dozen* (New York: Warner, 1991): 47–48.

16. Ziv, A., and Gadish, O. *Journal of Social Psychology* 129 (1990): 759–768.

17. Imber-Black and Roberts. *Rituals for Our Times*; Imber-Black, E., Roberts, J., and Whiting, R., eds. *Rituals in Families and Family Therapy* (New York: Norton, 1988).

18. Imber-Black and Roberts. *Rituals for Our Times*: 15, 45.

19. Ibid.

20. Mackoff. *The Art of Self-Renewal*: 57–59.

21. Ibid.: 61–62.

PART III

PERMANENT WEIGHT CONTROL AND DO-IT-ANYWHERE FITNESS

Turn on Your Morning "Fat-Burning Switch"

Give Your Metabolism a Wake-Up Call and Start the Day with More Energy

---

Nearly half of all Americans skip breakfast, do little if any morning exercise and wait to eat until noon—or later. This "calorie-saving" habit backfires—*slowing down* your metabolism and energy, triggering binges and promoting *fat storage*.

In this section of *The Power of 5* you will learn how to permanently lose excess body fat and stay fit for life *without dieting*. You know it as well as we do: Every time you buy into another diet plan, chances are you're in for a nasty struggle, some brief signs of success and then an inescapable return to your old weight, or more. The failure, however, lies not in your weak will or genetics. Instead, it's because dieting is one of the worst forms of weight control—and a major cause of body fat *gain* and stress-induced eating.[1]

When compared to nondieters, chronic dieters are more easily upset, have more mood swings, are more likely to eat when anxious, have trouble concentrating, have lower self-esteem and are preoccupied with weight dissatisfaction or body self-hatred, says Janet Polivy, Ph.D., professor of psychology and psychiatry at the University of Toronto, who has researched the effects of dieting for nearly two decades.[2]

Yes, *The Power of 5* is an anti-diet program—because the "be thin at all costs" mindset is killing us. However, this is not a book about surrendering to fat, as some diet-backlash groups are clamoring for us to do, since that ignores the fact that being overweight can seriously hurt your health and shorten your life.[5,6] *Dieting* is a full-scale, runaway national problem and a key reason that millions of us are trapped in a disheartening day-to-day struggle and have lost our zest for living.

Cutting calories—which is *still* how 82 percent of women and 77 percent of men say they're trying to lose weight[7]—is painful and health-harming, and it doesn't even work.[8] Low-calorie dieting backfires by slowing your resting metabolism—your body's principal way of burning calories instead of storing them as fat—in some cases by as much as 15 to 45 percent,[9] and this fall-off in metabolism can last long after you've gone off the diet and gets lower each time you diet.[10,11] You're trapped—despite the fact that you're cutting calories, the pounds go right back on.

> Whenever we're "on a diet," most of us actually eat more high-fat foods than when we're not on a diet, regardless of our weight.[3] You'd be more likely to recover from almost any form of cancer than you would be to succeed, permanently, with weight loss from dieting.[4]

Scientific studies have sought out those very few people who have had lasting success at weight loss.[12] For example, the men and women in one study, who had lost an average of 53 pounds of body fat and kept it off for an average of six years, approached their excess weight as a symptom of an undesirable lifestyle (and, in some cases, slowed metabolism) and focused on *living* in a more active, desirable way, trusting that it would improve their bodies in successive small steps.[13] Therefore, they were *not* on a diet and did not have to worry about relapsing or regaining, and this contributed to lasting success.

A recent Gallup poll found that 90 percent of Americans feel that they are overweight.[14] And other national surveys show that we've never been so preoccupied and dissatisfied with our bodies—over the past 15 years the number of American men dissatisfied with their bodies has doubled to 34 percent, well over half of us are unhappy with our weight or abdomen size,[15] and nearly all women—even those who seem to have bodies that match Hollywood's ideal—have become obsessed with feelings of not liking their appearance. On surveys these women almost always endorse items such as, "I am terrified of gaining weight" or "I am always on a diet."[16]

Right now, today, as many as half of all adult Americans are on a diet, and nearly two out of every three of us will try to lose weight at least once this year,[17] running up an annual tab predicted to reach $51 billion in 1995.[18] And the results are horrendous: With dieting failure rates as high as 98 percent,[19] and a 33 to 73 percent chance of winding up *fatter* than you were when you started the diet,[20] a recent conference organized by the National Institutes of Health questioned the effectiveness of widely promoted weight-loss programs and products.[21]

The next five chapters of *The Power of 5* draw together the pieces of the puzzle for permanent weight control and no-strain lifelong fitness. In this opening chapter, we'll start with what happens once you wake up in the morning. Contrary to popular wisdom, there's no point trying to "save" calories by skipping breakfast. It doesn't work, and it actually changes your biology so you *gain more body fat*. Fine, you may be thinking, but I'm the exception. I feel great without breakfast, so why eat when I'm not hungry? Because it's easy to get lulled into thinking that you don't need a morning meal, when what's actually happening is that you've inadvertently slowed your metabolism, and you've taught your biochemistry to protect excess body fat and crave more high-fat foods.

This problem is compounded when you stay physically inactive all morning, since your body interprets this as added biological and psychological pressure and responds by trying to "save you" from semi-starvation. How? By driving you to overeat, and eat more high-fat foods, during the rest of the day and into late evening. And once you've skipped breakfast, whenever you *do* eat, there's a greater tendency for your body to store fat at a frightening rate.

With *The Power of 5*, you can reverse this trend. There are two key parts to this "wake-up call" to your metabolism: (1) Eat a great-*tasting*, low-fat breakfast, and (2) go through 5 minutes or more of physical activity or exercise.[22] Together, these two simple actions turn on your body's "thermic switch"[23]—as it has been called by Peter D. Vash, M.D., endocrinologist and internist on the faculty of the UCLA Medical Center, who specializes in obesity and eating disorders, and by dietitians Cris Carlin, R.D., and Victoria Zak, R.D. You move your body's natural biological rhythms into higher metabolism (and higher fat-burning).

POWER ACTION: FIRST OPTION
Enjoy a 5-Minute Power Breakfast Every Morning

Here's how breakfast can "fire up" your fat-burning power:

1. The major function of your morning meal is to break your overnight food fast. Some dietitians theorize that while you sleep, your body's metabolism slows down and you burn calories at a reduced rate.[24] Of course, you don't have to eat the minute you get out of bed.

(continued on page 88)

POWER KNOWLEDGE: WEIGHT CONTROL

MYTH #1: Skipping breakfast saves calories and will help me control my weight.

POWER KNOWLEDGE: Studies show that 40 percent or more of all adults leave the house in the morning without eating breakfast, often because of a mistaken belief that skipping this meal will help them control their weight. However, recent research shows that the opposite is true.[29]

Here's why: When you awaken from sleep, your body responds to the signals you give it. According to some authorities, from the moment you get out of bed, your brain cues the body's metabolism to match your physical demands.[30] If your morning ritual takes place in slow motion, your brain may have little incentive to push your metabolism much higher than near-hibernation rate. If you extend this "sleepwalk" activity level on into the morning—and skip breakfast in the process—you unwittingly fail to turn on your "fat-burning switch" and stimulate the fat-preserving and fat-storing processes instead.[31]

MYTH #2: If I skip breakfast, I'll eat less all day.

POWER KNOWLEDGE: Not likely. Skipping meals can lead to a ravenous appetite, writes obesity researcher C. Wayne Callaway, M.D. "People who skip breakfast or lunch then tend to binge in the evening, instead of eating moderately. It's a common problem among chronic dieters."[32] In addition, says Lawrence E. Lamb, M.D., in *The Weighting Game: The Truth about Weight Control*, "in the morning your liver will be about 75 percent depleted of glycogen [glucose-derived energy fuel]. It will already be sacrificing your body protein to manufacture glucose. If you want to protect your body protein [including muscle tissue], you had better provide some carbohydrate food early in the morning to replace that glucose. Your brain will function better, too, as it needs that glucose to maintain its ability to do all the complex tasks required of it."[33]

MYTH #3: If I'm not overweight, I don't get any real benefits from eating breakfast.

POWER KNOWLEDGE: Research reports that breakfast eaters are usually leaner, have lower blood pressure, eat fewer overall fat calories throughout the day,[34] have an easier time maintaining balanced blood sugar, have a greater sense of energy and strength and have an easier time maintaining a healthful, balanced diet.[35] A recent study at Memorial University of Newfoundland also suggests that eating breakfast is a possible shield against morning heart attacks.[36] According to this research, skipping breakfast increases platelet stickiness, which may promote clotting and contribute to heart attacks. Eating a good breakfast seems to help reduce platelet stickiness and thereby seems to provide some protection against heart attacks.

MYTH #4: Your metabolism is preset by genetics. If you're stuck with "slow calorie burning," you have to live with excess body fat. It's that simple.

POWER KNOWLEDGE: No, it's not that simple. While it's true that resting rate of calorie burning is influenced by genetics, there are many specific ways you can healthfully raise your own *metabolism*— which may be defined as the various ways your body burns calories to produce energy to carry out essential functions. Metabolism generates heat, a process called thermogenesis. As individuals, we each have naturally differing metabolic needs,[37] but here's an estimate of the contribution made by your three major calorie-burning processes:[38]

Resting metabolic rate: 50 to 70 percent of calories burned.

Thermic effect of exercise/physical activity: 20 to 40 percent of calories burned.

Thermic effect of food: 10 to 15 percent of calories burned.

Your resting metabolic rate (RMR) is the body's basic, nonstop calorie burning when you're sitting still or sleeping. It tends to decrease with age—due primarily to loss of muscle mass and diminished physical activity. As your muscles atrophy and you expend fewer and fewer calories, your RMR decreases—and, if your food intake remains the same, it's easier than ever to gain body fat. You help keep your

(continued)

83

POWER KNOWLEDGE: WEIGHT CONTROL—*CONTINUED*

RMR higher not by doing any serious calorie cutting but by building and maintaining strong muscles (see chapter 12)—which drives up your RMR and helps "burn off" fat as fuel 24 hours a day.

The thermic effect of exercise (TEE) relies on increased physical activity to give your metabolism a boost. In some cases (see chapter 11) this extra calorie burning, from aerobics, for example, can last for a few hours, but the effect quickly diminishes. The one primary exception to this happens when your fitness activity builds muscular strength, which, as noted above, increases your RMR.

Whenever you eat, you initiate the thermic effect of food (TEF), whereby your metabolism increases to help with digestion and absorption of nutrients. The TEF is greatest following a meal or snack that is high in complex carbohydrates and moderate in protein, and the TEF is much lower when you consume high-fat foods.[39] This fact has led some authorities to say that complex carbohydrates and protein are "heat-generating" foods, but dietary fat is not. And "when you eat 'hotter calories,'" say weight-loss researchers, "you *burn* more calories—by the simple act of eating."[40]

"Researchers have found that when you eat a complex carbohydrate, it stimulates a greater thermogenic loss of calories than when you eat fat," explains Elliot Danforth, M.D., director of clinical research at the University of Vermont School of Medicine in Burlington. "In scientific terms, we say carbohydrate is thermogenic; fat is non-thermogenic, that is, it generates much less heat for the same number of calories."[41] This thermic effect of food has been repeatedly verified—and some researchers suggest that merely by switching from a diet with 40 percent of total calories from fat (the current American average) to a diet with only 20 to 25 percent fat (a sensible level for most of us), an average, active person may steadily, permanently lose body fat *without cutting back on overall calories.*[42]

MYTH #5: Weight control is easy if you find the right diet.
POWER KNOWLEDGE: Diets don't work! The lure of a new

diet is the promise of rapid weight loss. The hook is the fact that any kind of diet can work for some of us—at first. But then we fail—again and again. Why? Here are seven scientific reasons we all should know.

1. By their very nature, diets mean deprivation and semistarvation. When you're forced to try to stop eating foods you love, eventually the cravings for these "forbidden" or "bad" foods become so powerful and unbearable that your resistance breaks down and, chances are, you binge, stuffing yourself with the not-allowed foods. In fact, it's most likely *the act of dieting itself* that leads to the compulsion to eat excessive amounts of fattening foods,[43] and all the positive self-talk in the world won't stop binge eating when it's the result of the biological rebound effect of semistarvation. One of the keys to *The Power of 5* is understanding an important principle: What you resist persists; what you accept *lightens.*[44]

2. Dieting leads to lowered metabolism—by as much as 45 percent![45] This fall-off in calorie burning is especially pronounced in women, whose metabolism—for genetic reasons—is generally slower than that of men.[46] Yale University studies indicate that breaking your diet by eating high-fat foods is not due to a failure of your willpower—it's because your own biology is fighting against the diet and working to replenish lost weight the quickest and easiest way possible: by driving you to eat lots of fat.[47]

3. Dieting fosters a sense of helplessness, shame and guilt. This is due to the fact that, rather than being based on flexible personal choice, diets typically call for rigid rules. This sets you up for repeated failures—and chances are, each time you regain lost weight you feel a deep shame that drains your energy, attacks your self-esteem and may lead to depression. As psychologist Susan Wooley, Ph.D., has pointed out, "*If shame could cure obesity, there wouldn't be a fat person in the world.*"[48] With dieting, whenever you perceive yourself as having violated the rules of the diet, you tend to unconsciously interpret this as being *off* the diet and therefore *out of control.* The logical consequence is to overeat and then feel terrible about it.

In contrast, lasting, no-guilt weight loss depends on having flexible, practical strategies for keeping your energy and self-image high

(continued)

POWER KNOWLEDGE:
WEIGHT CONTROL—*CONTINUED*

and an unshakable knowledge that momentary lapses are points of learning, of greater awareness, and are *not* personal failures.[49] Unfortunately, millions of us, especially women, still buy into the notion that happiness lies on the other side of the next diet, and so we keep delaying doing good things for ourselves until we have a body that is more deserving. With dieting, any weight loss is fleeting. The "I'll be happy when I lose weight" syndrome is self-defeating.

4. Diets are a painful, exhausting process. More than half of all dieters experience depression, nervousness, weakness or irritability,[50] and as many as 20 to 40 percent of American women have become compulsive eaters.[51] At the start of a new diet many of us report "success" in losing some weight and then, seemingly without any warning, we binge, with weekend eating splurges that some researchers have measured at 8,000 to 10,000 calories.[52] No matter what the trigger—tempting foods, feeling bad, feeling good or boredom—something happens and, when we're on a diet, we have an intense desire to stuff ourselves. In part, this is because under the stress of dieting there's an overwhelming desire to seek comfort through food.

5. Dieting makes you feel like a criminal. By forbidding between-meal snacks and labeling certain foods as "good" or "bad," allowed or not-allowed, you're forced to ignore your inner voice, and this suppression raises the fear of breaking down and losing control. It can also make you feel like a horrible glutton for eating otherwise-modest amounts of food—even though statistics show that people who are overweight usually eat no more, and often less, food than people who are at their "normal" weight.[53] In fact, large database studies indicate that normal-weight and overweight persons eat about the same total number of calories.[54] And research from Stanford University shows no correlation between how many calories you eat and your body fatness.[55] Even more surprising, studies at Indiana University's Weight Loss Clinic indicate that those people who restricted calories were the *least* successful in losing weight and keeping it off.[56]

6. Dieters are victimized by incomplete exercise. Participating in an aerobics class a few times a week—or even once every day—can certainly be good for your health, but it's not the best way to boost your metabolism 24 hours a day. When you join a fitness class, on average you probably go through 30 minutes or more of aerobics three or four times a week, and during those "fitness minutes" your fat-burning metabolism rises. However, it falls back near resting levels soon after you cool down, and if, like most of us, you think you're "finished" with any need for exercise until the next class, you're mistaken.

What most dieters don't realize is that the body's metabolism responds to your physical activity *every hour of the day*, not just once a day or once every few days. Your 24-hour-a-day calorie-burning power depends much more on increasing your *lean muscle mass* through strengthening exercises than on your aerobics classes. And if you join a health club and then quit (*as 50 percent of all people do after the first session at a health club or exercise class*[57]), you've probably said "forget it" to the minute-here, 5-minutes-there kinds of physical activity that are convenient but aren't "real exercise"—so why bother. But that's a mistake! Because there are certain times of the day—for example, within an hour or so of arising in the morning, within 15 to 30 minutes after eating each meal, and in the early evening—when as little as 5 minutes of walking or other do-it-anywhere kind of physical activity may actually *double* your calorie burning for the next 3 hours or more.

7. Diet-caused weight fluctuations (weight loss and regain) can be a serious health risk. The anti-diet movement and size-acceptance movement each have many merits, but let's face it, in our image-driven, be-thin culture, few of us can simply accept ourselves unconditionally, extra fat and all. Obesity rates are going higher and higher, and being overweight through middle age can double your mortality risk, say scientists at the National Center for Health Statistics,[58] leading to such health problems as high blood pressure, cardiovascular disease, diabetes, digestive diseases, certain cancers, stroke, gallstones, sleep apnea and other conditions.[59] A recent study published in the *New England Journal of Medicine* suggests that weight fluctuations that result from so-called yo-yo dieting are associated with increased risk for heart disease and all-cause mortality.[60]

You can wait for a half hour or even an hour—but just don't skip this important meal, thinking you'll make up for it later. Your metabolism doesn't work that way.

As an added benefit, when your breakfast is low in fat and contains a moderate amount of metabolism-boosting protein[25] (such as some skim milk, low-fat cottage cheese, nonfat yogurt or nonfat cream cheese) and plenty of fiber-rich complex carbohydrates (such as whole grains), studies suggest that you'll be less likely to overeat or eat high-fat foods at lunch, and you'll have fewer impulsive, high-fat snacks.[26] "Always remember that skipping a meal leads to binge eating," explains dietitian Kathy Stone, R.D., author of *Snack Attack*. "Eating breakfast is also essential to help control eating after dinner. Surprising, but true. What you eat in the morning affects how full you feel at the end of the day. If you think that breakfast makes you hungrier, that you are actually better off on the days when you go as long as possible without eating, think again. What happens when you finally start eating? Most times you lose control."[27]

2. Eating a wholesome, low-fat breakfast gives you more lasting energy all morning—so it's easier and more enjoyable to further "fire up" your metabolism by being physically active or going through an exercise session with greater vigor and less frustration or resentment.

But what if you don't feel hungry for breakfast? It's probably because you've learned to override your morning body clock. Once you reestablish your normal, healthy metabolic rate, you'll begin to feel hungry when you get up in the morning. In addition, says C. Wayne Callaway, M.D., former director of the Nutrition and Lipid Clinic at the Mayo Clinic in Rochester, Minnesota, "you will be hungry at appropriate times throughout the day and will lose the urge to binge in the evenings."[28] If you've long avoided this morning meal, you might simply begin with a piece of fruit (an apple, banana or orange or half a grapefruit, for example) and some whole-grain toast or a whole-wheat bagel with nonfat cream cheese or all-fruit preserves. Or you might choose a 1-ounce serving of low-fat, whole-grain cereal with skim milk or a low-fat, whole-grain muffin and a serving of low-fat or nonfat cottage cheese. On some mornings you may enjoy mixing your whole-grain cereal with a 4-ounce serving of nonfat or low-fat yogurt. Include a beverage such as coffee or tea.

> Permanent weight loss means making small, manageable changes and sticking with them for life.
>
> **—Michael Hamilton, M.D.,**
> director, Duke University Diet and Fitness Center

POWER ACTION: MORE OPTIONS
Within an Hour of Arising, Enjoy at Least 5 Minutes of Physical Activity

We know, we know. Perhaps like many people you find it very hard to get enthused about doing *any* kind of exercise early in the morning. Make it a daily habit to *slowly* get out of bed, get dressed and *gradually* increase your activity level. Before or after you eat breakfast, go through a gentle warm-up period and then do a few minutes of light to moderate-intensity physical activity—such as taking a comfortable 5-minute walk or watching the morning news as you pedal *at an easy, moderate pace* on a stationary cycle or go through some smooth, balanced oar strokes on your rowing machine. Or for variety you might do some moderate strengthening or abdominal toning exercises. We think you'll soon enjoy this "active time" so much that on some days 5 minutes will turn into 10 or 15 or 20 (see chapter 11 to learn the latest aerobic exercise guidelines).

Resources

Obesity and Health: A Journal of Research, News, and Contemporary Issues (402 S. 14th St., Hettinger, ND 58639; 701-567-2646). A concise, enlightening professional journal that is popular with nonprofessionals as well.

The Weight Control Digest (The LEARN Education Center, 1555 W. Mockingbird Lane, Suite 203, Dallas, TX 75235; 800-736-7323). A scholarly but accessible newsletter with articles by leading experts.

PERSONAL POWER NOTES
A Quick-List of This Chapter's Power-Action Options

Enjoy a 5-minute Power Breakfast every morning.

Within an hour of arising, enjoy at least 5 minutes of physical activity.

PERSONAL NOTES

_____

_____

_____

_____

_____

_____

_____

_____

_____

_____

_____

_____

_____

_____

_____

_____

Snack-and-Ice-Water Breaks

Stop Going Hungry—And Increase Your Calorie-Burning Power All Day

Eating delicious, low-fat snacks *increases* your metabolism and reduces the urge to overeat, especially at night. And drinking ice-cold water actually *burns* calories. As one researcher puts it: "Water will do more to generate fat loss than any other single thing you can do."[1]

Eating great-tasting between-meal snacks is the most enjoyable way to rev up your metabolism and help you lose weight for good. But to get even greater results, your Power-Snack breaks include something extra—drinking *ice water*. Surprised? Most people are. But do you know that ice-cold water is a calorie-*burning* fluid? It is—requiring more than 200 calories of metabolic heat to warm it to body temperature.[2] In fact, *"water may be the simplest, most powerful key to fat loss,"* says Ellington Darden, Ph.D., exercise scientist and, for the past 20 years, director of research for Nautilus Sports/Medical Industries.

Let's begin with a closer look at between-meal snacks. No matter what you've been told all these years about avoiding snacks, there's just no reason to starve yourself hour after hour in a futile attempt to "save" calories.[3] It won't work: Each of us has an underlying physiological need to eat every 2 to 2½ hours or so throughout the day.

During the day, when you go for 4 or 5 hours without eating, your blood sugar levels drop and your energy wanes. This can force you to fight off needless tension and tiredness, and it may take a huge dose of willpower to force yourself to exercise, or in some cases, just to get up out of your chair. Far too many of us experience this kind of fatigue every day—caused, at least in part, by going too long without eating.

> Guard against genera-
> tion of new fat cells by
> avoiding large intakes of
> food at one time. Space
> smaller meals throughout
> the day. This tactic re-
> duces the hormonal sig-
> nal that causes fat cells
> to divide and multiply.
>
> **—Peter D. Vash, M.D.,**
> endocrinologist and
> eating disorders
> specialist at the UCLA
> Medical Center

And then, chances are, late in the day, after hours of deprivation, your hunger takes over and you're hit with an irresistible urge to nibble—and then fall victim to a nighttime eating binge.

Consider the alternative: Each time you pay attention to your natural hunger and eat snacks, you accomplish three vital things—you nourish your body, fire up your metabolism to burn more calorie, and nurture yourself emotionally—and together, these help end feelings of deprivation and reduce cravings for "forbidden" foods. And in *this* book "snack" doesn't mean a dry, Styrofoam-like rice cake or a fake "diet candy bar."

Now let's turn to the other part of your Power-Snack break: *ice water*. By sipping a tall glass of cold water several times a day, you burn extra calories in one of the easiest ways of all. Furthermore, explains Dr. Darden, "if you don't drink enough water, your body's reaction is to retain the water it does have. This, in turn, hampers kidney function, and waste products accumulate. Your liver is then called on to flush out impurities. As a result, one of your liver's main functions—metabolizing stored fat into usable energy—is minimized."[4]

"Drinking generous amounts of water is overwhelmingly the number one way to head off food cravings and reduce appetite," says George L. Blackburn, M.D., Ph.D., associate professor at Harvard Medical School and director of the Center for the Study of Nutrition and Medicine at New England Deaconess Hospital in Boston.[5] When you drink plenty of water throughout the day, it takes up room in the stomach, helping you feel full and reducing the desire to eat when under stress or by habit. And research by Wayne C. Miller, Ph.D., and his colleagues at Indiana University's Weight Loss Clinic indicates that high daily water consumption is related to successful, lasting weight loss.[6]

POWER ACTION: FIRST OPTION
Enjoy a 5-Minute Power Snack at Midmorning and Midafternoon

Whenever possible, eat between-meal snacks when you first begin to feel an energy drop or notice some initial pangs of hunger. It's very important to have your favorite healthy snacks readily available at mid-morning and midafternoon. There are three main points about healthy, metabolism-boosting snacks:

First, make certain they're low in fat (less than 3 grams) and low in sweeteners.

Second, eat a modest serving. This is particularly important because when we're overweight, there seems to be an increased tendency to eat quickly, to eat much larger snacks in late evening instead of spread more evenly throughout the day, and to keep eating without being aware of it.[7]

Third, keep great-tasting snacks readily available—so you're not as likely to unconsciously reach for high-fat junk food. For starters, here are some good choices to consider.

- A few whole-grain crackers or unsalted pretzels, or several cups of plain air-popped popcorn (or, until your tastes become accustomed to the natural flavor of air-popped corn, not more than 1½ cups—half a bag—of PopSecret's By Request microwave popcorn, with 2 grams of fat, or Orville Redenbacher's Smart Pop, with 2½ grams of fat).
- A whole-grain bagel, English muffin or hard roll or a piece or two of whole-grain bread (you might feel like it's more of a treat if you add some nonfat cream cheese).
- A low-fat muffin or several low-fat cookies.
- A serving of fresh fruit or juice, vegetable sticks or vegetable juice, with a small portion of low-fat or nonfat yogurt or cottage cheese.
- A handful (not a bagful) of dried fruit-and-nut mix.
- A cup of vegetable, lentil or bean soup.

POWER ACTION: MORE OPTIONS
Sip Ice Water throughout the Day to Burn Extra Calories and Aid Weight Control

When drinking water during the day you can "maximize calorie burn by keeping the water ice cold," explains Dr. Darden. "A gallon (128 ounces or eight 16-ounce glasses) of ice-cold (40°F) water requires over 200 calories of heat energy to warm it to core body temperature (98.6°F)."[26]

By not drinking enough water you *slow down fat loss*. Beyond the weight-loss benefits, it's a vital health concern to take in *plenty* of water, even when you're not thirsty (thirst can be an unreliable signal during

(continued on page 96)

POWER KNOWLEDGE: SMART SNACKS

MYTH #1: To lose weight you need to "save calories" by avoiding between-meal snacks.

POWER KNOWLEDGE: The exact opposite is true. As discussed in chapter 8, whenever you skip breakfast, your metabolism remains sluggish during the morning hours and your biology gets primed to store more of your lunch and dinner as body fat and to compel you to eat higher-fat snacks all evening. If you want to "burn off" excess body fat—and think, feel and perform at your best all day—it's a priority to take 5 at midmorning and midafternoon to rev up your energy and metabolism with a 5-minute Power Snack.

To get fat out of storage in your fat cells, a process called lipolysis needs to take place—and glycerol and fatty acids need to be broken apart so that the free fatty acids can then be transported to other cells, especially muscle cells, to be burned to release energy. But when you skip between-meal snacks, your blood sugar falls, you experience increased fatigue and tension[8] and your biochemistry primes you to stuff yourself at lunch and dinner. Your body responds with larger-than-normal amounts of insulin, which inhibits lipolysis, making it more difficult for your body to mobilize fat deposits, and instead you inadvertently promote fat *storage*.[9] Between-meal snacks can help keep calorie burning going and minimize the blood sugar drops that can prompt overeating.[10] In addition, they help reduce body fat storage,[11] perhaps due to changes in the secretion of insulin.[12]

Large meals stimulate excessive insulin production—and insulin is the body's strongest pro-fat hormone and promoter of fat storage. It also speeds the conversion of sugar to body fat.[13] Moderate meals and between-meal snacks bring a smaller, healthier insulin response. "Eating frequently without overeating will actually assist you to lose weight rather than hinder your weight loss as promoters of very-low-calorie dieting would like you to believe," says Wayne C. Miller, Ph.D., of Indiana University's Weight Loss Clinic.[14]

"For every meal we eat, we have actually missed one small meal that our body wants," adds psychobiologist Ernest Lawrence Rossi, Ph.D. "By skipping [these] calls for sustenance, we incur significant energy deficits and become much hungrier than we should be. Eating six times a day helps spare us from the wide swings of alertness and fatigue that can occur by eating too many calories in a single large meal. Eating smaller, nutritious meals and snacks helps to stabilize blood sugar levels, which in turn optimizes memory, learning and performance."[15]

Research published in the *New England Journal of Medicine* and the *American Journal of Clinical Nutrition* suggests that moderate-sized meals plus small between-meal snacks may help lower blood cholesterol levels, reduce body fat, enhance food digestion, lessen the risk of heart disease and increase metabolism.[16,17] Interestingly, in one study the people who ate more frequently had lower cholesterol levels despite eating more food overall.[18] And, remember the *added* benefit for weight control: By eating low-fat snacks in midmorning and midafternoon, you're less likely to stuff yourself at main meals or lapse into stress-related eating binges in the evening.

MYTH #2: A snack is a snack. If the total calories are equal, then a doughnut or some ice cream is a perfectly acceptable, "healthy" snack.

POWER KNOWLEDGE: A calorie isn't just a calorie any more. When it comes to snacks, metabolic *efficiency* is what sets one kind of calorie apart from another. Since dietary fat is already fat, it takes very little energy "cost"—only about 3 calories—to convert 100 calories of fat into new body fat.[19] So gaining new body fat from dietary fat is amazingly easy. In contrast, it "costs" about 23 calories to turn 100 calories of carbohydrate into fat, estimates Jean-Pierre Flatt, Ph.D., professor of biochemistry at the University of Massachusetts Medical Center in Worcester.[20] In other words, it's considerably easier for your body to convert dietary fat into body fat than it is to convert complex carbohydrates into fat.

Compounding the lower calorie-burning effect of eating high-fat foods are the facts that they tend to stimulate you to eat *more* high-fat foods in the hours that follow,[21] and the body fat you gain seems to be preferentially deposited around your waist and stomach areas.[22] Complex, fiber-rich carbohydrates—including whole grains and legumes—have been shown to assist in reducing body fat.[23] On the other hand, consuming large amounts of refined carbohydrates—sweeteners such as sugar, honey and syrup—is linked to gaining body fat.[24] The most potent fat-promoting foods seem to be those that are high in both fat and sugar.[25]

the early stages of dehydration). "The fatigue, simple headaches, lack of concentration and dizziness you feel at the end of a workday can result simply from not drinking enough water," explains Liz Applegate, Ph.D., nutritional science lecturer at the University of California, Davis, and nutrition columnist for *Runner's World* magazine.[27] These are symptoms that too many of us have come to expect—and worse, to *accept*. Don't! In addition, the best way to rid the body of excess retained water is to drink *more* water, says dietitian Kathy Stone, R.D., author of *Snack Attack*. "When an individual senses he is retaining fluid, then cuts back on his water intake to compensate, the body just responds by retaining more fluid."[28]

Begin the day with a glass of cold, fresh water. "When you open your eyes in the morning, your body is already facing a water deficit," warns Dr. Applegate.[29] So make it an enjoyable habit to drink 8 to 16 ounces of cold, fresh water as soon as you arise in the morning, plus some extra water or juice with breakfast. This, and every glass of water you drink, should be as pure as you can get (see chapter 16 for details).

Make it convenient to drink ice water wherever you are. Head off the symptoms of mild dehydration by making it a point to sip a tall 16-ounce glass of water every hour or two throughout the day on each of your work breaks. Drink even more frequently if the air is noticeably hot or dry or when you're engaged in active physical work. By keeping the water *ice cold*, you will burn more calories, since your metabolism will increase to warm the water to body temperature. Admittedly this provides a relatively minor calorie-burning benefit, but drinking more water—warm, cool *or* cold—is a simple and healthful habit that helps reduce cravings, and if you keep the water ice cold, you benefit from an added metabolic boost every day. By the way, in case you're thinking this calorie-burning principle may also apply to frozen desserts (ice cream, frozen yogurt and so on), there's a catch: Eating ice-cold foods dulls your sense of taste[30]—and you often end up overeating the frozen treat. So stick with ice water as a calorie-burning aid.

Notice—and respond—to the symptoms of fluid loss. Drink some extra water whenever you notice dryness of the eyes, nasal passages or mouth. These can be vital signs that you're starting to become dehydrated. Develop new water-drinking habits by ensuring that water is readily accessible in your work area—and monitor how much you consume. Keep a glass or cup of water next to you during work hours and at home, and sip extra water during exercise. Consider going to a local department store, sporting goods store or fitness center and purchasing an insulated 16- or 32-ounce plastic container with a straw. This makes it easy to keep the water ice cold and to sip it through the straw instead of gulping it down every hour or two. You can also keep track of your daily water-drinking habits by putting eight rubber bands on your 16-ounce container or four on a 32-ounce container and then removing a rubber band each time you refill the container. For some extra taste, try adding a slice of lemon, lime or orange or a sprig of mint to your water. And make it a point to drink most of your day's water before 5:00 P.M., so you aren't as likely to have to get up in the middle of the night to urinate.

Limit your intake of caffeinated beverages and alcohol. Caffeine-containing beverages—such as coffee, tea and some sodas—and alcoholic drinks act as diuretics, increasing urine production and prompting loss of fluids. In addition, according to a recent study published in the *New England Journal of Medicine*, even moderate amounts of caffeine consumed on the job during the week can leave you feeling out of sorts on weekends if you suddenly withdraw from the caffeine on Saturday and Sunday.[31]

Claims that caffeine revs up your metabolism are overstated. "Caffeine stimulates in a negative way," says Judith Rodin, Ph.D., former professor of psychology and psychiatry at Yale University, "because it provokes insulin release and may in fact enhance the storage of what is eaten as fat. . . . Try to stay away from too many caffeinated beverages. Countless women drink caffeinated diet sodas to help them through their days of [diet] fasting or eating very little. This practice may lead them to feel even more hungry, and it prepares their bodies for maximally storing [as body fat] whatever food they eat."[32]

Eat snacks and meals high in complex carbohydrates. To aid in your body's absorption and handling of water, be certain to eat plenty of complex carbohydrates as part of each meal and snack. "The only way to avoid extreme water loss is to eat enough complex carbohydrates to produce sufficient glucose for your brain and red blood cells," says C. Wayne Callaway, M.D., former director of the Nutrition and Lipid Clinic at the Mayo Clinic in Rochester, Minnesota. "When your liver is forced to make sugar from stored glycogen or protein, water loss is inevitable."[33]

If you're hungry between a snack and a meal, drink a glass of cold water. Many of us mistakenly perceive our thirst drive as hunger and eat additional snacks when we're really thirsty, not hungry. A good way to distinguish the two is to drink a glass of ice-cold water when you feel hungry and then wait for a few minutes. If you're still hungry, then go ahead and eat an appropriate light snack.

Limit Alcohol Consumption—"Beer Bellies" Are Real!

On the subject of fluids and weight loss, here's a recent discovery worth noting: It seems there really *is* such a thing as a "beer belly." Researchers at Stanford University School of Medicine and the University of California, San Diego, report an apparent link between drinking alcohol and having a protruding belly. In a study of men and women, those who had more than two alcoholic drinks a day had the largest hip-to-waist ratio, the measurement of a potbelly.[34] In fact, the drinkers had nearly twice as many large ratios as nondrinkers had.

A recent Swiss study, reported in the *New England Journal of Medicine,* indicated that drinking alcoholic beverages causes the body to burn fewer *fat* calories—which, in turn, favors fat storage and weight gain, particularly in the abdomen, and is a risk factor for obesity.[35] Compounding the problem is the fact that even for moderate drinkers, when alcohol is consumed, meals tend to be larger and last longer, say Georgia State University researchers.[36] Because alcohol is absorbed through the stomach wall without emptying into the intestine, it may not trigger intestinal satiety ("full") signals, say the scientists, so you eat more. When you have alcohol at a meal, you'll consume an average of 350 calories more than if you don't. The Swiss researchers recommend that anyone wishing to reduce weight without totally giving up alcohol should decrease dietary fat to help offset the fat-storing stimulus of the alcohol.

Note: Few of us realize that there's also a link between uncontrolled—or mismanaged—*stress* and abdominal fat (see chapter 12 for details).

Resources

Eat More, Weigh Less by Dean Ornish, M.D. (HarperCollins, 1993). A well-rounded collection of healthful, low-fat recipes.

The Fat Attack Plan by Annette B. Natow, R.D., Ph.D., and Jo-Ann Heslin, R.D. (Pocket Books, 1990). A practical guide to reducing fat in the diet—at breakfast and every other meal.

The LEARN Program for Weight Control by Kelly D. Brownell, Ph. D. (The LEARN Education Center, 1555 W. Mockingbird Lane, Suite 203, Dallas, TX 75235; 800-736-7323). One of the best-balanced guidebooks on lifelong weight control.

PERSONAL POWER NOTES
A Quick-List of This Chapter's Power-Action Options

Enjoy a 5-minute Power Snack at midmorning and midaftenoon.

Sip ice water throughout the day to burn calories and aid weight control.
- *Begin the day with a glass of cold, fresh water.*
- *Make it convenient to drink ice water wherever you are.*
- *Notice—and respond—to symptoms of fluid loss.*
- *Limit your intake of caffeinated beverages and alcohol.*
- *Eat snacks and meals high in complex carbohydrates.*
- *If you're hungry between a snack and a meal, drink a glass of cold water.*

Limit alcohol consumption—"beer bellies" are real!

PERSONAL NOTES

ENJOY HIGH-TASTE, LOW-FAT MEALS

Increase Your Digestive Power, Savor the Tastes You Love and Prevent High-Fat Snack Attacks

With *The Power of 5* there are *no* "forbidden" foods . . .

The pleasures of eating are vanishing, or so it may seem—especially if you want to lose weight. Like never before, we're scrutinizing food labels and dissecting menus, counting grams of fat and milligrams of cholesterol and patting ourselves on the back for eating a healthier diet—yet all the while we're still craving the fattening, "forbidden" foods that, over the years, we've come to love.

According to a recent Gallup Survey commissioned by the American Dietetic Association, nearly 50 percent of Americans believe that the foods they like and enjoy are not good for them, and 36 percent feel guilty about eating the foods they *do* enjoy.[1] Unfortunately, while the experts have been busy monitoring fat and fiber, they've forgotten about *taste*—ignoring the findings that bland or monotonous meals may be poorly digested, may drive up yearnings for high-fat foods and may even *slow down* your metabolism so you burn less dietary fat (and store more of it as body fat).

The message in this chapter is straightforward: Stop counting calories. Stop labeling foods as "bad" or "forbidden" (since this will make you crave them even more). Emphasize the *tastes* you love and bring back a genuine *pleasure in eating*. In fact, for most of us the only number that really matters for permanent weight loss is *grams of fat*—how much fat you eat throughout the day. In the preceding chapter we discussed why this makes so much sense and how eating a typical high-fat diet promotes unhealthy weight gain.

The Power of 5 program is designed to help reduce fat intake *without* feelings of deprivation or boredom. There is good evidence, for example, that regular physical activity and exercise help blunt your cravings for high-fat foods.[2] And research indicates that within a few months of eating lower-fat foods you may actually lose your taste for fat.[3] For example, over half the women in one recent major study reported that they soon disliked the taste of fat, and nearly two-thirds said that within a few months on a low-fat menu, they soon felt physically uncomfortable after eating high-fat foods.[4]

However, we certainly realize that ending the habit of labeling foods either "good" or "bad" isn't easy. "It's promoted by the food industry, the diet business and our own psyches," says Judith Rodin, Ph.D., former professor of psychology and psychiatry at Yale University. "Often we believe that *healthful* and *delicious* are mutually exclusive. . . . Although there certainly are foods that are 'nutritional nightmares,' high in fat and salt or high in fat and refined sugar, there are many healthful foods that taste delicious. Unfortunately, however, . . . we have [been led] to believe that eating healthful foods is a burden. According to most studies, adults now express the same confusion and lack of control over their weight and food choices as adolescents do."[5]

First and foremost, our nutritional goal with *The Power of 5* is to put *great taste* back in eating—without all the fat and with none of the guilt. In addition, it's time to make peace with the "fattening" foods you have tried so hard to avoid. If you don't, there's no avoiding the fact that your food bans can lead to compulsive overeating binges, the *real* source of dieting heartache and weight gain. A favorite food—even a high-fat food—eaten occasionally is successful management, *not* a loss of control.

POWER ACTION: FIRST OPTION
Plan Your Meals and Snacks for More Taste and Less Fat

"There's the idea that you either lead a sensual, rich life and die young, or you avoid life and eat boring food," says heart specialist Dean Ornish, M.D., assistant clinical professor at the University of California, San Francisco, School of Medicine and president and director of the

Preventive Medicine Research Institute, whose program of exercise, stress reduction and a very-low-fat diet has been shown to reverse heart disease. "That isn't the choice at all. You can be sensually satisfied without abusing yourself."[6] "Boring is bad," adds Dr. Rodin. "Taste is a good cue for regulating food intake, so don't eat foods that don't taste good enough."[7]

POWER KNOWLEDGE: ACTIVE NUTRITION

MYTH #1: Overweight is caused by over*eating*.

POWER KNOWLEDGE: Not usually. "The high-fat American diet . . . [and/or] a diet high in refined sugar can cause obesity *without* overeating,"[20] says Wayne C. Miller, Ph.D., director of the Weight Loss Clinic at Indiana University, who, along with his colleagues, has done extensive research on the subject.[21] Other studies have reached similar conclusions.[22] There is growing evidence that the longer you eat a high-fat diet, the more your body actually begins to shift its metabolism further toward storing fat instead of *burning* it for energy.[23] This undesirable transformation involves an enzyme called lipoprotein lipase (LPL), whose job it is to break down fat molecules into components (fatty acids) small enough to get through the walls of your body's fat cells. The more fat you eat, the more activated this fat-storing enzyme becomes.

Compounding the lower calorie-burning effect of eating high-fat foods is the fact that they tend to make you feel driven to eat more high-fat foods in the hours that follow,[24] and the body fat you gain seems to be preferentially deposited around your waist and stomach areas.[25] In addition, high-fat foods don't switch off the "eat" message as effectively as foods that are high in complex carbohydrates, perhaps because dietary fat cannot be converted into glycogen (stored carbohydrate), and glycogen—especially that stored in the liver—seems to help turn off feelings of hunger.[26] One of the first benefits of a lower-fat diet may be abdominal fat loss. In a recent study of 124 women who each lost 10 to 15 pounds by cutting dietary fat, 64 percent lost the most fat from their abdomen.[27]

The challenge is to eat foods high in *taste* but low in *fat*. "Ninety-seven percent of all fat calories are converted to body fat," explains Robert E. T. Stark, M.D., author of *Controlling Fat for Life* and past president of the American Society of Bariatric Physicians, a group of doctors who specialize in treating overweight people.[8] By eliminating excess fat from your diet and increasing your intake of fiber-rich com-

MYTH #2: To get thinner and stay that way, you've got to totally avoid high-fat "forbidden" foods you love.

POWER KNOWLEDGE: Your biology won't let you. Depriving yourself of pleasure from food isn't fun, and it doesn't work. When you try to force yourself to stop eating "forbidden" or "bad" foods you love, eventually your cravings for them become so powerful and unbearable that your resistance breaks down, and chances are, you'll binge, stuffing yourself with the not-allowed foods. In *The Power of 5* you break out of this trap by taking 5 minutes of "Taste Time" to savor your meals and then add 5 minutes of walking or some other pleasurable activity after eating (see chapter 11). Together, these quick strategies enable you to go ahead and healthfully *enjoy* small portions of your favorite higher-fat foods as well as making it easier to gradually substitute lower-fat, high-taste alternatives.

MYTH #3: "Starches" are the most fattening carbohydrates.

POWER KNOWLEDGE: Complex, fiber-rich carbohydrates have been shown to assist in reducing body fat.[28] However, eating large amounts of refined carbohydrates—sweeteners such as sugar, honey and syrup—is linked to obesity,[29] and even drinking large quantities of beverages high in refined carbohydrates can cause obesity.[30] And the most potent fat-promoting foods of all seem to be those that are high in both fat and sugar[31]—because sugar can substantially boost LPL activity. Sugar, by calling up insulin in your bloodstream, makes fat cells hypersensitive for storage and *encourages calories to be stored as fat rather than burned for energy.* This seems to make fat cells "open up"—and the LPL drives the circulating fat molecules right in.[32]

plex carbohydrates, you help halt the increase in body fat.

The single most important factor in enjoying lower-fat meals and snacks is *taste*. To an astonishing extent, "the brain is more interested in what's happening on the tongue than in the body," explains Harvey Weingarten, Ph.D., chairman of the psychology department at McMaster University in Hamilton, Ontario.[9] Giving up your favorite foods and switching to a very healthy but very boring diet won't work, says Kelly D. Brownell, Ph.D., a leading researcher on obesity who is professor of psychology at Yale University and co-director of the university's Eating and Weight Disorders Clinic.[10] If you want to eat healthy for a lifetime, you either have to find low-fat foods that taste great or learn to prepare your own.

A healthy, high-pleasure meal plan includes a variety of different fresh *fruits and vegetables*, *whole grains* (eaten as breads, pasta or side dishes and in soups or casseroles), a variety of *legumes* (beans, peas and lentils), low-fat or nonfat *dairy products*, limited amounts of *nuts*, *seeds*, *eggs*, *fish*, *lean poultry* and little if any *beef* or *pork*.

Beyond your choice of *what* to eat, one of the most important nutritional decisions you make is *how* you eat—especially at main meals. When you take the first 5 minutes to slow down your fork—and use this brief time to feel thankful for the meal and to savor the special tastes and textures of what you're eating—you'll feel more satisfied and will be less likely to overeat higher-fat foods. Here are some ideas on how to get the most out of the healthy habit of "Taste Time" at every meal.

Emphasize the food tastes you love. Take out a piece of paper and make some notes: What are your *favorite* main courses, side dishes, fresh vegetables, fruits, soups, breads and pasta? Pinpoint the *tastes* you love and start searching out—or creating—recipes that accentuate those tastes while gradually reducing fat, refined sugar and cholesterol. There's little point in trying to force yourself to eat "healthy meals" if they make you gag. Turn this taste challenge into a family affair. Get everyone involved. If the focus is first on savory flavors and second on lowering the fat, it's easier to shift into healthier, lifelong low-fat eating habits.

The mere sight, smell and taste of low-fat food you love may help increase your metabolism and stimulate your body to burn more calories than when eating bland, boring food.[11] You may even get a calorie-burning benefit from liberally sprinkling your meals with your favorite fat-free seasonings and spices. For example, meals laced with hot chili pepper and mustard have been shown to help boost the body's metabolic rate and actually *burn more calories*. In one study, the subjects ate identical 766-calorie meals. Some of the meals contained 3 grams of chili and 3 grams of mustard sauce, while the other meals were spiceless. After the meal, the subjects' metabolic rate was tracked for 3 hours. The spicy meals boosted metabolism by an *average of 25 percent*.[12] (Apparently this isn't true for all spices, however—ginger, for example, does not seem to influence metabolic rate.)

Researchers in Quebec performed repeated studies, first on rats and then on people, to compare nutritionally identical meals—one tasty and one bland—and found that the smell and taste of flavorful food seemed to stimulate the thermic effect of food—the amount of calories burned digesting, absorbing and utilizing it.[13]

Enjoy every bite—with few distractions. According to researchers, when compared to lean persons, those who are overweight are more likely to eat fast, to eat secretly, to nibble at food without being aware of it and to continue eating when full.[14] When you don't get fully involved with the *conscious pleasures of eating*—savoring, smelling, admiring and tasting each bite of food—there's a tendency to mindlessly pack in bite after bite for 20 minutes or so until the first "I'm full" signal can be given off by the brain. Therefore, except for enjoying a pleasant conversation at mealtimes, *when you eat, do nothing else but eat*. In most cases, that means no eating while watching television, driving the car, reading a newspaper or magazine, writing a letter or talking on the telephone.

Second, most of the time it makes sense to *eat only in one or two places at home*—at the kitchen table or dining room table, for example. When you eat anywhere and everywhere—in bed, at your desk, in front of the television or while you read in your easy chair—it's too easy to eat unconsciously and not really enjoy a single bite. It's fine to eat one of your favorite low-fat snacks while watching a movie or special television program, but clearly choose, in advance, the food and the quantity—and take that specific serving, not the whole bag or container, to your seat.

Third, take a few seconds before eating to *look at your food and smell it*. This starts the thermogenic calorie-burning effect even before you eat the first bite,[15] and that makes you feel that you're capturing more of the full pleasure of eating. Fourth, *chew thoroughly*, since the way you eat plays a role in how much pleasure you derive from each low-fat calorie.

And fifth, *slow down your fork, especially during the first 5 minutes of eating*. A recent study by Theresa Spiegel, Ph.D., and her colleagues at the University of Pennsylvania in Philadelphia reported that those eaters who increased the length of their meal—by an average of about 4 minutes—lost more body fat than those who ate more quickly.[16] In addition, those who paused for 15 minutes before eating second helpings felt fuller and more satisfied—without needing to eat any more. There is also evidence that slow, soothing music during meals may make you less likely to wolf down your food or to reach for unconscious second helpings. In contrast, lively, fast-tempoed music may make you eat *more*. Volume also matters, say scientists at northern Ireland's University of Ulster. The higher the volume, the more food consumed.[17] Other studies also report that fast or loud music or loud noise increases the rate of eating, the amount eaten and/or preference for refined sugar (sucrose).[18]

Note: If necessary, *eat before you eat*. What we mean is that if you find yourself going from feeling starved to feeling stuffed without experiencing that "just right," satisfied feeling in between, consider preceding your meals with some ice water and then eating an extra-small, low-fat, high-fiber appetizer (such as some fruit, vegetables, whole-grain crackers or rye crisps or ½ cup of skim milk or nonfat yogurt).[19]

POWER ACTION: MORE OPTIONS
Know Your Target Fat-Gram Budget—And Other "New Basics" of Weight-Control Nutrition

Overall, your most important nutritional decision is how to control the amount of dietary fat you consume. Unfortunately, the average American diet still includes about 40 percent of its total calories from fat—nearly twice the amount recommended by many experts. In general, a reasonable dietary goal for adults is an average of between 20 and 25 percent of total daily calories from fat, including about one-third as polyunsaturates, one-third or less as saturates and the balance as monounsaturates.[33] (More than 90 percent of dietary fat is composed of complex molecules consisting of three fatty acids—saturated, monounsaturated and polyunsaturated. Animal fats usually contain a high percentage of saturated fatty acids, while most vegetable fats—which include many vegetables, grains, legumes, nuts and seeds—contain mainly monounsaturated or polyunsaturated fatty acids.)

Limit dietary fat intake—with a Target Fat-Gram Budget divided evenly throughout the day. To calculate 25 percent of total daily calories in grams of fat per day, multiply your total daily calorie intake

---

TARGET FAT-GRAM BUDGET:
AVERAGE DAILY TOTAL GRAMS OF DIETARY FAT

Examples (figures are given as estimates only):
Moderately active adult woman: Maximum of 40 to 60 grams of fat.
Moderately active adult man: Maximum of 50 to 70 grams of fat.

Using the example of 50 grams of fat per day:
Breakfast: Maximum 10 grams of fat.
Midmorning snack: Maximum 3 grams of fat.
Lunch: Maximum 10 grams of fat.
Midafternoon snack: Maximum 4 grams of fat.
Supper: Maximum 20 grams of fat.
Light evening snack: Maximum 3 grams of fat.

---

by 0.25 and divide the result by 9. Examples: At 1,800 calories per day for a typical moderately active woman (who is neither pregnant nor breastfeeding an infant), total fat shouldn't exceed *50 grams*, and at 2,200 calories, fat should top out at *60 grams*; for a typical active man eating 2,500 calories, the fat limit is *70 grams*.[34] At 20 percent of calories from fat, a woman eating 1,800 calories shouldn't exceed *40 grams* of fat, and at 2,200 calories, her fat should top out at *49 grams*; for a man eating 2,500 calories, the fat limit is *56 grams*. Some researchers even suggest that merely by switching from a diet with 40 percent of total calories from fat to a diet with only 20 to 25 percent of its total calories from fat (a sensible level for the ***The Power of 5*** program), an average, active person may lose body fat *even without cutting back on overall calories.*[35]

Take a moment to make an estimate of your own Target Fat-Gram Budget and then divide this evenly throughout the day, such as one-fifth at breakfast, one-fifth at lunch, two-fifths at supper (if you eat the larger meal at midday, you can switch the fat allotment for lunch and supper) and the final one-fifth divided among midmorning, midafternoon and evening snacks.

All across America, it's becoming easier to count the grams of fat in each meal. Many recipe books and restaurant menus list fat grams per serving, and pocket-size fat-gram counters (see Resources) list totals for thousands of popular foods. With the Target Fat-Gram Budget, your allocation of fat intake helps you avoid the widespread dieter's habit of starving in the morning and then, feeling ravenously hungry later in the day, ending up overeating high-fat foods far into the evening—precisely at the time when your activity level is lowest and when overeating may add the most body fat.[36] In contrast, when you eat the same total daily number of fat grams but consume them in smaller amounts throughout the day (see chapter 9), you are healthier, have more effective digestion and metabolism and will not gain as much body fat. Remember our discussions about how complex carbohydrates and proteins burn much "hotter" than fats and aren't stored as easily in the body.

Note: In chapters 11 and 12, we'll explain how regular fitness activities may be instrumental in controlling dietary fat intake by helping to neutralize your natural cravings for high-fat foods.[37]

Use "food swap" ideas to increase the taste and lose much of the fat. One of the simplest ways to save grams of fat is by steadily reducing the quantity of high-fat foods you eat and simultaneously increasing your portions of lower-fat or nonfat alternatives that still provide vital taste satisfaction. Here are some ideas for reducing your intake of dietary fat.

• Read labels and use recipes that list the grams of fat in each serving.

• Use low-fat or fat-free salad dressings and mayonnaise. Salad dressing is the number-one source of fat in the diets of American women aged 19 through 50, accounting for almost one-third of their fat intake, according to the National Cancer Institute and the U.S. Department of Agriculture (USDA) Human Nutrition Information Service.

• Poach, bake or steam vegetables, fish and other foods instead of frying them.

• Cook or lightly sauté with vegetable broths and a very small amount of oil, and help keep the fat content low by using nonstick sprays and pans.

• Accentuate recipe tastes—and help reduce the need for fat as flavoring—by seasoning foods with pepper, parsley, basil, oregano, jalapeños, garlic, onions, shallots, curry, ginger, horseradish, tarragon and other fresh spices and herbs.

• Drink skim milk or 1 percent low-fat milk instead of whole milk, and choose nonfat yogurt, cream cheese, cottage cheese and sour cream and reduced-fat or nonfat cheeses.

• Eat less red meat and pork. Substitute beans, peas, lentils, pasta, rice, potatoes, vegetables and low-fat cottage cheese or small servings of fish (all finfish, canned salmon, water-packed tuna and shellfish), turkey (skinless breast, drumstick or thigh, or ground without the skin) or chicken breast without the skin. Enjoy tasty international recipes—Italian, Japanese, Mexican, Chinese, Greek and Middle Eastern, for example—that combine vegetables or fruit with whole grains, beans and little or no meat. On occasion, include small amounts of tofu, nuts, almond butter or peanut butter.

• Choose canned tuna packed in spring water instead of oil.

• Eat more whole grains—in breads, crackers, rolls, bagels, tortillas, brown rice, bulgur, pasta and breakfast cereals. On occasion, eat whole-grain, low-fat muffins, waffles, pancakes or granola cereals.

• On top of bread, rolls, bagels or crackers, add all-fruit preserves, nonfat fruit yogurt, apple butter or nonfat cream cheese instead of margarine, butter or traditional high-fat cream cheese.

• Increase your intake of fresh fruits and vegetables, potatoes and unsweetened applesauce. On occasion, eat avocados, dried fruit, canned fruit (in its own juice instead of syrup), fruit juice or canned vegetables.

• For dessert, choose fresh fruit or a small serving of nonfat frozen yogurt or low-fat or nonfat baked goods instead of higher-fat treats.

Eat more health-building foods—and weigh less. According to William J. Evans, Ph.D., chief of the Human Physiology Laboratory at the USDA Human Nutrition Research Center on Aging at Tufts University in Boston, and Irwin H. Rosenberg, M.D., a healthful diet for adults of all ages includes up to 60 percent of total daily calories from fiber-rich complex carbohydrates.[38] Other authorities agree.[39] Yet carbohydrates are still one of the most misunderstood nutrients. There are many reasons for this, including the widespread fear that "starchy" foods are responsible for obesity. But *exactly the opposite is true*: To lose excess body fat, the most important foods to eat are moderate amounts of protein and plenty of complex carbohydrates (which are high in starches and fiber). For the latter, the best choices are vegetables, fruits, whole grains and legumes—all of which are digested slowly and efficiently, providing a steady source of energy without the biochemical roller-coaster effect of concentrated sugars,[40] and are also excellent sources of vitamins, minerals and other protective nutrients.[41] By including more of these nutrient powerhouses in your meals and snacks you'll automatically be reducing your intake of fat and cholesterol (which come primarily from animal foods such as meat and dairy products), and you'll feel fuller and more satisfied.

Guide your "sweet tooth"—and don't use artificial sweeteners as a crutch. Experiments indicate that the taste of sweet can increase general appetite, sometimes to the point of obesity, and that this is true for artificial sweeteners as well as for caloric sweeteners (such as sucrose and fructose).[42] This may be due in part to the fact that the liver increases hunger by lowering blood sugar and increasing storage of ingested fuels as fat.[43] "Studies conducted on the effects of artificial sweeteners have shown no evidence that they contribute to an overall reduction in calories or to weight loss," says C. Wayne Callaway, M.D., former director of the Nutrition and Lipid Clinic at the Mayo Clinic in Rochester, Minnesota. "It appears that the calories simply get replaced by other foods. It has also been demonstrated that sweets (even artificial ones) stimulate an appetite for fats in some people."[44]

Refined white sugar—sucrose—tops the list of "empty calories," along with its counterparts corn syrup, brown sugar, dextrose, fructose, maltose and cane syrup. It makes sense to moderate your consumption of sweeteners and of highly sweetened foods—*especially* when they're eaten with higher-fat foods, because, as explained in the "Power Knowledge" section of this chapter, the sugar/fat combo *increases* the chances of gaining more body fat.[45] In place of highly sweetened foods, and instead of loading up on artificial sweeteners, choose more of your favorite snacks and meals that include whole grains, fresh fruits, vegetables and legumes.

Take advantage of the fact that what warms you up may help slim you down! Do a little personal taste-testing to see if you can take advantage of the metabolic boost that some spices seem to create. Increase your affection for "hotter" meals by gradually stepping up your use of such seasonings as chili peppers and mustard—and start including a greater variety of other tasty spices and natural flavorings in your meals and snacks.

When Dining Out, Choose Great-Tasting, Low-Fat Foods

Let's face it, your weight control is not only in your own hands but also in the pots, pans and buffets controlled by chefs in America's 620,000 restaurants.[46] Chances are that your tight schedule often makes it necessary for you to eat meals and snacks away from home. But there's no reason that dining out has to be a dietary disaster. While many menu items are still loaded with fat and cholesterol, making healthy choices is becoming easier. Restaurants are adding more fresh salads, seafood, baked potatoes, grain/legume casseroles and side dishes, whole-grain breads and lower-fat pasta recipes to their menus. Nonetheless, you still need to watch out for hidden fats, especially in prepared cookies, muffins, pie crusts, cream sauces and soups and cheeses.

High-quality, low-fat dining begins with your selection of restaurant. Skip all-you-can-eat buffets and smorgasbords. Order á la carte, since full-course bargain dinners encourage overeating and tend to be too high in fat and protein. If possible, look over the menu in advance or call ahead to ask about featured recipes and daily specials.

Don't be shy about making requests over the phone or in person to the waiter, waitress or chef—many restaurants will eliminate salt, cook with half the amount of fat (or no added fat at all) and cut back on cheese, eggs and whole-milk dairy products. Regional offices of the American Heart Association (7300 Greenville Ave., Dallas, TX 75231) print lists of local restaurants that serve low-fat meals. Write for details. Choose entrées that are steamed, poached, broiled, roasted, baked or cooked in their own juices. Pass up anything fried or sautéed. Good restaurants will broil seafood or poultry dry (without fat) and unsalted and have or will create a special low-fat sauce to your liking. Salads and salad bars can be good choices if the vegetables are actually *fresh*, but steer clear of prepared salads with a cream or heavy oil base, since they are usually high in fat. Instead, choose a variety of fresh raw vegetables or fruits, legumes and whole-grain bread. As a salad dressing, use a very small amount of olive oil with vinegar or lemon added.

The best restaurant soups are vegetable-based, since cream- and meat-based soups are usually high in fat. Pasta can be a good choice if served with tomato, wine or other low-fat sauces. Whole-grain breads, rolls, bagels and low-fat muffins are delicious sources of fiber and complex carbohydrates, but skip the nut spreads, mayonnaise, butter and margarine. Hot cereals such as oatmeal and multigrain varieties and whole-grain dry cereals can be a good breakfast choice when served with skim milk and fruit. And when you choose to have dessert, make the portion small. A slice of home-baked pie or cake is all right as a once-a-month option, but on a more frequent basis fresh fruit tops the list, followed by fruit-based frozen sorbet, nonfat frozen yogurt and low-fat or nonfat puddings.

If you eat out often, you run the risk of consuming excessive fat and protein. Watch quantities—many eateries serve extra-large portions of food. If you're dining with other people, consider having a fresh salad, vegetable/grain/legume side dish and a piece of whole-grain bread and then splitting a main dish with another person.

Many ethnic restaurants offer exquisite-tasting cuisine featuring whole grains, legumes, vegetables and fruit and recipes supplemented with fish or poultry. Here are several insights about ethnic cuisine.

Italian. Delicious, low-fat foods with a pleasing array of tastes make Italian restaurants a good choice for dining away from home. Pasta with meatless marinara (tomato-based), vegetable, red clam or wine sauce is first-rate. Shrimp al vino blanco (sautéed in white wine) gets high marks, too, for its low fat content. Pollo cacciatore (boneless chicken breast served in a tomato-and-mushroom sauce) is another option. The list also includes nonmeat (vegetable) lasagna and cioppino— fisherman's stew with a variety of seafood and vegetables in a tomato-based stock (make certain it's low in fat). If you enjoy pizza, order it vegetarian (go very light on the olives) with extra vegetables and half or one-third the normal amount of cheese. Onions, green peppers and mushrooms are standard fare, but try fresh spinach, garlic, tomatoes, artichoke hearts, beans, seafood, skinless turkey or chicken breast and other ingredients for an inviting change of pace.

Mexican. When chosen with care, Mexican food is inexpensive, delicious, high in complex carbohydrates and low in fat. Beans, rice, unfried corn tortillas, fish and salads are common staples. Vegetable/bean burritos, fresh fish marinated in lime sauce and beans with rice are low-fat specialties. A good practice when selecting a new Mexican-style restaurant is to call ahead and ask if the chef uses lard, coconut oil or other oils in the refried beans. Many establishments have switched to small amounts of soybean oil or, ideally, no added fat at all. Skip the sour cream, guacamole, meat and egg dishes and fried foods, and request no more than half the usual amount of cheese.

French. Traditional French restaurants offer rich, delicious foods that are high in fat, calories and cholesterol. Fortunately, more and more French chefs are preparing nouvelle cuisine, including a special variety called *cuisine minceur* (cuisine of slimness). Cuisine minceur uses culinary techniques such as steaming or poaching seafood or poultry in vegetable juices and wine and serving side dishes of fresh vegetables, potatoes and grains. For dessert, skip the usual fare and request fresh fruit or fruit (usually peaches or pears) poached in a light wine sauce, which gives a delightful taste with few calories.

Indian. The recipes used in Indian restaurants often include vegetables, legumes, yogurt and lots of spices. Avoid the dishes soaked in coconut oil or ghee (clarified butter). One popular recipe is *murg jalfraize*—chicken or legumes flavored with fresh spices and sautéed (request no butter or oil) with onions, tomatoes and bell peppers.

Chinese. Some menu items at Chinese restaurants are good choices because of the emphasis on rice and vegetables, with only small amounts of seafood or poultry. Bypass the fried appetizer dishes such as egg rolls and spring rolls. And don't choose duck—3½ ounces of Peking duck has 30 grams of fat. Stir-fried dishes like moo goo gai pan—a combination of mushrooms, bamboo shoots, water chestnuts and chicken, seafood or tofu served over rice—generally get good ratings. At Chinese restaurants, stir-fried dishes tend to be cooked quickly in a lightly oiled, very hot wok, and the vegetables retain more vitamins than those cooked the traditional American way. The oil is usually peanut oil, which is high in monounsaturates.

Japanese. Generally low in fat, Japanese cuisine is based on protein-rich soybean products (such as tofu and tempeh), seafood, vegetables, noodles and rice. The seaweed used in Japanese soups and stews is high in minerals. One top entrée choice is *yosenabe*, a vegetable dish with seafood.

American. Traditional American restaurants have contributed some healthful dishes to the array of dining options, including New England and West Coast seafoods, fresh salad bars, Cajun gumbos and a variety of new "California cuisine" specialties.

Vegetarian. Although vegetarian restaurants serve nonmeat and even nondairy meals, many dishes tend to be high in fat. Limit your consumption of cheeses and avoid items that are heavy with oil, butter or cream. Choose fresh whole-grain breads, cooked grain/legume casseroles and side dishes and rice or pasta with low-fat sauces and a variety of vegetables.

Give Up Guilt—And Allow Yourself
Small Servings of "Forbidden" Foods

As we advised at the outset of this chapter, it's essential to stop labeling foods as "bad" or "illegal"—because there's strong evidence that "what you resist persists." That is, your unwanted cravings cannot be suppressed for long and, sooner or later, they'll loom up more powerful than ever.[47] Besides, more important than the type of food you eat is the quantity and frequency. You can have some of anything you want; just manage the amounts. And once you stop labeling high-fat foods "forbidden," chances are you'll start talking about them less, and fantasizing about them less, and they'll cease to be a serious nutritional problem—especially if you allow yourself a small serving every once in a while and follow the other guidelines in *The Power of 5*.

Choose several high-taste, low-fat cookbooks (see Resources) for your kitchen library. In many cases, you may even find that new low-fat or nonfat substitutes can taste *more* delicious than your favorite old, full-fat recipes.

Maintain a Daily Food Record

An awareness of what and when you eat may seem like a trivial matter. However, chances are you are not aware of much of what you consume—especially from 5:00 P.M. on into the evening. Research by Albert F. Smith, Ph.D., a cognitive psychologist who studies memory at the State University of New York at Binghamton, says everyone has trouble remembering how much and what they've eaten.[48] "The first, and perhaps most important, lifestyle behavior is to keep records," says Dr. Kelly Brownell, co-director of the Eating and Weight Disorders Clinic at Yale University.[49] A recent study in the *Journal of the American Dietetic Association* reveals that impressive body fat losses are associated with record-keeping—on average, those who kept the most accurate food records lost the most weight.[50]

Resources

Cooking Light Magazine (P.O. Box 830549, Birmingham, AL 35282; 800-336- 0125). Features health-conscious, lower-fat recipes.

Dean and Deluca (560 Broadway, New York, NY 10012; 800-221-7714; 212-431-1691). A great mail-order source for high-taste foods and ingredients from around the world.

Eating Well Magazine (P.O. Box 52919, Boulder, CO 80322; 303-447-9330). Emphasizes the connection between food and health.

The Fat Counter by Annette B. Natow, R.D., Ph.D., and Jo-Ann Heslin, R.D. (Pocket Books, 1989). Fat and calorie values for over 10,000 foods.

The Fat Tooth Fat-Gram Counter by Joseph C. Piscatella (Workman, 1993). An excellent pocket-size fat-gram counter. A version for restaurants and fast-food eating is also available.

G. B. Ratto, International Grocers (821 Washington St., Oakland, CA 94607; 800-325-3483; 800-228-3515). A wonderful mail-order source for specialty foods for meatless meals and snacks.

Gourmet Light 2nd ed., by Greer Underwood (Globe Pequot, 1993). Health-conscious cooking concepts.

Great Good Food by Julee Russo (Crown, 1993). Lots of ideas for lower-fat meals.

High-Flavor, Low-Fat Cooking by Steven Raichlen (Camden House, 1992). An innovative cookbook with foods that are visually appealing and delicious.

In the Kitchen with Rosie by Rosie Daley (Knopf, 1994). A small book filled with recipes for low-fat, low-sugar, low-salt eating.

Mediterranean Light (Bantam, 1989) and *Entertaining Light* (Bantam, 1991) by Martha Rose Shulman. These cookbooks are endorsed by Dean Ornish, M.D., president and director of the Preventive Medicine Research Institute.

The 99% Fat-Free Cookbook by Barry Bluestein and Kevin Morrissey (Doubleday, 1994). *Very* low-fat recipes.

100% Pleasure by Nancy Baggett and Ruth Glick (Rodale Press, 1994). A well-designed high-taste, low-fat recipe book.

Recipe Rescue Cookbook by *Eating Well Magazine*, edited by Patricia Jamieson and Cheryl Dorschner (Camden House, 1993). An excellent guidebook to reviving old favorite recipes in new, lower-fat form.

Southwest Gourmet Gallery (Sinagua Plaza, Suite D, 320 N. Highway 89A, Sedona, AZ 86336; 800-888-3484; 602-282-2682). Far and away our favorite mail-order source for fresh, flavor-packed salsas, sauces, marinades and spices.

The T-Factor Fat-Gram Counter by Jamie Pope-Cordle and Martin Katahn (Norton, 1994). This inexpensive pocket-size guide lists fat-gram counts for more than 2,000 foods and includes a three-week recording diary.

The Wellness Lowfat Cookbook by the editors of the *University of California at Berkeley Wellness Letter* (Rebus/Random House, 1993). An eating plan to help reverse heart disease.

PERSONAL POWER NOTES
A Quick-List of This Chapter's Power-Action Options

Plan your meals and snacks for more taste and less fat.
- *Emphasize the food tastes you love.*
- *Enjoy every bite—with few distractions.*

Know your Target Fat-Gram Budget—and other "new basics" of weight-control nutrition.
- *Limit dietary fat intake—with a Target Fat-Gram Budget divided evenly throughout the day.*
- *Use "food swap" ideas to increase the taste and lose much of the fat.*
- *Eat more health-building foods—and weigh less.*
- *Guide your "sweet tooth"—and don't use artificial sweeteners as a crutch.*
- *Take advantage of the fact that what warms you up may help slim you down!*

When dining out, choose great-tasting, low-fat foods.

Give up guilt—and allow yourself occasional small servings of "forbidden" foods.

PERSONAL NOTES

_____

_____

_____

_____

_____

_____

_____

_____

5-Minute, Do-It-Anywhere "Fit Times"

The Easy, Super-Effective "Active Minutes" That Give You Up to Twice the Metabolic Benefits

What you do—or *don't* do—in the first half hour after eating each meal or snack may make a surprising difference in how much energy you have and how many calories you burn.

Who can find the time to spend an hour a day at a fitness club or follow a full-length weight-loss exercise video at home? Answer: Not many of us. And the idea of using fitness to slim down is even more discouraging when you hear the old argument that it takes an inordinate amount of time just to lose one pound of body fat, as for example, chopping wood for 10 hours, doing calisthenics for 22 hours or playing volleyball for 32 hours.[1] Looking at these numbers, it's hard not to say "Forget it" to fitness—and to try instead to lose weight by what has long seemed the easier route: starving yourself by cutting calories. Don't!

According to some leading researchers, there's now a whole new way of looking at the "fitness factor": First, the calorie-expending effects of physical activity and exercise are cumulative. That is, *every minute adds up*. Second, when you build strength, your newly toned muscle fibers increase your resting metabolism and fat-burning power—night and day, not just during the time you do the exercise. And third, researchers re-

(continued on page 120)

POWER KNOWLEDGE:
ACTIVE LIVING

MYTH #1: Calorie counting is more important than exercise to control my weight.

POWER KNOWLEDGE: Research indicates that physical exercise—not calorie counting—may be the number-one key to *successful, long-term* weight management. In one study at the University of California, 90 percent of the individuals who reached and maintained a goal weight reported exercising regularly, compared to only 34 percent of the relapsers.[16] Exercise may also help you reduce dietary fat intake by offsetting your natural cravings for high-fat food,[17] and studies indicate that lipoprotein lipase (a key fat-storing enzyme) is restricted by exercise—and this helps reduce excess body fat.[18]

Yet nationwide surveys estimate that as many as eight out of ten U.S. adults don't exercise on a regular, fitness-enhancing basis.[19] And the older we get after age 40, the less active we become,[20] even though *physical inactivity* is now ranked as a major risk factor for coronary heart disease by the American Heart Association.[21]

According to recent studies published in the *New England Journal of Medicine*, for men, starting to exercise can have as big an effect on all-cause mortality as stopping smoking.[22] Yet sedentary lifestyles are now rampant with working couples whose hectic schedules allow virtually no time for formal exercise. In addition, one-half of all people who begin vigorous exercise programs never return after the first workout.[23] Many more drop out within 6 to 12 months,[24] and more intense, vigorous activities are associated with higher dropout rates.[25]

MYTH #2: I'm stuck with weight problems because I can't join a health club and get on a schedule of regular exercise workouts.

POWER KNOWLEDGE: Not true. If you're sick and tired of being told to follow some arbitrary fitness program, we have good news—*just being more physically active throughout the day can really* *pay off.* According to George L. Blackburn, M.D., Ph.D., director of the Center for the Study of Nutrition and Medicine at New England Deaconess Hospital, rather than worry so much about planned exercise, we need to think of ways to naturally get more activity into our lives.[26] And even if you *do* follow a weekly exercise regimen, your weight management and vitality get a boost by adding 5 minutes of activity here and there.

The thermic, metabolism-boosting effect of physical activity usually returns to a near-resting level within approximately one hour after exercise. Yet studies report that the combined metabolic lift of eating and exercise—when they take place within a half hour of each other—may, in some cases at least, extend this calorie-burning rise for more than 10 hours.[27] Every bit of physical activity and exercise helps.[28] Judith Rodin, Ph.D., former professor of psychology and psychiatry at Yale University, and Thomas Plante, Ph.D., of Yale have reported that people in a weight-control program who did only 10 minutes of jumping jacks three times a week lost more body fat than their counterparts who did not exercise.[29] New data also suggests that three 10-minute exercise "mini-sessions" spread over the day produce essentially the same gains in fitness—and perhaps a greater improvement in your overall daily energy level—as one 30-minute session.[30] Research shows that a single *10-minute walk* may trigger a 2-hour boost in your sense of well-being by raising energy levels and lowering tension,[31] and may also help prevent cravings for high-fat foods.[32]

"Repeated short exercise sessions *have the same physiological or metabolic effect in a weight-loss program as a single long workout with the same caloric cost,*" adds Steven N. Blair, M.D., director of epidemiology at the Cooper Institute for Aerobics Research in Dallas, "and the multiple-short-bouts approach to increasing energy expenditure . . . may be easier to build into a person's daily schedule than freeing a large block of time for a workout."[33]

(continued)

POWER KNOWLEDGE: ACTIVE LIVING—*CONTINUED*

Three leading weight-loss experts at Yale University's Eating and Weight Disorders Clinic even go so far as to make the following recommendation: "Specifically, we propose that the typical exercise prescription involving the three-part cardiorespiratory equation (comprised of frequency, intensity and duration) be avoided with overweight individuals."[34]

MYTH #3: As long as my blood cholesterol and blood pressure readings are fine, I don't need to be concerned about exercise.

POWER KNOWLEDGE: There are literally *dozens* of documented benefits from "active living" and regular exercise. For example, a moderate, enjoyable exercise session in early evening promotes deeper, more rejuvenating sleep—which in turn helps you awaken the next day with more energy and a greater likelihood that you'll maintain a physically active day. "If you can increase your body temperature with exercise about 5 or 6 hours before going to bed," explains Peter Hauri, Ph.D., director of the Mayo Clinic Insomnia Program in Rochester, Minnesota, "the temperature then will drop most as you are ready to go to sleep . . . and sleep becomes deeper, with fewer awakenings."[35]

In addition, a lifestyle filled with frequent physical activities also helps lessen the odds of your becoming—or staying—depressed or overwhelmed by stress. Numerous surveys, some by government health agencies, report that physically fit people—including those who exercise regularly—are generally more self-confident, self-disciplined and psychologically resilient—and less likely to become, or remain, anxious and depressed.[36]

port that physical activity and exercise can produce body fat losses even *without* caloric restriction[2] and may be the single most important factor in *maintaining* weight-loss success.[3]

POWER ACTION: FIRST OPTION
Get Moving after Each Meal and Snack:
Every Minute Counts!

Whether or not you follow a regular, formal fitness program, begin taking a 5-minute "mini-walk" or other enjoyable form of physical activity every morning near breakfast time and again after your midmorning snack, at lunch time, after your midafternoon snack, and again in early evening. If you enjoy variety—and it *is* the spice of life—look for a host of different ways to increase your energy level (and burn more calories) by being active. You don't have to break out in a sweat. By choosing pleasurable ways to be physically active and "pulling oxygen into the body within a half hour of eating," explains Bryant A. Stamford, Ph.D., exercise scientist and director of the Health Promotion and Wellness Program at the University of Louisville in Kentucky, these short bouts of increased physical activity can make "food burn hotter, in a sense, with fewer calories being available for fat storage."[4]

Here are some other possibilities.

Walk someplace at least 5 minutes from your work area to eat your lunch—so that, after eating, you can enjoy a 5-minute return walk to work. Three or four times a day, climb a flight or more of stairs instead of taking the elevator (you burn ten times more calories climbing stairs than you do resting).

When walking through the shopping mall, walk up the escalators instead of riding like a mannequin. Several times during the workday, head across the hall or next door to talk to someone. Stand up and move around while reading letters or talking on the telephone.

At home, make this the time to take a walk with loved ones, friends or the dog, shovel snow from the sidewalk or driveway, take out the trash, bring in some firewood, hand wash the dishes, rake some leaves, head outside to check on your plants, pets or children or pedal on a stationary bicycle while watching television or talking on the telephone. If you've got 5 minutes to wait for the start of a favorite television show, spend the time pedaling at a moderate, comfortable pace and then

> Middle-aged Americans who are overweight only move their bodies for an average of 50 minutes a week, and they need to move them for 200 minutes a week.
>
> **—George L. Blackburn, M.D., Ph.D.,** director, Center for the Study of Nutrition and Medicine, New England Deaconess Hospital

> A good exercise prescription for the 30 to 50 million mostly sedentary and unfit Americans is "turn off the television, get up off your fanny, go out the door and move around a bit." We have learned from research that it often doesn't matter what you do. Any activity that increases your metabolic rate and burns more calories provides benefits.
>
> —**Steven N. Blair, M.D.,** *Living with Exercise*

add some extra "active minutes" during commercials.

In that first half hour after eating, are you ever waiting for the laundry to finish its last cycle or for the bathtub to fill? Take the chance to go up and down the stairs an extra time or to go through some smooth strokes on a rowing machine.

Feel ready to yell at someone? Instead, you could do some light dumbbell exercises or release some of your frustrations by gliding through a hundred strides on your cross-country ski machine. Whenever possible, make this an enjoyable "active family time"—when your loved ones or friends join you in the exercise or activities.

This strategy works best when you keep your home fitness equipment in a *convenient location*—that is, where it can be used. If you only have a few extra minutes here and there, you don't want to waste them taking equipment from the closet or trudging to a distant corner of the basement or garage. Even if your fitness equipment doesn't match the decor in the "action area" of your home, keep in mind that this discrepancy may be well worth accepting: Research indicates that the happiest people—at *every* age—tend to be those whose bodies stay healthy and fit.[5]

So dance to your favorite music. Play doubles tennis. Take short bicycle rides. Play a game of Frisbee or shoot some baskets. Join a walking club. Whenever you can, make this session 10 to 20 minutes, but if you can only squeeze in 5 minutes, then by all means do it. The point is to keep moving—not just once in a while, but throughout the day, *every* day, in ways that are as enjoyable and convenient as possible. Just as important, you'll be fending off the urge to sink into your chair and stay there. To a significant extent, "creeping obesity"—a common complaint for many of us over 40—is the result of "creeping inactivity," especially after eating.

In general, physical activity is advisable *any* time it fits into your schedule—and the goal of this ***Power of 5*** shortcut is to help you gradually increase the number of enjoyable, active minutes you spend each day and to include comfortable aerobic exercise whenever it's convenient. But it pays to know that there are three key times when you may get up to *twice* the usual calorie-burning benefits for each active exercise minute.

1. Within an hour of arising in the morning. As discussed in chapter 8, according to national surveys, many of us are quite sedentary in the morning hours, and this keeps our metabolism sluggish. Whether you do it before or after breakfast, morning physical activity helps to increase your morning metabolism.[6] And there's another consideration: Moderate exercise in the morning before you eat breakfast may give you even more of a boost in burning off excess body fat, based on the theory that after a full night's sleep there is little glycogen (stored carbohydrate) in your muscles to supply energy, and therefore more fat is used as fuel.[7] One study of runners directed by Anthony Wilcox, Ph.D., at Kansas State University in Manhattan reported that two-thirds of the calories burned during prebreakfast workouts were from fat, while fat calories accounted for slightly less than half of those burned during afternoon runs.[8]

2. Within 15 to 30 minutes after eating your midmorning snack, lunch and midafternoon snack. Research indicates that your body's metabolic rate goes up by about 10 percent after a meal or snack as a result of the chemical processes that are activated to get that food digested. And there's evidence that this 10 percent can be increased—and at least in some cases, may be *doubled*[9]—if 5 to 20 minutes of moderate (not vigorous) physical activity such as walking takes place while these initial digestive processes are still going on.[10]

3. In the early evening—within 30 minutes after eating. You can help further increase your body's fat-burning power by scheduling some kind of enjoyable physical activities in the early evening. As physiologist Melanie Roffers puts it: "Exercising at this time of the day elevates the metabolic rate just as it's winding down."[11] Exercising after eating has been shown in some studies to increase your calorie-burning by 30 percent to 50 percent for at least 3 hours following the meal.[12, 13] And since overeating high-fat foods in the evening is associated with weight gain, evening exercise may help ease this appetite drive and reverse other factors responsible for the increase in body fat.[14] As an added benefit, a brief, early-evening fitness activity may increase your comfort in forgoing high-fat foods during the key evening hours when most binges tend to occur.[15]

Now you can stop feeling guilty if you miss a formal exercise session; you can add "active minutes" in other ways, and see and feel the benefits. Start emphasizing *active living* to take the dread and drudgery out of fitness. As science learns more about exercise, fewer of the old hard-and-fast rules apply.

POWER ACTION: MORE OPTIONS
Make Aerobic Exercise a Pleasurable
Option, not a Rigid Rule

When you can realistically fit it into your weekly schedule, go ahead and enjoy a 20- to 30-minute session of your favorite aerobic exercise. In those weeks when you have a few extra minutes here and there, it makes sense every other day to extend one of your physical activity times into 20 to 30 minutes of aerobic exercise in order to gain valuable cardiovascular benefits. Here are some important considerations.

Guideline #1: Warm Up

Precede each aerobic session with at least 5 minutes of gentle warm-up time that mimics your activity or sport, moving around at an easy pace. If you stretch, do it gently, without any bouncing movements, *after* your muscles are warmed up—otherwise you may cause injuries to your joints.[37]

Guideline #2:
Use Major Muscles at a Rhythmic Pace

Exercise at a rhythmic, comfortable pace using major muscle groups such as the thighs.[38] Begin gradually. Listen to your body. Stop at any sign of pain.

Guideline #3:
Choose a Safe, Sensible Intensity

Choose an exercise intensity that allows you to work steadily while still being able to talk without gasping for breath. This is known as the "talk test." During aerobic exercise your physician may recommend that you stay in your "target heart rate zone"—the range of heartbeats per minute where you're most likely to gain safe, solid benefits. For many of us, a sensible aerobic intensity level is 60 to 75 percent of our predicted maximal heart rate (PMHR). For best fat-loss results, some authorities suggest exercising near the *lower end* of this range.[39] That's based on the theory that when you drive your heart rate high in the target heart rate zone and your muscles are pushed to high intensity levels, not only are you at increased risk of injury but you use more blood glucose for energy and provide lowered stimulus to fat-metabolizing processes—so you burn less fat.

Here's the math to calculate your PMHR and target heart rate zone. First subtract your age from 220. This number is your PMHR. Then multiply your PMHR once by 0.60 and once by 0.75 to find the lower and upper limits of your target heart rate zone. Take your pulse at the radial artery of the wrist (or, with very gentle pressure, at the carotid artery in the neck) shortly after beginning to exercise, again at a midway point in the aerobic session and once more when cooling down. Count for 15 seconds (starting with the first beat as 0, not 1) and then multiply by 4. This gives you an estimate of your heart rate per minute.

Guideline #4:
Respect "Ideal" Duration—But Value Every Minute

Whenever it fits your schedule, perform aerobic exercise for 20 to 30 minutes (and generally *not more than 45 minutes*) three to five times a week. But don't get stuck counting minutes. For some people, it's most convenient to schedule an early-morning session of walking or cycling while listening to music or an educational tape or watching the morning news, and then another 15- to 20-minute session in early evening.

But remember, if on some days you can't find the time you had hoped to spend on aerobic exercise, don't worry about it—just go ahead with a few 5- to 10-minute "mini-walks" or climb several flights of nearby stairs once in the morning and again after lunch.

Guideline #5:
Know When to Vary the Pace

In a recent study at the University of Washington, 15 older men (average age 68) followed an aerobics program that totaled 45 to 60 minutes a day, five days a week, for six months, and the men lost fat *preferentially* from their abdomen.[40] According to Dr. Stamford, to burn off more fat, aerobic-type exercise must do two things. First, it must begin gradually, working up to enough comfortable vigor to trigger a substantial adrenaline release. "One of the jobs of adrenaline is to increase the free fatty acids in the bloodstream so the body can use them as fuel for activity."[41] Second, this higher-but-still-comfortable level of activity must be followed by prolonged, moderate aerobic-type exercise that will burn up the liberated fat molecules. Even walking can be effective. "Just step up the pace or even jog a bit now and then to boost adrenaline output," advises Dr. Stamford, who notes that with other common activities like gardening, the same principle can be applied. You might start out hoeing or digging, which are more vigorous, and then follow with some raking or other sustained aerobic activity.

Guideline #6: Cool Down

At the end of each aerobic activity, keep moving for enough extra minutes to allow your heart rate to *gradually* return to normal.

Resources

Fitness without Exercise by Bryant A. Stamford, Ph.D., and Porter Shimer (Warner, 1991). A refreshing and sensible alternative to rigid exercise regimens.

Living with Exercise by Steven N. Blair, M.D. (The LEARN Education Center, 1555 W. Mockingbird Lane, Suite 203, Dallas, TX 75235; 800-736-7323). A well-documented and practical plan to make *every minute of physical activity count.*

PERSONAL POWER NOTES
A Quick-List of This Chapter's Power-Action Options

Get moving after each meal and snack: every minute counts!

Make aerobic exercise a pleasurable option, not a rigid rule.
- *Guideline #1: Warm up.*
- *Guideline #2: Use major muscles at a rhythmic pace.*
- *Guideline #3: Choose a safe, sensible intensity.*
- *Guideline #4: Respect "ideal" duration—but value every minute.*
- *Guideline #5: Know when to vary the pace.*
- *Guideline #6: Cool down.*

PERSONAL NOTES

_____

_____

_____

_____

_____

_____

_____

_____

_____

_____

_____

_____

_____

_____

_____

5-Minute Muscle-Toning Shortcuts

Fast, at-Home Ways to Stay Stronger and "Burn Off" Excess Fat 24 Hours a Day— Even while You Sleep

---

You get tremendous metabolism-boosting power from strong, well-toned muscles[1]—and it takes as little as *5 minutes of at-home exercise to get results.* "To wage war effectively against body fat," says one research team, "you need to be a good calorie-burning machine 24 hours a day, and having adequate muscle tissue is the only way to do that."[2]

Okay, let's get to the waistline first: Without a doubt, a slim, toned abdomen is the most sought-after symbol of weight-loss success. But the two most popular traditional exercises—sit-ups and leg-lifts—don't work, and can cause or aggravate lower back pain! We need new alternatives because there's increasing evidence that those of us who store much of our excess body fat *above the hips* have a higher risk for developing heart disease, stroke and diabetes.[3] One explanation, according to researchers at the University of Washington School of Medicine, is that cholesterol levels are closely linked to the areas where people carry fat on their torso.[4] And, in women, carrying fat in front may raise the risk of both breast and endometrial cancer.[5] Unfortunately, this extra body fat doesn't just sit there—it seems to alter hormonal patterns.

Sad to say, most of us seem to have accepted the "fact" that we're fighting a losing battle against waistline flab. We have one response: Don't give up! To remain slim and fit, however, you have to look past your abdomen—to all your other major muscles. Here's why: If you're like most sedentary adults (and *even if you have exercised regularly for many years with an aerobic activity such as walking, jogging or cycling*), you began losing muscle in your midtwenties, up to a pound a year. Then, as your "lean mass" steadily decreased, so did your resting metabolism. As a result, because your body now needs fewer calories to function, excess calories—especially dietary fat calories—are more easily stored as body fat.

A number of healthy lifestyle habits contribute to reducing body fat and lowering associated disease risks, but one of the most important is strength training.[6] Strong, well-toned muscles keep your circulation high, draw in more oxygen, rev up calorie burning and increase your overall metabolism—helping you to "burn off" stubborn layers of excess body fat.[7] Best of all, *it's never too late to get stronger— and stay stronger.*

> Of all the calories burned in the body, 50 to 90 percent are burned by your muscles—even when you sleep.
>
> **—Covert Bailey,**
> *Fit or Fat*

POWER ACTION: FIRST OPTIONS
Determine Your Waist-to-Hip Ratio

From a health perspective, how important is it, really, for *you* to trim and tone your waistline? One of the simplest ways to find out is using a waist-to-hip ratio. Here's how to check your own ratio.[8]

1. Measure your waist (it's the smallest measurement below your rib cage and above your navel) while standing relaxed, without pulling in your abdomen or stomach. Using the chart on page 132, make a mark along the left-hand scale next to your waist measurement.

2. Measure your hips (it's the largest measurement around the widest part of your buttocks and upper leg joints). On the chart, make another mark along the right-hand scale next to your hip measurement.

3. Draw a line connecting the marks. The point at which the line crosses the Waist-to-Hip Ratio scale down the middle of the chart is your ratio. (You can also obtain this number by dividing your waist measurement by your hip measurement.)

(continued on page 132)

POWER KNOWLEDGE: MUSCLE TONE

MYTH #1: By doing lots of sit-ups or leg-lifts you can melt fat from your stomach.

POWER KNOWLEDGE: Not a chance. First of all, spot reducing doesn't work, and traditional sit-ups and leg-lifts not only won't trim your abdomen but can contribute to lower back pain, a potbelly and poor posture. To have a slim, strong waist, the first priority is a 5-minute "stomach flattening" set of simple exercises (see "Power Action: First Options") that you can perform at home. Next you can attack excess abdominal fat by raising your metabolism—which gets fired up by 5-minute toning activities to strengthen your major muscles and by a host of other tips given throughout *The Power of 5*.

When strong and balanced, the abdominal muscles flatten your waist, help hold your internal organs in place and stabilize your lower back at its most vulnerable point—the lumbosacral angle of the pelvis.[17] Most of us still don't realize that America's two most popular abdominal exercises, traditional sit-ups and leg-lifts, don't slim the waistline, no matter how many you do (even as many as 5,000 a month).[18] In fact, they often cause or aggravate lower back pain by pulling on the front of the lower spine, which causes pelvic tilt.[19] When this happens, your back is swayed inward and your lower abdomen pushes out—spotlighting the "potbelly" appearance.

MYTH #2: To lose weight, *aerobics*—such as running, swimming, stairclimbing, dancing or cycling—is more important than other kinds of exercise.

POWER KNOWLEDGE: Participating in an aerobics class a few times a week—or even once a day—can be good for your health and is an aid to weight management, but it's not the best way to boost your metabolism 24 hours a day. What most people don't realize is that your metabolism responds to your physical activity *every hour of the day*, not just once a day or once every few days. More than aerobics, your 24-hour-a-day calorie-burning power depends on increasing your *lean muscle mass.* More than 400 muscles make your body firm—or let it sag. If these muscles aren't made strong and balanced in relationship with each other—and kept that way—they slowly wither away, and one of the prices you pay is reduced metabolism.[20]

Although aerobics (chapter 11) is the most effective exercise for burning calories *during the time you're doing the exercise*, lean muscle mass consumes calories 24 hours a day, just to maintain itself. In one eight-week study of 72 men and women conducted by Wayne L. Westcott, Ph.D., consultant to the National YMCA, the American Council on Exercise and the National Academy of Sports Medicine, an aerobics-only group lost an average of 3 pounds of fat and also *lost* ½ pound of muscle in eight weeks.[21] However, in the group that combined brief strength training sessions and aerobics, each person lost an average of *10 pounds of fat* and *gained 2 pounds of muscle!* Several followup studies reported similar results.[22]

MYTH #3: Strong muscles are more important for men than for women.

POWER KNOWLEDGE: Muscle-strengthening exercises are just as vital for women as they are for men, says Barbara Drinkwater, Ph.D., past president of the American College of Sports Medicine. "It's healthy that women are now accepting muscles as part of a normal human body."[23] A recent study published in the *Archives of Internal Medicine* reported that strength-training exercises for premenopausal women were associated with decreases in levels of "bad" LDL cholesterol (chapter 15 contains a discussion of cholesterol).[24] For both sexes, the basic fact of strength training is simple: Stress your muscles by making them work against resistance, and they'll get stronger to meet the challenge. Muscles respond immediately—and at any age—so each of us has the lifelong capacity to develop more strength and tone. There's absolutely no truth to the idea that, for women, getting stronger means getting "huge" muscles.

MYTH #4: If you start getting stronger but stop training for more than a few days, your muscles will begin to "turn into fat."

POWER KNOWLEDGE: Muscle cells and fat cells are completely different. One cannot turn into the other.

The goal for women is a ratio below 0.95, and for men, below 0.85. When your ratio is higher than that number, you may be at greater risk for certain health problems—whether or not your bathroom scale says you are at an "ideal weight." And even if you don't have a high waist-to-hip ratio, you'll certainly want to keep your abdominal muscles toned, since this helps your posture—which makes you look and feel thinner and reduces your chance of suffering from lower back pain. For a sample weekly schedule listing all the 1- to 5-minute muscle-toning options, see page 138.

2-Minute "Stomach-Flattening" Exercise Sets

Here are several of the easiest, most effective abdominal exercises.

"Transpyramid" breathing exercise. Do this exercise ten times a day—in the car, at your desk or wherever it's most convenient. It's a simple, often-overlooked waist exercise that can be very effective in helping you build a toned, fit *lower abdominal area*.[9] Sometimes called "voluntary contractions" by exercise experts, as Lawrence E. Lamb, M.D., explains, these "are the most important exercises to flatten your abdomen."[10]

Do the transpyramid exercise right now: Sit or stand with balanced posture. Place your hands on your hips, with your thumbs pointing toward the back. Slowly exhale and, as you reach the place where you normally finish breathing out, smoothly and forcefully breathe out *more*, using the power of your *lower* abdominal muscles (the transversalis and pyramidalis). At first you might use your hands to gently push up on the lower abdomen during the exhalation part of the exercise. Work up to doing ten of these exercises each day. Fit them in wherever you can, such as doing one or two right before each meal and snack, at each stoplight on your commute to and from work or each time you sit down at your desk.

Abdominal roll-ups and reverse trunk rotations. As a goal, do a 2-minute set of 25 abdominal roll-ups and 6 reverse trunk rotations three times a week (Tuesday-Thursday-Saturday, for example), but don't worry if you can only manage to get in one or two sets—every abdominal exercise repetition counts!

Abdominal roll-ups—also called crunches or curls—are one of the easiest and most effective exercises for toning your upper abdominal area.[11]

As shown in Illustration 12-1, lie on your back with your knees bent and your legs and feet free. (Do *not* secure your feet or legs under a heavy object or have them held by a partner, since this lets the power-

12-1

12-2

ful hip-flexor muscles take over the movement and stress your lower back.) You can bend your legs at the knees or place them over a bench or chair seat. Cross your arms on your chest or clasp your hands *lightly* behind your head. Don't let your arms whip upward, since this may cause injury to the neck.

Leaving your middle and lower back flat on the floor, as shown in Illustration 12-2, slowly raise your head and shoulders off the ground about 30 to 45 degrees. Pause for a second at the top of the motion and then slowly lower yourself to the original position. Begin very gradually and, as long as there is no serious discomfort or pain, over a period of weeks work your way up to 25 or more repetitions three times a week. For some extra effectiveness, slowly twist your shoulders to the left (by gently reaching with both hands toward your left knee) at the top of one repetition and to the right at the top of the next.

Reverse trunk rotations are another proven exercise for abdominal fitness and good posture.[12] This movement involves the external and internal obliques, a set of midsection rotation muscles that help keep your abdomen slim and toned. This exercise also strengthens the deep spinal muscles (multifidus and rotatores), posterior spinal surface muscles (erector spinae) and an important lower back muscle, the quadratus lumborum. The full range of motion of this exercise builds both flexibility and strength in the waist and lower back, an ideal combination for helping to prevent injuries and back pain.

As shown in Illustration 12-3, lie on your back on the floor. Extend your arms out to the sides, perpendicular to your torso so that, if viewed from above, your body forms the letter T. Raise your knees up in a sharp angle (pulling your heels toward the buttocks) and hold your legs together. As you get in great shape, you may raise your legs to a 90-degree angle, vertical to the floor.

As shown in Illustration 12-4, maintain your leg/trunk angle as you slowly lower your legs to the left and touch the floor with the outside of the knee and foot of your lower leg. Smoothly raise your legs back up to the starting position and repeat the movement to the other side. Your arms and shoulders should remain in contact with the floor throughout the exercise to stretch and strengthen the internal and external obliques. If

> There's a myth that we lose the ability to respond to exercise as we age; that we can't get stronger or make muscles bigger. That's not true. We can make people aged 65 stronger than they've ever been in their lives. We can make a 90-year-old stronger than a 50-year-old. Our oldest exerciser is 100 years old. We can triple muscle strength in old people.
>
> **—William J. Evans, Ph.D.,** chief, Human Physiology Laboratory, Human Nutrition Research Center on Aging at Tufts University

your shoulders come off the ground as you lower your legs to the side, you may wish to have a friend *gently* hold your shoulders down as you do the exercise. If you still find the exercise difficult, use more knee bend and, as rehabilitative medicine authority Rene Cailliet, M.D., suggests, you may also wish to bring your knees up toward your shoulder as you gently lower them to the side.[13] If you have any doubt about being able to do this exercise effectively, begin by having a partner support your knees as you gently lower them down to one side and then the other to test your current strength and flexibility levels.

Begin with very few repetitions and gradually, over a period of weeks, work your way up to ten repetitions three times a week (Tuesday-Thursday-Saturday, for example). Over time, gradually straighten your legs as you do the exercise.

Reduce Stress, Reduce Abdominal Fat!

For a number of years, researchers at Yale University's Department of Psychology have been studying the relationship between stress and tummy fat.[14] Judith Rodin, Ph.D., and Marielle Rebuffe-Scrive, Ph.D., and their colleagues recently concluded a study of 42 overweight women, aged 18 to 42, and reported one of the likeliest reasons why,

12-3

12-4

even with regular exercise and a low-fat diet, some of us—women *and* men—have so much trouble with abdominal fat.[15] What seems to be happening is this: Uncontrolled stress initiates the release of a hormone called cortisol, which stimulates preferential depositing of body fat around your waist. Other researchers are reporting similar findings.[16] "Uncontrolled stress," as explained in chapters 3 and 24, is negative and is linked to other health risks such as high blood pressure and heart attack. Negative stress is often characterized by a nagging feeling of time-urgency, hostility, anger, aggression or worry and a general sense of pessimism or helplessness. Under this kind of pressure, it seems we secrete excessive amounts of cortisol and store increasing amounts of fat in the abdomen.

Chapters 3 and 24 offer many simple, proven ways to take charge of the stresses in your life. For additional ideas on how to rev up your fat-burning, waist-slimming potential, see chapters 8, 9, 10 and 11.

POWER ACTION: MORE OPTIONS
Target Key Body Areas for 5-Minute Muscle-Toning Sets

Like most of us, you may assume that building strength and muscle tone requires dozens of exercises and hours in the gym. The truth is, it doesn't. If you select some basic exercises, listen to your body, maintain good posture and begin with light resistance and smooth, well-controlled movements, you'll quickly feel and see the results. Begin with whatever types of strengthening exercises interest you. Perhaps this will mean doing more activities—gardening, playing ball, wrestling with the kids or grandkids, swimming, cross-country skiing or some other choices that build and maintain muscle tone. Scan the following 5-Minute Muscle-Toning sets and schedule those target areas that are most appealing to you.

Whatever your natural body type, is there a difference between the physique you want and the one that faces you in the mirror every morning? If you're hoping for a change, you may be blocked from the results you want for the simple reason—noted in the opening of this chapter—that you lack *balanced muscular strength*, and with each passing year your metabolism continues to slow down as your lean body mass (muscle) atrophies from disuse. As we've already noted, when combined with a low-fat diet and "active living," *building muscle tone* through strengthening exercises is a vital factor—for both men *and* women—to increase your metabolism to "burn off" stubborn layers of body fat.

Getting started is simple. No long warm-ups (you might go through a muscle-toning set right after a 5-minute "mini-walk"—discussed in chapter 11). No need for special exercise clothes. No reason to waste time driving to and from a fitness club or gym. No call for expensive equipment (most of the exercises in this chapter require *no* equipment, and the rest call for only a few simple weights and a sturdy bench or chair). Best of all, you can begin in the privacy of your own living room, den or office. Simply select whatever body area you want, first and foremost, to shape and strengthen:

• Abdomen
• Lower back
• Chest-shoulders-upper back
• Upper arms
• Thighs-buttocks
• Lower legs

Then start with a 5-Minute Muscle-Toning Set targeted to that area. There are sections in this chapter for each of these six major muscle groups of the body.

With *The Power of 5*, that's all it takes to get started. See the sample schedule on page 138 for ideas on which days of the week to include the body area(s) you're toning. Add new areas whenever you want. Remember, it takes only 5 minutes to try the illustrated exercises in any section of this chapter. If, like many other readers of this book, you get enthused about the quick results you get, you may want to add 5-Minute Muscle-Toning Sets for each of the six major areas of the body covered in *The Power of 5*. You can divide your strengthening sets throughout the day—one 5-minute routine in the morning, another at lunch and a final quick set on your own or with your spouse or kids right after supper; or you might squeeze in several 5-minute sets during family TV time. Eventually, you might even feel inclined to join a health club or gym. Whatever you choose, it's entirely up to you.

Even on days when you have no special time to devote to muscle toning, you can keep in better shape by noticing the many different ways you can safely, *gradually* build more strength while pushing, pulling, turning, lifting and bending during everyday activities. Try to switch sides to balance your actions—alternately carrying groceries or your briefcase or a young child with your *left* and then your *right* arm, for example, or changing your weight-bearing leg and arm from time to

SAMPLE WEEKLY MUSCLE-TONING TARGET SCHEDULE

Select the options that are most appealing to you. If you miss a day, don't feel guilty. Add 1- to 5-Minute Muscle Toning Sets whenever they fit into your schedule—which might be before or after the 5-minute "mini-walks" from chapter 11. Above all, remember that every minute of strengthening exercise pays off!

Daily

1-minute *abdominal* toning set:
> Ten repetitions of the "transpyramid" breathing exercise—in your car, at your desk, or wherever it's most convenient.

Monday-Wednesday-Friday

5-minute *chest-shoulders-upper back* strengthening set:
> Modified pushups: 6 to 25 repetitions.
> Chest and shoulder raises: 6 to 10 repetitions.
> Chest crosses: 6 to 10 repetitions.

5-minute *upper-arm* strengthening set:
> Arm curls: 6 to 25 repetitions.
> Back-of-the-upper-arm extensions: 6 to 10 repetitions.

Tuesday-Thursday-Saturday

2-minute *abdominal* toning set:
> Roll-ups: 25 repetitions.
> Reverse trunk rotations: 6 repetitions.

3-minute *lower-back* toning set:
> Single knee-to-chest lifts: 6 to 10 repetitions.
> Seated low-back stretch: 6 to 10 repetitions.
> Pelvic tilt movement: 6 to 10 repetitions.

5-minute *thigh-buttocks* strengthening set: Select two or three of the following:
> Modified knee bends: 6 to 25 repetitions.
> Seated leg extensions: 6 to 25 repetitions.
> Standing side leg raises: 6 to 25 repetitions.
> Hip raises: 6 to 10 repetitions.

5-minute *lower-leg* strengthening set:
> Standing calf raises: 10 to 50 repetitions with each leg.
> Repeat twice for each leg.

time as you work at a counter or weed your lawn or shovel snow or dig in the garden.

In short, building and maintaining muscle tone is an integral part of a "total fitness" program—and the benefits go far beyond having a more attractive physique. With healthy, strong muscles, your body is better balanced and coordinated and more vigorous, and research indicates you'll help slow—*or even reverse*—the aging process. And for the thousands of Americans who are already eating a healthy, low-fat diet and doing daily aerobic exercise but are *still* having a difficult time losing weight, getting stronger means healthfully increasing your metabolism to "burn off" more excess body fat 24 hours a day, even while you sleep!

We've already discussed exercises for firming and slimming your abdomen. Here are optional 3- to 5-Minute Muscle-Toning Sets for the other five major areas of the body.

3-Minute Lower-Back Toning Set

Your posture and back strength can influence how much your abdomen protrudes and also whether or not you can safely, enjoyably perform other exercises without injury or tension-related fatigue. Here are several simple exercises, each recommended by at least one medical specialist on back care,[25] that may prove very helpful in gently stretching and strengthening your back. If possible, perform these exercises two or three times a week on the days when you do a 2-minute set of abdominal-toning exercises. A word of caution: It's best to do these movements after you've warmed up with at least 5 minutes of walking (see chapter 11), and start with only one or two repetitions of each exercise. (If you have a history of back problems or are currently experiencing back pain, consult your physician before doing these or any other exercises.)

12-5

Single knee-to-chest lift. This easy-does-it exercise helps stretch the muscles and connective tissues of your back and hip.

As shown in Illustration 12-5, lie on your back with both knees bent. Using both hands, grasp one leg and gently pull it toward your chest for a slow count of 5. Relax. Now slowly return to the starting position. Repeat with the other leg. Do six to ten repetitions.

Seated low-back stretch. From a seated position in a chair with your feet and knees apart, slowly and gently bend forward toward the floor, as shown in Illustration 12-6, as far as you comfortably can without bouncing. Hold the down position for up to 20 seconds. Do six to ten repetitions.

"Pelvic tilt" movements. This simple, relaxing exercise helps strengthen some of the front spine structures and stretch the back ones. As shown in Illustration 12-7, lie on your back with your knees bent and gently press your lower back flat against the floor. Hold for a few seconds. Do six to ten repetitions.

12-6

12-7

5-Minute Chest-Shoulders-Upper Back Strengthening Set

Modified push-ups (with your knees on the floor if necessary). This revision of a classic exercise strengthens muscles in your arms, chest, shoulders and back.

To begin, lie face-down on the floor with your knees together and the palms of your hands flat on the floor at either side of your chest, near the front of each shoulder. As indicated in Illustration 12-8, support the weight of your upper body on your arms and keep your knees in contact with the floor as you slowly raise your body upward, keeping your back as flat as you can. Smoothly return to the starting position, as in Illustration 12-9. (To increase the strengthening effect on your upper arms and back, keep your hands beneath your shoulders during the push-up movements; to increase the strengthening focus for your chest, keep your hands slightly wider than your shoulders.) Do 6 to 25 repetitions.

Chest and shoulder raises. To begin this exercise, sit upright in a

12-8

12-9

chair with one arm at your side, holding a weight such as an adjustable dumbbell (where small, round weight "plates," in 2-, 5-, or 10-pound increments, can be slipped on and off to achieve the desired level of poundage or resistance in the dumbbell) or a plastic milk or juice container filled with water to a comfortable weight level. *Note:* The key in selecting a starting weight is to experiment until you find the heaviest weight you can use to safely, effectively go through at least the mini-mum number of specified repetitions of the exercise—which is usually 6. If you can't perform 6 correct repetitions without getting too tired to lift the weight, then the weight is too heavy and you should reduce the number of pounds. However, if you can easily perform more than the specified maximum repetitions—usually 10 or 25—then you should gradually increase the weight.

For this exercise, the starting position is shown in Illustration 12-10. Keeping your elbow straight, slowly raise your arm forward and up. Pause when your arm is fully extended above and slightly in front of your head, as indicated in Illustration 12-11. Then slowly return to the starting position. Do six to ten repetitions.

Chest crosses. Lie on your back on a flat, stable bench or on a car-

12-10

12-11

peted floor, with your knees bent and your feet and lower back firmly against the bench or floor. As shown in Illustration 12-12, hold a weight—such as a dumbbell or small water jug—in each hand. Experiment to find your ideal starting weight (as noted in the preceding exercise). Then extend your arms to the sides, keeping them level with your shoulders. Keep your elbows slightly bent and raise your arms *very slowly* in an arc toward each other until the weights gently touch above the center of your chest, as indicated in Illustration 12-13. Slowly lower the weights in a reverse arc to the starting position. Do six to ten repetitions.

5-Minute Upper-Arm Strengthening Set

Arm curls. This is a popular, easy exercise to strengthen the biceps muscle in the front of your upper arm and to help tone your forearms.

12-12

12-13

You can use dumbbells or a plastic milk or juice container filled or partially filled with water.

As shown in Illustrations 12-14 and 12-15, holding a weight in your hand, with your palm up, raise your arm to your shoulder, bending at the elbow, and then return slowly to the starting position. Experiment (as noted in chest and shoulder raises) to find your ideal starting weight. In this exercise, you can either lift both arms at once or alternate left and right. Vary the exercise by doing it with your palms down. Do 6 to 25 repetitions.

Option: Although some exercise scientists advise against doing isometric-type exercises (pushing against an immovable object like a wall),[26] Bryant A. Stamford, Ph.D., exercise scientist and director of the Health Promotion and Wellness Program at the University of Louisville in Kentucky, suggests varying your routine by including bicep curls isometric-style by pulling up against the lip of your desk or a countertop. He finds that simple exertions of just 6 seconds each, repeated five to ten times, will aid muscle tone.[27]

Back-of-the-upper-arm extensions. This basic exercise will help tone the triceps muscles at the back of your upper arms.

To begin, grasp a dumbbell—or a plastic jug filled with water—in your right hand and bend your body forward at the hips, with your

12-14   12-15

right arm bent at a 90-degree angle at the elbow, until your torso is parallel to the floor, as shown in Illustration 12-16. Experiment (as noted in chest and shoulder raises) to find your ideal starting weight. Place your left palm on a flat bench or sturdy chair to support or stabilize your body. Lightly press the inside of your upper right arm against your torso along a line parallel to the floor.

Slowly straighten your arm, bringing the weight to the rear and up from its starting position (see Illustration 12-17). Then slowly return to the starting position. Repeat the exercise motion with your left arm. Alternate right and left. Do a total of six to ten repetitions for each arm.

5-Minute Thigh-Buttocks Strengthening Set

Select two or three of the following exercises. Your choices will depend on time—on how long it actually takes you to go through each exercise correctly—and which of the exercises seem most targeted to your personal muscle-toning needs.

Modified knee bends. These are great do-it-anywhere leg-strengthening exercises.

Begin in a standing position, with your feet flat on the floor and shoulder-width apart, as shown in Illustration 12-18. Holding on to a desk or counter for support, slowly bend at the knees and lower your

12-16   12-17

weight until your thighs are almost parallel to the floor—as if you're sitting in an imaginary chair, as indicated in Illustration 12-19—and then return to the starting position. End the movement by raising up on the balls of your feet, with your heels off the ground. Do 6 to 25 repetitions.

Seated leg extensions. For this exercise, you'll need a set of ankle weights for your lower legs. Most sporting goods stores sell them. Select a pair that is comfortably padded and easy to adjust to fit the diameter of your lower leg just above the ankle. Make certain the poundage in each ankle weight is adjustable (usually this is accomplished with ½-pound or 1-pound rectangular sacks of sand that you can slide into and out of side-by-side compartments on the ankle weight, thereby varying the weight resistance). If you have strong legs, you may want to use two ankle weights on each leg.

For this exercise, sit on the edge of a chair or a flat bench with your posture erect and both feet firmly on the floor, as shown in Illustration 12-20. Raise your right knee slightly to lift your right foot off the floor and then extend your lower right leg to the front, as indicated in Illustration 12-21, holding tension in your leg muscles throughout the exercise. Slowly return to the starting position. After 6 to 25 repetitions, switch legs.

Standing side leg raises. Stand at a right angle to your desk, a door

12-18   12-19

frame or a countertop (holding on for support) and raise one leg as shown in Illustration 12-22. Slowly raise it higher to the side (Illustration 12-23) until you feel tension along the outer muscles of your thigh. Hold this position for several seconds and then slowly lower your leg down a foot or so (but do not touch the floor) and then repeat the lifting movement. After 6 to 25 repetitions, change to the other side and lift the other leg. As your legs get stronger, you may wish to place an adjustable ankle weight (or eventually two ankle weights) on the lifting leg.

Hip raises. This simple, effective exercise uses body weight and voluntary contractions to help tone the buttocks area.

As shown in Illustration 12-24, lie face-up on the floor with your arms extended, palms down, on either side of your shoulders and bend your knees with your feet flat on the floor beneath them. Then, as indicated in Illustration 12-25, slowly raise your hips upward, while keeping your head, shoulders, hands and arms on the floor. Arch your lower back slightly and tense your buttocks muscles. Then slowly return to the starting position. Do six to ten repetitions.

5-Minute Lower-Leg Strengthening Set

Standing calf raises. This easy movement helps tone your lower leg muscles. Here's how to get started. As shown in Illustration 12-26, stand

12-20

12-21

12-22

12-23

12-24

12-25

between two sturdy chairs and place your toes and the balls of your feet on a solid block of wood (a sturdy piece of 2-by-6 or 2-by-8 would be fine). Point your toes straight ahead and grasp the backs of the chairs to maintain balance. Keeping your legs straight (with only a *slight* bend at the knees), sag your heels as far below the level of your toes as comfortably possible (your heels don't need to touch the floor). Then slowly rise

(continued on page 152)

12-26

12-27

STRENGTH-TRAINING GUIDELINES

It doesn't take long to produce results with strength training. According to the latest guidelines from the American College of Sports Medicine, all it takes for solid, progressive strength-training results is a *total* of 15 minutes of strengthening exercises three or four times a week—using free weights, supported weight machines or bodyweight calisthenic exercises.[28]

Want to know more about muscle-toning? Here are six important guidelines.

1. Precede every strength-building session with some smooth, comfortable motions to increase blood flow and loosen up your muscles and joints.

2. Know your one-repetition maximum (1RM) for each formal exercise and then *choose a resistance level that is 80 percent of your 1RM.* "In our studies at Tufts [University's Human Physiology Laboratory]," writes William J. Evans, Ph.D., chief of the laboratory at the USDA Human Nutrition Research Center on Aging at Tufts in Boston and Irwin H. Rosenberg, M.D., "we exercise our subjects at 80 percent of their one-repetition maximum (1RM) because we recognize that *to build strength appreciably a person must work out at that level.*"[29]

One RM is the most weight you can lift with a single movement or muscle contraction. It's a weight so heavy that you cannot lift it again without resting for a while. The amount of this weight varies from person to person. Once you know your 1RM, be certain to keep checking it every two to four weeks and then recalculate the 80 percent level so, whenever appropriate, you can make upward adjustments in the resistance level.

3. Listen to your body. If you feel any pain during a particular movement, stop immediately. Continue only if the pain subsides, but only after reducing the amount of weight you are lifting. A *mild* burning sensation is usually acceptable discomfort; pain of any kind is not. A slight soreness the next day is common when beginning to exercise. Consult your physician with any questions.

4. During each strengthening exercise, use good posture, smooth, controlled movements and even breathing. Don't hold your breath while exercising, since this may cause an unhealthy rise in blood pressure. Breathe evenly and steadily. Maintain balanced posture throughout every movement—don't arch your back or use any twisting or turning motions that are not part of the exercise. Each exercise has a concentric (lifting) portion and an eccentric (return) portion. "Without the eccentric component in an exercise, you don't get much muscle growth," says Maria Fiatarone, M.D., of the Tufts University Human Physiology Laboratory and Harvard Medical School.[30] Therefore, be sure to go through each exercise slowly and smoothly from start to finish. This also helps prevent injuries.

5. Once you've worked up to it, go through two sets of five to ten repetitions of each exercise (which should require a total of about 5 minutes per body part—such as chest, shoulders, arms, back or other area). For example, using 80 percent of your 1RM resistance level for a given exercise, go through a first "set" of five to ten repetitions (a "rep" is a complete motion of an exercise). It may be helpful to rest a few seconds between repetitions. You'll know the resistance level is correct when, after five to ten repetitions, your muscles are too tired to continue without resting. At the end of the first set, rest for a full minute or two to let your muscles recover. Then go through a second set of five to ten reps; rest; and then, if you have the ability, desire and an extra few minutes, add a third set.

6. Cool down for at least several minutes. Don't stop suddenly or sit still after exercising. Keep moving as you ease back into your normal routine and let your heart rate and blood flow return gradually to their preexercise state.

How about some face-to-face professional guidance? Since safety and proper form are very important in strength-building exercises—especially when using resistance machines in a gym or as you become more advanced and the amount of weight resistance increases—it's a good idea to consider working with a qualified instructor. But if you opt for one-on-one guidance, choose it wisely. Never assume that a "staff member" shirt or a good physique signify professional competence. The most qualified fitness instructors are usually certified (through comprehensive practical and written examinations) by one or more of the following organizations:

• American College of Sports Medicine (P.O. Box 1440, Indianapolis, IN 46206)

• Institute for Aerobics Research (12330 Preston Rd., Dallas, TX 75230)

• National Strength and Conditioning Association (P.O. Box 81410, Lincoln, NE 68501) up as high as you can on the balls of your feet, as indicated in Illustration 12-27. Slowly return to the starting position, with your heels lowered as close to the floor as possible. Be certain your ankles do not roll outward. Perform 10 to 50 repetitions, depending on your ability level. Then switch legs.

For a more advanced version of this exercise, you might try one leg at a time instead of two, and to tone additional lower-leg muscles, you might proceed as noted above but keep your leg straight—continuing repetitions until your calf area feels too tired to continue. Then alter the exercise by bending your knee during the downward motion (as you sag your heels below the edge of the wood) and then straightening your leg during the upward motion. Continue for 10 to 50 repetitions.

PERSONAL POWER NOTES
A Quick-List of This Chapter's Power-Action Options

Determine your waist-to-hip ratio.

2-minute "stomach-flattening" exercise sets.
- Do the "transpyramid" breathing exercise ten times a day.
- Do a 2-minute set of 25 abdominal roll-ups and 6 reverse trunk rotations.

Reduce stress, reduce abdominal fat!

Target key body areas for 5-minute muscle-toning sets.

3-minute lower-back toning set.
- Single knee-to-chest lift.
- Seated low-back stretch.
- "Pelvic tilt" movements.

5-minute chest-shoulders-upper back strengthening set.
- Modified push-ups (with your knees on the floor if necessary).
- Chest and shoulder raises.
- Chest crosses.

Resources

Be Strong: Strength Training and Muscular Fitness for Men and Women by Wayne Westcott, Ph.D. (Brown & Benchmark, 1993). A succinct, scholarly resource on designing a serious personal muscle-building program.

Fitness without Exercise by Bryant A. Stamford, Ph.D. and Porter Shimer (Warner, 1990). Contains a wide range of do-it-anywhere muscle-toning options.

Getting Stronger: Weight Training for Men and Women by Bill Pearl and Gary T. Moran, Ph.D. (Shelter, 1986). A comprehensive, illustrated guide to lifelong strength training, filled with dozens of exercise options for each area of the body. A must-have reference book for all of us who love variety in exercise.

5-minute upper-arm strengthening set.
- *Arm curls.*
- *Back-of-the-upper-arm extensions.*

5-minute thigh-buttocks strengthening set.
- *Modified knee bends.*
- *Seated leg extensions.*
- *Standing side leg raises*
- *Hip raises.*

5-minute lower-leg strengthening set.
- *Standing calf raises.*

PERSONAL NOTES

_____

_____

_____

_____

_____

_____

POWER VISION: BUILDING INNER STRENGTH AND WILL

Accentuating Your Progress, Rising
above Cravings and Setbacks and
Gaining Support from Others

Most people live—whether physically, intellectually, or morally—in a very restricted circle of their potential being. We all have reservoirs of life to draw upon, of which we do not dream.
—**William James, M.D.**, founder of modern psychology, *The Energies of Men*

This chapter targets two issues that are crucial to lifelong good health and weight control: First, how to build on and then sustain your day-to-day successes by focusing your mind and building inner strength each evening with "Power Vision," and second, how to quickly regain your momentum whenever you have had a setback or think you've "blown it."

POWER ACTION: FIRST OPTION
Make a 5-Minute Assessment
of Your Current Body Image

Let's begin by identifying one of the common hurdles to lasting weight loss—a maddening feeling most of us know well: Just when things seem to be going fine, you catch a glimpse of yourself in a mirror or get hit with a stressful situation—and suddenly you find yourself feeling down, hating how you look, skipping exercise (and probably feeling guilty about it) and then eating a few brownies and feeling even worse because now you've cheated on your "diet." Next, it's likely you say something like, "Oh, what's the use, I just don't have any willpower—and I've already blown it. I might as well do whatever I please." Then all hell breaks loose—and you consume the whole *package* of brownies and perhaps a quart of ice cream or a bag or two of your favorite chips. It feels good for a few minutes, but then you feel terrible about that, too. Before you know it, a small lapse has turned into a big dietary collapse.

This failure cycle is often rooted in something most of us have today, whether we realize it or not: a *negative body image*. To what extent does it affect you? Here are several clues: Do you compare yourself to everyone else who walks into the room? Do you make nasty remarks to yourself when you see yourself in a mirror? Do you spend lots of time concerned about how you look—and then feel ashamed for spending all that time worrying about your appearance? Have you spent much of your adult years either on a diet or thinking about going on one?

To gain a better understanding of your own body image, use the self-discovery inventory on page 158. It was developed by a leading expert on the subject, Thomas F. Cash, Ph.D., professor of psychology at Old Dominion University in Norfolk, Virginia, in *Body-Image Therapy: A Program for Self-Directed Change*. To interpret your score, see the chart on page 160.

Even among the "normal weight" population in the United States, the majority of women and many men perceive themselves to be overweight. Instead of *being* fat, these self-classified overweight men and women are *thinking* fat, say researchers, and this creates a poor body image, more frequent binge eating, chronic dieting attempts to lose "extra" weight and weakened health.[1] "At least one-fourth of our self-

(continued on page 158)

POWER KNOWLEDGE: ACTIVE IMAGERY

MYTH #1: I hate my body. But everyone else hates their body, too. That's part of life.

POWER KNOWLEDGE: It doesn't have to be part of *your* life. "Individuals with a negative body image are more susceptible to other unhappy experiences," says Thomas F. Cash, Ph.D., professor of psychology at Old Dominion University, "such as getting depressed, . . . struggling with eating behavior or having difficulties achieving sexual satisfaction. Clearly, body image is a core part of our personalities and affects our lives in many ways."[12]

"We are witnessing an epidemic whose victims are the millions of people who obsess about their bodies," says Judith Rodin, Ph.D., former professor of psychology and psychiatry at Yale University, and author of *Body Traps*.[13] A number of studies suggest that *dieting* is a better predictor than obesity for determining if you'll eat under stress or when feeling depressed.[14] Dieters, but not nondieters, tend to eat more when anxious or depressed.[15] So once again, we see why one of the clear advantages of **The Power of 5** is that it isn't a diet. Instead, we're focusing, 5 seconds to 5 minutes at a time, on healthfully increasing your metabolism and reducing those diet-related behaviors that promote obesity. It's no wonder that the American Medical Association,[16] the California Dietetic Association[17] and the International Congress on Obesity[18] have all concluded that behavior modification—making simple, specific changes in how you think and feel about yourself, food and fitness—is necessary for successful, lasting weight loss.

"Our negative feelings about our bodies really create difficulties in our intimate relationships with either men or women," explains psychologist Marcia Germaine Hutchinson, Ed.D., in *Transforming Body Image*. "We are brainwashed to believe that we have to be beautiful or at least thin in order to be sexual and sexually desirable. Therefore many of us deny ourselves the pleasures of love and intimacy. . . . With such strong feelings of inadequacy, the fear of rejection becomes very powerful, to be avoided at all costs. . . . We strive for the time 'when I'm thin enough' or 'when I get my body under control.' Then we will be worthy of the pleasures of intimacy."[19]

MYTH #2: The more I dislike my appearance, the more I'll stick with a diet to lose weight.

POWER KNOWLEDGE: That's doubtful. Negative emotions contribute to dieters' inability to maintain weight loss.[20] And there is support for the premise that, while under increased stress, many of us eat more foods high in fat and sugar.[21] Furthermore, high levels of work stress seem to trigger overeating of high-fat foods: In a study published in *Psychosomatic Medicine*, intake of calories, total fat and percentage of calories from fat was significantly higher during periods of high workload and stress than during periods of low workload and stress.[22]

Anger, anxiety, guilt, worry, frustration, boredom, social pressures and loneliness can all trigger the urge to eat inappropriately and skip exercise. Hormones produced by stress—including cortisol and epinephrine—appear to make body cells resistant to insulin, and in some cases, may actually increase the amount of stored body fat.[23]

MYTH #3: All it takes to stay on a diet is positive thinking.

POWER KNOWLEDGE: That's rarely, if ever, true. When it comes to weight control, is the influence of positive thinking always positive? Not according to a recent study at the Max Planck Institute for Human Development and Education in Berlin, where researchers reported that pessimistic expectations interfere with weight-loss success.[24] But, surprisingly, so do positive fantasies—imagining yourself with a perfect, Hollywood-type body. In contrast, the most effective mental attitudes in this study were *optimistic expectation about weight management* combined with *"realistic" fantasies*—where the imagined outcome was less than perfect and more in line with modest, step-by-step improvements.

Dieters frequently get stuck trying to make losing weight the solution to their life's problems. But this common kind of problem solving is an attempt to escape reality, says psychologist Gary Emery, Ph.D. "In general, you may use problem solving as a manipulation into temporary action ('I must solve my problems'), an inhibition to going through obstacles ('I have to solve my problems first') and as a justification for an unfulfilled life ('I had too many unsolvable problems').

"Problem solving reinforces the mistaken notion that you must be problem-free to be happy. Actually, as you become healthier, you give up the need to be problem-free and are willing to take on more real problems and real challenges. You define yourself as capable by your willingness to embrace rather than avoid problems," Dr. Emery says.[25]

SELF-DISCOVERY OF BODY IMAGES: SAMPLE ASSESSMENT

The following items are adapted from Dr. Thomas Cash's *Body-Image Therapy: A Program for Self-Directed Change*. Complete the two sections below and turn to page 160 to interpret your scores.

The Body Areas Satisfaction Scale

Indicate your dissatisfaction or satisfaction with each listed physical area or aspect.

1	2	3	4	5
		Neither		
Very	Mostly	Satisfied nor	Mostly	Very
Dissatisfied	Dissatisfied	Dissatisfied	Satisfied	Satisfied

_____ 1. Face (facial features, complexion)

_____ 2. Hair (color, thickness, texture)

_____ 3. Lower torso (buttocks, hips, thighs, legs)

_____ 4. Mid torso (waist, stomach)

_____ 5. Upper torso (chest or breasts, shoulders, arms)

_____ 6. Muscle tone

_____ 7. Weight

_____ 8. Height

_____ 9. Overall appearance

_____ TOTAL SCORE (Sum of Ratings)

The Situational Inventory of Body-Image Distress

A number of situations are listed below. How often do you have *negative feelings about your appearance* in each situation? There may be situations listed that you have not been in or that you avoid. For these situations, simply indicate how often you believe that you

esteem is the result of how positive or negative our body image is," says Dr. Cash.[2]

Studies also confirm an alarming trend among adolescents: There is so much pressure to have a "perfect" body—in the Hollywood image—that 61 to 77 percent of high school girls are dieting, as are 28 to 42 per-

would experience negative feelings about your appearance *if* you were in the situation.

0	1	2	3	4
		Moderately		Always or
Never	Sometimes	Often	Often	Almost Always

_____ 1. At social gatherings where I know few people.

_____ 2. When I look at myself in the mirror.

_____ 3. When I am with attractive persons.

_____ 4. When someone looks at parts of my appearance that I dislike.

_____ 5. When I try on new clothes at the store.

_____ 6. When I am exercising.

_____ 7. After I have eaten a full meal.

_____ 8. When I am wearing certain revealing clothes.

_____ 9. When I get on the scale to weigh.

_____10. When I think someone has ignored or rejected me.

_____11. When anticipating or having sexual relations.

_____12. When I'm already in a bad mood about something else.

_____13. When I think about how I looked earlier in my life.

_____14. When I see myself in a photograph or videotape.

_____15. When I think I've gained some weight.

_____16. When I think about what I wish I looked like.

_____17. When I recall any kidding or unkind things people have said about my appearance.

_____18. When I'm with people who are talking about appearance, weight or dieting.

_____ TOTAL SCORE (Sum of Ratings)

cent of high school boys.[3] As we pointed out earlier, national surveys show that we've never been so preoccupied and dissatisfied with our bodies—over the past 15 years the number of American men dissatisfied with their bodies has doubled to 34 percent, well over half of us are unhappy with our weight or abdomen size,[4] and nearly all women—

HOW TO SCORE AND INTERPRET THE SELF-DISCOVERY

After you have completed the Self-Discovery of Body Images: Sample Assessment on page 158, use the following guide to help you interpret your scores. The two sections listed below correspond to the two sections on the Sample Assessment.

The Body Areas Satisfaction Scale

Sum your ratings for all nine items. Your total score should fall somewhere between 9 and 45. Locate your score and its interpretation (depending on your sex) below.

Female	Male	Interpretation
35–45	36–45	Your satisfaction with many aspects of your appearance places you in the top 20–25 percent of peers of your sex. Congratulations!
26–34	30–35	Your level of body-image satisfaction is similar to most of your peers. This average level means that there are some areas of your body that you should appreciate more.
9–25	9–29	Your discontent with your looks exceeds about 75 percent of your peers. You really need to learn to like more aspects of your appearance.

even those who seem to have bodies that match Hollywood's ideal— have become obsessed with feelings of not liking their appearance and on surveys almost always endorse items such as, "I am terrified of gaining weight" or "I am always on a diet."[5]

And such nagging voices in your subconscious hold considerable self-harming power, especially when they keep you trapped in old, sabotaging behavior patterns.[6] Time and again we hear people say, "When I feel bad, I overeat." "When I'm angry at myself, I punish myself by

The Situational Inventory of Body-Image Distress

Sum your ratings for all 18 items. Your total score should fall somewhere between 0 and 72. Locate your score and its interpretation (depending on your sex) below.

Female	Male	Interpretation
0–20	0–11	Your experience of negative body-image emotions is relatively infrequent and seldom interferes with your life. At least 75 percent of persons your sex have more body-image distress than you do.
21–36	12–23	Your body-image distress is somewhat frequent, yet is comparable to most of your peers. Sometimes it adversely affects your feelings about yourself. A little improvement would be worthwhile.
37–50	24–36	Your negative body-image emotions occur more often than most of your peers. Distress erupts and disrupts many situations, and it undermines the quality of your life and your self-esteem. Help yourself by improving your body image.
51–72	37–72	Body-image distress is clearly a pervasive problem in your daily life, more troublesome for you than for about 90 percent of your peers. Improving your body image should definitely be a goal!

eating." "When someone makes me feel fat, I use food to get even." Scientists have discovered that when you're on a diet and then feel out of control and no longer restrict what you eat, this feeling of failure is usually not based on reality—that is, a certain number of extra calories or grams of fat. Instead it's triggered by your own *perception* that you've lapsed or cheated, and it can be prompted by emotional distress—especially from ego threats that attack your self-image or bring up feelings of low self-esteem and unattractiveness.[7] As a result, "body shame leads to poor posture—rounded shoulders, drooping head—which is not only unattractive but unhealthy, and interferes with our ability to breathe properly," says psychologist Marcia Germaine Hutchinson, Ed.D.[8]

One of the simplest ways to shake off this negative mindset and start creating a constructive, self-supporting alternative is by choosing a variety of the quick, practical daily habit changes offered to you in *The Power of 5*. By using do-it-anywhere fit times and snack-and-ice-water breaks, for example, you can turn up your energy and calorie-burning power, and there's good scientific evidence that, in addition, your mood will tend to stay more positive and it will be easier to manage stress and hold on to a higher vantage point.[9]

Toss out your bathroom scale! In the weight-control battle, much discouragement—and many a binge—comes from allowing ourselves to become emotionally dependent on the readings we receive each morning from the bathroom scale. Among the reported 70 percent of all dieters who regularly weigh themselves,[10] most forget that their "body weight" reflects an intricate combination of water, muscle, fat, bone and related tissues. It varies from minute to minute, hour to hour, day to day. It can be manipulated with remarkable ease, even with no fat loss occurring. Bathroom scales cannot distinguish between water weight and fat weight. A sudden added pound or two may be just water and may vanish in a day or so. There's just no good reason to weigh yourself every day, or even every week.[11] Besides, as you become more physically fit, you'll gain muscle. Muscle weighs more than fat and, to no surprise, you may actually *gain* weight on the scale while losing fat, changing your body proportions, getting healthier and increasing your energy.

If you're a stickler for mathematical progress checks, measure your waist, hips, thighs and arms—which will begin to change as you lose excess fat. Checking these measurements every month or two can provide a simple indication of progress. The fit of your clothing is, in many cases, another valid sign of improvement. You may want to try on a tight pair of jeans now and put them away, without washing or wearing them again, for future comparison.

Accept yourself right now, just as you are. A few moments is all it takes to give yourself a comforting emotional hug—and it can really pay off. One reason this is so important is that the "if onlys" tend to tie us in knots. For example, most dieters live in a tightening web of "if only" statements: "If only I could lose that 15 pounds." "If only I had more willpower, I could change." Often, when we say, "If only I were thin," what we're really saying is, "I hate myself the way I am." To move forward, you first need to forgive yourself, today, for not looking the way society has coerced you into thinking you *should* look. It's difficult enough to be overweight in our thinness-driven culture, without adding to the problem by abusing yourself. It's also essential for you to distinguish between *having* a body and *being* that body. Remind yourself that the best of who you are, as a human *being*, is in your head and heart. The fact that you *have* a body to live in is something to be thankful for—rather than ending up with the distorted and negative feeling that all *you* are is your *body*, or more precisely, your chunky thighs or protruding abdomen!

Of course we recognize that, chances are, you want to be different than you are right now. But accepting overweight is not the same as resigning yourself to it. And ironically, research shows that you must first take steps to fully accept yourself as a prerequisite to changing. You don't have to *like* your body if you really don't, but it's important to acknowledge your own self-worth and current reality in order to move forward in a healthy, self-supporting way.

It also pays to remember that, for the most part, any contempt you feel for your body or appearance wasn't your own idea in the first place. Our culture put that notion in your head; you learned it. It's time for all of us to fully recognize that self-hatred can hold us at a miserable standstill. To ease its grip, get in the habit of looking in your own full-length mirror, for at least a few minutes a day, in a different way. Make a conscious effort to appreciate your own unique features—your eyes, your facial expressions, your general presence—steadily developing a healthy sense of inner pride and seeing yourself *without saying anything negative about your appearance.* If you've been avoiding mirrors for a long time, this can be a challenging step, but it's an important one.

With these and other supportive changes from *The Power of 5* under way, it's important to consider the final strategy—*Power Vision*—a brief break each evening to acknowledge your specific accomplishments and plan for tomorrow. It works well because it helps your mind "jump the tracks" and keep from getting caught up obsessing over what's wrong with you (which, in turn, prevents you from moving forward with your life). Power Vision begins with a realistic acceptance of who you are and what you've accomplished today, and this serves as a mental springboard to keep moving ahead.

POWER ACTION: MORE OPTIONS
Take Charge of Inner Dialogues and Respond Constructively to Environmental Cues

Successful, long-term weight management requires thinking differently,[26] and one of the most important steps to take each evening before you go to sleep is to take some time to better recognize—and guide—your *self-talk*, the small, chattering "voices" you hear in the back of your mind. Like a nonstop rain of darts, your self-talk—which you may sometimes speak aloud but usually utter silently—pokes away at your subconscious. On top of that, *environmental cues*—social pressure, sabotage from relatives or friends, emotional twists and turns and advertising stimuli from television, radio, billboards, newspapers and magazines—bait you to overeat or choose poor-quality foods even when you're not hungry. But by becoming more aware of your self-talk patterns and the environmental signals that affect you the most, you can gradually control their influence.

> We cannot change anything unless we accept it. Condemnation does not liberate, it oppresses.
>
> —Carl Jung, M.D., Swiss psychologist

Here are some examples: When you notice self-talk turning negative—and putting you down—make it a point to pause and say something more helpful to yourself. Then follow up that statement with some action step to bring out more inner strength and self-pride. The first step in taking control of your mental imagery and self-talk is to become more aware of your current habits. "If you find that your self-talk, that little, nagging voice in the back of your mind, is highly critical and judgmental, or self-discounting, or self-indulgent, or emotionally upsetting, you need to retrain the way you are thinking," says psychologist Joyce D. Nash, Ph.D. "You need to teach your little voice to be more objective and supportive—like a coach for a team. When you allow your self-talk to be negative, you allow it to sabotage you, to rob you of motivation, to enmesh you in painful emotions."[27]

Negative self-talk is often triggered by a critical comment from a friend about your appearance or a glimpse of your physique in a mirror, an upswell of self-doubt or impatience when "final results" are slow in coming, or a sudden urge to eat high-fat foods. You might increase your results by taking a few extra minutes once a month or so to use a well-proven method for identifying and changing self-talk habits: the double column technique. Divide a piece of paper down the middle and label the left column "saboteur" or "negative self-talk" and the right column "voice of truth" or "coach." Then you record negative self-statements you've noted over the past several hours or so—"shoulds," put-downs, and so on—in the left column and then replace them in your mind and heart with true statements that you enter in the right column. It is often simplest to make entries in general categories, as suggested in the following examples.

In goal-setting, an extreme statement such as "I'm *never* going to overeat or eat high-fat foods again" can be replaced with "It's perfectly all right to occasionally eat some high-fat foods. That's because most of the time I'm eating the lower-fat, high-*taste* foods I'm coming to love."

In anticipating results, comments such as "I've got so far to go, and I've tried and failed so many times before, why should things be any different now?" can be exchanged for "Maybe the things I tried before weren't effective—or maybe they just weren't right for me. And this time there's more to it than simply losing fat. I'm building up my health and fitness—5 seconds to 5 minutes at a time."

In gauging progress, appraisals such as "I'm not losing weight fast enough" or "My God! It looks like I gained a few pounds; I might as well quit right now" might be traded for "The most permanent way to lose fat is slowly and steadily" or "If I keep making good *Power of 5* choices, the extra weight will steadily come off. Besides, I'm getting stronger and more toned from exercise—and muscle helps burn off excess body fat night and day."

Weak rationalizations like "I deserve a treat now and then and this rich dessert looks great—besides, I just finished exercising and I can afford it" need to be jettisoned in favor of "Yes, I really *do* deserve regular rewards for making healthy choices in my life, but they don't always need to be food. Today, I feel like _____ (curling up with a favorite new book later this evening; taking a quiet stroll; buying a new music CD or audiotape or some special flowers; snuggling with my spouse, child, grandchild or special friend; window shopping or looking through catalogs for ideas on a new piece of clothing; and so on)."

A catastrophic statement such as "Like the irresponsible person I am, I didn't even take the time to go to exercise class today. I might as well give up right now" should be cast off in favor of "Every active minute counts! I'll get in a few short walks this evening instead. Besides, what I am doing most of the time will carry me through."

Enlist Support and Avoid Sabotage

For some of us, changes are easier to make and maintain when we are part of a group of similarly focused people. If you enjoy participating in physical activities with friends, for example, by all means do them. You may wish to create an informal support group to review and apply the principles of *The Power of 5*. This may also be helpful in fending off conscious or unconscious sabotage attempts from others, since it's estimated that nearly one-third of those who are involved with body-fat control efforts encounter sabotage from family members or friends.[28]

This sabotage can take many forms, such as bringing you food gifts, teasing you by leaving high-fat treats around the house, badgering you to stop at fast-food restaurants that serve only high-fat foods and not supporting your exercise efforts. Why do we experience this sabotage from others? According to Kelly D. Brownell, Ph.D., a leading researcher on obesity who is a professor of psychology at Yale University and co-director of the university's Eating and Weight Disorders Clinic, spouses and friends may fear that you will become too attractive or that you'll begin making more physical or emotional demands, start meeting new friends, launch a social life that excludes them or become more independent or successful.[29] Even when mates and close friends want to help, they often don't know how. They assume the role of body-fat "police officers," delivering warnings and catching violations. This increases tension and undercuts your self-esteem.

If your spouse or close friends feel threatened by your new weight-control program, you may need to reassure them. Then it's time to enlist their true support. First communicate warmly, clearly and firmly, letting them know you want their help. Be specific, leaving nothing to chance. Refuse offers of inappropriate food without offending. Be ready to increase your assertiveness if necessary—it's *your* health and well-being at stake here. Choose your words carefully and state requests positively, since this tends to turn saboteurs into supporters, making people feel good and more willing to help. Instead of saying something like "You make it so hard for me to eat slowly when you stare at your newspaper and wolf down your meal like that" (a negative, indirect request), say "Please help me by eating more slowly and talking with me during the meal" (a positive, direct request).

If You "Blow It," Use a Quick Turnaround

By learning to be kinder to yourself and, on occasion, to eat small amounts of formerly "forbidden" foods, you'll be much less likely to have full-blown binges, and if you *do* happen to overeat and don't automatically yell at yourself, you'll likely eat less and recover more quickly. Here are some quick steps to take.

• Forgive yourself for not being perfect; everybody "blows it" sometimes.

• Become more active—head out the door for a 5-minute "mini-walk"

• Continue with your regular meals and snacks—do *not* eat less today and tomorrow trying to compensate for overeating. You'll simply confuse your body's metabolism.

• In tonight's Power Vision time (see the upcoming section), pay special attention to scheduling a few extra *Power of 5* choices and shortcuts for tomorrow. This helps you let go of guilt and sleep more deeply— and *that* will give you more energy to get things off to a great start first thing in the morning.

Enjoy 5 Minutes of "Power Vision" Each Evening

One of the most useful strategies for lifelong weight control is to make it a daily habit to take 5 minutes each evening—once the household chores are finished and things settle down a bit—to sit in a comfortable chair, breathe deeply, relax your body and focus your mind in what we call Power Vision, a concept introduced in this chapter and discussed further in chapters 29 and 31. Power Vision is a quick, effective way to accentuate your progress and the successes you've had today and then to direct your attention to how best to use *The Power of 5* at specific times tomorrow. Here are some of the considerations for making the most of your Power Vision time.

1. Acknowledge today's specific accomplishments. With *The Power of 5*, it's easy to feel good about whatever 5-minute steps you've taken today to keep your metabolism and energy levels higher. Pause now to reflect on which *Power of 5* choices and shortcuts you used today, as well as other constructive, pleasant experiences in the past 24 hours.

2. Make specific *Power of 5* plans for tomorrow— say yes to more of what matters most, and no to more of what doesn't. This is an ideal time to look ahead in your mind to tomorrow's schedule. When, specifically, would it make the most sense to use the choices and tips from *The Power of 5*? Was there a time today—after lunch, for example, or right before supper, when you probably would have felt more energetic or satisfied if you'd used a *Power of 5* strategy?

3. Identify simple, healthy ways to have more fun— both tonight and tomorrow. "A lot of people who think they want food really want pleasure, solace, comfort and

POWER VISION

1. Acknowledge today's accomplishments.

2. Make specific **Power of 5** plans for tomorrow.

3. Identify simple, healthy ways to have more fun.

4. Choose to be the architect of your future.

> Things which matter
> most should never be at
> the mercy of things
> which matter least.
>
> **—Johann von Goethe,**
> German poet and
> dramatist

relief from boredom," says Howard Flaks, M.D., a weight-loss specialist. "Food is only one of an infinite number of pleasures. I give my clients a list of 150 pleasures: taking a hot bath, calling a friend, getting a pedicure, planning a fantasy vacation. Anything to take their mind off wanting to eat constantly."[30] On a practical level, you plan some brief pleasure-boosting times tomorrow which might include:

• Pausing each hour to be certain you're taking the best care of yourself and supporting the people around you.

• Watching less television—and in its place, spending more hours reading and reflecting as well as increasing your time with loved ones and friends. Surprisingly, watching TV may reflect a slowed metabolism. Researchers at Memphis State University monitored 32 girls watching a half-hour television program, and their metabolic rates *dropped as much as 16 percent below resting metabolic rate*. In other words, they *burned fewer calories watching television than they did by just sitting*.[31]

• Taking some time on the weekend to help others or to initiate or support a cause you deeply believe in.

• Pursuing a craft or hobby that sounds like fun and interests you.

• Stopping to notice nature—to smell a flower, marvel at birds in flight or children playing, gaze up at the stars, admire the clouds and watch the sun rise or set.

• Writing a note or postcard to a loved one or friend, a politician, a school board member, a person in charge of a cause you believe in or someone who has done something worthwhile in your community.

• Cultivating more humor and encouraging laughter. As we discussed in chapter 7, humor relieves tension and helps you stay more relaxed and flexible—instead of rigid or anxious.[32] Start looking for more of the ridiculous, incongruous events that go on around you all the time. Point them out to others. Make up short stories about the funniest things you see or hear, and use them to spice up family discussions at the end of the day. This simple appreciation of life's paradoxes and absurdities is known as "cosmic humor," and sometimes it's the most fun of all.

> Organize and execute
> around priorities.
>
> **—Stephen Covey, Ph.D.,**
> author of *The Seven
> Habits of Highly Effective
> People*

4. Choose to be the architect of your future. Use the final minute of your Power Vision time to plan ahead on a deeper level. This corresponds to the inner longing that most of us feel—to get more out of each minute of life, to give more back, to gain a deeper under-standing of whatever matters most. To move effectively away from the self-limiting "diet trap," it's imperative to take increased conscious con-trol of where your life's heading, one day at a time.

Let's face it, none of us can make time. We can only make *choices*. All the dreaming in the world won't get you anywhere without action. Whether your plans are big or small, whether you're reaching for seri-ous weight control or simply a better way to handle day-to-day living, identifying the specific steps to achieve your objectives really pays off. Big dreams are fine, of course, but it's essential to make your step-by-step daily goals reachable. And, during each evening's Power Vision time, take a few moments to savor your small wins, the one-at-a-time choices and changes you made today, as well as your other efforts and accomplishments. Then do some quick planning for tomorrow.

Your goals can be divided into short-term and long-term categories. *Long-term goals* include your chosen mission—your values and life-path—and far-off dreams ("I want to travel from island to island in the Caribbean," "I want to earn another college degree," "I want to write a novel," "I want to help end world hunger," "I want to provide for my children's future"). But the truth is, to achieve a long-term goal, it must first be divided into small, specific steps, or *short-term goals*. Each must be stated in posi-tive terms, describing what, precisely, you *want*, not what you *don't want*. *Note*: Make sure your goals deal with things you can change di-rectly rather than things that depend on other people making changes. One of the most powerful ways to unlock personal focus and energy is to create a detail-rich, crystal-clear picture of whatever it is that you want to accomplish. Power Vision time is ideal for doing this.

> Planning is bringing the future into the present so that you can do some-thing about it now.
>
> **—Alan Lakein,** time management specialist

Back to *long-term goals* for a moment: During Power Vision, you can take a fresh, hard look at your work and your life. Right now you may wish to write out a personal purpose statement or mission state-ment. Here's how: First define what you want to *be*—what character strengths you want to have and what qualities and skills you want to de-velop. Then describe what you want to *do*—specify in detail what you want to accomplish and what specific contributions you want to make.

Next, reflect on what you've written and make any revisions that come to mind. Ask yourself, Do my goals represent the best within me? Do I feel motivated when I read them or think about them? Am I aware of the strategies and skills I'll need to accomplish my objectives? Then, and most important of all, ask, What, specifically, do I need to do today to reach where I want to be tomorrow? What are the most important activities for me to do now to reach my longer-term goals? In my work? As a husband/father or wife/mother? In weight control and health? Each evening, several minutes of Power Vision can help you keep in touch with these specific, important priorities, instead of letting them slip away in the rush of daily life. (For more highly practical ideas on being the architect of your future, see chapter 31.) Remember, purpose is energy. It's the single most motivating force there is.

Resources

Body Traps by Judith Rodin, Ph.D. (Morrow, 1992). A leading psychologist's enlightening guide to breaking the bonds that keep us from feeling good about our bodies.

Emotional Eating: A Practical Guide to Taking Control by Edward Abramson, Ph.D. (Lexington Books, 1993). A practical, readily understandable action plan by a professor of psychology at California State University.

First Things First by Stephen R. Covey, Ph.D. A. Roger Merrill and Rebecca R. Merrill (Simon & Schuster, 1994). Fresh, doable ideas that transcend traditional approaches to time management.

The Weight Maintenance Survival Guide by Kelly D. Brownell, Ph.D. and Judith Rodin, Ph.D. Sage advice from two Yale University psychology professors on making lifelong weight control a reality.

PERSONAL POWER NOTES
A Quick-List of This Chapter's Power-Action Options

Make a 5-minute assessment of your current body image.
- *Toss out your bathroom scale.*
- *Accept yourself, right now, just as you are.*

Take charge of inner dialogues and respond constructively to environmental cues.

Enlist support and avoid sabotage.

If you "blow it," use a quick turnaround.

Enjoy several minutes of Power Vision each evening.

PERSONAL NOTES

_____

_____

_____

_____

_____

_____

_____

_____

_____

_____

_____

_____

References

CHAPTER 8

1. Ruderman, A. J. "Dietary Restraint: A Theoretical and Empirical Review." *Psychological Bulletin* 99 (1986): 247–262.
2. Polivy, J., quoted in *Obesity and Health* 6 (5)(Sept./Oct. 1992): 86.
3. Studies by Polivy, J. *Environmental Nutrition* 15 (3)(Mar. 1992): 1.
4. Brownell, K. D. "Obesity: Understanding and Treating a Serious, Prevalent and Refractory Disorder." *Journal of Consulting and Clinical Psychology* 50 (1982): 820–840.
5. Rosencrans, K. "Health Risks of Obesity." *Obesity and Health* 6 (2)(May/June 1992): 45–47, 51; Harris et al. *Journal of the American Medical Association* 259(1988): 1520–1524; Polivy, J., quoted in *Obesity and Health* 6 (5)(Sept./Oct. 1992): 86. According to Dr. Polivy, professor of psychology and psychiatry at the University of Toronto, dieting can lead to gallstones, cardiac disorders, weakness, fatigue, anemia, gouty arthritis, nausea, hair loss, elevated cholesterol, hypertension, aching muscles, loss of lean (muscle) tissue, changes in liver function, constipation, amenorrhea and decreased sex drive and even death.
6. J. E. Manson et al. "Body Weight and Longevity." *Journal of the American Medical Association* 257 (3)(1987): 353–358.
7. Williamson, D. F. Centers for Disease Control report given to Congress on Sept. 24, 1990, reported in *Obesity and Health* 6 (2)(May/June 1992): 49.
8. D. M. Dreon et al. "Dietary Fat: Carbohydrate Ratio and Obesity in Middle-Aged Men." *American Journal of Clinical Nutrition* 47 (1988): 995–1000; Ries, W. "Feeding Behavior in Obesity." *Proceedings of the Nutrition Society* 32 (1973): 187–193; L. E. Braitman et al. "Obesity and Caloric Intake: The National Health and Nutrition Examination Survey (Hanes I)." *Journal of Chronic Disease* 38 (9)(1985): 727–732; Miller, W. C. *The Non Diet Diet* (Englewood, Colo.: Morton Publishing, 1991): 64.
9. C. A. Geissler et al. "The Daily Metabolic Rate of the Post-Obese and the Lean." *American Journal of Clinical Nutrition* 45 (1987): 914–922; T. A. Wadden et al. "Responsible and Irresponsible Use of Very Low Caloric Diets in the Treatment of Obesity." *Journal of the American Medical Association* 262 (1990): 83–85; W. Garner et al. "Psychoeducational Principles in the Treatment of Bulimia and Anorexia Nervosa," in *Handbook of Psychotherapy for Anorexia Nervosa and Bulimia*, eds. Garner, D. M., and Garfinkel, P. E. (New York: Guilford Press, 1985): 513–575; B. J. Stordy et al. "Weight Gain, Thermic Effect of Glucose and Resting Metabolism Rate during Recovery from Anorexia Nervosa." *American Journal of Clinical Nutrition* 30 (1977): 138.
10. D. T. Elliot et al. "Sustained Depression of the Resting Metabolic Rate after Massive Weight Loss." *American Journal of Clinical Nutrition* 49 (1989): 93–96.
11. G. L. Blackburn et al. "Weight Cycling: The Experience of Human Dieters." *American Journal of Clinical Nutrition* 49 (1989): 1105–1109.
12. Schachter, S. "Recidivism and Self-Cure of Smoking and Obesity." *American Psychologist* 38 (1982): 346–354; Colvin, R. H., and Olson, S. C. *Keeping It Off: Winning at Weight Loss* (New York: Simon & Schuster, 1985); Wolfe, B. L. "Long-Term Maintenance Following Attainment of Goal Weight: A Preliminary Investigation." *Addictive Behaviors* (in press).
13. Colvin and Olson. *Keeping It Off.*
14. Gallup poll, cited in Brownell, K. D., and Stein, L. J. "Metabolic and Behavioral Effects

of Weight Loss and Regain: A Review of the Animal and Human Literature," in *Perspectives in Behavioral Medicine: Eating, Sleeping, and Sex*, eds. Stunkard, A. J., and Baum, A. (Hillsdale, N.J.: Erlbaum, 1989): 39–52.

15. Kimbrell, A. *The Human BodyShop* (New York: HarperCollins, 1992).

16. Rodin, J. *Body Traps* (New York: Morrow, 1992).

17. Calorie Control Council Report. *Obesity and Health* 4 (9)(Sept. 1990): 1.

18. "Experts Speak Out: It's Time to Give Up Dieting." *Environmental Nutrition* 15 (3)(Mar. 1992): 1.

19. Wadden, T. University of Pennsylvania 5–Year Study, quoted in the *New York Times* (Apr. 1, 1990).

20. Ibid.

21. National Institutes of Health Conference. *Newsweek* (Aug. 17, 1992): 57.

22. D. G. Schlundt et al. "The Role of Breakfast in the Treatment of Obesity." *American Journal of Clinical Nutrition* 55 (1992): 645–651; *Obesity and Health* 6 (12)(Nov./Dec. 1992): 103.

23. Zak, V., Carlin, C., and Vash, P. D. *Fat-to-Muscle Diet* (New York: Berkley, 1988): 30.

24. "Body-Trimming Breakfasts." *Prevention* (Apr. 1992): 67–74.

25. Stone, K. *Snack Attack* (New York: Warner, 1991): 169.

26. A. S. Levine et al. "Effect of Breakfast Cereals on Short-Term Food Intake." *American Journal of Clinical Nutrition* 50 (1989): 1303–1307.

27. Stone. *Snack Attack*: 33, 87.

28. Callaway, C. W. *The Callaway Diet* (New York: Bantam, 1991): 192.

29. Hager, D. L. "Why Breakfast Is Important." *Weight Control Digest* 3 (1)(Jan./Feb. 1993): 225–226.

30. Stamford, B. A., and Shimer, P. *Fitness without Exercise* (New York: Warner, 1990); Zak, Carlin, and Vash. *Fat-to-Muscle*: 30; Natow, A. B., and Heslin, J. *The Fat Attack Plan* (New York: Pocket Books, 1990): 42, 165.

31. Zak, Carlin, and Vash. *Fat-to-Muscle*: 30.

32. Callaway, C. W., quoted in *Prevention* (Sept. 1992): 56.

33. Lamb, L. E. *The Weighting Game: The Truth about Weight Control* (New York: Lyle Stuart, 1988): 265.

34. Special Report. *Tufts University Diet and Nutrition Letter* 10 (4)(June 1992): 6.

35. Natow and Heslin. *The Fat Attack Plan*: 42; Schlundt. "The Role of Breakfast": 645–651.

36. "Health after 50." *The Johns Hopkins Medical Letter* 4 (5)(July 1992): 1.

37. Brownell and Stein. "Metabolic and Behavioral Effects": 39–52.

38. Ravussin, E., and Swinburn, B. A. "Energy Metabolism," in *Obesity: Theory and Therapy*, 2nd ed., Stunkard, A. J., and Wadden, T. A. (New York: Raven Press, 1992): 97–123; McArdle, W. D., Katch, F. I., and Katch, V. L. *Exercise Physiology: Energy, Nutrition, and Human Performance*, 3rd ed. (Philadelphia: Lea & Febiger, 1991): 159; Foster, G. D. "Causes of Obesity: Resting Metabolic Rate." *Weight Control Digest* 1 (3)(Mar./Apr. 1991): 42–44.

39. Jequier, E. "Energy Utilization in Human Obesity," in *Human Obesity*, eds. Wurtman, R. J., and Wurtman, J. J. (New York: New York Academy of Sciences, 1987).

40. Zak, Carlin, and Vash. *Fat-to-Muscle*: 17–18.

41. Danforth, E. "Diet and Obesity." *American Journal of Clinical Nutrition* 41 (May 1985): 1132–1145; Danforth, E. "Calories: A Scientific Breakthrough." *Shape* (Mar. 1991): 47.

42. A. Kendall et al. "Weight Loss on a Low-Fat Diet." *American Journal of Clinical Nutrition* 53 (1991): 1124–1129.

43. Callaway. *Callaway Diet*: 5.

44. Wegner, D. M. *White Bears and Other Unwanted Thoughts* (New York: Viking, 1989); Uleman, J. S., and Bargh, J. A., eds. *Unintended Thought* (New York: Guilford Press, 1989).

45. C. A. Geissler et al. "The Daily Metabolic Rate of the Post-Obese and the Lean." *American Journal of Clinical Nutrition* 45 (1987): 914–922; Wadden. "Responsible and Irresponsible Use": 83–85; Garner. "Psychoeducational Principles": 513–575; Stordy. "Weight Gain, Thermic Effect": 138.

46. Callaway. *Callaway Diet*: 47.

47. Brownell and Stein. "Metabolic and Behavioral Effects": 39–50.

48. Wooley, S., quoted in Sternhell, C. "We'll Always Be Fat, but Fat Can Be Fit." *Ms.* (May 1985): 143.

49. S. Kayman et al. "Maintenance and Relapse after Weight Loss in Women." *American Journal of Clinical Nutrition* 52 (1990): 800–807; Brownell, K. D. *The LEARN Program for Weight Control*, 2nd ed. (Dallas: LEARN Education Center, 1991); J. P. Mooney et al. "The Abstinence Violation Effect and Very Low Calorie Diet Success." *Addictive Behaviors* 17 (1992): 319–324; Blackburn, G. L., and Rosofsky, W. "Making the Connection between Weight Loss, Dieting, and Health." *Weight Control Digest* 2 (1)(Jan./Feb. 1992): 127.

50. Rodin. *Body Traps*: 182.

51. R. H. Streigel-Moore et al. "Toward an Understanding of Risk Factors for Bulimia." *American Psychologist* 41 (1986): 246–263.

52. A. Keys et al. *The Biology of Human Starvation* (Minneapolis: University of Minnesota Press, 1950): 63–78.

53. Wooley, S., and Wooley, W. *Journal of Applied Behavior* 12 (1979); Callaway. *Callaway Diet*: 7.

54. Ries, W. "Feeding Behavior in Obesity." *Proceedings of the Nutrition Society* 32 (1973): 187–193; L. E. Braitman et al. "Obesity and Caloric Intake: The National Health and Nutrition Examination Survey (Hanes I)." *Journal of Chronic Disease* 38 (9)(1985): 727–732.

55. D. M. Dreon et al. "Dietary Fat: Carbohydrate Ratio and Obesity in Middle-Aged Men." *American Journal of Clinical Nutrition* 47(1988): 995–1000.

56. Miller. *Non Diet Diet*: 98.

57. Anderson, M. A. "The Leader's Forum: Helping Clients Begin an Exercise Program." *Weight Control Digest* 1 (6)(Sept./Oct. 1991): 93.

58. Harris et al. *Journal of the American Medical Association* 259 (1988): 1520–1524.

59. Rosencrans, K. "Health Risks of Obesity." *Obesity and Health* 6 (2)(May/June 1992): 45–47, 51.

60. L. Lissner et al. "Variability of Body Weight and Health Outcomes in the Framingham Population." *New England Journal of Medicine* 324 (1991): 1839–1844.

CHAPTER 9

1. Darden, E. *A Day-by-Day 10-Step Program* (Dallas: Taylor Publishing, 1992): 43.

2. Darden. *Day-by-Day*: 43; Darden, E. Personal communication (Oct. 19, 1992).

3. Lamb, L. E. *The Weighting Game: The Truth about Weight Control* (New York: Lyle Stuart, 1988). "There are millions of people in the United States who are suffering from *undernutrition*—a simple lack of calories because they have been on unwise diets . . . ," says Dr. Lamb, cardiologist and medical consultant to the President's Council on Physical Fitness. "As metabolism slows, there is less demand for oxygen. [And] fatigue is the single most commonly experienced symptom by individuals on a diet overly restricted in calories."

4. Darden. *Day-by-Day*: 41.

5. Blackburn, G. L., quoted in *Prevention* (Sept. 1992): 50.

6. Miller, W. C. *The Non Diet Diet* (Englewood, Colo.: Morton Publishing, 1991): 83–84.

7. *Obesity and Health* 3 (2)(Feb. 1989): 4; Brandon, J. E. *Health Values* (May/June 1987).

8. Lamb. *The Weighting Game*: 95–96.

9. Ibid.: 56.

10. Leveille, T. "Adipose Tissue Metabolism: Influence of Eating and Diet Composition." *Federation Proceedings* 29 (1970): 1294–1301; Lukert, B. "Biology of Obesity," in Wolman, B., ed., *Psychological Aspects of Obesity: A Handbook* (New York: Van Nostrand Reinhold, 1982): 1–14; Szepsi, B. "A Model of Nutritionally Induced Overweight: Weight 'Rebound' Following Caloric Restriction," in Bray, G., ed., *Recent Advances in Obesity Research* (London: Newman, Ltd., 1978).

11. Mirkin, G. *Getting Thin* (Boston: Little, Brown, 1983): 62.

12. Logue, A. W. *The Psychology of Eating and Drinking* (New York: W. H. Freeman, 1991): 215.

13. Mirkin. *Getting Thin*: 62–65, 195; Darden. *Day-by-Day*: 26.

14. Miller. *Non Diet Diet*: 88.

15. Rossi, E. L., with Nimmons, D. *The 20-Minute Break* (Los Angeles: J. P. Tarcher, 1991): 122–123.

16. D. A. Jenkins et al. "Nibbling versus Gorging: Metabolic Advantages of Increased Meal Frequency." *New England Journal of Medicine* 321 (4)(Oct. 5, 1989): 929–934.

17. Jones, P. J., Leitch, C. A., and Pederson, R. A. "Meal-Frequency Effects on Plasma Hormone Concentrations and Cholesterol Synthesis in Humans." *American Journal of Clinical Nutrition* 57 (6)(1993): 868–874; S. L. Edelstein et al. "Increased Meal Frequency Associated with Decreased Cholesterol Concentrations." *American Journal of Clinical Nutrition* 55 (1992): 664–669.

18. Edelstein et al. "Increased Meal Frequency."

19. Danforth. "Diet and Obesity." *Proceedings of the National Academy of Sciences U. S. A.* 82 (1985): 4866.

20. "Is Fat More Fattening?" *Tufts University Diet and Nutrition Letter* 4 (12)(Feb. 1987): 1–2; *Metabolism* 31 (1982): 1234–1242.

21. A. Trembley et al. "Impact of Dietary Fat Content and Fat Oxidation on Energy Intake in Humans." *American Journal of Clinical Nutrition* 49 (1989): 799–805.

22. Bouchard, C. "The Response to Long-Term Overfeeding in Identical Twins." *New England Journal of Medicine* 322 (1990): 1477–1482.

23. M. K. Fordyce-Baum et al. "Use of an Expanded-Whole-Wheat Product in the Reduction of Body Weight and Serum Lipids in Obese Females." *American Journal of Clinical Nutrition* 50 (1989): 30–36; S. D. Rossner et al. "Weight Reduction with Dietary Fibre Supplements—Results of Two Double-Blind Randomized Studies." *Acta Medica Scandinavica* 222 (1988): 83–88.

24. Miller. *Non Diet Diet*: 75–77.

25. Ibid.: 77.

26. Darden. *Day-by-Day*: 43.

27. Applegate, L. *Power Foods* (Emmaus, Pa.: Rodale Press, 1991): 2.

28. Stone, K. *Snack Attack* (New York: Warner, 1991): 145.

29. Applegate. *Power Foods*: 8.

30. "Accounting for Taste." *University of California at Berkeley Wellness Letter* 7 (2)(Nov. 1990): 7.

31. R. Griffiths et al. *New England Journal of Medicine* (Oct. 15, 1992).

32. Rodin, J. *Body Traps* (New York: Morrow, 1992): 194.
33. Callaway, C. W. *The Callaway Diet* (New York: Bantam, 1991): 191.
34. A. Laws et al. "Behavioral Covariates of Waist-to-Hip Ratio in Rancho Bernardo." *American Journal of Public Health* 80 (Nov. 1990): 1358–1362.
35. P. M. Suter et al. "The Effect of Ethanol on Fat Storage in Healthy Subjects." *New England Journal of Medicine* 326 (April 1992): 983–987.
36. *American Journal of Clinical Nutrition* 52 (1990): 246–253.

CHAPTER 10

1. Gallup Survey commissioned by the American Dietetic Association. *Weight Control Digest* 1 (7)(Nov./Dec. 1991): 100.
2. Grilo, C. M., Wilfley, D. E., and Brownell, K. D. "Physical Activity and Weight Control: Why Is the Link So Strong?" *The Weight Control Digest* 2 (3)(May/June 1992): 153–160; Grilo, C. M., Brownell, K. D., and Stunkard, A. J. "The Metabolic and Psychological Importance of Exercise in Weight Control," in *Obesity: Theory and Therapy*, eds. Stunkard, A. J., and Walden, T. A. (New York: Raven Press, 1992); Piscatella, J. C. *Controlling Your Fat Tooth* (New York: Workman, 1991): 100–104.
3. A. R. Kristal et al. "Nutrition Knowledge, Attitudes, and Perceived Norms as Correlates of Selecting Low-Fat Diets." *Health Education Research* 5 (1990): 467–477; A. R. Kristal et al. "Long-Term Maintenance of Low-Fat Diets: Durability of Fat-Related Dietary Habits in the Women's Health Trial." *Journal of the American Dietetic Association* (in press).
4. N. Urban et al. "Correlates of Maintenance of a Low-Fat Diet among Women in the Women's Health Trial." *Preventive Medicine* 21 (1992): 279–291.
5. Rodin, J. *Body Traps* (New York: Morrow, 1992): 191–192.
6. Ornish, D., quoted in *Newsweek* (May 27, 1991): 53.
7. Rodin. *Body Traps*: 163.
8. Stark, R. E. T., quoted in "Good, Better, Best Weight Loss Ideas from the American Society for Bariatric Physicians." *Prevention* (Jan. 1988): 35–41; 115–124.
9. Weingarten, H., quoted in Goldberg, J. "The Taste of Desire." *American Health* (Oct. 1990): 52.
10. "Medical Consensus Survey of 300 Nutrition Experts," reported in Zarrow, S. *Men's Health* (Apr. 1992): 72–73.
11. Schiffman, S. "The Use of Flavor to Enhance the Efficacy of Reducing Diets." *Hospital Practice* 21 (7)(1986): 44H-44R.
12. Henry, C. J. K., and Emergy, B. "Effect of Spiced Food on Metabolic Rate." *Human Nutrition: Clinical Nutrition* 40C (1986): 165–168.
13. Schiffman. "The Use of Flavor": 44H-44R; Quebec studies cited in Bricklin, M., ed. *Prevention's Lose Weight Guidebook* (Emmaus, Pa.: Rodale Press, 1992): 64.
14. Brandon, J. E. *Health Values* (May/June 1987); "What Is a Slender Eating Style?" *Obesity and Health* 3 (2)(Feb. 1989): 4.
15. *International Journal of Obesity* 13 (1)(1989): 10.
16. Spiegel, T. A., Wadden, T. A., and Foster, G. D. "Objective Measurement of Eating Rate during Behavioral Treatment of Obesity." *Behavior Therapy* 22 (1991): 61–67.
17. *Tufts University Diet and Nutrition Letter* 9 (4)(June 1991): 1–2.
18. Ferber, C., and Cabanac, M. "Influence of Noise on Gustatory Affective Ratings and Preference for Sweet or Salt." *Appetite* 8 (1987): 229–235; McCarron, A., and Tierney, K. J. "The Effect of Auditory Stimulation on the Consumption of Soft Drinks." *Appetite* 13 (1989): 155–159; T. C. Roballey et al. "The Effect of Music on Eating Behavior." *Bulletin*

of the Psychonomic Society 23 (1985): 221–222.

19. Stone, K. *Snack Attack* (New York: Warner, 1991): 156.

20. Miller, W. C. *The Non Diet Diet* (Englewood, Colo.: Morton Publishing, 1991): 70, 91.

21. Oscai, L. B., Brown, M. M., and Miller, W. C. "Effect of Dietary Fat on Food Intake, Growth, and Body Composition in Rats." *Growth* 48 (1984): 415–424; Oscai, L. B., Miller, W. C., and Arnall, D. A. "Effects of Dietary Sugar and of Dietary Fat on Food Intake and Body Fat Content in Rats." *Growth* 5 (1987): 64–73.

22. B. E. Levin et al. "Metabolic Features of Diet-Induced Obesity without Hyperphagia in Young Rats." *American Journal of Physiology* 251 (20)(1986): R433–R440; D. M. Dreon et al. "Dietary Fat: Carbohydrate Ratio and Obesity in Middle-Aged Men." *American Journal of Clinical Nutrition* 47 (1988): 995–1000.

23. C. N. Sadur et al. "Fat Feeding Decreases Insulin Responsiveness of Adipose Tissue Lipoprotein Lipase." *Metabolism* 33 (1984): 1043–1047; Stamford, B. A., and Shimer, P. *Fitness without Exercise* (New York: Warner, 1990): 186–187; N. Torbay et al. "Insulin Increases Body Fat Despite Control of Food Intake and Physical Activity." *American Journal of Physiology* 248 (1985): R120–R124.

24. A. Trembley et al. "Impact of Dietary Fat Content and Fat Oxidation on Energy Intake in Humans." *American Journal of Clinical Nutrition* 49 (1989): 799–805.

25. Bouchard, C. "The Response to Long-Term Overfeeding in Identical Twins." *New England Journal of Medicine* 322 (1990): 1477–1482.

26. "10 Appetite Cutoffs." *Prevention* (Sept. 1992): 52.

27. D. Schapiro et al. "Estimate of Breast Cancer Risk Reduction with Weight Loss." *Cancer* 67 (10)(May 1991).

28. M. K. Fordyce-Baum et al. "Use of an Expanded-Whole-Wheat Product in the Reduction of Body Weight and Serum Lipids in Obese Females." *American Journal of Clinical Nutrition* 50 (1989): 30–36; S. D. Rossner et al. "Weight Reduction with Dietary Fibre Supplements—Results of Two Double-Blind Randomized Studies." *Acta Medica Scandinavica* 222 (1988): 83–88.

29. Miller. *Non Diet Diet*: 75–77.

30. Ibid.: 92.

31. Ibid.: 77.

32. Drewnowski, A. *Environmental Nutrition* 16 (10)(Oct. 1993): 6; Oscai, Miller, and Arnall. "Effects of Dietary Sugar": 64–73; Oscai, L. B., and Miller, W. C. "Dietary-Induced Severe Obesity: Exercise Implications." *Medicine and Science in Sports and Exercise* 18 (1)(1985): 6–9; Oscai, Brown, and Miller. "Effect of Dietary Fat": 415–424.

33. "Are You Eating Right? What 68 Nutrition Experts *Really* Think about Diet and Health." *Consumer Reports* (Oct. 1992): 644–653; J. Hallfrisch et al. "Modification of the United States' Diet to Effect Changes in Blood Lipids and Lipoprotein Distribution." *Atherosclerosis* 57 (2–3)(Nov. 1985): 179–188; Connor, S. L., and Connor, W. E. *The New American Diet* (New York: Simon & Schuster, 1986); Alabaster, O. *The Power of Prevention* (New York: Fireside, 1985): 87–88, 107.

34. Hellmich, N. "Midlife Middles Are Prime for Reducing." *USA Today* (Mar. 30, 1992).

35. A. Kendall et al. "Weight Loss on a Low-Fat Diet." *American Journal of Clinical Nutrition* 53 (1991): 1124–1129.

36. Stone. *Snack Attack*: 33.

37. Grilo, Wilfley, and Brownell. "Physical Activity and Weight Control": 153–160; Grilo, Brownell, and Stunkard. "The Metabolic and Psychological"; Piscatella. *Controlling Your Fat Tooth*: 100–104.

38. Evans, W., and Rosenberg, I. H. *BioMarkers* (New York: Simon & Schuster, 1991): 222.

39. S. M. Grundy et al. "Rationale of the Diet-Heart Statement of the American Heart Association, Report of the Nutrition Committee." *Circulation* 65 (4)(1982): 841A; Cooper, K. H. *Controlling Cholesterol* (New York: Bantam, 1988): 12, 83.

40. Special Report. *Tufts University Diet and Nutrition Letter* 10 (4)(June 1992): 4.

41. *Diet and Health: Implications for Reducing Chronic Disease* (National Academy of Sciences): 8 (1989).

42. J. E. Blundell et al. "Paradoxical Effects of an Intense Sweetener (Aspartame) on Appetite." *Lancet* (May 10, 1986): 1092–1093; Brala, P. M., and Hagen, R. L. "Effects of Sweetness Perception and Caloric Value of a Preload on Short-Term Intake." *Physiology and Behavior* 30 (1983): 1–9; Porikos, K. P., and Friedman, M. I. "Drinking Saccharin Increases Food Intake and Preference." *Appetite* 12 (1989): 1–10.

43. D. G. Bruce et al. "Cephalic Phase Metabolic Responses in Normal Weight Adults." *Metabolism* 36 (1987): 721–725; Geiselman, P. J. "Sugar-Induced Hyperphagia: Is Hyperinsulinemia, Hypoglycemia, or Any Other Factor a 'Necessary' Condition?" *Appetite* 11 (Supplement) (1988): 26–34; Rodin, J. "Insulin Levels, Hunger, and Food Intake: An Example of Feedback Loops in Body Weight Control." *Health Psychology* 4 (1985): 1–24; J. Rodin et al. "Effect of Insulin and Glucose on Feeding Behavior." *Metabolism* 34 (1985): 826–831; C. Simon et al. "Cephalic Phase Insulin Secretion in Relation to Food Presentation in Normal and Overweight Subjects." *Physiology and Behavior* 36 (1986): 465–469; Tordoff, M. G., and Friedman, M. I. "Drinking Saccharin Increases Food Intake and Preference." *Appetite* 12 (1989): 37–56; VanderWeele, D. A. "Hyperinsulinism and Feeding: Not All Sequences Lead to the Same Behavioral Outcome or Conclusions." *Appetite* 6 (1985): 47–52; Vasselli, J. R. "Carbohydrate Ingestion, Hypoglycemia, and Obesity." *Appetite* 6 (1985): 53–59.

44. Callaway, C. W. *The Callaway Diet* (New York: Bantam, 1991): 194.

45. Drewnowski, A. *Environmental Nutrition* 16 (10)(Oct. 1993): 6; Oscai, Miller, and Arnall. "Effects of Dietary Sugar": 64–73; Oscai and Miller. "Dietary-Induced Severe Obesity": 6–9; Oscai, Brown, and Miller. "Effect of Dietary Fat": 415–424.

46. This section adapted from Cooper, R. K. *Health and Fitness Excellence* (Boston: Houghton Mifflin, 1989).

47. Wegner, D. M. *White Bears and Other Unwanted Thoughts* (New York: Viking, 1989); Uleman, J. S., and Bargh, J. A., eds. *Unintended Thought* (New York: Guilford Press, 1989).

48. Smith, A. F., cited in DeAngelis, T. "On a Diet? Don't Trust Your Memory." *Psychology Today* (Oct. 1989): 12.

49. Brownell, K. D. *The LEARN Program for Weight Control*, 2nd ed. (Dallas: The LEARN Education Center, 1991): 15.

50. K. J. Streit et al. "Food Records: A Predictor and Modifier of Weight Change in a Long-Term Weight Loss Program." *Journal of the American Dietetic Association* 91 (1991): 213–216.

CHAPTER 11

1. McArdle, W. D., Katch, F. I., and Katch, V. L. *Exercise Physiology: Energy, Nutrition, and Human Performance*, 3rd ed. (Philadelphia: Lea & Febiger, 1991): 684–685.

2. Grilo, C. M., Wilfley, D. E., and Brownell, K. D. "Physical Activity and Weight Control: Why Is the Link So Strong?" *Weight Control Digest* 2 (3)(May/June 1992): 53–60.

3. K. N. Pavlou et al. "Exercise as an Adjunct to Weight Loss and Maintenance in Moderately Obese Subjects." *American Journal of Clinical Nutrition* 49 (1989): 1115–1123; S. Kayman et al. "Maintenance and Relapse after Weight Loss in Women." *American Jour-*

nal of Clinical Nutrition (in press).

4. Stamford, B. A., and Shimer, P. *Fitness without Exercise* (New York: Warner, 1990): 44.

5. Myers, D. G. *The Pursuit of Happiness* (New York: Morrow, 1992): 76; 77–79; 206–207.

6. Zak, V., Carlin, C., and Vash, P. D. *Fat-to-Muscle Diet* (New York: Berkley, 1988); Stamford and Shimer. *Fitness*: 41, 44.

7. Sheats, C. *Lean Bodies* (Dallas: Summit Group, 1992): 25.

8. Wilcox, A., study cited in "Fat Burns as Sun Rises." *Prevention* (Oct. 1986): 67.

9. Stamford, B. "Meals and the Timing of Exercise." *The Physician and Sports Medicine* 17 (11)(Nov. 1989): 151.

10. Stamford and Shimer. *Fitness*: 44, 128; Stamford. "Meals and the Timing": 151; J. M. Davis et al. "Weight Control and Calorie Expenditure: Thermogenic Effects of Pre-Prandial and Post-Prandial Exercise." *Psychology of Addictive Behavior* 14 (3)(1989): 347–351; Poehlman, E. T., and Horton, E. S. "The Impact of Food Intake and Exercise on Energy Expenditure." *Nutrition Reviews* 47 (5)(May 1989): 129–137.

11. Roffers, M. "Nutrition Myths." *Medical Self-Care* (Mar./Apr. 1986): 52.

12. Davis et al. "Weight Control": 347–351.

13. Davis et al. "Weight Control"; Gleeson, M. "Effects of Physical Exercise on Metabolic Rate and Dietary-Induced Thermogenesis." *British Journal of Nutrition* 47 (1982); R. Bielinski et al. "Energy Metabolism during the Postexercise Recovery in Man." *American Journal of Clinical Nutrition* 42 (1985); Darden, E. *A Day-by-Day 10-Step Program* (Dallas: Taylor Publishing, 1992): 75.

14. Stamford, B. A. "What Time Should You Exercise?" *The Physician and Sports Medicine* 14 (8)(Aug. 1986): 162.

15. Stamford. "Meals and the Timing"; Roffers. "Nutrition Myths."

16. S. Kayman et al. "Maintenance and Relapse after Weight Loss in Women: Behavioral Aspects." *American Journal of Clinical Nutrition* 52 (1990): 800–807.

17. Piscatella, J. C. *Controlling Your Fat Tooth* (New York: Workman, 1991): 100–104.

18. Tremblay, A. in *International Journal of Obesity* 13 (1989): 4.

19. C. J. Caspersen et al. "Status of the 1990 Physical Fitness and Exercise Objectives." *Public Health Reports* 101 (1986): 587–592.

20. Piscopo, J. *Fitness and Aging* (New York: Wiley, 1985).

21. G. F. Fletcher et al. "Benefits and Recommendations for Physical Activity Programs for All Americans: A Statement for Health Professionals by the Committee on Exercise and Cardiac Rehabilitation of the Council on Clinical Cardiology, American Heart Association." *Circulation* 86 (1992): 340–344.

22. R. S. Raffensberger et al. "The Association of Changes in Physical Activity Level and Other Lifestyle Characteristics with Mortality among Men." *New England Journal of Medicine* 328 (1993): 538–545; R. S. Raffensberger et al. "Changes in Physical Activity and Other Lifeway Patterns Influencing Longevity." (submitted for publication).

23. Anderson, M. A. "The Leader's Forum: Helping Clients Begin an Exercise Program." *Weight Control Digest* 1 (6)(Sept./Oct. 1991): 93.

24. Dishman, R. K. "Exercise Compliance: A New View for Public Health." *The Physician and Sports Medicine* 14 (1986): 127–145.

25. J. Pekkanen et al. "Reduction of Premature Mortality by High Physical Activity: A 20-Year Followup Study of Middle-Aged Finnish Men." *Lancet* 1 (1987): 1473–1477.

26. Blackburn, G. L., quoted in Hellmich, N. "Simple Lifestyle Strategies." *USA Today* (Apr. 2, 1992).

27. Davis et al. "Weight Control": 347–351; Gleeson. "Effects of Physical Exercise": 173; Bielinski et al. "Energy Metabolism": 69–82.

28. Danforth, E. "Diet and Obesity." *American Journal of Clinical Nutrition* 41 (May 1985): 1132–1145.
29. Rodin, J., and Plante, T. J. "The Psychological Effects of Exercise," in *Biological Effects of Physical Activity*, eds. Williams, R. S., and Wallace, A. (Champaign, Ill.: Human Kinetics, 1989).
30. R. F. DeBusk et al. "Training Effects of Long versus Short Bouts of Exercise in Healthy Subjects." *American Journal of Cardiology* 65 (1990): 1010–1013.
31. Thayer, R. E. "Energy, Tiredness, and Tension Effects of a Sugar Snack versus Moderate Exercise." *Journal of Personality and Social Psychology* 52 (1987): 119–125.
32. Grilo, Wilfley, and Brownell. "Physical Activity": 153–160; Grilo, C. M., Brownell, K. D., and Stunkard, A. J. "The Metabolic and Psychological Importance of Exercise in Weight Control," in *Obesity: Theory and Therapy*, eds. Stunkard, A. J., and Walden, T. A. (New York: Raven Press, 1992); Piscatella. *Controlling Your Fat Tooth*: 100–104.
33. Blair, S. N. "Ask the Expert: Fat Burn and Exercise." *Weight Control Digest* 1 (3)(Mar./Apr. 1991): 47.
34. Grilo, Wifley, and Brownell. "Physical Activity": 53–60.
35. Hauri, P., and Linde, S. *No More Sleepless Nights* (New York: Wiley, 1991): 130–131.
36. Stephens, T. "Physical Activity and Mental Health in the United States and Canada: Evidence from Four Population Surveys." *Preventive Medicine* 17 (1988): 35–47; Hogan, J. "Personality Correlates of Physical Fitness." *Journal of Personality and Social Psychology* 56 (1989): 284–288; Tucker, L. A. "Physical Fitness and Psychological Disorders." *International Journal of Sports Psychology* 21 (1990): 185–201.
37. Yessis, M. *Secrets of Soviet Sports Fitness and Training* (New York: M. Evans, 1987): 71–78; Lawrence, R. M., and Rosenzweig, S. *Going the Distance* (Los Angeles: J. P. Tarcher, 1987): 26–27; Shellock, F. G. "Physiological Benefits of Warm-Up." *The Physician and Sports Medicine* 11 (10)(Oct. 1983): 134–139; Shyne, K. "To Stretch or Not to Stretch?" *The Physician and Sports Medicine* 10 (9)(Sept. 1982): 137–140.
38. Sharkey, B. J. *New Dimensions in Aerobic Fitness* (Champaign, Ill.: Human Kinetics, 1991): 25–26.
39. Bailey, C., and Bishop, L. *The Fit or Fat Woman* (Boston: Houghton Mifflin, 1989): 44–45.
40. R. S. Schwartz et al. "The Effect of Intensive Endurance Exercise Training on Body Fat Distribution in Young and Older Men." *Metabolism* 40 (5)(May 1991): 545–551.
41. Stamford, B. A., quoted in *Prevention* (May 1992): 35.

CHAPTER 12

1. Evans, W., and Rosenberg, I. H. *BioMarkers* (New York: Simon & Schuster, 1991): 44.
2. Stamford, B. A., and Shimer, P. *Fitness without Exercise* (New York: Warner, 1990): 71.
3. R. P. Donahue et al. "Central Obesity and Coronary Heart Disease in Men." *Lancet* 8537 (1987): 821–824.
4. R. E. Ostlund et al. "The Ratio of Waist-to-Hip Circumference, Plasma Insulin Level, and Glucose Intolerance as Independent Predictors of the HDL (sub 2) Cholesterol Level in Older Adults." *New England Journal of Medicine* 322 (1990): 229–234.
5. D. Schapiro et al. "Estimate of Breast Cancer Risk Reduction with Weight Loss." *Cancer* 67 (10)((May 1991): 2622–2625.
6. Evans, W., quoted in "Bodybuilding for the Nineties." *Nutrition Action Health Letter* (June 1992): 1–7.
7. Wilmore, J., in "Ask the Expert." *The Weight Control Digest* 1 (5)(July/Aug. 1991); Westcott, W. L. "Exercise Sessions Can Make the Difference in Weight Loss." *Perspec-*

tive 13(1987): 42–44; Westcott, W. L. *Strength Fitness*, 3rd ed. (Dubuque, Iowa: Wm. C. Brown, 1991): 3, 74–75; Westcott, W. L. "Strength Training: How Much Is Enough?" *IDEA Today* (Feb. 1991): 33–35; Westcott, W. L. "The Magic of 'Fast Fitness': They Enjoy It More and Do It Less." *Perspective: The Journal of Professional Directors of YMCA* (Jan. 1992): 14–16; Wilmore, J. H. "Alterations to Strength, Body Composition and Anthropometric Measurements Consequent to 10-Week Weight Training Program." *Medicine and Science in Sports and Exercise* 6 (1974): 133–138; Westcott, W. L., Toomey, K., and Doherty, A. "Strength Training, Body Composition, and Spot Reducing." 1992.

8. *Tufts University Diet and Nutrition Letter* 10 (4)(June 1992): 5; Schardt, D. "Lifting Weight Myths." *Nutrition Action Health Letter* 20 (8)(Oct. 1993): 8.

9. Daniels, L., and Worthingham, C. *Therapeutic Exercise for Body Alignment and Function* (Philadelphia: W. B. Saunders, 1977): 77; Yessis, M. "Kinesiology." *Muscle and Fitness* (Feb. 1985): 18–19, 142.

10. Lamb, L. E. *The Weighting Game: The Truth about Weight Control* (New York: Lyle Stuart, 1988): 201.

11. Pirie, L. *Getting Built* (New York: Warner Books, 1984): 146–148.

12. Lagerwerff, E. B., and Perlroth, K. A. *Mensendieck Your Posture and Your Pains* (New York: Anchor/Doubleday, 1973): 148–150; Yessis, M. "Back in Shape." *Sports Fitness* (June 1986): 46 and 76; Yessis, M. "The Midsection: Your Essential Link." *Sports Fitness* (Apr. 1985): 91–93; Daniels and Worthingham. *Therapeutic*: 59.

13. Cailliet, R. *Understand Your Backache* (Philadelphia: F. A. Davis, 1984): 116.

14. Rebuffe-Scrive, M., Walsh, U. A., McEwen, B., and Rodin, J. "Effect of Chronic Stress and Exogenous Glucocorticoids on Regional Fat Distribution and Metabolism." *Physiology and Behavior* 52 (1992): 583–590.

15. Moyer, A., Rodin, J., Grillo, C. M., Larson, L. M., and Rebuffe-Scrive, M. "Differential Stress-Induced Cortisol Response in Women with Abdominal vs. Gluteal-Femoral Fat Distribution." *Annals of Internal Medicine* PA04A* Abstracts from Scientific Meeting (Mar. 10–13, 1993).

16. *Obesity Research* 1 (3)(1993): 206–222; Berg, F. S. "Risks Focus on Visceral Obesity, May Be Stress Linked." *Obesity and Health* (5)(Sept./Oct. 1993): 87–89; Bjorntorp, P. Paper submitted at NATO-NIH Conference: "Obesity Treatment" (June 2–5, 1993, New York).

17. Cailliet. *Understand Your Backache*: 118–121; Mensendieck, E. M. *Look Better, Feel Better* (New York: Harper & Row, 1954): 48.

18. F. I. Katch et al. "Effects of Sit-Up Exercise Training on Adipose Tissue Cell Size and Activity." *Research Quarterly for Exercise and Sport* 55 (1984): 242–247; Clark, N. "Sit-Ups Don't Melt Ab Flab." *Runner's World* (Mar. 1985): 32.

19. Sharkey, B. J. *Physiology of Exercise* (Champaign, Ill: Human Kinetics, 1984): 336; Cailliet. *Understand Your Backache*: 122–124; Cailliet, R., and Gross, L. *The Rejuvenation Strategy* (Garden City, N.Y.: Doubleday, 1987).

20. Lamb. *Weighting Game*: 147–148.

21. Westcott "Exercise Sessions"; Westcott. *Strength Fitness*.

22. Westcott. "Strength Training": 33–35; Westcott. "The Magic."

23. Drinkwater, B., quoted in Hogan, C. "Strength." *American Health* (Nov. 1988): 55–59.

24. T. W. Boyden et al. "Resistance Exercise Training Is Associated with Decreases in Serum Low-Density Lipoprotein Cholesterol Levels in Premenopausal Women." *Archives of Internal Medicine* 153 (1)(Jan. 11, 1993): 97–100.

25. Cailliet. *Understand Your Backache*; Cailliet and Gross. *The Rejuvenation Strategy*;

White, A. A., III *Your Aching Back* (New York: Bantam, 1984); Imrie, D., and Barbuto, L. *The Back Power Program* (New York: Wiley, 1990); Swezey, R. L., and Swezey, A. M. *Good News for Bad Backs* (New York: Knightsbridge, 1990).

26. Evans and Rosenberg. *BioMarkers*: 127.
27. Stamford and Shimer. *Fitness*: 88
28. American College of Sports Medicine. *Guidelines for Exercise Testing and Prescription*, 4th ed. (Philadelphia: Lea & Febiger, 1991): 112–113.
29. Evans and Rosenberg. *BioMarkers*: 119.
30. Fiatarone, M., quoted in *Prevention* (Feb. 1992): 55.

CHAPTER 13

1. Cash, T. F., and Hicks, K. L. "Being Fat versus Thinking Fat: Relationships with Body Image, Eating Behaviors, and Well-Being." *Cognitive Therapy and Research* 14 (3)(1990): 327–341.
2. Cash, T. F. "Body Images and Body Weight: What Is There to Gain or Lose?" *Weight Control Digest* 2 (4)(July/Aug. 1992): 169–176.
3. L. Emmons et al. *Journal of the American Dietetic Association* 92 (3)(1992): 306–312; Centers for Disease Control, Youth Risk Behavior Surveillance System: *Journal of the American Medical Association* 266 (1991): 2811–2812.
4. Kimbrell, A. *The Human BodyShop* (New York: HarperCollins, 1992).
5. Rodin, J. *Body Traps* (New York: Morrow, 1992).
6. King, G. A., Polivy, J., and Herman, C. P. "Cognitive Aspects of Dietary Restraint: Effects on Person Memory." *International Journal of Eating Disorders* 10 (3)(May 1991): 313–321.
7. Heatherton, T. F., Polivy, J., and Herman, C. P. "Dietary Restraint: Some Current Findings and Speculations." *Psychology of Addictive Behaviors* 4 (2)(1990): 100–106; Heatherton, T. F., Polivy, J., and Herman, C. P. "Effects of Distress on Eating: The Importance of Ego-Involvement." *Journal of Personality and Social Psychology* 62 (5)(May 1992): 801–803.
8. Hutchinson, M. G. *Transforming Body Image* (Trumansburg, N. Y.: The Crossing Press, 1985): 35.
9. Thayer, R. E. *The Biopsychology of Mood and Arousal* (New York: Oxford University Press, 1989); Rossi, E. L., and Nimmons, D. *The 20-Minute Break* (Los Angeles: J. P. Tarcher, 1991); "Move Your Moods." *Prevention* (Jan. 1993): 8–9.
10. National Institutes of Health report, cited in Hellmich, N. "Most Battle the Bulge without a Strategy." *USA Today* (Mar. 30, 1992).
11. "Swear Off the Scales for Good and Still Lose." *Environmental Nutrition* 16 (11)(Nov. 1993): 3.
12. Cash. "Body Images and Body Weight": 169–176.
13. Rodin. *Body Traps*: 12.
14. Ruderman, A. J. "Dietary Restraint: A Theoretical and Empirical Review." *Psychological Bulletin* 99 (1986): 247–262.
15. Logue, A. W. *The Psychology of Eating and Drinking* (New York: W. H. Freeman, 1991): 196.
16. Council on Scientific Affairs, American Medical Association. "Treatment of Obesity in Adults." *Journal of the American Medical Association* 260 (17)(1988): 2547–2551.
17. Rock, C. L., and Coulston, A. M. "Weight Control Approaches: A Review by the California Dietetic Association." *Journal of the American Dietetic Association* 88 (1988): 44–48.

18. R. R. Weinsier et al. "Recommended Therapeutic Guidelines for Professional Weight Control Programs." *American Journal of Clinical Nutrition* 40 (1984): 865–872.

19. Hutchinson. *Transforming Body Image*: 22–23.

20. Sternberg, B. "Relapse in Weight Control: Definitions, Processes, and Prevention Strategies," in *Relapse Prevention: Maintenance Strategies in the Treatment of Addictive Behaviors*, eds. Marlatt, G. A., and Gordon, J. R. (New York: Guilford Press, 1985): 521–545.

21. M. A. Rookus et al. "Changes in Body Mass Index in Young Adults in Relation to Number of Life Events Experienced." *International Journal of Obesity* 12 (1988): 29–39.

22. B. S. McCann et al. "Changes in Plasma Lipids and Dietary Intake Accompanying Shifts in Perceived Workload and Stress." *Psychosomatic Medicine* 52 (1)(1990): 97–108.

23. Mirkin, G. *Getting Thin* (Boston: Little, Brown, 1983): 62–63, 84–85.

24. Oettingen, G., and Wadden, T. A. "Expectation, Fantasy, and Weight Loss: Is the Impact of Positive Thinking Always Positive?" *Cognitive Therapy & Research* 15 (2)(Apr. 1991): 167–175.

25. Emery, G. "Beyond Problem Solving." *Emery News: A Psychological Newsletter* 8 (1991).

26. Foster, G. D. "Changing the Way You Think: A Challenge for Long-Term Weight Control." *Weight Control Digest* 2 (1)(Jan./Feb. 1992): 130–132; "Cognitive Orientation: Understanding Behavior." *Obesity and Health* 3 (8)(Aug. 1989): 57–60.

27. Nash, J. D. *Maximize Your Body Potential* (Palo Alto, Calif.: Bull Publishing, 1986): 206.

28. Nash, J. D., and Ormiston, L. *Taking Charge of Your Weight and Well-Being* (Palo Alto, Calif.: Bull Publishing, 1978): 381–473.

29. Brownell, K. D. *The LEARN Program for Weight Control*, 2nd ed. (Dallas: The LEARN Education Center, 1991).

30. Flaks, H., quoted in *Prevention* (Jan. 1992): 112.

31. Klesges, R. C. Report to the Society of Behavioral Medicine, cited in *Environmental Nutrition* 15 (6)(June 1992): 1.

32. Lefcourt, H. M., and Martin, R. A. *Humor and Life Stress* (New York: Springer-Verlag, 1986); A. M. Nezu et al. "Sense of Humor as a Moderator of the Relation between Stressful Events and Psychological Distress: A Prospective Analysis." *Journal of Personality and Social Psychology* 54 (1988): 520–525.

PART IV

STAYING YOUNGER, LIVING LONGER

AGEPROOF LIVING WITH "MENTAL CROSS-TRAINING"

New Keys to Dying Young—*As Late as Possible*

> The goal in life is to die young—as late as possible.
> —**Ashley Montagu, Ph.D.**, British anthropologist

Who wants to look and feel old—at *any* age? Answer: No one. And the most recent national surveys by the Alliance for Aging Research in Washington, D.C., indicate that two out of every three of us in America want to live 100 years—and that we're willing to "do whatever it takes to stay healthy and increase our chances of living longer."[1] You hold in your hands an immediate, unprecedented action plan for doing just that: With *The Power of 5* you can begin looking and feeling younger no matter *how* busy your schedule and no matter what your age—not only today but throughout your potential 100- to 120-year life span.[2] That's because, to a surprising extent, *how rapidly you age is up to you.*

"Changes associated with growing older may be much more reversible and preventable than we recently thought," says John Rowe, M.D., president of Mount Sinai Medical Center in New York City.[3] "We are designed to last a remarkable 120 years, but most of us die in late middle age, around age 75," explains Walter M. Bortz II, M.D., former president of the American Geriatrics Society, co-chair of the American Medical Association Task Force on Aging and a clinical professor at Stanford University Medical School.[4] "Only one thing is certain—we are *not* dying of old age."[5]

To a great extent, what lies ahead of you—at *every* age—will be the result of the choices you make today, 5 seconds to 5 minutes at a time. Each of us deserves to know the latest scientific insights on how to keep looking and feeling younger. But here's the key question: Are you ready to act on these new discoveries? If so, this section of *The Power of 5* will give you tools for ageproof living.

> How old would you be if you didn't know how old you were?
>
> —Satchel Paige, baseball star

Old age doesn't take you by surprise, like a frost. It takes hold in stages—and you can break its grip whenever you choose, and the sooner the better. Byron once wrote, "Years steal fire from the mind as vigor from the limbs." He was right only in the sense that it *is* common to see minds decay and muscles wither away with the passing years. But these losses are in no way predestined. Barring a neurological disease, by and large, if there's any theft of your muscle mass, it's because you stopped using your muscles; if there's any disappearance of your mental powers, it's the result of conventional expectations of senescence.

Here's why: One of the most widely feared—and accepted—beliefs about "aging" is the notion that after you reach maturity your mind steadily, irrevocably deteriorates, until you finally end up stuck in some inevitable web of confusion, frailty and despair. This common mindset powerfully affects your thinking—resulting in hundreds of small but insidious "premature cognitive commitments" that can shape your later life in a self-fulfilling prophecy.[6] Fortunately, each of us can choose ageproof living. In fact, recent research published in the *Journal of the American Medical Association* suggests that *regularly exercising your brain may help protect against the debilitation of Alzheimer's disease.*[7] Scientists have discovered that with a broad range of active intellectual interests and a vigorous lifestyle, your mind can keep developing toward its full potential and, for nearly all of us, be as sharp—or *sharper*—at age 70, 80 and even 90 as at age 20.[8]

How is this possible? In part, because whenever your brain cells are activated—by new sights, sounds, conversations, creative pursuits or problem solving, for example—they instantaneously begin to change. They take in more electrochemical energy, form new connections, remodel nerve endings, improve receptor networks and revitalize brain function.[9] With varied neural stimulation, you become more capable, "smarter" and more vibrantly involved with life. "Best of all, it doesn't matter what age you are when you start—improvement is always possible," says Michael D. Chafetz, Ph.D., a research neuropsychologist at the University of New Orleans.[10] The key to ageproof living is "brain fitness"—you must regularly challenge all aspects of your brain to expand its performance and slow or prevent its aging.[11]

And what about your memory power? Certainly it's one of the most crucial lifelong mental attributes. "What use is a perfectly healthy heart if the brain is unable to remember how to cross a street without being hit by a car?" warns Jonathan D. Lieff, M.D., past president of the American Association for Geriatric Psychiatry.[12]

It is now quite widely accepted that memory is not stored in a single cell but is spread throughout an extensive nerve-cell network. "Even the simplest memory is spread over millions of neurons," says neurobiologist Charles Stevens, Ph.D., of the Salk Institute in La Jolla, California.[13] And memory recall seems to involve multiple parts of the brain. "Memory is like a piece of music," says neuroscientist Marcus Raichle, Ph.D., of Washington University in St. Louis. "It has lots of different parts that come together to create the whole."[14]

Your most important memory power is known as vital memory, and it's "one of the most basic and necessary functions of our brains," explains Massachusetts General Hospital neurosurgeon Vernon H. Mark, M.D. "It is at the core of our being, representing the essential you, your personality, your feelings."[15] Here's how it works: Each new experience elicits a *memory trace*, which is registered in the brain in a certain sequence—transferred from the *senses* into your *working memory*. Whether or not something will make it into your *vital memory*—sometimes called *long-term memory*—depends on how intently you pay attention during that particular experience. As discussed in chapter 4, *The Power of 5* provides many specific ways to turn on your biological "switches" of energy and alertness. Once this happens, you're able to effectively focus your attention on whatever experience is at hand. Amazingly, everything, *everything*, you experience in life, every impression that impinges on your consciousness, causes some degree of physical changes in your brain. Within moments of reading a passage in this book, for example, or having a conversation or walking around the block or gazing out the window, new nerve circuits are formed, igniting memories, and memories of memories, that can alter forever the way you look at the world—or at yourself. In this chapter and throughout *The Power of 5* program, we've included "mental cross-training" activities and techniques that can directly or indirectly promote lifelong brain growth and an ageproof vital memory.

> Once stretched by a new idea, man's mind never returns to its original dimensions.
>
> **—Oliver Wendell Holmes,**
> U.S. Supreme Court Justice

POWER KNOWLEDGE: AGELESS MIND

MYTH #1: Over your lifetime, you use only about 10 percent of your brainpower—and mental decay is a natural, inescapable part of getting older. Why fight it?

POWER KNOWLEDGE: Here's why: Neuroscientists now estimate that we each use only about 1/10,000, or 1/100 of 1 percent, of our potential brainpower over the course of our lifetime![19] And researchers have found that senility is *not* a normal part of aging. According to Marian Cleeves Diamond, Ph.D., professor of neurosciences at the University of California, Berkeley, there's mounting evidence that as long as disease does not intervene, the brain retains its capacity to grow new anatomical connections, to learn and to function at high levels throughout our entire lives.[20] In fact, with some easy 1- to 5-minute mental cross-training, you can help age-proof your vital memory and may increase the size, number and function of many types of brain cells. Gene Cohen, M.D., Ph.D., acting director of the National Institute on Aging, is among the growing number of scientists who would like to quash the myth that our mental powers inevitably wither away with age.[21]

MYTH #2: I'm getting older. I shouldn't "strain" my mind.

POWER KNOWLEDGE: "The less we ask of our brain," says Monique Le Poncin, Ph.D., brain researcher at the French National Institute for Research on the Prevention of Cerebral Aging, "the less it gives us, and eventually there are signs of what I call cerebral hypo-efficiency: memory difficulties, absentmindedness, little quirks, inability to handle certain details of everyday life. . . . But, contrary to widespread opinion, people are capable of good cerebral efficiency *regardless of their age.*"[22] As the myths of mental aging have been cast aside, we have learned that brain function is remarkably changeable and that we possess nearly unfathomable capacities for learning, achieving and remembering. This quality is called neuroplasiticity.[23] "Throughout our lives we only use a fraction of our thinking ability," wrote the prominent Russian scholar Ivan Yefremov. "We could, without any difficulty whatever, learn 40 languages, memorize a set of encyclopedias from A to Z and complete the required courses of dozens of colleges."[24]

Brain experts report that mental calisthenics make the mind more alert and agile and help keep it that way.[25] Learning actually changes the qualities of nerve cell endings and increases the strength of nerve impulse transmission,[26] and a major part of the neurological deficits attributed to "aging" may actually be the result of a *lack* of stimulation of the nerves involved with lifelong learning.

MYTH #3: Physical fitness is fine for the body, but it doesn't do anything for the brain.

POWER KNOWLEDGE: The essence of life and of brain function is *movement*. In recent years, a number of scientists have reported that regular exercise may help keep the brain sharp as we age—improving and protecting such cognitive processes as memory, sensory acuity, reaction speed, learning abilities, practical intelligence and emotional control.[27] In a study of 55- to 70-year-olds by Robert Dustman, Ph.D., and his colleagues at the Veterans Administration Medical Center in Salt Lake City, exercise of three hours a week for four months led to "clear improvement" in intelligence test scores.[28] These studies were extended by Theodore Bashore, M.D., of the Medical College of Pennsylvania in Philadelphia, with similar results.[29] Research at Scripps College in Claremont, California, found that very active men and women, aged 55 to 91, did substantially better on cognitive and reaction tests than did a similar group of nonexercisers. The researchers suggested that "cardiovascular benefits from exercise may help forestall degenerative changes in the brain associated with normal aging."[30]

Medical researchers in Texas studied 90 healthy subjects who had reached retirement age, finding that regular physical exercise/activity helps sustain cerebral blood flow, reducing stroke risk.[31] In those subjects who were generally inactive, there was a steady decline in cerebral blood flow—which means increased vulnerability to stroke and other cerebrovascular disorders—during the four-year course of the study. And, as in other studies, tests given at the end of the research

(continued)

POWER KNOWLEDGE:
AGELESS MIND—*CONTINUED*

showed superior cognitive ability among those subjects who remained physically active.

It seems that insufficient oxygen supply to cerebral nerve cells leads to a decline of certain neurotransmitters and diminished brain function.[32] At both young and older ages, individuals with excellent physical fitness have reportedly displayed higher levels of "fluid intelligence"—the ability to actively, creatively use their minds.[33] And a study reported in the *American Journal of Cardiology* found that after a 12-week aerobic exercise program, volunteers had less cardiac reactivity to stressful mental tasks and tended to secrete less of the stress hormone epinephrine.[34]

MYTH #4: Memory loss is an unavoidable part of aging.

POWER KNOWLEDGE: "When your mental and physical conditions are poor, your *entire* memory functions under par," explains Douglas J. Herrmann, Ph.D., an authority on scientific approaches to memory enhancement and a research psychologist at the National Institute of Mental Health in Rockville, Maryland. "Attention, a key to memory performance, is diminished. Long-term memory suffers. Ideas and images are not likely to be registered strongly. Memory traces become fainter. It's harder to get them into or out of long-term memory."[35]

Studies show that the memory power of people over 60 may in many cases be greater and more accurate than that of younger people. In one study of nearly 1,500 people in three age groups—under 60, 60 to 69 and 70 or older—independent verification confirmed a high degree of memory accuracy in people over 60.[36] And, in many circumstances, the memories of people over 70 were just as sharp as those of people under 60. Memory loss, often considered an unavoidable part of growing older, may actually be due to such relatively simple factors as lack of intellectual stimulation.[37]

POWER ACTION: FIRST OPTION
Reject "Aging Brain" Stereotypes!

"The regular and 'irreversible' cycles of aging that we witness in the later stages of human life may be a *product* of certain assumptions about how one is supposed to grow old," explains Ellen J. Langer, Ph.D., professor of psychology at Harvard University. "If we didn't feel compelled to carry out these limiting mindsets, we might have a greater chance of replacing years of decline with years of growth and purpose."[16] Whenever you hear statements about the inevitability of memory loss or assumptions about mental decay due to "getting older," challenge them.

In one research project at Yale University, Dr. Langer and Ann Mulvey, Ph.D., found that for young, middle-aged and elderly people, there appeared to be a clear stereotype of being "old" that included a fairly well defined and negative idea of senility[17]—envisioning it as a condition of physical deterioration causing memory loss, mental incompetence, loss of contact with reality and helplessness. In addition, "a full *90 percent* of elderly subjects felt that there was a good chance that they would become senile, even though, according to medical accounts, only 4 percent of those over 64 suffer from a severe form of senility, and only another 10 percent suffer from a milder version."[18]

POWER ACTION: MORE OPTIONS
Practice 1- to 5-Minute "Mental Cross-Training" Exercises

To enrich your mind in as many ways as possible, some authorities recommend "mental cross-training," a process in which you blend studying languages, sculpture or painting and playing mental games of every conceivable type, as well as various physical activities, in order to stretch your mind in different directions. "The more variety, the better," says Danielle Lapp, Ph.D., who has researched and taught memory skills at UCLA.[38]

The following mental activities highlight some of the quick, varied ways to increase your brain fitness for the rest of your lifetime.[39] But do them *only* at those times when you're feeling rested and energetic, because to be effective, these exercises must grab your attention and focus you in the moment with a sense of enjoyment. Otherwise, say researchers, you probably won't bring your brain the extra surge of oxygen and nutrients that help make experience most rewarding.[40] Weave these simple, do-it-anywhere mental activities into your daily schedule—while traveling to and from work, shopping, waiting in line, doing housework and so on, 1 to 5 minutes at a time. Here are some of the most practical and enjoyable ways for you to expand and protect your mind with mental cross-training.

Perceptual flexibility. Be more observant of the people, places and objects that enter and leave your awareness during the day. Notice shapes, textures, colors, shadowing, movement and the other distinguishing features of each image. Can you draw sketches of an image right after seeing it (short-term memory) or at the end of the week (long-term memory)? On the telephone, practice recognizing voices the moment you hear them, and stretch your skill at recognizing different sounds, touches, tastes and smells.

Feature calisthenics. Use this kind of "visuospatial activity" to increase your ability to make quick and accurate estimates of areas, distances, volumes and other proportions of things you encounter. When you walk into a room, immediately notice the number and placement of people, furniture and other objects. On occasion, sit down and draw a map of what you've seen. Have fun mentally rearranging the furniture. And if a meeting or travel delay allows it, doodle—connecting whatever seems to grab your interest, such as geometric shapes, irregular line contours and so on. For an added challenge, use your nondominant hand. If you have access to a personal computer, video games are another good way to heighten your visuospatial abilities.

Integrative swiftness. Here you want to sharpen your ability to create coherent wholes from divergent pieces. For example, select a sentence at random from a newspaper, book or magazine. Try to make another sentence with the same words. Practice fitting together jigsaw puzzles as quickly as you can. Or cut up a newspaper page into various shapes, scatter them and see how quickly you can reassemble the page.

Get logical. Games of all kinds involve logical, reasoning-oriented activities. Alone and with various partners, play a variety of amusements—bridge, pinochle, chess, checkers, Japanese Go, crossword puzzles, math games and so on.

Expanded language skills. "The more words you know and recognize in English and other languages, and the more words you can use intelligently, the greater will be your brain capacity," says Dr. Vernon Mark in *Brain Power*. "And all other things being equal, the more resistant your brain will be to injury and disease."[41] Whether or not you learn a second (or third) language, the broader your vocabulary and the more precisely you can use your mother tongue in referring to concrete and abstract concepts, the more you strengthen your short-term and long-term memory. Each time you meet someone new, practice coming up with an anagram of his or her name. Find enjoyable ways to study the language, use your dictionary and thesaurus, read aloud, engage in mind-stretching conversations, listen to books on tape while you drive and strive to be more accurate and descriptive whenever you write and speak. Play word games such as Scrabble and get immersed in crossword puzzles—both playing them and making them. Sometimes when you hear a radio or television program, practice distilling the key points as briefly and clearly as you can. Whenever you come to the end of a chapter in a book, imagine that you must summarize it—aloud or in writing—for someone who has not read it.

More creativity—"outside the walls." Creativity involves not a single type of brain activity but a wide-ranging, ever-changing collection of skills. In addition to the preceding mental exercises, spice up your experiences by asking "What if . . . ?" questions, writing your own mysteries (on paper or in your mind), creating limericks and enjoying punning and humor—which, at their best, push you into looking at familiar things in different ways, escaping from one pattern of thought into another. Puns, for example, can spur you to think of words or word patterns that sound alike but have a humorous twist.

Get physical. It may sound surprising: You can also strengthen your mind by developing your body. One of the reasons is that the more sensitively aware the surface of your body is, and the more fit your muscles, the larger the active involvement of the related areas of your brain. For example, you can augment the area of the brain assigned to your fingers simply by increasing and varying the use of your fingers.[42] Consider giving some special attention to those physical activities that challenge your balance and coordination. Playing the piano, stacking coins, using tweezers to pick up small objects, playing jacks, completing puzzles that require tracing from dot-to-dot, connect-the-numbers, mazes and so on, are among the exercises recommended by some neuroscientists for improving hand dexterity and hand/eye coordination.[43]

Lighten up. "Overwork is a prime cause of mental impairment," says Monique Le Poncin, Ph.D., brain researcher at the French National Institute for Research on the Prevention of Cerebral Aging. "Our brain, like the whole cerebral mechanism and the body in general, works better when it respects a certain biological rhythm. If we force it to work at an excessive rate for too long, it causes mental strain."[44]

Beyond the mind-numbing problems of overwork is the daily on-slaught of "useless" information. In essence, everything you see, hear, smell, taste and touch throughout the day bombards your mind with stimulation. We all need techniques that periodically free us from this assault that jams up our creative circuits, warns Richard Restak, M.D., neurologist and author of *The Brain Has a Mind of Its Own*. For example, "too much nonessential news . . . may be hazardous to your health," says Dr. Restak. "Much of the information bombarding us from our televisions and radios lacks redeeming nutritional value [for the mind], dulls our sensibilities and leaves us, idea-wise, bloated with trivia yet at the same time intellectually deprived."[45] Dr. Restak suggests a new kind of healthy, "enlightened" illiteracy—periods of rest and re-covery each day and week freed up by an unwillingness to be exposed to mind-numbing subjects that we really don't need—or want—to know anything about. It's time to take action. Neurobiologist Richard F. Thompson, Ph.D., of the University of Southern California recently demonstrated that high levels of uncontrolled stress may create mem-ory disruptions and learning deficits.[46] And Stanford University psy-chiatrist Jerome Yesavage, M.D., and his colleague Dr. Lapp have discovered that many people can restore their memory by simply learn-ing relaxation techniques. "Anxiety clutters the channels of memory," says Dr. Lapp. "Relaxation opens these channels."[47]

With *The Power of 5*, you can use 5-second rest pauses and 5-minute escapes throughout the day to consistently revitalize your brain and better protect it from information onslaughts and fatigue-related declines in function.[48] From chapter 3 onward, this book offers you a wide range of practical 5-minute escapes to choose from—such as various forms of exercise, snacks, mental "vacations," and so on. Five-second rest pauses might include such strategies as One-Touch Re-laxation (see chapter 3) and One-Breath Meditation (see chapter 4), to name just two of the many choices in *The Power of 5*. For the work-place, there is another highly effective technique known as a *5-second strategic pause*. It encompasses three steps:

1. Take a deeper-than-usual breath (this signals the parasympathetic nervous system to bring added calmness to the body and mind).

2. Change your position (push back from your desk or work sur-face, loosen your shoulders or increase blood flow by going through a gentle neck circle as you open and close your hands; if possible, turn to look out a nearby window) as you simultaneously . . .

3. Think of something humorous (a quick flash of silent humor can come from simply imagining a funny face, glancing at a favorite cartoon or remembering something humorous from earlier in the day.

Note: Whenever possible, *follow the pause with a switch in your work focus for the next few minutes*. For example, you might return that one positive-looking or positive-sounding phone message, file some papers or go through some brief maintenance activity. All you have to do is make certain this action shifts your mind *away* from what you were thinking about before the pause.

Get deep, memory-protecting sleep. There are two principal ways that sleep protects the brain. First, according to some researchers, as we grow older, the blood/brain barrier, which helps protect the brain against toxic substances that may harm it, becomes more permeable.[49] Therefore, because irritants and poisons may pass through it with less resistance, it becomes more vital than ever to promote peak brain function with deep, rejuvenating sleep (see chapter 6).[50]

Second, while sleeping, your brain reinforces memories and makes sense of your daily experiences.[51] "During this extra neuronal activity during sleep," explains neuropsychologist Dr. Michael Chafetz, "proteins are manufactured by nerve cells. These proteins, like those produced by the stimulation from directed brain exercise, help restore cellular memories. It is important that you get enough sleep time to allow such protein production to occur, because part of the 'wear and tear' of daily life is a continual breakdown of the cellular proteins. If the proteins in the brain were to decay without being replaced, all memory would gradually be lost. Sleep thus serves to retain memories (or memory fragments) through protein replacement which counteracts the continual wear and tear."[52] Make it a personal priority to get the regular, deep sleep your brain needs to take care of retaining cellular memories and helping your mind sort out the information input from the preceding hours of your life.

Resources

Brain Fitness by Monique Le Poncin, Ph.D. (Fawcett, 1990). A tested program used at the French National Institute for Research on the Prevention of Cerebral Aging for revitalizing and expanding mental abilities.

Brain Power: A Neurosurgeon's Complete Program to Maintain and Enhance Brain Fitness throughout Your Life by Vernon H. Mark, M.D., with Jeffrey P. Mark (Houghton Mifflin, 1989). An excellent, well-founded program.

A Common Reader: A Selection of Books for Readers with Imagination (141 Tompkins Ave., Pleasantville, NY 10570; 800-832-7323; 914-747-3388) and **Daedelus Books** (P.O. Box 9132, Hyattsville, MD 20781; 800-395-2665; 301-779-4224). Far and away our favorite sources of uncommon books of the hour and books of all time. Call or write for a free catalog.

Computer games. For exercising the brain's spatial abilities, "computer games have so many brain stimulation advantages, I could not be more enthusiastic about them," says Dr. Michael Chafetz.[53] Among those recommended: Simon, Caverns, Mazes and Tetris.

Enriching Heredity: The Impact of the Environment on the Anatomy of the Brain by Marian Cleeves Diamond, Ph.D. (Free Press, 1988). A fascinating scientific tale of Dr. Diamond's decades of pioneering brain research.

Get Thee to a Punnery by Richard Lederer (Wyrich, 1988). A treasury of puns and wordplay.

Mathematical Carnival by Martin Gardner (Knopf, 1975). A collection of math games by the puzzle maven for *Scientific American.*

The Play of Words: Fun and Games for Language Lovers by Richard Lederer (Pocket, 1990). A great volume of mind-turning linguistic revelry.

Puzzlegrams by Pentagram (Fireside, 1989). A fun, brain-boggling set of colorful puzzles.

Reversing Memory Loss: Proven Methods for Regaining, Strengthening and Preserving Your Memory by Vernon H. Mark, M.D., with Jeffrey P. Mark (Houghton Mifflin, 1992). An excellent resource on identifying and correcting many common types of memory loss and on strengthening your vital memory power.

Smart for Life: How to Improve Your Brain Power at Any Age by Michael D. Chafetz, Ph.D. (Penguin, 1992). Compelling current insights on memory enhancement.

Super Memory: A Quick-Action Program for Memory Improvement by Douglas J. Herrmann, Ph.D. (Rodale Press, 1990). A complete memory-building approach by one of the leading researchers in the field.

The Teaching Company (P.O. Box 3370, Dubuque, IA 52004; 800-832-2412). The best source for renting or purchasing audio and video programs by some of America's most celebrated university lecturers, on subjects ranging from "The Great Minds of the Western Intellectual Tradition" to the "Superstar Teachers" series that offers various programs on ancient and intellectual history, religion/psychology, literature, history/politics and science. If you want to be a lifelong learner with the help of the masterfully entertaining teachers you wish you'd had in school but probably never did, take the time to write or call for this exceptional catalog.

Thinkertoys by Michael Michalko (Ten Speed Press, 1991). A manual of idea-generating exercises for business purposes.

PERSONAL POWER NOTES
A Quick-List of This Chapter's Power-Action Options

Reject "aging brain" stereotypes.

Practice 1- to 5-minute "mental cross-training" exercises
- *Perceptual flexibility*
- *Feature calisthenics*
- *Integrative swiftness*
- *Get logical*
- *Expanded language skills*
- *More creativity—"outside the walls"*
- *Get physical*
- *Lighten up*

Get deep, memory-protecting sleep.

PERSONAL NOTES

_____

_____

_____

_____

_____

_____

_____

_____

_____

_____

_____

_____

_____

_____

LIFE-EXTENDING NUTRITION

Making Sensible Vegetarian
or Semi-Vegetarian Choices

Tell me what you eat, and I will tell you what you are.
—**Anthelm Brillat-Savarin**, French gastronome

To live a long, *young* life, a number of researchers and health organizations now advise moving toward a vegetarian diet (including whole grains, beans and legumes, fruits, vegetables and low-fat or nonfat dairy products) or a semi-vegetarian diet (a vegetarian diet plus limited amounts of skinless poultry or fish and little, if any, beef or pork).[1] A healthful, life-extending diet includes a wide array of fresh, seasonal *fruits* and *vegetables*, *whole grains* (eaten as breads, pasta, side dishes and in soups or casseroles), a variety of *legumes* (beans, peas and lentils), low-fat or nonfat *dairy products* and limited amounts of *nuts, seeds, eggs, fish* and *lean poultry.*

For many years, most Americans were openly critical of vegetarians, but scientific findings have begun to change that attitude. "We tend to scoff at vegetarians, call them the nuts among the berries," says William Castelli, M.D., director of the federal government's respected Framingham Heart Study in Massachusetts, "but the fact is, they're doing much better [healthwise] than we [nonvegetarians] are."[2] In a study at the University of Kuopio, Finland, medical researchers followed new vegetarians for seven months and found that total blood cholesterol levels dropped by an average of 9 percent and ratios of HDL (a "good" type of cholesterol) to total cholesterol improved by going up 2.5 percent.[3] After seven months, *38 percent of the new vegetarians reported feeling more alert and vigorous and less fatigued.* In another recent study, researchers in a five-year Family Heart Study in Portland, Oregon, report that, over time, many people who have adopted a diet low in fat and fried foods and rich in low-fat whole grains, fruits, vegetables and legumes suffer fewer day-to-day feelings of "the blues," as well as less anger.[4] The study suggests that healthful low-fat eating—tending toward more vegetarian meals or snacks—may help people cope more effectively with everyday stresses.

Vegetarianism falls into several categories. *Vegans* eat vegetables, whole grains, legumes, fruits, nuts and seeds but no animal products—not even milk or eggs. *Lacto-vegetarians* include dairy products in their diet. *Lacto-ovo-vegetarians* include both dairy products and eggs. *Semi-vegetarians* may include dairy products, eggs and occasional fish, poultry or meat in their diet.

Medical researchers have carefully studied tens of thousands of vegetarians (in most cases lacto-vegetarians or lacto-ovo-vegetarians) over decades and have found that they are generally well nourished and have *significantly less chronic, degenerative disease than the rest of the U.S. population.*[5] As a group, vegetarians have been found to have lower blood pressure and more ideal blood cholesterol levels; less incidence of heart disease, osteoporosis, obesity, arthritis, diabetes and kidney disease; a lowered risk of certain cancers; and a generally stronger immune system.[6] A lacto-vegetarian or lacto-ovo-vegetarian diet is also now considered a positive part of many prevention and treatment programs for obesity, constipation, diverticular disease, coronary artery disease, diabetes, high blood pressure and, to some degree, breast cancer, colon cancer and gallstones.[7]

Researchers have discovered that vegetarians and semi-vegetarians don't just eat less meat—they also tend to eat more whole grains, legumes, vegetables and fruits than do nonvegetarians. The fiber, vitamins, minerals and other substances in these foods may help prevent vegetarians from developing cancers. And millions of Americans are discovering that vegetarian and semi-vegetarian diets not only are nutritious but are relatively inexpensive and offer a tremendous variety of delicious meal and snack options. When statistically compared with Americans, the Japanese—whose traditional diet tends to be vegetarian-oriented and very low in fat—experience only about one-fifth as much breast and colon cancer.[8] "Our working hypothesis is that mutagens in fried and broiled meat *initiate*, and high-fat diets *promote*, cancers of the breast, prostate and colon," say scientists at the American Health Foundation in Valhalla, New York. "Fried potatoes and similar foods contain some mutagens, but meats contain one thousand times more."[9]

The more meat there is in your diet, the more likely you are to consume agricultural and industrial chemical carcinogens. One particular class of insecticides, chlorinated hydrocarbons, is known to accumulate in the body fat of animals and humans. But, you may be wondering, aren't vegetarians deficient in iron and vitamin B_{12}?

There is no doubt that beef is richer in iron than most other foods, but new research reports that many plant foods, such as lentils, beans and green leafy vegetables, are also excellent sources.[10] While some cases of anemia have been reported in vegetarians,[11] this may have been due to a lack of variety in their diets.

Recent discoveries show that iron absorption from grains and legumes can be significantly enhanced when vitamin C is present—in the form of tomatoes, green peppers, potatoes, chili peppers and lemons. One international group of experts reports: "The effect of ascorbic acid [vitamin C] on [nonmeat-source] iron absorption has been tested in a number of dietary settings and in every case has been shown to be profound. It plays a particularly critical role in diets in which little or no meat is present."[12] One recent study showed that iron absorption was quadrupled in meals that contained enough vegetables to provide 65 milligrams of vitamin C.[13] Lactic acid (contained in yogurt and other cultured dairy products) is also thought to perform a role similar to that of ascorbic acid in increasing assimilation of iron.[14]

It was also thought for many years that vegetarians were deficient in vitamin B_{12}. But by the early 1980s, these conclusions were judged premature or based on scientific oversights.[15] Sophisticated research techniques have revealed that vitamin B_{12} is made by bacteria high enough in the human intestinal tract that it can be absorbed into the body.[16] And the absorption of vitamin B_{12} is reportedly as high as 70 percent for vegans, compared to 16 percent in meat eaters.[17] Excess fat and protein in the diet—commonly seen in meat eaters—increases the need for B_{12}. Although the American Dietetic Association still recommends that vegans include a reliable B_{12} source (either supplements or fortified foods) in their diets, vegetarians with widely varied diets high in complex carbohydrates and fiber, moderate in protein and low in fat appear to run little risk of vitamin B_{12} deficiency.[18]

> Clogged with yesterday's excess, the body drags the mind down with it.
>
> **—Horace,**
> Roman poet

A growing number of athletes—including Super Bowl–champion football players—are making the transition to vegetarianism or semi-vegetarianism[19] and report improvements in strength, performance and endurance. In one study, athletes placed on a high-fat, high-protein diet promptly found that their endurance had been cut in half, according to U. D. Register, Ph.D., professor of biochemistry and nutrition at Loma Linda University and one of America's leading authorities on vegetarianism. In contrast, with a high-carbohydrate vegetarian diet, the athletes' endurance levels doubled over their normal levels.[20] Some people have become vegetarians for religious reasons, others for a moral or ethical rationale: To them, meat not only contributes to health problems but also represents an extravagant style of life in a world of shortages and poverty.[21] According to the Worldwatch Institute, the average 1-pound feedlot steak costs the world 5 pounds of grain, 2,500 gallons of water, 1 gallon of gasoline and at least 35 pounds of eroded topsoil.[22]

POWER ACTION: FIRST OPTION
Quick Steps to Eating Less Meat— And Enjoying More High-Taste Meals

The best advice for readers who are not yet vegetarians or semi-vegetarians is this: *Change gradually*. No matter what your current dietary habits, one of the simplest ways for you to receive a broader range of life-extending nutrients is to *eat less meat and expand the variety of fruits, vegetables, legumes and grains in your diet.*

Expanding on the suggestions given in chapter 10, here are some of the simplest, easiest ways to *gradually, day by day,* make the transition toward a vegetarian diet. You'll soon discover that what starts out as a challenge will slip into an enjoyable, healthy new habit.

Eat more fresh-baked bread and rolls. Look in the Yellow Pages for your nearest whole-grain bakery (Great Harvest Foods is one nationwide chain), and try some of the delicious fresh-baked breads, rolls, bread sticks and low-fat (if it's not on the label, ask how many grams per serving) cookies and muffins. Whole-grain baked goods are a healthy, life-extending way to quickly have you looking forward to meals with less meat that include an *extra* serving or two of fresh bread (the taste is so good, you'll be able to go light on the margarine or butter, and then, best of all, skip it entirely).

Cut back on the portion sizes of red meat. Begin mathematically. Eat one-fifth less red meat this week. Take off another fifth next week. Perhaps, at the same time, you can substitute low-fat chicken or turkey breast or fresh fish for beef or pork, and then, as you continue to reduce your flesh-food portions, you can gradually, painlessly, turn meat into a mealtime "garnish." A realistic step? Yes it is, at least for most of us. You might set an initial goal of having no more than one serving of lean meat, fish or poultry a day and limiting your portion size to 3 or 4 ounces (the size of a deck of cards). And it's easier than you may think once you shift meal plans toward satisfying your hunger with a variety of high-taste, nutrient-packed, low-fat dishes.

Go for more garlic, spices, salsas, chutneys and chowchows. As

POWER KNOWLEDGE: HEALTHFUL EATING

MYTH #1: Lots of people in their eighties and nineties have never eaten a "healthful diet." And this proves there's no point to it—it's an overrated concern.

POWER KNOWLEDGE: Here's the point: Healthful eating might enable millions *more* Americans to live into their nineties. And the true scientific question about those fortunate individuals who survive to be 90 on a high-fat, high-cholesterol diet is this: How much healthier and more vigorous *might* they be at 80 and 90 on a health-promoting diet?

Environmental factors such as diet and smoking are thought to contribute to 80 to 90 percent of all human cancers in America,[26] with dietary factors alone contributing to an estimated 60 percent of cancers in women and 40 percent in men.[27] A report in the *Journal of the National Cancer Institute* estimated that 90 percent of deaths from colon cancer (the leading cause of cancer death) in the United States might be prevented by dietary modifications.[28] The American Heart Association has identified strong links between diet and heart disease.[29]

High-fat diets are linked to cancers of the breast, colon, prostate, endometrium (uterus lining), ovary, pancreas and lung,[30] as well as cardiovascular diseases including atherosclerosis (buildup of plaque in the arteries) and high blood pressure.[31] High-fat diets have also been associated with poor calcium absorption.[32]

In countries where the consumption of fiber-rich, complex carbohydrate foods is low, people experience up to eight times the incidence discussed in chapter 10, no one wants to change their diet unless the new meals and snacks have fresh, knockout *tastes*. Make it a point to sample the full range of low-fat and fat-free intensely flavored "little dishes" from around the world (see the mail-order sources in the Resources), and include high-taste seasonings in all new recipes.

Add different fresh vegetables to your salads—and put new zip in your dressings. Look for vegetables with color, and great new flavors. Walk through your local produce stand or farmer's market and

---

of colon cancer as in countries where intake is high.[33] Studies have linked diets high in carbohydrate-rich foods—such as fruits, vegetables, whole grains or legumes—with lower risks of coronary heart disease and cancers of the lung, stomach, colon and esophagus.[34] The National Cancer Institute (NCI) recommends eating at least five daily servings of fruits and vegetables ("For many cancers, persons with high fruit and vegetable intake have about half the risk of people with low intakes," says Peter Greenwald, M.D., of the NCI[35]). The benefits are further highlighted by research from Harvard University suggesting that one daily serving of a vegetable or fruit such as carrots, apricots or leafy greens lowers the risk of suffering from a stroke by 40 percent and decreases the risk of heart disease by more than 20 percent.[36] Furthermore, complex carbohydrates are digested slowly and efficiently, providing a steady source of energy without the biochemical roller-coaster effect of concentrated sugars. Another benefit is that by choosing more foods high in complex carbohydrates, you'll automatically be reducing your intake of fat and cholesterol (which come primarily from animal foods such as meat and dairy products).

MYTH #2: Most Americans eat "healthy" meals and snacks.

POWER KNOWLEDGE: Despite increased awareness about the basic principles of a good diet, a recent Gallup poll sponsored by the American Dietetic Association indicates that only 5 to 8 percent of people are actually eating more whole grains, legumes, fruits and vegetables.[37] A recent survey sponsored by the NCI indicated that 77 percent of adults don't eat the recommended five or more servings of fruit and vegetables per day.[38]

sample the hundreds of possible additions to mealtime salads. Deep green spinach or kale or purple arugula lettuce are several increasingly popular options. Carrots, tomatoes, onions, broccoli and cauliflower are a few of the other great ideas (see the listings in the section on "Variety" on page 208), plus a sprinkling, perhaps, of diced apples, chopped nuts or very-low-fat shredded cheese for added taste. Look for fat-free salad dressings or make your own oil-and-vinegar dressing (with a *very* small amount of olive oil followed by a good splash of balsamic vinegar and/or lemon juice, plus your favorite seasonings).

Add "fill-in" fruits and veggies in the easiest possible ways. What many people like is adding fresh produce to foods they already enjoy. Love tuna or chicken salad? Try it with fat-free mayonnaise and consider adding some chopped green or red peppers, plus slices of tomatoes, onions or cucumbers (or all three) and some fresh greenleaf or Romaine lettuce on top. In less than a minute, you can have an extra serving of vegetables while preserving the main part of your favorite-tasting sandwich. When it's time for dessert, slip in some fruit—as topping on frozen yogurt or something quick and easy on the side, such as a crisp apple or perfectly ripe banana. In stews and casseroles, add less flesh-meats and put in some extra vegetables, grains or pasta. For snacktime in front of the television, replace the high-fat chips-and-dip with a full plate of crispy fresh slices of cucumber, carrots, celery or zucchini and some broccoli or cauliflower florets, along with some guiltless, fat-free corn chips. Set out several varieties of spicy salsas and low-fat or fat-free creamy dips. Enjoy!

Update your cookbook selection. See Resources for several of the high-taste, low-fat vegetarian and semi-vegetarian low-fat cookbooks available.

Shop the specialty foods section of your grocery or health food store. Plan more low-meat or meatless meals with your favorite ethnic foods—flavorful Mexican, Tex-Mex, Chinese, Italian and others. Experiment with new ideas (see the mail-order selections in the Resources). Keep your kitchen well stocked with vegetable soups, fat-free canned beans, whole-grain low-fat crackers, pasta, rice and tortillas, frozen fruit juice, fresh fruits, nuts and seeds (such as sunflower seeds) and fresh spices. Broaden your menus with small sample servings of side dishes, soups or casseroles containing "exotic" new foods such as basmati rice, kasha, bulgur wheat, couscous, quinoa, soy tempeh and tofu. Consider trying some quick meals by stir-frying in a wok without meat and with little oil. Your taste preferences may change far faster than you think!

Eat a delicious vegetarian breakfast! If you're still in the habit of skipping breakfast (as noted in chapter 8, by doing this you fail to turn on your morning "fat-burning switch") or eating fat-dense meat products and eggs, it's time for a healthy change. You might choose a 1-ounce serving of low-fat, whole-grain cereal with skim milk, or a whole-wheat bagel or two pieces of whole-grain bread with all-fruit preserves and perhaps a small spreading of nonfat cream cheese, or a low-fat, whole-grain muffin and a serving of low-fat or nonfat cottage cheese. Include some fresh fruit and a beverage. On some mornings you may enjoy mixing your whole-grain cereal with a 4-ounce serving of nonfat or low-fat yogurt.

Choose meatless dishes that include more vegetables. Some pasta-only dishes, for example, are higher in fat than pasta choices that feature spinach or tomatoes or zucchini, because the pasta-only versions are often covered by high-fat sauces.

Watch out for hidden meat, hidden fat! The latest government surveys indicate that fewer Americans than ever are eating steak and pork chops.[23] But this apparent drop in meat consumption is at least part illusion: Meat is now hidden in casseroles, sandwiches and mixtures such as chili and tacos. In fact, according to government surveys, as much as 60 percent of meat (and 75 percent of beef) is now consumed this way. For many people, this hidden meat means hidden fat. Take steps to change this: First, choose extra-lean meats, then substitute, for example, ground turkey breast (extremely lean and available in grocery stores nationwide) or textured soy protein or soy tempeh (a bit high in fat, so count the grams per serving), then keep reducing the amount of meat per recipe and gradually make the transition to nonmeat alternatives (fat-free beans for tacos and stews, more veggies and spicy salsas for great seasoning).

Go meatless more often in restaurants—but beware. A recent Gallup survey found that 20 percent of American adults are likely to choose a restaurant that serves meatless meals.[24] And at least 30 percent are likely to order specific favorite vegetarian items when they are on the menu. Although limiting meat consumption can be a good way to reduce dietary fat and cholesterol, just because a dish is listed as vegetarian does not mean it's low in fat or cholesterol. Take a minute to review the "Dining Out" guidelines given in chapter 10. Beware of dishes made with traditional high-fat cheeses, eggs or nuts. Steer clear of large helpings of accompaniments such as avocado, nut butters, full-fat sour cream or salads with full-fat mayonnaise or cream-based salads or soups. Instead, go for meals with plenty of fresh vegetables and rice and other whole grains. Ask for vegetables to be steamed or stir-fried with little oil, and then well seasoned with herbs and spices. Other healthy options include veggie pizza with little or no cheese, fresh pasta with marinara or tomato sauce and vegetable-based soups.

Go for high-taste *variety*! Research suggests that a diet lacking in variety is also likely to lack nutrients essential to good health and longevity.[25] "Eat 30 or more different kinds of food each day," the Japanese government recommends to its people, and the rest of the world would do well to heed such advice.

Take a minute right now to review your daily meal and snack choices of yesterday, then the day before. Look back over the past month. Are you in a rut? What old favorites have you been missing? What fruits and vegetables are freshest or in season now? What taste sensations sound especially appealing? Are there some new tastes you'd like to try? Can you accentuate these tastes while keeping the fat content low? Expand your search by scanning the list below. Which of the following sampling of nutrient-rich foods have you been missing this past month?

Vegetables: Arugula, asparagus, beans (green, yellow and string), beets, bok choy, broccoli, carrots, cauliflower, garlic, green onions, jícama, kale, greenleaf lettuce, mushrooms, onions, peppers (red, green or yellow bell, chili, jalapeño), potatoes, pumpkin, radishes, spinach, squash, sweet potatoes, tomatoes and yams.

Fruits: Apples, bananas, blackberries, blueberries, cherries, dates, figs, grapefruit, grapes, kiwi fruits, mangoes, melons, oranges, plums, raisins , raspberries and strawberries.

Whole grains. Whole wheat is only one part of the whole-grain picture; how about barley, buckwheat, couscous, millet, oats, quinoa, rice and rye?

Legumes: Aduki beans, black beans, black-eyed peas, chick-peas (garbanzo beans), lentils, lima beans, navy beans, pinto beans, soybeans (and tofu, tempeh, grits or soy flour) and split and whole dried peas.

Once you've begun to expand the *variety* of foods in your meals and snacks, the *way you eat* also plays a role in how much pleasure you derive from each low-fat calorie. Your sense of taste and smell tend to become fatigued and less responsive when faced with bite after bite of the same flavor or texture—so vary each mouthful, alternating between different parts of the meal. In addition, chewing your food thoroughly breaks it down to release all of the succulent high-flavor molecules. And, in general, avoid ice-cold foods, since they reduce satisfying aromas and dull your senses—which may cause you to keep eating even when you're not hungry.

POWER ACTION: MORE OPTIONS
Limit Dietary Fat and Sweeteners

As previously discussed, a reasonable dietary goal for adults is an average of between 20 and 25 percent of total daily calories from fat, with about one-third as polyunsaturates, one-third or less as saturates and the balance as monounsaturates.[39] Please refer to the guidelines in chapter 10 to determine your personal Target Fat-Gram Budget, and be sure to take advantage of that chapter's specific, practical ideas on reducing dietary fat in your meals and snacks. But remember, there's no reason why cutting back on meat and fat means ending up with bland, boring recipes. Quite the contrary. And, as the cookbooks in the Resources attest, at last there are quick and easy menus and recipes designed to painlessly reduce *fat* and *cholesterol* at the same time you gain new, highly pleasurable *taste*.

Research continues to confirm the benefits of low-fat eating. And some of those benefits may be more immediate than scientists have yet realized. For example, eating a single high-fat meal on Sunday night may increase your risk of having a heart attack on Monday morning! That's according to a recent series of studies published in the *Lancet* and other respected journals,[40] suggesting that high-fat foods unbalance the body's blood-clotting system, pushing it into high gear and increasing the chances of an artery-blocking clot and resulting heart attack. British researcher George Miller, M.D., believes that a high-fat diet, or even a single fat-rich meal, leads to high fat levels in the blood and triggers the production of a blood-clotting protein known as factor VII, which is linked to increased risk of heart attack.

At the present time, it's still unclear if saturated fats in the diet raise factor VII more than unsaturated fats. But reducing dietary fat in general appears to quickly lower the level of factor VII, and choosing a low-fat meal may benefit you and your loved ones as much tomorrow morning as in ten years![41]

Note: Beware of snacks and other packaged foods listing "pure vegetable oil" as an ingredient. Coconut, palm kernel and palm oils are 86, 81 and 49 percent saturated, respectively.[42] The first two are even more saturated than beef fat and lard. And don't be misled by the claim that these oils are "cholesterol-free." While they don't contain cholesterol, they do raise cholesterol levels in the blood.

Reduce Dietary Cholesterol

Elevated blood cholesterol is one of the greatest threats to your health because it can clog arteries and set the stage for heart attacks. The cholesterol in your blood—measured in milligrams per deciliter (mg/dl)—is characterized by three major types of lipoproteins, the compounds that transport the cholesterol around the body: high-density lipoproteins (HDL), low-density lipoproteins (LDL) and very-low-density lipoproteins (VLDL). The total cholesterol content in the blood—referred to as total serum cholesterol—is the sum of all three types of lipoproteins.

LDL cholesterol is generally regarded as the predominant culprit in heart disease.[43] When teamed with a villainous chemical called apolipoprotein B, LDLs adhere to the coronary artery walls as part of the formation of a complex substance called plaque. In general, the higher the LDL level in the blood, the greater the risk of heart disease.

VLDL cholesterol is manufactured by the liver and transports various fatty substances such as triglycerides and LDLs. The higher the VLDL level, the more LDL the liver can produce.

HDL cholesterol, often referred to as "good cholesterol," is the protective type. It actually draws cholesterol away from the coronary arteries. In general, therefore, the higher your HDL level, the greater your protection against heart disease.

What's a "good" total serum cholesterol reading? 200 mg/dl has been the target advised by both the American Heart Association and the National Institutes of Health in recent years.[44] However, the results of a major study published in the *Journal of the American Medical Association* suggest that a lower level may be better—for the average adult, this may mean total cholesterol in the range of 180 to 190 mg/dl or lower. The total-cholesterol-to-HDL ratio (which some health authorities now consider the most important cholesterol number) should generally be below 4.6 for men and below 4.0 for women.[45] In addition to providing protection against coronary heart disease, reducing elevated levels of serum cholesterol may also help reduce your risk of colorectal cancer.[46]

What are the best ways to control your cholesterol level? According to researchers, LDL production is decreased by a widely varied vegetarian or semi-vegetarian diet that is low in fat (especially saturated fat) and refined sugar and includes soluble fiber-rich foods such as vegetables, beans and legumes, grains and fruits.[47] Other factors include regular aerobic exercise (which, as noted in chapter 11, provides the additional benefit of raising protective HDL levels) and effective stress management.

The U.S. Senate Select Committee on Nutrition and Human Needs recommends limiting dietary cholesterol intake to less than 100 milligrams per 1,000 calories, not to exceed 300 milligrams per day. But a number of authorities recommend lower limits—in certain cases a total of 100 milligrams per day or less.[48]

What about oils for cooking and baking? Based on recent research, two of the best choices seem to be olive oil and canola oil.[49] Both are high in monounsaturated fatty acids that, like polyunsaturates, have been found by researchers to help lower LDL cholesterol levels. But unlike polyunsaturates, which also lower protective HDL cholesterol levels, monounsaturate-rich oils don't seem to lower the beneficial HDLs.[50] Some nutritionists recommend extra-virgin (from the first pressing) and virgin (from the second pressing) olive oils because they may be less affected by heat-generated refining (which may increase oxidation and produce more harmful "free radicals").[51]

It's also important to note that there is growing evidence warning us to limit dietary intake of *trans fatty acids*, most of which come from partially hydrogenated vegetable oils. Partial hydrogenation may interfere with the production of hormone-like chemicals called prostaglandins, may raise serum cholesterol levels[52] and interfere with several of the body's protective mechanisms.[53] Recently, Dutch researchers found that trans fats are linked to unhealthy changes in blood lipid balance—causing a rise in "bad" LDLs and a drop in "good" HDLs.[54] Two new studies, one by the U.S. Department of Agriculture and the other part of the Harvard Nurses' Health Study, provide strong evidence suggesting that partially hydrogenated vegetable oils contribute to heart disease.[55]

In biochemical terms, oils in their natural state consist of a variety of fatty acids arranged in a precise natural molecular pattern. When oils are partially hydrogenated (have hydrogen artificially pumped in to "stiffen" them and make them more spreadable—a desirable quality for margarine), their molecular architecture becomes, in the words of a biochemist, "completely disorganized." Widespread use of hydrogenated oils in cakes, cookies, fried foods, mayonnaise, salad dressings, puddings, shortenings, crackers, snack chips, candies, bread, breading and frostings causes unintentional changes to occur in the fatty acids that remain unsaturated—in biochemical terms, the molecules are rearranged from a natural "cis" pattern into an unnatural "trans" position. Evidence suggests that the average adult may be consuming several times the government's average per capita estimate (used to determine dietary cautions) of 8 grams per day.[56] What's the best advice? Go easy on margarine, using as little as you can, and choose soft tub margarine over stick. In recipes, try substituting a small amount of olive or canola oil for margarine, or—if your diet's already very low in meat and other sources of saturated fat—you might use very small amounts of butter. Finally, become an avid label reader—and minimize your consumption of foods that contain hydrogenated fats.

Go Easy on Extra Protein

Research shows that, contrary to popular wisdom, if you think the more protein you eat, the better . . . you're wrong. In truth, few of us in America ever have to worry about not eating enough protein.[57] In fact, many of us eat more than twice as much as we actually need. And since your body cannot store excess protein, it must eliminate it as toxic wastes or convert it to glucose or fat for storage.[58] For healthy adults, the U.S. Senate Select Committee on Nutrition and Human Needs recommends that 12 percent of total daily calories come from protein (at 4 calories per gram).

Slow Down Your Fork—And Eat in a Relaxed, Enjoyable Atmosphere

"Make all activities pertaining to food and eating as pleasurable as possible," advises a special report in the *Tufts University Diet and Nutrition Letter*. "This recommendation, which appears in the Japanese dietary guidelines (but not those for the United States), emphasizes that the social aspects of eating can be as beneficial to health as food itself."[59] Therefore, it's important to slow down your eating speed (besides, the faster you eat, the more likely you are to *over*eat) and focus on pleasant, relaxing mealtime conversations. And, perhaps best of all, this provides a natural opportunity to increase your health-promoting *social* connections with loved ones and friends.

Resources

Cooking for a New Earth by Carl Jerome (Henry Holt, 1993). A healthful, back-to-basics cookbook.

Cooking Light Magazine (P.O. Box 830549, Birmingham, AL 35282; 800-336- 0125). Features delicious lower-fat recipes.

Dean and Deluca (560 Broadway, New York, NY 10012; 800-221-7714; 212-431- 1691). A great mail-order source for high-taste foods and ingredients from around the world.

Eating Well Magazine (P.O. Box 52919, Boulder, CO 80322; 303-447-9330). Emphasizes the connection between food and health.

Food for Life: How the New Four Food Groups Can Save Your Life by Neal Barnard, M.D. (Harmony Books, 1993). With a foreword by Dean Ornish, M.D., and backed by hundreds of scientific and medical references, this book—written by a faculty member at the George Washington University School of Medicine—offers a serious new call for low-fat vegetarian eating.

Frieda's by Mail (P.O. Box 58488, Los Angeles, CA 90058; 800-241-1771). Specialty and exotic produce.

G. B. Ratto, International Grocers (821 Washington St., Oakland, CA 94607; 800-325-3483; 800-228-3515). A wonderful mail-order source for specialty foods for meatless meals and snacks.

Mediterranean Light by Martha Rose Shulman (Bantam, 1989) and **Entertaining Light** (Bantam, 1991). Cookbooks endorsed by Dean Ornish, M.D., president and director of the Preventive Medicine Research Institute.

The 99% Fat-Free Cookbook by Barry Bluestein and Kevin Morrissey (Doubleday, 1994). *Very* low-fat recipes.

Nutrition Action Healthletter (Center for Science in the Public Interest [CSPI], Suite 300, 1875 Connecticut Ave., N.W., Washington, DC 20009; 202-332-9110). A well-documented, highly readable newsletter on better nutrition.

100% Pleasure by Nancy Baggett and Ruth Glick (Rodale Press, 1994). A low-fat recipe book filled with many savory ideas.

Southwest Gourmet Gallery (Sinagua Plaza, Suite D, 320 N. Highway 89A, Sedona, AZ 86336; 800-888-3484; 602-282-2682). Far and away our favorite mail-order source for fresh, flavor-packed salsas, sauces, marinades and spices.

Vegetarian Journal's Guide to Natural Foods Restaurants in the U.S. and Canada by the Vegetarian Resource Group (Avery Publishing, 1993). A detailed handbook listing more than 2,000 eateries featuring semi-vegetarian or vegetarian fare, plus a vacation guide that includes resorts, spas, camps, bed-and-breakfasts and tour groups that cater to those who eat little or no meat.

Walnut Acres (Penns Creek, PA 17862; 800-433-3998). An organic grocery store by mail order. Lots of meatless ideas and healthful convenience foods.

The Wellness Lowfat Cookbook by the editors of the *University of California at Berkeley Wellness Letter* (Rebus/Random House, 1993). An eating plan to help reverse heart disease.

PERSONAL POWER NOTES
A Quick-List of This Chapter's Power-Action Options

Quick steps to eating less meat—and enjoying more high-taste meals.
- *Eat more fresh-baked bread.*
- *Cut back on portion sizes of red meat.*
- *Go for more garlic, spices, salsas, chutneys and chowchows.*
- *Add different fresh vegetables to your salads—and put new zip in your dressings.*
- *Add "fill-in" fruits and veggies in the easiest possible ways.*
- *Update your cookbook selection.*
- *Shop the specialty foods section of your grocery or health food store.*
- *Eat a delicious vegetarian breakfast!*
- *Choose meatless dishes that include more vegetables.*
- *Watch out for hidden meat, hidden fat!*
- *Go meatless more often in restaurants—but beware.*
- *Go for high-taste variety!*

Limit dietary fat and sweeteners.

Reduce dietary cholesterol.

Go easy on extra protein.

Slow down your fork—and eat in a relaxed, enjoyable atmosphere.

PERSONAL NOTES

EMPHASIZE "PROTECTOR FOODS"

Slow Aging and Strengthen
Your Resistance to Disease

How often does your diet include nutrient-rich Protector Foods that may give an extra boost to your body's defenses against disease and aging?[1] And do you know the simplest ways to reduce your exposure to pesticides, bacteria and other food contaminants?

Which specific fruits, vegetables, whole grains and legumes are researchers calling Protector Foods? Most of us don't know the answer. Yet there is a growing scientific awareness that if these nutrient-packed foods are included regularly as part of a low-fat, high-fiber diet, they may significantly strengthen your body's resistance to disease-related aging. And there is also growing evidence that there are anti-aging benefits to making "safe" food choices—reducing your exposure to pesticides, bacteria and other food and water contaminants. This chapter presents some of the latest insights.

POWER ACTION: FIRST OPTION
Eat More Protector Foods

In *The Power of 5*, one of the smartest, quickest and simplest ways to ageproof your nutritional health may be to add a pleasing variety of anti-aging Protector Foods to a sensible low-fat, low-cholesterol, vegetarian or semi-vegetarian diet (discussed in chapters 10 and 15). According to the latest scientific and medical research, Protector Foods offer your body and brain more than just vitamins and minerals, more than just fiber and complex carbohydrates. In fact, there are a whole range—perhaps thousands in all—of *phytochemicals* (*phyto* is derived from the Greek word for plant) and other unique protective factors found in these powerhouse natural foods. You may have heard some of these anti-aging, anti-disease chemicals mentioned in the news: *limonenes* in citrus fruits, *indoles* and *isothiocyanates* in broccoli, *flavones* in dried beans, *flavonoids* in nearly every fruit and vegetable and *genistein* in soybeans. It may be time to start learning some of these new names. That's because a growing number of scientists are contending that the disease-preventing potential of these phytochemicals may be even greater than that of vitamins.[2]

Protector Foods can easily be added to side dishes, salad fixings, sandwich toppings, soups, dips, flavor-rich seasonings, snacks and desserts, and you can quickly find any of a dozen other tasty ways to enjoy them. For fruit and vegetable Protector Foods, fresh is usually best. Yet some researchers insist that, at least for those people who just don't like raw produce or can't find good-quality produce (for help in this, see the mail-order companies listed in the Resources), there's no reason not to consume cooked, frozen, canned or juiced Protector Foods, since they may still retain much of their potential protective value. (As a point of interest, when you cook broccoli, for example, you're likely to produce *more* indoles due to an enzymatic effect during steaming or cooking.) With that in mind, here is a brief sampling of some of these powerhouse Protector Foods.[3] Scientists are regularly adding to this list—which may, it seems, eventually include nearly the full spectrum of fresh vegetables, fresh fruits, whole grains and legumes.

Researchers have compared the eating habits of people with and without lung, esophageal and other cancers. Those who ate the most fruits and vegetables were about half as likely to have cancer as those who ate the least.[4] There are now at least 150 of these kinds of human studies. In almost every one of them, some plant food is associated with a lower risk of some type of cancer.[5]

Anti-Aging Protector Foods I:
Fresh Fruits

Apples contain *ellagic acid* and *caffeic acid*, which bolsters the production of enzymes that make carcinogens more soluble in water and may aid in eliminating them from the body. Another phytochemical in

(continued on page 220)

POWER KNOWLEDGE: PROTECTOR FOODS

MYTH #1: The idea of "protector foods" is pure advertising hype.

POWER KNOWLEDGE: Over the past several decades, scientists have identified more and more nutritive substances—found in a wide range of specific foods—that may extend your life and enhance its quality.[33] One of the reasons is that these foods help neutralize damaging free radicals, the prevalent and destructive mutagens that rank among the primary contributors to degenerative disease and premature aging.

Free radicals are unstable, highly reactive, "pyromaniac" molecular fragments that can harm cells throughout the body. A by-product of normal cellular activity, free radicals are also created in the body by exposure to sunlight, x-rays, ozone, tobacco smoke, car exhaust and other environmental pollutants. They set off chain reactions that convert fats to peroxides, which produce more and more free radicals. This leads to a destructive effect that biochemists call a cascade. Beyond altering biochemical compounds, corroding cell membranes and killing cells outright, the predominant damage caused by free radicals may be to mutate DNA. Scientists increasingly believe that this destructive power may play a significant role in the development of ailments such as cancer, heart or lung disease and cataracts.

In optimal health, with an optimal diet, your body would ideally possess the proper nutrients to neutralize free radicals at just the right times, before they can do serious damage.[34] These free radical quenchers, some called antioxidants, include carotenoids such as beta-carotene (a precursor to vitamin A that's found in carrots, pumpkins and many red, yellow and deep green vegetables), lycopene (the carotenoid that makes red peppers and tomatoes red), vitamins C, E, B_1 (thiamine) and B_6, lecithin, zinc, selenium (found in wheat, rice, oats, corn, garlic, onions, chicken, turkey and some fish), catechols (a class of chemicals in potatoes and bananas), isoflavones (found in soybeans), flavonoids (found in citrus fruits and some berries), indoles (protective substances found in cabbage-family foods), and chlorophyll-related substances (found in most fresh green vegetables).

Research also indicates that legumes (including lentils and dried beans), for example, can have a remarkable balancing effect on insulin that lasts for hours, helping the body stabilize blood sugar levels, metabolize excess fat and keep LDL serum cholesterol levels low.[35] Legumes may also be helpful in protecting against certain cancers, according to researchers at the Harvard University School of Public Health and other institutions.[36]

In addition, between 5 and 40 percent of the fat in seafood is omega-3 fatty acids,[37] and research suggests that omega-3's may help reduce heart disease and heart attack risk by helping to streamline the blood platelets' clotting actions, reducing LDL cholesterol and increasing HDL.[38]

MYTH #2: The health risks from consuming food or water containing pesticides, chemical additives and contaminants is greatly exaggerated by the vitamin and health food industries. There's really nothing to be concerned about.

POWER KNOWLEDGE: The destructive health effects of toxic agricultural chemicals—pesticides, herbicides, fungicides and others (which in this chapter we will collectively refer to as pesticides)—are well documented and include genetic mutations and cancer. It is important to determine that the foods we eat are free of these chemicals. Many are so dangerous to human health that they're banned by the Food and Drug Administration (FDA) yet are still manufactured in America and sold to foreign countries, where they're sprayed on crops that, in some cases, are then imported and consumed in America. According to recent estimates,[39] an average of 27 tons of pesticides leave the United States for shipment overseas every hour of the day, and this figure doesn't include the huge quantities of pesticides transported by truck and train to Mexico and Canada.

Between 71 and 80 percent of all pesticides sold in the United States have not been sufficiently tested for cancer-causing potential, according to a report by the National Academy of Sciences.[40] For genetic mutations, 21 to 30 percent of all pesticides have not been adequately tested; for adverse effects on the nervous system, 90 percent.

(continued)

POWER KNOWLEDGE:
PROTECTOR FOODS—*CONTINUED*

Although some critics claim that pesticide risks are exaggerated, scientists at the Environmental Protection Agency (EPA) believe the risk is real. In a recent report, *Unfinished Business: A Comparative Assessment of Environmental Problems*, a group of 75 EPA experts and professionals rated pesticide residues among the top three environmental cancer risks. When the USDA recently monitored pesticide residues in foods, it found that 58 percent of 2,859 samples tested had at least one detectable residue.[41]

Studies suggest that exposure to low levels of pesticides for years may be serious enough to cause health problems. In one study conducted by researchers at Mount Sinai School of Medicine and the New York University Medical Center in New York City, blood samples from 58 women with breast cancer were compared with blood samples of 171 women without breast cancer.[42] The women who had the highest levels of DDE (which comes from the pesticide DDT) were four times more likely to have breast cancer.

Children may be especially vulnerable. Researchers at the Natural Resources Defense Council (NRDC) and other organizations are finding that children aged one to five, for example, may receive 6 to 12 times greater exposure to pesticides than adults.[43] There are two main reasons: Children tend to eat more for their body weight, and they eat more pesticide-laden foods such as fresh fruits, vegetables and juices.

Many commercially available salt-cured, salt-pickled or smoked foods contain nitrites and/or nitrates that are added as curing agents

apples and other fruits is *ferulic acid*. It binds to nitrates in the stomach, which may help block them from changing into cancer-causing nitrosamines. A third protective factor in apples is *octacosanol*, a substance that may be linked to boosting protection against Parkinsonism.

Apricots contain at least six *carotenoids*, which may help prevent various forms of cancer.

Bananas contain *catechols*, substances that may benefit immune function.

and for coloring and flavoring. These chemicals promote the formation of cancer-causing substances called nitrosamines. In addition, "burned/brown foods are perhaps the major sources of dietary carcinogens," warns Sheldon Saul Hendler, M.D., Ph.D., biochemist, internal medicine specialist and professor at the University of California at San Diego School of Medicine. "There are substances in protein that when . . . browned or burned become highly mutagenic."[44] In barbecuing meats, the incomplete combustion of animal fat creates potent carcinogens called polycyclic hydrocarbons.[45] And more than 700 contaminants have been found in public drinking water—including pesticides, solvents (including the carcinogen benzene), lead and other metals, radon and harmful microbes.

MYTH #3: Water impurities are overrated as a health concern.

POWER KNOWLEDGE: According to one of the most comprehensive studies of drinking water ever conducted, millions of Americans are being exposed to dangerous waterborne contaminants.[46] Here are several of the disturbing findings.

• It's estimated that nearly one million Americans become sick each year from waterborne diseases. One percent die.

• Nearly 50 million Americans drink water that contains cancer-causing radioactive materials such as radon and radium.

• Between 1991 and 1992, more than 250,000 violations of the Safe Drinking Water Act affected nearly 120 million people.

• More than 90 percent of these violations were the result of water suppliers failing to: (1) test water for contaminants; (2) report contamination to the EPA; (3) use proper treatment methods; and (4) notify the public of violations.

Blueberries contain *anthocyanosides*, which may help prevent heart disease.

Cantaloupe is a source of *beta-carotene*, which may help prevent cancer.

Citrus fruits (oranges, lemons, limes, and grapefruits) contain *limonene*, a phytochemical that stimulates the production of certain enzymes that may help neutralize or dispose of potential carcinogens. Oranges also contain protective substances such as *terpenes*, which may aid in preventing lung cancer, and *beta cryptoxanthin*, an anti-cancer carotenoid.

Figs contain *benzyaldehyde*, which appears to be an anti-cancer substance, and *psoralens*, which may help the body guard against lymphoma and help prevent psoriasis.

Grapes contain *ellagic acid*, which scavenges carcinogens and may help block them from damaging DNA (cellular genetic material).

Mangoes contain *beta-carotene,* provides anti-cancer benefits.

Papaya an antioxidant that also contains *beta-carotene,* which provides anti-cancer benefits.

Pineapple contains *bromelain*, which may help prevent cancer and inflammation.

Strawberries, blackberries and raspberries contain one or more of the anti-carcinogens *ellagic acid, p-coumaric acid* and *chlorgenic acid,* plus *pectin*, a potential cholesterol-reducing substance found in a wide range of fruits and vegetables.

Watermelon contains the carotenoid *lycopene*, which may help prevent cancer.

Anti-Aging Protector Foods II: Fresh Vegetables

Artichokes contain the phytochemical *cynarin*, which may help lower high cholesterol levels.

Broccoli contains *sulphoraphane*, which stimulates the body's own enzyme systems that help protect against disease, the antioxidants *luetin* and *zeaxanthin*, which are only two of the ten known carotenoids in broccoli, and *dithiolthiones*, which promote the formation of glutathione S-tranferase and other enzymes that may block carcinogens from damaging a cell's DNA.

Cabbage (even when steamed or chopped into coleslaw or cooked into sauerkraut) contains the phytochemical *phenethyl isothiocyante (PEITC)*, as do turnips, and this compound seems to inhibit the development of lung cancer.

Carrots are rich in *alpha-carotene* and *beta-carotene* (discussed in chapter 17), protective substances which may act as antioxidant cancer preventers in the body.

Celery contains *psoralens,* which may help the body prevent psoriasis and protect against lymphoma.

Cruciferous vegetables (including bok choy, broccoli, brussels sprouts, cabbage, cauliflower, collards, kohlrabi, mustard greens, rutabaga, turnip greens, turnips, radishes and watercress) each contain protective factors, such as *indoles*, which prompt the production of enzymes that make the hormone estrogen less effective, which may reduce the risk of breast cancer, and *isothiocyanates*, which boost the formation of glutathione S-transferase and other body enzymes that may stop carcinogens from damaging the DNA in cells.

Kale is a rich source of the carotenoids *luetin* and *zeaxanthin*, which may help prevent cancer.

Potatoes contain *catechols*, substances which may benefit immune function.

Pumpkin is one of the best sources of *beta-carotene*, which helps prevent cancer.

Red cabbage is a good source of *indoles* and *carotenoids*, which may help prevent cancer.

Red peppers contain *lycopene*, a cancer-fighting carotenoid.

Spinach contains several *carotenoids*, which help prevent cancer.

Sweet potatoes are one of the best sources of *beta-carotene*, which may help prevent cancer.

Tomatoes contain an estimated 10,000 phytochemicals, including *lycopene*, one of five known *carotenoids* in tomatoes which help prevent cancer; *p-coumaric acid* and *chlorgenic acid*, which both neutralize cancer-causing substances; and *gamma amino butyric acid*, a substance that may aid in preventing high blood pressure.

Anti-Aging Protector Foods III: Whole Grains

In countries where the consumption of fiber-rich foods is low, people experience up to eight times the incidence of colon cancer as in countries where fiber intake is high.[6] Digestive and gastrointestinal tract diseases afflict nearly half of all Americans,[7] cancer of the colon is a leading cause of cancer death, and constipation is a daily problem for an estimated 100 million U.S. citizens.

In comparison, the people of underdeveloped nations with an average of five or six times the amount of fiber and complex carbohydrates in their diets have virtually no incidence of these disorders. In recent years, the U.S. Department of Health and Human Services, the Surgeon General, the Public Health Service, the National Cancer Institute and the National Institutes of Health all have urged Americans to eat less fat and refined carbohydrates and to consume more healthful foods high in starch and fiber.

The term *dietary fiber* refers to all plant material resistant to digestion. It isn't actually "roughage," although fiber does help to produce a smooth, prompt transit through the digestive tract. Fiber is divided into two categories. Water-insoluble fibers include celluloses (found in wheat bran), lignin and hemicelluloses (found in whole grains and vegetables). Although they can't be dissolved in water, they absorb water, which means they swell up and add bulk, making it easier for the intestines to pass along waste products.

Other dietary fibers are called water-soluble fibers and include pectins (found in apples, citrus fruits, legumes and certain vegetables), gums and mucilages (found in oats and legumes). These fibers perform very differently from the crude, water-insoluble fibers.

All fibers help slow down the absorption of glucose into the bloodstream, since they are bound to digestible carbohydrates in whole foods. Pectins and gums slow sugar absorption from the intestines. Both fiber properties appear helpful to people with diabetes[8] and can aid us all in keeping blood sugar levels more even. Water-soluble fibers also bind with bile acids, which are produced by the gallbladder from cholesterol. As the body uses bile acids, it produces more, pulling cholesterol out of the bloodstream and thereby lowering serum LDL cholesterol levels.[9] High fiber intake has also been shown to aid in losing excess body fat and may even lower blood pressure by about 10 percent.[10]

How much total fiber should you consume per day? The National Cancer Institute recommends 20 to 35 grams, although the average American consumes only about 10 grams. Other authorities suggest that average-size adults should consume between 30 and 60 grams of total fiber per day,[11] and it is generally best to get your daily fiber from food rather than supplements. And remember, wheat bran is only a small part of the fiber picture.

Here are several examples of Protector Foods that are good sources of fiber (with the amount of total dietary fiber in parentheses).[12]

For water-insoluble fiber: One-third cup (1 ounce) All-Bran cereal (9 grams); ½ cup cooked pearled barley (4.4 grams); ½ cup boiled, drained brussels sprouts (3.4 grams); one biscuit (1 ounce) shredded wheat (2.2 grams); ½ cup cooked broccoli (2 grams); ½ cup cooked asparagus (1.8 grams); ½ cup cooked, drained carrots (1.1 grams); and ½ cup cooked, drained green beans (0.9 gram).

For water-soluble fiber: One-half cup cooked, drained black-eyed peas (8.3 grams); ½ cup cooked dried split peas (3.1 grams); one apple, with skin (3 grams); ½ cup cooked oatmeal (2.6 grams); ½ cup cooked oat bran (2 grams); 2 tablespoons raw oat bran (1.9 grams); ½ cup strawberries (1.9 grams); and one banana (1.8 grams).

In addition to the various healthful fibers and phytochemicals found in the preceding lists of fruit and vegetable Protector Foods, whole grains are another outstanding source of these anti-disease, anti-aging factors. Unfortunately, the standard grain choices for most families are still white, bleached, all-purpose wheat flour and polished white rice. Traditional whole-grain recipes offer a wide range of delicious tastes and textures, and we can each benefit by expanding the variety of dietary whole grains that we consume.

Cooked or baked foods that are high in amaranth, barley, brown rice, buckwheat, bulgur (cracked wheat), corn, millet, oats, quinoa, rye, triticale or whole wheat can be good sources of various types of health-protective insoluble and/or soluble fiber (as can many fruits, vegetables and legumes), and they may also contain significant amounts of the anti-cancer trace mineral *selenium*. In addition, whole grains contain *phytic acid,* which binds to iron and may help prevent this mineral from creating cancer-causing free radicals and may also prove to be of some benefit in reducing risk of heart disease. Fresh-baked breads and rolls, pasta and tortillas and low-fat or nonfat muffins, biscuits, cereals, chips, crackers and cookies are nutrient-rich foods that can play a valuable role in a health-enhancing, life-extending diet. Each of the following whole grains can be considered a Protector Food and offers a special taste, texture and nutrient profile. All are available in natural food stores and grocery stores.

Amaranth was a staple grain of the Aztec civilization and is used by the country people of Mexico, South America, China, India and Africa.

Barley, a favorite in ancient Egypt, Rome and Greece, was cultivated in China as early as 2000 B.C. It is favored today in western China, Tibet and other Himalayan countries, and the southern and southeastern mountainous regions of the former Soviet Union.

Brown rice has been cultivated for centuries in China and surrounding countries.

Corn originated in Central and South America.

Millet, a staple grain of the ancient Egyptians, has been eaten for more than a thousand years in northern China, the Himalayan region and parts of Russia, India and Africa.

Oats are a relative newcomer to the grain family, thriving in cooler countries such as Scotland, Ireland, Great Britain, the northern United States and Canada.

Quinoa (pronounced *keen-WAH*) is botanically a fruit, yet, like buckwheat and wild rice, it has been consumed for centuries as a cereal grain. It's an ancient staple food from the South American Andes and the mountainous regions of Ecuador, Peru, Bolivia, southern Colombia, northern Argentina and Chile.

Rye and buckwheat are the primary grains for more than one-third of the countries in northern Europe, including Scandinavia and the former Soviet Union.

Triticale is a hybrid of wheat and rye.

Whole wheat is now cultivated on more acres than any other grain in the world, and America has made it the most popular grain. But wheat's nutritional profile is insufficient to warrant choosing it as the solitary grain in anyone's diet.

Wild rice is botanically related to brown rice. It grows in cool freshwater lakes and rivers in the northern part of the midwestern United States, New Brunswick (Canada) and some areas of the Rocky Mountains.

Anti-Aging Protector Foods IV: Legumes

Legumes, by definition, are the edible mature seeds that grow inside the pods of leguminous plants. This important food group includes dried beans, peas and lentils. Known for centuries as "poor man's meat," legumes are a diet staple of many of the world's healthiest, longest-lived peoples.

In today's hurry-up society, legumes are appearing in countless new recipes, and they provide fast and easy opportunities to break meal-plan boredom. They are an inexpensive, nutrient-rich food source, high in complex carbohydrates, fiber, good-quality proteins (though they are deficient in one or more essential amino acids, they are ideal as complementary proteins when eaten with grains), minerals and several B vitamins. They are free of cholesterol, low in simple sugars and sodium and, with the exception of soybeans, very low in fat (an average of only 3 percent).

Medical research indicates that legumes are beneficial for people with diabetes because they have a remarkable balancing effect on insulin that lasts for hours, helping the body stabilize blood sugar levels, metabolize excess fat and keep LDL serum cholesterol levels low.[13] Legumes may also be helpful in protecting against certain cancers, according to researchers at the Harvard University School of Public Health and other institutions.[14]

Which legumes can qualify as Protector Foods? Perhaps nearly all. *Soybeans*, for example, contain the natural chemical *genistein*, which seems to help prevent small cancerous tumors from growing. Unaccustomed to eating soybeans? They are available in grocery and health food stores either fried or canned or as miso paste, tempeh or tofu. They may be conveniently added to your favorite soups and casseroles and used as main ingredients in main courses and a variety of side dishes.

Beyond the genistein in soybeans, virtually all legumes—*soybeans, lentils and dried or canned beans* (*black beans, garbanzo beans, kidney beans, lima beans, navy beans, pinto beans* and *white beans*) contain several, or all, of the following potential protective factors.

• *Isoflavones*, which block the entry of the hormone estrogen into cells, which may reduce the risk of breast or ovarian cancer.

• *Phytosterols*, which slow down the reproduction of cancer cells in the large intestine, thereby helping to prevent colon cancer. Phytosterols have also been shown to slow or prevent the absorption of cholesterol in the body, which may have a very minor effect on blood cholesterol regulation.

• *Protease inhibitors*, which suppress the production of certain enzymes in cancer cells and may thereby slow tumor growth.

• *Saponins*, which block some of the abnormal processes by which DNA reproduces and may therefore aid in preventing cancer cells from multiplying.

Anti-Aging Protector Foods V:
Omega-3 Sources

Studies suggest that eating omega-3-rich fish just once or twice a week may reduce the level of triglycerides in the blood and provide some modest yet significant protection against heart disease and possible benefits in lowering blood pressure.[15] The best options include *salmon* (sockeye, coho, chinook or pink), *albacore* or *bluefin tuna, mackerel, halibut, herring* or *sardines*.[16] For vegetarians, reports in the *New England Journal of Medicine* and the *American Journal of Clinical Nutrition* indicate that some other sources of omega-3's, such as *green leafy vegetables, broccoli, fruits, dry beans* (see "Legumes" above), *soy tofu or tempeh, butternuts* or *walnuts*, can be an excellent alternative.[17] These sources are more biochemically stable than the omega-3 molecules in fish, which can readily turn into damaging free radical fragments, as discussed in "Power Knowledge" on page 218.

Anti-Aging Protector Foods VI: Yogurt

Lactobacillus bulgaricus, Streptococcus thermophilus and *Lactobacillus acidophilus* are three of the health-promoting bacteria that digest lactose, the milk sugar that about one-quarter of American adults (especially African-Americans, Native Americans, Asians and people of Mediterranean heritage) have difficulty handling.[18] The beneficial bacteria in yogurt break down the lactose into glucose and galactose, two sugars that nearly all adults can absorb. Several European studies report that populations that eat large amounts of yogurt or other fermented milk products seem to have a significantly lower risk of developing breast cancer and perhaps other forms of cancer as well.[19]

Although the evidence is preliminary, studies in animals and humans shed light on the way these beneficial bacteria work: In the large intestine, acidophilus can block certain dangerous bacteria from creating carcinogens from food or from bile that the liver secretes to help digest fat. In a study conducted by researchers at the New England Medical Center in Boston, 21 people were given milk with *L. acidophilus* every day for four weeks, and the harmful bacteria in their stools were two to four times *less* active than when they were given milk without *L. acidophilus* for four weeks.[20] Researchers in Sweden studied 11 volunteers who had been regularly eating fried beef patties. After three days of continuing to eat the beef patties but also consuming milk with *L. acidophilus*, the subjects had *half* the potentially cancer-causing substances in their stools and urine than they had after three days of consuming fried beef patties and milk with no *L. acidophilus*.[21]

Anti-Aging Protector Foods VII:
Selected Spices and Herbs

Here's a surprise. Could a cancer prevention aid be as near as your spice rack? A growing body of research says yes.[22] Not only do common and exotic spices and herbs add memorable flavors to recipes—and thereby encourage us to eat healthier meals that include fruits, vegetables, legumes and whole grains—but spices may also bolster the body's immune resistance to disease. Although much of the research is ongoing and not conclusive, the findings are both promising and compelling—and warrant our attention. Here are some examples.

Garlic, onions and company. Garlic, the popular and pungent wonder clove, may offer many valuable health benefits, including help in the prevention of both heart disease and cancer.[23] The *allyl sulfides* in garlic increase the production of glutathione S-transferase, which may make carcinogens easier to excrete. Other allium compounds may decrease reproduction of tumor cells. Garlic has also been found to have natural antibiotic properties,[24] and onions—botanically related to garlic—contain oils that have mild potential anti-cancer and cholesterol-lowering properties.[25]

"I think you've got a compelling argument to use lots of garlic with the food you eat," says James Scala, Ph.D., a member of the American Dietetic Association who has taught nutrition and biochemistry at

Georgetown University Medical School, the University of Oklahoma Medical School, the Ohio College of Medicine and the University of California, Berkeley. "I prefer to use fresh garlic, onions, leeks, shallots, chives and asparagus (all are botanically related to garlic)."[26] *Spice-up-your-life suggestions:* To get the most from garlic, use fresh cloves and mash, chop or squeeze the garlic through a hand-held garlic press. To maximize the health-promoting effect of garlic, add it to dishes just prior to serving. Favorite uses include adding it to fresh and marinated salads, sautéeing it with onions for sauces and soups and using it as a seasoning for poultry. *Note:* Don't use garlic salt; it's nearly 100 percent salt and can create problems for sodium-sensitive people.

Beyond the many popular uses of common white and yellow onions, enjoy adding zest to recipes with an extra amount of sweet Bermuda onions, small pearl onions, leeks, scallions, shallots and chives.

Black pepper, jalapeño peppers, mustard and hot red pepper. As mentioned in chapter 10, some intriguing studies indicate that spices such as hot pepper and mustard may actually increase your metabolic rate—and potentially aid your body's fat-burning power—for up to several hours after eating.[27] Researchers have reported that black pepper may be associated with a lower rate of cancer—and this finding seems to be supported by research in India on mice.[28]

Studies also suggest that *capsaicin*, the chemical that gives hot red pepper its fire, may be helpful in keeping toxic molecules from attaching to DNA and initiating some forms of cancer, and that it may also help fend off migraine headaches and serve as a protective aid against arthritis, asthma and bronchitis. But one study has also suggested that capsaicin might, in some cases, have a mild *pro*-cancer effect.[29] More data is needed to know for sure, but it makes sense not to go overboard by deluging recipes with peppers, or any other herb or spice. *Spice-up-your-life suggestions:* When cooking with black pepper, grind whole pepper cloves as needed, since once it's ground, black pepper rapidly loses its flavor. For added zip in ethnic meals, gradually introduce mild and then hot jalapeño peppers—and, when you're ready, you might try adding a dash of the roaring hot habanero pepper (see Southwest Gourmet Gallery in the Resources).

For a pleasant, mouth-tingling change of pace, you might also enjoy adding a pinch of hot red pepper powder to a batch of low-fat microwave popcorn.

Cinnamon. Richard A. Anderson, M.D., of the U.S. Department of Agriculture (USDA) Human Nutrition Research Center, is adding cinnamon to his daily bowl of oatmeal because of initial laboratory findings—yet to be proven in human subjects—that cinnamon and turmeric (the yellow spice used in rice and curry mixtures) effectively triple the ability of insulin to metabolize glucose.[30]

Basil, cumin and turmeric. In response to the growing popularity of ethnic foods, all across America these three spices are appearing at dining tables. Preliminary findings from researchers in Israel suggest that these spices may have anti-cancer properties, specifically toward cancer of the bladder or prostate.[31] Scientists in India report that all three of these spices may offer mild cancer-preventive properties, and turmeric may give an extra boost to the immune system.[32] Some preliminary animal studies indicate that it may also boost the ability of insulin to metabolize glucose. *Spice-up-your-life suggestions*: Mix plenty of fresh basil with fresh garlic, some olive oil and Parmesan cheese to make pesto sauce, which is delicious over pasta. Basil leaves can also spice up poultry, shellfish and vegetable/grain dishes. Cumin seeds are ground up as part of chili powder, the core ingredient in popular Tex-Mex cooking, and are used in Indian recipes featuring curry powder. Turmeric's rich, peppery flavor adds snap to Moroccan dishes and may be used as an inexpensive substitute for saffron.

Parsley. This common, inexpensive, flavorful green plant can offer a wonderful dietary source of small but significant amounts of trace elements—including copper, magnesium, molybdenum and zinc. Sprinkle it liberally into soups, stews, sauces, vegetable side dishes and salads, and serve it with cooked potatoes and main courses. Fresh parsley is far more flavor-packed than dried.

What's the bottom line? Go ahead and spice up your meals and snacks—there are many possible benefits and few, if any, cautions. Accentuate the tastes you love by including more of your favorite fat-free spices and seasonings.

POWER ACTION: MORE OPTIONS
Drink *Pure* Water

Usually this is easier said than done. It doesn't have to be. Let's begin with some quick facts: More than 700 contaminants have been found in public drinking water—including solvents (including such potent carcinogens as arsenic and benzene), trihalomethanes (by-products of chlorine), pesticides, lead, other metals, radioactive radon and harmful microbes (such as disease-causing bacteria). The list of contaminants identified in private wells can be even worse. Unfortunately, the Environmental Protection Agency (EPA) has set legal limits—called "maximum contaminant levels"—for inspection and monitoring of just 77 of the 700-plus contaminants.[47]

There are three specific situations where you may want to have your family drinking water tested:

1. If your water comes from a private well (which, due to variables in underground water sources, could be contaminated even if neighbors' wells have tested contaminant-free).

2. If you have any reason to suspect the presence of lead, solvents or other contaminants.

3. If your water utility serves less than 3,300 people (rated a "small" system by the EPA and therefore subject to fewer water-purity checks; according to government records, nearly 90 percent of all violations of federal drinking water standards involve these small systems).

Before you decide to drink bottled water or invest in a home water purifier, it's a good idea to have your tapwater tested. Pollution danger signs include brown, cloudy or murky-looking water; smelly or bad-tasting water; foam; and sudden changes in appearance or taste. However, many toxic chemicals are invisible, odorless and tasteless. Laboratory analysis is the only sure way to identify safe drinking water.

When testing your water, it's vital to use only independent, state-certified laboratories for water testing. If you don't know whom to contact, call the EPA's Safe Drinking Water Hotline (1-800-426-4791 or 1-202-382-5533) for on-the-phone help and to request the free booklet, "Is Your Drinking Water Safe?" If you drink municipal water, you can compare your utility's water-testing results (which you should be able to readily obtain from their local office) with the EPA's legal limits.

If you find contaminants in your tapwater, select either bottled water or a home treatment method that best removes the contaminants you have identified (for a listing of your most reliable water-treatment options, contact the National Sanitation Foundation, P.O. Box 1468, Ann Arbor, MI 48106; 313-769-8010). If you cannot find a reputable analysis lab locally (check with your community health department), contact WaterTest (P.O. Box 186, New London, NH 03257; 800-426-8378). For more information on water filters, send a $3 check or money order for Reprint #R0126 to *Consumer Reports*, Bulk Reprints, P.O. Box 53016, Boulder, CO 80322. North Americans now spend nearly $2 billion each year for bottled water and almost that much for water filters.[48]

Eat "Safe" Foods

Conventional government and industry propaganda asserts that America has the safest food supply in the world. But a surprising percentage of what is sold here isn't safe. Food contaminated with pesticides, antibiotics, hormones, bacteria, molds and additives has become a concern in recent years as overuse, misuse and abuse of these toxic chemicals and animal drugs has escalated. Ironically, the foods that health-conscious Americans are striving to eat more of—fresh vegetables and fruits—are among those most likely to be contaminated.

Our food supply can and should be made safer. Some problems can be solved by each of us as individuals, while others need to be addressed politically. One place to start is with ecologically sound farming and gardening.

The words *natural* and *organic* have been greatly abused in the food industry and in fad diet books. What do they really mean? In *The Nutrition Debate: Sorting Out Some Answers*, Joan Dye Gussow, Ed.D., chairperson of the Department of Nutrition Education at Columbia University in New York City and a member of the Diet, Nutrition and Cancer Panel and the Food and Nutrition Board of the National Academy of Sciences, says that even the food technologists and scientists who consider the word *natural* to be undefinable "were in 'reluctant agreement' that *natural* referred to treatment after the harvest and that it had something to do with 'minimal processing and the absence of artificial or synthetic ingredients or additives.'. . . [And] *organic* was acknowledged, 'albeit often reluctantly,' to have a popularly agreed-upon meaning having to do with how the food was produced."[49]

As health professionals and authors of *The Power of 5*, we are both in favor of organic gardening and farming, first simply because of the environment-conserving agricultural practices it employs. It is a sustainable, biological approach to farming. "The fundamental concept of growing 'organically' is that the farmer uses practices that are in harmony with nature, and avoids the use of chemically synthesized herbicides, fungicides, pesticides or acidulated fertilizers," says organic farming advocate Frank Ford. "For example: the grower may introduce beneficial insects to control harmful ones; apply natural mulches, mechanical cultivation, or even tolerate weeds; he may apply compost, manure, seaweed, etc. or depend on the natural fertility of the soil."[50]

Note: Before we discuss food safety, it's important to keep the risks in perspective. Avoiding pesticides and other food additives ultimately—by itself—may not protect you from cancer or heart disease if you continue to eat a diet that's high in fat, cholesterol, sodium and alcohol or eat too few fresh fruits, vegetables or whole grains. With fresh produce, for example, the riskiest thing you could do would be to stop eating fruits and vegetables because you're concerned that they may have been treated with pesticides. A somewhat more sensible approach would be to eat plenty of them, pesticides and all. But the best choice of all would be to buy certified organic produce and to wash and prepare your fruits and vegetables in ways that reduce your exposure to potentially harmful chemical residues. With that in mind, here are some basic suggestions.

Buy the freshest, cleanest food you can—"certified organic" may be best. The Food, Agriculture, Conservation and Trade Act of 1990 (the 1990 "Farm Bill"), scheduled for implementation in 1995, requires the first national standards for producing, growing and processing organic foods. It includes a mandatory certification program, to be administered by the states, with third-party certifying agents to be accredited by the USDA, to ensure compliance with the standards. With these new national standards, you can more confidently select fresh, certified organic, locally grown, minimally processed foods. For quick and easy mail-order sources, see Resources.

Get the most nutritional value from the produce you grow or buy. Be alert for freshness—don't buy or eat wilted, discolored, bad-smelling food of any kind. Cut up fresh produce at the last minute before eating to avoid possible nutrient loss related to oxidation—which means the "combining with oxygen" in the air that can lead to the production of harmful free radicals (as discussed in "Power Knowledge" on page 218). Cover pans when boiling or steaming to shorten cooking time and preserve nutrients.

Wash fresh vegetables and fruits before eating them. This practice can help remove some—but not all—of the chemical residues, as well as any dirt and harmful bacteria that may be present. "Adding a drop of mild dishwashing soap to a pint of water is more effective than plain water at removing pesticides," explain Michael F. Jacobson, Ph.D., Lisa Y. Lefferts and Anne Witte Garland, coauthors of *Safe Food: Eating Wisely in a Risky World*. "Just choose a soap brand that isn't loaded with dyes and perfumes. Don't use salt water or vinegar—they won't help. . . . Use a vegetable brush, and be sure to rinse completely.

"Here are some tips for handling specific types of produce (short of buying organic food): For leafy vegetables like lettuce and cabbage, discard the outer leaves and wash the inner leaves. Wash celery after trimming off the leaves and tops. For recipes calling for grated peel, buy organic fruit if possible. Peel carrots (you won't be losing out on fiber, since it is found throughout). Peel the skins off potatoes (contrary to popular belief, nearly all nutrients are in the *center* of a potato, and the skin is where toxic solanine spreads, and is where sprout-inhibitors end up—and these chemicals, which accumulate in the body, have not been tested for safety in humans.)[51] Peel cucumbers if they're waxed. Peel all nonorganic apples, peaches and pears, since these are most likely to contain risky surface residues of pesticides. Wash eggplants, peppers, tomatoes, potatoes, green beans, cherries, grapes and strawberries. Cut or chop up cauliflower, broccoli and spinach before you wash them, since pesticides may be hard to wash off otherwise."[52]

Avoid moldy foods. Don't eat nuts or seeds that have the least suspicion of moldiness or rancidity. Use the sensitive receptors of your eyes, nose and mouth to detect bitterness, moldiness, discoloration or "old" appearance of foods—and then don't buy them, or discard them if you find these signs in foods you already have at home. Cut out and throw away green spots on potatoes.

Handle and prepare animal flesh-foods with care. If you eat meat, poultry or fish, choose the leanest varieties. Preferably before cooking, remove all the visible fat and the skin from poultry and fish. This will help lower your fat intake and reduce your exposure to pesticides and other chemicals that accumulate in fatty tissues. If possible, buy meat produced without the routine use of antibiotics and other veterinary drugs. Choose fish caught far from shore—such as cod, haddock and pollock—since these are less likely to be contaminated with chemicals found close to shore. (Salmon, a top source of heart-healthy omega-3 fatty acids, is usually safe even though it's caught near shore.) Thoroughly cook all meat, fish and poultry to kill harmful bacteria that may be present. Use a *wooden cutting board*—since, much to the surprise of scientists, dangerous bacteria such as *E. coli*, *Listeria* and *Salmonella* from raw flesh-foods didn't remain on wood surfaces but multiplied on plastics and rubber surfaces.[53]

Say no to burned and many barbecued foods. In general, avoid all burned foods. If you choose to eat barbecued foods on occasion, here are several important guidelines. Don't use high-fat meats. Avoid basting foods with high-fat mixes—baste instead with lemon juice, wine or tomato-based barbecue sauces to add flavor. Wrap vegetables and fish in foil to preserve flavor and protect them from smoke. After cooking, scrape off any charred material on the surface of foods before eating them.

Resources

The Complete Guide to Anti-Aging Nutrients by Sheldon Saul Hendler, M.D., Ph.D. (Simon & Schuster, 1988). This remains one of the best documented books on the nutrients that may extend and enrich human life.

Diamond Organics (P.O. Box 2159, Freedom, CA 95019; 800-922-2396). A mail-order source for organic varieties of vegetables and fruits.

Environmental Nutrition (P.O. Box 420451, Palm Coast, FL 32142; 800-829-5384). A well-referenced monthly newsletter written by a staff of registered dietitians.

Green Groceries: A Mail-Order Guide to Organic Foods by Jeanne Heifetz (HarperCollins, 1992). A handy resource for ready access to trustworthy quick-ship sources of fresh, certified organic foods.

Nutrition Action Healthletter (Center for Science in the Public Interest [CSPI], Suite 300, 1875 Connecticut Ave., N.W., Washington, DC 20009; 202-332-9110). A well-documented, highly readable newsletter on better nutrition.

Prescription for Longevity: Eating for a Long Life by James Scala, M.D. (Dutton, 1992). A referenced guide to "protector" foods written by a former professor of nutrition and biochemistry at Georgetown Medical School, the University of Oklahoma Medical School, the Ohio College of Medicine and University of California, Berkeley.

Safe Food: Eating Wisely in a Risky World by Michael F. Jacobson, Ph. D., Lisa Y. Leffert and Anne Witte Garland (Living Planet Press, 1991). The best book to date about protecting yourself and your family against pesticides, bacteria and other hidden hazards in food.

Southwest Gourmet Gallery (Sinagua Plaza, Suite D, 320 N. Highway 89A, Sedona, AZ 86336; 800-888-3484; 602-282-2682). Far and away our favorite mail-order source for fresh, flavor-packed salsas, sauces, marinades, and spices.

Starr Organic Produce (P.O. Box 561502, Miami, FL 33256; 305-262-1242). A mail-order source for fresh, organically grown tropical fruits.

Staying Healthy in a Risky World by Arthur C. Upton, M.D., and Eden Graber (Simon & Schuster, 1993). A comprehensive guide from the New York University Medical Center.

Think before You Drink (Environmental Resources Defense Council, 40 W. 20th St., New York, NY 10011; 1993). One of the most comprehensive studies on drinking water ever conducted.

Walnut Acres (Penns Creek, PA 17862; 800-433-3998). One of America's oldest and most trusted mail-order sources for organic foods.

PERSONAL POWER NOTES
A Quick-List of This Chapter's Power-Action Options

Eat more anti-aging Protector Foods.
- *Fresh fruits*
- *Fresh vegetables*
- *Whole grains*
- *Legumes*
- *Omega-3 sources*
- *Yogurt*
- *Selected spices and herbs*

Drink pure water.

Eat "safe" foods.
- *Buy the freshest, cleanest food you can—"certified organic" may be best.*
- *Get the most nutritional value from the produce you grow or buy.*
- *Wash fresh fruits and vegetables before eating them.*
- *Avoid moldy foods.*
- *Handle and prepare animal flesh-foods with special care.*
- *Say no to burned and many barbecued foods.*

PERSONAL NOTES

_____

_____

_____

_____

_____

_____

_____

"Nutritional Insurance"

Why It Makes Sense to Take
a Broad-Spectrum, Moderate-Dosage
Vitamin/Mineral/Antioxidant Supplement

"A poor diet plus vitamins is still a poor diet," warns Art Ulene, M.D. And he's right. But more and more nutritional scientists, aware of the latest research, are themselves taking vitamin/mineral supplements—in addition to a good diet, not in place of one.

You may already be taking a daily multivitamin/mineral supplement. Or maybe you've said "forget it" after hearing so many contradictory, vehement views on the subject. The truth is, your decision may play a small but significant role in how long you live and how young you stay along the way. Even if you eat a well-balanced diet, manage stress and lead a physically active lifestyle, you may still want to take a multivitamin/mineral supplement, if only as a form of nutritional insurance.

Surveys indicate that up to one-half of the American population regularly takes some form of daily vitamin/mineral supplement (as do nearly 60 percent of the dietitians in Washington State and 14 percent of the faculty of Harvard Medical School[1]), and, contrary to fears expressed by some professionals, most people seem to realize that a basic vitamin/mineral pill is no substitute for a good diet. Apparently, Americans are using supplements as part of an overall approach to a healthy lifestyle. In this respect, supplements may be appropriate. Furthermore, most vitamin and mineral supplements seem to be taken safely. "Few if any individuals consume nutrients in amounts considered toxic," says Amy Subar, Ph.D., a National Cancer Institute researcher.[2]

POWER ACTION: FIRST OPTION
A Comprehensive, Synergistic Vitamin/Mineral Supplement

For greatest benefits, cost-effectiveness and safety, vitamins and minerals should generally be taken together in a balanced formula and consumed along with healthy meals. That's because taking large doses of certain isolated nutrients may put you at increased risk of developing a nutritional imbalance. Although each vitamin and mineral has its own biochemical functions in the body, they work synergistically—that is, they help each other. A well-balanced supplement is a highly efficient supplement, one in which dosages of all nutrients can be kept optimal but as low as possible, and costs can be minimized.

A growing number of medical and health authorities are admitting that there is no harm, and may in fact be a variety of real and potential benefits, in taking a broad-spectrum vitamin/mineral/antioxidant supplement that provides up to 150 percent of the Recommended Dietary Allowances (RDAs) for nutrients.[7] Here are several added considerations in selecting a supplement.

> Nutrients always act as a team. Comprehensive nutritional science must rise above the traditional piecemeal approach.
>
> —Roger Williams, Ph.D., nutritional biochemist

Choose a supplement with calcium. It's of special importance that women receive the RDA of at least 800 milligrams of calcium. The National Institutes of Health and the National Osteoporosis Foundation recommend up to 1,500 milligrams of total calcium every day—from foods and supplements—for postmenopausal women (the average calcium intake from food sources is only between 560 and 600 milligrams a day, and many women fall below the 400-milligram mark), and suggest combining adequate calcium intake with bone-strengthening weight-bearing exercise.[8] In supplement form, *calcium citrate* appears to be the most absorbable form of calcium, and there is some evidence suggesting the citrate part of the molecule may also aid in preventing the formation of calcium kidney stones.[9] (See chapter 22 for important related information on vitamin D.)

Folic acid is vital for women. Also called folate, this B vitamin has been shown to prevent certain birth defects,[10] and increased intakes of folic acid are now recommended for *all* women in their childbearing years unless they are absolutely certain of not becoming pregnant. Folic acid has also been linked to cancer protection, in particular cervical cancer. Dosage: 400 micrograms (and up to 800 micrograms for pregnant women[11]) from food (leafy greens, beans, whole grains, broccoli, asparagus and citrus fruits and juices) and supplements. *Note*: Do note take supplemental folic acid if there is a suspicion that you have vitamin B_{12} anemia. Discuss this with your physician—if you do have B_{12} anemia, folic acid make be taken as soon as the B_{12} deficiency is treated.[12]

Make sure it's iron-free. After decades of popularity in the public mind, iron's reputation has recently taken a serious plunge. While iron indeed helps the blood transport oxygen, in excess, iron actually *encourages* the formation of oxygen-related free radicals (the dangerous, cancer-causing, age-accelerating fragmented molecules discussed in chapter 16). According to Randall B. Lauffer, Ph.D., a biochemist at Harvard University, any extra iron in the body catalyzes the production of free radicals, which then damage the tissue around them—and this damage has been linked to both heart disease and cancer, in addition to speeding up the aging process.[13] Do nearly all of us have extra iron in our bodies? Unfortunately, yes. Men accumulate iron throughout adulthood; for most women, some iron is lost each month with menstruation, and therefore iron accumulation is generally not a problem until menopause.

"In general, as you age, you accumulate iron," explains Dr. Lauffer. "Your body is really a sort of dead end for iron. There's no way to get rid of it in a regulated fashion. We can always get rid of extra sodium if we eat too many potato chips. But with iron, there's really no way to get rid of it. It stays in your body . . . just waiting to stir up trouble."[14] *Trouble* may be an understatement, warns Neal Barnard, M.D., president of the Physicians Committee for Responsible Medicine, author of *Food for Life* and a faculty member at the George Washington University School of Medicine in Washington, D.C. "Iron-catalyzed free-radical damage is now thought to be the spark that can set off both heart disease and cancer, in addition to aggravating the aging process."[15] Where does most of the iron come from? Meat in the diet, first of all. Meat contains a form of iron that is more easily absorbed than the iron in vegetables, fruits, grains and beans. This used to be seen as a nutritional advantage to eating meat.

Not anymore. This adds another piece of strong scientific evidence in support of semi-vegetarian and vegetarian diets. Iron in vitamin/mineral supplements may contribute to iron-related health problems—although iron in supplements may still be indicated for

POWER KNOWLEDGE: SUPPLEMENTS

MYTH #1: The government establishes the optimum levels for each vitamin and mineral. That's what the Recommended Dietary Allowances (RDAs) are for.

POWER KNOWLEDGE: That's *not* what the RDAs are for. The Food and Nutrition Board of the National Academy of Sciences (NAS) appoints a committee every five years or so to update the RDAs, which include recommended dosages for many vitamins and minerals for specific age and sex groups. (The U.S. Recommended Daily Allowances, or U.S. RDAs, issued by a division of the U.S. Department of Health and Human Services, are based on the RDAs and were developed to be used on supplement and food labels. The Daily Values now shown in the Nutrition Facts on food labels are the same as the U.S. RDAs.) RDA decisions are a political fulcrum affecting hundreds of corporate, federal and state programs. A heated debate continues about choosing RDAs that prevent dire *clinical deficiencies*—conditions where uncommonly low levels of a nutrient quickly lead to disease (a diet with no vitamin C produces the ailment called scurvy, for example)—versus establishing those that may also safely *promote optimal health.* In other words, this means that *even if you get the RDA for every nutrient, you may not be adequately protected against disease and premature aging.*

"Dietary/nutritional imbalances and deficiencies contribute significantly to the premature deaths of millions of Americans annually," says Sheldon Saul Hendler, M.D., Ph.D., professor at the University children and pregnant and nursing mothers (consult your physician or registered dietitian for the latest guidelines).

A Sample of a Comprehensive "Insurance" Supplement

A nutritional supplement "insurance" formula, at its best, strives for a balance of nutrients that seems optimal given present scientific knowledge. Despite the fact that there are literally hundreds of dif-

of California at San Diego School of Medicine and author of *The Complete Guide to Anti-Aging Nutrients.* "Moreover, our changing world has placed new demands on our bodies, exposing them to environmental stresses and insults that were not previously so prevalent, stresses and insults that deplete our tissues of protective micronutrients as never before."[3] *Even with an optimal diet, there's growing evidence that it's getting harder all the time to protect your health with RDAs of vitamins and minerals.*

MYTH #2: Health professionals are opposed to taking nutritional supplements.

POWER KNOWLEDGE: In January 1994, the public health editorial board of the prestigious *University of California at Berkeley Wellness Letter*, headed by Sheldon Margen, M.D., recommended supplementary vitamins on a broad scale, even for people eating healthy diets.[4] This follows similar advice in the *Nutrition Action Health Letter*: "I believe there is now sufficient evidence to warrant people taking supplements—some at many times the U.S. RDA—*in addition to an excellent diet*,"[5] says Michael F. Jacobson, Ph.D., executive director of the Center for Science in the Public Interest.

"I recommend that people take a multivitamin-multimineral supplement at one to two times the RDA as nutritional insurance," says Tufts University nutrition professor Jeffrey Blumberg, Ph.D. "In addition, I choose to take vitamin E because of the studies that suggest that antioxidants reduce the risk of heart disease, cataracts and cancer. The evidence on antioxidants is still equivocal and the trials under way could prove no benefit, but it could take ten or more years before the results are published."[6]

ferent vitamin/mineral formulas available, we agree with the candid assessment of Sheldon Saul Hendler, M.D., Ph.D., biochemist, internal medicine specialist, professor at the University of California at San Diego School of Medicine and author of *The Complete Guide to Anti-Aging Nutrients*, that "there are very few products that qualify as insurance formulas."[16] Perhaps in the coming years, dozens of such broad-spectrum, moderate-dosage formulas will emerge.

In the meantime, what suggestions can we share with you?

After much discussion, we've decided to give you the level of nutrients in the product Dr. Hendler helped develop as an example of a sample comprehensive "insurance" formula—something you can use for comparison with other supplements you might consider buying in your health food store or pharmacy. Keep in mind that there are many variables and considerations in selecting a well-balanced nutritional supplement. Also, remember that new research updates continue to result in modifications and additions to what individual scientists consider an "ideal" formula. Over the past decade, many supplement formulas have been revised based on the latest scientific discoveries. It stands to reason that there will be continued updating in the years ahead. Therefore, we strongly suggest that you use this sample formula merely as a starting point for comparison.

We want to make it clear that neither of us nor any member of our families has any direct or indirect financial interest in the product mentioned here. We also want to point out that there is no one "perfect" formula for everyone, and perhaps you can find other supplements that are as good or even better than the one we have chosen. We encourage you to become an aware, informed consumer (see Resources for several good places to begin), to compare prices and formulas of the supplements available from many respected companies in your health food store or pharmacy, and to keep abreast of new discoveries published in respected journals.

The product Dr. Hendler helped design (as a nonfee consultant) is called Broad Spectrum and consists of the nutrient ingredients shown at right.

Note: This formula has the benefit of being designed for use in divided doses—two tablets taken with each meal, thus providing more continuous nutrient protection, especially with antioxidants.

An added note: *freshness matters*. Make certain that any supplements you choose to take have an expiration date on the bottle. Certain nutrients interact with others (for example, thiamine may hasten the decomposition of folic acid and vitamin B_{12}). Because of this, vitamin formulas can lose potency over time. Store supplements in a cool, dark, dry place, but not in the refrigerator.

BROAD SPECTRUM
(Daily dose: 6 tablets)

Nutrient	Amount	% U.S.RDA
Beta-carotene	25,000 IU	500
Vitamin A	5,000 IU	100
Vitamin B_1	10 mg.	667
Vitamin B_2	10 mg.	588
Niacinamide	100 mg.	500
Calcium pantothenate	50 mg.	500
Vitamin B_6	20 mg.	1,000
Vitamin B_{12}	30 mcg.	500
Folic acid	800 mcg.	200
Biotin	100 mcg.	33
Vitamin C	1,000 mg.	1,667
Vitamin D	400 IU	100
Vitamin E	400 IU	1,333
Vitamin K	100 mcg.	*
Calcium	800 mg.	80
Magnesium	400 mcg.	100
Zinc	30 mg.	200
Manganese	6 mg.	*
Copper	3 mg.	150
Selenium	200 mcg.	*
Chromium	400 mcg.	*
Iodine	150 mcg.	100
Molybdenum	150 mcg.	*
Silicon	20 mg.	*
Boron	3 mg.	*

*No U.S.RDA established

POWER ACTION: MORE OPTIONS
Special Antioxidant Protection:
Beta-Carotene, Vitamins C and E

Scientists are intrigued with the health-protective potential of *antioxidants*[17] (the free radical neutralizers discussed in chapter 16)—especially beta-carotene and vitamins C and E. "The data suggests that supplementary intakes beyond what dietary guidelines advise may provide protection against cardiovascular disease, cancer, infectious diseases and so on. But the evidence is not so clear that one can say 'This is what you ought to do,' " says Jeffrey Blumberg, Ph.D., professor of nutrition at Tufts University in Boston and associate director of the U.S. Department of Agriculture's Human Nutrition Research Center on Aging at the university. "But there is some very compelling data, and some people may . . . choose to act now rather than wait 10 or 20 years until clear-cut recommendations can be made. Vitamin C, beta-carotene and vitamin E are extraordinarily safe. Even at supplementary intakes that approach five to ten times the U.S. RDA for these three nutrients, there is virtually no harm whatsoever and no interactions that would lessen the efficacy of any other nutrients or of any medications."[18]

In a study recently reported in the *Journal of the National Cancer Institute*, a combination of three antioxidants—beta-carotene, vitamin E and selenium (a trace mineral with antioxidant effects that complement those of vitamin E)—dramatically reduced the cancer death rate among a rural, malnourished population group of 30,000 people studied in China.[19] The researchers studied the effects of supplementation in an area of China where stomach cancer and cancer of the esophagus are rampant. In a five-year controlled study, the overall cancer rate was 13 percent lower among individuals receiving the three antioxidants, and stomach cancer rates in that group dropped a remarkable 21 percent.

A new study by researchers at the Washington University School of Medicine in St. Louis suggests that antioxidant supplements may be very important for protecting the body against free radicals produced during exercise.[20] Here's why: The body's increased need for oxygen, especially during aerobic exercise (see chapter 11), seems to produce free radicals which, in a chemical process called lipid peroxidation, can damage muscle cell membranes, making cells more susceptible to disease and aging. Antioxidants disarm free radicals before they can do their damage, and in this study, 11 men—all joggers—

were given about 600 international units of vitamin E, 1,000 milligrams of vitamin C and 30 milligrams (50,000 international units) of beta-carotene. Nine other men—also regular joggers—were given identical-looking but inactive supplements (placebos). At the beginning of the study, all of the men ran on a treadmill for 35 minutes and then had free radical levels measured. When free radical measurements were again taken after they exercised on a treadmill six months later, the antioxidant takers formed 17 to 36 percent *fewer* free radicals than the men who took the placebos.

A recent cover report in the *University of California at Berkeley Wellness Letter* states, "The role that [the antioxidants beta-carotene, vitamin C, vitamin E, and the B vitamin folic acid] play in disease prevention is no longer a matter of dispute,"[21] and another report in the same publication echoes the safety message: "Supplements of beta-carotene and vitamin E seem to have no significant side effects, even in large amounts. Up to 1,000 milligrams of vitamin C also produces no ill effects."[22]

Note: Scientists were surprised by some recently published results of a Finnish study on beta-carotene and vitamin E that seemed to indicate that instead of protecting against lung cancer as expected, beta-carotene tablets seemed to increase the risk of disease among smokers.[23] However, according to Allan Smith, M.D., professor of epidemiology at the University of California at Berkeley, the study findings are "dangerously misleading. . . . It borders on ludicrous to expect antioxidants to reduce cancer risk in six years of follow-up."[24] Any single study must be reviewed in the context of other studies, and this one clashes with all other research.

According to scientists, this particular study appears *too short* (the development of most cancers takes decades, and it's highly doubtful that six years is long enough to halt the course of cancer brought on by a lifetime of smoking). It also *makes little if any biological sense* (while there are good explanations of why beta-carotene, and other antioxidants, may help prevent cellular damage and cancer, "it's inconceivable," says Dr. Smith, that it causes cancer—much larger doses of beta-carotene have been used in other studies with no adverse effects). The results *may be the result of chance* (the Finnish scientists were themselves surprised at the findings), and the study was *limited to one homogeneous group* (white, middle-aged men who had smoked for decades and continued to smoke; and, among those men who took no supplements, those with a diet highest in beta-carotene and/or vitamin E had the lowest risk for developing lung cancer).

Several longer clinical studies are under way, and additional results will be known in the years ahead. Meanwhile, as the editors of the *University of California at Berkeley Wellness Letter* recently concluded: "We continue to believe that beta-carotene supplements are safe and offer some protection against heart disease and cancer if taken over the long haul. Of course, you're better off getting beta-carotene from foods than from a pill, since foods contain other nutrients and substances that may also protect against cancer and other diseases. So among your five (minimum) daily fruits and vegetables, include a carrot, a sweet potato, some leafy greens, or other foods rich in carotenoids. But to hedge your bets, take a beta-carotene pill. We stick by our recommendations about daily antioxidant supplements:
• 6 to 15 milligrams (10,000 to 25,000 international units) of beta-carotene.
• 200 to 800 international units (133 to 533 milligrams) of vitamin E.
• 250 to 500 milligrams of vitamin C."[25]

While these protective factors—vitamins C and E and beta-carotene—may be included in a broad-spectrum vitamin/mineral supplement, you might choose instead to take a moderate extra supplement of each (if you have questions, check with your physician or registered dietitian). Here's more about each of these important antioxidants.

Beta-carotene. This is the deep orange compound that is naturally abundant in sweet potatoes, pumpkin, carrots and cantaloupes. Beta-carotene is turned into vitamin A by the body as needed (this makes it exceptionally safe, since large doses of vitamin A can lead to liver damage and other effects). More than a dozen studies suggest that beta-carotene may be "moderately preventive" against cancer of the stomach, colon and rectum, bladder and cervix, and, to a minor extent, breast cancer.[26]

Researchers at Harvard Medical School who have been following 22,000 male physicians as part of a ten-year study found that those men with a history of cardiac disease who were given beta-carotene supplements of 50 milligrams every other day suffered half as many heart attacks, strokes and deaths as those taking placebo pills. No heart attacks occurred among those in the study who received aspirin along with the beta-carotene.[27] The Harvard research team has begun a study of 45,000 postmenopausal women to see if a similar effect occurs.

Many of us receive plenty of beta-carotene through our daily diet—by eating more red or orange vegetables, fruit with colored flesh and green leafy vegetables every day. Some scientists also suggest including a moderate amount of beta-carotene as part of a daily nutritional supplement. Kenneth H. Cooper, M.D., prevention authority and author of *The Antioxidant Revolution*, takes a daily supplement of 15 milligrams (25,000 international units) of beta-carotene.[28] "As a potential preventive against certain diseases," writes Dr. Hendler in his well-documented book *The Doctor's Vitamin and Mineral Encyclopedia*, "take a daily supplement of 5,000 to 25,000 international units of beta-carotene. This amount can be safely used by children as well as adults."[29]

Vitamin C. Ascorbic acid, as vitamin C is known to chemists, is an essential nutrient and antioxidant, aiding the immune system and virtually every cell in the body in neutralizing dangerous free radicals. Along with other nutrients, vitamin C also helps protect the body from certain carcinogens and toxic environmental chemicals.

One recent large-scale ten-year study of 11,348 U.S. adults aged 25 to 74 looked at vitamin C and mortality.[30] When compared with subjects receiving under 50 milligrams per day of vitamin C, men in the highest vitamin C group (getting 50 milligrams or more a day in food plus a supplement averaging 500 milligrams) had a 35 percent lower mortality rate and a 43 percent lower death rate from heart disease and stroke—suggesting a gain in life span of about five to six years. Women in the highest vitamin C group were 25 percent less likely to die of heart disease or stroke and had 10 percent less mortality—suggesting a gain of a year in life span. Epidemiologist James Enstrom, Ph.D., of the UCLA School of Public Health, who headed the study, points out that other dietary changes, such as lowering cholesterol, have never been shown to reduce mortality by the margins seen in this study.[31]

"There is good evidence that supplements of ascorbic acid greater than the amount needed for its vitamin function may be useful in combating some of the effects of both physical and emotional stress," says Hans Fisher, M.D., chairman of the Nutrition Department at Rutgers University and contributing editor to *Nutrition Reviews* and *Nutrition Reports International*. "There is evidence that emotional stress can reduce blood ascorbic acid levels, suggesting the body has a greater need for vitamin C at that time. A potentially important finding has been reported by researchers at the Massachusetts Institute of Technology that ascorbic acid at levels of 2 grams [2,000 milligrams] a day blocked the formation in the intestine of potent cancer-forming compounds called nitrosamines."[32]

According to Oliver Alabaster, M.D., associate professor of medicine and director of cancer research at George Washington University Medical Center in Washington, D.C.: "Since it is very difficult to achieve levels of vitamin C much above 250 to 500 milligrams with modern dietary habits, we probably should be taking supplements to achieve the cancer-protecting levels of vitamin C that we need. . . . After considering all the evidence carefully, I have come to the conclusion that a reasonable vitamin C intake, which might lower your cancer risk and is completely safe, is 1 gram [1,000 milligrams] a day, preferably in divided doses (250 milligrams four times a day). This should be achieved by combining a 1-gram daily supplement with a diet that is rich in vitamin C."[33]

"The best available data," says Dr. Hendler, "suggest that adults and children over ten years of age may benefit from a daily intake of 250 to 1,000 milligrams of vitamin C . . . which will be best utilized by the body if taken in divided doses, preferably with each meal."[34] Dr. Cooper reports that, based on current research on antioxidants, he takes a daily dose of 1,000 milligrams of vitamin C.[35]

Vitamin E. This vitamin occurs naturally in a variety of higher-fat food sources, including wheat germ oil, seed oils, seeds and nuts.

LOW-DOSE ASPIRIN—THE ULTIMATE "DAILY SUPPLEMENT" FOR PROTECTING YOUR HEALTH?

For a number of years now, leading researchers in cardiovascular disease have been calling aspirin "the greatest preventive medical bargain of all time." Recently, new studies have prompted both top cancer researchers and scientists investigating senility, migraines and arthritis to proclaim the preventive power of low-dose aspirin. Based on current medical research, aspirin appears to offer the following benefits.[43]

- It can reduce heart attack risk 30 to 40 percent.
- It can reduce stroke risk 18 percent.
- It may reduce colon cancer deaths by up to 50 percent.
- It may reduce the likelihood of migraine attack by 20 percent.
- It may help stave off certain forms of senility.
- First aid for a heart attack might include calling 911 and taking half an aspirin tablet (crushed, chewed or dissolved in water)—because studies indicate that this may reduce damage and improve chances of survival.

It's imperative to realize, however, that aspirin is not a cure-all for these or other conditions. And it's absolutely no substitute for a low-

---

Numerous studies have looked at vitamin E's antioxidant properties. Preliminary findings suggest that vitamin E plays a significant role in the prevention of cancer, coronary artery disease and cataracts.[36] Two new studies published in the *New England Journal of Medicine* strongly suggest that men and women who regularly take vitamin E supplements can cut the risk of heart attacks by about 40 percent.[37] According to researchers at the Harvard School of Public Health and Brigham and Women's Hospital in Boston, of the more than 120,000 people they studied, those who regularly took 100 international units or more of vitamin E daily for two years received the greatest benefits. The results of a recent study at the University of Texas Southwestern Medical Center in Dallas indicate that the LDLs (low-density lipoproteins, discussed in chapter 15) of men receiving 800 international units of vitamin E a day were only half as likely to become oxidized (becoming the "bad" LDL that is believed to clog arteries) as those of men receiving no supplements of vitamin E.[38] Even though their total cholesterol levels remained the same during the study, it is

fat, high-fiber diet, regular exercise, stress management, smoking cessation, regular medical checkups or any of the other priorities noted in *The Power of 5*. Having stated that, we'd like to add that physicians now urge hundreds of thousands of Americans to take a low-strength dosage of aspirin every day or every other day as part of a preventive health program. More and more physicians take low-dose aspirin themselves (acetaminophen and ibuprofen have not been shown to provide similar benefits). As of this writing (May 1994), studies seem to indicate that the best regular daily preventive dose of aspirin may fall between 81 milligrams (one-quarter of a standard 325-milligram aspirin tablet) and 162 milligrams (half a standard tablet).

The key question here, however, is should *you* take some form of aspirin regularly? Quite possibly—but *only* after discussing this with your personal physician and then, if he or she recommends aspirin, tailoring a minimal dosage that may offer you, individually, the greatest chance for health protection. Besides, there *are* side effects—stomach upset, gastrointestinal bleeding and other problems—although for many individuals, physicians believe the benefits may far outweigh the risks. (To learn more about recent research on aspirin, see Resources.)

contended that the men taking the vitamin E were at lower risk for heart disease because of their lower levels of oxidized or "bad" LDLs.

According to one review of the research literature, "there is evidence sufficient to suggest that vitamin E may play an important role in helping to prevent the development of several degenerative processes associated with aging. Supplementation, however, should not exceed 600 international units daily for adults,[39] . . . since vitamin E in higher doses has been shown to interfere with beta-carotene absorption. The benefits of vitamin E—and there are many—can be obtained with daily doses up to 400 international units."[40]

"When your dietary fat intake is . . . reduced to approximately 20 percent of total calories," says Dr. Alabaster, "your [dietary] access to vitamin E will naturally fall. Unlike with other vitamins, there is no need to make a special effort to increase your intake from natural sources, for two reasons. First, there is no evidence that dietary vitamin E is better than a simple supplement. Second, there is every reason to reduce your fat intake, not increase it. For those who decide to take supplements, I recommend 400 international units of vitamin E daily."[41]

The *University of California at Berkeley Wellness Letter* recently stated that, "200 to 800 international units of vitamin E [are] advised for everybody; you can't get that much from food, especially on a low-fat diet. [There are] no serious side effects at that level, though diarrhea and headaches have been reported."[42]

Note: Vitamin E supplements should not be taken by those with vitamin K deficiency or with known blood coagulation defects, or by those receiving anticoagulation therapy.

Resources

The Antioxidant Revolution by Kenneth H. Cooper, M.D. (Thomas Nelson, 1994). A well-referenced, up-to-date guidebook on smart, responsible supplementation with antioxidants by a leader in the preventive medicine movement.

An Aspirin a Day: What You Can Do to Prevent Heart Attack, Stroke, and Cancer by Michael Castleman (Hyperion, 1993). A medical journalist's well-organized, highly readable review of the known and potential benefits— and risks—of aspirin as a preventive health aid. More than 200 medical studies cited.

The Aspirin Handbook: A User's Guide to the Breakthrough Drug of the '90s by Joe Graedon and Tom Ferguson, M.D. (Bantam, 1993). This pharmacologist/physician team has compiled an exhaustive and valuable guidebook on aspirin's documented and potential uses in preventive care. Hundreds of medical references.

The Complete Guide to Anti-Aging Nutrients by Sheldon Saul Hendler, M.D., Ph.D. (Simon & Schuster, 1988). An enlightening, scientifically based reference guide to many of the nutrients that may extend and enrich human life.

The Doctor's Vitamin and Mineral Encyclopedia by Sheldon Saul Hendler, M.D., Ph.D. (Simon & Schuster, 1991). Perhaps the most comprehensive, best documented manual on nutritional supplements yet written. A valuable resource.

Nutrition Action Health Letter (Center for Science in the Public Interest [CSPI], Suite 300, 1875 Connecticut Ave., N.W., Washington, DC 20009; 202-332-9110). A well-referenced, highly readable newsletter on better nutrition.

University of California at Berkeley Wellness Letter (P.O. Box 420148, Palm Coast, FL 32142; 904-445-6414). A top-rated newsletter that includes well-founded advice on nutrition.

PERSONAL POWER NOTES
A Quick-List of This Chapter's Power-Action Options

A comprehensive, synergistic vitamin/mineral supplement.
- *Choose a supplement with calcium.*
- *Folic acid is vital for women.*
- *Make sure it's iron-free.*

Special antioxidant protection: beta-carotene, vitamin C and vitamin E.

PERSONAL NOTES

AGELESS AGILITY AND FLEXIBILITY

Enjoying the Benefits of 5-Minute Scientific Stretches

Those who think they have not time for bodily exercise will sooner or later have to find time for illness.
—**Edward Stanley**, Earl of Derby, 1873

Once you're enjoying some *Power of 5* aerobic "fit times" (see chapter 11) and your muscles are getting "quick-toned" (see chapter 12), you're on your way to feeling younger and more vigorous. But to live long and well, there's another vital aspect of fitness to consider.

What if we told you that you could look and feel several *decades* younger than your age by spending a few *minutes* a week sharpening some underrated skills—flexibility, agility, balance and coordination? And what if you knew that these skills could, in turn, encourage you to stay more active and keep you light on your feet long after people half your age are sitting down and shaking their heads in wonder? Well, it's true.

Why do most longevity approaches overlook agility and flexibility? Because to the majority of us in the Western world, good flexibility, balance, agility and coordination seem "good" mostly because of how everyone else moves around. Elegantly coordinated people—elite dancers, gymnasts, yogis, martial artists and others—are indeed rare to behold. But brain scientists have found that each of us could establish a greater sense of physical mastery—flexibility, balance, agility and coordination—than we normally imagine.[1] How? By progressively developing your mind, senses and muscles in some new ways, with 5-minute scientific stretches.

Furthermore, flexibility, balance, agility and coordination are essential if you expect to avoid many of the common falls that are the chief late-life accident menace (nearly all harmful falls occur in the home as a result of tripping during normal activities, not as the result of climbing on ladders). And there's more: Once you start to expand these skills beyond normal limits, you experience a cascade of pleasurable benefits. New levels of *physical* flexibility and balance have a way of turning into greater *life* flexibility and balance. What a great way to help turn back the clock!

> Health is aliveness, spontaneity, gracefulness, and rhythm.
>
> **—Alexander Lowen, M.D.,** author of *Bioenergetics*

POWER ACTION: FIRST OPTION
1-Minute "Balan-sations"[5]

Here are several of the easiest, do-it-anywhere ways to develop and maintain greater balance, flexibility, agility and coordination in just 1 minute at a time combining *relaxing, balanced movements and heightened sensations of agility and coordination.*[6] Do a *balan-sation exercise* anytime it's convenient—when talking on the phone, on the way back from the refrigerator with a low-fat snack for TV, when winding down in the evening or whenever you feel like doing a minute of gentle, relaxing exercise.

"Moving Balance"

Stand comfortably with your feet about shoulder-width apart, your knees slightly bent, your elbows flexed 30 to 60 degrees, and your arms held in a relaxed and balanced position (grasp a solid object with one hand for support if necessary). Keeping both feet on the ground, slowly and smoothly raise and lower your vertical torso, bending at the knees. In this exercise, your upper body moves as a whole—up and down, left and right, forward and back—with your head properly extended on a straight neck. Next, bending at the knees and hips (not the waist or lower back), smoothly lean your torso in an oblique (diagonal) angle halfway between straight ahead and left, then return to center. Now

> Two of the worst pieces of advice an older person can receive are: What do you expect at your age? and Take it easy.
>
> **—Robert Butler, M.D.,** chairman, Department of Geriatrics and Adult Development, Mount Sinai Medical School

lean halfway between straight ahead and right, then back again, and so on in each direction.

Be creative, moving in as many different directions as capture your interest, while keeping your feet on the ground. Imagine standing on footprints painted on the ground. You may come up on the balls of your feet or heels, but don't twist or slide completely off the footprints.

Then change your foot positions, with your feet placed wider or narrower than shoulder-width or with one foot farther in front of the other, with your toes pointing straight ahead or off to the left or right, and so on, and begin a new series of movements. If you find a certain

POWER KNOWLEDGE: LOOSENING UP

MYTH #1: Bounce-type stretches, the kind we all learned years ago in physical education classes, are the way to loosen up and stay flexible.

POWER KNOWLEDGE: Over the years, exercise authorities have recommended many different ways to increase flexibility. Ballistic stretching (bounce-stretching), ballistic and hold, passive lift and hold, prolonged stretch, active PNF (proprioceptive neuromuscular facilitation), passive PNF and relaxation methods of stretching have all been popular to varying degrees. Some work well in specific therapeutic circumstances. Others don't work at all. Some, rather than relaxing the body, make it more tense. Beyond that, the most commonly taught stretching exercises in America are dangerous. These gymnastic-type "bounce-stretches" include bouncing toe touches, side-bends and traditional hurdler's stretches.

"The rapid bounce-stretch releases a nerve reflex that signals the muscle to contract," explains Sven-A. Solveborn, M.D., a sports medicine expert from Sweden and author of *The Book about Stretching*. "This stretch-reflex is a protective mechanism that prevents the joint from getting hurt when a stretch is going too far. Every bounce-type stretch activates the stretch reflex. Since the created muscle contraction works against the stretching movement, the muscle fibers are position is uncomfortable or painful, work gently around it. For long-term benefits, you only need to spend a minute or so on this exercise several times a week.

"Expanding Circles"

This is a pleasantly challenging, smooth but fast exercise in which you add hand and upper body movements to the double-leg moving balance exercise. Here's the image: You are standing inside a beautiful sphere of soft, sparkling lights, all about the size of a silver dollar. Keep your knees bent, moving from unlocked straight legs to very bent

torn. When they heal, scar tissue is created, which makes the muscle elasticity worse. The muscle becomes sore and stiff."[2]

For many of us, a far more practical, safe and useful method of building and sustaining healthy, lifelong flexibility is through comfortable, relaxed *dynamic flexibility exercises*[3] such as those presented in this chapter.

MYTH #2: Balance, agility and coordination are one and the same. As long as you do some kind of aerobic exercise, these things take care of themselves.

POWER KNOWLEDGE: Although aerobics and strengthening exercises promote balance, agility and coordination, there's more to it than that.

Balance is the dynamic ability to control shifts in your body's center of gravity. It isn't a gift; great balance must be *learned, developed* and *maintained.*

Agility is the competence to smoothly and precisely change position and direction without loss of balance. Agility, like balance, is developed and sustained through regular activity and practice. It increases your adaptability and resilience and helps prevent many common physical injuries.

Coordination is "a harmonious relationship of movements, a smooth union or flow of motion in the execution of a task," writes exercise physiologist Brian Sharkey, Ph.D. "Coordination . . . *is achieved by practice."*[4]

knees. Your posture is aligned from your hips to your neck, and your whole body moves fluidly with each arm motion. At first, you may want to hold on to a solid object with one hand for support.

Create this exercise in your own way. It is a flowing, silken movement, nothing abrupt, nothing tense. As smoothly as you can—maintaining complete control of your balance and moving a little more quickly each time you practice—reach to touch different points with one hand, then the other, again and again; up high, down low; forward, backward; left, right; in straight lines, inside circles, outside circles. Reach to touch all parts of the imaginary sphere surrounding you.

As soon as it's comfortable, go ahead and try combining the preceding exercise with this one—putting the moving balance leg exercise beneath you as you touch dozens of points with your hands in 30 seconds. Each time you do this exercise, encourage yourself to be a little smoother, a little more relaxed, a little faster, reaching a few new points in the sphere.

Note: Wherever possible—with comfort and safety—movements to the left should be balanced with complementing movements to the right; motions up with motions down; inside to outside; front to back; circles moving up and to the right with circles moving down and to the left; and so on. This will help expand your flexibility and coordination and bring the body into greater overall balance.

In an alert, relaxed way, preplan your movements so that your whole body takes on a kind of fluid integration and unity—feet guiding legs, legs guiding waist, waist guiding torso, torso guiding shoulders, shoulders guiding arms, arms guiding hands. Avoid the random leg-here, hip-there, where-are-my-hands-supposed-to-be-anyway kind of motions.

"Staying on Top"

This is a more advanced technique to be performed only after the "free and easy" movements feel comfortable. The movement orientation is the same, but only one leg is in contact with the ground. Once again, grasp a solid object for support whenever necessary.

Begin by elevating one foot only an inch or two off the ground, which allows a quick, safe recovery if you should momentarily lose your balance. In a relaxed and controlled way, move slowly within the imaginary sphere of directional possibilities, reaching high, low, forward, backward, left and right with the whole body; bend the knee of the support leg smoothly up and down while moving the free leg in complementing directions to preserve and enhance balance. Then rest for a moment and switch legs. Begin again. This kind of exercise can feel great whenever you find an extra minute here or there during the day.

POWER ACTION: MORE OPTIONS
Dance to the Music!

When you can't get in the mood for other types of exercise, or if you just happen to love stepping to music, put on your favorite record or audiocassette for 5 minutes, and then, on your own or with a partner, twist and shake, glide and turn or rock 'n' roll. This type of dancing can be a great way to maintain and improve your balance, agility and coordination. And dancing is a wonderful way to build fitness into a social activity with your spouse or friends. Ballroom and folk dancing are on the upswing all across America, and one of the reasons is that you can start out with simple, slow steps and gradually work up from there. And while you're having fun, you'll also be gaining some aerobic benefits. Thomas Allison, M.D., of the Mayo Clinic's Cardiovascular Health Clinic in Rochester, Minnesota, says dancing can burn as many calories as walking, swimming or riding a bicycle.[7]

30-Second Dynamic Flexibility Stretches[8]

These dynamic flexibility exercises are smooth, easy movements that increase circulation and range of motion (the optimal movement pattern) for the joints of your body. This convenient stretching method gives a surprisingly fast and effective increase in flexibility and can work well for people of all ages. Dynamic flexibility exercises—performed slowly and smoothly, without any bouncing movements—may also be included as part of a general exercise warm-up. Do each exercise at least twice, and perhaps three to ten times—spending a total of approximately half a minute. With practice, all ten exercises can be completed in a total of just 5 minutes or less. Even better, if you're especially tight for time, is what we do: fitting in one of these 30-second stretches on work breaks during the day—at your desk, while on hold on the telephone and so on—or during TV time at home. As with do-it-anywhere "fit times" (see chapter 11) and some of *The Power of 5*'s simple strengthening exercises (see chapter 12), staying in better shape can be easier and more convenient than ever. *Note*: Whatever form of stretching you choose, if you have a history of back injury or pain, have your physician approve your stretching routine.

NECK

Neck Ovals

Starting position: Assume a comfortable sitting or standing position, with your neck and shoulders relaxed. Use your hands to lightly support your neck, jaw and the base of your skull.

Movement performance: As indicated in Illustrations 18-1 and 18-2, *smoothly* and *slowly* move your head in clockwise and then counter-clockwise ovals (with the far points out to the sides) of varying radii, starting with tiny ovals where your neck remains almost vertical and then making the ovals wider. Don't attempt to stretch to the maximum in any direction, but if you feel any points of tension, pause a moment or two as you let the muscles relax. Do *not* extend your neck straight back, since this can place excessive stress on the cervical spine area.

18-1

18-2

SHOULDERS

"Hanging in There"

A "brachiated stretch" is a simple exercise in which you hang by your hands from a pull-up bar. This action relaxes the midsection muscles, gently stretches and aligns the spine and brings welcome relief to overtaxed back muscles.[9] This can be a good home exercise, using a door-frame pull-up bar (available in sporting goods stores). Select one with strong brackets that can be installed in any door frame.

Starting position: Stand beneath a secure pull-up bar and reach up to hold on firmly with your hands. If you are not certain whether your grip is strong enough to hold your body weight, keep your feet on the floor (or on a sturdy chair if the bar is high) and bend your knees, shifting as much weight to your hands as you can comfortably handle.

Movement performance: As shown in Illustration 18-3, hang by your hands (in the down position of a pull-up exercise) for up to 10 seconds, then rest. Repeat several times. This exercise feels wonderful toward the end of the day and can help release accumulated tension in the shoulder area.

18-3

18-4

Shrugs and Rolls

This quick, simple exercise increases shoulder flexibility.[10]

Starting position: Sitting or standing with your arms relaxed.

Movement performance: As indicated in Illustration 18-4, slowly roll your shoulders up toward your ears, down in back, then forward and up toward your ears again in a circular manner. Reverse the direction and repeat.

Advanced version: Gently vary the circular angles from front-back and back-front circles to more inside-outside (toward the midline, away from the body's center) and outside-inside circles.

Freestyle Swim Circles

This exercise promotes good shoulder flexibility.[11]

Starting position: Begin in a standing position with balanced posture and your knees slightly bent.

Movement performance: Bend your torso slightly forward at the hips, *with your knees bent*. Smoothly perform a swimming motion using the shoulders, similar to the freestyle or "crawl" stroke (see Illustrations 18-5 and 18-6). As your arms circle with the center of the axis at the shoulder joint, let your knees bend and your hips shift to help make each circle as smooth and flowing as possible. Then "swim backward," reversing the direction of the arm motions.

18-5   18-6

CHEST AND UPPER BACK

Ribcage Lifts and Expansions

This exercise helps increase the elasticity of your ribcage and may aid your breathing power.[12]

Starting position: Sit up or lie flat, face-up, on the floor. Relax your body as you flatten your lower back (gently pressing it toward the floor) and keep your head properly aligned, with your neck long and your chin slightly in. Place your hands on either side of your ribcage, with your palms and fingers pressing lightly against the ribs.

Movement performance: Inhale slowly and deeply, using your diaphragm. Lift and expand the chest fully as you maximize the inhalation. Exhale slowly. Rest for several moments, breathing normally. Repeat the exercise, expanding your chest out against some light hand pressure, lifting your ribs a little higher. Some people find this exercise more effective if they inhale using a series of short in-breaths until the chest is completely expanded.

ARMS

Elbow Circles

Starting position: In a sitting or standing position, with your neck and shoulders relaxed, hold your upper right arm out to the front of your body; support it under the elbow with your left hand.

Movement performance: Begin a series of slow clockwise and counterclockwise circular rotations at the elbow joint, gently turning and twisting your right forearm, wrist and hand. The motion looks a bit like the circular action of washing a small window at face height. When finished with your desired number of repetitions (two or more) with the right arm, switch to the left.

WRISTS AND HANDS

Wrist Circles

Starting position: This exercise is best performed by using your left hand to hold your right forearm just in back of the wrist.

Movement performance: Move your free right hand smoothly in clockwise and counterclockwise circles of varying diameters, with the movement originating at the wrist joint. Repeat with the other hand and wrist.

"Globes of Light"

Starting position: In a comfortable standing or sitting position, hold your right hand out in front of you and gently grasp your right wrist with your left hand.

Movement performance: Be creative, performing a series of circular finger movements to increase the flexibility of your hands and fingers. Imagine inserting your hand through an opening into the middle of a small crystalline sphere or globe and then gently reaching with your fingers—each moving freely and independently—to touch as many places as possible on the surface of this globe while your wrist stays relatively still, held by the opposite hand. Repeat with the fingers on the left hand.

WAIST AND LOWER BACK

Mountain Circles

This type of unique exercise has been used for centuries to develop flexibility and strength in the waist and lower back area—the upper-body/lower-body "bridge"—which assists in many fitness movements and is essential to good posture. Variations are recommended by several researchers.[13] Seek your physician's advice before doing this exercise if you have a history of back injury or pain.

Starting position: Assume a comfortable standing position with your back erect and straight, your neck relaxed and your head aligned with your spinal column. Your feet should be spread at shoulder-width or a little wider, *with your knees moderately bent.* Lightly clasp your hands together and extend your arms over your head as shown in Illustration 18-7.

Movement performance: Inhale a normal breath, then *slowly* and *smoothly* begin to exhale as you rotate your torso down and to the right as if you were lightly swinging an axe in slow motion (See Illustration 18-8).

Allow your torso to bend as your arms swing in a slow, gentle arc toward the floor and then on up to the left and back to the hands-over-head starting position. As you move, your knees should bend to eliminate stress on the lower back. Pause for a moment with a natural

18-7

18-8

inhalation at the top of the arm motion, and then repeat the circle in the opposite direction—down to the left and back up to the right.

Don't swing too hard or too fast. This exercise should be comfortable, and you must remain in full control at all times. As you become proficient, try varying the arc of the circle. For example, begin the exercise in the same position (see Illustration 18-7) and then swing down to the right, but more to the front of your body than to the side (that is, at a more oblique angle). Continue the circle from the bottom of the motion in front of your right knee, back past your left knee and then more to the rear of your body as you complete the circle with your arms passing your left hip and continuing to the top of the motion. After pausing briefly, repeat this motion in a complementary manner, going down and to the left.

HIPS AND KNEES

Alternate Leg-Ups

Starting position: Standing on a padded surface, such as a grassy lawn or carpet.

Movement performance: Slowly jog in place, using high, smooth lift-ups of your knees at the top of the motion.[14]

Imaginary Pedaling

Starting position: Stand, holding on to a countertop or other secure object for stability.

Movement performance: Go through a slow series of smooth, circular movements centered at the hips. Lift one leg and move it from the hip as if pedaling an imaginary bicycle. Then vary the leg motion as if the pedaling circles were shifted a little toward the right or the left (keeping your torso in the original position). Rest for a moment and then repeat with the other leg. Be gentle and creative, progressively expanding the flexibility of your hips and knees.

ANKLES AND FEET

"Globes of Light"

Some of the simplest exercises for developing flexibility in your ankles, feet and toes approximate those for the wrists, hands and fingers.

Starting position: Sitting in a chair, lift your right leg several inches off the floor and extend it to the front about 6 inches. You may wish to support your right knee by cradling it in your right and left hands, with your fingers intertwined.

Movement performance: Perform slow, circular movements, clockwise and counterclockwise for both ankles, flexing and extending the foot. Move your toes in as many directions as comfortably possible. Imagine inserting your foot through an opening into the middle of a small crystalline sphere or globe and then gently reaching with your toes—moving freely and independently—to touch as many places as possible on the surface of this globe while your lower leg stays relatively still. Repeat with your other ankle, foot and toes.

PERSONAL POWER NOTES
A Quick-List of This Chapter's Power-Action Options

1-minute "balan-sations."
- *Moving balance*
- *Expanding circles*
- *Staying on top*

Dance to the music!

30-second "dynamic flexibility stretches."
- *Neck: neck ovals*
- *Shoulders: hanging in there; shrugs and rolls; freestyle swim circles*
- *Chest and upper back: ribcage lifts and expansions*
- *Arms: elbow circles*
- *Wrists and hands: wrist circles; "globes of light"*
- *Waist and lower back: mountain circles*
- *Hips and knees: alternate leg-ups; imaginary cycling*
- *Ankles and feet: "globes of light"*

PERSONAL NOTES

_____

_____

_____

_____

_____

_____

_____

Positive Posture

Sitting, Standing and Moving
with Ease instead of Effort

The truth is, to live a long, active, energetic life, few things matter more than good posture. When you're stooped over, you not only look old, but you tend to feel that way too.[1] When, instead, you uplift and relax your body alignment, you can actually help prevent or reverse the aging process—not just cosmetically but functionally, says Rene Cailliet, M.D., a leading authority on rehabilitative medicine.[2]

If the idea of someday seeing yourself collapsed in a wheezing heap in a nursing home rocking chair alarms you, you're not alone. For many of us between the ages of 30 and 70, this is one of the gnawing worries about what "getting old" holds in store for us. One of the most destructive myths of aging concerns the supposed inevitability of bodily decrepitude, as if at age 40 or 50 or 60 some invisible web draws tight against your frame and then slowly, unstoppably drags you toward the ground. Reject that image! Collapsing posture descends on your frame in slow stages, and you can reverse its downward pull—starting right now. And even if you're already 80 and feel trapped with slumping posture, you can probably make some real headway in lifting yourself back upright against the physical weight of gravity and the mental weight of what society wrongly thinks an "aging" body is supposed to look like.

Research suggests that how you sit and stand may exert a powerful influence not only on how rapidly you age but also on your mind and mood. It makes scientific sense when you realize that slouching or hunching over in your chair creates 10 to 15 times as much pressure on your lower back as does sitting up straight.[3] And when you're slumped in your seat, it also restricts your breathing and impedes circulation.[4]

PEANUTS ®   **By Charles M. Schulz**

But here's the key: Sitting and standing with upright, relaxed posture is a choice you make—or fail to make—every minute of your life. Whether consciously controlled or not, your sitting position creates its own momentum. If gravity gets a grip on your tilted head or drooping shoulders, your body starts to feel like a slow wave moving downhill; slouching gradually becomes slumping, and ease turns into effort. Fortunately, at any point in your life—and what better time than now?—you can turn the tide.

Consider the mental benefits: "Posture is not solely the manifestation of physical balance," writes occupational medicine specialist David Imrie, M.D. "It's also an expression of mental balance. Think about the way you stand when you are depressed or tired: You stand with your shoulders rounded and drooping. Your body represents your emotions by giving up the fight against gravity, sagging just as low as you feel. . . . It's also notable that the term 'well-balanced' is used to describe someone who 'won't go over the edge' and whose emotions are 'on an even keel.' "[5]

As you are drawn into the future by the arrow of time, you have considerable choice as to what happens to your posture and freedom of movement. You can allow your body, through inattention and neglect, to sag, bulge, twist, stiffen and spread. Or you can stand and move with grace and vigor. Along with food, water and oxygen, your body depends on movement to sustain its vitality and to preserve its natural, graceful function. As the days and decades advance, your moving posture takes its cues from the habits you etch into memory each time you stand, turn, bend and walk.

POWER ACTION: FIRST OPTION
5-Second Head Lift

Great posture begins with your head and neck position, which strongly affects the placement—and comfort—of your shoulders, chest and back. At the crest of your spine is a small muscle called the rectus capitus anterior.[6] It flexes and rotates your head, and perhaps most important, it is one of the overlooked keys to maintaining good neck posture.[7]

One of the simplest ways to tone this muscle is with a gentle "head nod" exercise. Starting in a comfortable sitting or standing position, place your hands (thumbs facing to the rear) on the base of your skull just behind and above your earlobes. Let your neck lengthen, gently extending upward as if it's being lifted by an imaginary cord attached to the top of your skull. With your neck in this slightly elevated position, nod your head as if in agreement, bringing your forehead a little forward and your chin slightly in. Repeat the nodding motion about a dozen times each day.

POWER ACTION: MORE OPTIONS
Take 30 Seconds to Breathe—And "Think Taller"

The best posture isn't forced; it's unlocked. Your head weighs between 10 and 15 pounds. To avoid placing undue stress on your neck, shoulders and spine, your head must be poised in a comfortable, centered position. Here's one way to become more aware of that ideal placement.

Sit comfortably. If this is the first time you're doing this exercise, you'll want to leave your eyes open as you read the instructions. With a bit of practice, it's easy to remember the simple guidelines and receive the greatest benefit by doing the exercise with your eyes closed.

Instructions: Breathe naturally and comfortably. Lengthen your neck and let your head move upward, with your chin slightly in, your shoulders broadening and your lower back flattening. Now gently lean your head to the left and then to the right, returning to the most central, balanced spot you can sense. Next move your head slightly forward and then back, finding the precise center once again.

Here's an alternative image: If you put an imaginary 5-pound weight on your head, and you gently push up against the resistance, your neck posture will improve. This image of weight gives your senses instant, valuable signals that help balance and stabilize your head and neck.[16]

We suggest you use this awareness exercise several times a day, in particular whenever you sit down or step up to a counter to begin—or resume—work. The movements in this technique relax the neck and enable you to quickly and consciously choose where to hold your head with the least strain during work.

Beyond this exercise, begin to "think taller," to encourage your head to float upward. Don't push or strain your neck; simply bring your head back over your shoulders, with your chin slightly in. You'll sense the difference. You might even want to try this in front of a mirror, where you can actually see the difference.

It's also important to realize that your head does more than simply rest atop your neck. Whenever possible, your head should lead your body motions: As you begin any movement or act, move your whole head upward and away from your whole body, and let your whole body lengthen by following that upward direction.[17] The process gives you a new way to use your body, with smoothness and ease.

> Most of the muscles of the respiratory system are connected to the cervical and lumbar vertebrae, and breathing therefore affects the ability and posture of the spine, while conversely the position of the spine will affect the quality and speed of breathing. Good breathing also means good posture; just as good posture means good breathing.
>
> **—Moshe Feldenkrais, Ph.D.,** author of *Awareness through Movement*

30-Second Neck-Toning Exercise

These exercises are recommended by authorities on neck and back pain and use isometric—unmoving—tension to improve your neck strength and resiliency.[18] Throughout each movement, maintain a verti-

(continued on page 272)

POWER KNOWLEDGE:
POSTURE AND VITALITY

MYTH #1: Good posture is automatic. You simply force yourself to sit and stand up straight.

POWER KNOWLEDGE: "Stand up straight!" was an admonition you probably heard often over the years from your parents and physical education teachers. And you tried—with your shoulders broad and pulled back, buttocks tucked, back ramrod straight, stomach sucked in. Pure military. The advice was well intended, but it doesn't work. By tightening muscles you end up stiff and braced—a tiring, unnatural position to maintain for very long. The truth is, good posture can't be forced—and it isn't instinctive or automatic. "We're not born knowing how to do it right," says Wilfred Barlow, M.D., medical director of the Alexander Institute in Great Britain. "No reflex system sets up good posture. We have to learn it."[8] Of the nearly 700 muscles in your body, excellent, natural posture relies on only 4 or 5 key muscles to hold your chest, shoulders, neck and head upright, buoyantly, comfortably. This chapter will help teach you simple ways to establish and sustain excellent, health-promoting posture.

MYTH #2: Poor posture just looks bad—it doesn't hurt health.

POWER KNOWLEDGE: Poor posture distorts the alignment of bones and chronically tenses muscles, and researchers report that it also contributes to conditions such as loss of lung capacity (as much as 30 percent or more); increased fatigue; reduced blood and oxygen to the brain and senses; limited range of motion, stiffness of joints and pain syndromes (headaches, jaw pain, muscular aches); reduced mental alertness, reaction speed and work productivity; premature aging of body tissues; faulty digestion and constipation; back pain (perhaps 80 percent of all cases); and a tendency toward cynicism, pessimism, drowsiness and poor concentration.[9] In addition, poor posture may diminish blood flow to your brain and magnify feelings of panic and helplessness—and in some cases, it may even help cause depression.[10]

MYTH #3: Slumped posture might make me a little tired by the end of the day, but it doesn't affect my work quality.

POWER KNOWLEDGE: "It's extremely difficult to work in a technological society and not develop a forward head," says rehabilitative medicine expert Rene Cailliet, M.D.,[11] If you're sitting in front of a typewriter or at a computer, or working behind a counter or on an assembly line, chances are that you have one. Even cooking, cleaning, reading and desk work can produce one. And this constant postural stress contributes to tension headaches, vision problems and jaw and neck pain.[12]

In addition, compared with people with relaxed, upright posture, those who slump may have a greater tendency toward feelings of helplessness and frustration during tasks and to perceive themselves to be under greater stress.[13] Other studies indicate that poor sitting posture decreases mental alertness and increases work errors.[14]

MYTH #4: It's normal to have slumped posture as you get older.

POWER KNOWLEDGE: No, it isn't. "The bodily decrepitude presumed under the myth of aging is not inevitable," writes Thomas Hanna, Ph.D., director of the Novato Institute for Somatic Research in Novato, California. "It is, by and large, both avoidable and reversible. The fact is that, during the course of our lives, our sensory-motor systems continually respond to daily stresses and traumas with specific muscular reflexes. These reflexes, repeatedly triggered, create habitual muscular contractions. . . . These muscular contractions have become so deeply involuntary and unconscious that, eventually, we no longer remember how to move about freely. The result is stiffness, soreness and a restricted range of movement.

"This habituated state of forgetfulness is called sensory-motor amnesia. It is a memory loss of how certain muscle groups feel and how to control them. Our image of who we are, what we can experience, and what we can do is profoundly diminished by sensory-motor amnesia. And it is primarily this event, and its secondary effects, that we falsely think of as 'growing older.' "[15]

cal "best posture" position. Your head and neck don't actually move—the resistance is provided by your gradual, controlled attempt to move your head in the direction indicated while you resist equally with tension in the muscles of the arms and hands.

Begin by placing both hands against your forehead. Slowly and smoothly push forward with your head as you simultaneously push back with equal pressure from your hands. Gently and gradually increase the resistance, but do not exceed half of your maximum tensing strength—which means the hardest you can push. Hold for 2 to 5 seconds, then release and relax. Next place your hands behind the center of your head with your fingers interlaced. Slowly and smoothly push backward with your head as you simultaneously push against your head with gentle, equal pressure from your hands. Hold the tension for 2 to 5 seconds. Release and relax. You can perform this exercise two or three times a week. At no point should it be the least bit painful.

5-Second Posture Check: Sit Tall and "at Ease"

Whenever you sit down, it pays to briefly pause and choose the most balanced, comfortable sitting position. Here's how: First of all, seat yourself squarely; don't slump. Center your buttocks and upper legs on the seat. Leaning to one side or becoming off-center in any other way shifts the line of gravity and causes tension and restricted circulation if you stay in that unbalanced position for very long. Armrests on a chair can relieve about 25 percent of the load on the lower back[19] and help provide stability and support when you're changing positions.

Avoid sitting on your wallet, car keys, pen, comb or checkbook. The *New England Journal of Medicine* published a study showing that, in a number of cases, chronic back pain was completely alleviated for male patients once they simply stopped carrying fat wallets in their back pockets.[20]

After you're seated squarely, let your chest and shoulders come forward as you bend at the thigh/hip joints (not the lower spine). This ensures that your buttocks and lower back are centered and far back in the chair. Then smoothly bring your upper body back against the seat back (once again "hinging" the movement at your thigh/hip joints, not your lower spine). If you must cross your legs, do it at the ankles. Crossing at the knees misaligns the pelvis and can lead to back tension and pain if you don't change positions frequently enough. Whenever possible, place your feet flat on the floor. Another good option is keeping one foot elevated on a chair rung or placing it slightly forward of the other foot on a small stool.[21]

To find your own best sitting position, first balance your neck:

With your eyes closed, gently lean your head to the left and to the right, then return to center. Next lean your head slightly forward and then back, returning to the spot you sense as the exact central position. To balance your torso, repeat these instructions, bending at the hips/thighs.

Read *Up!*

When you read—at your desk, on the commuter train or during air travel—bring your reading material up to your field of vision and avoid the strain of dropping your head. Try a bookstand (see Resources) to hold books at a comfortable slant, and consider buying a small reading light that clips onto the book (available at bookstores). And when talking on the telephone, bring the handset up to your ear and mouth; don't bend your head and neck down to the phone or cradle it between your ear and shoulder by forcing your neck to the side.

Choose—And Adjust—Your Chairs with Care

Especially for prolonged hours of work, choose adjustable seating. For best support and comfort, your chair must fit the length, size and contours of your body, and the height of the chair seat should precisely match the position of the desk, work station or countertop where you work. If you sit in various chairs at work during the day or if another person uses your chair, adjust it each time you use it, just as you adjust your car seat, steering wheel and mirrors after someone else has driven your car.

Then, sometimes even more important, once you've found a chair you love, leave it—often. That's because sitting down all day is stressful, no matter how ideal the design of the chair and work surface. Make it a priority to get up from your desk at least once every half hour or so to take a short break that lasts at least a minute or two.

De-tense in 5 Seconds—Whenever You Need To!

"In our world," warn posture specialists Joseph Heller and William A. Henkin, "tension and stress are realities; they impinge upon our bodies all the time. When we ignore these pressures or pretend they do not affect us, we are prone to absorb them into our physical forms, which is why your personal levels of tension and stress rise when you are out of touch with—unaware of—your body."[22] The longer a muscle area stays tense, the more your awareness of it will dim and the greater the tendency will become to "lock in" that tension. So whenever you notice a stiffening or tightening in your body—usually because of stress or postural slumping—you should immediately release it by lightly shaking the muscles, shifting your position and taking several deep breaths. For more on-the-spot stress-relief techniques, see chapter 3.

Walk Tall—And with Comfort

As you walk, hold your head high, with your neck and shoulders relaxed and lower back flat. Walk with your heel coming down lightly on the ground first, roll your weight forward across the sole of your foot and then gently push off with your toes. Keep your feet pointed straight ahead and don't hyperextend the leg (let it lock straight). Use a "heterolateral" walking pattern, moving your left arm forward as your right leg advances and your right arm forward as your left leg steps.

Finally, there's a cardinal rule for everyday work movements: Whenever you turn to reach for something, take a step in that direction. This helps coordinate and focus your power, integrating the body as it moves and taking strain off back muscles by better using the legs and trunk. When you're reaching, bending or turning, lead the movement with your head floating upward, followed by your whole body.

Resources

CEQUAL Products (1328 16th St., Santa Monica, CA 90404; 800-350-2998). Offers reliable, medically tested products for improved posture and back care, including *Good News for Bad Backs* by Robert L. Swezey, M.D., and Annette M. Swezey (an expertly written book), *21 Days to Back Pain Relief* (Dr. Swezey's home video program), and *Drive Away Back Pain* (a drive-time self-help audiocassette).

Levenger: Tools for Serious Readers (975 South Congress Ave., Delray Beach, FL 33445; 800-544-0880 or 407-276-4141). A catalog of innovative furniture, lights and accessories that can help take much of the stress and strain out of sitting and reading.

The Rejuvenation Strategy by Rene Cailliet, M.D. and Leonard Gross (Doubleday, 1987). A collection of posture-building exercises from a trusted expert in physical and rehabilitative medicine.

Somatics by Thomas Hanna, Ph.D. (Addison-Wesley, 1988). A compelling book on reawakening your mind's control of better posture, movement, and flexibility.

PERSONAL POWER NOTES
A Quick-List of This Chapter's Power-Action Options

5-second head lift.

Take 30 seconds to breathe—and "think taller."

30-second neck-toning exercise.

5-second posture check: sit tall and "at ease."

Read up!

Choose—and adjust—your chairs with care

De-tense in 5 seconds—whenever you need to!

Walk tall—and with comfort.

PERSONAL NOTES

_____

_____

_____

_____

_____

_____

_____

_____

_____

_____

_____

_____

_____

_____

_____

ON-THE-SPOT TRIGGER POINT THERAPY

Put an End to Many Common Aches and Pains with This Safe, Effective Self-Treatment

We are bound to our bodies like an oyster to its shell.
—**Plato**, Greek philosopher

As the years pass, many of us are beset with body aches and stiffness. But chances are, say researchers, the tension and pain you feel are *not* due to getting older; they're caused by poor posture and by hidden myofascial "trigger points" in your muscles and tendons. (*Myo* means muscle and *fascial* refers to a protective tissue that wraps the muscles.) According to specialists, almost any one of your body's hundreds of muscles can develop trigger points.

Active trigger points can cause debilitating, sometimes incapacitating, pain. *Latent* trigger points cause stiffness and restricted movement but are not painful except when pressure is applied to them. Usually, the discomfort occurs at or near the trigger point itself. But in some cases, the actual pain shows up at a site in the body far distant from where the trigger point actually originates. For example, a hidden trigger point in the shoulder muscles might cause neck pain or headaches. This is called referred pain.

"Trigger points are extremely common and become a distressing part of nearly everyone's life at one time or another," say two national experts, Janet G. Travell, M.D., emeritus clinical professor of medicine at George Washington University School of Medicine in Washington, D.C., and David G. Simons, M.D., clinical professor in the Department of Physical Medicine and Rehabilitation at the University of California, Irvine.[1] Dr. Travell and Dr. Simons are coauthors of *Myofascial Pain and Dysfunction: The Trigger Point Manual*. One study of adults found latent trigger points in the shoulder muscles in 54 percent of women and 45 percent of men.[2] Another research team discovered that the greatest number of trigger points are found in people who are between the ages of 31 and 50.[3]

"Individuals of either sex and of any age can develop trigger points," observe Dr. Travell and Dr. Simons. "It is our impression that the likelihood of developing pain-producing active trigger points increases with age to the most active, middle years. As activity becomes less strenuous in later years, individuals tend to exhibit chiefly the stiffness and restricted motion of latent trigger points."[4]

Fortunately, in many cases you can easily learn to locate and relieve these trigger points right away (the scientific evidence suggests that if you ignore them, they may simply keep getting worse). Of course, at any age, arthritis or injuries to your bones or joints may limit your movements or leave you with pain, but here too, trigger points may be involved.

One simple, drug-free way to relieve many common conditions of tension and pain is a method of pressure-point therapy that you can do right where you are. It has different scientific names, but we'll call it Direct Pressure Therapy (DPT). It's a method that, in just 5 to 30 seconds, can treat a predominant cause of tension, aches and pain. DPT is gentle, easy to learn and apply and based on principles supported by scientific and medical research.[5]

POWER ACTION: FIRST OPTION
Find Several Key Trigger Points

To do this, first be certain that your muscles are warm and relaxed. Otherwise it's difficult to distinguish tense bands of muscle—where trigger points are usually located—from adjoining slack muscles. Once you have located a tight band or cord of tense muscle fibers, press or squeeze it with light to moderate pressure until you're able to locate the spot of maximum tenderness with minimum pressure; this is the trigger point.

In most areas of the body, you can gently press the muscle against the underlying bone by using your fingertip or thumb. Even a tennis ball placed behind you in a chair may be used to reach some points on your back.

With practice, you can learn to readily notice when trigger points are aggravated—sensing your muscles becoming tense from poor posture or an uncomfortable sitting position, for example—and then take

POWER KNOWLEDGE: TRIGGER POINTS

MYTH #1: Aches and pains are part of life. They don't affect most people that much.

POWER KNOWLEDGE: As many as 65 million Americans may be suffering the isolation that can be a result of chronic pain.[7] Three-fourths of us have headaches, over half of the American population has backaches, and more than 10 percent of us experience serious back pain at least 30 days a year.[8] Stress-related headaches are the leading cause of lost work time in the United States,[9] followed by back pain.[10] And on any given day, nearly 7 million Americans are undergoing some form of treatment for lower back pain.[11] These figures may be doubled if we include related disorders, such as fatigue and depression, that may be brought on by chronic tension and pain syndromes.[12]

MYTH #2: Chronic tension and stiff, aching muscles require medical treatment.

POWER KNOWLEDGE: Not usually. Many, or even most, trigger point problems can be relieved by simple detection and therapy, researchers say. But there's a problem—few health professionals have been trained to recognize or treat trigger points. The total cost of this oversight "is enormous," say Janet G. Travell, M.D., of George Wash-immediate action to relax the affected area by rebalancing your posture and relaxing tight muscles. If necessary, you can use simple, direct pressure to help relieve trigger point areas.

In many cases, DPT gives immediate benefits, including reduced tenderness or stiffness in the muscles. Relief is likely to be more lasting if the area is kept warm after treatment and if you balance your posture (see chapter 19) and go through several gentle range-of-motion exercises for the affected area.[6]

Note: All persistent or severe pain requires medical attention.

---

ington University School of Medicine in Washington, D.C., and University of California professor David G. Simons, M.D., "When patients mistakenly believe that they must 'live with' trigger point pain because they think it is due to arthritis or a pinched nerve that is inoperable, they restrict activity in order to avoid pain. Such patients must learn that the pain comes from muscles, not from nerve damage, and not from permanent arthritic changes in the bones. Most important, they must know it is responsive to treatment."[13]

MYTH #3: Unless you've been in a serious accident or had some other form of traumatic injury, minor aches and pains are something you just have to live with.

POWER KNOWLEDGE: Not usually. What causes trigger points? Injuries, including life's bumps, bruises, twists and strains; imbalanced posture; chronically tensed muscles; fatigue from overwork; emotional distress; poor sitting or sleeping positions; or a lack of sleep. Trigger points vary in irritability from hour to hour and day to day. But once formed, they tend to remain in your muscles unless treated and released. The reason is that, when injured, most body tissues heal, but muscles "learn" to avoid pain. Trigger points cause you to hold tension and "guard" muscles by limiting their motion. In addition to producing pain, stiffness, fatigue and restricted range of motion, trigger points also restrict circulation and can cause weakness in the affected muscles, loss of coordination and dizziness, as well as other symptoms.

POWER ACTION: MORE OPTIONS
"Press Away" Your Trigger Points[14]

Now it's time to help relieve any trigger points you may have found while following the instructions given under the first Power Action in this chapter. Remember, trigger points can occur in any of the major muscle areas of the body—the back of the head, the neck, jaw, shoulders, arms, forearms, hands, upper back, lower back, hips, buttocks, upper and lower legs, ankles and feet. If you feel tense, tight or uncomfortable in one of these areas, review the preceding Power Action option and take a few moments to use finger, thumb or knuckle pressure to find the precise location of any trigger points.

Now it's time to use "direct pressure" to relieve the irritation. Here's the essence: Once you have located a trigger point, apply pressure that is gentle enough so that it creates only mild discomfort. Hold the trigger point for 5 to 10 seconds and then release. Go on to another trigger point, treat and then release, and so on. You may repeat the therapy at each trigger point twice in one day if desired.

Note: Most trigger points may respond well to this brief pressure. For those that don't, one simple alternative that may improve results is to apply a modified version of DPT. It's what some professionals call *direct compression,*[15] a 30- to 60-second technique of gradually increasing direct pressure on the trigger point. With some practice, and an increased awareness of your own tension-holding patterns and common trigger-point locations (see the "Quick-Map" section on page 281), you'll probably soon find it relatively easy to determine which trigger-point areas of your own body respond best to brief DPT and which benefit from the longer-lasting compression technique.

One method of DPT uses the pad of the thumb or knuckle of the index or middle finger. In the temple areas of the forehead and the hinge joint of the jaw, the pad of the index finger is used to apply pressure. (You can reinforce the index finger by putting the adjoining middle finger over the nail side of the index finger.) In addition to straight-on pressure, certain muscle areas may be checked for trigger points using a spiral pattern of pressure: first press down in the center and then press down successively on different points in a circular pattern until you have checked the whole area. Each time you locate a trigger point, treat it by holding steady pressure for 6 to 10 seconds and then releasing.

Here are several examples of common trigger point locations and treatments: First, place your right forearm, palm down, on the desk or table in front of you. With the pad of your left thumb or the knuckle of your left index or middle finger, press straight down on the top of your forearm about 1 inch toward the wrist from the fold of skin at the elbow. Apply pressure slowly but firmly.

In many cases, you may find a sensitive spot that becomes more sensitive the harder you press on it. Hold moderate pressure here for 6 to 10 seconds, and then release. You have just located and relieved a trigger point.

Now move your left thumb or knuckle several inches toward your right wrist and press again on this new spot on your right forearm. When an area of your body is free from trigger points, all you will feel when you press down on the muscles is pressure, not sensitivity or pain.

A second area to explore for trigger points is at the base of the skull—the site of trigger points in many headaches. Gently place the pad of your right thumb—or, if you have weak thumbs, use your index finger reinforced or covered by your adjoining middle finger—on the back of your neck just to the right of your spine. Glide up to find the natural "notch" at your hairline at the base of the skull. Apply moderate pressure upward against the bone to locate any trigger points.

Search the area from right next to the spine outward along the base of the skull to just behind your ear. Relieve any trigger points by applying pressure for 6 to 10 seconds, and then release. Repeat the process for the matching area on the left side of your neck where it meets the skull.

A third area where trigger points are commonly found is the trapezius muscle that attaches from your shoulders to your neck. Reach up and, using your thumb on one side of the muscle and index and middle fingers on the other side, squeeze the uppermost muscle midway between the crest of your shoulders and the sides of your neck. Apply pressure with your thumb on the front side and your index and middle fingers on the back side of this muscle. Squeeze slowly and firmly. If you find a sensitive area, hold the pressure on that spot for 6 to 10 seconds and then release. Move a finger-width at a time toward the sides of your neck and then out toward your shoulder crests, locating and relieving any trigger points along the way.

Make a Map of Your Body's Trigger Points

Once you know what trigger points feel like and have identified several of the common places where they're located, every month or two it makes sense to record a quick-map of the areas of your body that seem to have the most trigger points. This is an excellent means

20-1

20-2

20-3

of raising your awareness for detecting zones of tension and specific trigger points as they appear in the future. Do your "tight spots" tend to recur in the same general areas? Make a photocopy of illustrations 20-1, 20-2 and 20-3. Write the date on each page and, using a red pen, search your major muscle areas and mark a red dot or "X" wherever you find a trigger point.

The first time through, begin by pressing your thumbs firmly along the base of your skull—beginning near the ears along the bony lower ridge of the skull and moving, thumb press after thumb press, along this ridge to the back of your neck at the spine. Pause to make a note of any trigger points you find. Next reach up and press against the muscles of the "hinge" of your jaw joint (you can feel this joint move by pressing from the outside of your jaw at a site an inch or two forward from your earlobes and then opening and closing your mouth while you adjust the pressure site). Note any trigger points you discover.

Move on in a rapid, similar pressure-search to the shoulders, upper arms, elbows, forearms and hands, firmly pressing each muscle area, searching for tender spots. Then go through the muscles of your lower back (reaching around to press on them with your thumbs) and continue, checking the buttocks area (a site where sciatica-like pain or tingling can occur from trigger points) on down the outer muscles of your thighs, around the knees and then to the calves and feet. For convenience, you might have a family member or friend press on the muscles of your upper and middle back, helping you identify any trigger points in these areas. Be particularly watchful for tender spots above and between the shoulder blades and between the upper border of the shoulder blade and the base of your skull.

DPT is a simple, useful *Power of 5* technique that, like improved posture, can help free you from much of the common tension and pain that, if unabated, takes the joy out of life and pushes us ever too quickly into old age.

PERSONAL POWER NOTES
A Quick-List of This Chapter's Power-Action Options

Find several key trigger points.

Press away your trigger points.

Make a map of your body's trigger points.

PERSONAL NOTES

_____

_____

_____

_____

_____

_____

_____

_____

_____

_____

_____

_____

_____

_____

_____

_____

_____

_____

HEIGHTEN THE POWER OF YOUR 5 SENSES

Stimulate Greater Pleasure and Learning

> Youth is happy because it has the ability to perceive beauty. Anyone who keeps the ability to perceive beauty never grows old.
> —**Franz Kafka**, German writer

How often has a beautiful sunset filled you with awe? Or a starry night sky lifted your spirits? When have you felt deeply moved by a piece of music, an epicurean meal, a compassionate—or passionate— embrace, or by the sight and smell of a fresh bouquet of wildflowers? What soothes and sparks your senses gives distinct signals to your mind. As the perimeters of consciousness, your senses are the most ancient gateways to the brain.[1]

At first thought, it would seem that we live in a blessed era that might be described as a sensory extravaganza. Day in and day out, we're exposed to the myriad sights, sounds, smells, tastes and touches of an information-packed existence. But beneath it all, a blanketlike numbness has wrapped itself around many of us, and in our scramble to get ahead, we're falling out of touch with our senses. And we're paying for it. Without regular, varied, sense-stimulating "exercises," research indicates that the brain slows, and even stalls, in its powers, and mind and body experience symptoms of premature aging and greater susceptibility to disease.[2]

Consider the alternative—what might be possible if *all* of your senses were extended and honed to their utmost? How vital and mentally alert might you stay? How much longer—and *younger*—might you be able to live? Thus far, few people have the benefit of full sensory enrichment. But we've all had glimpses of what might be possible. Take, for example, the fact that one of the most influential people of all time was a handicapped woman with several senses gone.[3] Blind, deaf and mute, Helen Keller's remaining senses were so exceptionally attuned that she was more vigorously alive than most people of her generation. When she put her hands on the radio to enjoy music, she could tell the difference between the strings and the coronets. She listened to colorful stories of life along the Mississippi from the lips of her friend Mark Twain. She communicated with the rest of the world in every way she could about the richness of life's feelings, touches, tastes and aromas.

Your senses are the doors and windows on your world. They give your life richness and coherence—or, through disuse and imbalance, press you into ever-narrowing corridors of emptiness and frustration. The expression "to sense" means that *all* of your senses are being drawn upon to create perception, to inform your mind about everything you experience.

In 1901, a small book was published entitled *The Education of the Nervous System*. It was written by Reuben Halleck,[4] and the central message was that the best education we can provide the nervous system is one of stimulating all of the five known senses. Halleck warned that, in nearly every case, the person who commonly has only one or even two senses properly trained is at best "a pitiful fraction of a human being."

Over the past century, scores of studies have added credence to these words. According to Marian Cleeves Diamond, Ph.D., professor of neurosciences at the University of California, Berkeley, and author of *Enriching Heredity: The Impact of the Environment on the Anatomy of the Brain*, it is highly desirable—and very practical—for each of us to conscientiously train our senses, all of them, throughout our lives. Dr. Diamond was one of the neuroscientists who studied Albert Einstein's brain (he died at the age of 76) in the late 1970s, and her finding that, for the tissues studied, Einstein had unusually high levels of certain active brain cells, further inspired her research—research that strongly suggests that the richer your sensory experience, the more slowly you will age.[5]

This subject is all the more intriguing when we consider the fact that Einstein's approach to learning emphasized using and integrating *all of the senses*, and this may indeed have provided a rare richness and comprehensibility to his work—and life—as he grew older. Einstein had been a poor and resistant student in school and, upon applying for admission to the Polytechnic Institute in Zurich, was turned down. It was then that he spent a year in the provincial Swiss Pestalozzi Institute, founded in 1770 by Johann Heinrich Pestalozzi, who was a passionate advocate of *enlisting all the senses in each and every learning experience.*[6] Despite the derision of his contemporaries, Pestalozzi firmly believed that the absolute foundation of knowledge came from teaching each student to observe (*anschauen*). The importance of this word extended far beyond merely "looking"—it meant observing intently with each sense—handling, smelling, listening to and looking at every experience from a variety of angles. You learned the name of something only after you had absorbed all of its properties that the senses could observe. The creation of *form*, said Pestalozzi, simply follows the ability to draw together all of the sensory information that has been gathered into a coherent whole.

According to psychoanalyst Erik H. Erikson, although Einstein did eventually go on to attend the Polytechnic Institute in Zurich, his "resistance against enforced instruction, far from ever being 'broken,' became a deep and basic character trait that permitted [Einstein] to remain free in learning, no matter how slowly or by what sensory or cognitive steps he accomplished it. I see a connection here with what he later emphasized as *Begreiflichkeit* (comprehensibility), that is, an active and intuitive 'beholding' as a necessary step in thinking. . . . And remember, one of his later most childlike and yet wisest sayings is that the most incomprehensible aspect of the world is its comprehensibility."[7]

Through varied, sense-stimulating activities, it seems the nerve cells in the brain can be expanded or enriched—at *every* age. As Dr. Diamond explains, studies "caution us against entering into inactive lifestyles that reduce the sensory stimuli reaching our brains, and they provide hope, if we continue to stimulate our brains, for healthy mental activity throughout a lifetime."[8]

POWER ACTION: FIRST OPTION
Appreciate Nature's Beauty

Scientific studies indicate that when individuals view beautiful nature scenes—for example, of water, sky, trees, flowers or green plants—they often feel reduced anxiety, greater work effectiveness and an emotional lift, and they can relax more easily.[9] They may also be less likely to have negative thoughts or experience stressful symptoms in the body.[10]

"There is mounting evidence that even brief exposures to a natural scene can be an excellent antidote to *mental fatigue*," write Robert Ornstein, Ph.D., and David Sobel, M.D., in *Mental Medicine Update*. "In studies of workers with desk jobs, [access to] natural scenes nearly doubled satisfaction ratings. Workers with a view of nature felt less frustrated and more patient, found their job more challenging and

POWER KNOWLEDGE: "SENSATIONAL" LIVING

MYTH #1: The mind and senses are separate.
POWER KNOWLEDGE: "In our research," writes Jean Houston, Ph.D., psychologist and director of the Foundation for Mind Research in Pomona, New York, "we have found that there is a real equation between the ability to entertain and sustain complex thinking processes and *the richness of sensory . . . awareness.*"[14]

MYTH #2: It's the *muscles*, not the senses, that are subject to the rule "use them or lose them."
POWER KNOWLEDGE: According to researchers, the full development—and continued energetic use—of your senses may help promote lifelong physical, emotional and mental well-being.[15] In response to heightened sensory activity, the nerve cells in the brain's cortex apparently grow larger[16] and become more resistant to certain aging processes.[17] In addition to the traditional five senses—touch, sight, hearing, taste and smell—scientists have now identified at least a dozen other sensory systems in the human body.[18] "If we learn to modulate our senses," says neurosurgeon Arthur Winter, M.D., in *Build Your Brain Power*, "and develop them even in advanced years, we increase our pleasure in living and we maintain normal function in the cells that receive and respond to sensual input. A decrease in sensory input due to changes in the sense organs or to social isolation is reflected in reduced metabolism and blood flow within the brain."[19]

interesting, expressed greater enthusiasm for their work, and reported greater overall life satisfaction and health."[11]

You might begin by including some simple yet enticing changes of scene on each of your daily work breaks. Examples: Gazing at fish swimming back and forth in an aquarium; looking out your window at nearby trees or flowers; watching clouds form and swirl against the sky; enjoying the antics of birds or squirrels in a stand of trees; staring into the fire of a burning log; or looking at photographs or paintings of nature—waterfalls, canyons, forests, snow-covered mountains or meadows brimming with wildflowers.

It also makes sense to take one of your daily—or at least a weekly—"mini-walks" in your favorite nearby park (why not schedule a few of your 5-minute aerobic "fit times" from chapter 12 here?) and perhaps to cultivate a small window box of flowers or a backyard garden. At the very least, you might bring some flowering plants into your home and office. And, if your work limits you to gray urban environs, consider setting aside some time every once in a while to view nature scenes on videotape accompanied by relaxing music.

More than half of your body's sense receptors are clustered in your eyes. When people view slides or pictures of bright, beautiful scenes of Nature, they report much higher levels of positive energy and friendliness and a reduction in anxiety and fear.[12] When compared to pictures of treeless urban streets and modern architecture, pictures of lakes, ponds, streams, trees and flowers produce lower levels of stress arousal and higher alpha brain waves, a state associated with calm alertness and wakeful relaxation.[13]

> Through the window of the eye, the soul regards the world's beauty. . . . Who would believe that a small scene of nature could contain the images of the universe?
> —**Leonardo da Vinci,**
> Italian painter and architect

POWER ACTION: MORE OPTIONS
Enjoy 5-Second to 5-Minute "Sensory Stimulations"[20]

The key here is to begin to sharpen your senses and turn up your self-awareness. How many daily tasks do you perform on "autopilot"? To stimulate a greater involvement of *all* your senses, ask yourself questions: What, precisely, does this feel like—on my fingertips, on the skin of my arm? How, exactly, is this sound different than it was before?

How has the lighting changed the image I see before me? And so on. In short, begin to "sense" more of what you experience each day—both the unusual and the mundane.

Turn up the lights. For a mental and emotional lift, experiment with turning on some added lights or, if possible, moving your work closer to a window. As discussed in chapter 3, research at Harvard University indicates that many people report increased calmness or alertness when exposed to bright sunlight or some extra indoor light (even at the intensity level of normal room lamps[21]). Or, on other occasions, you may want to draw the shades or turn down the lights for a restful pause during your break time.

Seek out pleasant scents. As we discussed earlier, scientists have long known that pleasing fragrances prompt us to take slower, deeper breaths and become more relaxed and refreshed. Your sense of smell contains "all the great mysteries," says physician and essayist Lewis Thomas.[22] Every breath you take passes currents of air molecules over the olfactory sites in your nose. Odors flood the nerve receptors in your nasal cavities, where five million cells fire impulses directly to the brain's cerebral cortex and limbic system—the mysterious, ancient, intensely emotional area of the brain where you experience feelings, desires and wellsprings of creative energy. Certain scents seem to activate specific chemical messengers, or neurotransmitters, in the brain.[23]

And remember that teams of researchers in the United States, Europe and Japan have published dozens of new studies on the behavioral influence of smell.[24] Tests at the University of Cincinnati indicate that fragrances added to the atmosphere of a room can help keep people more alert and improve performance of routine tasks.[25] Controlled brain-wave studies by professors at Toho University in Japan have produced surprising indications about which scents tend to stimulate and which relax, and which promote significantly fewer errors on the job.[26] Research at Rensselaer Polytechnic Institute in Troy, New York, shows that people who work in pleasantly scented areas perform an average of 25 percent better than those not exposed[27] and also carry out their tasks more confidently, more efficiently and with greater willingness to resolve conflicts.[28]

Which natural scents do you enjoy the most? Which invigorate? Which are calming? Research indicates the potential value of bringing

> I should like to raise the question whether the inevitable stunting of the sense of smell as a result of man's turning away from the earth, and the organic repression of the smell-pleasure produced by it, does not largely share in his predisposition to nervous diseases.
>
> **—Sigmund Freud, M.D.,**
> Austrian neurologist

fresh flowers or a potted evergreen or some piquant herbs or potpourri into your home and work areas. Or you might add a few drops of an "essential oil"—such as lemon, peppermint, pine, jasmine, rose, vanilla, lavender or orange to a small scent dispenser. However, here's a note of caution: Very mild "doses" are probably best, since scents are quite person-specific—what is enjoyable for you may not be as pleasing to others who live or work next to you.

> The eye takes a person into the world. The ear brings the world into a human being.
>
> **—Lorenz Oken,** German naturalist and philosopher

Take pleasure in music. Listening to music you love is like receiving a terrific massage from the inside. The right melody at the right time can bring you feelings of joy and serenity and soothe frayed nerves.

"The primary importance of your hearing is to *charge* your nervous system," says Alfred A. Tomatis, M.D., French otolaryngologist, psychologist and educator, after 50 years of research.[29] A number of experts on the auditory system now agree that listening and hearing are powerful sensory pathways "for problems related to energy level (tension or fatigue), loss of enthusiasm and depressive tendencies."[30] Music, for example, influences respiratory rate, blood pressure, stomach contractions and the level of stress hormones in your blood,[31] and research suggests it may also help strengthen your immune response.[32] The mind processes music in ways that are intertwined with perception, memory and language,[33] and music speaks to us so powerfully that one Harvard psychologist, and a number of other scientists, think it may be an actual language that we're born with.[34] In an essay in *New Literary History*, composer George Rochberg argues that "music is a secondary 'language' system whose logic is closely related to the primary alpha logic of the central nervous system. . . . We listen with our [whole] bodies."[35]

The main point is to find your own comfort tones, but vary them often, because some scientists believe that after 20 minutes or so, the nervous system may become oversensitized to a specific tune and react with symptoms of distress.[36]

Stay in closer touch—with loved ones and friends. Touch is the oldest sense and the most urgent. Any new touch or a change in feeling sends the brain into a rush of activity. In contrast, touch receptors are dulled by tedium. When we speak of something being "touching," it suggests a close relationship between touch and the

> We are spectacular, splendid manifestations of life. We have language. We have affection. And finally, and perhaps best of all, we have music.
>
> **—Lewis Thomas, M.D.,** physician and essayist

emotional reactions of the heart.[37] You can enrich your sense of touch in many ways—by such simple, healthful habits as hugging loved ones, pats on the back, petting your family pet and periodically exchanging a backrub or gentle massage with family members and close friends. In addition, one of the simplest, most comforting self-help techniques is the Direct Pressure Therapy (DPT) explained in chapter 20.

Pique—and expand—your tastes. Earlier in *The Power of 5*, we discussed a variety of research on "taste power" (in chapters 10 and 15). Think back to those discussions. What specific flavors do you love in your meals and snacks? Which lively tastes perk you up first thing in the morning? Or help you feel refreshed or relaxed at midafternoon? Taste is a vast territory, and there seem to be health-related benefits from exploring every part of it.[38]

Resources

Enriching Heredity: The Impact of Environment on the Anatomy of the Brain by Marian Cleeves Diamond, Ph.D. (Free Press, 1988). A pioneering, scholarly work.

Healthy Pleasures by Robert Ornstein, Ph.D., and David Sobel, M.D. (Addison-Wesley, 1989). Scholarly, entertaining teachings on the influence of the senses in health and well-being.

The Light Book: How Natural and Artificial Light Affect Our Health, Mood, and Behavior by Jane Wegscheider Hyman (J.P. Tarcher, 1990). A scientifically based review of the powerful effects of light.

A Natural History of the Senses by Diane Ackerman (Random House, 1990). A superb exploration of the role senses play in human life.

Touching: The Human Significance of the Skin 3rd ed., by Ashley Montagu, Ph.D. (Perennial Library, 1986). The single most influential book on the lifelong need for touching.

Two sources for nature-scene videotapes are **Windham Hill Productions, Inc.** (Box 9388, Stanford, CA 94309) and **Source Cassette Learning Systems** (Emmett E. Miller, M.D., P.O. Box W, Stanford, CA 94309; 415-328-7171).

Wisdom and the Senses by Joan M. Erikson (Norton, 1988). A wonderful book that explores the key role played by the senses at every stage of psychological development—from birth through old age.

PERSONAL POWER NOTES
A Quick-List of This Chapter's Power-Action Options

Appreciate Nature's beauty.

Enjoy 5-second to 5-minute "sensory stimulations."
- *Turn up the lights.*
- *Seek out pleasant scents.*
- *Take pleasure in music.*
- *Stay in close touch—with loved ones and friends.*
- *Pique—and expand—your tastes.*

PERSONAL NOTES

_____

_____

_____

_____

_____

_____

_____

_____

_____

_____

_____

_____

_____

_____

_____

_____

REDUCE THE RISKS OF SUN AND NOISE

Neutralize Two Common Causes of Rapid Aging

Since ancient times, our lives have been bathed in light and surrounded by sounds. But there's a downside to sun and noise, and new guidelines to know.

There is something very exhilarating about spending a few minutes outside on a bright day. Light is one of the most powerful forces in coordinating the body's biological rhythms and the chemicals that govern the way you sleep, feel and behave.

Yes, sunlight is powerful—and it has a darker side. There's now unequivocal evidence that unless we use skin and eye protection, the sun's rays cause or contribute to premature skin aging, cataracts and skin cancer. Yet we can't hide away in dark, sunless rooms—and we shouldn't. Life's outdoor brilliance lifts our moods and invigorates both body and mind. You *can* enjoy the benefits of sunlight while still protecting your skin and eyes.

The facts are much the same with sound. On the one hand, pleasant music, sounds of nature and engaging conversations are invigorating. On the other hand, loud noise rattles the emotions and disorients the mind. Worse, it can progressively destroy your hearing and obfuscate your ability to learn, and it may even increase your blood pressure.[1] To stay younger longer, it's vital to not only surround ourselves with uplifting sounds but to identify—and then start reducing—the din in our lives.

POWER ACTION: FIRST OPTION
Protect Your Skin and Eyes from Sun Damage

The risk of skin damage from the sun is now considered so great that it's imperative to wear an effective sunscreen on all exposed skin surfaces *at all times* when you're outside during the peak exposure period—10 A.M. to 3 P.M., Standard Time. And it also may be wise to don a sunscreen if you're outside for more than 5 minutes or so at nonpeak times. Don't assume that because your skin isn't getting red, it isn't getting burned. At first you often won't see, or even feel, sunburn. And don't assume that you're safe when the sun's behind clouds. On overcast days, the sun's rays are almost as damaging as on bright days, since as much as 85 percent of ultraviolet (UV) rays can penetrate clouds.

Sunscreens are rated according to an SPF (sun protection factor) scale, ranging from 2 to over 30; the higher the number, the greater the protection. Suncreens with an SPF of 15 or above are most universally recommended by dermatologists. Unfortunately, at the current time the SPF only pertains to ultraviolet B (UVB) rays—not UVA. Although UVB may be mainly responsible for sunburn and skin cancer, it now appears that UVA radiation can damage the skin's connective tissue, prompting premature aging, and that UVA also plays a role in causing skin cancer.[2] For a sunscreen to offer "broad spectrum" skin protection, it must block UVB *and* UVA rays. The chemical compound avobenzone presently offers the fullest UVA protection.

Note: Be certain to protect your ears from sun damage. According to research conducted at Brown University, squamous cell carcinoma accounts for half of all nonmelanoma skin cancer deaths—and half of these deadly squamous cell cancers are located on the ears.[3] Moreover, sun-smart people often unwittingly overlook the ears when applying sunscreen. Be sure to apply sunscreen to all exposed areas, including the ears, hairline, back of the neck and hands. Wear a broad-brimmed hat when gardening, hiking, fishing or playing golf or tennis. And report any unexplained skin changes to your doctor immediately.

Wear good-quality sunglasses when you're outside in bright sun—all year round, not just in summer. For protecting your eyes, many ophthalmologists recommend sunglasses that filter out all ultraviolet rays, plus most or all of the blue and violet wavelengths. Since excess light can damage the retina, it's important that lenses are tinted enough to block 75 to 90 percent of visible and infrared light. Consult your eye-care professional for current recommendations.

POWER ACTION: MORE OPTIONS
Get 5 Minutes a Day of Nonpeak
Sun without Sunscreen

"Sunlight is a powerful natural cue, or *zeitgeber*, that sets your inner circadian clock and makes its rhythm more regular," explains psychologist and sleep researcher James Perl, Ph.D., a member of the Sleep Panel at the Presbyterian/St. Luke's Medical Center in Denver. "A strong circadian rhythm helps you sleep more soundly at night. To take

POWER KNOWLEDGE:
SUN AND SOUND

MYTH #1: The risks from sun exposure are overstated.

POWER KNOWLEDGE: The Skin Cancer Foundation reports that one of every seven Americans will develop skin cancer.[4] Rates for the most common skin cancers have at least doubled in the United States since the 1970s. Within the last 60 years the incidence of malignant melanoma, by far the deadliest form of skin cancer, has gone from 1 in 1,500 white Americans to 1 in 138. By the year 2000, it may be 1 in less than 100,[5] and at least 95 percent of the risk is related to the sun. There's a double payoff to protecting your skin from sun damage. Not only are you cutting your chances of developing skin cancer but you also help preserve the skin's youthful elasticity and beauty. Excessive tanning makes blood vessels more prominent and turns the skin stiff, dry, yellow and mottled and promotes wrinkling.

Lifetime exposure to sunlight is also a major factor in blindness, reports Richard Young, M.D., of UCLA's Jules Stein Eye Institute.[6] Ultraviolet light can damage the eye's transparent coating, the cornea, as well as the lens. Sunglasses that block UV rays may provide important protection from lifelong damage contributing to cataracts.[7] Long-term exposure to the sun's violet and blue wavelengths also appears to damage the retina of the eye. Called age-related macular degeneration, this condition affects perhaps 30 percent of elderly Americans and is a advantage of sunlight's effect on your sleep/wake cycle, get outside during the day as often and for as long as you can. On your lunch hour and at breaks, try to get outdoors at least for a short while. . . . You don't need to expose your skin directly to the sun. Even on a cloudy day, if you are outside, you will receive enough light to provide alertness cues to your internal clock."[11]

You can actually accomplish this in "no time" by combining this 5 minutes of nonpeak sun exposure with a "mini-walk" (see chapter 11) and "getting closer to nature" (see chapter 21). Total time required for all three health enhancements: 5 minutes.

Getting out in the sun offers another advantage: vitamin D, which is

major cause of blindness. Yet it's preventable if your eyes are protected when you are outside in bright light.

On the other side of the sunlight issue, some scientists have suggested that there are health benefits from a few brief minutes of daily exposure to sunlight during nonpeak hours (the best times to be outside are early morning, late afternoon and early evening).[8] This may provide a good source of vitamin D for the body, says Michael F. Holick, M.D., director of the Vitamin D and Bone Metabolism Laboratory at the U.S. Department of Agriculture Human Nutrition Research Center on Aging at Tufts University in Boston.[9]

MYTH #2: Except for those few people who work in a loud jobsite like a construction zone, the rest of us aren't at risk from noise-related hearing damage.

POWER KNOWLEDGE: The American Speech and Hearing Association estimates that 40 million Americans live, work or play every day around noise that is dangerously loud. According to the Environmental Protection Agency booklet "Noise around Our Home," nearly half of all Americans are regularly exposed to levels of noise that interfere with speaking, listening or performing tasks. Half of all Americans over 65 and two-thirds of those over 80 suffer some form of hearing impairment. For many of us, this hearing loss is not an inevitable part of aging, because in less industrialized, quieter societies, hearing is as keen at 75 years as at 17 years.[10]

synthesized in the skin when it's exposed to sunlight. Unfortunately, as we grow older our skin becomes less efficient at making vitamin D. Compounding the problem is evidence suggesting that many adults don't get out in the sun very often and consume very few foods that are rich in vitamin D—milk, for example, or fatty fish such as salmon, herring, mackerel and swordfish. In one study by scientists at Tufts University, over half of a group of elderly people living in New Mexico were found to be consuming less than 50 international units of vitamin D, or one-fourth of the Recommended Dietary Allowance (RDA). The researchers also found a low vitamin D intake when they looked at a group of more than 300 women with an average age of 58, in which the average daily consumption of vitamin D was only 112 international units, just over half the RDA. They also discovered that only those women who were taking at least 10 percent more than the RDA for vitamin D—a minimum of 220 international units—were free from what researcher Elizabeth Krall, Ph.D., called "a seesaw of hormones" that can lead to weakened bones.[12] This seesaw effect has to do with the fact that vitamin D is needed to aid calcium absorption from food for use not only in the bones but also in the blood.

Those who are already taking in enough calcium with their food (see chapter 17) may need to increase their intake of vitamin D. A good place to start is with at least one glass of nonfat milk per day and a moderate portion of fatty fish several times a week. In addition, suggest researchers at the University of Texas Health Center, "set aside time to go out and enjoy the sun at least a little bit."[13] Research evidence indicates that a small amount of daily sunlight may help reverse marginal vitamin D deficiency and thus slow or stop calcium loss from your bones.[14] Unless your physician advises against it, it seems that about 5 minutes per day of nonpeak sun exposure—such as a brief morning stroll or late afternoon walk *without* sunscreen or sunglasses—may help maintain vitamin D levels without increasing the risk of skin cancer. If it's impossible to get some sun, and milk and fish are not part of your diet, consult your physician about a vitamin D supplement.

Give Quick, Careful Attention to Daily Skin Care

Beyond sunbathing and smoking, skin-cleansing practices may cause the most harm to your appearance. "The face is constantly assaulted," says University of Pennsylvania dermatologist Albert Kligman, M.D. "Harsh soaps, buff puffs, alcohol astringents—when I take a patient's cosmetics history I can't believe how much insult she's causing to her own face. We're a society of detergent fanatics who are injuring our skin cells."[15] Dr. Kligman recommends washing once a day with warm—not hot—water and a mild soap (stay away from perfumed or deodorant soaps, since they may be too drying for facial skin). Wash gently with a washcloth but avoid rough pads and harsh scrubbing grains that irritate the skin. If you live in an area of heavy air pollution, clean your face a second time. Then, if your skin feels dry, use a moisturizer right after washing to hold in skin moisture. The right moisturizer is the one you like (petroleum jelly is recommended by many dermatologists, but it's messy). It also pays to drink at least eight glasses of water every day (see chapter 9), since this aids skin health and plumps up the skin so wrinkles are less obvious. And finally, get plenty of regular exercise, since this helps increase blood flow to the skin and adds a natural, healthy glow to your complexion.

Reduce Obvious—And "Hidden"—Noise

Your auditory system influences the frontal lobe of the brain, which plays a primary role in personality and intellectual functions. Loud noise (above 80 decibels—which includes the roar of traffic or factory machinery) and noise that may be soft but irritating can produce harmful physical and mental effects.[16] The sustained low-level din of urban life—rush-hour traffic, for example—can gradually destroy your hearing. This "hidden noise" has an insidious cumulative effect. Even noises from common household appliances—food processors, electric shavers, vent fans, garbage disposals, dishwashers, electric mixers, knife sharpeners, vacuum cleaners—produce heightened body arousal and general nervous tension, according to a University of Wisconsin study.[17] Home noise can reportedly contribute not only to noise-related health damage but also to conflicts between household members.[18] Therefore, it may really pay off to reduce loud noises whenever you can. Here are some steps to consider.

• Become sound-conscious, reducing or eliminating noise whenever and wherever it is reasonable to do so.

• Before buying new appliances and electronic equipment, compare noise levels and select a quieter model.

• When looking for your next home or apartment, do some detailed "sound" research before making your decision. Remember that carpeting, rugs and extra wall insulation help reduce noise levels.

• Put foam pads under small kitchen appliances and office machines such as typewriters and computer printers.

• Use noise-absorbing insulation and vibration mounts for dishwashers, garbage disposals and office machines such as computer printers and typewriters.

• Wear hearing protection whenever it's necessary to be near loud or even moderately loud noises.

• Have your hearing tested regularly, and if you notice any hearing loss, consult your family physician, who can refer you to a specialist such as an otologist or otolaryngologist.

Resources

Hearing Helpline (The Better Hearing Institute, 5021-B Backlick Rd., Annandale, VA 22003; 800-327-9355; 800-424-8576 in Va.). Free telephone information service on hearing loss symptoms and treatment options.

A free hearing test by telephone is available from **Johns Hopkins Hospital Hearing and Speech Clinic** (301-955-3434) or from **Occupational Hearing Services** (800-222-EARS; 800-345-3277 in Pa.).

The Light Book: How Natural and Artificial Light Affect Our Health, Mood, and Behavior by Jane Wegscheider Wyman (J.P. Tarcher, 1990). A scientifically based book that reviews light's effects on depression, insomnia, diet, stress and productivity.

Sound Advice and *Have You Heard?* are two free booklets on dealing with the problems of noise and hearing loss, available from: AARP, 1909 K St., N.W., Washington, DC 20049.

To learn more about sunlight research, send a stamped, self-addressed envelope for a free copy of *Sun and Skin News* (Skin Cancer Foundation, P.O. Box 561, New York, NY 10156; 212-725-5176).

PERSONAL POWER NOTES
A Quick-List of This Chapter's Power-Action Options

Protect your skin and eyes from sun damage.

Get 5 minutes a day of nonpeak sun without sunscreen.

Give quick, careful attention to daily skin care.

Reduce obvious—and "hidden"—noise.

PERSONAL NOTES

ELIMINATE POISONS FROM YOUR HOME

Reduce Your Exposure to Toxic Chemicals, Radiation and Electromagnetic Fields

Contrary to popular opinion, the greatest health dangers from pollutants are commonly found *inside* our homes.

Chances are, your home contains 100 to 200 air contaminants. That's the estimated average by the Environmental Protection Agency (EPA). Radon is emitted from the ground, formaldehyde outgasses from plywood and other building materials, carbon monoxide and nitrogen dioxide enter the air from cigarette smoke and gas appliances. Molds, fungi and bacteria can breed and be spread from air conditioners. And toxic chemicals seem to come from everywhere—from shoe polish to dry-cleaned clothes, paint to insect repellents, mothballs to room deodorizers, drain openers to furniture polish and a staggering array of cleaners, disinfectants, glues and adhesives.

Even at low levels, repeated contact with these substances is suspected of causing an increased risk of illness or disease, in some cases including cancer, liver damage or brain injury. Accidental exposure comes through ingestion, skin contact or inhalation of vapors and sprays, and some chemicals can even be absorbed through the skin and cause internal damage without any noticeable injury to your skin surface. All told, researchers have found that indoor toxic pollutants can reach levels 100 times higher than those found outdoors,[1] where they can disperse more readily. Even though the odds of developing cancer from indoor contaminants other than cigarette smoke are relatively small, since many of us spend most of our time indoors, these risks are now being taken seriously.

First, some general tips: Reduce your exposure to indoor pollutants by taking frequent brief breaks during the day to relieve eyestrain, increase circulation and get some fresh air. Improve your nutritional health (and thus increase your body's protection against pollutants) by eating regular, healthful small meals and light snacks and perhaps taking a moderate-dosage, broad-spectrum multivitamin/mineral/antioxidant supplement (see chapter 17). Help reduce your risk of fatigue and respiratory infections by drinking extra water to prevent dehydration. And begin learning more about local pollution risks. Plan action steps—in your neighborhood, workplace and community—to legally or politically rectify the *causes of pollution* where you live and work. On a personal and family level, here are several specific steps you might take.

POWER ACTION: FIRST OPTION
Monitor—And Reduce—Your Radiation Risks

The effects of high-frequency *ionizing* radiation are cumulative—they keep adding up throughout your lifetime—and they can cause cancer and genetic mutation.

The first thing to do is test your home and office for *radon gas* concentrations (see Resources), since radon is the number two cause of lung cancer, second only to smoking. You can buy easy-to-use short-term test kits at many hardware stores and home improvement centers. If the test shows that radon concentrations are high, you can reduce the risks by using fans and heat exchangers, which vent the radon into the outside air, where it rises and disperses into the atmosphere. In some extreme cases, buildings require more elaborate measures such as installation of a perforated pipe system beneath the building to vent the radon away. If you've tested the air and found a radon problem, and your drinking water comes from a well, have your water tested for radiation by a laboratory that's qualified to do such tests (see the discussion of water safety in chapter 16).

A number of authorities are also warning about health dangers from low-frequency *nonionizing* radiation.[13] There are two basic types—microwave and electromagnetic. Here are several ways to reduce your potential risk.

• If your job requires frequent video display terminal (VDT) time or if you use a home computer regularly, position your VDT monitor at arm's-length (a minimum of 30 inches away) and at least twice that far away from the side or rear of any people nearby.[14]

• Whenever possible, turn off your computer terminal whenever it's not in use and, if you're pregnant, either strictly limit VDT time to less

POWER KNOWLEDGE: CHEMICALS AND RADIATION

MYTH #1: Health harm from cigarette smoke is overstated.

POWER KNOWLEDGE: Data on the health damage caused by cigarette smoke continue to mount. In addition, the National Research Council, National Academy of Sciences, American Heart Association and Environmental Protection Agency (EPA) have published research reports documenting many of the ways that "passive smoking" (also called slipstream smoking, secondhand smoke, environmental tobacco smoke and involuntary smoking) is linked to health risks—including lung cancer, respiratory problems and heart disease—among nonsmokers.[2]

MYTH #2: There are few facts to show that everyday sources of radiation are harmful to people.

POWER KNOWLEDGE: Over half of the average American's exposure to damaging ionizing radiation may come from radon, a colorless, odorless, naturally occurring radioactive gas that causes up to 10 percent of all lung cancer deaths and a total of 20,000 to 30,000 cancer deaths each year.[3] Radon is emitted from natural underground uranium deposits in soil and bedrock into at least 10 percent of all American homes, and the EPA also estimates that about one-fourth of all U.S. homes and businesses have water that is radon-contaminated.[4]

In addition, scientists have discovered that, at least in some cases, microwave radiation seems to cause unhealthy alterations to cell structures and functions.[5] There is also evidence suggesting that electromagnetic radiation—from power lines, video display terminals (VDTs), televisions and other sources—may cause subtle damage by interfering with delicate electromagnetic force fields involved with than 20 hours a week or request assignment to a job that doesn't require you to use a VDT.

• If you cook with a microwave oven, use a recent model (since current designs have much lower emission levels) and be very aware of

---

brain and nervous system functions in the body[6] and may also stimulate human colon cancer cells to grow faster, proliferate and survive longer.[7] Other studies show that electromagnetic fields may reduce immune system white cell activity and lower resistance to disease.[8]

MYTH #3: As long as I eat a good diet and exercise, there's no call to worry about the so-called toxic chemicals in the air, food or water that "health nuts" warn about.

POWER KNOWLEDGE: It makes sense to avoid whatever toxic chemicals you can. There are a variety of reasons and examples. The use of aluminum in cooking, storage, condiment preparation, antacids and antiperspirants is on the rise, despite increasing evidence that aluminum may be involved in several brain and nerve disorders, including Alzheimer's disease.[9] Studies published in the *Lancet* and other respected medical and scientific journals suggest that it may be prudent to reduce or avoid aluminum exposure.[10]

There are many other chemicals to avoid whenever possible. For example, formaldehyde—a strong irritant to the respiratory, sensory and nervous systems that may also cause brain damage—is a preservative chemical used in embalming fluids. It can be given off ("outgassed") by hundreds of consumer products in America, ranging from cosmetics, perfumes and soaps to permanent-press fabrics, upholstery fabrics, resin-treated drapes, carpets, dry-cleaning fluids and paper towels. It is also used in building materials such as laminated wood paneling, plywood, particleboard and urethane foam insulation.[11]

Solvents and other volatile organic compounds—used in many commercial cleaners, adhesives, finishes, paints, art supplies, spot removers, furniture-stripping solutions and some cosmetic and hair-care products—are linked to brain malfunctions and may contribute to other debilitating behavioral changes.[12]

---

safety procedures such as keeping the seals clean and never standing directly in front of the oven while it is operating.

• To reduce other potential health risks, some experts recommend avoiding the use of electric blankets, heating pads[15] and perhaps other devices that generate electromagnetic fields. In *Crosscurrents*, Robert O. Becker, M.D., an orthopedic surgeon and professor at the State University of New York, Upstate Medical Center, and Louisiana State University Medical Center, gives the following advice: "The basic concept we need to apply is dose rate. For example, the electric razor produces an extremely high-strength magnetic field if it is line-operated (that is, plugged into a wall socket rather than battery operated). . . . When such a razor is in use, the tissues within a few inches of its surface are exposed to a high magnetic field. Because 60-Hz fields of only 3 milligauss have been shown to be significantly related to increases in cancer rates, the safety of using this device—with a field 100 times greater—becomes questionable.

"However, the dose-rate concept must enter the picture. The electric razor is used for just a few minutes once a day, so the total exposure, or dose, to the user is minimal. . . . The electric blanket, however, is applied almost as close to the body surface as the electric razor, [but] because it is used for several hours at a time, the dose is much higher. . . . Obviously, the risks involved in using an electric blanket are quite significant, while using an electric razor [if possible, a battery-operated one] is probably safe. . . . However, for both devices there are obvious alternatives that satisfactorily serve the same function."[16]

An electric clock plugged into a wall socket, warns Dr. Becker, produces an "amazingly high magnetic field because of the small electric motor that runs it. . . . If the bedside table is placed close to the bed, so that the sleeper's head is within [2 feet of the clock], the dose rate is considerable for the average 8 hours per night. Battery-operated clocks have a negligible field, and I recommend their use as a substitute."[17]

With these facts in mind, check to see that none of the beds in your home is near a concentrated source of electromagnetic fields—such as a wall with a TV on the other side or near the point where the electric power cable enters the house. Place items such as electric clocks, fans, humidifiers, baby monitors and stereos at least 30 inches from the nearest bed, chair, sofa or desk. Whenever possible, use battery-powered versions of these devices. In the kitchen, don't let family members make a habit of standing near a running dishwasher or microwave or beside a running refrigerator or freezer. Limit time spent using personal appliances such as hair dryers.

POWER ACTION: MORE OPTIONS
Open Windows and Ban Indoor Smoking

In energy-efficient homes and offices, one of the simplest and most effective ways to reduce airborne pollutants is to regularly open windows and use exhaust fans in the kitchen and bathroom whenever you use these rooms. It's also important to make certain that all gas appliances in your home and office are well maintained and efficiently vented to the outside. When gas appliances—using natural gas, oil, propane or kerosene—aren't expertly maintained and adjusted, they can be a major, hidden source of carbon monoxide (CO).[18] Stoves and heaters that burn charcoal and wood can also give off CO.

Ventilation isn't enough, however, when it comes to cigarette smoking. It's a health threat to both the smoker and to everyone else who breathes smoke-contaminated air. We suggest you take the necessary steps to make your home and office smoke-free. At the same time, be supportive of others who smoke—and help them quit (see Resources).

Reduce Your Exposure to Aluminum and Lead

Are you absorbing aluminum without knowing it? According to Michael D. Chafetz, Ph.D., a research neuropsychologist at the University of New Orleans and author of *Smart for Life*, here are some of the potential ways it may be getting into your body and brain.[19]
• From contaminated groundwater or drinking water.
• By wrapping acidic foods such as cut tomatoes or lemons in aluminum foil.
• By cooking acidic foods (including tomatoes, vinegar and applesauce) in aluminum pots or scraping an aluminum pot with a metal utensil while cooking.
• By taking certain aspirin products or antacids for an upset stomach (check the list of ingredients to see if aluminum is used). Also be aware that aluminum silicate compounds are used to keep table salt and condiments free-flowing and aluminum anti-wetness compounds are found in many popular deodorants and antiperspirants.

Lead is a toxic metal that is found in drinking water, paint chips, food, dust and soil. It is widely considered the leading environmental health threat to children in the United States—where, according to the U.S. Department of Health and Human Services, an estimated 15 percent of children under the age of six have been exposed to lead levels high enough to potentially impair their learning ability. The most common source of exposure comes from inhaling or ingesting small particles of lead-based paint found in many homes built before 1980. A recent EPA study noted that more than 800 water systems serving 30 million Americans exceed the permissible level of lead: 15 parts per billion.

If you suspect that your children have been exposed to lead (sometimes there are no obvious symptoms; at other times the early effects include fatigue, irritability, headaches and abdominal pain), see your physician for a blood test to detect lead. The EPA recommends that all families with young children have their drinking water tested for lead (laboratories are discussed in chapter 16). If your home was constructed before 1980, be especially careful during remodeling, when scraping or sanding painted walls. To learn more, see Resources.

Keep Your Air Clean with Some Simple Strategies

Air conditioners and humidifiers are common breeding spots for molds, viruses, fungi and bacteria. Because of this, it's highly important to change filters regularly and have each unit inspected—and cleaned, if necessary—at least once a year. 3M's Filtrete High Performance Clean Air Filters (available at hardware stores or by calling 800-388-3458) are an example of high-technology filters that are 20 times more efficient than ordinary furnace/air filters at attracting and removing a wide range of airborne pollutants.

Other simple household strategies may also be beneficial, such as making it a point to wash your bedding every week in *hot* water. This reduces the chances that dust mites will be able to give you itchy eyes and nose or contribute to asthma attacks. Also, household plants can play a useful role in protecting you and your family members against toxic and potentially toxic chemicals. Common, low-light house plants—such as spider plants, philodendrons, golden pothos, bamboo palms (or other palms), dracaenas, chrysanthemum, English ivy, gerbera daisy, peace lily or a fern (such as Boston fern)—not only add a pleasing dash of greenery to your indoor environment but may also help reduce the levels of certain indoor contaminants—such as benzene, formaldehyde and tetrachloroethylene. A good guideline seems to be to select at least one of these easy-care houseplants for every 100 square feet of floor space in your home and work area.

It may also be sensible to avoid the use of mothballs and solid home deodorizers. These common household products usually contain paraperidichlorobenzene, a chemical that is given off into the air and is suspected of causing cancer. As an alternative to mothballs and chemical deodorizers, open windows more often and mothproof your woolens by dry-cleaning them, hanging them outside in the sun for several hours and then sealing them in airtight bags or storing them in a cedar chest or closet. The reason for this is that the chemical dry-cleaning process often uses tetrachloroethylene, which has been linked to cancer in animals and may be harmful to humans. The greatest source of exposure is on the clothes themselves. To reduce the risk, as soon as you pick up dry-cleaned clothes, air them out for a few hours on your clothesline, porch or balcony.

Whenever Possible, Choose Nontoxic Cleaning Products

"The easiest way to begin your transformation to a nontoxic home," suggests Debra Lynn Dadd in *The Nontoxic Home and Office*, "is by replacing cleaning products—ammonia, oven cleaners, furniture polish, scouring powder, disinfectant, glass cleaner—all the heavy-duty chemicals we use to maintain our homes. The replacement products are simple and inexpensive—in fact, most cleaning jobs can be done quite well using natural materials you probably already have in your kitchen. These substances are odorless or have natural fragrances and work *every bit as well* as the chemicals you are accustomed to cleaning with."[20]

If for any reason it's necessary to use toxic cleaning chemicals, do so with protective gloves and a mask in a well-ventilated space, preferably outdoors. Inside areas must be ventilated from the ground up with an exhaust fan, since solvent fumes are heavier than air and accumulate near floor level.

Resources

Bug Busters: Poison-Free Pest Controls for Your House and Garden by Bernice Lifton (Avery, 1991).

CrossCurrents: The Perils of Electropollution and the Promise of Electromedicine by Robert O. Becker, M.D. (J.P. Tarcher, 1990). A thoughtful look at a serious issue.

Earth in the Balance: Ecology and the Human Spirit by Al Gore (Houghton Mifflin, 1992). A strong call for taking charge of our environmental future.

The Environmental Protection Agency has a hotline for radon information (800-334-8571, ext. 713). EPA booklets, available at public libraries and local health offices, include "A Citizen's Guide to Radon" (OPA-86-004) which describes what radon is and how to test for it, and "Radon Reduction Methods" (OPA 86-005) which explains how to decrease radon pollution if it exists.

Consumer Reports (May 1994) "Electromagnetic Fields." A summary of what studies have shown; provides some prudent advice.

Electropollution: How to Protect Yourself against It by Roger Coghill

(Thorsons, 1990). A referenced review of electromagnetic radiation risks and practical steps individuals may take to protect themselves and loved ones.

Guide to Hazardous Products around the Home by Household Hazardous Waste Project (1031 East Battlefield, Suite 214, Springfield, MO 65807). Describes toxic products and safe alternatives.

Healthy Computing: Risks and Remedies Every Computer-User Needs to Know by Ronald Harwin and Colin Haynes (Amacom, 1992). Offers practical prevention techniques for several common computer-related health problems such as repetitive-motion injuries, eyestrain and backaches.

Indoor Pollution by Steve Coffel and Karyn Feiden (Fawcett, 1990). Features a quick checklist of common hazards and what you can do about them.

To learn more about lead pollution and its solutions, contact the **National Safety Council's National Lead Information Center** (800-424-LEAD).

The No-Nag, No-Guilt, Do-It-Your-Own Way Guide to Quitting Smoking by Tom Ferguson, M.D. (Ballantine, 1989). The best nonjudgmental guide to date for health-concerned smokers who want to quit.

The Nontoxic Home and Office by Debra Lynn Dadd (J.P. Tarcher, 1992). A popular guidebook that identifies proven and potential hazardous substances and offers simple, safer alternatives.

PERSONAL POWER NOTES
A Quick-List of This Chapter's Power-Action Options

Monitor—and reduce—your radiation risks.

Open windows and ban indoor smoking.

Reduce your exposure to aluminum and lead.

Keep your air clean with some simple strategies.

Whenever possible, choose nontoxic cleaning products.

PERSONAL NOTES

_____

_____

_____

_____

_____

References

CHAPTER 14

1. "Looking Forward to the Good Life at Age 100." Report on survey results from the Alliance for Aging Research, in *USA Today* (Dec. 21, 1992).
2. Cutler, R. "Evolution of Longevity in Primates." *Journal of Human Evolution* 5 (1976): 169–202; Bortz, W. M., II. *We Live Too Short and Die Too Long* (New York: Bantam, 1991): 1; Butler, R. N., quoted in "Slowing Down the Clock." ABC News *20/20* (May 19, 1988).
3. Rowe, J., quoted in "The Search for the Fountain of Youth." *Newsweek* (Mar. 5, 1990): 42.
4. Bortz. *We Live Too Short*: 1.
5. Ibid. 47.
6. Langer, E. J. *Mindfulness* (Reading, Mass.: Addison-Wesley, 1989): 95–98.
7. Y. Stern et al. "Influence of Education and Occupation on the Incidence of Alzheimer's Disease." *Journal of the American Medical Association* 271 (13)(Apr. 6, 1994): 1004–1010.
8. "Neuroscientists Explore the Benefits of Brain 'Calisthenics'." *Life* (July 1994): 62–70; Kra, S. *Aging Myths* (New York: McGraw-Hill, 1986); Le Poncin, M. *Brain Fitness* (New York: Fawcett, 1990); Chafetz, M. D. *Smart for Life* (New York: Penguin, 1992); "Building a Better Brain." *Omni Longevity* 1 (1)(Nov. 1986): 1–2; Schaie, K. W., ed. *Longitudinal Studies of Adult Psychological Development* (New York: Guilford Press, 1983); Task force sponsored by the National Institute on Aging, Bethesda, Md. "Senility Reconsidered: Treatment Possibilities for Mental Impairment in the Elderly." *Journal of the American Medical Association* (July 18, 1980): 259–260; R. Duara et al. "Cerebral Glucose Utilization as Measured with Positron Emission Tomography in 21 Resting Healthy Men between the Ages of 21 and 83 Years." *Brain* 106 (1983): 761–775; Rosenzweig, M. R. "Experience, Memory, and the Brain." *American Psychologist* (Apr. 1984).
9. Le Poncin, M. *Brain Fitness* (New York: Fawcett, 1990): 65; M. Y. Zhang et al. "The Prevalence of Dementia and Alzheimer's Disease in Shanghai, China: Impact of Age, Gender, and Education." *Annals of Neurology* 27 (4)(Apr. 1990): 428–437; Research by Robert Katzman of the University of California, San Diego, and Richard Mayeux, of Columbia University, cited in *Psychology Today* (Sept./Oct. 1992): 45.
10. Chafetz. *Smart for Life*: xii-xiii.
11. Schaie, K. W. "Late Life Potential and Cohort Differences in Mental Abilities," in *Late Life Potential*, ed. Perlmutter, M. (Washington, D.C.: The Gerontological Society of America, 1990): 43.
12. Lieff, J. D. Foreword to *Reversing Memory Loss* by Mark, V. H., and Mark, J. P. (Boston: Houghton Mifflin, 1992): xii.
13. Stevens, C., quoted in *Psychology Today* (Sept./Oct. 1992): 46.
14. Raichle, M., quoted in *Psychology Today* (Sept./Oct. 1992): 46.
15. Mark. *Reversing Memory Loss*: 1–3.
16. Langer. *Mindfulness*: 112–113.
17. Mulvey, A., and Langer, E., as discussed in Rodin, J., and Langer, E. "Aging Labels: The Decline of Control and the Fall of Self-Esteem." *Journal of Social Issues* 36 (1980): 12–29.
18. Katzman, P., and Carasu, T. "Differential Diagnosis of Dementia," in *Neurological and Sensory Disorders in the Elderly*, ed. Fields, W. S. (Miami, Fla.: Symposia Specialist Medical Books, 1975): 103–104.

19. Winter, A., and Winter, R. *Build Your Brain Power* (New York: St. Martin's Press, 1986): 1.
20. "Successful Aging." *University of California at Berkeley Wellness Letter* 7 (11)(Aug. 1991): 1.
21. Cohen G., quoted in Laurence, L. "Jogging the Mind." *Self* (Mar. 1992): 110.
22. Le Poncin. *Brain Fitness*: 40, 60.
23. I. B. Black et al. "Neurotransmitter Plasticity at the Molecular Level." *Science* 225 (4668)(1984): 1266–1270; Kandel, E. R., and Schwartz, J. H. "Molecular Biology of Learning: Modulation of Transmitter Release." *Science* 218 (4571)(1982): 433–443; *Treatise on Neuroplasticity and Repair in the Central Nervous System* (Geneva, Switzerland: World Health Organization, 1983).
24. Nightingale, E. "Our Changing World." Radio program. (Chicago: Nightingale-Conant Corporation, 1974).
25. "Mental Calisthenics to Keep Your Mind in Shape." *University of Texas Health Science Center Lifetime Health Letter* 3 (12)(Dec. 1991): 7.
26. Kandel and Schwartz. "Molecular Biology of Learning": 433–443; Clark, G. "Cell Biological Analysis of Associative and Non-Associative Learning." Paper presented at the annual meeting of the American Association for the Advancement of Science (New York, May 26, 1984); News feature, University of Illinois at Urbana (May 26, 1984).
27. Sime, W. E. "Psychological Benefits of Exercise." *Advances* 1 (4)(Fall, 1984): 15–29. Ninety references cited; Roth, D. L., and Holmes, D. S. "Influence of Aerobic Exercise Training and Relaxation Training on Physical and Psychological Health following Stressful Life Events." *Psychosomatic Medicine* (July/Aug. 1987); Morgan, W. P., and Goldston, S. E. *Exercise and Mental Health* (Washington, D.C.: Hemisphere Publishing, 1987).
28. R. Dustman et al. "Aerobic Exercise Training and Improved Neuropsychologic Function of Older Individuals." *Neurobiology of Aging* 5 (1984): 35–42.
29. Bashore, T. "Age, Physical Fitness, and Mental Processing Speed," in *Clinical and Applied Gerontology* vol. IX of the *Annual Review of Gerontology and Geriatrics*, ed. Lawton, M. P. (Spring 1989).
30. Clarkson-Smith, L., and Hartley, A. A. "Relationships between Physical Exercise and Cognitive Abilities in Older Adults." *Psychology and Aging* 4 (2)(1989): 183–189.
31. R. L. Rogers et al. "After Reaching Retirement Age, Physical Activity Sustains Cerebral Perfusion and Cognition." *Journal of the American Geriatrics Society* 38 (1990): 123–128.
32. Spriduso, W. W. *Journal of Gerontology* 35 (1980): 850.
33. M. Elsayad et al. "Intellectual Differences of Adult Men Related to Age and Physical Fitness before and after an Exercise Program." *Journal of Gerontology* 35 (May 1980): 383–387.
34. "Exercise and Mental Health." *University of Texas Health Science Center Lifetime Health Letter* (Aug. 1990): 2.
35. Herrmann, D. J. *Super Memory* (Emmaus, Pa.: Rodale Press, 1990): 35–36.
36. Rodgers, W. L., and Hertzog, A. R. "Interviewing Older Adults." *Journal of Gerontology* 42 (1987): 387–394.
37. Rowe, J. W., and Kahn, R. L. "Human Aging: Usual and Successful." *Science* 237 (1987): 143–149.
38. Lapp, D., quoted in *University of Texas Health Science Center Lifetime Health Letter* 3 (12)(Dec. 1991): 7.
39. In highlighting these mental activities, I've relied heavily on two primary references: Le Poncin. *Brain Fitness* and Chafetz. *Smart for Life.*
40. Chafetz. *Smart for Life*: 68.
41. Mark, V. H., and Mark, J. P. *Brain Power* (Boston: Houghton Mifflin, 1989): 183.

42. R. J. Nelson et al. "Variations in the Proportional Representations of the Hand in So-matosensory Cortex of Primates." Paper presented at the Society for Neuroscience meeting (Boston, Nov. 13, 1980); W. M. Jenkins et al. Coleman Memorial Laboratories, University of California at San Francisco. Paper presented at the Society for Neuro-science meeting (Anaheim, Calif., Oct. 13, 1984).

43. Winter and Winter. *Build Brain Power*: 17–43.

44. Le Poncin. *Brain Fitness*: 36–37.

45. Restak, R. *The Brain Has a Mind of Its Own* (New York: Harmony Books, 1991): 60–61.

46. J. J. Shors et al. "Unpredictable and Uncontrollable Stress Impair Neuronal Plasticity in the Hippocampus." *Brain Research Bulletin* 24 (5)(May 1990): 663–667; Thompson, R. F. Study, cited in *Psychology Today* (Sept./Oct. 1992): 44.

47. Yesavage, J., and Lapp, D., quoted in Toal, J. "The Fear of Forgetting." *American Health* (Oct. 1986): 77–86.

48. Rossi, E. L., with Nimmons, D. *The 20-Minute Break* (Los Angeles: J. P. Tarcher, 1991): 27–28; Chafetz. *Smart for Life*: 63–65.

49. Le Poncin. *Brain Fitness*: 38.

50. Chafetz. *Smart for Life*: 63–65.

51. Ibid.: 64; Davis, B. *Perspectives in Biology and Medicine* 28 (1985): 457–464.

52. Chafetz. *Smart for Life*: 64.

53. Ibid.: 94.

CHAPTER 15

1. Snowdon, D. A., and Phillips, R. L. "Does a Vegetarian Diet Reduce the Occurrence of Diabetes?" *American Journal of Public Health* 75 (5)(May 1985): 507–512; "Position of the American Dietetic Association: Vegetarian Diets." *Journal of the American Dietetic Association* 88 (3)(Mar. 1988): 351; Ballentine, R. *Transition to Vegetarianism* (Hones-dale, Pa.: Himalayan Institute, 1987); Liebman, B. "Are Vegetarians Healthier Than the Rest of Us?" *Nutrition Action Health Letter* (June 1983): 8; Burr, M. L., and Sweetnam, P. M. "Vegetarianism, Dietary Fiber, and Mortality." *American Journal of Clinical Nu-trition* 36 (5)(Nov. 1982): 873–877; Dwyer, J., quoted in *Environmental Nutrition* (May 1987).

2. Liebman. "Vegetarians": 8.

3. P. Maenpaa et al. "Effects of a Low-Fat Lactovegetarian Diet on Health Parameters of Adult Subjects." *Ecology of Food and Nutrition* 25 (3)(1991): 255–267.

4. "Better Eating Goes to Your Head." *Tufts University Diet and Nutrition Letter* 11 (1)(Mar. 1993): 2.

5. Burr and Sweetnam. "Vegetarianism, Dietary Fiber": 873–877; Liebman. "Vegetarians."

6. Snowdon and Phillips. "Does a Vegetarian Diet": 507–512; "Position of the American Dietetic Association": 351; *Australian and New Zealand Journal of Medicine* (Aug. 1984); Ballentine. *Transition to Vegetarianism*; Liebman. "Vegetarians"; *British Medical Journal* 291 (July 6, 1985); *Journal of the Royal Society of Medicine* 79 (June 1986).

7. Dwyer, J., quoted in *Environmental Nutrition* (May 1987); "A.D.A. Report: Position Paper on the Vegetarian Approach to Eating." *Journal of the American Dietetic Associa-tion* 77 (1)(1980): 61–69; *Journal of the American Dietetic Association* 88 (3)(Mar. 1988): 351.

8. Liebman. "Vegetarians."

9. *Mutagen Research* 72 (1980): 511.

10. D. D. Truesdell et al. "Nutrients in Vegetarian Foods." *Journal of the American Dietetic Association* 84 (1984): 28–36.

11. H. C. Heinrich et al. "Nutritional Iron Deficiency Anemia in Lacto-Ovo Vegetarians." *Klinische Wochenschrift* 57 (1979): 187–193; J. T. Dwyer et al. "Nutritional Status of Vegetarian Children." *American Journal of Clinical Nutrition* 35 (1982): 204–216.

12. International Nutritional Anemia Consultative Group. *The Effects of Cereals and Legumes on Iron Availability* (Washington, D.C.: Nutrition Foundation, 1982): 8, 16–19.

13. Hallberg, L., and Rossander, L. "Improvement of Iron Nutrition in Developing Countries: Comparison of Adding Meat, Soy Protein, Ascorbic Acid, Citric Acid, and Ferrous Sulphate on Iron Absorption from a Simple Latin American-type of Meal." *American Journal of Clinical Nutrition* 39 (1984): 1469–1478.

14. International Nutritional Anemia Consultative Group. *Effects.*

15. Ballentine. *Transition*: 168.

16. M. J. Albert et al. "Vitamin B-12 Synthesis by Human Small Intestine Bacteria." *Nature* 283 (1980): 781–782.

17. National Academy of Sciences, National Research Council, Food and Nutrition Board. *Recommended Dietary Allowances*, 9th ed. (National Academy Press: Washington, D.C., 1980): 112–120.

18. *Journal of the American Dietetic Association* 88 (3)(Mar. 1988): 351; Ballentine. *Transition*: 168–175.

19. "Real Men Eat Broccoli—and Bananas and Oranges." *Tufts University Diet and Nutrition Letter* 11 (9)(Nov. 1993): 8.

20. Register, U. D., quoted in Zucker, M. *Sports Fitness* (Oct. 1985): 28.

21. Lappe, F. M., and Collins, J. *Diet for a Small Planet* (New York: Ballantine, 1982); Lappe, F. M., and Collins, J. *Food First: Beyond the Myth of Scarcity* (New York: Ballantine, 1978); Lappe, F. M., and Collins, J. *World Hunger: Twelve Myths* (New York: Grove Press, 1986).

22. Worldwatch Institute. *State of the World 1993* (Washington, D.C.: 1993).

23. *Environmental Nutrition* 16 (7)(July 1993): 8.

24. "Eating Out the Vegetarian Way." *Environmental Nutrition* 16 (12)(Dec. 1993): 6.

25. "Variety." *Tufts University Diet and Nutrition Letter* 11 (10)(Dec. 1993): 1.

26. Higginson, J., in *Proceedings of the Eighth Canadian Cancer Research Conference* (Oxford, England: Pergamon Press, 1969): 40–75; B. Reddy et al. "Nutrition and Its Relationship to Cancer." *Advances in Cancer Research* 32 (1980): 237–345; "How to Cut the Risk of Cancer." *FDA Consumer* (Apr. 1988): 22–29.

27. Wynder, E. L., and Gori, G. B. "Contribution of the Environment to Cancer Incidence: An Epidemiologic Exercise." *Journal of the National Cancer Institute* 58 (1977): 825–832.

28. Doll, R., and Peto, R. "The Causes of Cancer: Quantitative Estimates of Avoidable Risks of Cancer in the United States." *Journal of the National Cancer Institute* 66 (1981): 1192.

29. American Heart Association. *Heart Facts 1986.*

30. Willett, W., and MacMahon, B. "Diet and Cancer—An Overview." *New England Journal of Medicine* 310 (1984): 633–638; Alabaster, O. *The Power of Prevention: Reduce Your Risk of Cancer through Diet and Nutrition* (New York: Simon & Schuster, 1985); *Journal of the National Cancer Institute* 77 (1)(1986): 33–42.

31. Berenson, G. *American Journal of Diseases of Children* 133 (1979): 1049; *Atherosclerosis* 5 (1985): 404; Report of the American Heart Association Nutrition Committee. *Atherosclerosis* 4 (1982): 177–191; P. Puska et al. "Controlled Randomized Trial of the Effect of Dietary Fat on Blood Pressure." *Lancet* (1)(1983): 1; *Journal of Hypertension* 4 (4)(1986): 407–412.

32. Williams, H. *Kidney International* 13 (1978): 410; D. Kromhout et al. *New England Journal of Medicine* 312 (May 9, 1985): 1205.

33. Burkitt, D., in *Colorectal Cancer: Prevention Epidemiology and Screening*, eds. Winawer et al. (New York: Raven Press, 1980): 13–18; Jensen, O. "Colon Cancer Epidemiology," in *Experimental Colon Carcinogenesis*, eds. Atrup and Williams (Boca Raton, Fla.: CRC Press, 1983): 3–23.

34. *Diet and Health: Implications for Reducing Chronic Disease* (NAS) 8 (1989).

35. Greenwald, P., quoted in *USA Today* (July 2, 1992): 1D.

36. Special Report. *Tufts University Diet and Nutrition Letter* 10 (4)(June 1992): 4.

37. "No Fast Fix for a Bad Diet." Gallup poll for the American Dietetic Association reported in *USA Today* (Feb. 21, 1990).

38. National Cancer Institute. "They're Good for You, but Many Still Shun Fruit, Veggies." *USA Today* (June 2, 1992): 1D.

39. J. Hallfrisch et al. "Modification of the United States' Diet to Effect Changes in Blood Lipids and Lipoprotein Distribution." *Atherosclerosis* 57 (2–3)(Nov. 1985): 179–188; Connor, S. L., and Connor, W. E. *The New American Diet* (New York: Simon & Schuster, 1986); Alabaster. *The Power of Prevention*: 87–88, 107.

40. Reports at the American Heart Association's 20th Science Forum (Jan. 17–20, 1993).

41. "Sunday Dinner May Trip Monday Heart Attack." *Environmental Nutrition* 16 (3)(Mar. 1993): 1; "The Immediate Benefits of Low-Fat Eating." *University of California at Berkeley Wellness Letter* 9 (7)(Apr. 1993): 1.

42. *Tufts University Diet and Nutrition Letter* 5 (3)(May 1987): 1–2.

43. E. J. Schaefer et al. "The Effects of Low-Cholesterol, High-Polyunsaturated Fat and Low-Fat Diets on Plasma Lipid and Lipoprotein Cholesterol Levels in Normal and Hypercholesterolemic Subjects." *American Journal of Clinical Nutrition* 34 (1981): 1158–1163; Cooper, K. H. *Controlling Your Cholesterol* (New York: Bantam, 1988).

44. *Tufts University Diet and Nutrition Letter* 5 (1)(Mar. 1987): 2.

45. Cooper. *Controlling Cholesterol*: 42, 44.

46. S. A. Tornberg et al. "Risks of Cancer of the Colon and Rectum in Relation to Serum Cholesterol and Beta-Lipoprotein." *New England Journal of Medicine* 315 (26)(Dec. 25, 1986): 1629–1634; G. Mannes et al. "Relation between the Frequency of Colorectal Adenoma and the Serum Cholesterol Level." *New England Journal of Medicine* 315 (26)(Dec. 25, 1986): 1634–1638.

47. J. M. Hoeg et al. "An Approach to the Management of Hyperlipoproteinemia." *Journal of the American Medical Association* 255 (4)(Jan. 24/31, 1986): 512–521; Anderson, J. W., and Chen, W. L. "Plant Fiber: Carbohydrate and Lipid Metabolism." *American Journal of Clinical Nutrition* 32 (1979): 346–363; J. W. Anderson et al. "Hypocholesterolemic Effects of Oat-Bran or Bean Intake for Hypercholesterolemic Men." *American Journal of Clinical Nutrition* 40 (1984): 1146–1155; R. W. Kirby et al. "Oat-Bran Intake Selectively Lowers Serum Low-Density Lipoprotein Cholesterol Concentrations of Hypercholesterolemic Men." *American Journal of Clinical Nutrition* 34 (1981): 824–828.

48. *Tufts University Diet and Nutrition Letter* 5 (1)(Mar. 1987): 2; Cooper. *Controlling Cholesterol*: 80–83.

49. Grundy, S. M. "Comparison of Monounsaturated Fatty Acids and Carbohydrates for Lowering Plasma Cholesterol." *New England Journal of Medicine* 314 (12)(Mar. 20, 1986): 745–748; S. M. Grundy et al. "Rationale of the Diet-Heart Statement of the American Heart Association, Report of the Nutrition Committee." *Circulation* 65 (4)(1982): 841A; Mensink, R. P., and Katahn, M. B. "Effect of Monounsaturated Fatty Acids vs. Complex Carbohydrates on High-Density Lipoproteins in Healthy Men and Women." *Lancet* (Jan. 17, 1987): 122–124; "Guide to Heart-Healthy Oils." *Environmental Nutrition* 12 (8)(Aug. 1989): 1–6.

50. Mensink and Katahn. "Monounsaturated"; "More Good News for Olive Oil Lovers."

Environmental Nutrition (Mar. 1987): 2; "Heart-Healthy Oils": 6.

51. Blume, E. "Why Oxidized Fats Are in Your Food and Why You Wish They Weren't." *Nutrition Action Health Letter* (Dec. 1987): 1–6.

52. Fletcher, D., and Rogers, D. *Postgraduate Medicine* 77 (5)(1985): 319–328; "Trans Fatty Acids in Processed Foods." *Environmental Nutrition* (Feb. 1988): 6–7; Kritchevsky, D. *Federation Proceedings* 41 (Sept. 1982): 2813; Smith, E. *Lancet* (Mar. 8, 1980): 534.

53. M. G. Enig et al. "Dietary Fat and Cancer Trends—A Critique." *Federation Proceedings* 37 (1978): 2215–2220; M. G. Enig et al. *Journal of the American Oil Chemists Society* (Oct. 1983): 1788; J. E. Kinsella et al. "Metabolism of *trans* Fatty Acids with Emphasis on the Effects of *trans*, Trans-Octadecadienoate on Lipid Composition, Essential Fatty Acid, and Prostaglandins: An Overview." *American Journal of Clinical Nutrition* 34 (1981): 2307–2318.

54. "Trans Fatty Acids Hidden in Foods May Raise Cholesterol Levels." *Environmental Nutrition* 16 (7)(July 1993): 1–6.

55. "Trans Fatty Acids." *Environmental Nutrition* 16 (7)(July 1993): 6.

56. *Nutrition Week* (Sept. 17, 1987): 4.

57. "The Problem with Protein." *Nutrition Action Health Letter* 20 (5)(June 1993): 1–7; "Balancing Protein Needs Is Easy." *Environmental Nutrition* 16 (6)(June 1993): 7.

58. Blume, E. "Overdosing on Protein." *Nutrition Action* 14 (2)(Mar. 1987): 1–6; Morgan, B. L. G. "Protein and Your Body." *Columbia University Nutrition and Health* 8 (1)(1986): 1–6; Carroll, K. K. "Dietary Protein in Relation to Plasma Cholesterol Levels and Atherosclerosis." *Nutrition Reviews* 36 (1978): 1–5; Brenner, B. M., and Meyer, T. W. "Dietary Protein Intake and the Progressive Nature of Kidney Disease." *New England Journal of Medicine* 307 (1982): 652–654.

59. Special Report. *Tufts University Diet and Nutrition Letter* 10 (4)(June 1992): 6.

CHAPTER 16

1. The health risks from cigarette smoking, excessive alcohol consumption, drug abuse, a low-fiber, high-saturated-fat diet, not wearing seat belts, and unsafe sex each may statistically outweigh the increased disease risks you may face from lacking a variety of Protector Foods in your diet, or the risks from eating pesticide-laden foods. But, assuming you've taken action steps (including eating a lower-fat, higher-fiber diet) to help control the more significant and pressing health risks, to us it makes scientific sense to minimize unsafe foods and accentuate Protector Foods.

2. "Will Phytochemicals Fight Cancer?" *Environmental Nutrition* 16 (3)(Mar. 1993): 1–6; Schardt, D. "Phytochemicals: Plants against Cancer." *Nutrition Action Health Letter* 21 (3)(Apr. 1994): 1, 9–11.

3. The listing of Protector Foods was drawn from the following resources: Schardt. "Phytochemicals: Plants against Cancer": 1, 9–11; "Beta-Carotene's Extended Family." *University of California at Berkeley Wellness Letter* 10 (6)(Mar. 1994): 2; Begley, S. "Beyond Vitamins." *Newsweek* (Apr. 25, 1994): 44–49; "Will Phytochemicals Fight Cancer?" *Environmental Nutrition* 16 (3)(Mar. 1993): 1–6; Scala, J. *Prescription for Longevity* (New York: Dutton, 1992); *Cancer Research* (Supp.) 52 (1992): 2085s; "Spicing Up Your Isoflavones and Phytosterols." *University of California at Berkeley Wellness Letter* 10 (10)(Oct. 1993): 1–2; *Journal of the American Cancer Institute* 83(1991): 541; "What's the Best Diet?" *Nutrition Action Health Letter* 18 (10)(Dec. 1991): 1–9; "Nutrition and Aging." *Nutrition Action Health Letter* 19 (4)(May 1992): 1–7; Jacobson, M. F., Lefferts, L. Y., and Garland, A. W. *Safe Food* (Los Angeles: Living Planet Press, 1991): 47; "'Super-Foods' to Fight Cancer: The National Cancer Institute Is Now Trying to Harness Na-

ture's Most Powerful Preventives." *Prevention* (Nov. 1991): 44–47; 121–122; Jacobson, M. F. *Eater's Digest and Nutrition Scoreboard*, rev. ed. (New York: Doubleday, 1985).

4. *Cancer Causes and Control* 2 (1991): 324, 427.

5. Potter, J., quoted in Schardt, "Phytochemicals: Plants against Cancer": 1, 9–11.

6. Burkitt, D., in *Colorectal Cancer: Prevention Epidemiology and Screening*, eds. Winawer et al. (New York: Raven Press, 1980): 13–18; Jensen, O. "Colon Cancer Epidemiology," in *Experimental Colon Carcinogenesis*, eds. Atrup and Williams (Boca Raton, Fla.: CRC Press, 1983): 3–23.

7. Alabaster, O. *The Power of Prevention: Reduce Your Risk of Cancer through Diet and Nutrition* (New York: Simon & Schuster, 1985): 36.

8. Weininger, J., and Briggs, G. M. "Nutrition and Diabetes." *Nutrition Update* (New York: John Wiley & Sons, 1985): 59–60.

9. Anderson, J. W. "Medical Benefits of High-Fiber Intakes." *The Fiber Factor* (Quaker Oats Co., Chicago, Ill., Aug. 1983); Anderson, J. W. *Plant Fiber in Foods* (Lexington, Ky.: HCF Diabetes Research Foundation, Inc., 1986); Kinosian, B. P., and Eisenberg, J. M. "Cutting into Cholesterol." *Journal of the American Medicine Association* 259 (15)(Apr. 15, 1988).

10. Anderson. "Medical Benefits."

11. Connor, S. L., and Connor, W. E. *The New American Diet* (New York: Simon & Schuster, 1986): 38; Alabaster. *The Power of Prevention*: 127.

12. Anderson. *Plant Fiber*.

13. F. Grande et al. "Effect of Carbohydrates of Leguminous Seeds, Wheat and Potatoes on Serum Cholesterol Concentration in Man." *Journal of Nutrition* 86 (1965): 313–318; D. J. A. Jenkins et al. "The Glycaemic Index of Foods Tested in Diabetic Patients: A New Basis for Carbohydrate Exchange Favouring the Use of Legumes." *Diabetology* 24 (1983): 257–264; D. J. A. Jenkins et al. "Leguminous Seeds in the Dietary Management of Hyperlipidemia." *American Journal of Clinical Nutrition* 38 (1983): 567–573.

14. Gori, G. B. "Dietary and Nutritional Implications in the Multifactorial Etiology of Certain Prevalent Human Cancers." *Cancer* 43 (1979): 151–161.

15. Odeleye, O. E., and Watson, R. R. "Health Implications of the Omega-3 Fatty Acids." *American Journal of Clinical Nutrition* 53 (1991): 89S–93S; Kinsella, J. E. *American Journal of Clinical Nutrition* 53 (1991): 178; Hunter, J. E. "Omega-3 Fatty Acids from Vegetable Oils." *American Journal of Clinical Nutrition* 51 (1990): 809–814; Weiner. *New England Journal of Medicine* 315 (13)(Sept. 25, 1986): 833; Berry, E. M., and Hirsch, J. "Does Dietary Linolenic Acid Influence Blood Pressure?" *American Journal of Clinical Nutrition* 44 (1986): 336–340.

16. Scala, J. *Prescription for Longevity* (New York: Dutton, 1992): 168.

17. Odeleye and Watson. "Health Implications of the Omega-3 Fatty Acids": 89S–93S; Kinsella. : 178; Hunter. "Omega-3 Fatty Acids from Vegetable Oils": 809–814; Weiner.: 833; Berry and Hirsch. "Does Dietary Linolenic Acid Influence Blood Pressure?": 336–340; F. N. Hepburn et al. "Provisional Tables on the Content of Omega-3 Fatty Acids and Other Fat Components of Selected Foods." *Journal of the American Dietetic Association* 86 (6)(June 1986): 788–793.

18. Schardt, D. "Yogurt: Bacteria to Basics." *Nutrition Action Health Letter* 20 (7)(Sept. 1993): 8–9.

19. "Effects of Dairy and Fermented Milk Products." *Foods, Nutrition and Immunity* 1 (1992): 77.

20. Goldin, B. R., and Gorbach. S.L. "The Effect of Milk and Lactobacillus Feeding on Human Intestinal Bacterial Enzyme Activity." *American Journal of Clinical Nutrition* 39(5)(1984): 756.

21. *Microbial Ecology in Health and Disease* 5 (1992): 59.
22. "Herbs and Spices May Be Barrier against Cancer, Heart Disease." *Environmental Nutrition* 16 (6)(June 1993): 1–4.
23. "Research: Garlic May Be Wonder Bulb against Disease." *Environmental Nutrition* 17 (1)(Jan. 1994): 1–6; "Herbs and Spices": 1–4; Block, E. "The Chemistry of Garlic." *Scientific American* 252 (3)(1985): 114–119; Lin, R. I. "Proceedings of the First World Congress on the Health Significance of Garlic and Garlic Constituents" (Irvine, Calif.: Nutrition International, in press). Sumiyoshi, H., and Wargovich, M. J. "Garlic (Allium Sativum): A Review of Its Relationship to Cancer." *Asia Pacific Journal of Pharmacology* 4 (1989): 133–140; Kendler, B. S. "Garlic and Onion: A Review of Their Relationship to Cardiovascular Disease." *Preventive Medicine* 16 (1987): 670–685; Y. Wei-Cheng et al. "Allium Vegetables and Reduced Risk of Stomach Cancer." *Journal of the National Cancer Institute* 81 (1989): 162–164; *Proceedings of the American Association for Cancer Research* (Mar. 1991).
24. *Environmental Nutrition* 16 (6)(June 1993): 1–4.
25. Ibid.
26. Scala. *Prescription for Longevity*: 227–228.
27. Henry, C. J. K., and Emergy, B. "Effect of Spiced Food on Metabolic Rate." *Human Nutrition: Clinical Nutrition* 40C (1986): 165–168.
28. "Plant Products as Protective Agents against Cancer." *Indian Journal of Experimental Biology* 28 (Nov. 1990): 1008–1011; "Tumor Reducing and Anticarcinogenic Activity of Selected Spices." *Cancer Letters* 51 (1)(May 15, 1990): 85–89.
29. "Will Phytochemicals Fight Cancer?" *Environmental Nutrition* 16 (3)(Mar. 1993): 1–6.
30. Anderson, R. A., U. S. Department of Agriculture Study, quoted in Bricklin, M. "The Spice of Longer Life." *Prevention* (June 1992): 37–38.
31. Bitterman, W. A. "Environmental and Nutritional Factors Significantly Associated with Cancer of the Urinary Tract among Different Ethnic Groups." *Urologic Clinics of North America* 18 (3)(Aug. 1991): 501–508.
32. *Environmental Nutrition* 16 (6)(June 1993): 1–4.
33. Scala. *Prescription for Longevity*; "What's the Best Diet?" *Nutrition Action Health Letter* 18 (10)(Dec. 1991): 1–9; "Nutrition and Aging." *Nutrition Action Health Letter* 19 (4)(May 1992): 1–7; Jacobson, Lefferts, and Garland. *Safe Food*: 47; "'SuperFoods' to Fight Cancer": 44–47; 121–122.
34. Hendler, S. S. *Complete Guide to Anti-Aging Nutrients* (New York: Simon & Schuster, 1985); Scala. *Prescription for Longevity*.
35. F. Grande et al. "Effect of Carbohydrates of Leguminous Seeds, Wheat and Potatoes on Serum Cholesterol Concentration in Man." *Journal of Nutrition* 86 (1965): 313–318; D. J. A. Jenkins et al. "The Glycaemic Index of Foods Tested in Diabetic Patients: A New Basis for Carbohydrate Exchange Favouring the Use of Legumes." *Diabetology* 24 (1983): 257–264; D. J. A. Jenkins et al. "Leguminous Seeds in the Dietary Management of Hyperlipidemia." *American Journal of Clinical Nutrition* 38 (1983): 567–573.
36. Gori, G. B. "Dietary and Nutritional Implications in the Multifactorial Etiology of Certain Prevalent Human Cancers." *Cancer* 43 (1979): 151–161.
37. Exler, J., and Weihrauch, J. L. "Comprehensive Evaluation of Fatty Acids in Foods. VIII. Finfish." *Journal of the American Dietetic Association* 69 (3)(Sept. 1976): 243–248; Exler, J., and Weihrauch, J. L. "Comprehensive Evaluation of Fatty Acids in Foods. XII. Shellfish." *Journal of the American Dietetic Association* 71 (5)(Nov. 1977): 518–521.
38. *New England Journal of Medicine* 312 (19)(May 9, 1985): 1205–1224; 1253; Nestel, P. J. "Fish Oil Attenuates the Cholesterol-Induced Rise in Lipoprotein Cholesterol." *American Journal of Clinical Nutrition* 43 (5)(May 1986): 752–757.

39. Foundation for the Advancement of Science and Education. *FASE Reports* 11 (1)(1993): S1.
40. National Academy of Sciences. *Regulating Pesticides in Food* (1987).
41. "Red Flag on Pesticides: What's Being Done?" *Environmental Nutrition* 16 (10)(Oct. 1993): 1–4.
42. Wolff et al. "Blood Levels of Organochlorine Residues and Risk of Breast Cancer." *Journal of the National Cancer Institute* 85 (8)(1993): 648–652.
43. Mott, L., and Snyder, K. *Pesticide Alert: A Guide to Pesticides in Fruits and Vegetables* (New York: National Resources Defense Council, 1988).
44. Hendler. *Anti-Aging Nutrients*: 54.
45. National Research Council. *Diet, Nutrition, and Cancer* (Washington, D.C.: National Academy Press, 1982): chapter 13.
46. "Study Warns: Don't Take Safe Water for Granted." *Environmental Nutrition* 16 (11)(Nov. 1993): 2; *Think Before You Drink* (New York: Environmental Resources Defense Council, 1993).
47. "Is Your Tap Water Safe to Drink?" *University of Texas Health Science Center Lifetime Health Letter* 5 (11)(Nov. 1993): 4–5.
48. EPA Report in *Ultrasport* (July 1987): 80.
49. Gussow, J. D., and Thomas, P. R. *The Nutrition Debate: Sorting Out Some Answers* (Palo Alto, Calif.: Bull Publishing, 1986): 261–262.
50. Ford, F. "A Grain of Truth." *New Age Journal* (Mar. 1986): 18.
51. "Peel Your Potatoes to Avoid Toxins, Says Cornell Researcher." *Environmental Nutrition* 16 (2)(Feb. 1993): 8.
52. Jacobson, Lefferts, and Garland. *Safe Food*: 69.
53. *Tufts University Diet and Nutrition Letter* 11 (3)(May 1993): 2.

CHAPTER 17

1. Worthington-Roberts, B., and Breskin, M. *Journal of the American Dietetic Association* 84 (7)(1984): 795–800; *Nutrition Action Health Letter* 18 (8)(Oct. 1991): 5.
2. Subar, A., quoted in "Taking Supplements Seriously." *Nutrition Action Health Letter* 18 (8)(Oct. 1991): 6.
3. Hendler, S. S. *Complete Guide to Anti-Aging Nutrients* (New York: Simon & Schuster, 1985): 12.
4. "Our Vitamin Prescription." *University of California at Berkeley Wellness Letter* 10 (4)(Jan. 1994): 1–2 ;4–5.
5. Jacobson, M. J. *Nutrition Action Health Letter* 19 (4)(May 1992): 3.
6. Blumberg, J., quoted in "Taking Supplements Seriously." *Nutrition Action Health Letter* 18 (8)(Oct. 1991): 5.
7. "Can Taking Supplements Help You Ward Off Disease?" *Tufts University Diet and Nutrition Letter* 9 (2)(Apr. 1991): 3–6; "Taking Supplements Seriously." *Nutrition Action Health Letter* 18 (8)(Oct. 1991): 1–7; Toufexis, A. "The New Scoop on Vitamins." *Time* (Apr. 6, 1992): 54–59.
8. "Dramatic Support for Calcium." *The Johns Hopkins Medical Letter* 2 (11)(Jan. 1991): 1.
9. Hendler, S. S. *The Doctor's Vitamin and Mineral Encyclopedia* (New York: Simon & Schuster, 1990): 402.
10. For a review of the scientific literature on folacin, see Hendler. *Vitamin and Mineral Encyclopedia*, or *University of California at Berkeley Wellness Letter* 9 (2) (Nov. 1992) or 10 (4)(Jan. 1994).
11. Hendler. *Vitamin and Mineral Encyclopedia*: 401.

12. Ibid.: 78.
13. Lauffer, R. B. *Iron Balance* (New York: St. Martin's Press, 1991).
14. Ibid.
15. Barnard, N. *Food for Life* (New York: Harmony Books, 1993): 11.
16. Hendler. *Anti-Aging Nutrients*: 317.
17. "Growing Old Healthfully: Are Antioxidants the Answer?" *Environmental Nutrition* 15 (1)(Jan. 1992): 1–3.
18. Blumberg, J., interviewed in "Can Taking Supplements Help You Ward Off Disease?" *Tufts University Diet and Nutrition Letter* 9 (2)(Apr. 1991): 3–6.
19. W. J. Blot et al. "Nutrition Intervention Trials in Linxian, China: Supplementation with Specific Vitamin/Mineral Combinations, Cancer Incidence, and Disease-Specific Mortality in the General Population." *Journal of the National Cancer Institute* 85 (18)(Sept. 15, 1993): 1483–1492.
20. Kanter, M. M., Nolte, L. A., and Holloszy, J. O. "Effects of an Antioxidant Vitamin Mixture on Lipid Percolation at Rest and Postexercise." *Journal of Applied Physiology* 74 (1993): 965–969.
21. "Our Vitamin Prescription: The Big Four." *University of California at Berkeley Wellness Letter* 10 (4)(Jan. 1994): 1.
22. "Free Radicals and Antioxidants: Finding the Key to Heart Disease, Cancer, and the Aging Process." *University of California at Berkeley Wellness Letter* 8 (10)(Oct. 1991): 4–5.
23. *New England Journal of Medicine* 330 (1994): 1029, 1080.
24. Smith, A., quoted in "We're Still Taking Our Beta-Carotene." *University of California at Berkeley Wellness Letter* 10 (10)(July 1994): 1–2.
25. "We're Still Taking Our Beta-Carotene." *University of California at Berkeley Wellness Letter* 10 (10)(July 1994): 2.
26. Bendich, A., and Olson, J. A. "Biological Actions of Carotenoids." *Federation of American Societies for Experimental Biology Journal* 3 (8)(1989): 127–132; N. Potischman et al. "Breast Cancer and Dietary Plasma Concentrations of Carotenoids and Vitamin A." *American Journal of Clinical Nutrition* 52 (5)(1990): 909–915; Willet, W. C. "Vitamin A and Lung Cancer." *Nutrition Reviews* 48 (5)(1990): 201–211; Ziegler, R. G. "A Review of Epidemiologic Evidence That Carotenoids Reduce the Risk of Cancer." *Journal of Nutrition* 119 (1989): 116–122; Scala, J. *Prescription for Longevity* (New York: Dutton, 1992): 126–127.
27. J. E. Manson et al. "Baseline Characteristics of Participants in the Physician's Health Study: A Randomized Trial of Aspirin and Beta-Carotene in U. S. Physicians." *American Journal of Preventive Medicine* 7 (3)(1991): 150–154.
28. Cooper, K. H., quoted in *USA Today* feature article on nutritional supplements (Mar. 25, 1994): 4D.
29. Hendler. *Vitamin and Mineral Encyclopedia*: 48.
30. J. E. Enstrom et al. "Vitamin C Intake and Mortality among a Sample of the United States Population." *Epidemiology* 3 (1992): 194–202.
31. Enstrom, J. Comments cited in "Health: Live Longer with Vitamin C." *Newsweek* (May 8, 1992).
32. Fisher, H. "Nutrition in Your Life." *Prevention* (May 1987): 123–124.
33. Alabaster O. *The Power of Prevention: Reduce Your Risk of Cancer through Diet and Nutrition* (New York: Simon & Schuster, 1985): 153–154.
34. Hendler. *Vitamin and Mineral Encyclopedia*: 93.
35. Cooper, K. H., quoted in *USA Today* feature article on nutritional supplements (Mar. 25, 1994): 4D.

36. E. B. Rimm et al. "Vitamin E Consumption and the Risk of Coronary Disease in Men." *New England Journal of Medicine* 328 (20) (May 20, 1993): 1450–1456; M. J. Stampfer et al. "Vitamin E Consumption and the Risk of Coronary Disease in Women." *New England Journal of Medicine* 328 (20) (May 20, 1993): 1444–1449; "Vitamin E." *University of Texas Health Science Center Lifetime Health Letter* 3 (3)(Mar. 1991); Smith, S. M. "Vitamin E Lives Up to Its Image as Protective Nutrient." *Environmental Nutrition* 12 (1): 1–2; Lloyd, J. K. "The Importance of Vitamin E in Human Nutrition." *Acta. Paediatrica Scandinavia* 79 (1)(1990): 6–11; Bendich, A., and Machlin, L. J. "Safety of Oral Intake of Vitamin E." *American Journal of Clinical Nutrition* 48 (1988): 612–619.

37. Rimm et al. "Vitamin E Consumption and the Risk of Coronary Disease in Men": 1450–1456; Stampfer et al. "Vitamin E Consumption and the Risk of Coronary Disease in Women": 1444–1449.

38. "Research News: Vitamin E Prevents 'Good' LDLs from Turning 'Bad.'" *Environmental Nutrition* 16 (4)(Apr. 1993): 8.

39. Hendler. *Anti-Aging Nutrients*: 127.

40. Hendler. *Vitamin and Mineral Encyclopedia*: 107.

41. Alabaster. *The Power of Prevention*: 158–159.

42. "Our Vitamin Prescription: The Big Four." *University of California at Berkeley Wellness Letter* 10 (4)(Jan. 1994): 5.

43. Castleman, M. *An Aspirin a Day: What You Can Do to Prevent Heart Attack, Stroke, and Cancer* (New York: Hyperion, 1993); Graedon, J., and Ferguson, T. *The Aspirin Handbook: A User's Guide to the Breakthrough Drug of the '90s* (New York: Bantam, 1993).

CHAPTER 18

1. Evarts, E. V. "Brain Mechanisms in Voluntary Movements." *Scientific American* (Sept. 1979): 164–179; Ehrenberg, M., and Ehrenberg, O. *Optimum Brain Power* (New York: Dodd, Mead, and Company, 1985): 223–224; Winter, A., and Winter, R. *Build Your Brain Power* (New York: St. Martin's Press, 1986): 47–63.

2. Solveborn, S. A. *The Book about Stretching* (New York: Japan Publications, 1985): 19.

3. For further details on various forms of flexibility exercise, see: Cooper, R. K. *Health and Fitness Excellence* (Boston: Houghton Mifflin, 1989).

4. Sharkey, B. J. *Physiology of Exercise* (Champaign, Ill: Human Kinetics, 1984): 63.

5. To learn more, see: Cooper. *Health and Fitness Excellence.*

6. Ibid.

7. Allison, T., quoted in *Prevention* (Dec. 1991): 94–99.

8. To learn more, see: Cooper. *Health and Fitness Excellence.*

9. Corbin, C. B., and Lindsey, R. *The Ultimate Fitness Book* (Champaign, Ill.: Leisure Press, 1984); Pollock, M. L., Wilmore, J. H., and Fox, S. M. *Exercise in Health and Disease* (Philadelphia: W. B. Saunders, 1984): 278.

10. Kraus, H. *Clinical Treatment of Back and Neck Pain* (New York: McGraw-Hill, 1970): 64–65; Daniels, L., and Worthingham, C. *Therapeutic Exercise for Body Alignment and Function* (Philadelphia: W. B. Saunders, 1977): 69.

11. Solveborn. *Stretching*: 20.

12. Daniels and Worthingham. *Therapeutic Exercise*: 58

13. Pollock, M. L., Wilmore, J. H., and Fox, S. M. *Exercise in Health and Disease* (Philadelphia: W. B. Saunders, 1984): 278; Borysenko, J. *Minding the Body, Mending the Mind* (Reading, Mass.: Addison-Wesley, 1987): 77.

14. Solveborn. *Stretching*: 20.

CHAPTER 19

1. Cailliet, R., and Gross, L. *The Rejuvenation Factor* (Garden City, N.Y.: Doubleday, 1987): 3–5.
2. Cailliet and Gross. *Rejuvenation*: 62; Hanna, T. *Somatics* (Reading, Mass.: Addison-Wesley, 1988); Heller, J., and Henkin, W. A. *Bodywise* (Los Angeles: J. P. Tarcher, 1986).
3. "Don't Be Slack about Good Posture." *University of California at Berkeley Wellness Letter* (Oct. 1986): 6.
4. Roach, M. "Do You Fit into Your Office?" *Hippocrates/In Health* (July/Aug. 1989): 44.
5. Imrie, D., with Dimson, C. *Good-Bye to Backache* (New York: Fawcett, 1983): 128–129.
6. Warfel, J. H. *The Head, Neck, and Trunk*, 4th ed. (Philadelphia: Lea & Febiger, 1973): 46.
7. Binder, T. *Position Technic: The Science of Centering* (Boulder, Colo.: Binder, 1977).
8. Barlow, W., quoted in *Somatics* (Spring/Summer, 1987): 11.
9. V. Bhatnager et al. "Posture, Postural Discomfort, and Performance." *Human Factors* 27 (2)(Apr. 1985): 189–199; "Remedies for a Painful Case of Terminal-itis." *U. S. News and World Report* (Jan. 9, 1989): 60–61; Cailliet and Gross. *Rejuvenation*: 52–54; Grandjean, E. *Fitting the Task to the Man*, 4th ed. (London: Taylor and Francis, 1991): 11; Migdow, J. A., and Loehr, J. E. *Take a Deep Breath* (New York: Villard, 1986): 97. Kraus, H. *Backache, Stress and Tension* (New York: Pocket Books, 1969): 40; Imrie. *Good-Bye to Backache*: 128–129; Astrand, P. O., and Rodahl, K. *Textbook of Work Physiology: Physiological Bases of Exercise* (New York: McGraw-Hill, 1986): 112; Hanna, T. *The Body of Life* (New York: Knopf, 1980).
10. Riskind, J. H., and Gotay, C. C. "Physical Posture: Could It Have Regulatory or Biofeedback Effects on Motivation and Emotion?" *Motivation and Emotion* 6 (3)(1982): 273–298; Weisfeld, G. E., and Beresford, J. M. "Erectness of Posture as an Indicator of Dominance or Success in Humans." *Motivation and Emotion* 6 (2)(1982): 113–131; Wilson, E., and Schneider, C. "Static and Dynamic Feedback in the Treatment of Chronic Muscle Pain." Paper presented at the Biofeedback Society of America meeting (New Orleans, Apr. 16, 1985); Winter, A., and Winter, R. *Build Your Brain Power* (New York: St. Martin's Press, 1986); *The Neuropsychology of Achievement* (Newark, Calif.: Sybervision Systems, Inc., 1985).
11. Cailliet and Gross. *Rejuvenation*: 56.
12. Heller and Henkin. *Bodywise*: 92; Cailliet and Gross. *Rejuvenation*: 56.
13. Riskind and Gotay. "Physical Posture."
14. V. Bhatnager et al. "Posture, Posture Discomfort, and Performance." *Human Factors* 27 (2)(Apr. 1985): 189–199.
15. Hanna. *Somatics*: xii-xiii.
16. Cailliet and Gross. *Rejuvenation*: 64–65.
17. Barker, S. *The Alexander Technique* (New York: Bantam, 1978): 24.
18. Cailliet and Gross. *Rejuvenation*: 86–87.
19. Ibid.: 127.
20. Gould, N. "Back-Pocket Sciatica." *New England Journal of Medicine* 290 (1974): 633.
21. Lettvin, M. *Maggie's Back Book* (Boston: Houghton Mifflin, 1976): 131.
22. Heller and Henkin. *Bodywise*: 43.

CHAPTER 20

1. Travell, J. G., and Simons, D. G. *Myofascial Pain*: 5. Drs. Travell and Simons are co-authors of *Myofascial Pain and Dysfunction: The Trigger Point Manual*, vol. I and II. (Baltimore: Williams and Wilkins, vol. I: 1983; vol. II: 1992).

2. A. E. Sola et al. "Incidence of Hypersensitive Areas in Posterior Shoulder Muscles." *American Journal of Physical Medicine* 34 (1955): 585–590.

3. G. H. Kraft et al. "The Fibrositis Syndrome." *Archives of Physical Medicine and Rehabilitation* 49 (1968): 155–162.

4. Travell and Simons. *Myofascial Pain*: 13.

5. The standard medical text in this field is Travell and Simons, *Myofascial Pain*. These highly technical manuals, complete with several thousand scientific and medical references, are the result of decades of research by the authors and are strongly endorsed by the author of the foreword to the first volume, Dr. Rene Cailliet, professor and former chairman of the Department of Physical Medicine and Rehabilitation at the University of Southern California School of Medicine. Several studies on myofascial pain and dysfunction include: Simons, D. G. "Myofascial Pain Syndromes." *Archives of Physical Medicine and Rehabilitation* 65 (9)(Sept. 1984): 561; Simons. D. G. "Myofascial Pain Syndromes: Where Are We? Where Are We Going?" *Archives of Physical Medicine and Rehabilitation* 69 (3) (Pt. 1)(Mar. 1988): 207–212; Simons, D. G. "Familial Fibromyalgia and/or Myofascial Pain Syndrome?" *Archives of Physical Medicine and Rehabilitation* 71 (3)(Mar. 1990): 258–259; Simons, D. G. "Trigger Point Origin of Musculoskeletal Chest Pain" *Southern Medical Journal* 83 (2)(Feb. 1990): 262–263; Smythe, H. "Referred Pain and Tender Points." *American Journal of Medicine* 81 (3A)(Sept. 29, 1986): 7–14; Fisher, A. A. "Documentation of Myofascial Trigger Points." *Archives of Physical Medicine and Rehabilitation* 69 (4)(Apr. 1988): 286–291; Mennell, J. "Myofascial Trigger Points as a Cause of Headaches." *Journal of Manipulative and Physiological Therapeutics* 11 (2)(Apr. 1989): 63–64; Friction, J. R. "Myofascial Pain Syndrome." *Neurological Clinics* 7 (2)(May 1989): 413–427; Campbell, S. M. "Regional Myofascial Pain Syndromes." *Rheumatic Diseases Clinics of North America* 15 (10(Feb. 1989): 31–44.

6. Travell and Simons. *Myofascial Pain*: 18.

7. Linchitz, R. M. *Life without Pain* (Reading, Mass.: Addison-Wesley, 1987): 3.

8. Ibid.

9. Matteson, M. T., and Ivancevich, J. M. *Controlling Work Stress: Effective Human Resource and Management Strategies* (San Francisco: Josey-Bass, 1987): 6; M. S. Linet et al. "An Epidemiological Study of Headache." *Journal of the American Medical Association* 261 (15)(Apr. 21, 1989): 2211–2216.

10. Monmaney, T. "Bouncing Back from Bad Backs." *Newsweek* (Oct. 24, 1988): 69; Zamula, E. "Back Talk: Advice for Suffering Spines." *FDA Consumer* (Apr. 1989): 28–35.

11. Zamula. "Back Talk": 28.

12. R. Haynes et al. "Increased Absenteeism from Work after Detection and Labeling of Hypertensive Patients." *New England Journal of Medicine* 299 (14)(1978: 741–744.

13. Travell and Simons. *Myofascial Pain*: 31.

14. To learn more, see: Cooper, R. K. *The Performance Edge* (Boston: Houghton Mifflin, 1991).

15. Referred to as *ischemic compression* in Travell and Simons. *Myofascial Pain and Dysfunction*: 87.

CHAPTER 21

1. Ornstein, R. *The Evolution of Consciousness* (New York: Prentice-Hall, 1991).

2. Diamond, M. C. *Enriching Heredity: The Impact of the Environment on the Anatomy of the Brain* (New York: Free Press, 1988); Winter, A., and Winter, R. *Build Your Brain Power* (New York: St. Martin's Press, 1986).

3. Ackerman, D. *A Natural History of the Senses* (New York: Random House, 1990): xviii.

4. Halleck, R. *The Education of the Nervous System* (New York: Macmillan, 1901).
5. Diamond, M. C. *Enriching Heredity: The Impact of Environment on the Anatomy of the Brain* (New York: Free Press, 1988).
6. Holton, G., ed. "Albert Einstein Autobiographical Notes," in *Albert Einstein: Philosopher-Scientist*, ed. and trans. by P. A. Schilpp (Evanston, Ill.: Library of Living Philosophers, 1949); Erikson, J. M. *Wisdom and the Senses* (New York: Norton, 1988): 30–33.
7. Erikson, E. H. *Psychoanalytic Reflections of Einstein's Centenary* (Princeton, N.J.: Princeton University Press, 1982).
8. Diamond. *Enriching Heredity*: 114.
9. Kaplan, R. "The Role of Nature in the Context of the Workplace." *Landscape and Urban Planning* 26 (1993): 193–201; Ulrich, R. S. "Natural versus Urban Scenes: Some Physiological Effects." *Environment and Behavior* 13 (5)(1981): 523–556; Ulrich, R. S. "View through a Window May Influence Recovery from Surgery." *Science* 224 (4647)(1984): 420–421.
10. Justice, B. *Who Gets Sick?* (Los Angeles: J. P. Tarcher, 1988): 262.
11. *Mental Medicine Update* 2 (2)(Fall, 1993).
12. Ornstein, R., and Sobel, D. *Healthy Pleasures* (Reading, Mass.: Addison-Wesley, 1989): 53
13. Ulrich, R. S. "Human Responses to Vegetation and Landscapes." *Landscape and Urban Planning* 13 (1986): 29–44.
14. Houston, J. *The Possible Human* (Los Angeles: J. P. Tarcher, 1982): 32.
15. Erickson, J. M. "Vital Senses: Sources of Lifelong Learning." *Journal of Education* 167 (3)(1985).
16. Justice, B. *Who Gets Sick? Thinking and Health* (Houston: Peak Press, 1987): 259.
17. Diamond, M. C. *How the Brain Grows in Response to Experience* (Series on the Healing Brain Cassette Recording No. T55; Los Altos, Calif.: Institute for the Study of Human Knowledge, 1983); *Brain/Mind Bulletin* 12 (7)(Mar. 1987): 1–5; S. Kiyono et al. *Physiology and Behavior* 34: 431–435; Hwang, H. M., and Greenough, W. T. Paper presented at the annual meeting of the Society for Neuroscience (1986).
18. Rivlin, R., and Gravelle, K. *Deciphering the Senses: The Expanding World of Human Perception* (New York: Simon & Schuster, 1984).
19. Winter, A., and Winter, R. *Build Your Brain Power* (New York: St. Martin's Press, 1986): 17.
20. To learn more, see: Cooper, R. K. *Health and Fitness Excellence* (Boston: Houghton Mifflin, 1989).
21. Weaver, R. A. "Characteristics of Circadian Rhythms in Human Functions." *Journal of Neural Transmission* 21 (Supp.)(1986): 351; C. A. Czeisler et al. "Bright Light Induction of Strong (Type O) Resetting of the Human Circadian Pacemaker." *Science* 244 (1989): 1328–1333; Czeisler, C. A. "Biological Rhythm Disorders, Depression, and Phototherapy: A New Hypothesis." *Psychiatric Clinics of North America* 10 (4)(Dec. 1987): 699; I. McIntyre et al. *Life Sciences* 45 (1990): 327–332; *Brain/Mind Bulletin* (Jan. 1990): 7.
22. Thomas, L., quoted in *Vis-a-Vis* (Apr. 1988): 28.
23. Kallan, C. "Probing the Power of Common Scents." *Prevention* (Oct. 1991): 39–43.
24. Van Toller, S., and Dodd, G. H. *Perfumery: The Psychology and Biology of Fragrance* (London: Chapman and Hall, 1991); Kallan, C. "Probing the Power of Common Scents." *Los Angeles Times* (May 13, 1991); "24th Japanese Symposium on Taste and Smell: 64 Scientific Studies." *Chemical Senses* 16 (2)(1991): 181–208; "Renaissance of Fragrance." *Age of Tomorrow* 113 (Dec. 1989).
25. Dember, W., and Warm, J. University of Cincinnati studies, reported at a meeting of the American Association for the Advancement of Science (Washington, D. C., Jan. 1991).

26. Torii, S. *The Futurist* (Sept./Oct. 1990): 50.
27. Baron, R. A. Research paper presented at the annual meeting of the American Psychological Association. In *USA Today* (August 14, 1992).
28. Baron, R. A. Research cited in *The Futurist* (Sept./Oct. 1990): 50.
29. Tomatis, A. A. *The Conscious Ear* (Barrytown, N.Y.: Station Hill Press, 1991); T. M. Gilmor et al. *About the Tomatis Method* (Toronto, Ontario, Canada: The Listening Centre, 1989).
30. Gilmor et al. *The Tomatis Method*: 11.
31. Rosenfeld, A. H. "Music: The Beautiful Disturber." *Psychology Today* (Dec. 1985): 48–56; Karsh, S., and Merle-Fishman, C. *The Music within You* (New York: Simon & Schuster, 1985); Hodges, A., ed. *Handbook of Music Psychology* (Dubuque, Iowa: Kendall-Hunt, 1985).
32. M. S. Rider et al. "The Effect of Music, Imagery, and Relaxation on Adrenal Corticosteroids." *Journal of Music Therapy* 22 (1)(1985): 46–58; Ryder, M. S., and Achterberg, J. "The Effect of Music-Mediated Imagery on Neutrophils and Lymphocytes." Unpublished manuscript, 1987.
33. "The Musical Brain." *U. S. News and World Report* (June 11, 1990): 55–62.
34. Ackerman. *Natural History of the Senses*: 209.
35. G. Rochberg, quoted in Ackerman, *Natural History of the Senses*: 212.
36. Winter and Winter. *Build Your Brain Power*: 30.
37. Lynch, J. J. *The Broken Heart* (New York: Basic Books, 1979).
38. "Accounting for Taste." *University of California at Berkeley Wellness Letter* 7 (2)(Nov. 1990): 7.

CHAPTER 22

1. Gilbert, S. "Noise Pollution." *Science Digest* (Mar. 1985): 28.
2. "Full Sun Protection." *University of California at Berkeley Wellness Letter* 9 (9)(June 1993): 4–5.
3. "Neglecting Your Ears Can Be Deadly." *University of Texas Health Science Center Lifetime Health Letter* 4 (4)(Apr. 1992): 2.
4. Lasden, M. "Sunblock Bingo." *Hippocrates* (July/Aug. 1987): 86.
5. *FDA Consumer* (June 1987): 21–23.
6. Young, R. W. "Solar Radiation and Age-Related Macular Degeneration." *Survey of Ophthalmology* 32 (1988): 252–269.
7. F. S. Rosenthal et al. "The Effect of Prescription Eyewear on Ocular Exposure to Ultraviolet Radiation." *American Journal of Public Health* 76 (10)(Oct. 1986): 1216–1220.
8. Liebmann-Smith, R. "The Man Who Patented Sunlight." *American Health* (Dec. 1985): 33–35; Kunz-Bircher, R. *The Bircher-Benner Health Guide* (Santa Barbara, Calif.: Woodbridge, 1980): 66; Lillyquist, M. J. *Sunlight and Health: The Positive and Negative Effects of the Sun on You* (New York: Dodd, Mead, 1985); Kime, Z. R. *Sunlight Could Save Your Life* (Penryn, Calif.: World Health Publications, 1980); Hollwich, F. *The Influence of Ocular Light Perception on Metabolism in Man and in Animal* (New York: Springer-Verlag, 1979); Okudaira et al. *American Journal of Physiology* 254 (1983): R613–615.
9. Holick, M. F., quoted in *Prevention* (Mar. 1986): 122–123; Holick, M. F. *Journal of Clinical Endocrinology and Metabolism* (1987).
10. "How Today's Noise Hurts Body and Mind." *Medical World News* (June 13, 1969): 42–43.
11. Perl, J. *Sleep Right in Five Nights* (New York: Morrow, 1993): 231–232.

12. "Over 50? Chances Are You Need More Vitamin D." *University of Texas Health Science Center Lifetime Health Letter* 8 (4)(June 1990): 2.
13. Ibid.
14. D. T. Villareal et al. "Subclinical Vitamin D Deficiency in Postmenopausal Women." *Journal of Endocrinology and Metabolism* 72 (3)(Mar. 1991): 628–634.
15. Kligman, A., quoted in "Okun, S. "Facing Your Future." *Health* (Apr. 1992): 28–29.
16. Safranek, M. D. "Effect of Auditory Rhythm on Muscle Reactivity." *Physical Therapy* (Feb. 1982): 161–188.
17. Halpern, S., and Savary, L. *Sound Health* (New York: Harper & Row, 1985): 31–40.
18. Westman, J. C., quoted in Halpern and Savary. *Sound Health*: 31–40.

CHAPTER 23

1. Rice, F. "Do You Work in a Sick Building?" *Fortune* (July 2, 1990): 86–88; "EPA: Pollution Higher Indoors." *USA Today* (Sept. 11, 1986).
2. "American Heart Association: Passive Smoke Seen as Environmental Toxin and Major Risk Factor for Heart Disease." *USA Today* (June 11, 1992); "EPA Panel: Passive Smoke Toxic." *USA Today* (July 23, 1992); "Poison at Home and at Work." *Newsweek* (June 29, 1992): 55.
3. Shabecoff, P. "Issue of Radon Peril: New National Focus on Ecology." *New York Times* (Sept. 10, 1986); Eckholm, E. "Radon: Threat Is Real." *New York Times* (Sept. 2, 1986).
4. Shabecoff. "Radon Peril"; Eckholm. "Radon."
5. Becker, R. O. *CrossCurrents* (Los Angeles: J. P. Tarcher, 1990); Baranski, S., and Czerski, P. *Biological Effects of Microwaves* (Stroudsburg, Pa.: Dowden, Hutchinson, and Ross, 1976); Samuels, M., and Bennett, H. Z. *Well Body, Well Earth* (San Francisco: Sierra Club, 1984): 122; Coghill, R. *Electropollution: How to Protect Yourself against It* (London: Thorsons, 1990).
6. Adey, W. R. "Tissue Interactions with Non-Ionizing Electromagnetic Fields." *Physiological Review* 61 (1981): 435–514; Singer, S. J., and Nicholson, G. L. "The Fluid Mosaic Model of the Structure of Cell Membranes." *Science* 175 (1972): 720–731; M. T. Marron et al. "Mytotic Delay in Heterokaryons and Decreased Respiration." *Experientia* 24 (1978): 589–590; M. T. Marron et al. "Cell Surface Effects of 60-Hz Electromagnetic Fields." *Radiation Research* 94 (1983): 217–220; Hansson, H. A. "Lamellar Bodies in Purkinje Nerve Cells Experimentally Induced by Electric Field." *Brain Research* 216 (1981): 187–191. Bawin, S., and Adey, W. "Sensitivity of Calcium Binding in Cerebral Tissue to Weak Environmental Electrical Fields Oscillating at Low Frequency." *Proceedings of the National Academy of Sciences U. S. A.* 73 (1976): 1999; Wiltschko, W., and Wiltschko, R. "Magnetic Compass of European Robins." *Science* 176 (1972): 62; Larkin, R. P., and Southerland, P. J. "Migrating Birds Respond to Project Seafarers's Electromagnetic Field." *Science* 195 (1977): 777; Samuels and Bennett. *Well Earth*: 125.
7. J. L. Phillips et al. "Transferrin Binding to Two Human Carcinoma Cell Lines: Characterization and Effect of 60-Hz Electromagnetic Fields." *Cancer Research* 46 (1986): 239–244; Winters, W. D. "Biological Functions of Immunologically Reactive Human and Canine Cells Influenced by *in vitro* Exposure to 60-Hz Electric and Magnetic Fields (1986)," cited in A. Ahlbom et al. "Biological Effects of Power Line Fields, New York State Power Lines Project Scientific Advisory Panel Final Report." *State of New York Department of Health* (July 1, 1987).
8. H. Konig et al. *Biological Effects of Environmental Electromagnetism* (New York: Springer-Verlag, 1981): 218.
9. Chafetz, M. D. *Smart for Life* (New York: Penguin, 1992): 59–61.

10. "Growing Evidence for Aluminum/Alzheimer's Link." *Clinical Psychiatry News* (Dec. 1988): 2; Jackson et al. "Aluminum from a Coffee Pot." *Lancet* 1 (1989): 781–782; A. B. Graves et al. "The Association between Aluminum-Containing Products and Alzheimer's Disease." *Journal of Clinical Epidemiology* 43 (1)(1990): 35–44; G. Farrar et al. "Defective Gallium-Transferrin Binding in Alzheimer's Disease and Down Syndrome: A Possible Mechanism for Accumulation of Aluminum in the Brain." *Lancet* 335 (1990): 747–750; C. N. Martyn et al. "Geographical Relation between Alzheimer's Disease and Aluminum in Drinking Water." *Lancet* 1 (1989): 59–62; Birchall, J. D., and Chappell, J. S. "Aluminum, Water Chemistry, and Alzheimer's Disease." *Lancet* 1 (1989): 953.
11. "Formaldehyde: Assessment of Health Effects." National Academy of Sciences Commission on Toxicology (Mar. 1980): vi; Fawcett, S. "Formaldehyde: If It Smells, Watch Out!" *Medical Self-Care* (Summer 1984): 21–23.
12. Waldbott, G. L. *Health Effects of Environmental Pollutants*, 2nd ed. (St. Louis: C. V. Mosby, 1978): 256.
13. "Electromagnetic Fields." *Consumer Reports* (May 1994): 354–359.
14. "Danger from a Glowing Screen." *U. S. News and World Report* (June 18, 1990): 76; Special Report. *Macworld* (July 1990); Poch, D. I. *Radiation Alert* (Garden City, N.Y.: Doubleday, 1985); DeMatteo, P. *Terminal Shock: The Health Hazards of Video Display Terminals* (Toronto: NC Press Ltd., 1985).
15. "Are Electric Blankets Safe?" *Consumer Reports* (Nov. 1989): 715–716.
16. Becker, R. O. *CrossCurrents* (Los Angeles: J. P. Tarcher, 1990): 269–278.
17. Ibid.: 278.
18. *Western Journal of Medicine* 146 (1986): 1.
19. Chafetz. *Smart for Life*: 60–61.
20. Dadd, D. L. *The Nontoxic Home* (Los Angeles: J. P. Tarcher, 1986): 17.

PART V

LOVE FITNESS: IMPROVING YOUR EMOTIONAL HEALTH, INTIMACY AND SEX

LOVE FITNESS

A Special Introduction

Few people recognize how out of shape they are when it comes to intimate communication and therefore their ability to love. When communication in a relationship begins to sour, bigger problems are not far off. Love Fitness helps you avoid or reverse emotional damage that erodes love, friendship and work relationships. The key is to stop repeating past emotional mistakes. Love Fitness can prevent further problems in a relationship just as physical fitness can prevent chronic disease.

Over the past decades, there has been a resurgence of interest in fitness. Many people now recognize that the rewards of getting in shape, improving diet and giving up destructive habits, such as smoking or excessive drinking, far outweigh the effort and sacrifice required. So too, we are confident that the time has come for people to apply the same principles of self-improvement to their relationships.

There is much you can accomplish with the right emotional workouts to make the changes you desire, both in how you respond to your lover and how he or she responds to you. Great relationships are created, not simply found!

There are certain additional parallels worth noting between the Love Fitness program and a physical fitness program. First and foremost, Love Fitness is intended to develop emotional strength. Too many people feel defeated and discouraged about their ability to create vibrant relationships. The emotional workouts we describe are aimed at enabling each person in a relationship to take 100 percent responsibility for the quality of the relationship. Blaming and complaining are out! Love Fitness also develops emotional grace, the ability to accept other people's strengths and limitations. The intense enjoyment of true heart-to-heart communications replaces the idealized effort to make another person into something he or she is not. Love Fitness also develops emotional vitality. If you are bored in your relationship, one of the problems may be that you have let yourself become boring. The same holds true for your lover, friends and co-workers. We describe emo-

Everything that lives

lives not alone,

not for itself.

—**William Blake,**
British poet

tional workouts to escape from that trap. Finally, Love Fitness develops emotional agility and timing. You learn when to confront and when to hold back and how to express strong feelings, such as anger or rage, in effective rather than destructive ways.

In exploring Love Fitness, we uncovered four basic misconceptions about personal growth, each of which can make the whole process unnecessarily laborious and complicated. Changing these misconceptions is the first step toward taking full charge of your personal relationships.

#1: Psychological growth is a mysterious process of gaining insight. Perhaps the most common myth about psychological growth is that it is intricate, unconscious and mysterious. We never cease to be amazed at how pervasive the idea has become that psychological growth requires a search for repressed childhood traumas that, when recognized, will bring sudden insight and transformation. For most people, psychological development just does not happen that way. This myth is often destructive because it reinforces a magical expectation that relationship problems can be solved through a search for a Holy Grail of "in-depth" psychological insight.

The fact is that poor modeling, rather than emotional trauma, is responsible for most problems in relationships. Whether the issue is an inability to make a commitment, express anger or reveal intimate feelings, the problem can be traced to poor emotional habits developed during childhood. Few people have grown up in families where the basic communication skills necessary for creating vibrant love relationships were modeled. Most people with problems in their relationships are basically mature and emotionally healthy. The problem is usually not some deep psychological disorder but rather a simple lack of emotional strengths and communication skills.

Deep psychological insight does not have to precede behavior change; on the contrary, change most often precedes insight! The whole process can thus be accelerated, and you can look back and see why and how you were locked into emotional patterns that were not beneficial.

#2: Psychological development requires lengthy investigation to reveal "what's wrong." One of the most dangerous misperceptions about psychological development is that a person is more deeply and thoroughly served through three or four sessions of psychotherapy a week. The fact is that such a practice is just as likely to be destructive as it is to be helpful. For most people, a lengthy examination of their personal problems just makes them more preoccupied with those problems and reinforces a fear that there is something deeply wrong with them.

A key principle about psychological development: *What you put your attention on in life grows stronger.* For example, if you place attention on successes rather than failures, your self-esteem will grow stronger. Similarly, placing attention on negative feelings you may have about yourself or problems you may have in your relationships is likely to cause those bad feelings and problems to dominate your awareness. The more you think there is something deeply wrong, the more your problems will persist. Low self-esteem decreases your capacity to love and be loved, thus perpetuating a vicious cycle.

There will always be "reasons" why you've developed emotional habits that don't serve you, and an inventory of reasons alone will not help empower you to change. Love Fitness focuses your attention on "stretching"—expanding your emotional strengths and intimacy skills.

#3: The right therapist or seminar will provide the answers. The boom in psychotherapy and personal development seminars has created a new myth. Some people seem to believe that if they just keep hopping from one psychotherapist or personal growth seminar to another, they will eventually find one that will give them the ultimate key to happiness. On the one hand, competent therapy and good seminars can be valuable. On the other hand, becoming a therapy or seminar "junkie" reinforces the myth that someone else can do it for you.

Love Fitness is based on the premise that the greatest therapist lies within. Your body has enormous physical regenerative abilities: Just think of the healing energy it mobilizes to mend a broken bone. That same healing and regenerative capacity exists emotionally.

A fundamental premise of Love Fitness is that only you can change your emotional habits. Even the most skilled therapist or seminar leader or the best self-help book can only assist in identifying what emotional habits are not serving you and suggest appropriate skills and exercises to learn new emotional and communication skills. Ultimately you alone are responsible for your personal development. In some cases, this responsibility means finding the right therapist as a consultant.

#4: Psychological growth involves pain and turmoil. This is the most damaging misperception. Many people believe that challenging their emotional status quo may involve pain or the risk of unacceptable emotional turmoil. Love Fitness shatters this myth. Physical workouts can involve effort, but they can also be a source of fun, excitement, energy and even pleasure. Likewise, many of the emotional workouts that constitute Love Fitness are enjoyable. They will expand your emotional horizons and help you gain a new perspective on yourself and others.

ANGER WORKOUTS

Quick, Healthy Ways to Manage Anger and Defuse Hostility

We boil at different degrees.
—**Ralph Waldo Emerson**, American essayist and poet

*A*nger and hostility can kill.[1] When you chronically lose your cool, you lose your perspective, your health and eventually maybe even your life. We aren't referring to the anger that provokes some people to beat, stab or shoot others. Instead, we're talking about the everyday kind of anger, annoyance, irritation and hostility that runs through the heart and mind of the average person. If you're quick to blame or feel anger when faced with everyday delays and frustrations—waiting in line, slow-poke drivers, lethargic elevators, rude teenagers—and if this blaming flashes into heated irritation and the urge (controlled or not) to take aggressive action, then getting angry can be like taking a small dose of *slow-acting poison*, and chances are, it will eventually destroy your relationships and harm your health.[2] These are two of the reasons that we decided to put this chapter at the beginning of the section on "Love Fitness." Healthy anger workout skills are a key to enduring, loving relationships. In fact, without effective anger-management capabilities, most other relationship-building efforts never get off the ground.

Anger may be defined as the thoughts, feelings, physical reactions and actions that result from a blame-worthy or attack-worthy physical, emotional or mental provocation—"a demeaning offense against me and mine."[3] In many cases, anger is a straight track to *hostility*, the expression of aggression or even attack. It's essential to point out that anger is certainly an instinctive and normal emotion, *and sometimes anger is highly adaptive and reflective of a healthy sense of indignation.* Assertively speaking out against attacks or transgressions against your personal beliefs and values can be warranted and healthy. Feeling anger and rage when defending yourself against a violent physical assault can be both necessary and justified.

However, the problem arises when anger occurs frequently, is triggered by very minor hassles or perceived slights and is *chronically mismanaged*—leading to feelings or reactions of hostility. For years, researchers have known that mismanaged anger and hostility can contribute to high blood pressure and the risk of sudden cardiac death (an unexpected fatal heart attack).[4] Marital discord is strongly correlated to depression.[5] And there may be a link between anger, or helplessness, and certain forms of cancer.[6] Perhaps worst of all, anger is the emotion that tends to fuel violence.

In a recent study published in *Psychosomatic Medicine*, researchers noted that in married couples, angry or hostile behaviors—including criticizing, blaming, denying responsibility, making excuses and frequent interruptions during dialogue—were linked to increased blood pressure and heart rate and a fall-off in immune response.[7] Women were even more likely to show negative immunological changes than men. According to this study, dealing *effectively* with anger and conflict is a key to a healthy relationship and your physical and mental health. Tragically, over a lifetime, many of us wreck dozens, perhaps hundreds, of relationships in the heat of runaway anger.[8] As a group, hostile people are unhappy people, with more hassles and negative life events and less social support.[9]

Another impact of anger, far subtler but nearly as destructive, is that a climate of unmanaged anger—and violent arguments—between parents is the most disturbing and depressing event that children witness. Studies suggest that when parents chronically or frequently fight—not when they *disagree,* but when they *argue* and *verbally fight* each other in anger—their children "become unbridled pessimists."[10] In general, these children see bad events in life as permanent and pervasive, and they see themselves as responsible. Years later, research indicates that, on average, this pessimism persists, even after the parents are no longer fighting. It's time for a change.

> Often the first indication of heart disease is sudden death.
> **—Robert S. Eliot, M.D.,** *From Stress to Strength*

"Our research has shown that intimate partners must learn how to manage their anger and control the exchange of negative behavior by

---

WHEN YOU FIGHT IN FRONT OF THE CHILDREN . . .

The truth is, at one time or another we all fight in front of our children. Fights happen. Solid research suggests that when that happens—despite honestly using the strategies in this chapter to defuse the impact and fight as infrequently as possible—*go through a visible resolution in front of your children.*[14] Children who view films of adults fighting are much less disturbed when the argument ends with a clear resolution in the spirit of friendship. When fights happen—and children are near enough to see or hear—make it a point to *resolve the conflict*, clearly and in front of your children.

---

finding a way to express their feelings in a constructive manner," say Howard Markman, Ph.D., professor of psychology at the University of Denver and director of the Center for Marriage and Family Studies, and Clifford Notarius, Ph.D., professor of psychology at Catholic University in Washington, D.C. "Constructive expression of gripes, criticisms and annoyances is a matter of knowing how to express oneself and *choosing the appropriate time and place for the conversation.*"[11]

Anger has three core components: First, there is a *thought* that you are being trespassed against. Your angry reaction may be launched so rapidly that you fail to notice this mental turning point, but it's always there.[12] "I'm never appreciated." "*Another* delay!" "He never helps; he just complains." "That idiot changed lanes without signaling!" "Why does this *always* happen to me . . ." "Here we go again . . ."

The second component of anger is your *bodily reaction*. Your blood pressure soars; your heart rate accelerates. Your muscles tense up for physical assault. Brain centers go into a warfare mode. And you're swamped with a subjective feeling of anger or hostility.

The third element of anger is the *attack*, which is what the thought and bodily reaction have readied you to make. You lash out, to blame or accuse, in words or body language or with some form of physical aggression. Or, on the other extreme, you struggle to suppress your angry feelings. There are those who say that telling off other people "gets things off your chest," but studies indicate that, rather than relieving aggression, such *anger-out* reactions amplify it, creating more hostility, not less.[13]

POWER ACTION: FIRST OPTION
Use Quick-Checks to Identify
Your Anger "Hot Spots"

Perhaps you already realize that "anger-out" makes things worse, not better. Many of us don't. In the course of a typical day and week, what *specific* kinds of incidents trigger your anger? Injustices? Frustrations or annoyances? Interruptions? Threats to your income? Rush-hour traffic? Rudeness? Discourteous drivers? Waiting in lines? Slow-moving co-workers or employees? Unsolicited romantic advances? Snubbed romantic advances? A partner's anger? Family disagreements? A nagging financial or legal issue? The perception that your spouse or parents or mother-in-law or neighbor is nagging or criticizing you? Does ranting and raving make you feel better or worse? How *long* did the feelings of anger or hostility last? After the incident, do you feel guilty, ashamed or remorseful? Did you accomplish what you wanted? Do others seem to like you more, or less? In short, *what are your patterns of anger?* To gain some valuable insights, for the next week record a daily Anger Log—a sample is given on page 339—and, right now, calculate your Struggle Index score (page 344).

THE HOSTILITY ROADMAP

My Cynical Thought, Angry Feeling, or Aggressive Action:

Is the matter worth my continued attention?

Yes

Am I justified? ⟶ No

Yes

Do I have an effective response?

Yes

By using the Hostility Roadmap on page 337, it's clear to see that we *don't* mean you're never going to have angry feelings, or that you shouldn't—in certain, specific cases—act on those feelings with assertive behavior. At those times when the issue at hand is *not* trivial, your angry thoughts and reasonable actions may indeed be justified. The challenge, however, is to take "reasonable" action, without lashing out, becoming violent or sabotaging your relationships.

With both of these examples, the key point is this: Only when you're clearly *aware* of your own anger and hostility patterns, and your "hot spots" or "triggers," can you effectively choose the tactics to dampen or dissolve your hostile reactions, turning negative emotional energy into something more healthful and constructive. The following strategies complement those in chapter 3.

POWER ACTION: MORE OPTIONS
Become an Emotional A.C.E.:"Own What You're Feeling" and Choose Your Response

Anger is fast and furious. We're primed to accuse or deny, blame or feel victimized. The content of anger, unchecked, is volatile and potentially harmful. More often than ever, in our modern society people say and do things they later regret. Yet the effect of these words and hurtful actions cannot be undone or erased simply by saying, "I'm sorry." When you're provoked to anger, the time between the trigger and your reaction is often extremely brief.

Chances are, when you're upset you tell yourself, "I'm angry *because* that person made a critical remark," or "I'm angry *because* my wife doesn't understand me," or "I'm angry *because* that person cut in front of me in line." The problem is that automatic comments such as these set the blame for feeling angry on something *outside* ourselves. This *perception* forces you to wait to feel better until some outside event happens or someone else changes—and these things are often beyond your control.

When you blame some*one* or some*thing* else for how you're feeling, you give this person or thing the power to cause *your* emotional state. In contrast, if at the first moment you feel yourself getting upset or angry, you pause for 5 seconds, without saying a word, to take

> Every great mistake has a halfway moment, a split second when it may be recalled and perhaps remedied.
>
> **—Pearl S. Buck,** American writer

(continued on page 342)

WHAT TRIGGERS MY ANGER?[15]

Time	Trigger	Intensity	Duration	Action/Sequel
7:25 A.M.	Speeding jerk cut me off on highway.	7 (of 10)	40 min.	Cursed at him and laid on horn. Imagined his car blowing up. Glared at parking attendant. Felt distracted, guilty.
12:05 P.M.	Co-worker late for lunch meeting	9	15 min.	Confronted him. Got apology, dirty look.
12:55	Soda machine broken. Kept my quarters.	8	5 min.	Kicked it. Put in more money and got soda.
5:55	More traffic delays and discourteous drivers.	6	10 min.	Honked. Turned up radio. Ate a cookie. Tuned out stress.
6:45	I find out my son "forgot" to give me a teacher's warning note about missed homework.	9	3 hr.	Blew up. Grounded son. Feelings of incompetence and shame as parent.

POWER KNOWLEDGE: MAKING ANGER WORK FOR YOU

MYTH #1: The best way to deal with anger is to vent it—to yell, rant and rave, and immediately get your feelings out in the open.

POWER KNOWLEDGE: Recent studies report that suppressing anger *and* explosively venting it may both be linked to a death rate (from all causes) that is over two times greater than that related to "reflective coping." Three standard responses to anger are (1) "anger-in"—suppressing your angry feelings altogether; (2) "anger-out"—explosively venting your anger immediately; and (3) "reflective coping"—waiting until tempers have cooled to rationally discuss the conflict with the other person or sort things out on your own. Reflective coping is often the best choice because, as researchers have discovered, it restores a sense of control over the situation and helps resolve it. Those people who kept their cool—who acknowledged their anger but were not openly hostile, physically or verbally—felt better faster and had superior health. While venting anger does relieve tension, it can also contribute to guilt feelings, which become an added source of stress.

MYTH #2: Anger is a *feeling*. What I *think* has nothing to do with it.

POWER KNOWLEDGE: Your brain uses neurochemicals, electrical impulses and trillions of special receptors to spread the influence of your thoughts to every cell in your body. These chemicals change in response to the way we each perceive ourselves and interact with the people and events in our lives. Every pressure triggers a host of questions: Can I handle this? What happens if I can't? What are my options?

Researchers have discovered a number of ways that thinking can distort or magnify the stressful effects of experiences in your life. When you blame yourself for bad events but feel powerless to change them, feelings of distress rise sharply. A pessimistic view of life events makes them more stressful and thus more likely to produce illness.[18] Some researchers call this phenomenon *cognitive distortion*—the automatic, negative thoughts that lead to distress and conflict.[19] Each one encourages and amplifies others. It's easy to end up trapped in a labyrinth of pessimism, and it takes dedication to break out.

"Much of our stress is due to conversations we have with ourselves," explains Robert S. Eliot, M.D., professor of cardiology at the University of Nebraska Medical Center in Omaha and author of *Is It Worth Dying For?* "Unfortunately, we often talk ourselves into the ground. Our mental tapes are always running, and if they are programmed with negative messages, they become a prime cause of stress. . . .

"The result: feelings become heated up and exaggerated; energy that could be used elsewhere gets tied up in self-talks that make life seem hopelessly out of control; and behavior becomes counterproductive and self-defeating as stress carries the day. . . . Replacing certain negative and irrational self-talks with more constructive, helpful ones lets you cultivate a 'thick-skinned' reaction to stress. People who respond in thick-skinned ways pay the minimum psychological and physical price for stress."[20]

MYTH #3: Why should I care if other people are angry? Their feelings don't affect me.

POWER KNOWLEDGE: Like it or not, it is a natural part of human interactions to be affected by the moods and emotions of the people around you. This is sometimes very beneficial—when the feelings are positive and constructive—but it can be very alarming when the emotions are negative and destructive. Contagious emotions, such as depression, create an atmosphere that breeds unending loops of hostility, tension, turmoil and gloom.[21]

"When we begin to share the negative emotions of another person," explains Ronald M. Podell, M.D., assistant clinical professor at UCLA's Neuropsychiatric Institute, "we begin to act differently toward that person, and here's where the destructive forces gather steam. When confronted with the hardships or pessimistic thoughts of another person, it is a natural reaction to feel a threat to your own well-being. . . . A depressed person is 'radioactive' . . . and poses threats to you, threats that cause you to react defensively despite your wishes to be helpful. This, in turn, confuses, frustrates, angers and further depresses your partner, and an emotional interplay very analogous to a nuclear reaction gets in motion. Energy is released— very negative and hurtful energy—which can leave both of you injured, and angrier than ever."[22]

full responsibility for how you feel and respond, it's easier to see how many *choices* you have, and to realize that you can choose *not* to feel like a victim of outside circumstances. To *acknowledge and understand your anger*, you must accept it as a signal that something significant is happening. Transforming your anger requires *responding* in such a way as to express yourself honestly while preserving and nurturing your relationship rather then reacting, arguing and attacking each other. This chapter provides many quick, practical options for accomplishing this.

For some people, acronyms are helpful devices to remember specific skills under pressure. Here's one example of a useful acronym— Emotional A.C.E.—for recalling constructive anger-management skills whenever you feel the first rush of anger.

A: Assess Accurately
C: Choose Constructively
E: Express Effectively

For example:

*A: **Assess Accurately.*** Especially with a loved one, it's easy to assume inaccurately that he or she is angry. Instead, the loved one may be rushed and tense due to the pressures of school or work or accumulated daily hassles. He or she may not actually be anxious or short-tempered. Ask clarifying questions, such as, "I'm sensing that things are tense for you right now, is that right?" "Are you upset with *me* about something? Or is it work . . . or school . . . or . . . ?" It's important to be able to quickly and readily distinguish between everyday stress-related "baggage" and genuine interpersonal anger and to avoid assuming that your loved one *intends* to ignore you or snap at you because of anger at something *you've* done or haven't done. Unfortunately, if you fail to assess things accurately and jump to the conclusion that there's a fight already under way or keep pressing this person for what he or she simply cannot give right then, your pressure itself can be hurtful and trigger an angry reaction. Many anger-generated arguments have little to do with the issues or concerns being discussed. For instance, you and a loved one or friend may quarrel over finances, the children, politics, housecleaning, errands or even your reactions to a recent movie or book. Yet the anger and heated words are often less about the issue being discussed and more about the frustration that comes from a failure to listen and acknowledge each other's needs, feelings and points of view.

C: **Choose Constructively.** Don't say, "Why are you *always*. . . ?"

> If you are patient in one moment of anger, you will avoid a hundred days of sorrow.
>
> **—Tibetan proverb**

or "There you go, getting *angry* again!" Rather say, "Did something at work make you late for . . . ?" Don't say, "That's an ugly, cheap-looking outfit." Rather say, "You are a handsome man (or great-looking woman), and *I* don't happen to like this outfit on you." Don't say, "Get off my back—I hate your guts!" Rather say, "Right now I'm really feeling (upset, stressed, worried) and I'm getting (or I'm not) angry at *you.*"

E: Express Effectively. Stop for a moment *whenever you feel a surge of anger* and ask yourself, "Why am I starting to feel angry, and what, specifically, do I want to change?" Rather than being "right" (and the other person "wrong"), you must be committed to being *effective.* Ask yourself, "How can I best express my anger to get the results I/we want?" Remember, it's essential to *be specific.* For example: "You keep promising to come home for dinner at 7:00, but it's been 7:30 or 8:00 almost every day the past week. Not once did you call to let me know you'd be late. It makes me feel like you don't care, and that hurts; I'm angry." It would have done no good to say, "You make me furious because you're *always* late. You don't love me and you're a selfish, inconsiderate slob!" Effective anger management asks for an acknowledgment of your hurt *and* moves on to a commitment to avoid the same frustrations or mistakes in the future.

Becoming an Emotional A.C.E. is not a competition. Instead, the goal is to make stress and anger into opportunities for you and your lover, for example, or friend, or child, to learn more about each other, to meet each other's needs and to affirm your bond by working out conflicts *together*—in ways that make both of you feel good about the outcomes of interactions that involve anger. This requires skill in expressing your own anger and also acceptance of the other person's anger. Acknowledge and reaffirm each other's efforts to clarify irritations and manage anger effectively.

Practice the three A.C.E. skills. Rehearse imaginary dialogues geared toward specific frustrating situations at work, school or home. Write things down, if that feels helpful to you. Of course, there are many "proper" or "psychologically correct" styles of anger management, and they vary according to the dynamics of each unique relationship.

Take 5 Seconds to Quick-Stop Negative or Distorted Thinking

"But what can I do about it?" many of us ask when anger keeps throwing us off-balance and threatens our relationships. One thing you can do is to change the way you *think* about the events of your life. Nearly all of us tend to make some very *specific* mistakes in thinking—mistakes that make us angry or hostile, that create prob-

THE STRUGGLE INDEX

Indicate how strongly you agree with each of the following statements.

4 = All of the time   3 = Often   2 = Sometimes   1 = Never

_____ I am regularly exhausted by daily demands at work and home.
_____ My stress is caused by outside forces beyond my control.
_____ I am trapped by circumstances that I just have to live with.
_____ No matter how hard I work to stay on top of my schedule, I never feel caught up.
_____ I have financial obligations that I cannot meet.
_____ I dislike my work but cannot take the risk of a career change.
_____ I'm dissatisfied with my personal relationships.
_____ I feel responsible for the happiness of the people around me.
_____ I am embarrassed to ask for help.
_____ I do not know what I really want out of life.
_____ I am disappointed that I have not achieved what I hoped for.
_____ No matter how much external success I have, I feel empty inside.
_____ If the people around me were more competent, I would be happier.
_____ Many people have let me down in the past.
_____ I "stew" in my anger rather than express it.
_____ I become enraged and resentful when I am hurt.
_____ I can't take criticism.
_____ I'm afraid I'll lose my job (home, finances, etc.).
_____ I do not see the value of expressing sadness or grief.
_____ I do not trust that things will work out.

_____ **Total number of points**

Scoring

80–70: Life has become one crisis after another.
69–50: Your options are often clouded and you feel trapped.
49–30: You have an awareness that your life is in your hands.
29–20: You are your own best ally with a high degree of control, self-esteem, and identity.

lems or block us from finding solutions.[23] These mistakes in thinking cause us to *misinterpret* what we're experiencing, *misjudge* others and *misjudge* ourselves.[24]

These mistakes in thinking often involve *distorted thought patterns*—rigid, unrealistic ways of perceiving what's happening to us. In an instant, distorted thought patterns can make you jump to conclusions—or provoke you to anger or worry, for example, or doubt or resentment. Or they may impart a nagging sense of frustration, impatience or helplessness. No matter how irrational they are, distorted, automatic thoughts are almost always believed, and they often appear in incomplete sentences—several key words or a visual image flash. Emerging research also suggests that, in many cases, the amount of *emotional arousal* you feel when negative thoughts arise may be influenced by a variety of additional factors, including excessive muscle tension, tiredness or even low blood sugar from going more than 2 or 3 hours without eating.[25] (In this respect, you may find many of the 5-second to 5-minute guidelines throughout *The Power of 5* helpful in heading off anger and hostility.)

> Men are disturbed not by things, but by the view which they take of them.
>
> **—Epictetus,** Greek philosopher

Fortunately, there are some rapid, well-proven ways to *identify—and correct—distorted, unproductive thoughts*. Let's begin with a review of some of the most common distorted thought patterns[26] (listed alphabetically).

Availability. When you accept and advocate an explanation or solution that comes quickly to mind without considering other less obvious or less readily available solutions.

Argumentum populum. "If everyone else thinks this way, it must be right."

Being right. You believe confessing ignorance or confusion makes you look ineffective, so you pretend to know things you really don't. You need to always prove that your statements and actions are right. You are quick to launch into defensive rationalizations whenever your "rightness" seems in question.

Blaming. Your problems are either *never* your fault (other people and situations cause whatever goes wrong) or *always* your fault.

Change illusion. Your happiness and success depend on other people changing their bad habits—"bad" from your perspective of reality—and you believe they will make these changes if you keep pressuring them enough.

Composition illusion. With this fallacy, you reason that what is

THE "WHAT A . . ." HUMOR TECHNIQUE

Whenever you find yourself feeling a surge of anger or hostility, shift your attention. Ask yourself: Is this *really* a deliberate affront? Try to reframe the provocation and see things from the other person's view:

- There's no need to get upset about this.
- Maybe he's angry about something else and is letting off steam.
- This could turn into a difficult situation, so stay calm.

Finally, be sure you cope with any effects of antagonism. Relax tense muscles. Slow your breathing. Whenever possible, use humor. If someone has failed to signal and cut into the lane ahead of you during rush-hour traffic, you think, "What a clown!" Envision a huge bodiless clown face, red lips and nose pressed to the wheel, fumbling to steer down the road. Or, as suggested by University of Pennsylvania psychologist Martin E. P. Seligman, Ph.D., if you say, "What an ass!" go ahead and visualize a pair of buttocks steering the car ahead. Decorate them with some feathers or glitter paint. Get into the image. Or visualize yourself as a bomb disposer. Your job is to slowly and coolly defuse the bomb of anger. Then move on with some kind of action without attacking. In conversations, you might rely on a short list of "defusing lines" to reduce anger on the part of your spouse, children, boss, difficult co-workers or irritating neighbors.[17]

What if your spouse comes home after a rough day at work and takes out frustrations by yelling at you or the kids? Instead of becoming angry and emotionally off-balance, try a dose of humor or fun: Imagine your spouse as a grouchy, irritable-yet-cuddly Teddy bear in need of a hug or a kiss or a kind word. Hear your spouse saying he or she needs your help because of the difficult day at work. You can take the grumpiness less seriously because what he or she really needs is your support and care, rather than yelling, a confrontation and a ruined evening or weekend. If the grouchiness is a chronic behavior, then other strategies may be called for. But if it happens only occasionally (even if, in the heat of the moment, it *feels* as if it *always* happens), your willingness to be compassionate and have fun can be contagious. Humor and good jokes, well timed and backed with kind words and providing a chance for your spouse to "cool off," can lighten almost anyone's burden.

true of parts of a whole is necessarily true of the whole itself.

Control illusion. You feel either externally controlled—and therefore victimized—by other people and circumstances or internally controlled, which leaves you feeling that you cause everyone else's unhappiness.

Disqualifying the positive. You reject positive experiences on the grounds that they somehow "don't count" when compared with the endless list of problems at your job and in your life.

Division illusion. You assume that what is true of the whole is necessarily true of each individual part of that whole.

Either/or thinking. There is no middle ground—things are either good or they're bad. Either you perform perfectly or you're a total failure.

Emotional reasoning. You automatically assume that your feelings are facts and therefore must reflect the way things really are. If you *feel* incompetent or indecisive, then you must *be* incompetent or indecisive.

Failure to make distinctions. Distinctions are subtle differences among things.

Fairness illusion. You think you know exactly what's fair in all situations but feel victimized when other people often don't agree with you.

Filtering. You find negative details in any situation and dwell on them so exclusively—ignoring the positive—that no matter how bright an experience may initially be, it soon looks bleak.

Invalid disjunction. Here you only examine one or several possible solutions to a question or problem and assume that these are the only solutions that could possibly be relevant.

Jumping to conclusions. You quickly leap to negative interpretations of statements and situations even though you usually lack the facts to support your conclusion. This includes *mind reading*—without checking to find out the truth, you assume that you know precisely why other people are thinking, feeling and acting the way they are—and *fortune telling*—you anticipate that a future event will turn out badly and act as if this is a predetermined fact.

Justification of effort. This is a powerful force in human thought and action. Once you've invested a substantial amount of time or other resources in a given course of action, you seek reasons to justify that investment and become overly defensive if anyone questions it.

Labeling and mislabeling. This is an extreme version of overgeneralization. When you make an error or become irritated with others, you emotionally assign a label to yourself ("I'm a loser"; "I'm an idiot"), another person ("He's a quitter"; "She's a liar") or situation ("It's a lost cause.").

Magnification (catastrophizing) and minimization. You exaggerate risks, anticipating disaster; you overplay your mistakes or the importance of someone else's achievements; or you erroneously shrink your positive attributes or another person's imperfections until they appear insignificant.

Overgeneralization. You make a sweeping assumption based on only a shred of evidence—a single negative event turns into a never-ending pattern of defeat.

Oversimplification. Simplification can be valuable and enlightening. However, in oversimplification, you omit certain essential information or ignore complexity. Oversimplification distorts reality and confuses discussion.

Personalization. You see yourself as the cause of some negative work occurrence for which you were not primarily responsible. You think that everything other people say or do is a reaction to you. You keep comparing yourself to others, wondering who's smarter, more successful, better looking and so on.

Resistance to change. Old beliefs provide a sense of comfort and security. New ideas are resisted simply because they are new.

"Shoulds." You try to motivate yourself and others with guilt, using statements filled with "shoulds" and "shouldn'ts," "musts," and "oughts." When you or others break your rules, you feel anger, resentment and frustration.

Ultimate-reward illusion. You talk and act as if monumental daily sacrifices and self-denial are what will ultimately bring you great rewards. You feel resentful when the rewards don't seem to come.

Distorted thinking is contagious—the habit spreads. "If you consistently respond to events pessimistically," says Martin E. P. Seligman, Ph.D., professor of psychology at the University of Pennsylvania in Philadelphia, "that negative style can actually *amplify* your feelings of helplessness and spread to other areas of your life."[27]

Therefore, resist the natural tendency to accept distorted thoughts as true simply because they seem reasonable or "feel right." Begin paying closer attention to the way you explain unpleasant situations and outcomes to yourself and others. Catch negative, stressful thoughts and examine them clearly and carefully, looking for supporting evidence, contradictory evidence, alternative explanations and more logical inferences. Derail the temptation to resort to habitual, self-defeating reactions, such as defensiveness, retaliation or withdrawal. The next time you feel yourself losing control, stop. Keep breathing and release physical tension. Reflect: Ask yourself questions, such as, What's going on here? Why am I so distressed? What's the worst thing that will happen if I'm late? Will worrying about it help? (For more insights on depression, see chapter 25.)

Take a 5-Second Pause to Value the Power of Feelings

In many cases, anger is fueled by judgments about others. Therefore, if you can learn to communicate in more caring, trusting, less judgmental ways, you may be able to prevent arguments and even extend your life.[28] Researchers have found, for example, that the frequency with which a person refers to himself or herself—that is, how often you use the words *I*, *me*, *my* and *mine* in ordinary conversations—actually may predict the recurrence of a heart attack.[29] "In short, *anything that promotes a sense of isolation leads to chronic stress and, often, to illnesses like heart disease*," says heart specialist Dean Ornish, M.D., assistant clinical professor at the University of California, San Francisco, School of Medicine and president and director of the Preventive Medicine Research Institute. "Conversely, *anything that leads to real intimacy and feelings of connection can be healing*."[30]

"How we approach other people each day can determine whether we experience isolation, chronic stress, suffering and illness, or intimacy, relaxation, joy and health," adds Dr. Ornish. "Of course, touching, hugging and massage are ways of increasing intimacy.... Another powerful technique is that we can learn to talk to each other in ways that allow the other person to hear us better."[31]

Dr. Ornish and other researchers recommend communicating our feelings in ways that are likely to be heard without causing the other person to feel attacked. The basic principle is this: Our *feelings* tend to help connect us to others; whereas our *thoughts*—especially judgments—tend to isolate us and increase distress. Thoughts connect our heads, feelings join our hearts.

That's because thoughts are more likely than feelings to be heard as criticisms. "I think you're stupid," or "I think you're wrong" puts the other person in the position of feeling verbally attacked—the walls go up ... and stress rises with them. As soon as we feel criticized by someone else, it's extremely hard to hear anything else the attacker has to say. In contrast, if you communicate feelings, such as "I feel hurt by what happened"

For some of the large indignities of life, the best remedy is direct action. For the small indignities, the best remedy is a Charlie Chaplin movie. The hard part is knowing the difference.

—Carol Tavris,
Anger: The Misunderstood Emotion

or "I feel upset by what you just said," you are less likely to be perceived as an attacker, and it's easier for both people to be better understood. It's important to note that although expressing feelings makes many of us feel somewhat vulnerable, it actually makes us safer.

Here are several ways to get closer—and reduce stress—by talking.

Pay greater attention to what you're feeling. Some common *feelings* that people have but often fail to identify include:

Abandoned	Calm	Disappointed
Adamant	Carefree	Dishonest
Affection	Caring	Disorganized
Afraid	Capable	Distracted
Agony	Centered	Distraught
Agreeable	Challenged	Disturbed
Alert	Charmed	Dominated
Alone	Cheated	
Ambivalence	Cheerful	Eager
Anger	Cherished	Ecstatic
Animated	Combative	Empathy
Annoyed	Competitive	Empathetic
Anxious	Condemned	Empty
Appreciated	Confident	Enchanted
Appreciative	Confused	Energetic
Apprehensive	Conspicuous	Envy
Argumentative	Content	Envious
Awed	Cozy	Exposed
Awful	Crazy	Exasperated
	Crushed	Excited
	Cruel	Exhausted
		Exhilarated
Beautiful		Explosive
Betrayed	Defeated	Expressive
Bitter	Delighted	Evil
Blissful	Desire	
Blue	Desirable	
Bold	Despair	Fascinated
Bored	Destructive	Fear
Brave	Determined	Fearful
Bright	Different	Flighty
Brilliant	Diffident	Flustered
Bubbly	Diminished	Foolish
Burdened	Disagreeable	Forgiving

Forgiven
Forgotten
Frantic
Frustrated
Frightened
Free
Full
Funny
Furious

Generous
Giving
Glad
Gratified
Greedy
Grief
Grounded
Guilty
Gullible

Happy
Hate
Hateful
Healthy
Heavenly
Helpful
Helpless
High
Homesick
Honored
Horrible
Humorous

Impatient
Impressed
Inadequate
Infatuated
Infuriated
Inspired
Insignificant
Integrated

Intimidated
Isolated

Jealousy
Jealous
Joy
Joyous
Jumpy

Kind
Kindness

Lazy
Lecherous
Left out
Light
Lively
Lonely
Longing
Loose
Love
Lovable
Loving
Low
Lust

Mad
Mean
Melancholy
Miserable
Mistreated
Mystical

Naughty
Neglected
Nervous
Nutty

Obnoxious
Obsessed
Odd

Panic
Panicked
Patience
Peaceful
Persecuted
Petrified
Pity
Pitiful
Playful
Pleasant
Pleased
Powerful
Pressured
Pretty
Proud

Quarrelsome
Quiet

Radiant
Rage
Rapture
Real
Refreshed
Rejected
Relaxed
Remorse
Resented
Resentful
Responsible
Responsive
Restless
Reverent
Rewarded
Righteous

Sad
Sassy
Sated
Satisfied

Scared	Stingy	Terrible
Secure	Strange	Terrified
Selfish	Stress	Threatened
Self-assured	Stressed	Thrilled
Serene	Strong	Tired
Shocked	Stunned	
Silly	Stupefied	Used
Skeptical	Stupid	United
Sleepy	Suffering	
Sneaky	Suppressed	Vibrant
Solemn	Surprised	Victorious
Sorrow	Sympathetic	Vile
Sorrowful		Vital
Sorry	Talkative	
Spiritual	Teary/Tearful	Warlike
Spiteful	Tempted	Weak
Spontaneous	Tenacious	Worried
Spunky	Tenuous	
Stable	Tense	Zapped
Startled	Tentative	Zesty

In contrast, some typical judgment-centered *thoughts* include: "I'm right"; "You're wrong"; "You're always . . ."; "You're never . . ."; "You're not listening"; "You're a jerk"; "You should have . . ."; and so on. Sometimes thoughts disguise themselves as feelings, such as: "I feel that you're wrong"; "I feel that I'm right"; "I feel you're being stupid and short-sighted"; "I feel you ought to . . . ." The words *that*, *like* or *as if* following *I feel* are a signal that what follows is probably a judgment thought instead of a feeling. Words like *you should*, *you ought to*, *you never* and *you always* are thoughts that are often heard as criticisms.

Be willing to express what you're feeling. In the opening chapters of *The Power of 5*, we stated an age-old observation: *What you resist persists; what you accept lightens.* It can be a healthy, healing experience to let a loved one or friend know what you're truly feeling—in the spirit of informing this person rather than judging or criticizing. Just as, similarly, it helps when you know what others are really feeling. To ask another person, "How are you *feeling* about . . . ?" can provide you with a very different insight than you may receive by asking the more common question, "What do you *think* about . . . ?" When two people share a greater willingness to express not only what they think but also what they feel, it helps them in many ways, including spending less time arguing and more time dealing with real issues in life, work and relationships.

Listen with openness and empathy. Stress pressures often ease when we listen to each other with empathy—trying to understand what the other person is feeling and acknowledging what we are sensing and hearing. (For practical strategies on this subject, see chapter 29.)

Make Regular Deposits in Your "Emotional Bank Accounts"

If you frequently find yourself getting angry, begin to identify practical prevention strategies. Relaxation and meditation (discussed in chapters 3 and 4) are two examples of techniques that have been shown to prevent angry arousal,[32] and they can prove just as useful for angry people as for anxious people.

Recall our discussion earlier in this chapter: In most cases, the events of life don't make us angry—our "hot thoughts" do. Anger is usually a defense against loss of self-esteem and comes from frustration and unmet expectations. Most thoughts that generate anger contain distortions, and most anger can be quickly defused if you take a moment to see the world through the other person's eyes. Remember, conflicts are rarely caused by only one. Although we all have the *right* to get angry whenever we want, in almost every case it's not to our advantage.

This brings us to another key point: Anger often arises from relationship imbalances in which one person perceives that he or she is *giving* more than *receiving*. In truth, every relationship is a balancing act. By this we mean that the basic, guiding principle in most relationships is that people give to get. We open a door or bestow a gift, we expect a thank-you or at least a smile in return. We work hard to earn money, we count upon visible appreciation from household members. We spend long hours caring for the family and doing housework, we feel entitled to appreciation on a par with that accorded the highest wage-earner.

But things start going wrong when you feel that what you've given does not equal what you have received in return. "Equity is not a matter of facts or reality," say researchers Richard C. Huseman, Ph.D., and John D. Hatfield, Ph.D., of the University of Georgia in Athens. "Instead, it's a matter of fragile, peculiar and sometimes slanted perceptions of reality."[33] Often, what matters most in a relationship is not what men and women *do* but what they say to each other and how they say it, according to sociologist Arlie Hochschild, author of *The Second Shift*.

There's an "economy of gratitude" in marriage, she says. "When couples struggle, it's seldom over who does what. Far more often it's over the giving and receiving of gratitude."[34]

"After having spoken with hundreds of couples," says James Fadiman, Ph.D., a consultant and former professor of psychology at San Francisco State University and Brandeis University in Waltham, Massachusetts, "I can safely say that most people think they know a number of ways in which their marriages might be improved. In most cases, however, each person can *only see how their spouse should change* and how that would make things better for both of them. But that's the wrong focus."[35]

In reality, the people we love are those to whom we should be most responsive and caring. But then why, so often, do so many of us lash out at our partner, neglect our children, snap at our parents and avoid our friends? In part, these behaviors reflect the tense-and-tired state discussed in chapters 4 and 6. But, just as important, these bearish acts signal that we feel we're giving far more than we're getting. As Adam Smith wrote, "Give me that which I want, and you shall have that which you want." Otherwise, problems and resentments tend to snowball.

"Our research has shown that it takes one put-down to undo hours of kindness you give to your partner," warn Dr. Notarius and Dr. Markham.[36] "We all know what a financial bank account is," adds Stephen R. Covey, Ph.D., author of *The Seven Habits of Highly Effective People*. "We make deposits into it and build up a reserve from which we can make withdrawals when we need to. An Emotional Bank Account is a metaphor that describes the amount of trust that's been built up in a relationship. It's the feeling of safeness you have with another human being.

"If I make deposits into an Emotional Bank Account with you through courtesy, kindness, honesty and keeping my commitments to you, I build up a reserve. Your trust toward me becomes higher, and I can call on that trust many times if I need to. I can even make mistakes and that trust level, that emotional reserve, will compensate for it . . .

"But if I have a habit of showing discourtesy, disrespect, cutting you off, ignoring you, becoming arbitrary, betraying your trust, threatening you or playing a little tin god in your life, eventually my Emotional Bank Account is overdrawn. The trust level gets very low. Then what flexibility do I have?"[37]

Here are several quick, focused steps to prevent some common causes of anger and, at the same time, improve your relationships.

Respect differences in personal perspective. You can better recognize others' perspectives by being an active listener and by asking questions about how the other person sees his or her inputs and outcomes in the relationship. Ask whether or not they feel underrewarded, and if so, why. Sometimes just bringing this out in the open improves the relationship. And remember another's perspective is reality through his or her eyes. If you try to deny or invalidate it, you'll simply start an argument. But by sharing your own perspective—as *your* view instead of *the* view—and learning about the other person's perceptions, you'll gain insights on how to increase trust in the relationship.

Rewrite the golden rule. According to Dr. Huseman and Dr. Hatfield, the Golden Rule for Relationships should be: "Do unto others as *they* would have you do unto them."[38] Before you invest time, energy and money in a relationship-building process, clarify what kinds of Emotional Bank Account deposits are valued most highly by the other person in the relationship. It's what *they* value that matters most here, not what you *think* they should value.

Build up your Emotional Bank Accounts—and avoid getting overdrawn. To prevent what Dr. Huseman and Dr. Hatfield call "trust bankruptcy," start an active, ongoing deposit program to build up a large balance in your Emotional Bank Account for each of your family relationships. Be more attentive to the needs of the other person, keep your commitments, attend to the little kindnesses and courtesies that pay such big dividends (See chapters 26 and 27), clarify your expectations, maintain personal integrity and apologize sincerely whenever you need to make a withdrawal. One final thought here: An Emotional Bank Account is not a license to get away with unkind or thoughtless deeds.[39] Some individuals excuse inconsiderate or rude behavior by saying, "Oh, I didn't mean it." The more often behaviors like this occur, the more negative the influence on relationships and the harder they are for others to forgive—no matter *how* many other kinds of deposits you may have made in Emotional Bank Accounts.

When You've Had a Tough Day, Be Careful How You "Come Home"

At the end of a difficult day, when you may be exceptionally tense or tired or hungry and your partner asks, "How was your day?" your answer may sound more negative than you intended because of your current mood and fatigue. Similarly, your partner may *hear* your question, "What's for dinner?" as an attack (it may sound more like, "Why isn't dinner ready yet?") and trigger an angry reaction and argument— and a "run" of withdrawals from your Emotional Bank Account. To avoid this common, counterproductive problem, take a different approach: Whenever you and your partner greet each other at the end of the day, make it warm and brief, as discussed in chapter 7, and then give each other a "buffer zone" lasting at least 5 minutes to wind down and relax. *Then* talk.

Take a 5-Minute "Anger-Release" Walk

For years, scientists have known that exercise can be one of the best stress relievers around. In fact, research suggests that, in many cases, it's a highly effective way to defuse anger, lift moderate depression, raise self-esteem and spark creative thinking.[40] And it's a pleasure to realize that the psychological benefits of physical activity can often be felt very quickly—in only 5 minutes or so of brisk walking.

The central idea here is to combine the brief bout of exercise with a *shift of mind*, by choosing something else—a natural outdoor scene, humming a pleasant song, taking a "mental vacation"—to capture your attention.[41] One of the reasons this can work so well is that the conscious mind has difficulty focusing on two things at once. It's hard work to hold on to the heat of anger when something else draws your focus away.

Use Reflective Coping

Conventional thinking contends that telling other people off "clears the air" and makes you feel less angry. But in truth, many times the opposite is probably true: Studies report that venting anger tends to make people more hostile and destructive, not less.[42] A 15-year controlled study of husbands and wives by the University of Michigan School of Public Health measured the effects of expression of anger, suppression and "cool reflection." The researchers discovered that ineffectively managed anger was linked to 2½ times greater risk of death from all causes.[43] The findings held true for both sexes and all age groups and education levels, regardless of whether the individuals smoked or had any other common risk factors for heart disease. "The key issue," says Ernest Harburg, M.D., one of the researchers, "is not the amount or degree of your anger, but *how you cope with it.*"

"Reflective anger-coping," explains Mara Julius, M.D., who headed the study, "not only promotes better problem solving but better health, and possibly longer life." And it affects our children, too. A recent study by researchers at the National Institute of Mental Health in Rockville, Maryland, confirmed that young children are especially susceptible to psychological problems from angry exchanges they see or hear in the home.[44] This "background anger" of heated arguments clearly distressed the children studied, causing them to freeze in place, cry, cover their ears or eyes or run away from the scene. Their reactions suggest that background anger may have a cumulative effect, perhaps even more detrimental than television violence.

Reflective coping means waiting until tempers have cooled to rationally discuss the conflict with the other person or sort things out on your own. In general, reflective coping is the best choice because it enables you to avoid hostility traps, restores a sense of control over the situation and helps resolve it. Studies show that those people who keep their cool—who acknowledged their anger but were not openly hostile, physically or verbally—feel better faster, solve problems more easily and have superior health.[45]

Of course, reflective coping does *not* mean ignoring your anger—since it's a signal worth listening to. "Our anger may be a message that we are being hurt, that our rights are being violated, that our needs or wants are not being adequately met, or simply telling us that something isn't right," says Harriet Goldhor Lerner, Ph.D., in *The Dance of Anger*. "Just as physical pain tells us to take our hand off the hot stove, the pain of our anger can motivate us."[46]

Aldous Huxley once remarked that it was a bit embarrassing to get to the end of his life and have no more profound advice than "Be a little kinder."[47] But what golden counsel that is. Indeed, one of the consummate ways to head off useless hostility and anger is to develop a more trusting heart, says Redford Williams, M.D., professor of psychiatry, associate professor of medicine and director of the Behavioral Medicine Research Center at Duke University Medical Center in Durham, North Carolina.[48] His research suggests that when you begin to feel angry, it really pays to pause for an extra moment to gently laugh at yourself, forgive others, put yourself in the other person's shoes, use some logic, and in short, find ways to keep things from getting blown out of proportion. Ask, Is my anger useful? Does it support my integrity and help me achieve my goals—or does it just defeat me?

Being there first (in evolution), emotions act as the driver of the human system. Their role in our life is much greater than we'd like to think. . . .

Emotions set our agenda. And they do so largely without our being aware of them. . . . They are the focal point of the mental system's activity: They govern our choices, they determine our goals, and they guide our lives. . . . The central readout within ourselves is an emotional appraisal of a change in the outside environment. . . . While there is much more to emotions than a simple positive/negative, stop/start, approach/avoid program, much more of our life is determined by these primitive appraisals than we, the conscious thinkers, might believe.

—Robert Ornstein, Ph.D., *The Evolution of Consciousness*

Take 5 Minutes to "Exorcise" Hostility and Rage

Hostility and rage can be destructive reactions to a perceived threat to survival, severe rejection, betrayal or abuse. For those instances when anger-management tactics don't succeed, it's essential to have a safe means of releasing hostility and rage. For this, one technique is to head out the door for a walk or run. Another is to go to a private place (the basement or garage, for example) with a soft "wiffle bat" and pound an old mattress, roll of carpet or padded punching bag.[49] Assume a balanced stance, take several deep breaths and begin striking the padded surface. Yell if you like: "You jerk! I hate you for what you did!" as you visualize the person's image superimposed on the striking surface. Give yourself permission to use the physical strikes to release your pent-up hostility and rage—to acknowledge and constructively vent the dark side of your emotions—until you are exhausted. Rage, which is characterized by the intention to destroy, must be appropriately and safely discharged. As long as you remember that you will never act out your rage on an actual person, this exercise can be healthy and healing.

Confide in Others, but Protect Yourself from "Chaindumping"

Misery often demands company. In "chaindumping," it's more like a distress parade—the same complaints get unloaded again and again with lots of exaggeration, blaming and symbols of helplessness (whining, sighing, groaning and looks of tiredness). As researcher Ann McGee-Cooper points out,[50] chaindumping occurs when someone heaps, or dumps, a string of problems—first on one person, then on the next, eventually pulling down everyone who will listen. This is distinctly different from "opening up to others," in which, at an appropriate time, you share your personal disappointments and anxieties with a trusted friend or loved one.

Of course, *all* of us have down moods and bearish, bad-tempered days. There are a host of reasons for this and no quick-fix solutions. The "Don't worry, be happy" rhetoric is fool's gold; and there just aren't enough exuberant, positive people for all the rest of us to cluster around them and try to "catch" *their* emotional uplifts, either. So what's the most realistic thing to do? Fortunately, there *are* some sensible new approaches you can take—including gentle verbal self-protection skills that enable you to be less upset with yourself when you're feeling low and less combative—and more helpful—to others when the dark cloud over their head starts moving your way.

First, some further clarity: In chaindumping, the person complaining is always the victim of the story being told. The listeners usually first express sympathy and then find themselves becoming distressed by the episode—and mentally distracted from their work tasks. The net result is mental and emotional fatigue—for the complainer and for all the listeners. And every time we "rescue" chaindumpers through sympathy or by offering to "help out" by taking over some of their responsibilities, we only make matters worse—encouraging more draining conversations.[51]

> Nothing on earth consumes a man more quickly than the passion of resentment.
> —**Friedrich Nietzsche,** German philosopher

The other side of the coin can sometimes be just as bad. When you make the mistake of choosing a chaindumper to act as a "listener," your own problems can quickly take on catastrophic proportions. The speed and power of this emotional downturn and mood "collapse" occurs in part because the subconscious mind—in both the dumper and the listener—can't distinguish between exaggerated or imaginary dilemmas and actual ones. Once we engage in unproductive thinking, it tends to steamroll if we don't intervene and break the cycle.

But what if some of these people who have a habit of chaindumping are your own loved ones or friends? Obviously you want to help them feel better. But most of us go about it in many of the wrong ways. For one thing, few people are aware of the latest insights on what research psychologists call "emotional contagion." That's the unconscious transmission of feelings—positive or negative—from one person to another that occurs in a flash (sometimes in a mere split-second).

When the mood is negative, it doesn't take long before your own feelings can go into a tailspin, as you rather mysteriously become anxious, frustrated, angry or trapped in a darkening mood. Especially when the other person is a relative or partner, each of you becomes convinced that what you think, feel, say and do is a logical response to what the other person is saying and doing. Conversations turn into arguments, which become circular—that is, each of you blames the other for causing problems and provoking bad feelings. Here are several ideas for opening up to others and bypassing the gridlock of chaindumping.

Recognize and respect emotional distance. "It's simply not possible to solve other people's life problems," says Ronald M. Podell, M.D., assistant clinical professor at UCLA's Neuropsychiatric Institute, "or give them the self-esteem they lack, or brighten their spirits when they're dark. By trying to do so, you only risk joining them in despair as a result. So what to do? You detach yourself, remain empathetic and set appropriate limits, not coldly or vindictively, but with wisdom and purpose."[52]

Whenever you feel an emotional drop, check to see if it's from being in the presence of a complainer. When you can't move away or find a more positive conversation focus, you might put on an imaginary "emotional raincoat" that creates a picture of protecting yourself from the energy-depleting "rain" of words. As often as you can, raise a clarifying question such as, "What do you plan to *do* about this situation right now, anyway?" and then move on. Blaming and complaining don't work; the dissatisfaction is contagious. If necessary, *break away from the interaction until you can calm down.* Make certain you've calmed down before returning. If not, you make get trapped by what researchers call the Zillmann Transfer of Excitation Effect.[53] Studies indicate that if you believe you're calmed down but are actually still angered when you reapproach the other person, *you'll be very susceptible to immediately taking on any emotion that he or she expresses.*

Don't take "dark cloud" words or actions too personally. When you allow irritating or hurtful words to get inside you and fester, you're torturing yourself—needlessly. Practice replacing distress-sustaining thoughts with more soothing, validating ones, such as: "Easy does it. Take some deep breaths."; "No need to take this personally, he/she is just feeling upset."; "This is just a stressful time—things are usually much better."; "He/she has so many great qualities to admire."; "Right now I'm upset, but this is basically a strong and good relationship."

The idea is to choose a higher vantage point and reassure yourself that the other person's mood has little or nothing to do with you. In this way, you're likely to be less vulnerable to contagious emotions, according to research by psychologists Chriss Hsee, Ph.D., of Yale University

---

THE FISHHOOK TECHNIQUE

In your first response to anger, you may be inclined to call upon the old saw to "count to ten." It's good advice—to a point. But by itself, pausing may do little to dampen the anger you feel. Go ahead and count to ten—better yet, when possible, sleep on it (see the "reflective coping" technique on page 356). During your pause, challenge and review the thoughts of trespass or affront that have made you angry. Envision yourself as a fish swimming along a stream.[16] Hundreds of fishhooks, symbolizing insults and criticisms, dangle in the water. Each offers you the *choice* of whether or not to bite.

---

and Elaine Hatfield, Ph.D., of the University of Hawaii.[54]

Don't add sparks to the process. Keep cool, look for chances to lighten things up with some humor and avoid making statements that: *blame* ("If you weren't so gloomy and grouchy, I wouldn't feel so stressed out all the time."); *instill guilt* ("You're so focused on yourself that the rest of the family hardly knows you anymore."); *make charges of incompetency or inadequacy* ("Only an idiot would say those things and act that way."); or *threaten abandonment* ("I'm sick of this—I'm ready to leave and never come back.").

Favor the positive. If you catch yourself repeating your own problems again and again or overstating them—to yourself or others—stop. Take a few minutes to distract yourself, perhaps by taking a short walk, and then replace negative, distorted statements with more accurate words and images. Relieve your own negative thoughts and feelings by using whatever works best for you from your own experience or the suggestions offered throughout *The Power of 5* program. Popular options include "mini-walks" or other types of exercise or physical activity, deep breathing, meditation or relaxation practices, a low-fat, high-carbohydrate snack, extra time with good friends or a pleasure-filled evening pursuing one of your favorite hobbies or watching a funny movie.

Resources

Anger Kills by Redford Williams, M.D., and Virginia Williams, Ph.D. (Times Books, 1993). Seventeen scientifically based strategies for controlling the hostility that can harm your—and your loved ones'—health.

Inner Joy by Harold Bloomfield, M.D., and Robert B. Kory (Wyden Books, 1980). Strategies for adding more pleasure to your life and relationships.

From Stress to Strength: How to Lighten Your Load and Save Your Life by Robert S. Eliot, M.D. (Bantam, 1994). Timely, well-founded advice by a pioneering cardiologist investigating the sudden cardiac deaths—unexpected fatal heart attacks—caused by mismanaged stress.

We Can Work It Out: Making Sense of Marital Conflict by Clifford Notarius, Ph.D., and Howard Markman, Ph.D. (Putnam, 1993). A well-proven approach to anger management in love relationships.

When Anger Hurts: Quieting the Storm Within by Matthew McKay, Ph.D., Peter D. Rogers, Ph.D. and Judith McKay, R.N. (New Harbinger Publications, 1989). A practical program of anger management based on cognitive-behavioral therapy.

Why Marriages Succeed or Fail by John Gottman, Ph.D. (Simon & Schuster, 1994). A variety of research-proven methods of anger management for couples.

PERSONAL POWER NOTES
A Quick-List of This Chapter's Power-Action Options

Use quick-checks to identify your anger "hot spots."
Become an Emotional A.C.E.: "own what you're feeling" and choose your response.
- *A: Assess Accurately.*
- *C: Choose Constructively.*
- *E: Express Effectively.*

Take 5 seconds to quick-stop negative or distorted thinking.
Take a 5-second pause to value the power of feelings.
- *Pay greater attention to what you're feeling.*
- *Be willing to express what you're feeling.*
- *Listen with openness and empathy.*

Make regular deposits in your "Emotional Bank Accounts."
- *Respect differences in personal perspective.*
- *Rewrite the Golden Rule.*
- *Build up your "Emotional Bank Accounts"—and avoid getting overdrawn.*

When you've had a tough day, be careful how you "come home."

Take a 5-minute "anger-release" walk.
Use Reflective Coping.
- *Acknowledge anger.*
- *Schedule time to deal with it later, not now—and then follow through.*

Take 5 minutes to "exorcise" hostility and rage.

Confide in others, but protect yourself from "chaindumping."
- *Recognize and respect emotional distance.*
- *Don't take "dark cloud" words or actions too personally.*
- *Don't add sparks to the process.*
- *Favor the positive.*

PERSONAL NOTES

WORKING THROUGH PAIN AND LOSS

Practical, Healing Ways to Deal
with Difficult Times

Life is not the way it's supposed to be. It's the way it is. The way
you cope with it is what makes the difference.
—**Virginia Satir**, marriage and family therapist

It's a universal truth. Sometimes life seems to fall apart. Grief spares
no one. It can strike suddenly, gripping your heart like a vise, and its
emotional pain can last for months or even years. Yet traumatic experiences are also life's turning points.

Whenever you're faced with a severe crisis—when a loved one or
friend dies, a major illness strikes, divorce occurs, a career is ended, life
savings disappear—your mind and heart are inundated with feelings of
helplessness, a sense of being defeated. You're pressed into a desperate
search for hope and a day-by-day (and sometimes minute-by-minute)
effort to reorganize your life. If left unresolved, these traumatic experiences may suppress the body's immune system and leave you more vulnerable to illness.[1]

Think back to the most traumatic day of your life. Do you remember feeling helpless or hurt or furious? Do you recall asking, Why me?
What did *I* do to deserve this? Will my life ever be normal again? How
can I handle this? In *Primitive Mythology: The Masks of God*, Joseph
Campbell shares an ancient Eskimo maxim: "The only true wisdom lies
far from Mankind, out in the great loneliness, and it can be reached only
through suffering. Privation and suffering alone can open the mind of
a man to all that is hidden to others."[2]

POWER ACTION: FIRST OPTION
For Now, Be with the Pain

Healthy coping with pain or loss begins with some straightforward steps.

Accept that your world has, for now, been turned upside down. According to Kathryn D. Kramer, Ph.D., health psychologist and founder of the Stress Center at St. Louis University, "To prepare yourself mentally to meet the demands of your stressful circumstance, you need: (1) *To accept* that your world has, indeed, been turned upside down by whatever traumatic event may have occurred; (2) *to believe* that opportunities for your growth do exist within your new circumstances; and (3) *to have confidence* that you will be able to take advantage of those opportunities and become healthier and happier as a result."[6]

Remember that grief is a process that takes time. Each of us experiences grief differently, but certain emotions are common. Denial, anger and symptoms of depression (loss of appetite, sleep problems and difficulty accomplishing daily activities) are "stages" that we each pass through. More distress usually follows a loss that is sudden and unexpected than one that has been anticipated. A loss is particularly hurtful when unresolved conflicts were present. Surprisingly, researchers at the State University of New York at Stony Brook found that people with a positive self-image and feelings of control experience more depression than others.[7]

"One of the most threatening aspects of disruption," says psychiatrist Frederic Flach, M.D., "is the loss of control that accompanies it. Our need to control our lives is a universal, fundamental need. . . . If a phase of disruption is especially severe or stretches over a long time span—years, perhaps—we can be certain that the meaning we have assigned to our lives is being challenged. We can also be sure that while we may be able to find some consolation in the values upon which we have already come to rely, we shall, if successful, in the end discover new meaning, one that will enrich our life and reshape, replace or confirm the meaning we had already given to it."[8] And it's important to recognize that every

> The last of the human freedoms is to choose one's attitude in any given set of circumstances, to choose one's own way.
>
> **—Viktor Frankl, M.D.,** Holocaust survivor

> Nobody, as long as he moves about among the chaotic currents of life, is without trouble.
>
> **—Carl Jung, M.D.,** Swiss psychologist

POWER KNOWLEDGE: PAIN AND LOSS

MYTH #1: Healthy people get over grief quickly.

POWER KNOWLEDGE: No matter how healthy you are, grief from severe change or loss can cause profound distress that's as painful as any experience life brings. But difficult as it is, grieving can't be avoided or hurried. It's a natural healing process that takes time and patience. Grief usually runs a long and tortuous route of emotions—sadness, hopelessness, fears, anxiety, sleep disorders, loss of appetite, crying, deep occupation with objects and locations associated with the person or job that was lost, and dreams of that person or experience. Yet all of these emotions and thoughts are normal, healthy responses, says Camille Lloyd, Ph.D., a professor of clinical psychiatry at the University of Texas Medical Center at Houston.[3] It's important to recognize this, since self-doubt about coping can contribute to feelings of depression. Perhaps more than anything else, grieving signifies how deeply we've been able to care about another person or an experience.

MYTH #2: If changes and losses are hard for me to handle, that's just the personality I was born with.

POWER KNOWLEDGE: Not necessarily. *Resilience* is the term psychiatrist Frederic Flach, M.D., uses to describe "the psychological

mourning process takes time. It's never easy to fully acknowledge, for example, the deep value of a loved one who has died. Sometimes it takes many months to pass through the acute stage of grieving.

POWER ACTION: MORE OPTIONS
Find Strength in 5-Minute Rituals

According to Steven Wolin, M.D., a psychiatrist and researcher at George Washington University in Washington, D.C., "Resiliency is the capacity to rise above adversity and forge lasting strengths in the struggle. . . . Even in the face of serious trouble, there are things families can do. The one I have been investigating has to do with protecting, cher-

and biological strengths required to successfully master change."[4] According to Dr. Flach's research, there are certain resilient personality traits that help sustain us through life's hard times. We can each develop these traits, including the ability to make and keep friends; creativity; the ability to tolerate pain; freedom to depend on others, with the skill to set proper limits on the depth of dependency; insight into ourselves, combined with an independence of spirit; self-respect and an ability to restore self-esteem when it is diminished or temporarily lost; and a perspective on life that offers a vital, evolving philosophy which helps us make sense from, and find meaning in, our difficult experiences.

"I came to realize," explains Dr. Flach, "that significantly stressful events, by their very nature, *must* shake us up and often disrupt the structures of the world around us as well. Moreover, such turbulence has to be accompanied by distress, which can range from mild unhappiness, anxiety or impatience all the way to a state of profound anguish in which we might seriously question who and what we are and the nature of the personal worlds we inhabit."[5] The points in life where such major shifts occur are *bifurcation points*—a term derived from the language of physics and representing moments of extreme change. And Dr. Flach believes that only through these times of great trauma and grief do we find the depth of character, health resources and perspective that produces wisdom and empathy throughout the rest of our lives.

ishing, altering and strengthening family rituals. In the face of trouble, families can evaluate, alter and improve family rituals, adopt new ones and revive old ones."[9]

These daily rituals might include some of the basic, health-bolstering suggestions from throughout *The Power of 5* program, such as regular meals, between-meal snacks, drinking plenty of water, getting enough rest and reducing tensions with whatever seems appealing—a warm bath, sipping your favorite tea, listening to music, watching television or movies, and in general finding sensible ways to comfort your mind and body. *Note*: Choose snacks (see chapter 9) that are low in fat, low in protein and high in complex carbohydrates. Judith J. Wurtman, Ph.D., nutritional researcher at Massa-

> I want to write, but more than that, I want to bring out all kinds of things that lie buried in my heart.
>
> **—Anne Frank,**
> *The Diary of a Young Girl*

chusetts Institute of Technology in Cambridge, and others have found they increase the brain chemical neurotransmitters which may help you feel less stressed, less anxious and more focused and relaxed.

Whenever possible, immerse yourself in activities that provide an outlet for your physical and emotional tensions at the same time they relax you and strengthen your inner resources. Examples include dance, music, sports, walking, movies, yard work or gardening, and hobbies.

Express Your Feelings through 5-Minute Daily Journaling

There is growing evidence—from studies involving thousands of people of all ages and backgrounds—that in many cases, a significant emotional uplift and healing effect can come from spending as little as 5 to 15 minutes a day for several days writing in a private journal about whatever issues and experiences are getting you down.[10]

"We encourage individuals to write for themselves [keeping the words anonymous and confidential] as opposed to writing for someone else," say two leading researchers in the field, James W. Pennebaker, Ph.D., and Martha E. Francis, Ph.D., of the Department of Psychology at Southern Methodist University in Dallas. "The benefits of writing lie in the act of letting go and expressing those deepest thoughts and feelings surrounding a personal upheaval. . . . By setting aside [up to] 15 to 20 minutes a day for several days to write down their deepest thoughts and feelings surrounding disturbing issues, individuals may gain new understanding and insight about their personal lives and, at the same time, foster their own physical health."[11] A similar benefit may come from talking, at the right time and in clear, honest ways, with a trusted friend (see chapter 26). You may also wish to read *How to Survive the Loss of a Love* (see Resources), a book that is often recommended by clinical psychologists.

Seek Periods of Solace—And Draw Help from Friends and Family

Identify what feels best to you for finding solace during times of grief. For some, spending time outdoors in a natural setting is uplifting. For others, hurts are resolved best by browsing through photo albums or old letters. Allow yourself to express your grief—and this means talking about the hurt with loved ones, close friends and perhaps your family physician or counselor. Chapter 26 offers a detailed look at when and how to most safely and effectively confide in others. You might also find it beneficial to talk with those who have experienced similar losses—by joining an organized support group (see Resources).

HEALING A BROKEN HEART

A broken heart requires at least as much care as a broken bone. With proper care, you can be confident that you will heal. The same powerful forces that mend a broken bone will heal your emotional pain, but a wounded heart needs time and proper care to heal.

Be with the pain. Admit you're hurting. The greater the loss, the more time you will take to heal. Don't worry about having ups and downs; these are a sign that you're healing.

You are more fragile now. There is no shame in that, so take it easy. Crying is a natural release. Remember you are not alone. You can't be a human being without suffering loss.

Here is some emotional first aid for a broken heart.

Do stay calm; treat yourself gently.
Do recognize your injury.
Do let yourself be with the pain.
Do take time to heal.
Do rest; nurture yourself.
Do accept comfort from friends and family.
Do stick to a routine.
Do take care in making important decisions.
Do accept understanding and support.

Do anticipate a positive outcome.
Don't panic.
Don't deny the hurt.
Don't dwell on the negative.
Don't abuse alcohol or drugs.
Don't stay isolated.
Don't create more chaos.
Don't make impulsive judgments; be wary of love on the rebound.
Don't be afraid to ask for help.
Don't lose faith.

Above all, spend some extra time with your closest friends and loved ones. Researchers have repeatedly demonstrated a vital link between the strength of our social support systems and our emotional and physical resilience under severe stress. Reviewing dozens of studies, Hebrew University psychiatrist Gerald Caplan, M.D., concluded that when stress is high, people without psychological support suffer as much as ten times the incidence of physical and emotional illness experienced by those who enjoy such support.[12]

Notice whenever you feel like blaming yourself for the trauma you are coping with. "If unchecked," explains psychologist Julius Segal,

Ph.D., author of *Winning Life's Toughest Battles*, "our natural tendency to blame ourselves for our suffering becomes unreasonable and immobilizing. The danger is especially great because our readiness to indict ourselves is often reinforced by the attitudes of people around us."[13] Therefore, be certain to assure your loved ones and friends that it's all right for you to take time to work through this—and that it's not helpful for them to sympathize or inadvertently accentuate your feelings of self-blame by saying things like: "Oh, you poor thing—it's just been one problem after another!" or "You've spent long enough feeling sorry for yourself" or "It's time to get on with your life" or "You'll get over it soon."

Know When and How to Get Professional Help

How much is your distress adversely affecting your personal life, your family or your work? Is your grief getting in the way of your ability to function? Certainly, most of life's difficulties and emotional crises do not require psychotherapy. However, if you feel you're not coping well with the pain or loss in your life, and/or have symptoms of lasting depression (see chapter 30), it's very important to seek help from a psychologist, psychiatrist or other qualified counselor.

Here are six clear and simple steps to finding the right therapy.[14]

1. Acknowledge that you need help. This is sometimes the most difficult step of all. If you are hesitating because you're uncertain what kind of help you can expect from therapy, go to your library or bookstore for a copy of *The Consumer's Guide to Psychotherapy* by Jack Engler, Ph.D., and Daniel Goleman, Ph.D. This is a well-founded and sensible resource filled with answers to common questions. .

2. Identify the core issue or problem you face. In the case of this chapter, the issue may be grief or loss. There are preferred therapy approaches for each major kind of problem or issue that therapy has been proven effective with. Organize in your mind—or, better yet, list on paper—what you want to talk over with a therapist.

3. Arrange for referrals to several therapists. Obviously, no referral guarantees a sensitive, competent therapist, but it may give you a better chance of finding an excellent professional who can give you the help you want. In this light, consider the following sources of referrals to obtain at least three names of prospective therapists.

• National professional associations and their state or local chapters:

For psychiatrists, the American Psychiatric Association (APA) (1400 K Street NW, Washington, DC 20005; 202-682-6142). The APA will provide information brochures on a variety of mental health topics and one explaining how to select a therapist. Callers are referred to the local district office, where they will talk with a psychiatrist. The nature of each caller's problem is assessed and a referral is then made to one or more practitioners in the caller's area. An effort is made to match the caller with a therapist who has experience with the caller's problem or issue.

For psychologists, the American Psychological Association (APA) (1200 17th St., NW, Washington, DC 20036; 202-336-5500). The APA will refer a caller to the state branch office, where the caller's name and number are taken. A referral coordinator returns the call and can provide a list of qualified psychologists and mental health centers in the caller's local area.

For clinical social workers, the National Association of Social Workers (7981 Eastern Ave., Silver Spring, MD 20910; 202-408-8600). The association provides callers with the names of members in its Clinical Registry and makes referrals to members in the caller's local area.

For marriage and family therapists, the American Association of Marriage and Family Therapy (1717 K Street NW, Suite 407, Washington, DC 20006; 202-452-0109). The association makes referrals to members in the caller's local area.

• Leading figures in the field. This is one of the best means of obtaining excellent referrals. Someone such as the director of a psychiatry department at a teaching hospital or head of a training institute is likely to know many therapists and may have a sense of who among them might be good prospects for you.

• Friends or relatives. This can be another excellent route to referrals if the friend or relative is connected to the therapist(s) on a professional, not personal, basis. This is because personal and social ties to a therapist may complicate or even jeopardize ther therapy.

• Self-help organizations. Groups such as Alcoholics Anonymous can sometimes be very helpful in recommending therapists who have a successful record of helping people with a specific type of problem.

4. Request an initial consultation. This is a no-obligation opportunity for you to meet and interview a prospective therapist. It provides a chance for you to ask questions, hear the therapist explain his or her approach to your problem—including strategy, goals and length of treatment—discuss fees and payment options and see what the therapist is like and if you feel you could work well together before any commitment is made. Would this be a therapist who can provide a safe, comfortable and secure setting for therapy that ensures your privacy and confidentiality and assures an exclusive focus on you and your concerns? Is the therapist honest, nondefensive and empathetic?

5. Consider your options and choose a therapist. After meeting with at least three therapists, weigh your findings and make a decision.

6. Contract for therapy. Once you've chosen a therapist, the first priority is for the two of you to agree on your specific goals for therapy and how, precisely, you will be working together to reach these goals. It's also the time to work out the details of how the therapy will be paid for: billing, insurance payment and third-party payment.

Help Others—It May Speed Your Own Healing

Researchers have discovered that, in many cases, the pain we feel, the losses we sustain, become far more bearable when we adopt a mission of caring.[15] This service can be volunteer work of any kind—and often the best is with children, suggests Dr. Segal. Self-sacrifice and thinking about others during an extended time of personal grief may even seem irrelevant or unhealthy, but it is neither. In the face of a crisis, one of the most courageous and healing steps is to practice empathy and compassion for other people in need. Once we've given ourselves a brief time to begin to come to grips with our own loss, then helping others "is eventually the best thing we can do for ourselves," says Dr. Segal.[16] (For a comprehensive look at this subject, see chapter 26.)

Resources

Consumer's Guide to Psychotherapy by Jack Engler, Ph.D., and Daniel Goleman, Ph.D. (Touchstone, 1992). The authoritative reference for making informed choices about all types of psychotherapy.

The Grief Recovery Institute (800-445-4808). Offers telephone counseling from 9 A.M. to 5 P.M. Pacific time, Monday through Friday, and makes referrals to affiliated outreach programs.

How to Survive the Loss of a Love by Melba Colgrove, Ph.D., Harold H. Bloomfield, M.D., and Peter McWilliams (Prelude, 1991). A practical, reassuring self-help book on coping with loss and enriching your life.

Making Peace with Your Parents (Ballantine, 1983) and *Making Peace with Yourself* (Ballantine, 1985) by Harold H. Bloomfield, M.D., with Leonard Felder. Clear advice on healing the hurts in life's important relationships.

Opening Up: The Healing Power of Confiding in Others by James W. Pennebaker, Ph.D. (Morrow, 1990). Documents the potential health benefits of self-disclosure—through private writing or, at the right time, through conversations with others.

Resilience: Discovering a New Strength at Times of Stress by Frederic Flach, Ph.D. (Fawcett, 1988). Illuminates the life-giving power of traumatic change.

Staying on Top When Your World Turns Upside Down by Kathryn D. Cramer, Ph.D. (Viking, 1990). An action plan developed by a well-known health psychologist and founder of the Stress Center at St. Louis University.

PERSONAL POWER NOTES
A Quick-List of This Chapter's Power-Action Options

For now, be with the pain.
- *Accept that your world has, for now, been turned upside down.*
- *Remember that grief is a process that takes time.*

Find strength in 5-minute rituals.

Express your feelings through 5-minute daily journaling.

Seek periods of solace—and draw help from friends and family.

Know when and how to get professional help.
- *Acknowledge that you need help.*
- *Identify the core issue or problem you face.*
- *Arrange for referrals to several therapists.*
- *Request an initial consultation.*
- *Consider your options and choose a therapist.*
- *Contract for therapy.*

Help others—it may speed your own healing.

PERSONAL NOTES

_____

_____

_____

_____

_____

_____

_____

_____

_____

_____

FROM CONFLICT TO CLOSENESS

Creating Greater Understanding
and Trust—Even When Others Resist

Everything that irritates us about others can lead us to an understanding of ourselves.
—**Carl Jung, M.D.**, Swiss psychologist

We live our lives as a mosaic of relationships, an ongoing series of dialogues and differing views. And at the core of each interaction, it's the thoughts and words—spoken and unspoken—that draw us together or drive us apart. And even when two people care deeply for each other, communication is often mishandled or gets mixed up—igniting arguments or soundlessly shattering our bond. We ask for help but no one answers. We talk, not understanding what needs to be understood. We listen, not able to hear what's in the other person's mind or heart.

Perhaps more than any other single factor, the way you handle misunderstanding and conflicts determines whether your relationships thrive or even survive.[1] One of the most difficult tasks in a loving relationship is managing differences and disagreements without arguments, anger and hostility. As we described in chapter 24, too often we fail: Suddenly you stop talking in a caring manner and start hurting each other—blaming, complaining, accusing, resenting, demanding and doubting. We live together under one roof, but we cope with problems like total strangers, you think to yourself. And it's true. We're married but speak different languages, you complain to your close friends. And you're right.

To appreciate and respect the unique "languages" of others, including loved ones, is one of life's steepest but most necessary climbs. It's also one of the most rewarding—because, to a major extent, your health and longevity are influenced by the success or failure of your relationships. In fact, says one medical researcher, "communication *is probably the single most important force that influences our health or lack of health.*"[2] We must either live together with hope and unfeigned support or face the growing possibility of dying prematurely and alone. In some startling respects, life and thoughts and dialogue are one and the same.

POWER ACTION: FIRST OPTION
Use 5-Second Reframing

One of the principal ways to keep relationships healthy and growing and head off arguments is this: No matter what problems we face together, we each naturally have different points of view, and those differences must at all times be respected rather than ignored or invalidated. In fact, some researchers are convinced that men and women use language so differently that they actually speak to each other with cross-cultural perspectives.

According to some researchers, *the single most important strategy to head off defensive communication is to consciously choose to hold on to a positive image of your partner and keep reintroducing praise and admiration in your relationship.*[3] It's up to you—as discussed in chapter 24—to be the architect of your own thoughts and to dispute and replace distorted thinking, irritation, contempt and regrets about what's *not* in your relationship. You can choose the opposite approach and make more of a point of acknowledging all the positive things that *are* in your relationship. If you arrive home to find clothing unwashed or on the floor, instead of ranting and raving about it, you can remember that your spouse was very tired last night and very busy all day. "We've been handling a hectic schedule recently," you might think to yourself or say aloud. "It's remarkable to me how many things *are* getting accomplished!"

Another powerful, on-the-spot way to get closer and stay closer is to *recognize—and adapt to—the other person's "conversational style."* For women, the key is intimacy and connection, explains Deborah Tannen, Ph.D., professor of linguistics at Georgetown University in Washington, D.C. "For men, it's about preserving independence and negotiating status," she says. To men, simply spending time together—eating at the same table, driving on errands or watching television—is part of being intimate, while having a conversation isn't. Whereas women often want to talk about what's happening in—or to—the rela-

POWER KNOWLEDGE:
CONFLICT AND CARING

MYTH #1: "Sticks and stones may break my bones but words can never hurt me."

POWER KNOWLEDGE: "While we speak with words, we speak also with our flesh and blood," says James J. Lynch, Ph.D., co-director of the Psychophysiology Laboratory and Clinic at the University of Maryland School of Medicine in Baltimore. "Study after study reveals that human dialogue not only affects our hearts significantly but can even alter the biochemistry of individual tissues at the farthest extremities of the body. . . . The entire body is influenced by dialogue. . . . New scientific data reveals the links between the spoken word and the human heart and show how that relationship influences two major cardiovascular disorders, [plus] hypertension and migraine headaches. Human dialogue is involved significantly in the development as well as the treatment of these diseases."[5]

When we open our mouths to speak, adds Dr. Lynch, we are, in a sense, "attempting to bring the hearer inside our own world. Ordinarily we tend to think of speech as words projected out, directed at or aimed toward someone else. Yet a moment of reflection would reveal that quite the opposite is true of *real speech*. For when a person speaks, he or she is inviting others to come inside his or her world, into his or her reality—that is, into his or her body and ultimately into his or her mind's heart. *Real speaking* is communication in the most profound sense: It is an act of communion."[6]

MYTH #2: In an ideal relationship, both partners agree on almost everything.

POWER KNOWLEDGE: In truth, different viewpoints and interests add spice and enjoyment to relationships—*if* they're appreciated by partners. Studies indicate that, over time, three of the most tionship, men usually just prefer to "be" in the relationship.

"To a woman, talking often means relaxing," says Dr. Tannen. "That's what she does with her friends. But a man sees talking as a kind of display—it involves competition, getting the edge, showing what you

---

damaging reactions to conflict are defensiveness, stubbornness and withdrawal from interaction. How *flexibly* a couple handles points of disagreement may be the key to the health and longevity of their relationship,[7] says University of Washington psychologist John Gottman, Ph.D.

Some of the elements once thought to be vital to relationship success—love, similar backgrounds, coming from well-adjusted families—are secondary to how well a couple communicates and even fights,[8] says Howard J. Markman, Ph.D., director of the Center for Marital and Family Studies in Denver. Exactly *why* it's often so difficult for one sex to communicate with the other is far less important than recognizing and learning to deal with this reality, says Georgetown University linguistics professor Deborah Tannen, Ph.D. "Whatever these differences [between men and women] come from, they're there and they're stubborn."[9]

MYTH #3: Friendships are great, but they have little to do with health or longevity.

POWER KNOWLEDGE: Human connectedness—a positive and supportive social network—helps us resist disease, enjoy life and live longer.[10] The existence of friendships is a good predictor of health and longevity,[11] and research indicates that people who do regular volunteer work show a dramatic increase in life expectancy over those who perform no such actions for others.[12] Even people with pets often seem to outlive people who do not have one to help keep them company.[13] And a recent 17-year followup study has revealed that the relationship between social ties and health continues into old age.[14]

At the University of New Mexico School of Medicine in Albuquerque, more than 250 elderly individuals participated in a study that evaluated the intimacy and intensity of their relationships. Researchers concluded that people who had strong, open friendships also possessed a number of physical characteristics (including low blood cholesterol levels and low uric acid levels) linked with reduced rates of disease.[15]

know." Example: A man says "I'm tired—it's been a long day." In reply, the woman says, "I had a hectic day, and I'm really worn out, too." Because conversation is usually perceived as a contest to men, he thinks she is trying to belittle him. But from her perspective, she's trying to make him feel better, showing empathy, deepening the connection. According to Dr. Tannen, when a woman asks, "What do you want to do tonight?" she's initiating "a free-flow give-and-take, but the man thinks she wants him to decide." Or, sometimes even more irritating, he simply responds: "I don't care, what do *you* want to do?"

"Nothing is more deeply disquieting than a conversation gone awry," says Dr. Tannen. "To say something and see it taken to mean something else; to try to be helpful and be thought pushy; to try to be considerate and be called cold . . . such failure at talk undermines your sense of competence and . . . can undermine your feeling of psychological well-being."

The main thing to do is simply take 5 seconds to clarify or "reframe" your dialogues, and *be flexible enough to adapt to the other person's inherent communication needs.* In truth, it's unrealistic to revamp your own conversational style or expect others to change theirs—especially since there's evidence that, to a significant extent, personal conversational style is a biologically centered *instinct* of the brain.[4] Therefore, what's called for is simply *greater flexibility*—in seeking out what, precisely, other people *really* mean, and in being more responsive to others' needs when trying to get your own meaning across. A good three-point guideline is this:

1. Listen attentively—and respect each individual's preferred "conversational style."

2. Get to the point early on.

3. Give enough details to ensure that what you *mean* to communicate comes through.

POWER ACTION: MORE OPTIONS
Meet Your Loved Ones and Friends Halfway:
Welcome Her Complaints, Confront Him Gently

One of the worst consequences of arguing is that it can quickly lead to what some researchers call *flooding*:[16] feeling so overwhelmed by your partner's negativity and your own reactions that you experience "systems overload." You're upset and distressed because you feel unfairly attacked, misunderstood or wronged. Within moments you may become defensive, hostile or withdrawn. Once you're feeling this far out of control—and some of us feel this far out of control *very often*—*constructive discussion is all but impossible.*

"In any intense exchange with a spouse," explains John M. Gottman, Ph.D., professor of psychology at the University of Washington in Seattle, who has spent more than a decade researching how men and women react to stress in relationships, "it's normal for some negative thoughts and feelings to arise. As long as they don't get too extreme, most people are able to handle them. We each have a sort of built-in meter that measures how much negativity accumulates during such interactions. When the level gets too high for you, the needle starts going haywire and flooding begins."[17] A few of us have very high thresholds for negativity. Others feel flooded at the mere hint of a complaint. Flooding is also influenced by how much pressure an individual is facing outside the relationship; the more stress, the more quickly flooding occurs. You may be surprised to learn that research indicates men become flooded far more easily than women. And the most common reaction is withdrawal—which represents a last-ditch effort to protect themselves from feeling trapped and overwhelmed.

To a large extent, the way you see yourself depends on the way you *assume* other people see you. As Aaron T. Beck, M.D., professor of psychiatry at the University of Pennsylvania in Philadelphia, explains it, such perceptions are shaped, in turn, by our interpretation of "signals" we get from others. But these interpretations can be biased by old, reactionary habits and by our current state of mind. For example, when you're feeling tense or tired (chapter 5), feelings of anxiety and doubt tend to be magnified.[18]

"When a partner doesn't live up to imagined expectations, the other becomes as upset as if a legal contract had been violated," explains Norman Epstein, Ph.D., associate professor at the University of Maryland in Baltimore. "It's as if a basic trust has been broken."[19] And once that trust is lost, *a catastrophic shift occurs in how you think about your partner and your relationship.* Even your *memory* gets altered—you come to recast your earlier, happier times together in a negative light. You start to react with dread to almost everything your partner says or does: "What *now*?" You feel continually on guard against attack. Your spouse says, "We have to talk," and you instantly think, "Here comes another fight," even if all he or she wanted was to invite some friends over this weekend.

You begin hesitating to say what you really mean and begin misreading each other's mind, imputing the worst possible motives to each other and overgeneralizing complaints: "You *always* ignore me." "You *never* help out around here." If this pattern isn't headed off, eventually hostility colors everything. (See chapter 25 for quick ways to overcome distorted, automatic thoughts that can hurt important relationships.)

Based on long-term research, here are two more important pieces of day-in, day-out advice for men and women.[20]

Men: Try not to avoid conflict. Sidestepping a problem or complaint won't make it disappear, it will just upset your partner more. Uncomfortable as it may be, by venting feelings she's able to help keep your relationship healthy and secure. To the best of your ability, stay detached and flexible—rarely is it her goal to attack you personally, even if frustrations prompt her to employ sarcasm or contempt. If you listen attentively to her complaints or criticisms without putting her down, she will feel validated and will likely calm down. If you refuse to listen, she'll be increasingly upset and may escalate the conflict, pushing you toward flooding.

Women: Confront him clearly but gently. Due to a host of genetic and cultural reasons, in most relationships it's up to the woman to raise the majority of important issues. But it's essential to be flexible enough to do so *in a calm, clear and gentle way*. If you don't, your partner will likely resist or withdraw. Be pleasantly persistent if he seems driven to keep changing the subject. Let him know you are *not* attacking him and that you need him to join with you in facing issues and conflicts in your relationship. You might say something like, "This may not seem so important to you right now, but it really *is* important for me—and we need to talk, *together*, about what's bothering me so we can keep the love alive in our relationship."

If He "Stonewalls," Give Him a Little Extra Space

At times, someone—usually a man—will suddenly stop communicating and become silent. Dr. Gottman, in *Why Marriages Succeed or Fail*, calls this emotional reaction stonewalling.[21] Apparently based in part on genetics and in part on learned behavior patterns, stonewalling occurs, for example, when a man hears—or just anticipates—criticism or senses that his wife is bringing up a difficult issue. He feels threatened—and withdraws. He avoids eye contact, barely moves his face, keeps his neck rigid and even neglects to say such simple acknowledgements as "Yes, I see" or "Uh-huh." Many women think out loud, sharing their struggles with an interested listener and to some extent discovering what they want to say through the process of talking.[22] But in many cases, men process information differently and tend to first silently "mull over" or think about what they've just heard or experienced.

Even though it's not fair, when a man stonewalls it often seems to be up to the wife to take control of what happens next. Dr. Gottman and other researchers have discovered that, in happy marriages, the wife usually interrupts the argument cycle.[23] She ignores a negative comment or says something positive in the face of stonewalling behavior. *It may surprise you to learn that it's less important to solve marital "problems" than to be able to deal with the emotions they bring up.* Distressed marriages are characterized by one, and often both, spouses getting flooded and escalating arguments into fights.

The man is likely to be too "rational" and downplay his partner's emotions. Experiencing his reaction, the woman is then more likely to complain and criticize her partner, feeling she must raise the intensity of the interaction to keep him responsive. Then, as the wife demands more emotional confrontation, the husband withdraws even more, which escalates the wife's demands. Often perceiving her husband's withdrawal as a lack of caring—which it usually isn't—she may become irate and further escalate the conflict, and trigger what Dr. Gottman calls kitchen-sinking—"bringing up all kinds of past and present complaints and mixing them with sarcasm and contempt."[24] This tactic, of course, immediately overloads most men and causes further withdrawal.

"The biggest challenge for women is to correctly interpret and support a man when he *isn't* talking . . . ," says John Gray, Ph.D., author of *Men Are from Mars, Women Are from Venus.* "Women need to understand that often when a man is silent, he is saying, 'I don't know what to say yet, but I am thinking about it.' What women *hear* is 'I am not responding to you because I don't care about you and I'm going to ignore you. What you have said to me is not important and therefore I am not responding.' "[25]

Pause for 5 Seconds and Say "It's Not Your Fault"

According to some researchers, men "hear" far better when they don't feel they're receiving unsolicited advice or being attacked. Often when a man feels challenged, his attention zeros in on being right and he forgets to be loving or to listen. And he is unaware of how uncaring he sounds or how hurtful this may be to his partner. Requests turn into commands; frustrations fireball into all-out attacks. He has no idea that by his response *he* is starting an argument; on the contrary, he thinks *she* is arguing with him. He defends his point of view while she defends *herself* from his barbed comments—which hurt her feelings.

To end this downspiral of misperceptions, pay careful attention whenever you're complaining about a problem to be sure that the listener *knows* that you're not blaming him or her for causing it. Whenever appropriate, say, "It's not your fault." And if you *feel* like the other person's complaining is really blaming, say, "It feels to me that you're saying this is my fault. Is that true?" Chances are, it isn't. By getting clear about it, you can avoid blowing things out of proportion in your mind and be a far better listener.

"In a sea of conflict," explains Dr. Gottman, "men sink while women can swim."[26] While neither men nor women enjoy conflict, women generally seem able to handle it better, whereas men are more likely to crumble under the stress.[27] "Men are less able to cope with negative expressions of emotion," says Howard J. Markman, Ph.D., director of the Center for Marital and Family Studies in Denver, who along with his colleagues has spent nearly two decades studying what makes successful marriages work. "As a result, men withdraw further and further and feed the vicious cycle."[28]

"A man commonly feels attacked and blamed by a woman's feelings, especially when she is upset and talks about problems," says Dr. Gray. "Many men don't understand the female need to share upset feelings with the people they love. With practice and awareness of our differences, women can learn how to express their feelings without having them sound like blaming."[29] She could use a comment such as: "It sure feels good to talk about this" or "I'm feeling so relieved that I can talk about this. Thank you." That kind of simple change can make a world of difference, and men need to work at remembering that complaining about problems does not mean blaming and that when a woman complains she is generally just letting go of her frustrations by talking about them. "The four magic words to support a man are 'It's not your fault,'" believes Dr. Gray.[30]

Fight Fair!

Even the most destructive relationship conflicts and fights begin with *good intentions*. The most important focus is how *to tap into these good intentions and the reservoir of hope*.[31] Evidence continues to mount that it's not *what* you fight about, it's the *way* you fight that's a key to either marital happiness or disaster.[32] "The more a couple is able to fight constructively, the higher their level of marital happiness," says researcher Susan E. Crohan, Ph.D., of the University of Wisconsin, Madison. "One of the most consistent predictors of marital unhappiness is destructive conflict."[33] Dr. Crohan bases this observation on her research with colleagues at the University of Michigan.[34]

The essence of genius is knowing what to overlook.

—William James, M.D., founder of modern psychology

And let's face it: Many of us have never learned how to express disappointments and frustrations and hurt feelings without all-out battles. It takes two to argue but only one to stop an argument. So get in the habit of asking yourself, Is this really worth arguing about? If the answer is yes, ask again.

One way to disengage from the start-up of an argument is with *no-fault communication phrases,*[35] such as: "We seem to be caught in a cycle" or "We seem to be out of sync" or "There seems to be a push/pull pattern going on right now in our relationship" or "We seem to have fallen into a pattern where you have this understandable reaction, which causes me to have an understandable reaction, which then causes you . . ."

When you and your partner can pinpoint whatever pattern you're locked in, you can recognize its power. Then it also becomes easier to see why blaming each other is a waste of time and energy. Even though every negative feeling occurs for some important reason, you can frame negative emotions as symptoms of problem patterns: "Lately I've been feeling (jealous, guilty, depressed, anxious, angry, critical) . . ." and then immediately add "and I think it's because we're starting to fall into a pattern of. . . . What do you think?" Healthy emotional intimacy requires knowing your own feelings and letting them be known—in a safe, caring "space" in your relationship.

Some other recommendations for easing relationship anger include making desposits in your relationship's "Emotional Bank Account" (see chapter 24), and avoiding using words and phrases that make your partner livid. But don't turn away from conflict at all costs, either, since there's evidence that "avoidance means couples never get to the issues, which blow up later," Dr. Crohan says. When conflict is handled constructively it can be positive, she explains. "You learn more about yourself and your spouse. You build a trust that you can weather the storms."

According to Dr. Crohan, constructive fighting means "calmly discussing issues; really listening; saying nice things and making your spouse laugh to defuse anger." And some hurtful tactics need to truly be off-limits—such as mud-slinging, playing psychologist, dumping loads of grievances on each other, acting like an ostrich and refusing to acknowledge that a problem exists, storming out of the room or maneuvering to pin the blame on each other.

As recommended in chapter 24, when things start to heat up, call a timeout and use Reflective Coping. Agree with your partner that either one of you can say "This is not a good time to talk" or "I'm getting upset and I don't want to argue, so let's not talk about this right now," as long as you choose another discussion time soon and keep your word. Pick a time *later* to talk about what's bothering you, and separate *discussing* the problem—bringing an issue into the open by describing behaviors that are upsetting to you but without calling your partner abusive names or criticizing his or her character—from *solving* the problem. Stretch your awareness so you can understand—not change—your partner's position or feelings, and refrain from mind-reading (see chapter 24) or anticipating what your partner will say. Instead of re-hashing the past, turn your attention toward the future.

One final note: Don't forget biology. "You can avoid a lot of rela-tionship conflicts if you both have had something to eat first," says William Nagler, M.D, psychiatrist and author of *The Dirty Half Dozen: Six Radical Rules to Make Relationships Last*. "Half the time, having a full stomach will prevent major fights. Blood-sugar battles are often what you are really fighting. . . . When your blood sugar is low, things that normally wouldn't bother you seem like major events."[36] For spe-cific snack recommendations, see chapter 9.

When You Want Support, Take 5 Seconds to Ask for It!

It's just not realistic to assume that if your partner loves you, he or she will always, instinctively, offer support without you having to ask for it, or that you can purposely "test" how much your partner loves you by *not* asking for support when you really want it.

Studies suggest that unless it's some kind of emergency, many of us are not intuitively driven to offer our support—we need to be asked.[37] This can be very frustrating, because if you ask in the wrong way—such as in a demanding tone of voice—no matter how politely you word your request, the other person may refuse to grant it. What often works best is a brief, direct request, put forth in a nondemanding way. "Would you pick up the groceries?" is very different from "We need groceries today and I can't do it" or "Please make the time to go pick up groceries today. It's about time you helped out in some way with the weekly er-rands!" And "Would you take us out to dinner tonight?" is heard very differently from "I can't take the time to fix dinner tonight" or "I've worked so hard, the least you could do is take us out to eat tonight!"

Take 5 Seconds to Disarm Dialogue "Landmines"

It's a sad fact of life that we often treat the ones we love worse than we treat nearly anyone else. "We are more likely to hurl insults at, push, shove, hit and slap our lovers than any other person in our life," explain Dr. Markman and Clifford Notarius, Ph.D., professor of psychology at Catholic University in Washington, D.C., authors of *We Can Work It Out: Making Sense of Marital Conflict*. "We are even more polite to acquaintances than we are to our mates."[38] Daily life is filled with interactions that can drive you crazy—or propel you toward your goals and dreams. Your minute-by-minute conversations—aloud and in your mind—are laced with *specific words and phrases* that can act like psychological "buttons," triggering frustration, anger, arguments, resentment, sabotage and self-doubt. In relationships, the truth is, "one 'zinger' can erase 20 acts of kindness," warn Dr. Notarius and Dr. Markman. "Our research has shown that it takes one put-down to undo hours of kindness you give to your partner. . . . The key: Intimate partners must learn how to manage their anger and control the exchange of *negative* behavior."[39]

Whenever you underestimate, mishandle or fail to disarm dialogue "landmines," you erode—and may even end up destroying—personal and business relationships. Yet researchers have recently discovered that *each of us has the power to stop this destructive communication pattern any time we want to*—in fact, you may only need to alter three or four exchanges to change the course of an entire conversation.[40] Few self-help skills may be more important, since studies suggest that, on average, we are communicating 5 out of every 10 minutes we're awake. Here, as much as in any other area of life, *small things make a big difference*. With awareness and practice, in more and more cases you can turn resistance into rapport, resentment into respect.

"Flash points" can trigger instant anger or alienation in other people—and can hit the listener's emotions like unexpected electric shocks. The resulting "fallout" ranges from the subtle to the explosive—including irritation, doubt, distraction, anger, mistrust, arguments, festering resentment and sabotage. And then, once the instigator (who may, in fact, be innocent of *intending* to provoke the listener) notices that things are awry, he or she may get caught up spending ridiculous amounts of time trying to soothe hurt feelings and "fix" misunderstandings.

Here, in random order, is a sampling of common button-pushing *thoughts*, *feelings* and *comments*. Which of them tend to make you irritated, distracted or angry? And, even more important, which are the most upsetting to you and to your loved ones, co-workers, employees or friends? (Unfortunately, many of us fail to recognize—and thereby alter—the precise, habitual words and "catch phrases" that pepper our daily use of the language and actually trigger much of the friction and many of the blowouts in our most important work and nonwork relationships.)

Once you start to notice these "flash points"—and dozens of other more innocuous but still maddening expressions—you can stop saying them and, when you hear others say them, you can head off your own negative reactions by pausing, separating people from problems, clarifying whatever feelings start to arise, switching perspectives and taking charge of the exact way you respond. Reflect on your recent conversations, disagreements and arguments. Psychologists sometimes refer to this as editing[41]—and it's a skill everyone in a relationship needs to master. Editing means *pausing for a split-second to make a deliberate effort to hold back destructive, negative comments in favor of something more polite.* Editing incorporates courtesy and politeness—two qualities that are sadly lacking in most relationships today. Can you identify any irritating words or expressions that distracted or frustrated you about the other person? Or can you remember what you were saying when you noticed the other person turn away or snap at you? Expand this list—or, best of all, create your own.

Nonwords

- Ummm . . .
- Ahhh . . . , uhhh . . .
- You know . . .
- Well . . .
- Sort of . . . , kind of . . .
- Like . . .
- Uhhh, well, you know, so, okay, like . . .

5-second alternatives: Use effective pauses, which emphasize what you've just said and provide the listener with a chance to enter the conversation. *Note*: If, when irritated, you tend to stonewall ("Talking to you is like talking to the wall") and present a blank face to your partner when a criticism or complaint is being aired, *make a conscious effort to stop stonewalling and start listening*, sending small signals that show you're paying attention. Psychologists call these signs *back channels*[42]— and they include focused (rather than glazed-over) eye contact, nodding your head periodically and asking clarifying questions or, if things seem clear, making brief vocal signals that you understand, using such nonwords as "uh-huhhh," "um-hmmmm," or a statement such as "I can see (hear, feel) that . . ."

Automatic Detours

- "Yes, *but* . . ."
- "I agree with you, *but* . . ."
- "That's a great idea, *but* . . ."
- "I respect your opinion, *but* . . ."

The conjunction *but* is often used—albeit sometimes unintentionally—to negate everything said before it. Notice how it feels to hear these statements: "I agree with you, *but* . . ."; "That's true, *but* . . ."; "I respect your opinion, *but* . . ."

According to communications experts, one way to solve this dilemma is something called an *agreement frame*. Certain phrases can be used to establish rapport, to share honest feelings and to minimize resistance to the opinions of others, thereby avoiding many conversational conflicts. You first point out something positive and specific about what the other person has done or said and then add your comments or ideas with the connection *and*.

Examples: "I agree with your basic idea (or a specific point you made), *and* here's another angle (thought/suggestion/resource) that might be helpful." Or "I respect your intense feelings about (a problem), *and* here are several of my thoughts." The process works just as effectively in self-talk: "I want to solve this conflict, *and* (not *but*) that looks very challenging to do." Or "I'm choosing not to get so upset over little things *and* (not *but*) it's taking me quite a while to learn how."

In each case, you're establishing rapport by acknowledging the communication rather than blocking, ignoring or denigrating it with trap words like *but* or *however*. You are bringing attention to areas of mutual agreement, a process that tends to form a positive bond. And you are creating the opportunity to redirect the conversation by avoiding and overcoming resistance wherever possible.

More examples of automatic detours:

- "Like I said, . . ."
- "That's *interesting*"; "That's an *interesting* idea."
- "Is that right?"
- "Something *just* like that happened to me—and here's what to do . . ."
- "What do you want to do?" Answer: "I don't care. What do *you* want to do?"
- "What happened?"; "What's wrong?"; "What's the matter?" Answer: "*Nothing*" or "It's no big deal" or "I'm okay."
- "Thanks for the compliment—but it was *nothing*."
- "Here's a little *constructive* criticism . . ."

Stinging Jabs

- "But you shouldn't *feel* that way!"
- "Are you having a *bad* day?" "Well, if you think *you're* having a bad day, . . ."

- "Why are you making this such a *big* deal?"
- "You shouldn't worry so much."
- "When are you going to get off it?"
- "How many times do we have to go *through* this?"
- "Why do you need to keep *talking* about it, anyway?"
- "So what are you *really* trying to say?"
- "Just *kidding*!"
- "But it's so *obvious*. Why don't you get it?"
- "You're not *listening* to me! If you were, you'd *understand*."
- "Okay, then, just forget it!"
- "Can't you agree with *anything*?"
- "But what can I *do* about it?" Answer: "*Nothing*—what makes you think I *want* you to do anything about it?"
- "But how can I *fix* it?" Answer: "You *can't*—what makes you think I *want* you to fix it, anyway?"
- "Stop *changing* the subject!"
- "Stop twisting my words! You *know* what I mean."
- "Stop *interrupting* me! You *always* do that!"
- "Well, if you'd let *me* say something for a change . . ."
- "That's *not* at all what I said!" "Yes it *is*. I *heard* you say it!"
- "Even a . . . could do *that*!"
- "There you *go* again. You're *such* a . . . !"
- "You *never* . . ."
- "You *always* . . ."
- "Stop nagging."
- "Don't tell *me* what to do."
- "If you *really* . . ."
- "I don't mean to upset you, but . . ."

5-second alternatives: In every relationship, there are times when we don't like something our partner has just said. If your relationship has become filled with button-pushing negativity, your reflexive reaction may be to lash back with criticism or contempt, which simply—and immediately—escalates the conflict and creates additional hard feelings. In short, *this response just doesn't work*. Instead, make it your goal to *be polite*—no matter what happens—and complain rather than make personal attacks. Before you say a word, acknowledge that *you have a choice to make*.

A complaint is specific, and limited to one situation. It expresses how you feel. ("I'm upset because . . .").

A *criticism* is more generalized and includes blaming or accusing your partner. (See the list of Stinging Jabs above—"You *never* . . ."

"You *always* . . ." "I can *never* count on your help when I need it!")

Contempt adds further insult to the criticism. ("You idiot . . ." "How *stupid* can a person get?" "Even a . . . could do *that!*").

For a successful, lasting relationship, stick with sharing *complaints*. Pay attention to your comments. Remove the blame, insults, mocking and sarcasm. Say how *you* feel: One effective technique is the *X,Y,Z statement*: "When you did (or didn't do) *X* in specific situation *Y*, I felt *Z.*" Don't let yourself criticize your loved one's personality or character. Be clear and precise: The more concrete and specific your complaint, the more you're likely to improve your partner's understanding of why you're irritated, confused or angry. Deal with one situation at a time. Don't make assumptions or mind-read.

Effectively controlling the "buttons" in relationship dialogues takes some concentration and practice. It's well worth the effort. Neurologist Richard Restak, M.D., author of *The Brain: The Last Frontier*, describes it this way: "Have you noticed that some people become slightly unglued—and sometimes a good deal more—whenever they hear certain words? *Tax audit, welfare, abortion, mistress, racial quotas*—merely mentioning them can produce marked alterations in personality. A person may stammer, blanch or go red in the face, turn argumentative and undergo erratic changes in blood pressure and pulse, all in response to a mere word. It's as if the offending term produced a kind of emotional short-circuit."[43]

With practice, says Dr. Restak, it's possible to learn to detect the emotional coloration that your mind—and your partner's mind—has given to certain words. Within a split second of hearing a word or phrase, you can detect the first subtle spark of emotion. For example, says Dr. Restak, "take the way words are sometimes used as weapons.

" 'I think I'll jam Tom's circuits by suggesting that he's a reactionary,' thinks Phil. 'That always gets a rise out of him. That'll end the argument.'

"But if Tom has learned to control his emotional responsiveness to being called a reactionary," says Dr. Restak, "the game is over. The two adversaries have no choice but to deal with the real issues and not simply one person's tendency to blow a fuse in response to another's vocabulary."[44]

Fortunately, you can use self-observation to strengthen your control over these automatic, counterproductive habits, says Robert Ornstein, Ph.D., psychologist and professor of human biology at Stanford University: "Your husband burns the toast. It's the last piece and he did it the previous Thursday as well. Of course, you're disappointed. And you want to give him a piece of your mind. You begin to describe how you were looking forward to the toast, and now you have to go off to work yet again without it. Why can't he simply watch the toaster more carefully, or even just set the darkness gauge a little lighter? He's a little abashed and a bit put out. A simple argument, so far.

"But now you are about to give him a piece of your mind that you didn't know about. All of a sudden you're thinking, automatically almost, how you don't like the way he's treated your friends when you're at dinner; he seems to patronize them. And he didn't make the car payment. He's too tired to be affectionate at night, you think. . . . All of these thoughts have appeared as a result of the agitation caused by the burnt toast . . .

"You may not be able to resist the moves of your mind the first or second time it happens, but after a while, you will be able to play the mind's game, learning to [take conscious control] instead of allowing the automatic routines to take over."[45]

Build More Trust in Your Friendships—5 Minutes at a Time

According to researchers, there is a vital link between the strength of our social support systems and our emotional and physical resilience under severe stress.[46] Simply having someone to talk to on a regular basis may be as important as costly medical treatment.[47] Studies indicate that deep, caring relationships really *do* matter, and that, as one medical researcher puts it, "they are desperately important to both our mental and physical well-being . . . because the rise of human loneliness may be one of the most serious sources of disease in the 20th century."[48]

Social support is the name scientists give to the combination of ongoing involvement with others, caring relationships, and an orientation of actively seeking friendship. Social support doesn't depend on the *number* of people you know but rather on the *quality* of your relationships, which above all must be based on the principle Ralph Waldo Emerson underscored in his 1841 essay on "Friendship": "The only way to have a friend is to be one."

A recent nine-year study of 1,368 patients initially admitted to Duke University Medical Center in Durham, North Carolina, for cardiac catheterization to diagnose heart disease showed that "those patients with neither a spouse nor a friend were three times more likely to die than those involved in a caring relationship,"[49] says Redford Williams, M.D., professor of psychiatry, associate professor of medicine and director of the Behavioral Medicine Research

Center at the medical center and lead author of the study.

A friend, said Emerson, "is a person with whom I may be sincere, before him I may think aloud." Authenticity is the basis of genuine friendship—and it enables both individuals to act freely and deeply as themselves. "Being with you," wrote E. B. White, "is like walking on a very clear morning—definitely the sensation of belonging there." Whereas a lack of trust poisons relationships,[50] a trusting heart strengthens them, says Dr. Williams, who suggests the following:[51]

• Reduce your cynical mistrust of the motives of others. Become a better listener, since this enables you to stave off jumping to conclusions and other "crystal ball"–gazing tendencies. To switch perspectives (see chapter 24), pretend this day is your last (see chapters 31 and 32). Turn to your friends whenever you need support or help, and give support and help to others whenever you can.

• Reduce the frequency and intensity with which you experience emotions such as anger, irritation, frustration and rage (see chapter 24). Learn to laugh at yourself, to step into the other person's shoes, to reason with yourself, to forgive.

• Treat others with greater kindness and consideration and develop your assertiveness skills for unavoidable confrontation situations. Follow through on whatever you agree to do; even the little things matter.

"Take 5" to Write in a Journal or Confide in Others

One of the most effective and meaningful ways to improve mind/body health can come from increasing your willingness to express your mistakes, secrets, hopes and fears.[52] This expression can either take the form of writing in a journal or confiding in loved ones, close friends or trained counselors. A study of 325 European managers, all male, found a strong relationship between "expressiveness" on the husband's part and marital happiness. Expressiveness was defined as taking an active interest in one's wife, talking with her about herself and her problems and concerns and expressing affection toward her. Eighty percent of the marriages in which the husband saw expressiveness as an important part of the relationship were happy. On the other hand, 80 percent of the marriages in which the husband did not value expressiveness were unhappy.[53]

When the National Opinion Research Center asked the question, "Looking over the last six months, who are the people with whom you discussed matters important to you?" those who named five or more friends or relatives were *60 percent more likely to feel "very happy"*[54] than those who could name no such confidants.

Researchers have discovered that suppressing deep guilt and misery—either consciously or unconsciously—requires such arduous physical effort that it takes a toll on your health. However, as we mentioned in chapter 25, those who confide their troubles in a private diary—writing as little as 5 to 15 minutes a day for three days—often experience marked improvements in their health, attitude and immune function.[55] "We encourage individuals to write for themselves as opposed to writing for someone else," say psychologists Martha E. Francis, Ph.D., and James W. Pennebaker, Ph.D., of Southern Methodist University in Dallas. "The benefits of writing lie in the act of letting go and expressing those deepest thoughts and feelings surrounding a personal upheaval. . . . And people who write about personally upsetting experiences report that it is important for their essays to be kept anonymous and confidential."[56,57] In fact, it may even be best to destroy what you have written to yourself. Planning to show it to someone else can affect your mindset while writing. "From a health perspective, you'll be better off simply making yourself the audience," says Dr. Pennebaker.[58]

When writing, focus on the issues that you are currently living with, and explore both the objective experience (what happened) and your feelings about it. Really let go, advises Dr. Pennebaker in his book *Opening Up*. Write about your deepest emotions. *What* do you feel about it and *why* do you feel that way? Don't be concerned about temporarily feeling worse. "As we have found in all of our studies," observes Dr. Pennebaker, "you may feel sad or depressed immediately after writing. These negative feelings usually dissipate within an hour or so. In rare cases, they may last a day or two. The overwhelming majority of our volunteers [who participated in the research studies], however, report feelings of relief, happiness and contentment soon after the writing studies are concluded."[59]

What about opening up to others? One of the reasons that Dr. Pennebaker and others suggest writing about upsetting experiences is that it's safe. You can be completely honest with yourself. No one else will judge you, criticize you or distort your perceptions. That doesn't change the fact that, ideally, we should each be able to express our most intimate thoughts to someone else—and sometimes this kind of sharing can forge a powerful and lasting bond with others and offer both physiological and psychological health benefits.[60] But the risk is that if you unburden yourself and are then rejected by the listener, you may become hostile, depressed or withdrawn. If you're contemplating opening up to a friend or loved one, here are several of the safeguards recommended by Dr. Pennebaker.[61]

• Know that self-disclosure will change the nature of your friendship—and your friend may be threatened or hurt by what you say.

• Hearing your traumas can be a trauma for the listener—and the listener may then feel the need to discuss what you said with someone else.

• Social blackmail is a risk—divulging your hurts can put the listener in a powerful position.

• The expectations of the listener can affect what you disclose.

• It's vital to ask yourself, Why am I choosing this particular listener? Dr. Pennebaker has found, for example, that some people have truly hurt others by confiding. Although they claim to be open and honest in their actions, their disclosures are clearly motivated by revenge.

Invest 5 Minutes a Week to Value and Expand Your Circle of Friends

"People with a rich network of supportive individuals to whom they can turn in trouble live longer and healthier lives," says Christopher Peterson, Ph.D., professor of psychology at the University of Michigan in Ann Arbor. "They are more robust in the face of stress and hassles in everyday life."[62] Here are several quick, practical suggestions for strengthening and enlarging your support network.

• Take three pieces of paper. In the center of one, draw a circle, and inside this circle, write your name. In circles near yours, write the names of the people with whom you have the strongest, closest bonds. Include those who have been sources of warmth and approval during earlier periods of your life, as well as those who actively support you now.

"List the people you have warm feelings for," suggests Tom Ferguson, M.D., a well-known medical writer. "People you are comfortable with. Nurturing people. People you would like to be able to talk with if you were having a hard time. Think of all the people you would feel comfortable hugging—or being hugged by. All the people you would enjoy sharing a meal with. All the people you'd enjoy receiving a letter from. Don't worry about being 'fair' or reasonable or logical—this exercise is for you alone."[63]

> When we learn not to judge others—and accept them, appreciate them, and not want to change them—we can simultaneously learn to accept ourselves.
>
> —Gerald Jampolsky, M.D., psychiatrist

• As you list the names, you may find yourself wishing you were in closer touch with some of them. If so, list these people on the second sheet of paper. Entries may include old friends you haven't seen in a long time or new friends you'd like to get to know better. There may be some people for whom you would like to do something special—a hug, a phone call, a letter or a gift to let them know they're really important to you. If such feelings come to mind, list them with the names of these friends on the third sheet of paper.

• When you've finished your drawing of your social support system, take several minutes to review each name, remembering the kinds of support you've received from and given to that person. Is there anyone you'd like to be in touch with right now? What ongoing use can you make of your lists?

Help Others in Need—5 Seconds to 5 Minutes at a Time— And Bring Out More of the Best in Yourself

In our everyday lives we all encounter other people struggling with adversity. In truth, how we each respond to this experience is about us, not about them. Do you reach out with empathy to those who are in poverty or sickness, despair or pain? Or do you turn away—not wanting to be distracted from your to-do lists and objectives, or with the attitude that "God helps those who help themselves"?

On any single day, we each witness innumerable gestures of empathy and caring—from small acts of kindness to heart-rending sacrifices—but rarely ever, while observing these actions, do we simply shrug and say, "Of course! That's just human nature to be concerned and generous." Why? Partly because there's a pervasive belief that our darker, selfish side is larger and more persistent that our brighter, compassionate side. And, to maintain that view, we unconsciously dismiss the volumes of research which confirm that the opposite is true.[64] It's high time that the worn-out cliché "I've got to look out for Number One" gets dumped, superseded by "What can I do to help?" Why? The answer can be philosophical. But instead let's be purely scientific about it: Altruism, charity, generosity, service and kindness contribute not only to a meaningful life but to a more satisfying, healthier and perhaps longer one as well. As noted in the "Power Knowledge" section of this chapter, doing good for others not only feels good, it is good for your well-being. The evidence clearly suggests that a regular weekly habit of helping others may be as important to your health and longevity as regular exercise and good nutrition[65]—and helping others offers value to the health of your community and the world as well. In fact, it may be a key to ending the deadly cycle of fear,

> I don't know what your destiny will be but one thing I do know: The only ones among you who will be happy are those who have sought and found how to serve.
>
> —Albert Schweitzer, M.D., French missionary physician and philosopher

isolationism and violence that is rampant in our individualistic society.

"The next revolution in health care," says Allan Luks, author of *The Healing Power of Doing Good*, "must be to bring to our awareness the health potential of helping others."[66] Lending a helping hand to other people may be good for your own vitality—and even for your heart and immune system,[67] and people—especially men—who do regular volunteer work show a dramatic increase in life expectancy over those who perform no such services for others.[68] And a study at the University of California at San Francisco Medical School uncovered evidence suggesting that self-centeredness may be a risk factor in coronary artery disease.[69] The most self-involved subjects—who emphasized such words as *I* and *me*—tended to have a more severe case of coronary artery disease as well as greater likelihood of depression and anxiety. A 13-year study of people between the ages of 60 and 94 concluded that maintaining a useful and satisfying role in society is one of the most important ways to enhance longevity.[70] French studies of 700 people (with documented ages of 100 or more) typically found these individuals to be enthusiastic and interested in public affairs.[71] Another study on altruism concluded that an attitude of selflessness made it 2.4 times more likely that an individual would be happy, whereas an attitude of selfishness made it 9.5 times more likely that the person would be unhappy.[72]

Focusing on others can help get you out of the common state of gridlock from self-centeredness or family, career and financial worries or stresses. Helping others tends to improve mood, deepen optimism and nourish us with a sense of genuine gratitude. Helping someone less capable can enhance your appreciation of your own skills, knowledge, competence and strengths. The primary benefits of helping seem to be in the *process* rather than the *outcome*. By that we mean the payoffs—for the one being helped and for you—arise primarily from the moment-to-moment interactions in helping rather than on whether a social condition is "fixed" or not.

Contrary to popular opinion, helping others doesn't require a huge commitment of time. All you need is a personal plan that can range from doing scheduled work with a volunteer organization to spontaneous acts of generosity and kindness throughout the week. In choosing a type of helping activity that will heighten good feelings and tend to keep you helping every week, Luks recommends personal contact with the people you help (especially strangers in need). To keep your enthusiasm high, make the helping activity something that appeals to your own interests or skills.

Here are several suggestions.[73]

Choose one-to-one volunteer activities. These could include tutoring children, reading to the blind, bringing food to house-bound neighbors or the homeless or visiting the elderly. Or you might choose to work on a telephone "hotline." These one-to-one activities offer a strong emotional connection, and this can be one of the best ways to benefit from "helper's high," increased self-esteem and reduced distress in your own life.

Make helping others a weekly habit. The more frequent the helping—even in small doses, at least once a week[74]—the more likely you'll experience the positive feelings and health benefits.[75]

Cancel guilt trips. Helping can backfire and become negative if you're doing it because you feel you *have* to.

Keep expectations modest. It may be possible to actually *harm* others with too much kindness or inappropriate helping—trying to make all the decisions yourself or "taking over"—especially if you get trapped in the role of "rescuer," expecting to be lavishly rewarded with thanks and praise. This can end up making those being "helped" feel more helpless and hopeless. Instead try empowering others, helping them to gain more control over their lives. Allow them to make choices, even about simple things. Divide complex tasks into clear, easy actions. Small successes create a growing sense of confidence, independence and pride. And know that *forced cheerfulness*—blind, unrelenting optimism (discussed in chapter 29)—is *not* helpful and blocks others from a healthy chance to express their anger, dreams, frustrations, hopes, disappointments, fears or sadness.

Practice "random acts of kindness." In a world plagued by random acts of violence, one of the simplest antidotes to fear and despair is to perform calculated and spontaneous acts of thoughtfulness and consideration—what have been recently been called random acts of kindness. Notice the innumerable 5-second opportunities each day to help others without expecting anything in return. Help with heavy packages, hold open a door, say a kind word, let someone who looks harried cut into line ahead of you, pick up litter, jot out a quick "thank you" note, give another driver that close-up parking space. Such unexpected thoughtfulness has a ripple effect and encourages others to help others, too.

If you love animals, consider adopting a pet. Several studies suggest that pet owners enjoy better health. One year after a heart attack, patients who have pets have *one-fifth* the death rate of those who do not have an animal companion.[76] The connection with pets may be explained in a number of ways. Pet owners frequently feel needed—since

pets such as dogs and cats can offer a source of unconditional, nonjudgmental affection and reliance—and petting a dog, seeing a kitten roll and tumble or observing
the amazing explorations of fish in an aquarium can help
prevent or reverse a down mood. Pets can also divert
our attention from our own problems for a while and
help us feel more connected to Nature and the rest of the
world. If you have the room in your home and heart for
a pet, a trip to the animal rescue shelter or Humane Society may prove, over time, to be a very rewarding one.

> We make a living by what we get, but we make a life by what we give.
>
> **—Winston Churchill,**
> British prime minister

Resources

The Brighter Side of Human Nature: Altruism and Empathy in Everday Life by Alfie Kohn (Basic Books, 1990). A lucid, scholarly look at this important subject.

The Broken Heart: The Medical Consequences of Loneliness (Basic, 1977) and *Language of the Heart: The Body's Response to Human Dialogue* (Basic, 1985) by James J. Lynch, Ph.D. Two classic works by a co-director of the Psychophysiological Clinic and Laboratories at the University of Maryland School of Medicine in Baltimore.

Center for Marital and Family Studies (2155 S. Race St., Denver, CO 80208; 303-750-8798). Provides information on the Prevention and Relationship Enhancement Program (PREP) and counselor referrals.

Dare to Connect: Reaching Out to Others in Romance, Friendship, and the Workplace by Susan Jeffers, Ph.D. (Fawcett, 1992). A warm, encouraging book.

The Evolution of Consciousness by Robert Ornstein, Ph.D. (Prentice-Hall, 1991). A compelling view on taking control of what we think, feel, say and do.

Guerilla Kindness: A Manual of Good Works, Kind Acts, and Thoughtful Deeds by Gavin Whitsett (Impact Publishers, 1993).

The Healing Power of Doing Good: The Health and Spiritual Benefits of Helping Others by Allan Luks with Peggy Payne (Fawcett, 1991). A sourcebook on helping others—with a nationwide directory of volunteer organizations.

Making Peace in Your Stepfamily by Harold H. Bloomfield, M.D. (Hy-
perion, 1993). A highly practical guide to managing the special tribulations and potential joys of being in a stepfamily.

Men Are from Mars, Women Are from Venus by John Gray, Ph.D. (Harper-
Collins, 1992). An insight-loaded, enjoyable book by a popular seminar leader.

Opening Up: The Healing Power of Confiding in Others by James W. Pennebaker, Ph.D. (Morrow, 1990). Documents the potential health benefits of self-disclosure—through private writing or, at the right time, through conversations with others.

Random Acts of Kindness by the Editors of Conari Press (Berkeley, 1993).

The Trusting Heart by Redford Williams, M.D. (Times Books, 1989).

An eye-opening review of medical reasons to reduce hostility and cynicism in our lives.

To link up with helping groups in your home area, talk to relatives, friends, psychologists, physicians, co-workers and community service offices. Or send a stamped, self-addressed envelope to **VOLUNTEER—The National Center** (1111 N. 19th St., Suite 500, Arlington, VA 22209; 703-276-0542). VOLUNTEER provides groups with information sharing, training and promotion.

We Can Work It Out: Making Sense of Marital Conflict by Clifford Notarius, Ph.D., and Howard Markman, Ph.D. (Putnam, 1993). A well-proven approach to improving love relationships.

Why Marriages Succeed or Fail by John Gottman, Ph.D. (Simon & Schuster, 1994). An enlightening, research-based collection of insights.

You Just Don't Understand: Women and Men in Conversation by Deborah Tannen, Ph.D. (Morrow, 1990). A modern relationship classic. This is must reading.

PERSONAL POWER NOTES
A Quick-List of This Chapter's Power-Action Options

Use 5-second Reframing.
1. Listen attentively—and respect each individual's preferred "conversational style."
2. Get to the point early on.
3. Give enough details so what you mean to communicate comes through.

Meet your loved ones and friends halfway: welcome her complaints, confront him gently.
• Men: try not to avoid conflict.
• Women: Confront him clearly but gently.

If he "stonewalls," give him a little extra space.

Pause for 5 seconds and say "it's not your fault."

Fight fair!

When you want support, take 5 seconds to ask for it!

Take 5 seconds to disarm dialogue "landmines."
• Nonwords
• Automatic Detours
• Stinging Jabs

PERSONAL POWER NOTES—*CONTINUED*

Build more trust in your friendships—5 minutes at a time.

"Take 5" to write in a journal or confide in others.

Invest 5 minutes a week to value and expand your circle of friends.

Help others in need—5 seconds to 5 minutes at a time—and bring out more of the best in yourself.

- *Choose one-to-one volunteer activities.*
- *Make helping others a weekly habit.*
- *Cancel guilt trips.*
- *Keep expectations modest.*
- *Practice "random acts of kindness."*
- *If you love animals, consider adopting a pet.*

PERSONAL NOTES

_____

_____

_____

_____

_____

_____

_____

_____

_____

_____

_____

_____

_____

_____

_____

_____

PUT LOVE FIRST TO MAKE LOVE LAST

How to Nurture a Powerful, Passionate
and Enduring Relationship

No partnership matters more. The relationship with the one you
marry provides 90 percent of your happiness and 90 percent of your
misery.
—H. Jackson Brown, Jr., *Life's Little Instruction Book*

Love is the most celebrated of emotions. Yet it is largely a mystery;
mocked and trivialized, looked for and longed for. But lasting love is
rarely found. The result is disappointment, and worse, bitterness and a
resounding sense of betrayal, cynicism and disillusionment. Look
around you. Look inside your heart. How do you define love?

In *The Power of 5*, it is our contention that love is an emotional
process that takes time and care. It is largely a matter of ideas and choices
in daily living. It is, as the late novelist Laurie Colwin wrote, "an amazing product of human ingeniousness, like art, like scholarship, like architecture." Love is neither fleeting nor purely romantic. It is not based
on novelty or restricted to youth. In fact, to a great extent, the way you
love defines the way you *live*. Love emerges from the self but is based,
first of all, in *caring* for another person as you care for yourself. If you
can come to better understand what love is and refuse to suffocate it or
take it for granted, then love becomes an invigorating force that reaches
into the future and sets a foundation for trust and excitement, for sharing
wholeheartedly with someone, for impassioned, meaningful living. And

researchers have confirmed two central truths: First, that loving relationships are built, not found. And second, they have little—if anything—to do with luck, and contrary to popular wisdom, have absolutely nothing to do with "being made for each other."

"Love is nothing less than the creation—or re-creation—of one's own most personal identity," says Robert C. Solomon, Ph.D., professor of psychology and philosophy at the University of Texas at Austin.[1] And the core, or essence, of love is the realization that *you are what you love; you are what you care about.*[2] "Only someone who is ready for everything, who doesn't exclude any experience, even the most incomprehensible, will live the relationship with another person as something alive and will himself sound the depths of his own being," wrote the German poet Rainer Maria Rilke. "For if we imagine this being of the individual as a larger or smaller room, it is obvious that most people come to know only one corner of their room, one spot near the window, one narrow strip on which they keep walking back and forth."[3] Lasting love—and with it, within it, the deep, often-exhilarating *shared experiences* of intimacy and romance—may be kindled and sustained in innumerable small and varied ways. This, truly, is one of life's most pleasing arts.

> Those who have not known the deep intimacy and the intense companionship of happy mutual love have missed the best thing that life has to give.
> **—Bertrand Russell,** British mathematician and philosopher

POWER ACTION: FIRST OPTION
Take 5 Minutes at Day's End to Get "in Sync" with Your Lover

There's just no denying it: Intimate relations are tied to a kaleidoscope of biological forces. And researchers have discovered a key relationship between sexual energy and the natural, ongoing influence of two biological cycles—the 24-hour circadian rhythm and the 60- to 90-minute ultradian rhythms. Successful, sexually satisfied couples tend to have overall activity patterns, appetite, need for diversion and sexual rhythms "all occurring in synchrony."

In contrast, unsynchronized sexual energy cycles produce some of the most frustrating sexual problems: When one of you is sexually aroused and sensually energetic, the other one isn't, or when one of you is in the mood for comforting, nonsexual cuddling, the other desires exciting, active sex.

The more you can align your daily energy cycles with those of your partner, the greater your chances for lifelong, mutually satisfying intimacy—the best of what sex can and should be. Couples with exceptionally intimate and lasting sexual relationships tend to unconsciously integrate their own individual ultradian and circadian rhythms. Couples complaining of lost sexual energy and unhappiness frequently report conflict and imbalance across these areas.

Years ago, at the end of the day in almost any town or village in Europe, America or Asia, you could see couples sitting together in rocking chairs or on a porch swing, gazing at the sunset, talking to each other, reflecting on the day. Without realizing it, says psychobiologist Ernest Lawrence Rossi, Ph.D., these couples were synchronizing their circadian and ultradian rhythms and increasing their sexual energy. The shared quiet time and rocking rhythm helped to lower their stress levels and reduced the odds that tensions or frustra-

POWER KNOWLEDGE: SHARED LOVE

MYTH #1: For things to improve in a troubled—or even a ho-hum—love relationship, extraordinary changes, bordering on a miracle, have to take place.

POWER KNOWLEDGE: Research confirms that by making *even small changes in ourselves, we can effect big, positive changes in our love relationships.*[4] Furthermore, it's time to rethink conventional thinking about romance. "By surveying more than 30 years of psychiatric literature, and submitting over a thousand studies on successful and unsuccessful relationships to a computerized factor analysis," writes psychiatrist William Nagler, M.D. "I found something curious: *There were [some] universal behavior patterns that were always present in relationships that fell apart.* And these were the exact behaviors that I and other psychiatrists had been *teaching* people for years: [such as] to always talk out their problems, to always tell the [whole] truth . . . and to ignore the little things that bugged them in their relationships."[5]

According to research studies, it seems there's a normal, predictable and universal challenge in marriage relationships, says Dean tions would be imposed from one mate to the other.

Today, more and more couples rush home, hurry to prepare dinner, flip through the newspaper, eat quickly and then either collapse for the evening in front of the television or plunge into another round of scheduled activities—nightly errands, exercise sessions, parental duties, catching up on paperwork, preparing reports or paying bills. What's missing is a transition period—15 or 20 minutes will do—to unplug from the commotion and sit together quietly, without the television on in the background, to tune into each other's energy rhythms and recover together from the day's pace. Here are some of the ways to increase sexual synchrony.

- Kissing and greeting each other whenever leaving

> Feelings of closeness and intimacy rise and fall on wavelike biological rhythms. When you and your partner are on opposite "waves," you're bound to experience more conflicts and frustrations.

C. Delis, Ph.D., clinical psychologist and associate professor of psychiatry at the University of California, San Diego, School of Medicine. "One partner is more in love (or 'emotionally invested' in the relationship) than the other. And the *more* love the loving partner wants from the other, the *less* the other partner feels like giving."[6] Dr. Delis calls this the passion paradox. "In balanced relationships," he adds, "*both* partners have secured the other's love. They're more or less equal in several ways: in their attractiveness to each other, in their emotional investment in the relationship and in the number of needs each will fill for the other. Neither one feels suffocated or emotionally shortchanged, and neither is inclined to take the other for granted."[7]

MYTH #2: It's common knowledge: Men have "problems with intimacy" and women tend to "overreact."

POWER KNOWLEDGE: Men and women differ little in their actual desire for intimacy and connection in love relationships.[8] But for a range of reasons, both cultural and genetic/biological, men often have a harder time handling relationship conflict, while women have a harder time handling emotional distance. Men, therefore, often feel the need to withdraw from uncomfortable marital discussions, while women frequently feel a need to immediately resolve every conflict through discussion.

> The Golden Rule of Love is: Relate first, resolve second. It is impossible to resolve relationship concerns if either partner feels misunderstood, unappreciated or ignored.
>
> **—Clifford Notarius, Ph.D., Howard Markman, Ph.D.,** *We Can Work It Out: Making Sense of Marital Conflict*

and arriving, thereby using the sensory power of touch to help align your energy cycles.

• Slowing down the pace of the main meal and enjoying each other's dining companionship.

• Going for a shared early-morning or evening stroll.

• Spending time together fixing meals, doing dishes or puttering around the lawn or garden.

• Sitting together quietly, listening to music you both enjoy, and sipping a cup of tea or a glass of wine.

• Sharing a warm bath or gentle, rhythmic massage for 15 to 20 minutes prior to sexual intimacy.

• Stretching out on the sofa and holding each other—fully clothed, with nothing unsnapped, unhooked or unzipped—in a "spoon" position, with one person wrapping arms around the other from behind; the warmth and comfort of this sensual embrace strengthens the closeness between you and helps release stress.

In each of these simple actions, powerful verbal and nonverbal cues are helping to synchronize your energy rhythms and renew and increase intimate bonds after time apart. In addition, the "break-away" time together and the mind/body connection of gentle touching can also serve as subtle aphrodisiacs (see chapter 28).

POWER ACTION: MORE OPTIONS
Enjoy 5-Second "Humor Breaks"

Every love relationship has its own unique reservoir of humor. Private jokes, shared laughter, ticklish spots on the body, comic faces, favorite funny experiences together. Make it a point to find more moments to ignite this humor each day, to remember some of the comical situations you witnessed, or created, during the day. Usually there are lots of humorous little events and situations. *Share these with each other*! A study by Avner Ziv and Orit Gadish, professors of psychology at Tel Aviv University in Israel, concluded by suggesting that *70 percent* of a married couple's satisfaction may depend in some way on humor—on making each other laugh and feel happy despite life's ups and downs.[9]

As Erich Fromm, M.D., stated in *The Art of Loving*, "Most people see the problem of love primarily as that of *being loved*, rather than of *loving*, of one's capacity to love." And clearly a part of that capacity to love comes from cultivating your ability to share laughter, to be a *loving* person with a sense of fun, of play, of humor.

"Take 5" to Relax Together

The experience of love takes time—time to relate to each other. Perhaps even more important, the experience of love is also tied to the experience *of* time.[10] By this we mean a deepening sense of *being* together, of *sharing* experiences together, weaving these events and memories into a narrative, a love story, moving through time. As noted in this chapter's first Power Action option, the intimacy and romance of love require biological alignment as much as they require emotional connection. To set the stage for a warmer bond with your loved one, spend a few key minutes when you greet your partner each morning and evening to hug, hold hands and kiss, thereby using touch to help entrain, or synchronize, your ultradian rhythms. Instead of rushing through supper and then plopping in front of the television, block out a few minutes to go for a walk, hand in hand, or sit side by side listening to music you both love, or take pleasure in some other activity together—such as gardening, enjoying a glass of wine or exchanging backrubs. These kinds of shared daily experiences provide significant verbal and nonverbal cues that help renew intimate bonds after a day apart. As simple as they seem, they're *vital* to keeping the closeness and passion in your relationship.[11]

In part, this reflects what psychiatrist William Nagler, M.D., has discovered: What makes people get along in a relationship is "*the ability to feel relaxed together*. . . . Do you want a relationship that is satisfying, makes you happy, and will last? The truth is that happy couples don't try to entertain each other, they relax and enjoy each other's company. . . . Tension reduction is the most important thing you can do to make your relationship last, and to make it better."[12]

Use Generous Listening—It's the Bridge to Intimacy

Friendship is one of the underappreciated foundations of love. Indeed, the bonds of friendship (discussed in chapter 26) are essential to make love last; without it love will falter.[13] Friendship encompasses loy-

> For all of the advice in the magazines on "How to Keep Your Love Alive," the salvation of love is not the prolongation of sexual desire but the shared lifelong cultivation of a romantic lightheartedness that softens conflicts and anxieties and focuses serious attention even as it undermines seriousness as such. It's hard to fall out of love so long as you're laughing together.
>
> **—Robert Solomon, Ph.D.,**
> *About Love*

Love becomes the ultimate answer to the ultimate human question.

—Archibald Macleish,
American poet

alty, trusting, caring, inspiring, sharing and wishing the other person well. And, not surprisingly, it adds a vital sense of meaning to sexual desire and satisfaction.

One of the reasons that love wanes is neglect, and one of the principal kinds of neglect is the inability *to listen well*—a subject we discussed in detail in the preceding chapter. In truth, in many cases the number one way a man may succeed in fulfilling a woman's primary love needs is through communication. "By learning to listen to a woman's feelings," explains John Gray, Ph.D., author of *Men Are from Mars, Women Are from Venus,* "a man can effectively shower a woman with caring, understanding, respect, devotion, validation and reassurance. . . . Just as men need to learn the art of listening to fulfill a woman's primary love needs, women need to learn the art of empowerment. When a woman enlists the support of a man, she empowers him to be all that he can be. A man feels empowered when he is trusted, accepted, appreciated, admired, approved of and encouraged. The secret of empowering a man is never to try to change him or improve him. . . when you try to change him or improve him, he feels controlled, manipulated, rejected and unloved. . . . And she mistakenly thinks he is not willing to change, probably because he does not love her enough."[14]

A related note: As mentioned in the previous chapter, one of the simplest, most effective ways to enhance your listening abilities and warm up your dialogues may be to ensure that you and your partner eat something *before* having important conversations. Low blood sugar, caused in many cases by skipping meals and not eating between-meal snacks, causes epinephrine (adrenaline) release in your bloodstream—which, according to some authorities, makes your temper short, your frustrations higher and reasoned thinking very difficult.[15] After eating a healthy meal or snack, you'll often be better able to head off arguments and listen more attentively and lovingly to each other.

Share a 5-Minute Snuggle—At Least Once a Day

Of all the ways in which people need each other, "holding" is the most primary, the least evident and the hardest to describe, says Ruthellen Josselson, Ph.D., professor of psychology at Towson State University in Maryland and author of *The Space between Us: Exploring the Dimensions of Human Relationships.* "Holding contains the invisible threads that tie us to our existence. From the first moments of our life to the last, we need to be held—or we fall."[16] There are physical and emotional aspects of holding, Dr. Josselson explains, and "the holding function of relatedness not only provides care and meaning; it also provides hope."[17] So make it a point to loosen up a bit and spend time just holding your partner—in a caring but nonsexual way.

Relate Eye-to-Eye

By now it should be clear that *caring* about each other—in virtually every imaginable way—is a central bond of identity in love. To help someone else grow can sometimes be the most difficult kind of caring, but it truly matters to love. In this respect, even the smallest changes from *The Power of 5* can boost your energy and attentiveness, free up new minutes for relationship-building and enable you to care for loved ones more effectively, from a higher vantage point.

One of the most important ways we affirm our connection to loved ones is eye-to-eye. No matter how old you become, you never cease to need unconditional, simple *valuing* in another's eyes—*and* in your own eyes. "These looks," says Dr. Josselson, "are far beyond words: eyes speak more profoundly than language the tenor of relatedness. They express, surely and absolutely, how much and in what way we matter to the Other. Words may lie; eyes cannot."[18] In short, *saying* "I love you" in words pales in contrast to the potential power of *expressing* "I love you" without any words, eye-to-eye.

End "Unconscious Exits"

A related way that many of us lose romance and kill intimacy is by making detours in and out of the time we spend together. Beyond eye-to-eye validation, reduce the other bothersome "exits" that drive people apart, such as staying up late, night after night, watching television while your partner is in bed; making long business calls in the evening and on weekends; watching hour after hour of sports on television during free time; not paying attention when your partner talks ("tuning out"); or making plans without consulting loved ones first. Consider bringing this out into the open by writing a simple agreement: "Beginning now, I agree to give our relationship more energy and attention. In particular, I agree to . . ." and then make a brief list of simple changes you could make that your partner would value.

Strengthen Your Love—With 5-Second Validations

For many of us, some of the best relationship advice is, Worry a bit less about what you think is important—money problems, career track, the annual vacation—and pay *more* attention to the little things. Begin with the *power of validation*. "Letting your spouse know in so many little ways that you understand him or her is one of the most powerful tools for healing your relationship," explains John M. Gottman, Ph.D., professor of psychology at the University of Washington in Seattle. "Validation is simply putting yourself in your partner's shoes and imagining his or her emotional state. It's then a simple matter to let your mate know that you understand those feelings and consider them valid, even if you don't share them. Validation is an amazingly effective technique. It's as if you opened a door to welcome your partner."[19]

Validations—some requiring as little as 5 seconds—can lead to genuine empathy and understanding. Few things make a person feel more valued and loved. You can increase your empathy in many ways, such as *acknowledging responsibility* ("Yes, I know this upsets you." "It feels like I really made you angry, didn't I?"), *apologizing* ("I'm sorry. I was wrong."), *expressing compliments* by honestly praising your partner, and saying that you really admire something specific about him or her (this can have a remarkably positive effect on the rest of the conversation).

Grow Closer—By Expressing 5 Seconds to 5 Minutes of Appreciation

Once you're making progress with validation, take a look at the *power of appreciation.* How many times has your day been brightened by one small, unexpected gesture of appreciation or caring? Unfortunately, many men think they make "points" with their partner when they do big things—like buying a car, replacing the refrigerator, setting up a new stereo or taking the family on a vacation. At the same time, many men assume that little things—opening doors, sharing loving glances, giving hugs or kisses, saying "I love you," sitting close together when watching a movie or television, checking with each other first before making plans, holding hands, saying "You look great," buying flowers or writing thank-you notes—count very little when compared to the "big things." But there is evidence that when many women keep score, no matter how big or small a gift of love or caring is, it scores a point.[20]

"You will survive major calamity, disaster and death," says Dr. Nagler. "You will not survive the top off the toothpaste tube, on a daily basis. The toilet seat left up, often enough, can kill you. That pile of clothes on the floor can be fatal. The little things are everything in terms of tension reduction. The casual details of everyday life are what allow long-term relationships to survive."[21]

One way to help bring this concern to the fore is for each of you to spend a few minutes doing sentence-completions,[22] such as: "I feel valued and loved when you . . ." and "I used to feel valued and loved when you . . ." and "To feel more valued and loved I would like you to. . . ."

When you're finished, exchange lists—and circle the items that are free of conflict for you and that you would be willing to start doing more of. You can add ideas to the lists as they arise and express appreciation to each other for each new caring behavior that results. Do not keep score—do your caring behaviors as gifts, not obligations, and do them no matter how you feel about your partner or how many caring acts he or she has done for you that day.

"I Appreciate You Because . . ."

Here's another love-building exercise: Arrange for 5 minutes in private to tell your partner many of the specific reasons you appreciate him or her. What meaning and inspiration can you and your spouse find in the detailed history of your relationship? Make a list ahead of time so you can "bathe" your loved one in appreciation. Some suggestions: What attracted you to your lover in the first place? What specific qualities about him or her do you admire the most? What were some of the highlights—and moments of laughter and fun—when you first began dating? What made the relationship worth pursuing? How did your partner help the two of you overcome any differences or obstacles along the way? What are your favorite memories of your first year in the relationship? What efforts by your partner have helped the relationship make it through the difficult times? Once you've made a list of specific experiences and qualities that you appreciate in your loved one, share the results. One rule: The partner who is listening must not make judgments or negate any of the appreciative comments ("I'm not *really* that considerate . . ." "I never looked *that* sexy; besides, now I've got to lose ten pounds . . ."). Then find another time to trade roles and give your spouse 5 minutes to express some of the specific things she appreciates about you. This simple exercise helps you stop taking each other for granted and can effectively reawaken an awareness of the qualities in your partner—and yourself—that form the shared, sometimes hidden, foundation of your love.

"Here's the Kind of Love and Appreciation I Want and Deserve . . ."

Perhaps, like many people, you have exaggerated images of your lover's bad habits, criticisms and contempt. In some cases, you may even remember nearly all of the hateful things said in every hostile argument you've ever had. As this inner script is played out over and over again, resentments grow deeper and it becomes nearly impossible to see any positive qualities in the person you once loved so dearly. Remember what we've said previously in *The Power of 5*: *What you place your at-*

tention on grows stronger. What if—in addition to periodically using a 5-second appreciation exercise—at the start of an argument, when the first barbs of criticism or contempt are being felt, you remembered your partner teaching you something valuable, a time when your lover did something really thoughtful and special for you or even the first time you passionately kissed and made love. This could have a great influence—*right now*—on how you treat the person you love and the outcome of your argument.

If you do not receive the respect and appreciation needed in a relationship, you are more likely to ignore, resist or feel victimized by your lover's requests and demands. Here's the point: *Although it may seem uncomfortable at first, if you feel your lover is taking you for granted, it is your responsibility to request the expression of love and appreciation you want and deserve.* We all deserve to be consistently and lovingly appreciated. Give this gift to your partner and ask for it in return. Take turns using heart-to-heart talks: "Something I really appreciate about you is . . ."; "Something I'd like to be appreciated for is . . ."; "One of the best things about our love relationship is . . ."; "One of the things I love most about our marriage is . . . ." No one ever tires of hearing how much they are appreciated or loved in specific ways.

Use "I Love You" as a Heartfelt Phrase—Not a Verbal Club

In most cases, to say "I love you" is not to report or express a feeling of intimacy or passion. "It is an aggressive, creative, socially definitive act," explains Dr. Solomon in his book *About Love: Reinventing Romance for Our Times*, "which among other things may place the other person in an unexpected and very vulnerable position. . . . It is not so terrible, of course, if he or she is willing and ready with the one acceptable response, namely, 'I love you, too.' But nothing else will do."[23] As Dr. Solomon observes, the expression "I love you" is essentially a plea, sometimes a demand, for a response in kind. Its uses and meanings are nearly as varied, or elusive, as lasting love itself. These three words can be an instrument—more powerful than the loudest noise—to interrupt a boring silence or painful conversation. Saying "I love you" can serve as a threat ("Don't push me on this; you might lose me"), a warning ("It's only because I love you that I'm willing to put up with this"), an apology ("I could not possibly have meant what I just said to you"), a verbal signal ("Pay attention to me!"), a disguised invitation for sex ("I love you" whispered while nodding at the bedroom door), an excuse ("It's only because I love you . . .") or an attack ("How can you do this to me?").

How you use the expression "I love you" can, by itself, be a significant force in defining and expressing the love in your relationship. The best advice? Initiate the reciprocal romantic exchange—"I love you"; "I love you, too."—only when you can mean it heart-to-heart. Find other ways—and alternative expressions—to draw closer to each other and clearly assert your needs.

Resources

About Love: Reinventing Romance for Our Times by Robert C. Solomon, Ph.D. (Littlefield Adams, 1994). An evocative, scholarly look at what it takes to make love last.

The Couple's Comfort Book by Jennifer Louden (HarperCollins, 1994). A creative resource on simple daily ways to renew passion and commitment to each other.

Intimate Connections by David D. Burns, M.D. (Signet, 1985). A clinically proven program for increasing self-esteem, making close friends and finding a loving partner.

Lifemates: The Love Fitness Program for a Lasting Relationship by Harold H. Bloomfield, M.D., and Sirah Vettese, Ph.D. (New American Library, 1989). A mutually supportive approach to keeping love alive.

Love Secrets for a Lasting Relationship by Harold H. Bloomfield, M.D., with poetry by Natasha Josefowitz (Bantam, 1992). An uplifting guide.

Men Are from Mars, Women Are from Venus by John Gray, Ph.D. (HarperCollins, 1992). Practical communication ideas.

The Passion Paradox by Dean C. Delis, Ph.D. (Bantam, 1990). A compelling exploration of the hidden tug-of-war in love relationships.

The Space between Us: Exploring the Dimensions of Human Relationships by Ruthellen Josselson, Ph.D. (Josey-Bass, 1992). A scholarly, enlightening look at the positive connections that make us whole.

We Can Work It Out: Making Sense of Marital Conflicts by Howard Markman, Ph.D., and Clifford Notarius, Ph.D. (Putnam, 1993). A collection of practical relationship-strengthening strategies from research conducted by these two pioneering psychologists.

Why Marriages Succeed or Fail by John Gottman, Ph.D. (Simon & Schuster, 1994). Valuable, research-based insights on lasting relationships.

PERSONAL POWER NOTES
A Quick-List of This Chapter's Power-Action Options

Take 5 minutes at day's end to get "in sync" with your lover.

Enjoy 5-second "humor breaks."

"Take 5" to relax together.

Use generous listening—it's the bridge to intimacy.

Share a 5-minute snuggle—at least once a day.

Relate eye-to-eye.

End "unconscious exits."

Strengthen your love—with 5-second validations.

Grow closer—by expressing 5 seconds to 5 minutes of appreciation.
- *"I appreciate you because . . ."*
- *"Here's the kind of love and appreciation I want and deserve . . ."*

Use "I love you" as a heartfelt phrase—not a verbal club.

PERSONAL NOTES

_____

_____

_____

_____

_____

_____

_____

_____

_____

_____

SECRETS FOR SUPERSEX

Creating Greater Sexual Intimacy and Pleasure

Joy in sex is experienced only when physical intimacy is at the same time the intimacy of loving.
—Erich Fromm, M.D., American psychoanalyst

When sex is great, it can be taken for granted, but when it's bad it can consume much of the consciousness of a relationship. As one of life's most exceptional pleasures, it's ironic that there are so many hidden obstacles to sexual fulfillment. Perhaps the most insidious of these impediments are the "aging sex life" stereotypes—the notion that sex is no longer great or frequent by age 35 or 45 or 60 or beyond. These myths persist despite recent studies showing couples in their nineties enjoying sex two or three times a week.[1] Trapped by misconceptions, few of us ever come close to realizing our lifelong potential for sexual energy, nor do we comprehend our capacity for extraordinary sexual pleasures and deeply satisfying intimacy. And that's deplorable.

This is because there's a growing awareness that great sex is not something that just happens—it comes no more naturally than great adult conversation. It has to be learned—in a shared, sensitive, open manner. What's emerging from scientific studies is a whole new model of human sexuality—one that emphasizes pleasure, closeness and self- and partner-enhancement rather than "performance."[2] Few of life's experiences yield greater rewards, since as our intimate relationships become more vibrant and aware, so in turn do we.

The energy of desire resides, and is nourished or confounded, in the mind. "It may be going too far to say that the mind is everything when it comes to sex," says psychologist Bernie Zilbergeld, Ph.D., author of *The New Male Sexuality*. "But if it's not everything, it's certainly far ahead of whatever is in second place."[3]

Every day, therapists nationwide treat countless cases of unwarranted anxiety and loss of sex drive in men and women. To a significant extent, the vanishing sexual energy and corresponding relationship struggles are brought on by popular misconceptions about sexual po-

POWER KNOWLEDGE: SUPERSEX

MYTH #1: Great sex is purely physical pleasure.

POWER KNOWLEDGE: Some of the most exceptional sexual orgasms happen way beyond "purely physical pleasure," say researchers.[10] It can include an uncommonly deep emotional connection, a sense of personal transformation and fulfillment, an expanded awareness of one of life's fundamental energies, a profound sense of timelessness and inner peace and even some degree of spiritual awakening. Investigations indicate that men and women of all ages and lifestyles can learn to experience "supersexual pleasure" in mind, body and spirit far more readily than most of us have ever imagined.

MYTH #2: As I get older, my sex drive and ability to achieve orgasms begins to wane. It's natural; there's nothing I can do about it.

POWER KNOWLEDGE: Two recent nationwide studies of nearly 6,000 people indicate that about four out of every ten married couples over age 60 are having sexual intercourse at least once a week.[11] The sexually active couples were more likely than other couples, young or old, to report happy marriages, personal happiness and exciting lives. They were also the most likely to say they "feel great joy after sex" and are more likely than younger couples to feel comfortable with nudity and find their spouses attractive.

Among 80- to 102-year-olds, a study at San Francisco State University found that 88 percent of the men and 71 percent of the women still had intimate thoughts about the opposite sex, 72 percent of the men and 40 percent of the women masturbated, and 63 percent of men and 30 percent of women enjoyed regular sexual intercourse.[12] The Starr-Weiner Report, one of the most accurate quantified studies on tency and intimacy. When we buy into these erroneous ideas, we can end up sexually incapacitated by our own thoughts.

Compounding all of this is the badly outdated image of men as continual, shameless seekers of sexual gratification. In a startling twist in gender roles, increasingly it's the man, not the woman, who is experiencing anxiety or apathy about sex.[4] More than ever before, we need to

(continued on page 420)

the sexuality of people across the country between the ages of 60 and 91, reported that 97 percent like sex; 75 percent think sex now feels as good or better than it did when they were younger; 72 percent are satisfied by their sexual experiences; and 80 percent think sex is good for their health.[13]

A study entitled "Love, Sex, and Aging"[14] reported on 4,246 men and women ranging in age from 50 to 93 and revealed some myth-breaking information about the quality and quantity of sexual activity and intercourse. Regular "sexual activity" (defined in this study as having sex at any time, including masturbation) was enjoyed by 93 percent of women and 98 percent of men in their fifties, 81 percent of women and 91 percent of men in their sixties and 65 percent of women and 79 percent of men in their seventies. "Sexual intercourse at least once a week" was reported by 73 percent of women and 90 percent of men in their fifties, 63 percent of women and 73 percent of men in their sixties and 50 percent of women and 58 percent of men in their seventies.

According to gerontologist Ruth B. Weg, Ph.D., of the University of Southern California in Los Angeles, sexual response in women changes over time. As the years move forward, the excitation phase, with vaginal lubrication and clitoral elevation, may take up to 4 or 5 minutes instead of 15 to 40 seconds. And, beginning about age 50, the orgasmic phase becomes shorter, "unless the woman has been extremely physically and sexually active," says Dr. Weg, adding, "If excitation is sufficient, women at *any* age can be sexually responsive."[15] In addition, scientists report that women often find that sex improves with age because of psychological factors such as greater self-assurance as well as confidence regarding the need for or use of contraceptives.

"With or without children, hormonal changes in women may work in favor of increased sex drive after menopause," writes Deborah S. Edelman in *Sex in the Golden Years*. "The libido-influencing

(continued)

POWER KNOWLEDGE: SUPERSEX—CONTINUED

hormone, androgen, is present throughout a woman's life, but its effects are masked by estrogen and progesterone during her reproductive years. After menopause, however, androgen circulates in the body unopposed, and may result in a woman's sex drive rising with age."[16]

Research by psychiatrist Eric Pfeiffer, M.D., reveals that 15 to 20 percent of older men actually report that their sex life has significantly *improved* in later life.[17] Psychiatrist Saul H. Rosenthal, M.D., director of the Sexual Therapy Clinic of San Antonio and clinical associate professor at the University of Texas Medical School in Houston, confirms that while it takes older men a longer time with more stimulation to achieve an erection and to climax, this is not an early sign of impotence (although when we mistakenly believe it is, the anxiety and frustration can cause impotence). "Now that your body is no longer pressuring you for quick ejaculations," explains Dr. Rosenthal, "you'll probably be able to enjoy intercourse longer than you could when you were younger. This can be a real plus for your partner. Women often require longer stimulation in order to become fully aroused and to climax. Your partner will thus enjoy your newfound sexual endurance, and you'll both enjoy being able to continue with longer, more sensual lovemaking."[18]

MYTH #3: Women are more likely than men to not want sex, to claim they "have a headache."
POWER KNOWLEDGE: Not true. "I have found that 50 to 60 percent of the time the complaint that one partner has fizzled out sexually comes not from the man, but from the woman," says psychologist Janet Wolfe, Ph.D., author of *What to Do When He Has a Headache*.[19] A survey of nearly 100,000 married women revealed that nearly 4 out of 10 felt they were not having sex often enough. A key reason: "He doesn't want to."[20]

Why are men losing interest in sex? Dr. Wolfe reports a number of reasons, including the observation that while many women see sex as a stress *reducer* and a means of connection and of shared joy, many men are more tense and tired than before and now view sex as an *added* stressor, one more area in which they have to "perform," especially if they're concerned about "giving" their partners an orgasm each time they're intimate. This anxiety raises the fear of sexual dysfunction or failure.

One of the paradoxes in a man's life, explains Dr. Rosenthal, author of *Sex after 40*, "is that he can order nearly every part of his body to do his will—but his penis, whose behavior is so important for his self-esteem, seems out of control and often behaves in ways that are very frustrating to him. In fact, the more he anxiously tries to control it, the more trouble he's likely to have. He can't get his penis erect by sheer will. He has to wait for the appropriate stimulation to make it happen. The more he worries or tries to get hard, the less likely he is to succeed."[21]

In contrast, for many women, emotional closeness is often the chief prerequisite for sexual arousal and passionate, enduring intimacy. Studies indicate that women often experience a strong need to establish and sustain this emotional closeness, and when this need isn't met, their own thoughts and feelings can subdue or block sexual desire.[22] The emotional bond is generally formed at three levels, says Patricia Schreiner-Engel, Ph.D., director of the Women's Sexual Health Program at Mount Sinai School of Medicine in New York City.[23] The most basic is *organizing*—interacting with your partner to schedule and handle joint chores and responsibilities (dealing with finances, meal planning, children, cleaning and other tasks). When these obligations are responsibly and consistently handled, the woman's emotional bond with her partner ascends to the next level, *sharing*—communicating feelings about your individual lives. Once this stage is satisfactorily explored, and only then, the third level, *intimacy*—holding, kissing and mutually passionate lovemaking—is possible.

When men fail to pay attention to these needs, women are offended by sexual advances, says Dr. Schreiner-Engel. Ironically, the more insistent the man's demand for sex, the less desire a woman feels, because her own female and sexual needs, based on emotional closeness, are not being met.

MYTH #4: You're just plain lucky if your love partner is turned on to make love at the same time of day or night you are.

POWER KNOWLEDGE: Couples with highly satisfying, lasting sexual relationships tend to spontaneously integrate their ultradian rhythms, says psychobiologist Ernest Lawrence Rossi, Ph.D.[24] "Getting

(continued)

POWER KNOWLEDGE:
SUPERSEX—*CONTINUED*

in touch with our ultradian rhythms can enhance both our sexuality and general well-being." In contrast, "unhappy couples invariably report conflict and desynchrony across these areas. . . . Sexual problems such as impotence, premature ejaculation, and dyspareunia (painful intercourse in women) may be at least partly caused by lack of attention to the crucial step of synchronizing the ultradian sexual rhythms of both partners."[25]

This poetry of intimacy has an underlying scientific basis, says University of Pennsylvania biologist Winnifred D. Cutler, Ph.D. "It has a cyclic harmony. And a 'time to embrace' is built into the biology of the human species. . . . How often a woman has sex with a man strongly affects her endocrine system. Regular weekly sex is vital for maintaining higher estrogen levels. . . . Women in their late forties who had regular weekly sex with a man showed almost twice as much estrogen circulating in their blood as women who were either celibate or sporadically active. . . . Higher estrogen has been associated with better bones, better cardiovascular health and a feeling of joy in life."[26]

MYTH #5: It's up to a man's partner to understand what he needs for satisfying sex.

POWER KNOWLEDGE: If men learned to make love the way most women say they prefer, many men's and women's sex problems would disappear. "When women are asked to critique the men in their love lives," says Michael Castleman, author of *Sexual Solutions*, "their chief complaints are that men make love too quickly, too mechanically and with too much attention focused on the genitals. Women say men are often so preoccupied . . . with the mechanics of intercourse that they often ignore what most women say really excites them— leisurely, playful, whole-body sensuality. Every square inch of the body is capable of sensual arousal through gentle, massage-style caresses. The body is a sensual wonderland. Most women say they like to explore all of it, and have difficulty understanding why so many men concentrate on a few small corners."[27]

When men are asked to critique women's lovemaking, reports

Castleman, their chief complaints are that women are too passive and unresponsive. An important reason for the lack of enthusiasm many women feel is that they tend to become aroused more slowly than men, and when a man rushes lovemaking it turns his partner off.

MYTH #6: Sex is natural. It's an instinct to be great in bed. You either have it or you don't.

POWER KNOWLEDGE: "The ability to make love well is not innate," explains Linda Perlin Alperstein, Ph.D., of the Department of Psychiatry at the University of California, San Francisco, Medical Center. "Most of us have to experiment and learn throughout our lives. But there's a myth that sex is 'natural,' that if people are *really* in love, they shouldn't have to negotiate."[28]

The idea that a lover should understand intuitively what pleases us is particularly destructive. It sets up a classic "damned if you do, damned if you don't" situation. If you ask what kinds of caress your lover enjoys, that proves you don't already "know," therefore you've failed. But if you don't discuss your lovemaking, you can't possibly know all the fine points of what your partner enjoys; therefore you won't be able to give the pleasure you otherwise might, and again, you've failed.[29]

MYTH #7: Sexual "fitness" has nothing to do with how often you have sex.

POWER KNOWLEDGE: Sex should always be pleasurable, not forced. Beyond this principle, however, some leaders in the field of sexual research stress the "consistency of lifestyle" as being highly de-terminative of late-life sexual capacity.[30] "The familiar refrain of 'use it or lose it' is heard once again," says Walter M. Bortz II, M.D., former president of the American Geriatrics Society and clinical associate professor at the Stanford University Medical School. "Sex is one form of exercise that no one should fault because of tedium. Research in-volving the testosterone levels in men has repeatedly shown that hor-monal levels remain unchanged as long as the individual maintains good health."[31]

Dr. Cutler, a pioneering researcher in reproductive biology, re-ports that from her studies with more than 700 women, consistent weekly sexual activity tends to help regularize menstrual periods, pro-

(continued)

POWER KNOWLEDGE: SUPERSEX—*CONTINUED*

motes good health and retards aging.[32] Julian Davidson, Ph.D., of the physiology department at Stanford University reports that regular sex helps cut down on hot flashes in menopause.[33]

MYTH #8: Menopause inevitably leads to a loss of sexual drive.
POWER KNOWLEDGE: *Menopausal and postmenopausal women should consult their physician about estrogen replacement therapy options.* According to Dr. Cutler, who founded the Stanford Menopause Study, there is strong scientific evidence that now supports personalized, minimum-dosage estrogen replacement therapy— prescribed by a physician based on each individual woman's needs. "When estrogen levels begin to wane at menopause, the bones, the cardiovascular health, the muscle tone and the skin all show signs of aging, and this aging process increases with time. The vagina dries out, and the capacity for sexual lubrication diminishes. The longer a woman has deficient levels of sex hormones, the further the deterioration in her bone mass and strength, muscle tone and cardiovascular health. Hormone replacement therapy, when appropriately dosed, can retard these processes of aging. . . . I see hormone replacement therapy

bypass pervasive misconceptions and learn the most effective "sexual rejuvenators." That's the focus of this chapter.

POWER ACTION: FIRST OPTION
Turn Sex into Loveplay—Instead of Foreplay and "the Act"

Unhurried, whole-body "loveplay" is a highly practical solution to both men's and women's primary complaints about the other's lovestyle. Sensitive, sensual intimacy helps give men the aroused, responsive lovers they want, while at the same time it gives women more as the natural evolution of civilization. It serves to prolong and enhance quality of life. I am very much in favor of it for those who can take appropriate levels."[34] Adds Dr. Bortz, "I believe the weight of scientific evidence today favors the use of estrogen replacement therapy after the menstrual periods stop. (This is not a simple matter, however, and it needs careful personal crafting.) While conjugal bliss is helped substantially by a little estrogen (either applied locally as a cream or taken orally in pill form), this therapy has a great deal to recommend it above and beyond its ability to promote satisfactory sex. Estrogens also help prevent osteoporosis and retard hardening of the arteries."[35]

MYTH #9: If I experience impotence, there's really nothing I can do about it.

POWER KNOWLEDGE: *Men experiencing impotence should consult their physician.* "I have probably done more good for my male patients' impotence problems by stopping medicines than by any other single maneuver," says Dr. Bortz.[36] Your physician may be able to treat impotence in a variety of ways, some quite simple—such as changing or reducing medications. Drugs commonly used for hypertension and certain gastrointestinal conditions, for example, have been linked to impotence, although there are many other possible contributing factors.

of the whole-body sharing they often desire. Extended loveplay means more variety, more playfulness and less likelihood of slipping into a boring routine.

Freud was wrong—the entire body is an erogenous zone.

While having sex or in the first few moments afterward, have you ever thought, Isn't there more to lovemaking than this? Many of us have. When the sexual experience is relegated to only a few square inches of the body's surface or exclusively to the genital organs, at best it's a pale shadow of the natural ecstasy that's possible. What makes lovemaking unforgettably vibrant is a combination of love (see chapter 27) and healthy, full-scale *sensuality*[5] (introduced in chapter 21).

"Until now most human beings have remained quite ignorant of their own loving potential," says Jolan Chang in *The Tao of the Loving*

421

Couple. "We human beings are able to make love more frequently and sensuously. . . .Yet we are often disappointed after love-making. Why? Because we are like owners of a precious Stradivarius violin that we have never learned to play."[6]

"Touch may be the most powerful sociobiological signal of all," according to psychobiologist Ernest Lawrence Rossi, Ph.D. "When we are touched gently and rhythmically, our brains release the feel-good messenger chemicals called beta-endorphins, and we slip into the psychologically receptive state [where we're] open to increased intimacy."[7]

In fact, from their late thirties on, women often develop their richest sensuality, reports Winnifred D. Cutler, Ph.D., reproductive biologist and co-founder of the Women's Wellness Program at the University of Pennsylvania in Philadelphia. "It is then that the capacity for sensual expertise most often expresses itself. By then men have become more patient, more capable of learning to control the timing of their own pleasure to enhance that of their partner."[8]

Sigmund Freud may have initiated much of the present public confusion about the sensuality/sexuality link by postulating that the body contains only three erogenous zones (areas that lead to sexual arousal when stimulated): the mouth, anal area and genitals. By implying that the rest of the body is unarousable, Freud ended up obfuscating the actual range of human sensuality. The fact is, the entire body can respond with tip-to-toe erotic energy during lovemaking, so there's no reason to let your sensual powers lie dormant. Explore your current sensual preferences—and identify those of your partner. Which sensations and images turn each of you on the most?

• Do you love *visual images* (seeing your partner in an erotic position, with the lights on bright or dim, or when making intimate eye contact)?

• Are you stimulated by *erotic sounds* (whispers, music, ocean waves, the rain)?

• How about your favorite *tantalizing smells* (do certain scents or aromas evoke sensual images for you)?

• Do you savor *special tastes* (for example, do you pay attention to the smell and taste of your partner during sex)?

• Are you turned on by *touch and movement* (the rhythm of massage, having your neck rubbed or hair stroked, the feel of the sheets beneath your skin, the precise sensations of your partner's touch wherever you enjoy it most)?

Learn your preferences—and those of your partner—and pay increased attention to respecting and deepening them. At the same time, discover or rediscover the wonders of your other senses. As you sharpen them and extend their reach, you'll be adding a new measure of resonant intimacy that can enrich your life, year after year. Here's one of the many ways to create more extraordinary sexual pleasure using the power of touch.

Take a 5-minute Sensory Body Tour with your sexual partner. This simple technique can help create a greater feeling of shared trust and a sensual and emotional bond between lovers. It can also heighten sexual energy during intercourse. To develop exceptional skill in sensual and sexual touch, one of the most effective exercises is the Sensory Body Tour.

First, choose a quiet, private room and choose a lighting level (bright, dim or dark) that is pleasing to *both* of you. If a certain smell arouses you (and is also enjoyed by your partner), create a hint of that scent in the room. If you *both* enjoy soft background music, put some on. Take the phone off the hook, put your favorite sheets on the bed and do whatever else you both wish to "set the scene" in a most enjoyable way.

Wearing as little or as much as you like, guide your partner's hands with your own on a special tour of every square inch of your body, showing him or her precisely the ways in which you like to be touched. Move in response to whatever touches you find most erotic, stimulating and desirable. (If you or your partner enjoy whispered love messages, then be certain that person receives them, but don't rely on the words and sound sensations alone to create erotic passion.) Once you have covered every part of your body, switch places and let your lover guide you.

"Touch," says Linda Perlin Alperstein, Ph.D., assistant clinical professor in the Department of Psychiatry at the University of California, San Francisco, Medical Center, "can be difficult to discuss with words. What does it mean if I tell you I like 'light' or 'medium' touch? That can mean different things to different people. It's much easier to demonstrate. You let your fingers do the talking. Of course, you can talk while conducting a Body Tour, but simple 'oohs' and 'ahhs' can be just as communicative as words. . . . If you feel ill at ease naming certain parts of the body, the Body Tour allows you to show your partner how you like to be touched there without saying anything."[9]

Some ancient Asian philosophers and physicians believed that exquisitely sensual, masterfully controlled sex replenished and strengthened the life force, or energy, of both men and women. The prevailing idea was that sexual vitality and potency depended, first and foremost, on *sensory* awareness and *sensual* expertise.

POWER ACTION: MORE OPTIONS
Take a 5-Minute "Transition Time" to Leave Work Stress Behind

If you arrive home from work and immediately dive into domestic chores, it's all but impossible to cultivate the level of intimacy that promotes extraordinary sex. You go from one type of stress to another. As discussed in detail in chapter 7, we suggest a 5-minute transition period—a regular daily "buffer zone" time for couples to release work tensions and simply be together—to chat, stroll, hug, hold hands and perhaps sip a single glass of wine. "A few minutes of peace and quiet can be worth 4 hours of foreplay," says Dr. Zilbergeld.[37]

Enjoy 5-Second "Sex Anticipations"

When researchers have analyzed moments of great, uninhibited passion, they have discovered that a great deal of planning usually precedes the sexual intimacy itself.[38] For most women and for many men, *anticipation*—with fantasizing thoughts, hormone-raising forefeelings and an uplifted mood—may be a more potent aphrodisiac than spontaneity. Thus the idea of securing private, scheduled times for "dating" your partner makes sense. This allows you a chance to shut out the rest of the rushing world at least a few times a week, long enough to share intimate affections and savor small islands of what some researchers call *sweet time*[39]—passionate, private, heart-to-heart love-bonding time—which, unfortunately, is usually the first thing to get lost in the hectic pace of everyday work and family life.

Create an Atmosphere of Intimate Safety and Trust

Lasting intimacy and extraordinary sex depend *at all times* on a genuine sense of safety and trust. This requires that you and your partner be honest and clear with each other every time you are making sensual or sexual contact—not just in body but in your minds and shared words—about what pleases and what displeases or hurts. Research indicates that extraordinary "supersex" is only possible when both partners feel completely safe and trusting in letting go and deepening pleasures above and beyond orgasm instead of holding back, feeling unsafe and being unwilling to cross the boundaries in the mind or heart.[40] This requires sharpening your skills in listening to your inner signals and having confidence in discriminating between times when it's all right to feel emotionally or mentally or sexually vulnerable in love-making and times when it's not. Limits can be gently set but must be firmly respected. A sense of safety also depends on the feeling that we, women and men, each create for ourselves by refusing to be involved with a partner who breaches our trust or will hurt us.

Light Up Your Mental Passion

Distractions and anxieties arise in the mind and manifest themselves in your mood and body responses, and even when you may have the physical energy for sex, your ability to enjoy, really enjoy, lovemaking may be hindered by thoughts that make you anxious and interfere with or undermine your arousal. Mental distractions, blue moods and fatigue all lower sexual energy and prevent many of us from getting in the lovemaking spirit or ruin sexual intimacy once we're close. In order to overcome these obstacles, the first thing to do is *recognize them.*

The mind/mood saboteurs of sexual energy appear in some basic patterns:[41]

Simple mental distractions: "What should we have for dinner?"; "Shhhh! We're probably making too much noise—someone will hear us."; "I forgot to put the laundry in the dryer."; "I have to get that report finished by tomorrow."; "I'm hungry."; "It's not the right temperature in here."

Anxious feelings about your appearance: "I didn't shave my legs."; "I wonder if I smell bad."; "I forgot to brush my teeth."; "It must feel gross to caress me."

Sexual performance worries: "Am I pleasing my partner?"; "Uh-oh, I'm not getting stimulated enough"; "What if I can't climax?"; "I'm taking too long—this is ridiculous."

Hurry-up stress and strain: "What was I thinking when I agreed to make love? I should be working on business right now—I'll never get caught up!"; "I forgot to call about that repair."; "Why is this taking so long? I'm going to miss out on some sleep."

Lingering resentments: "Why did I say yes to having sex? I'm still angry at him/her for what happened."; "The only times he or she acts nice and gives me attention is when there's sex attached to it."

To help overcome these—and many other—common cerebral stumbling blocks to extraordinary sex, the following Power-Action Options are some of the quickest, simplest suggestions we've found.

Clearly *Choose* to Enjoy Lovemaking

Negative, unwanted thoughts thrive when the mind and mood are uncommitted to the experience of the moment. Make it clear to yourself that the sensual and sexual intimacy is something you desire *right now* and that you don't want to spoil it with worry or resentments.

Whenever you find yourself mentally distracted during lovemaking, ask yourself, Does this thought or image make me feel better? Or help me behave the way I want to? Or help me think productively about the situation? Or reinforce positive images I have about myself? Or improve my relationship? "No matter what your problem or situation," explains Dr. Zilbergeld, "there are always two ways to go with it. The negative way leads to discouragement, despair and self-hate. The more positive way leads to useful thinking, good feelings and solutions. Just because something hasn't been working lately doesn't mean it will never work. You can make changes."[42]

Ironically, for years psychologists have advised us to use "thought-stopping" to block undesirable images or self-talk. But evidence (discussed in chapter 29) shows it doesn't work—in fact, the more you try to resist a thought, the more tenacious it becomes.[43] Paradoxically, the way to release unwanted cognitions is to stop trying—to let them enter your mind, observe them and then, on their own, they'll leave. The following Power-Action Options aid this process.

Align Your Breathing Patterns

There is some evidence that matching, or approximating, the respiration cycles of your lover can be a strong factor in creating heightened sexual rapport and erotic chemistry.[44] This may prove helpful in releasing your mind from self-centered anxious thoughts. Experiment with the effect of gently coming in sync with your partner's breathing rhythm. Don't try too hard, though, since you may hyperventilate and get dizzy. Instead, approximate the rhythms of your touch-strokes and movements to the cadence of your lover's inhalations and exhalations.

Focus on Sensations of Touch, Movement, Sight and Sound

Take a moment to remember what you have learned about the sensations that are most enjoyable and erotic to you and your partner (see "5-Minute Sensory Body Tour" earlier in this chapter). Keeping these preferences in mind, one of the simplest and most direct ways to light up sexual passion and disengage from mood downturns or unwanted thoughts is to focus intently on the *preferred sensations* you are giving and receiving—the feelings of softness or warmth in your partner's touch; the sensations you get from skin touching skin, fingers stroking hair, lips on skin, tongue on skin or kissing in other erotic ways; the smoothness of the pillow or sheets; the movement of your chest as you breathe; the sound of intimate whisperings; the look of your lover's features that you find sexiest; the feeling of increased warmth in the body and the rhythm of muscles tightening and relaxing as you gradually increase the level of sensuality and intimacy.

Take 5 Seconds to Adopt a "Beginner's Mind"

To enjoy supersex, it's essential to suspend judgment and certainty long enough to approach lovemaking in fresh, original, highly sensitive ways and to get out of ruts and routines as soon as they become so comfortable that your—or your partner's—sense of passion vanishes. Researchers have found, for example, that "supersexual women" have "learned to approach each moment with an openness to experience" referred to as a *beginner's mind*—approaching each sexual interlude as if it were the first.[45] All this requires is a bit of practice. Don't jump ahead with your thoughts. Instead, just keep pace with the wonderful information you receive through your senses. Follow whatever erotic thoughts emerge, responding spontaneously and naturally to your partner's body and touch and voice without "analyzing." Teach your mind to follow your fingertips and hands in discovering new sensations. Recreate the image you had when you first kissed your partner's lips passionately. Let your senses lead your mind.

Share Your Favorite Sensations—And Give Support

Sexual energy increases for many of us when we can feel free to relate how we are feeling, right now, in the changing, evolving experience of intimacy, and have our partner do the same. By describing sensations of closeness, we heighten feelings of sensuality. By using warm, sexually explicit dialogue, complimenting how the other person looks and feels and expressing your own sensations of arousal and pleasure, you can more easily distance yourself from unwanted thoughts. If you're having trouble focusing or concentrating on lovemaking, learn to tell this to your partner and ask for warm, supportive help in releasing distractions. Consider reexperiencing the 5-minute Sensory Body Tour.

Fantasize

Daydreaming can be used to rekindle the deeper levels of passion that promote exceptionally fulfilling sex. Fantasize with your favorite erotic images from the past and create new ones. Use mental imagery to visualize yourself in a stimulating scene—perhaps the most passionate previous experience with your partner, sex in some exotic position or place or some new twist on how you'd like to feel even more pleasure or make love right now. Many people are troubled by guilt feelings caused by sexual fantasies. It is quite natural, however, for both women and men to have a wide variety of sexual fantasies. Yet it's important to re-member that sexual fantasies are just that: fantasies. And as such, they require neither action nor guilt.

Take Advantage of 5-Second "Sex-Muscle Toning"

To get the most out of sex, at *every* age, you need to be in great shape for it—in mind and body. "Two powerful aphrodisiacs," write Robert N. Butler, M.D., of Mount Sinai Medical Center in New York, and Myrna I. Lewis, Ph.D., "are a vigorous and well-cared-for body and a lively personality. Much can be done to preserve the functioning of both."[46] In one recent nine-month study of 95 previously inactive but healthy men (average age 48), researchers found that those who engaged in regular moderate to vigorous exercise reported a 30 percent increase in frequency of intercourse, with a 26 percent increase in the frequency of orgasms. They also reported increases in other arousal measures, such as passionate kissing and caressing. In contrast, the control subjects, who didn't exercise, experienced no improvements and actually saw slight decreases in their sexual frequency.[47] Here are two sensible sug-gestions.

Stay physically fit. Regular exercise has been linked to heightened sensuality and sexuality (see chapters 11, 12 and 18).

Do the PC exercise regularly. Beyond a good, balanced approach to everyday physical activity, there's a valuable exercise that takes just a few seconds and can be done almost anywhere at any time, by both men and women, to strengthen the sex-related sphincter muscles of the pelvic floor and, at least in some cases, help improve sexual respon-siveness.[48] It's called the Kegel (*KAY-gill*) exercise, named after Arnold H. Kegel, M.D., the physician who discovered and developed it in the late 1940s and early 1950s.[49] In both men and women, the pubococ-cygeus (PC) muscle tends to progressively atrophy from disuse throughout our lives.

Studies report that, compared with women who have strong, toned

PCs, women with weak PCs—and this includes many, and perhaps most, women over age 45[50]—are more frequently troubled with incontinence (involuntary urination)[51] and are more often sexually dissatisfied.[52] Weak PCs in men may contribute to incontinence, inability to achieve and maintain an erection, poor ejaculatory control and perhaps even problems related to the seminal vesicles and prostate gland.[53] PC exercises have enabled some women to climax more readily and intensely, and the exercise may even assist men to achieve easier erections and more control of orgasm.[54]

To become toned, the PC must be exercised regularly. Dr. Kegel found that to learn the sensation of the PC contracting, you can start by interrupting urination. He recommended that to help the PC do most of the work itself, you should at first leave your knees spread when urinating and, once the flow has began, make an effort to stop it, let it start again, stop it, and so on. After a few trials, most people can consciously tense the PC by simple mental command, anytime and anywhere, and then should use the occasional interruption of urination only as a simple check.

Practice doing the PC exercise a number of times during the day. However, there is some evidence to suggest that performing it upon first awakening and before urinating, while the bladder is very full, may not be beneficial. Any other time is fine. Tense the PC strongly, holding for 1 to 2 seconds. Relax for several seconds. Repeat this cycle so that you complete 5 to 10 contractions in a set. You might also include quick flexing and relaxing sequences. As you gain strength and control, progressively increase the intensity of the PC exercise contractions, holding some for more than the usual 1 to 2 seconds. At first, the muscles may fatigue quickly. Don't overdo it. For many of us, 60 to 100 1-second to 5-second contractions performed inconspicuously throughout the day is a reasonable goal.

"Hot Dates": Plan for Extraordinary Sex at Least Once a Week

When you find your life especially busy, be careful not to let yourself feel that sexual overtures from your partner are an intrusion that wastes precious time. Warm, intimate, *shared moments* can often *save* you time overall by boosting vitality and feelings of well-being that, in turn, contribute to more effective work and less likelihood of arguments at home that arise from the perspective—in one or both partners—that "you never have time for *me*."

According to recent research, the reasoning for this goes far beyond enjoyment—which can be health-promoting in its own right.

Not only is there evidence that weekly sex may be health-promoting for premenopausal women,[55] there is also research showing that it may also reduce symptom distress for perimenopausal women—those going through the transition period into menopause. Hot flashes are rarer, and if they do occur, they tend to be milder than in women whose sexual encounters are infrequent. Other studies on post-menopausal women show that the adage "use it or lose it" may have a bearing on a woman's sensuality and sexuality. Vaginal atrophy (apparent deterioration of tissue) is a common problem for menopausal women. One study reported that there was significantly less vaginal atrophy in menopausal women who had more active sex lives.[56] For those women who did not have a partner, self-stimulation—masturbation—helped to reduce atrophy, apparently, theorizes Dr. Cutler, because the gentle stimulation increases blood flow to the area and helps delay the hormonally induced declines.

After more than two decades of research, Dr. Cutler concludes that having sexual intercourse "at least once in each nonmenstruating week (i.e., [at least] once in each seven-day span)" helps slow the aging process in women and promote naturally higher estrogen levels—especially from the late thirties through menopause and beyond. "Biology is teaching us an important lesson," she explains, and the lesson is that "sporadic sexual activity [having intercourse less often than once a week] is not good for a woman's endocrine system."[57]

Note: We *strongly* caution you against: (1) Making this another "have-to" habit in your relationship and feeling stressed or guilty if more than a week goes by without sex; (2) using—even once—Dr. Cutler's research as an excuse for promiscuous "sex as exercise"; (3) inferring that this research condemns the option of celibacy (there are studies suggesting potential health benefits from celibacy when compared, over the long term, to sporadic—less than weekly—sexual activity)[58]; or (4) assuming that if you live alone and presently do not have an intimate sexual relationship with another person, your health may suffer.

A 5-Second Choice for Men: Less Dietary Fat, Greater Sex?

The male hormone testosterone plays a major role in determining a man's sexual desire, his ability to get an erection and perhaps his ability to climax as well.[59] A study at the University of Utah Medical Center in Salt Lake City found that testosterone levels in men fell by about 30 percent during the 4 hours after eating a high-fat meal (57 percent of calories from fat), whereas hormone levels stayed the same for men who had consumed a carbohydrate/protein meal that was low in fat (2 percent of calories from fat).[60] Beyond the many health-promoting reasons for a low-fat diet cited in chapter 10, this preliminary but compelling evidence suggests that high-fat meals may affect sex hormones and their related functions in men. More research is needed to know for certain, but it makes sense—for many different reasons—to limit your intake of dietary fat.

> Lasting sexual intimacy has its own language, unique to each of us as individuals and couples. Without a learned, shared vocabulary of intimacy, sooner or later sexual dissatisfactions arise.

A 5-Minute Choice for Men: Do the Dishes!

Doing the dishes and other forms of housework and child care may seem like trivial concerns when compared to sexuality, yet studies show that *women see these as major issues affecting their sex life and the overall happiness of their relationship—and men who help more with housework have better sex lives, better health and happier marriages than others.*[61] To a large extent, women need to feel physical and emotional support, closeness and tenderness *before* wanting to have sex. Ironically, even for husbands who read this and say, "But that's not *me*. I do my share of housework," research indicates that almost every man *overestimates* the time he puts in at home. One study even reported that men who profess support for feminist ideas only put in an average of *4 minutes* more daily housework than those men at the opposite extreme—those with openly "macho" beliefs.[62]

Share the Benefits of 5-Minute Sexual "Pillow Talks"

Sex is intensely personal. We all feel vulnerable about it. Some of us may be able to have a satisfying love life without talking about it, but that's very rare, especially in long-term relationships. In a study of 805 nurses, for example, women with multiple orgasms didn't get them by accident: They identified what they liked, chose sensual/sexual touches and pacing that gave them maximum pleasure and communicated to their partners what aroused them most.[63]

It turns out that many of the most common sexual difficulties can be eased or overcome with open, sensitive, ongoing "pillow talk."

Acknowledge your awkwardness or anxiety. When you begin a discussion on sex with your loved one, says Dr. Alperstein, who teaches workshops called "Speaking Up while Lying Down: Assertive Communication in Sexually Intimate Relationships," acknowledge your fears: "This is difficult for me to say because I really love you and don't want to threaten our relationship, but . . ."[64]

Be specific. Don't say "I want more affection." Say "I want you to hug me and give me a special kiss when we first get together after work. I want to hold your hand when we go for a walk or sit side by side. And I want to be held for a little while each night without that always being interpreted as a sexual invitation."

Have sexual "heart talks." Consider taking turns sharing your innermost feelings and thoughts on one or two of the following sexual "heart talks." Be careful not to interrupt, and give your undivided attention. Be specific, caring, open and honest:

1. The best thing about our sex life is . . .
2. My father gave me the impression that sex . . .
3. My mother gave me the impression that sex . . .
4. What I find most sexually attractive about you is . . .
5. What I would like to add to our sexual and physical intimacy is . . .
7. I turn on to you most when . . .
8. It would be easier to express my sexual desires if . . .
9. I think our experience of sexual pleasure is . . .
10. A sexual delight I would like to indulge you in is . . .

Create a wish list. Over a week or two, you and your partner write down everything you wish the other would do for you sexually, from more cuddling, hugs and kisses to affectionate notes to specific intimate caresses. Next, rank your wishes in order from "easiest to ask for" to "the most difficult." Then, once or twice a month, you each reveal the "easiest" items on your lists and eventually work your way down to the more difficult requests. One ground rule: You both have the right to say no whenever you're uncomfortable with a request.

For most people, the sexual wishes that are easiest to request are also easiest to grant. Typically, they have to do with expressions of affection out of bed: hugs, kisses and light caresses in everyday situations. The combination of asking for affection and getting it can have a surprisingly positive impact on the relationship as a whole.

Resources

Couples seeking sex therapy should be very cautious in selecting a professional because of the large number of poorly trained individuals who call themselves therapists. For help in finding a qualified sex therapist near you, consult the human sexuality program at a nearby university medical center, ask your local medical society to recommend a medical sex therapist, send a stamped, self-addressed envelope to the **American Association of Sex Educators, Counselors, and Therapists** (435 North Michigan Ave., Chicago, IL

60611) or contact the **American Board of Sexology** (Registry of Diplomates in Sexology, P.O. Box 1166, Winter Park, FL 32789; 202-462-2122).

Going the Distance: Secrets to Lifelong Love by Lonnie Barbach, Ph.D., and David Geisinger, Ph.D. (Doubleday, 1991). A sensitive book designed to help monogamous couples communicate more effectively and deepen intimacy and trust.

Love Cycles: The Science of Intimacy by Winnifred B. Cutler, Ph.D. (Villard, 1991). A groundbreaking, scientifically based book.

The Magic of Sex by Miriam Stoppard, M.D. (Dorling Kindersley, 1991). A popular, color-illustrated guidebook to healthy sex for men and women.

Menopause: A Guide for Women and the Men Who Love Them by Winnifred B. Cutler, Ph.D., and Celso Ramon Garcia, M.D., 3rd ed. (Norton, 1993). An insightful, scientifically based book.

The New Joy of Sex by Alex Comfort, M.D., Sc.D. (Crown, 1991). The latest version of this classic.

The New Male Sexuality: The Truth about Men, Sex and Pleasure by Bernie Zilbergeld, Ph.D. (Bantam, 1992). An up-to-date, accurate guidebook for men and the women who love them.

Ordinary Women, Extraordinary Sex by Sandra Scantling, Ph.D. and Sue Browder (Dutton, 1993). An evocative, research-based view of exceptional sexual pleasure for women and their partners.

Sex after 50 (Better Sex Video Service, Suite 3635, 3600 Park Central Blvd. N., Pompano Beach, FL 33064; 800-866-1000). A sensitive and supportive video narrated by Lonnie Barbach, Ph.D., a faculty member in the Department of Psychiatry at the University of California Medical School in San Francisco.

Sex over 40 by Saul H. Rosenthal, M.D. (Tarcher, 1987). An encouraging book by a noted clinician in the field.

"Sex over 40" Newsletter (P.O. Box 1600, Chapel Hill, NC 27515; 800-334- 5474). An informative, up-to-date newsletter.

Sex in the Golden Years by Deborah S. Edelman (Donald Fine, 1992). A survey that concludes "What's ahead may be worth aging for."

Sexual Solutions: An Informative Guide by Michael Castleman (Touchstone, Revised Edition, 1990). A book for men and for the women who want to understand them and better communicate about sex. Advice in a wide range of sexual areas.

What to Do When He Has a Headache by Janet Wolfe, Ph.D. (Hyperion, 1992). Practical advice from a psychologist on how to overcome periodic male mental blocks to sexual intimacy.

PERSONAL POWER NOTES
A Quick-List of This Chapter's Power-Action Options

Turn sex into loveplay—instead of foreplay and "the act."
- *Take a 5-minute Sensory Body Tour with your sexual partner.*

Take a 5-minute "transition time" to leave work stress behind.

Enjoy 5-second "sex anticipations."

Create an atmosphere of intimate safety and trust.

Light up your mental passion.

Clearly choose to enjoy lovemaking.

Align your breathing patterns.

Focus on sensations of touch, movement, sight and sound.

Take 5 seconds to adopt a "beginner's mind."

Share your favorite sensations—and give support.

Fantasize.

Take advantage of 5-second "sex-muscle toning."
- *Stay physically fit.*
- *Do the PC exercise regularly.*

"Hot dates": plan for extraordinary sex at least once a week.

A 5-second choice for men: less dietary fat, greater sex?

A 5-minute choice for men: do the dishes!

Share the benefits of 5-minute sexual "pillow talks."
- *Acknowledge your awkwardness or anxiety.*
- *Be specific.*
- *Have sexual "heart talks."*
- *Create a wish list.*

PERSONAL NOTES

References

CHAPTER 24

1 Williams, R., and Williams, V. *Anger Kills* (New York: Times Books, 1993).

2. Ibid.

3. Lazarus, R. S. *Emotion and Adaptation* (Oxford, England: Oxford University Press, 1991): 222.

4. Williams and Williams. *Anger Kills*; Eliot, R. S. *From Stress to Strength* (New York: Bantam, 1994); Eliot, R. S., and Breo, D. *Is It Worth Dying For?* (New York: Bantam, 1989); Tavris, C. *Anger: The Misunderstood Emotion* (New York: Simon & Schuster, 1982).

5. "Marital Conflict Can Be Hazardous to Your Health." *Mental Medicine Update* II (3)(Winter 1993/1994): 2.

6. M. Watsom et al. *Psychological Medicine* 21 (1991): 51–57; Seligman, M. E. P. *Learned Optimism* (New York: Knopf, 1991): 167–178.

7. J. K. Kiecolt-Glaser et al. "Negative Behavior during Marital Conflict Is Associated with Immunological Down-Regulation." *Psychosomatic Medicine* 55 (1993): 395–409.

8. Seligman, M. E. P. *What You Can Change and What You Can't* (New York: Knopf, 1993): 130.

9. T. W. Smith et al. "Cynical Hostility at Home and Work: Psychosocial Vulnerability across Domains." *Journal of Research in Personality* 22 (Dec. 1988): 524–548.

10. Seligman. *What You Can Change*: 127–128.

11. Markman, H., and Notarius, C. *We Can Work It Out: Making Sense of Marital Conflict* (New York: Putnam, 1993).

12. Seligman. *What You Can Change*.

13. Berkowitz, L. "Experimental Investigations of Hostility Catharsis." *Journal of Consulting and Clinical Psychology* 35 (1970): 1–7; Tavris. *Anger: The Misunderstood Emotion* (New York: Touchstone, 1989); Seligman. *What You Can Change*: 130.

14. Seligman. *What You Can Change*.

15. Novaco, R. *Anger Control*. (New York: D. C. Heath, 1975).

16. Example is adapted from Powell, L., and Thoreson, C. "Modifying the Type A Pattern: A Small Groups Treatment Approach," in *Applications in Behavioral Medicine and Health Psychology: A Clinician's Source Book*, eds. Blumenthal, J. A., and McKee, D. C. (Sarasota, Fla.: Professional Resource Exchange, 1987): 171–207.

17. Seligman. *What You Can Change*.

18. Peterson, C., and Bossio, L. M. *Health and Optimism* (New York: Free Press, 1991): 53.

19. Beck, A. T. *Cognitive Therapy and the Emotional Disorders* (New York: New American Library, 1988); McKay, M., Davis, M., and Fanning, P. *Thoughts & Feelings: The Art of Cognitive Stress Intervention* (Richmond, Calif.: New Harbinger Publications, 1981); Burns, D. *Feeling Good: The New Mood Therapy* (New York: Signet, 1981).

20. Eliot, R. S., and Breo, D. L. *Is It Worth Dying For?*, rev. ed. (New York: Bantam, 1991): 95–96.

21. Podell, R. M. *Contagious Emotions* (New York: Pocket Books, 1992).

22. Ibid.: 50, 60.

23. Freeman, A., and DeWolf, R. *The 10 Dumbest Mistakes Smart People Make—and How to Avoid Them* (New York: HarperCollins, 1992); Suarez, R., Mills, R. C., and Stewart, D. *Sanity, Insanity, and Common Sense* (New York: Fawcett, 1987); Emery, G. "Rapid Cognitive Therapy of Anxiety." Research monograph. (Los Angeles: Los Angeles Cen-

ter for Cognitive Therapy, 1987): 39–52; Emery, G., and Campbell, J. *Rapid Relief from Emotional Distress* (New York: Fawcett, 1986).

24. Freeman and DeWolf. *The 10 Dumbest Mistakes.*

25. Vincent, J. D. *The Biology of Emotions* (Oxford, England: Basil Blackwell, 1990); Lazarus. *Emotion and Adaptation* (Oxford, England: Oxford University Press, 1991); Thompson, J. G. *The Psychobiology of Emotions* (New York: Plenum Press, 1988); Gray, J. A., ed. *Psychobiological Aspects of Relationships between Emotion and Cognition* (Hillsdale, N.J.: Lawrence Erlbaum, 1990).

26. Miller, R. C., and Berman, J. S. "The Efficacy of Cognitive Behavior Therapies: A Quantitative Review of the Research Evidence." *Psychological Bulletin* 94 (1983): 39–53; Beck, A. *Cognitive Therapy and the Emotional Disorders* (New York: New American Library, 1988); Beck, A., and Emery, G., with Greenberg, L. *Anxiety Disorders and Phobias* (New York: Basic Books, 1985); Burns. *Feeling Good: The New Mood Therapy*; McKay, Davis, and Fanning. *Thoughts & Feelings: The Art of Cognitive Stress Intervention.*

27. Seligman, M. E. P., in "Mind Over Illness: Do Optimists Live Longer?" *American Health* (Nov. 1986): 50–53.

28. Ornish, D. *Dr. Dean Ornish's Program for Reversing Heart Disease* (New York: Random House, 1991); Eliot and Breo. *Is It Worth Dying For?*; Williams, R. *The Trusting Heart* (New York: Times Books, 1989); Ornstein, R., and Swencionis, C. *The Healing Brain: A Scientific Reader* (New York: Guildford, 1991).

29. Ornish. *Reversing Heart Disease*; L. Scherwitz et al. "Self-Involvement and Coronary Heart Disease Incidence in the Multiple Risk Intervention Trial." *Psychosomatic Medicine* 48 (1986): 187–199; L. Scherwitz et al. "Speech Characteristics and Behavior-Type Assessment in the Multiple Risk Intervention Trial (MR FIT) Structured Interviews." *Journal of Behavioral Medicine* 10 (2)(1987): 173–195.

30. Ornish, D. "The Healing Power of Love." *Prevention* (Feb. 1991): 60–66.

31. Ibid.: 65–66.

32. Goren-Ost, L. "Applied Relaxation: Description of a Coping Technique and Review of Controlled Studies." *Behaviour Research and Therapy* 25 (1987): 397–410; Appendix of Clark, D. "Anxiety States: Panic and Generalized Anxiety," in *Cognitive Behaviour Therapy for Psychiatric Problems: A Practical Guide* eds. K. Hawton et al. (Oxford, England: Oxford University Press, 1989): 92–96; Eppley, K., Abrams, A., and Shear, J. "Differential Effects of Relaxation Techniques on Trait Anxiety: A Meta-Analysis." *Journal of Clinical Psychology* 45 (1989): 957–974; J. Kabat-Zinn et al. "Effectiveness of Meditation-Based Stress Reduction Program in the Treatment of Anxiety Disorders." *American Journal of Psychiatry* 149 (1992): 937–943.

33. Huseman, R. C., and Hatfield, J. D. *The Equity Factor* (Boston: Houghton Mifflin, 1989): 36.

34. Hochschild, A. *The Second Shift* (New York: Avon, 1989).

35. Fadiman, J. *Unlimit Your Life* (Berkeley, Calif.: Celestial Arts, 1989): 118.

36. Markman and Notarius. *We Can Work It Out.*

37. Covey, S. R. *The Seven Habits of Highly Effective People* (New York: Simon & Schuster, 1989): 188.

38. Huseman and Hatfield. *The Equity Factor*: 44–45.

39. Markman and Notarius. *We Can Work It Out*: 74.

40. "Exercise and Mental Health." *The University of Texas Health Science Center Lifetime Health Letter* 5 (3)(Mar. 1993): 7.

41. Williams and Williams. *Anger Kills*: 82–3.

42. Feshbach, S. "The Catharsis Hypothesis and Some Consequences of Interaction with Aggression." *Journal of Personality* 24 (1956): 449–462; Berkowitz, L. "Experimental In-

vestigations of the Hostility Catharsis." *Journal of Consulting and Clinical Psychology* 35 (1970): 1–7; Tavris. *Anger: The Misunderstood Emotion.*

43. M. Julius et al. "Anger-Coping Types, Blood Pressure, and All-Cause Mortality: A Follow-up in Tecumseh, Michigan (1971–1983)." *American Journal of Epidemiology* 124 (2)(1986): 220–233.

44. E. M. Cummings et al. *Developmental Psychology* 21 (3)(1985).

45. M. Julius et al. "Anger-Coping Types": 220–233.

46. Lerner, H. G. *The Dance of Anger* (New York: Harper & Row, 1985): 1.

47. Huxley, A., quoted in "Kindness Week." *Brain-Mind Bulletin* (June 1991): 3.

48. Williams. *The Trusting Heart*: xiii, 11.

49. Bloomfield, H. H., and Vettese, S. *Lifemates* (New York: New American Library, 1989): 163–165.

50. McGee-Cooper, A. *You Don't Have to Come Home from Work Exhausted* (New York: Bantam, 1992): 245–262.

51. Paul, J., and Paul, M. *Do I Have to Give Up Me to Be Loved by You?* (Minneapolis: CompCare, 1983).

52. Podell. *Contagious Emotions*: 15.

53. Gottman, J. M. *Why Marriages Succeed or Fail* (New York: Simon & Schuster, 1994): 178.

54. C. K. Hsee et al. "The Effect of Power on Susceptibility to Emotional Contagion." *Cognition and Emotion* 4 (4)(Dec. 1990): 327–340.

CHAPTER 25

1. Cramer, K. D. *Staying on Top When Your World Turns Upside Down* (New York: Viking, 1990).

2. Campbell, J. *Primitive Mythology: The Masks of God* (New York: Penguin, 1969): 54.

3. Lloyd, C., quoted in "Coping with Grief." *University of Texas Health Science Center Lifetime Health Letter* 4 (5)(May 1992): 1–6.

4. Flach, F. *Resilience* (New York: Fawcett, 1988): xi.

5. Ibid.: 14.

6. Cramer. *Staying On Top*: 54.

7. State University of New York at Stony Brook. Study cited in *University of Texas Health Science Center Lifetime Health Letter* 4 (5)(May 1992): 1.

8. Flach. *Resilience*: 255–256.

9. Wolin, S., quoted in "How to Survive (Practically) Anything." *Psychology Today* (Jan./Feb. 1992): 35–39.

10. Francis, M. E., and Pennebaker, J. W. "Talking and Writing as Illness Prevention." *Medicine, Exercise, Nutrition, and Health* 1 (1)(Jan./Feb. 1992): 27–33; Pennebaker, J. W. *Opening Up: The Healing Power of Confiding in Others* (New York: Morrow, 1990).

11. Francis and Pennebaker. "Talking and Writing."

12. Caplan, G. *Principles of Preventive Psychiatry* (New York: Basic Books, 1964); Lynch, J. J. *The Broken Heart* (New York: Basic Books, 1979).

13. Segal, J. *Winning Life's Toughest Battles: Roots of Human Resilience* (New York: McGraw-Hill, 1986): 80–81.

14. Adapted from Engler, J., and Goleman, D. *The Consumer's Guide to Psychotherapy* (New York: Touchstone, 1992): 48–49.

15. Segal. *Winning Life's Toughest Battles*: 109–110.

16. Ibid.: 105.

CHAPTER 26

1. Renick, M. J., Blumberg, S. L., and Markman, H. J. "The Prevention and Relationship Enhancement Program (PREP)—An Empirically Based Preventive Intervention Program for Couples." *Family Relations* 41 (2)(Apr. 1992): 141–147; Gottman, J. M., and Krokoff, L. J. "Marital Interactions and Satisfaction: A Longitudinal View." *Journal of Consulting and Clinical Psychology* 57 (1)(Feb. 1989): 47–52.

2. Lynch, J. J. "The Broken Heart: The Psychobiology of Human Contact," in *The Healing Brain: A Scientific Reader*, eds. Ornstein, R., and Swencionis, C. (New York: Guilford Press, 1990): 75–87.

3. Gottman, J. M. *Why Marriages Succeed or Fail* (New York: Simon & Schuster, 1994): 181–182.

4. Pinker, S. *The Language Instinct* (New York: Morrow, 1994).

5. Lynch, J. J. *Language of the Heart* (New York: Basic Books, 1985): 3–4.

6. Ibid.: 243.

7. Gottman and Krokoff. "Marital Interactions."

8. Renick, Blumberg, and Markman. "Prevention and Relationship Enhancement"; Markman, H. J., quoted in Blau, M. "Can We Talk?" *American Health* (Dec. 1990): 45.

9. Tannen D., quoted in Blau. "Can We Talk?": 37–45.

10. House, J. S., Robbins, C., and Metzner, H. L. "The Association of Social Relationships and Activities with Mortality: Prospective Evidence from the Tecumseh Community Health Study." *American Journal of Epidemiology* 116 (1)(1982): 123–140; Berkman, L. F., and Syme, L. O. "Social Networks, Host Resistance, and Mortality: A Nine-Year Follow-Up of Alameda County Residents." *American Journal of Epidemiology* 102 (2)(1979): 186–204; Eisenberg, L. "A Friend, not an Apple, a Day Will Keep the Doctor Away." *Journal of the American Medical Association* 66 (1979): 551–553; Syme, L. "People Need People." *American Health* (July/Aug. 1982): 49–51; Cohen, S., and Wils, T. "Stress, Social Support, and Buffering Hypothesis." *Psychological Bulletin* 98 (1985): 310–257; Russell, D. W., and Cutrona, C. E. "Social Support, Stress, and Depressive Symptoms among the Elderly: Test of a Process Model." *Psychology and Aging* 6 (2)(1991): 190–201; R. B. Oslon et al. "Social Networks and Longevity: A 14–Year Follow-up Study among the Elderly in Denmark." *Social Science and Medicine* 33 (10)(1991): 1189–1195.

11. J. S. House et al. "Social Relationships and Health." *Science* 241 (1988): 540–545.

12. House, Robbins, and Metzner. "The Association of Social Relationships": 123–140.

13. E. Friedmann et al. "Animal Companions and One-Year Survival of Patients after Discharge from a Coronary Care Unit." *Public Health Reports* 95 (1980): 307–312.

14. T. E. Seeman et al. "Social Network Ties and Mortality among the Elderly in the Alameda County Study." *American Journal of Epidemiology* 126 (4)(1987): 714–723.

15. Study cited in Kerman, A. *The H. A. R. T. Program* (New York: HarperCollins, 1991): 228.

16. Gottman. *Why Marriages Succeed or Fail*: 110.

17. Ibid.: 110.

18. Thayer, R. E. *The Biopsychology of Mood and Arousal* (New York: Oxford University Press, 1989).

19. Epstein, N., quoted in Gelman, D. "The Thoughts That Wound." *Newsweek* (Jan. 9, 1989): 46–48.

20. Gottman. *Why Marriages Succeed or Fail*; Markman, H., and Notarius, C. *We Can Work It Out: Making Sense of Marital Conflict* (New York: Putnam, 1993).

21. Gottman and Krokoff. "Marital Interactions"; Levenson, R. W., and Gottman, J. M. "Physiological and Affective Predictors of Change in Relationship Satisfaction." *Journal of Personality and Social Psychology* 49 (10)(July 1985): 85–94; Gottman, J. M., and Levenson, R. W. "Assessing the Role of Emotion in Marriage." *Behavioral Assessment* 8 (1)(1986): 31–48.

22. Gray, J. *Men Are from Mars, Women Are from Venus* (New York: HarperCollins, 1992): 67–68.

23. Levenson and Gottman. "Physiological and Affective Predictors."

24. Gottman. *Why Marriages Succeed or Fail*: 153.

25. Gray. *Men Are from Mars*: 68.

26. Gottman, J. M., quoted in Blau. "Can We Talk?": 41.

27. Gottman and Krokoff. "Marital Interactions."

28. Markman, H., quoted in Blau. "Can We Talk?": 42.

29. Gray. *Men Are from Mars*: 86.

30. Ibid.: 88.

31. Markman and Notarius. *We Can Work It Out.*

32. Peterson, K. S. "Fighting Fair Keeps Marriages Strong." *USA Today* (Feb. 20, 1992): 6D.

33. Crohan, S. E., quoted in Peterson. "Fighting Fair."

34. Crohan, S. E. "Marital Happiness and Spousal Consensus on Beliefs about Marital Conflict: A Longitudinal Investigation." *Journal of Social and Personal Relationships* 9 (1)(Feb. 1992): 89–102.

35. Delis, D. C. *The Passion Paradox* (New York: Bantam, 1990): 143–144.

36. Nagler, W. *The Dirty Half Dozen: Six Radical Rules to Make Relationships Last* (New York: Warner, 1991): 47.

37. Gray. *Men Are from Mars*: 245.

38. Markman and Notarius. *We Can Work It Out*: 77.

39. Ibid.: 28.

40. Ibid.: 115.

41. Ibid.: 183.

42. Gottman. *Why Marriages Succeed or Fail*: 186–187.

43. Restak, R. *The Brain Has a Mind of Its Own* (New York: Harmony Books, 1991): 158.

44. Ibid.: 160.

45. Ornstein, R. *The Evolution of Consciousness* (New York: Prentice-Hall, 1991): 239–240.

46. Segal, J. *Winning Life's Toughest Battles: Roots of Human Resilience* (New York: McGraw-Hill, 1986): 18.

47. R. B. Williams et al. "Prognostic Importance of Social and Economic Resources among Medically Treated Patients with Angiographically Documented Artery Disease." *Journal of the American Medical Association* 267 (4)(Jan. 1992): 520–524.

48. Lynch, J. J. *The Broken Heart: The Medical Consequences of Loneliness* (New York: Basic Books, 1977): 3.

49. Williams, R. B., quoted in *Prevention* (June 1992): 64.

50. Rempel, J. K., and Holmes, J. G. "How Do I Trust Thee?" *Psychology Today* 20 (2)(Feb. 1986): 28–34; Rempel, J. K., Holmes, J. G., and Zanna, M. P. "Trust in Close Relationships." *Journal of Personality and Social Psychology* 49 (1)(July 1985): 95–112.

51. Williams, R. *The Trusting Heart* (New York: Times Books, 1989).

52. Pennebaker, J. W. *Opening Up: The Healing Power of Confiding in Others* (New York: Morrow, 1990).

53. Bartolome, F., and Evans, P. *Must Success Cost So Much?* (New York: Basic Books, 1988); Kaplan, R. F. *Beyond Ambition: How Driven Managers Can Lead Better and Live Better* (San Francisco: Josey-Bass, 1991).

54. Burt, R. S. *Strangers, Friends, and Happiness*, GSS Technical Report No. 72 (Chicago: National Opinion Research Center, University of Chicago, 1986).

55. Francis, M. E., and Pennebaker, J. W. "Talking and Writing as Illness Prevention." *Medicine, Exercise, Nutrition, and Health* 1 (1)(Jan./Feb. 1992): 27–33.

56. J. W. Pennebaker et al. "Accelerating the Coping Process." *Journal of Personality and Social Psychology* 58 (1990): 528–537.

57. Francis and Pennebaker. "Talking and Writing."

58. Pennebaker. *Opening Up*: 50.

59. Ibid.: 51.

60. Pennebaker, J. W., Hughes, C. F., and O'Heeron, R. C. "The Psychophysiology of Confession." *Journal of Personality and Social Psychology* 52 (1987): 781–793.

61. Pennebaker. *Opening Up*: 124–125.

62. Peterson, C., and Bossio, L. M. *Health and Optimism* (New York: Free Press, 1991): 129.

63. Ferguson, T. "Social Support Systems as Self-Care." *Medical Self-Care* (Winter 1979–1980): 3.

64. Kohn, A. *The Brighter Side of Human Nature* (New York: Basic Books, 1990).

65. "Rx: Helping Others." *Mental Medicine Update* II (3)(Winter 1993/1994): 3–5.

66. Luks, A. *The Healing Power of Doing Good* (New York: Fawcett, 1991): 40.

67. Luks. *Healing Power of Doing Good*; Kohn. *Brighter Side of Human Nature*; House, Robbins, and Metzner. "Association of Social Relationships."

68. House, Robbins, and Metzner. "Association of Social Relationships."

69. L. Scherwitz et al. "Self-Involvement and the Risk Factors for Coronary Heart Disease." *Advances* 2 (2)(Spring, 1985): 6–18.

70. Palmore, E. B. "Physical, Mental and Social Factors in Predicting Longevity." *Gerontologist* 9 (2)(Summer, 1969): 103–108; Palmore, E. B. "Predicting Longevity: A Follow-Up Controlling for Age." *Gerontologist* 9 (4)(Winter, 1969): 247–250.

71. Beauvoir, S. *The Coming of Age* (New York: Putnam, 1972).

72. Rimland, B. "The Altruism Paradox." *Psychological Reports* 51 (2)(Oct. 1982): 521–522.

73. Adapted from "Rx: Helping Others." *Mental Medicine Update* II (3)(Winter 1993/1994): 3–5.

74. Peterson and Bossio. *Health and Optimism*: 49; House, Robbins, and Metzner. "Association of Social Relationships."

75. Luks. *Healing Power of Doing Good*: 82.

76. E. Friedman et al. "Animal Companions and Survival Rate." *Public Health Report* 95 (4)(July/Aug. 1980): 307–312; E. Friedman et al. "Social Interaction and Blood Pressure: Influence of Animal Companions." *Journal of Nervous and Mental Disease* 171 (8)(1983): 461–465; Ornstein, R., and Sobel, D. *Healthy Pleasures* (Reading, Mass.: Addison-Wesley, 1989).

CHAPTER 27

1. Solomon, R. C. *About Love: Reinventing Romance for Our Times* (Lanham, Md.: Littlefield Adams, 1994): 349.

2. Ibid.: 256.

3. Rilke, R. M., quoted in Mitchell, S., ed. *The Enlightened Mind* (New York: HarperCollins, 1991): 188.

4. Markman, H., and Notarius, C. *We Can Work It Out: Making Sense of Marital Conflict* (New York: Putnam, 1993).

5. Nagler, W. *The Dirty Half Dozen: Six Radical Rules to Make Relationships Last* (New York: Warner, 1991): 3–4.

6. Delis, D. C. *The Passion Paradox* (New York: Bantam, 1990): xviii.

7. Delis. *Passion Paradox*: 18.

8. Markman and Notarius. *We Can Work It Out*.

9. Ziv, A., and Gadish, O. "Humor and Marital Satisfaction." *The Journal of Social Psychology* 129 (6)(1989): 759–768.

10. Solomon. *About Love*: 264.

11. Rossi, E. L., with Nimmons, D. *The 20-Minute Break* (Los Angeles: J. P. Tarcher, 1991): 165–166.

12. Nagler. *Dirty Half Dozen*: 5–6, 17.

13. Solomon. *About Love*: 314.

14. Gray, J. *Men Are from Mars, Women Are from Venus* (New York: HarperCollins, 1992): 143.

15. Nagler. *Dirty Half Dozen*: 49.

16. Josselson, R. *The Space between Us* (San Francisco: Josey-Bass, 1992): 29.

17. Ibid.: 43.

18. Ibid.: 99.

19. Gottman, J. M. *Why Marriages Succeed or Fail* (New York: Simon & Schuster, 1994): 195.

20. Gray. *Men Are from Mars*: 177.

21. Nagler. *Dirty Half Dozen*: 113.

22. Adapted from Hendrix, H. *Getting the Love You Want* (New York: HarperCollins, 1988): 260–262.

23. Solomon. *About Love*: 36.

CHAPTER 28

1. Reinisch, J. "Communication Counters Misconceptions." *USA Today* (May 22, 1992): 9D.

2. Zilbergeld, B. *The New Male Sexuality* (New York: Bantam, 1992): 4.

3. Ibid.: 390.

4. Wolfe, J. *What to Do When He Has a Headache* (New York: Hyperion, 1992).

5. Scantling, S., and Browder, S. *Ordinary Women, Extraordinary Sex* (New York: Dutton, 1993): 200–207.

6. Chang, Y., quoted in Anand, M. *The Art of Sexual Ecstasy* (Los Angeles: J. P. Tarcher, 1989): 2.

7. Rossi, E. L., with Nimmons, D. *The 20-Minute Break* (Los Angeles: J. P. Tarcher, 1991): 174–175.

8. Cutler, W. B. *Love Cycles: The Science of Intimacy* (New York: Villard, 1991): 20.

9. Alperstein, L. P., quoted in Castleman, M. "Pillow Talk." *Medical Self-Care* (Spring 1985): 45–55.

10. Scantling and Browder. *Ordinary Women, Extraordinary Sex*.

11. Greeley, A. M. Follow-up to 1990 Gallup survey and research by National Opinion Research Center, University of Chicago; Reported in Painter, K. "Over 60 and Still in the Mood for Love." *USA Today* (Aug. 12, 1992).

12. Bretschneider, J., and McCoy, N. "Sexual Interest and Behavior in Healthy 80- to 102–Year-Olds." *Archives of Sexual Behavior* 17 (1988): 109–129.

13. Starr, B., and Weiner, M. *The Starr-Weiner Report on Sex and Sexuality in the Mature Years* (New York: Stein and Day, 1981).

14. Brecher, E. *Love, Sex, and Aging* (New York: Consumers Union, 1984).

15. Weg, R., quoted in Edelman, D. S. *Sex in the Golden Years* (New York: Donald Fine, 1992): 62.

16. Edelman. *Sex in the Golden Years*: 63.
17. Pfeiffer, E. study cited in Bortz, W. M., II. *We Live Too Short and Die Too Long* (New York: Bantam, 1991): 140.
18. Rosenthal, S. H. *Sex after 40* (Los Angeles: J. P. Tarcher, 1987): 8–9.
19. Wolfe. *What to Do*.
20. Survey cited in Wolfe. *What to Do*: 2.
21. Rosenthal. *Sex after 40*: 45.
22. Barchach, L., and Geisinger, D. L. *Going the Distance* (New York: Doubleday, 1991); Rosenthal. *Sex after 40*.
23. Schreiner-Engle, P., quoted in Siegel, P. M. "Can You Psych Yourself into Sex?" *Self* (Dec. 1990): 145.
24. Rossi. *The 20-Minute Break*: 165–166.
25. Ibid.: 164–175.
26. Cutler. *Love Cycles*: 22, 42.
27. Castleman, M. *Sexual Solutions*, rev. ed. (New York: Touchstone, 1990): 162.
28. Alperstein, L. P., quoted in Castleman. *Sexual Solutions*.
29. Castleman. *Sexual Solutions*: 145.
30. Masters, W., and Johnson, V. *Human Sexual Response* (New York: Bantam, 1966).
31. Bortz. *We Live Too Short*: 139–140.
32. Cutler. *Love Cycles*: 5, 11.
33. Davidson, J. *Gonadal Hormones and Human Behavior* (New York: Academic Press, 1978): 123–130.
34. Cutler. *Love Cycles*: 78.
35. Bortz. *We Live Too Short*: 153.
36. Ibid.: 149.
37. Zilbergeld, B., quoted in Wade, C. "Self-Help for Lovers: Relaxing for Romance." *American Health* (May 1985): 41–44.
38. Zussman, S., quoted in Siegel. "Can You Psych Yourself into Sex?": 144.
39. Mackoff, B. *The Art of Self-Renewal* (Santa Barbara, Calif.: Lowell House, 1992).
40. Scantling and Browder. *Ordinary Women, Extraordinary Sex*.
41. Adapted from Rosenthal. *Sex after 40*: 51–54.
42. Zilbergeld. *New Male Sexuality*: 394–395.
43. Wegner, D. M. *White Bears and Other Unwanted Thoughts* (New York: Viking, 1989): 173–174; Reed, C. F. *Obsessional Experience and Compulsive Behavior* (Orlando, Fla.: Academic Press, 1985).
44. Brooks, M. *Instant Rapport* (New York: Warner, 1989): 210.
45. Scantling and Browder. *Ordinary Women, Extraordinary Sex*: 198–199.
46. Butler, R. N., and Lewis, M. I. *Love & Sex after 60*, rev. ed. (New York: Harper & Row, 1988): 81.
47. J. B. White et al. "Enhanced Sexual Behavior in Exercising Men." *Archives of Sexual Behavior* 19 (3)(1990): 193–209.
48. Claes, H., and Baert, L. "Pelvic Floor Exercise versus Surgery in the Treatment of Impotence." *British Journal of Urology* 71 (1) (1993): 52–57; Rosenthal. *Sex after 40*: 125–133.
49. K. L. Burgio et al. "The Role of Biofeedback in Kegel Training." *American Journal of Obstetrics and Gynecology* 154 (1) (Jan. 1986): 58–64; Castleman. *Sexual Solutions*; Kegel, A. H. "The Physiological Treatment of Poor Tone and Function of the Genital Muscles and of Urinary Stress Incontinence." *Western Journal of Surgery, Obstetrics and Gynecology* (Nov. 1949); Kegel, A. H. "Active Exercise of the Pubococcygeus Muscle," in *Progress in Gynecology*, eds. Meigs and Sturgis (Orlando, Fla.: Grune and Stratton, 1950).
50. Cutler. *Love Cycles*: 203.

51. Burgio et al. "Kegel Training."
52. *Archives of Sexual Behavior* 14 (Feb. 1985): 13–28.
53. *British Journal of Urology* 71 (1993): 52–57; Britton, B., and Kiesling, S. "The Little Muscle That Matters." *American Health* (Sept. 1986): 59; Rosenthal. *Sex after 40*: 125–133.
54. Claes and Baert. "Pelvic Floor Exercise versus Surgery": 52–57; Graber, T., and Kline-Graber, G. "Female Orgasm: Role of the Pubococcygeus Muscle." *Journal of Clinical Psychology* 40 (1979): 348–351; Maly, B. J. "Rehabilitation Principles in the Care of Gynecologic and Obstetric Patients." *Archives of Physical Medicine and Rehabilitation* 61 (1980): 78–81; Perry, J. D., and Whipple, B. "Vaginal Atrophy," in *Circum-Vaginal Musculature and Sexual Function*, ed. Graber, B. (New York: S. Karger, 1982): 61–73; Britton and Kiesling. "The Little Muscle"; Rosenthal. *Sex after 40*: 125–133. .
55. W. B. Cutler et al. "Perimenopausal Sexuality." *Archives of Sexual Behavior* 16 (3)(1987): 225–234; Cutler, W. B., and Garcia, C. R. *Menopause: A Guide for Women and the Men Who Love Them*, 2nd ed. (New York: Norton, 1991).
56. S. Lieblum et al. "Vaginal Atrophy in Postmenopausal Women: The Importance of Sexual Activity and Hormones." *Journal of the American Medical Association* 249 (1983): 2195–2198.
57. Cutler. *Love Cycles*: 5, 11.
58. Ibid.: 249.
59. Rosenthal. *Sex after 40*: 16.
60. A. Meikle et al. "Effects of a Fat-Containing Meal on Sex Hormones in Men." *Metabolism* 39 (9)(1990): 943–946.
61. Gottman, J. M. *Why Marriages Succeed or Fail* (New York: Simon & Schuster, 1994): 154–155.
62. Ibid.: 155.
63. "Female Sexual Response: At Home with Multiple Orgasms." *Psychology Today* (July/Aug. 1992): 14; C. A. Darling et al. "The Female Sexual Response Revisited: Understanding the Multiorgasmic Experience in Women." *Archives of Sexual Behavior* 20 (6)(1991): 527–540.
64. Alperstein, L. P., quoted in Castleman. *Sexual Solutions*.

PART VI

HIGHER POWER OF 5: EXPANDING YOUR MIND AND SPIRIT

CHAPTER

29

HEALTHY OPTIMISM AND MENTAL RESILIENCE

Finding More Joy in Life and Rebounding More Quickly from Mistakes and Setbacks

A pessimist is someone who, when confronted with two unpleasant alternatives, chooses both.
—**Robert S. Eliot, M.D.,** *Is It Worth Dying For?*

It is through being wounded that . . . power grows and can, in the end, become tremendous," wrote philosopher Friedrich Nietzsche. As painful as our disappointments and failures may be, they can be a potent force for positive change—but only when we learn to perceive them, and all of life's other experiences, through the window of hopefulness. Unfortunately, few of us yet realize how much there is to be gained from cultivating an attitude of *healthy optimism*—which, like pessimism, refers to your expectations for what the future holds.

Let us be clear that when we use the word *optimism*, we're not talking about the vague or giddy "optimism" of Pollyanna, pop psychology or mental pep-talk jingles. Virtually all healthy people periodically experience the "blues"—short-term dips in mood that last for a few minutes, hours or even a day or two. And nearly all of us face periods of deep and abiding grief at the loss of a parent, spouse or child or some other tragic life event—and sometimes this anguish takes many months to pass (see chapter 25).

But overall, the mental attitude or outlook that pays the greatest dividends is characterized by *flexible, real-life optimism*—what some researchers simply call hopefulness—that prompts you to be *contemplative* and *sensitive* to the world's needs on the one hand and *active* on the other.[1] We must be able to use pessimism's sharp sense of reality when we need it, but without having to "dwell in its dark shadows."[2] Even dedicated pessimists can have more fun, stay healthier and be more successful by learning to use the *skills* of optimism, say researchers, and may permanently improve the quality of their lives.[3] In essence, the research literature now seems to strongly suggest that, although far from a panacea, optimism can help make us more resilient under stress, heighten our vantage points and help protect us against certain diseases. In contrast, pessimism makes a sense of helplessness and poor health more likely.

POWER KNOWLEDGE: OPTIMISM AND RESILIENCE

MYTH #1: "Think positive" pep talks are all it takes to be an optimist.

POWER KNOWLEDGE: Blind optimists spend their time telling others how they *should* feel about the misfortunes and pressures in their lives. A significant part of the time this not only doesn't work, it backfires and causes resentment and isolation. One study of cancer patients found that the majority felt that trite pep talks, no matter how well intended, only made them feel isolated and unable to air their true feelings in an open discussion.[5] The patients wanted to be able to talk about their frustrations and pain and anger and loneliness and fears—all the "bad" feelings. This clashed with the "glad game" being pushed by the Pollyanna-driven caregivers. Another survey of cancer patients asked the subjects what *they* viewed as most helpful on the part of family members and friends: Love, support and concern were cited often, along with practical actions such as providing transportation.[6] At the top of the list: Just "being there."

MYTH #2: Being pessimistic is a smarter way to look at life. Then you aren't so likely to be disappointed.

POWER ACTION: FIRST OPTION
Take 5 Seconds to Say No to Empty "Pep Talks"

Flexible optimists usually have one eye on reality—and they don't talk about how wonderful things are when in truth they're bad. Some men and women try to smile in the face of tragedies and difficulties and declare loud and clear that if everyone would just "be positive," everything will turn out grand. But in such cases, things do *not* turn out grand, because the big problems—when ignored—spread, and the small problems have a way of turning into big problems, too. And then things

POWER KNOWLEDGE: It's more involved than that. Positive, optimistic thoughts give rise to good moods, and good moods foster positive thoughts, in a mutually supportive interplay that tends to make positive moods fairly stable for those of us who are optimistic.[7] Furthermore, an optimistic view of life events makes difficulties less stressful and thus less likely to produce illness.[8]

Chronic pessimists exemplify what psychologists call neurotic paradox—that is, the tendency to make matters worse, to turn molehills into mountains, to let a single difficulty multiply into a dozen. In comparison, optimists more often respond mindfully and resiliently to situations one at a time—and they are usually able to bounce back from setbacks and shake off the negative effects of a failure in one area of life before moving on to another area. That is not to say, however, that optimism can be equated with mindless perseverance. It can't.

Research also shows that flexible optimists generally exhibit a pragmatic, goal-oriented attitude, a stance they assume in the face of difficulties, and that they set more *specific* goals for themselves than pessimists do.[9] This can be a distinct advantage, because research indicates that specific goals are associated with greater, more lasting achievements—in work, relationships and health—than are general goals.[10]

can *really* get out of hand. "Sometimes we don't realize how confusing and condescending it can be to tell people that if they simply lift up their chins and have the right attitude, life can be fine," explains Alan Loy McGinnis, Ph.D., director of the Valley Counseling Center in Glendale, California. "A phony pep talk is usually the last thing needed. What may be needed is a leader who says, 'We've got a mess on our hands, but if we all roll up our sleeves, we can do something about it.' "[4]

POWER ACTION: MORE OPTIONS
Use 5-Second Thought Screening

Listen to yourself. When describing hassles and hurts and difficulties in your work or life, what kinds of pessimistic, negative thoughts or statements do you use? One way your mind affects health is through *explanatory style*: the way you describe your difficult experiences to yourself and others. Evidence shows that when we consistently make certain assumptions about the cause of bad things that happen to us, we increase our risk of disease and undercut our performance.[11]

According to the results of more than 100 experiments involving nearly 15,000 subjects, people with negative explanatory styles tend to explain the bad things that happen to them in terms that are *internal* ("It's all my fault."), *stable* ("It's going to last forever."), and *global* ("It's going to spoil everything I do."). These individuals often exhibit what researchers have called learned helplessness[12] and may be at greater risk for depression, repeated mistakes and illness.

Your explanatory style is a mental habit. It's the way you routinely link bad events with perceived causes. In some cases it's positive, or optimistic. To look at a mistake and say, "It was just one of those things" and to realize that it's unlikely to be a problem tomorrow enables you to retain generally optimistic expectations for the future. In contrast, if you make what in truth is a minor mistake—one that is harmless and will not cost you your job, for example—but you say something like, "I'm a poor excuse for a manager and I'm a louse as a human being," there is a timeless, pessimistic quality to it. *Your explanatory style sets the parameters for your expectations about later events—the future. These expectations then determine the way you behave in the wake of the uncontrollable events—either helplessly or vigorously.*

"When someone explains bad events in terms of character flaws,"

> Pain is inevitable.
>
> Suffering is optional.
>
> **—M. Kathleen Casey**
> American sociologist

explains Christopher Peterson, Ph.D., professor of psychology at the University of Michigan in Ann Arbor, and Lisa M. Bossio in *Health and Optimism*, "he puts himself at risk for apathy, depression, failure, illness, and even death. Those who blame themselves for bad events *and* feel powerless to change them will find themselves in a particularly stressful situation. Prolonged stress weakens the immune system, which in turn makes illness more likely. An optimistic explanatory style makes this chain of events less likely."[13]

The first thing to do is become aware of your own typical explanatory style. One of the simplest ways to do this is to go through a sample self-test question from a survey that has been shown to reliably reflect personal explanatory style.[14] Remember, this question is only a sample. It's important to take a minute or two each time you respond to a "bad" event over the next few weeks in order to establish a more representative sampling of your explanatory style. Here's the question and a sensible format for such self-assessments, adapted from Dr. Peterson and Bossio's book, *Health and Optimism*.

ATTRIBUTIONAL STYLE SELF-TEST QUESTION

Event: You cannot get all the work done that your supervisor or boss has assigned.

Instructions: Try to vividly imagine yourself in this situation. If such a circumstance happened to you, what would you feel had caused it? Although events have many causes, in this case, pick only one—*the major cause if this event had happened to you*. Enter this answer in the blank space provided, and then answer three questions about the cause you wrote down.

A. Write down the one major cause:_____.

B. Is the cause of this something about you or something about other people or circumstances? (circle one number)
    totally due to others   1 2 3 4 5 6 7   totally due to me

C. In the future, will this cause again be present? (circle one number)
    never present   1 2 3 4 5 6 7   always present

D. Is this cause something that affects just this type of situation, or does it also influence other areas of your life? (circle one number)
    just this situation   1 2 3 4 5 6 7   all situations

Your answers fall in a range between pessimistic (internal, stable and global causes) and optimistic (external, unstable and specific). In some situations, of course, there *is* a clear, objective answer about the cause of an event—and there's little value in denying it. Yet most "mistakes" and "misfortunes"—"bad" events in everyday life—are far more ambiguous than that, where there really are no arguably correct or incorrect answers about causes. It's in these situations were a positive explanatory style can be most helpful and promote acknowledgment of a problem while sustaining a healthy, flexible sense of optimism. The following Power-Action Options offer you several quick-steps to consider.

Take 5 Seconds to Challenge Negative Thoughts

The goal of this strategy is to pay closer attention to the way you explain mistakes and unpleasant situations to yourself and others—and start catching distorted, pessimistic thoughts. Whenever possible, replace them with more constructive attributions. Be *specific, honest and constructive.* "My life is the pits" qualifies as a *global* attribution. "My boss hates Monday mornings and refuses to discuss my requests before midafternoon" is *specific*, less pessimistic and far more accurate. And be gentle to yourself. Sometimes pessimism is fine. Remember, we live in a difficult world, and few people truly want to be around a perpetual optimist.

To make it easier to notice the twists and turns of negative thinking, some psychologists suggest writing down your thoughts and feelings on a piece of paper—and enumerating a rational response next to each one. Or perhaps you'll find that talking aloud to yourself, instead of engaging in a silent dialogue, helps give you a better sense of perspective when you happen to be in a down mood.

Review chapter 24 to polish your skills in identifying, questioning and neutralizing these distorted thoughts, one by one. Set modest, very reachable goals—for example, cutting self-deprecating thoughts by a third or in half over the next month. Make it a personal priority to release yourself from what psychologist Karen Horney, Ph.D., calls The Tyranny of the Shoulds.[15] Whenever possible, step back and lighten your self-judgments whenever you find yourself feeling you should be able to:

> Argue for your limitations, and sure enough, they're yours.
>
> —**Richard Bach,**
> *Illusions*

- Never make mistakes.
- Be the perfect lover, parent or friend.
- Always look attractive.
- Be liked by everyone all the time.
- Always know what others are thinking and feeling.
- Handle every challenge perfectly.

Give Yourself Rewards for Reaching Small Goals

As you reach each modest, step-by-step objective for a brighter attitude, reinforce your progress with rewards that you enjoy—perhaps going to a movie, reading a novel, going out for a special dinner, buying a new piece of clothing you've been wanting for a while, ordering some fresh flowers or taking out an extra half hour to listen to your favorite music, snuggle with a loved one, go for a walk in a nearby park or garden or just sit on your porch watching the sun go down and the stars come out.

Note: Build your optimism in one life area at a time. Start with one aspect of your life where you find yourself feeling pessimistic—for example, you might begin by focusing on a strained family relationship or a difficult area of your work—where you'd like to increase your hopefulness and optimism.

Know When to Use 5-Second Thought Releasing

"Stand in the corner," his brother told young Leo Tolstoy, "until you stop thinking of a white bear." It seems a straightforward enough command, but as hard as Tolstoy tried, he was unable to do it. Instead, he stood helplessly in the corner, fighting against the imaginary white bear that loomed up, larger and larger in his mind, consuming his thoughts.

As children and adults, we rarely have much luck when we attempt to suppress unwanted thoughts, especially negative ones. The harder we try to push them away, the harder and larger and stronger they keep crowding back into the mind. Here's the paradox: The way the human mind works, when you attempt to suppress unwanted thoughts, you'll usually fail—and sometimes this struggle may even lead you into obsessions about the bleak or disturbing images you're trying to get rid of.[16]

Once you recognize this fact, you can use the simplest on-the-spot tactic we've found: *Let go of your effort to suppress the unwanted thought.* That's right. Stop trying to stop it and *ease off mentally.* Allow your unwanted thoughts to move, uncontested, through your mind. See yourself as a detached observer, watching these gloomy or mischievous images parade or race along your mental hallways. What you'll probably dis-

> Life is made up of small pleasures. Happiness is made up of those tiny successes. The big ones come too infrequently. And if you don't collect all these tiny successes, the big ones don't really mean anything.
>
> **—Norman Lear,**
> American television producer

cover in short order is that *when you stop resisting unwanted thoughts, they lose their power and soon diminish or fade away, and you'll quickly regain mental control.*[17]

Use 5-Second "Perspective Switches" to Foster Optimisim

We've found that one of the simple and effective ways to regain—and help sustain—a healthy sense of optimism is to practice using 5-second "perspective switches" whenever we're faced with irritating or difficult events involving other people (these techniques also work well when we're alone). Here are several examples.

Build Rapport with 5 Seconds of Empathy

Empathy is the ability to project yourself into the inner world of another person to thereby better understand the pressures and motivations that individual faces. As Montaigne wrote, "To each foot, its own shoe." Five seconds of empathy is a helpful strategy to create an *inner dialogue* as a means of talking yourself out of petty or unwarranted hostile thoughts or feelings. Start using this strategy whenever you find yourself making a negative assumption about the motives of another person. Pause a few seconds. Carry on a brief conversation in your mind and heart. There are times, of course, when there are *no* good reasons for another person to show discourteous or threatening behavior, and in these cases assertion may be called for. But most of the time it is not.

Reminder

Nothing changes until you change.

Therefore, before reacting, take a moment to genuinely attempt to see the world through this other person's eyes. Perhaps the grumpy salesman is overwhelmed by new job responsibilities and a shortage of help. Or maybe that co-worker who seems to be a "no-good lazy bum" today is in truth trying to cope with the fear of new corporate job cuts or the health problems of a young child. Perhaps your spouse's spiteful remarks or bleak humor are actually prompted by a pounding headache or worry about the safety of your teenage daughter. What if that slow elderly woman driver with her turn signal on block after block isn't deliberately ignoring your honking horn and trying to make you late for your appointment—what if she's hard of hearing or becoming senile or afflicted with severe arthritis?

Do considerations such as these make you feel less annoyed at these people? Each time you *apply* your empathy, your ability to empathize will grow—and, more often than before, you'll find yourself able to bypass cynical beliefs that generate needless anger, frustration or hostility. This may also encourage you to begin asking others more about themselves and their stresses and needs and dreams.

De-stress with 5 Seconds of Tolerance

What if you can empathize temporarily or listen to others for a short while, but you find it hard to actually *allow* other people to have beliefs and habits that are different from your own? Do you decide what the behaviors of the people important to you should be and then become angry or resentful when they don't measure up in your eyes? If so, you are showing signs of intolerance, perceiving others as misbehaving, which often makes you angry. Now, there *are* times when intolerance is warranted—and anger and assertion are called for in cases of personal and social injustice. But more often than not, tolerance is the healthier, more sensible path. The truth is, whenever you disapprove of the behavior of other people, the more isolated you become—and this places your health at risk.[18]

> The person who has stopped being thankful has fallen asleep in life.
>
> —**Robert Louis Stevenson,** Scottish writer

All that's necessary to practice 5 seconds of tolerance is to catch yourself beginning to feel angry or resentful at the behavior of a loved one, friend or stranger and pause for a moment *to accept them as they are, not as you want them to be.* For family members, this means unconditional acceptance and love. Ask yourself if this other person, in their own eyes and in good faith, may actually be *reasonable* in their position or behavior. Then, if the answer is yes, or probably yes, *allow this other person to be different from you.* Every time you succeed in doing this, you help defuse anger and will feel less threatened or stressed out. "If you are tolerant," say Redford Williams, M.D., and Virginia Williams, Ph.D., authors of *Anger Kills,* "your actions will almost always be more effective. By reducing the number of situations that elicit your righteous indignation, you will find your intimate acquaintances, your co-workers and the people of your community more likely to listen to and possibly even heed what you say when you are really adamantly opposed to something. Moreover, you can focus your assertion, money and time on the matters most important to you."[19]

Gain a Measure of Inner Peace with 5 Seconds of Forgiveness

To *understand* or *empathize* or *forgive* another person is not an *excuse* for the behavior that made you angry. There are times in all of our lives when another person has truly—and sometimes deliberately—wronged us. Unfortunately, in some of these situations asserting your-

> If we could reach the secret history of our "enemies," we should find, in each one's life, sorrow and suffering enough to disarm all hostility.
>
> **—Henry Wadsworth Longfellow,** American poet

REMINDER

Optimists accept what cannot be changed.

self is not going to help, especially if the one who hurt you was a stranger and the event happened long ago. Here there is little chance that anything you can do will change what has been done to you. Although the event is over, you still find yourself remembering it, feeling the hurt, the anger, the bitterness, the rage and a desire to lash out. When this happens, it makes good health sense to release your angry thoughts and feelings by forgiving this man or woman who wronged you.

To enact this strategy for 5 seconds of forgiveness, begin with small matters. Acknowledge that what this person did was wrong and *choose* to forgive him or her. Imagine yourself wiping a slate clean. This does not mean you have to forget what happened to you nor that you will in any way allow it to happen again; it simply means that you are forgiving the person for this one *specific* transgression. Major wrongs—sexual molestation or rape, desertion by a parent or spouse or any kind of violent crime—almost always require help from a qualified counselor (see chapter 25) in a safe, supportive environment where you can express your deepest feelings and work toward genuine, lasting forgiveness.

Enjoy 5 Seconds of Humor: Laughter Can Be the Best Medicine

There is increasing evidence that a good laugh can lift your mind and mood—and perhaps even give a healthy boost to your immune system.[20] In fact, light-heartedness and humor, which we've emphasized so often throughout *The Power of 5*, are vital to flexible optimism.[21] In part, this is because humor can be a good defense against regret and perfectionism. And, given that so much of our pessimism and anger is either petty or useless or unjustified, far too many of us miss golden chances to laugh at ourselves—and the comic occurrences in daily life around us. Laughter softens harsh judgments and helps us more readily accept our less-than-perfect selves in an often-unfair, always-changing world.

The principal suggestion here is to consciously choose to find more moments to *enjoy* a good laugh. An unexpected dose of humor can serve as a wonderful antidote to flashes of anger, frustration, annoyance and resentment. When a "bad" event or hassle has occurred—such as a personal mistake at work or another broken appliance at home—ask yourself to take 5 seconds for a "humor search" to uncover some inherent humor in what's happened (don't worry, there's almost *always* something funny about things). Can you laugh at yourself . . . or the crazy world we live in? Pretend you're looking down on your office or home from an airliner 35,000 feet above the earth, sipping some tea or lemonade. If you can find even a brief flicker of lightness, of humor, you'll be strengthening *flexible optimism*. *Note*: Even though chronic pessimists and hostile people may have difficulty seeking out and engaging in humorous moments, the attempt itself can prove very helpful to them.[22] For a list of specific tactics for promoting laughter, see chapter 24.

Use "Lessons of the Heart" to Make Sense of Bad Events

While optimism is associated with a state of vigor under stress, there are many events in life that we cannot control or change. Sometimes when loss and pain are severe, optimism can be completely at odds with reality. In these situations, some people become despondent, hopeless, depressed and ill. They may need professional help (see chapter 25). Yet in the same circumstances, other people continue to cope by accommodating themselves to the uncontrollable event or tragedy. "I learned what was really important in life," some of us say after a painful loss or a brush with death.

"To the extent that people can make sense of bad events," say Dr. Peterson and Bossio, "they can blunt their harmful effects."[23] This is called secondary control—and it's a strategy of seeking out the meaning and purpose in living through traumatic circumstances, trying to learn whatever we can from life's toughest hardships.[24] Psychologist Aaron Antonovsky, Ph.D., calls this a *sense of coherence*, which he defines as "the ability to find structure, meaning, and regularity in the events that one experiences."[25] Why did this happen? Why did it happen to me? How can this experience make me stronger or wiser or more compassionate or more tolerant or grateful for each moment from now on? Secondary control and a sense of coherence are life-enriching skills worth discovering, and calling forth, one event at a time.

Spend 5 Minutes with Young Children

When other strategies seem to come up lacking, or when you're unable to move to a higher vantage point or maintain a strong sense of hope for the future, one of the best pieces of advice may be to spend 5 minutes with young children. Wordsworth said that children come into this world "trailing clouds of glory," and it's almost impossible to stay in a dark mood or be pessimistic for long if there are small children around you. So you might enjoy making it a new habit to get down on the floor and spend 5 minutes—once a week, once a day or whenever you can—eye-to-eye, talking and playing with a toddler or youngster who's still filled with laughter and wonder at life. The love and exuberance can be truly contagious[26]—and, most of all during difficult times, are worth "catching."

Enjoy 5-Minute "Breakaway Walks" and Other "Positive Distractors"

Research now suggests that, in many cases, a brief bout of exercise may lift moderate depression as effectively as psychotherapy, and it can raise self-esteem and optimism when nothing else seems to work.[27] So test the value of this discovery in your own life. Next time a mental downturn begins to take hold, and it's time for a work break or meal break, take 5 minutes to head out the door for a brisk walk.

In some situations, you may gain similar benefits from *positive self-distraction*—such as interrupting a mental or emotional downturn by standing near a sunny window, going outside for some deep breaths of fresh air, enjoying a great-tasting snack, sipping a cup or glass of your favorite tea, looking at a positive scene, reading a comedy column in your newspaper or daydreaming about something humorous. Research suggests that having a ready list of your favorite *positive distractors* may prove helpful in staying more optimistic day in and day out.[28]

One reason that 5 minutes of exercise or another positive focus shift can work well is that there are times when you simply won't be able to just *think* or *talk* yourself into healthier optimism. Often it's necessary to first get up and go through the motions of *acting* optimistically and then let your mood and thoughts catch up.[29]

Use 5-Minute Mind Images for Greater Health and Healing Power

The ways you focus your mind—including your use of *mental imagery*—is an important factor in determining your health or illness, and perhaps life and death.[30] Mental imagery in healing and well-being is best known for its direct effects on physiology—stimulating changes in heart rate, blood pressure, respiration, oxygen consumption, brain wave rhythms and patterns, local blood flow and temperature, gastrointestinal motility and secretions, sexual arousal, levels of various hormones and neurotransmitters and immune system function.[31] Scientists have begun to discover what many people have suspected for centuries: Our thoughts and emotions influence our immune system's ability to protect us from disease.[32] "The relations between emotion and immunity may prove to be another strong argument for a return toward whole-person medicine," says an editorial in the *Lancet*, one of Great Britain's leading medical journals, reflecting growing support in some medical circles.[33]

Mental imagery is an inner representation of a flow of thoughts you can envision, hear, feel, smell and taste. Imagery is a powerful factor in the way your mind codes, stores, expresses and recalls information and experiences. "Imagery is the currency of dreams and daydreams; memories and reminiscence; plans, projections and possibilities," says Martin L. Rossman, M.D., a member of the scientific advisory council of the Institute for the Advancement of Health in New York City. "It is the language of the arts, the emotions, and most important, of the deeper self. Imagery is a window on your inner world; a way of viewing your own ideas, feelings and interpretations. But it is more than a window—it is a means of transformation and liberation from distortions in this realm that may unconsciously direct your life and shape your health."[34]

Mental imagery is not a panacea, however. Rather it is a valuable personal tool, not only for strengthening your resistance to illness and promoting healing but also for living the highest-quality life you possibly can.

Take a few minutes to review the relaxation techniques and imagery exercises presented in chapters 3 and 4. At first, the most effective mental imagery takes place when you have a quiet, private place to relax, with the phone off the hook, sitting in a favorite chair or lying down, face up. Make sure you are in loose, comfortable clothing and the room lighting is dimmed. Later, when you can deeply relax in a matter of moments, you can use brief mental imagery "focuses" almost anywhere, anytime you choose.

Here are two scripts for mental imagery practice. At first you will need to allow 10 to 15 minutes. Then, once you've practiced, you can condense the script in whatever ways you find useful so that the imagery sessions require 5 minutes or less. The least effective method of practicing mental imagery is by slowly reading the script aloud, pausing at the end of each phrase. Unfortunately, the act of reading draws part of your attention away from the experience. A better idea is to record, or have a good friend record, the script on an audiocassette recorder, using a calm, soothing tone of voice. Another option is to purchase a prerecorded audio tape (see Resources for Insight Publishing and Source Learning Systems). Whatever method you choose, keep in mind that mental imagery skill is *learned*, that it requires practice. Within a week or two, we expect that your comfort and confidence level will improve dramatically.

Healing Imagery Script

Begin by taking a couple of deep, full breaths . . . and let the breath out be a real "letting go" kind of breath . . . make sure you are comfortable . . . and that you won't be disturbed . . .

As you breathe comfortably and easily, invite your body to relax and let go of any unnecessary tension . . . take time to bring your attention to each part of your body, and invite it to release and relax as you have so many times before. . . .

Release and relax any tension you may have in your left foot . . . your right foot . . . your calves . . . your thighs and hamstrings . . . your hips . . . pelvis . . . genitals . . . low back . . . buttocks. . . .

Take your time and sense the comfortable feelings of deepening relaxation beginning in the lower half of your body . . . easily . . . naturally . . . invite your abdomen to release and relax and join in this more comfortable and pleasant state of relaxation . . . the organs within your abdomen . . . your midback and flanks . . . your chest . . . the muscles across and between your shoulder blades . . . deeper and more comfortably at ease . . . the organs in your chest . . . breathing easily and naturally . . . your shoulders . . . and neck . . . relaxing more deeply, more comfortably, more easily. . . .

As each part relaxes, you relax more deeply . . . and as you go deeper, it is easier to relax . . . .The relaxation is flowing down your upper arms . . . your elbows . . . forearms . . . wrists . . . and hands . . . sense the relaxation in the small muscles between your fingers . . . and all the way to the tips of the index fingers . . . the middle fingers . . . ring fingers . . . little fingers . . . and thumbs. . . .

Scalp and forehead soft and relaxed . . . the muscles of the face soft and at ease . . . the little muscles around the eyes relaxing more deeply . . . more pleasantly . . . more comfortably. . . .

And imagine yourself at the top of an imaginary staircase that leads to an even deeper and more comfortable state of mind and body . . . notice what it looks like today . . . and descend one step at a time . . . going deeper, more comfortably relaxed with each descending stair . . . let it be an enjoyable experience . . . head for that special inner place of peacefulness and healing you have visited before. . . .

Ten . . . nine . . . deeper, more comfortably relaxed as you go down the stairs . . . eight . . . seven . . . not being concerned at all with how deeply you go or how you go more deeply . . . six . . . easy . . . comfortable . . . five . . . just allowing it to happen . . . and four . . . comfortable and pleasant . . . three . . . two . . . body relaxed yet your mind still aware . . . one. . . .

And go in your mind to a special inner place of deep relaxation and healing . . . an inner place of great beauty, peacefulness and security for you . . . a place you have visited before, or one which simply occurs to you now. . . .

It really doesn't matter where you go now in your mind as long as the place is peaceful, beautiful and healing to you . . . take a few moments to look around this special inner place and notice what you see . . . what you hear . . . perhaps there's a fragrance or aroma there . . . and especially notice any feelings of peacefulness, safety and connection that you feel here. . . .

As you explore, find the spot where you feel the most relaxed, centered and connected in this place . . . become comfortable and quiet in this place. . . .

When you are ready, focus your attention on the symptom or problem that has been bothering you . . . simply put your attention on it while staying comfortably relaxed . . . allow an image to emerge for this symptom or problem . . . accept the image that comes, whether it makes sense or not . . . whether it is strange or familiar . . . whether you like it or not . . . just notice and accept the image that comes for now . . . let it become clearer and more vivid, and take some time to observe it carefully. . . .

In your imagination, you can explore this image from any angle, and from as close or as far away as you like . . . carefully observe it from different perspectives . . . don't try to change it . . . just notice what draws your attention. . . .

What seems to be the matter in this image? . . . What is it that represents the problems? . . .

When you know this, let another image appear that represents the healing or resolution of this symptom or problem . . . allow it to become clearer and more vivid . . . carefully observe this image as well, from different perspectives . . . What is it about this image that represents healing? . . .

Recall the first image and consider the two images together . . . how do they seem to relate to each other as you observe them? . . . Which is larger? . . . Which is more powerful? . . . If the image of the problem seems more powerful, notice whether you can change that . . . imagine the image of healing becoming stronger, more powerful, more vivid . . . imagine it to be much bigger and much more powerful than the other. . . .

Imagine the image of the problem or symptom turning into the image of healing . . . watch the transformation . . . how does it seem to happen? . . . Is it sudden, like changing channels on television, or is it a gradual process? . . . If it is a process, notice how it happens . . . notice if what happens seems to relate to anything in your life. . . .

End your imagery session by focusing clearly and powerfully on this healing image . . . imagine it is taking place in your body at just the right place . . . notice whether or not you can feel or imagine any changing sensations as you imagine this healing taking place . . . let the sensations be sensations of healing . . . affirm to yourself that this is happening now, and that this healing continues in you whether you are waking . . . sleeping . . . imaging . . . or going about your daily activities. . . .

When you are ready, prepare to return to your waking consciousness . . . imagine yourself at the bottom of your imaginary staircase . . . and begin to ascend . . . one . . . two . . . allowing this image to continue to work within you . . . three . . . becoming more and more aware of your surroundings . . . four . . . when you reach ten you may come wide-awake and alert, feeling refreshed and better than before . . . five . . . lighter and lighter . . . six . . . aware of the room you are in . . . seven . . . feeling refreshed and relaxed and better than before . . . eight . . . almost wide-awake now . . . nine . . . allow your eyes to open and come fully wide-awake . . . feeling refreshed, relaxed and better than before . . . and stretch and smile and go on about your day. . . .

Once you've gained experience with the preceding mental imagery exercise, here is a more advanced variation, in condensed form, requiring less time.

Wellness Imagery Script

Begin as usual by taking a comfortable position and loosening any restrictive clothing or jewelry . . . take a couple of deep, full breaths and let the out breath be a real "letting go" kind of breath . . . imagine that with each exhalation you begin to release and relax any unnecessary tension you feel. . . .

Allow your breathing to take its natural rate and rhythm . . . allow yourself to relax more deeply with each breath . . . allow the gentle movement of your chest and abdomen to take you more deeply inside . . . invite your body to relax and become comfortably supported by the surface beneath it. . . .

As you relax more deeply, your mind can become quiet and still . . . when you are ready, imagine yourself going inside to that special inner place of deep peacefulness and concentration you have visited before . . . take some time to notice what you see there today . . . what you hear in this special place . . . any aroma or fragrance that is there . . . and especially the sense of peacefulness, quiet, and security that you feel in this place. . . .

This is your special inner place . . . a place you can come to for rest . . . for healing . . . for learning things that will be helpful to you. . . .

Take some time and find the spot where you feel the most deeply relaxed, most quiet, centered and connected to the natural healing qualities of this special place . . . allow yourself to sense the healing qualities of this place supporting and nourishing your vitality and movement toward greater health and wellness. . . .

When you are ready, allow an image of you enjoying wellness to arise . . . welcome the image as it forms in your awareness, and allow it to become clear . . . take some time to notice what you observe . . . it may look like you or be a symbolic representation . . . What does it look like? . . . What is it wearing, if anything? . . . How does it move, and how does it hold itself? . . . What is its face like? . . .

How does the image seem to feel? . . . Notice what this image is doing . . . are there other people, places or things in this image of wellness? . . .

What are the qualities this image embodies? . . . What is it about this image that conveys a sense of wellness to you? . . . Are there particular qualities that seem to be intimately connected with its wellness? . . .

When you feel ready, imagine yourself becoming the image . . . notice how this feels . . . notice your posture, your face . . . especially notice the feelings of well-being you experience. . . .

Imagine looking out of the eyes of the image . . . How does the world look from here? . . . What is your world view? . . . If you had a motto, what would it be? . . .

Imagine looking back at yourself . . . How do you look from this perspective? . . . What do you think of the person you are looking at? . . . How do you feel about this person? . . . Is there anything you know that would be helpful for this person to know? . . .

Become yourself again, and continue to feel the qualities and feelings of wellness within you . . . observe the image of wellness once more . . . does it seem different in any way? . . . Is there anything you understand about it now that you didn't before? . . .

Is there anything that stands in the way of your moving more toward the experience of wellness in your daily life? . . .

What issues or concerns arise as you consider this? . . . How might you deal with them in a healthy way and take a step toward greater wellness today? . . .

When you are ready, slowly return to your waking consciousness, remembering what has been important to you in this experience . . . when you come fully awake. . . .

Take a 5-Minute "Depression Test"— And Get Help If You Need It

Everyone feels sad or hopeless from time to time, although even during a down mood—sometimes referred to as common, everyday depression—most of us still feel some control over our emotions and realize that the sad feelings will eventually pass. Throughout *The Power of 5*, we have presented many simple, practical ways to help lift your energy and mood—and these self-care techniques can be very valuable in coping with "everyday depression." But people with serious depression— often referred to as major depression or clinical depression— may feel that "a terrible heaviness and hopelessness has descended that

---

SIGNS OF DEPRESSION

According to the DEPRESSION Awareness, Recognition, and Treatment (D/ART) Program of the National Institute of Mental Health, symptoms of depression can include:
• Persistent sad or "empty" mood.
• Loss of interest or pleasure in ordinary activities, including sex.
• Decreased energy, fatigue, being "slowed down."
• Sleep disturbances (insomnia, early-morning waking or oversleeping).
• Eating disturbances (loss of appetite and weight, or weight gain).
• Difficulty concentrating, remembering or making decisions.
• Feelings of guilt, worthlessness and helplessness.
• Thoughts of death or suicide; suicide attempts.
• Irritability.
• Excessive crying.
• Chronic aches and pains that don't respond to treatment.
• Decreased productivity.
• Safety problems; accidents.
• Alcohol or drug abuse.
• Moral problems.
• Lack of cooperation.

A thorough diagnosis is needed if four or more of these symptoms persist for more than two weeks or are interfering with work or family life. Consult a qualified mental health professional (psychologist or psychiatrist) for a thorough diagnosis.

---

they are powerless to prevent or resist, and that it will go on and on. The intensity of despair that some people can feel in serious depression goes far beyond the lows of normal life. It destroys the person's ability to continue in life's usual roles and can lead to utter confusion, mental paralysis, or the brink of suicide," say researchers.[35]

Just because you may feel blue, therefore, does not mean you are suffering from a serious, or clinical, depression. Your feelings may be a normal, even healthy, reaction to a loss—at home or work. A key distinction is this: While the unhappiness of daily life or adjustment to a loss comes and goes, the unhappiness of serious depression stays on. With normal unhappiness, for example, going for a walk or to the movies may cheer you up, at least temporarily. With clinical depression, even your favorite comedy movie or a walk through a beautiful park will leave you unmoved. Will your family members or friends recognize if you're seriously depressed? In many cases, no, they won't. They may try to coax you into feeling better, but nothing they do will seem to help. All joy in life seems gone—and, day after day, it does not return.

"People are now recognizing clinical depression as an illness and not a character flaw," says Robert Hirschfield, M.D., chief of the Mood, Anxiety, and Personality Disorders Research Branch of the National Institute of Mental Health in Rockville, Maryland.[36] One significant shift in public attitudes about severe clinical depression—which affects an estimated 15 million Americans—is that it is a disease that is, at least in part, biologically based. Evidence suggests that many of us—perhaps 5 percent of Americans—may have an inherited vulnerability to depression, which may be triggered by environmental stresses or psychological distress. Fortunately, more than 80 percent of all cases of depression can be successfully treated.[37]

The first step in dealing with clinical depression is recognizing that you have it. There are some helpful self-tests for doing just that (see pages 464 and 466). If you discover, or even suspect, that you may have some form of serious depression, you should immediately seek professional help. The Resources list toll-free hotlines to call, and you can refer to chapter 26 for guidelines on knowing how to get some top-quality professional help.

Resources

American Imagery Institute (P.O. Box 13453, Milwaukee, WI 53213; 414-781-4045). A leading source for books and scientific research on mental imagery.

Anger Kills by Redford Williams, M.D. and Virginia Williams, Ph.D. (Times Books, 1993). A modern classic on defusing hostility and promoting healthy optimism.

(continued on page 470)

5-MINUTE SELF-TEST FOR DEPRESSION

For a thorough yet quick indication of how depressed you may be, here's a simple test—called the CES-D (Center for Epidemiological Studies—Depression)—that only requires about 5 minutes to complete. It was developed by Lenore Radloff, Ph.D., at the Center for Epidemiological Studies of the National Institute of Mental Health in Rockville, Maryland. Mark the answer that best describes how you have felt *over the past week*.

1. I was bothered by things that usually don't bother me.
    0   Rarely or none of the time (less than 1 day)
    1   Some or a little of the time (1 to 2 days)
    2   Occasionally or a moderate amount of time (3 to 4 days)
    3   Most or all of the time (5 to 7 days)

2. I did not feel like eating; my appetite was poor.
    0   Rarely or none of the time (less than 1 day)
    1   Some or a little of the time (1 to 2 days)
    2   Occasionally or a moderate amount of time (3 to 4 days)
    3   Most or all of the time (5 to 7 days)

3. I felt that I could not shake off the blues even with help from my family and friends.
    0   Rarely or none of the time (less than 1 day)
    1   Some or a little of the time (1 to 2 days)
    2   Occasionally or a moderate amount of time (3 to 4 days)
    3   Most or all of the time (5 to 7 days)

4. I felt I was not as good as other people.
    0   Rarely or none of the time (less than 1 day)
    1   Some or a little of the time (1 to 2 days)
    2   Occasionally or a moderate amount of time (3 to 4 days)
    3   Most or all of the time (5 to 7 days)

5. I had trouble keeping my mind on what I was doing.
    0   Rarely or none of the time (less than 1 day)
    1   Some or a little of the time (1 to 2 days)
    2   Occasionally or a moderate amount of time (3 to 4 days)
    3   Most or all of the time (5 to 7 days)

6. I felt depressed.
    0   Rarely or none of the time (less than 1 day)
    1   Some or a little of the time (1 to 2 days)
    2   Occasionally or a moderate amount of time (3 to 4 days)
    3   Most or all of the time (5 to 7 days)

7. I felt that everything I did was an effort.
- 0   Rarely or none of the time (less than 1 day)
- 1   Some or a little of the time (1 to 2 days)
- 2   Occasionally or a moderate amount of time (3 to 4 days)
- 3   Most or all of the time (5 to 7 days)

8. I felt hopeless about the future.
- 0   Rarely or none of the time (less than 1 day)
- 1   Some or a little of the time (1 to 2 days)
- 2   Occasionally or a moderate amount of time (3 to 4 days)
- 3   Most or all of the time (5 to 7 days)

9. I thought my life had been a failure.
- 0   Rarely or none of the time (less than 1 day)
- 1   Some or a little of the time (1 to 2 days)
- 2   Occasionally or a moderate amount of time (3 to 4 days)
- 3   Most or all of the time (5 to 7 days)

10. I felt fearful.
- 0   Rarely or none of the time (less than 1 day)
- 1   Some or a little of the time (1 to 2 days)
- 2   Occasionally or a moderate amount of time (3 to 4 days)
- 3   Most or all of the time (5 to 7 days)

11. My sleep was restless.
- 0   Rarely or none of the time (less than 1 day)
- 1   Some or a little of the time (1 to 2 days)
- 2   Occasionally or a moderate amount of time (3 to 4 days)
- 3   Most or all of the time (5 to 7 days)

12. I was unhappy.
- 0   Rarely or none of the time (less than 1 day)
- 1   Some or a little of the time (1 to 2 days)
- 2   Occasionally or a moderate amount of time (3 to 4 days)
- 3   Most or all of the time (5 to 7 days)

13. I talked less than usual.
- 0   Rarely or none of the time (less than 1 day)
- 1   Some or a little of the time (1 to 2 days)
- 2   Occasionally or a moderate amount of time (3 to 4 days)
- 3   Most or all of the time (5 to 7 days)

14. I felt lonely.
- 0   Rarely or none of the time (less than 1 day)
- 1   Some or a little of the time (1 to 2 days)
- 2   Occasionally or a moderate amount of time (3 to 4 days)
- 3   Most or all of the time (5 to 7 days)

(continued)

5-MINUTE SELF-TEST FOR DEPRESSION—*CONTINUED*

15. People were unfriendly.
- 0   Rarely or none of the time (less than 1 day)
- 1   Some or a little of the time (1 to 2 days)
- 2   Occasionally or a moderate amount of time (3 to 4 days)
- 3   Most or all of the time (5 to 7 days)

16. I did not enjoy life.
- 0   Rarely or none of the time (less than 1 day)
- 1   Some or a little of the time (1 to 2 days)
- 2   Occasionally or a moderate amount of time (3 to 4 days)
- 3   Most or all of the time (5 to 7 days)

17. I had crying spells.
- 0   Rarely or none of the time (less than 1 day)
- 1   Some or a little of the time (1 to 2 days)
- 2   Occasionally or a moderate amount of time (3 to 4 days)
- 3   Most or all of the time (5 to 7 days)

18. I felt sad.
- 0   Rarely or none of the time (less than 1 day)
- 1   Some or a little of the time (1 to 2 days)
- 2   Occasionally or a moderate amount of time (3 to 4 days)
- 3   Most or all of the time (5 to 7 days)

19. I felt that people disliked me.
- 0   Rarely or none of the time (less than 1 day)
- 1   Some or a little of the time (1 to 2 days)
- 2   Occasionally or a moderate amount of time (3 to 4 days)
- 3   Most or all of the time (5 to 7 days)

20. I could not get "going."
- 0   Rarely or none of the time (less than 1 day)
- 1   Some or a little of the time (1 to 2 days)
- 2   Occasionally or a moderate amount of time (3 to 4 days)
- 3   Most or all of the time (5 to 7 days)

The self-evaluation is easy to score—simply add up the numbers. Your total will be somewhere between 0 and 60. This test is merely an aggregation of the core symptoms of depression. The higher the number, the more likely that you are depressed. It's vital to realize, however, that a high score is *not the same thing as a professional diagnosis of major, or clinical, depression.* Instead, what it indicates is a "snapshot" of your level of depression *right now.* Some individuals with high scores are not, in fact, suffering from clinical depression, and some individuals with low scores can still be suffering from a "depressive disorder." A thorough diagnosis of depression—by a qualified psychiatrist or psychologist (see the referral guidelines in chapter 25)—takes into account how long you've had each symptom and whether the symptoms may be attributable to some primary source other than depression.

Here is a general interpretation of the scoring results: A score of 0 to 9 places you in the nondepressed range, below the mean (tested average score) of American adults. 10 to 15 suggests mild depression. 16 to 24 indicates moderate depression. If you scored over 24, there is a good chance that, right now, you are severely depressed. If you scored in this range—*25 or higher*—*we urge you to seek a diagnosis and possible treatment by a psychiatrist or psychologist.* If you feel suicidal—that is, if you feel you would kill yourself if you had a chance—*seek help from a mental health professional immediately, regardless of the scores you had on the other answers.* If you scored in the moderately depressed range, we suggest taking the test again in two weeks and again in a month. If you still score in this 16-to-24 range, we urge you to make an appointment with a mental health professional.

Note: As we grow older, "masked" or unrecognized depression (with complaints of aches and pains, listlessness and other symptoms that are often attributed to "aging" or hypochondria) are common. But it is never normal to feel unhappy day after day simply because you're growing older. Get medical attention. Treatment options may be as simple as cognitive psychotherapy, new coping skills, exercise or daily exposure to medically prescribed bright lights (which, in some cases, have proven very effective for depressions that are triggered or aggravated by what is called seasonal affective disorder, or SAD). Other cases of depression require individually tailored medication or counseling.

DEPRESSION/Awareness, Recognition, Treatment (D/ART): National Institute of Mental Health (Rockville, MD 20857; 301-443-4513). Free information.

Healing Yourself: A Step-by-Step Program for Better Health through Imagery by Martin L. Rossman, M.D. (Walker, 1988). A superb collection of mental imagery techniques.

Health and Optimism by Christopher Peterson, Ph.D. and Lisa M. Bossio (Free Press, 1991). One of the best-documented books on the health-related benefits of optimism.

How to Heal Your Depression by Harold H. Bloomfield, M.D., and Peter McWilliams (Prelude Press, 1994). A simple, user-friendly guide.

How to Survive the Loss of a Love by Melba Colgrove, Ph.D. , Harold H. Bloomfield, M.D. and Peter McWilliams (Prelude Press, 1991). A popular book filled with practical, reassuring advice.

Insight Publishing (Box 2070, Mill Valley, CA 94942). Audiotapes of mental imagery experiences designed by Martin L. Rossman, M.D., author of *Healing Yourself.*

Learned Optimism by Martin E. P. Seligman, Ph.D. (Knopf, 1991). A hopeful, inspiring book about *flexible*—not blind—optimism by a leading researcher in the field.

Living beyond Limits: New Hope and Help for Facing Life-Threatening Illness by David Spiegel, M.D. (Times Books, 1993). A fascinating guidebook written by a professor of psychiatry and behavioral sciences at Stanford University School of Medicine. Insights on effective uses of emotional support, mental imagery and self-hypnosis for those facing life-threatening illness.

National Foundation for Depressive Illness (20 Charles St., New York, NY 10014; 800-248-4344; 212-924-9171). Information and referrals for patients and families.

Overcoming Depression by Demitri Papolos, M.D., and Janice Papolos. Rev. ed. (Harper Collins, 1992). A popular, professionally endorsed reference.

Source Cassette Learning Systems (Emmett E. Miller, M.D., P.O. Box W, Stanford, CA 94309; 800-52-TAPES or 415-328-4412). One of the most popular and comprehensive collections of mental imagery audiocassette tapes available.

What You Can Change and What You Can't by Martin E. P. Seligman, M.D. (Knopf, 1993). Contains an excellent section on depression.

When the Blues Won't Go Away by Robert Hirschfield, M.D. (Macmillan, 1991). A practical, supportive approach to "dysthmic disorder" (and other forms of chronic low-grade depression).

White Bears and Other Unwanted Thoughts by Daniel M. Wegner (Viking, 1989). An enlightening work by a leading psychology researcher on suppression, obsession and the psychology of mental control.

PERSONAL POWER NOTES
A Quick-List of This Chapter's Power-Action Options

Take 5 seconds to say no to empty "pep talks."

Use 5-second Thought Screening.

Take 5 seconds to challenge negative thoughts.

Give yourself rewards for reaching small goals.

Know when to use 5-second Thought Releasing.

Use 5-second "perspective switches" to foster optimism.
- *Build rapport with 5 seconds of empathy.*
- *De-stress with 5 seconds of tolerance.*
- *Gain a measure of inner peace with 5 seconds of forgiveness.*
- *Enjoy 5 seconds of humor: laughter can be the best medicine.*

Use "lessons of the heart" to make sense of bad events.

Spend 5 minutes with young children.

Enjoy 5-minute "breakaway walks" and other "positive distractors."

Use 5-minute mind images for greater health and healing power.

Take a 5-minute depression test—and get help if you need it!

PERSONAL NOTES

_____

_____

_____

_____

_____

_____

_____

THE PURPOSE OF LIFE IS A LIFE OF PURPOSE

Create a Path of Least Resistance to Your Goals and Dreams

This is the true joy in life: To be used for a purpose recognized by yourself as a mighty one.
—**George Bernard Shaw**, British author

There is an inner longing that all of us feel—to get more out of each minute of life, to give more back, to gain a deeper understanding of whatever matters most. How many of us experience love, freedom, faith or devotion as deeply as we really want to? And how many of us cannot seem to feel these things at all and are left with guilt and blame instead?

A passion for life is more than some vague feeling of hopefulness or enjoyment of living. It is a deep, inner commitment to the experience of life that motivates you to pay attention, to extend a helping hand, to care deeply for the well-being of your family and to make some positive difference in the lives of other people and the planet. The search for meaning in life is as old as humanity, but in recent years this search has turned into a crisis, reflected in the large number of adults who are "isolated, self-centered, tolerant of everything and committed to nothing." Those are the words of University of Chicago professor Allan Bloom, Ph.D., author of *The Closing of the American Mind*. "There is philosophic wonderment," says Bloom. "Around us people say, 'I'm getting my act together,' 'I'm just being myself,' 'These are my values.' But there is an enormous sense of emptiness in our talking about what it means to live."[1]

"To be human," writes Robert Fulghum in *All I Need to Know I Learned in Kindergarten*, "is to keep rattling the bars of the cage of existence, hollering, 'What's it for?' "[2] Exhilaration and meaning in life are related to what some researchers are calling the creative spirit. No matter where you are or what you have or haven't done until now, more of this high-powered force of life can be part of your future, say Daniel Goleman, Ph.D., Paul Kaufman and Michael Ray, Ph.D., in *The Creative Spirit*. And, far from declining with age, the creative spirit "may actually gain in strength and vigor as an older man or woman . . . concentrates on what truly matters."[3]

> There is no heavier burden than a great potential.
>
> **—Charlie Brown,**
> cartoon character

POWER ACTION: FIRST OPTION
Enrich Yourself with a 5-Minute Reflection: "How I Want to Be Remembered at the End of My Life."

Will it take a heart attack to make you discover what really matters most to you in life? Being faced with your own mortality is a surefire way to focus more attention on your Higher Self, to uncover your heartfelt values, to find new ways to put more meaning into your life, one day at a time.

Here's a suggestion: Beginning this week, regularly—perhaps once a month—take 5 minutes to sit quietly in a relaxed position and enter your observations in a diary under the heading "How I want to be remembered at the end of my life." Vividly imagine what others would say about you in a eulogy if you died today. Be honest. Now envision the specific kinds of qualities and actions and contributions to the world you'd truly *wish* for them to feel and say and remember about you—if you could do some things differently between now and the day you die. Then ask yourself whether you are devoting some attention every single day to living that kind of life. If not, reexamine your priorities, dust off your hidden dreams and make specific, modest changes that draw the direction of your life more into line with the values and purpose in your heart. This can be one of the fastest,

> When you get to be older and the concerns of the day have all been attended to and you turn to the inner life. . . . Well, if you don't know where it is, you'll be sorry.
>
> **—Joseph Campbell,**
> *The Power of Myth*

(continued on page 476)

POWER KNOWLEDGE: MEANINGFUL LIVING

MYTH #1: Most adults have a crystal-clear awareness of their values.

POWER KNOWLEDGE: Far from it. Since values play such a central role in life, it would seem that most of us could clearly articulate our values. We can't. In fact, many of us seem to have only a vague idea of what is important to us and live our lives based on an imprecise understanding of values.[5] According to some researchers, when we suffer from inner conflict, it is often because we are unsure of our personal values and don't know how to determine which values are most important.[6]

MYTH #2: As I grow older, it's natural to hold rigidly to old values.

POWER KNOWLEDGE: What we think about reality can alter our relationship to it, just as what we perceive in the world around us can alter our thoughts. Once people over 40 begin to reject the mental stereotypes of aging (see chapter 14), there is growing evidence that it's then easier for them to clarify their values. "One of the most salient consequences of mental freedom is its effect on personal values," writes Catherine Chapman Pacheo in *Breaking Patterns*. "What was of earth-shattering importance during the old days suddenly seems trifling, and with this phenomenon a whole new set of values begins to emerge. Among the Pattern Breakers we know there has been a consistent thread that can be spotted throughout this reshuffling of values: a greater importance is attached to human relationships."[7]

MYTH #3: What I believe shapes my thoughts but not my health.

POWER KNOWLEDGE: Strong beliefs and a sense of purpose can have profound effects on health.[8] We are all motivated by a "will to meaning," says psychiatrist Viktor E. Frankl, M.D.[9] We reach out for activities and experiences that are of deep significance to our lives. When we are determined to reach value-oriented goals, make a cause our own or lovingly reach out to another person, we are prepared to make sacrifices because we see a reason for our efforts—and we have an inner happiness or satisfaction that only comes from intrinsically rewarding experiences. As Albert Einstein said: "Man is here for the sake of other men—above all for those upon whose smile and well-being our own happiness depends, and also for the countless unknown souls with whose fate we are connected by a bond of empathy. Many times a day I realize how much my own inner and outer life is built upon the labors of my fellowmen, both living and dead, and how earnestly I must exert myself in order to return or give as much as I have received."[10]

MYTH #4: What's the point of wrestling with life-values and struggling with the age-old search for meaning? It just leads to frustration and disappointment.

POWER KNOWLEDGE: Life-values are not some end point—they're part of a lifelong continuum of possibilities for growth and development. The humanistic psychologist Abraham Maslow, Ph.D., spent a large part of his career focused on the positive, growth-oriented aspects of human beings—including the quality that he called *self-actualization.* "As people become more self-actualized," explains Howard S. Friedman, Ph.D., professor of psychology and clinical professor of community medicine at the University of California at Los Angeles, "they become more concerned with issues of beauty, justice and understanding. They develop a sense of humor that is philosophical rather than hostile. They become more independent and march to the beat of a different drummer. They become more ethical and more concerned with harmony among members of the human race. These characteristics of the self-healing personality are not merely the opposite of such disease-prone characteristics as suspiciousness, bitter cynicism, despair and depression, or repression of conflicts. Rather, they are positive, meaningful motives, behaviors and goals in their own right."[11]

MYTH #5: For the lucky ones, life has no regrets.

POWER KNOWLEDGE: From the age of 30 or 35 on, there's evidence that *everyone* has regrets. "Regret is the painful sensation of recognizing that 'what is' compares unfavorably with 'what might have been,' " says psychologist Robert Sugden, Ph.D.[12] Used well, the fleeting pain of paths not taken and choices made poorly or not made at all can be a catalyst to forge a more meaningful life from today onward. But it is harder than ever because we're living in a complex,

(continued)

POWER KNOWLEDGE: MEANINGFUL LIVING—*CONTINUED*

technological landscape, with far more choices than our ancestors ever had to face. "Regret, which is inextricably linked to choice, has become a major malady of modern life," say Carole Klein and psychotherapist Richard Gotti, Ph.D., in *Overcoming Regret: Lessons from the Roads Not Taken*. "The more options there are to choose from, the more options we must relinquish at the moment of choice. . . . As we choose more, we give up more, and create more 'might have beens.' "[13]

MYTH #6: Creativity is, in truth, another name for problem solving.

POWER KNOWLEDGE: In *The Path of Least Resistance*, Robert Fritz writes, "There is a profound difference between problem solving and creating. Problem solving is taking action to have something go away—the problem. Creating is taking action to have something come into being—the creation."[14]

Problem solving is often an attempt to escape reality, explains psychologist Gary Emery, Ph.D. "In general, you may use problem solving as a manipulation into temporary action ('I must solve my problems'), an inhibition to going through obstacles ('I have to solve my problems first') and as a justification for an unfulfilled life ('I had too many unsolvable problems').

"Problem solving reinforces the mistaken notion that you must be problem-free to be happy. Actually, as you become healthier, you give up the need to be problem-free and are willing to take on more real problems and real challenges. You define yourself as capable by your willingness to embrace rather than avoid problems."[15]

most powerful ways to unlock the full powers of the creative process to bring into existence more of whatever you want. As one researcher in this field puts it, such "creating is the place where the human spirit shines its brightest light."[4]

As an alternative vision, you might pretend that you just received a call from your physician with the terrible news that you have a fatal, untreatable illness and have only a few days or weeks to live. Sit quietly and pretend you've just received the news. What do you think and feel as you go through those next days knowing you can count the moments until you're gone? Spend more time with the children or grandchildren? Walk in the woods or watch the sunrise? Gaze at the stars while hugging your loved ones? Slow down your daily pace? Few people would rush off to the office or want to launch into a tirade about some pet peeve.

> Most people live, whether physically, intellectually, or morally, in a very restricted circle of their potential being. We all have reservoirs of life to draw upon, of which we do not dream.
>
> **—William James, M.D.,** founder of modern psychology

The main point to remember is that *the things you think, feel and do today are the foundation of memories—yours and those of everyone who interacts with you—that you lay down for tomorrow.* When you're caught up in feeling more like a human *doing* than a human *being*, it's a clear sign to make different choices, or it's likely you'll end up with more to regret later on in your life. Admitting the deep importance of each day, every moment, in a limited life span can be frightening, but it is one of the best ways to illuminate more of your inner purpose, power and values *today*.

POWER ACTION: MORE OPTIONS
Gain the Benefits of 5-Minute Power Valuing

Life presents each of us with many possible courses of action, many possible ways to live. Anthropologist Carlos Casteneda gave this advice for whenever we stand at a crossroads: "Look at every path closely and deliberately, then ask yourself a crucial question: 'Does this path have a heart?' If it does, the path is good; if it doesn't, it is of no use.'"[16] In *Passion for Life*, Muriel and John James write: "A path with a heart is a course of action that calls us to respond with passion—to act on the basis of a positive emotional and intellectual commitment to someone or something. It calls us to devote positive energy and enthusiasm to an activity or a cause that has personal meaning. A path with a heart calls us to expand our horizons. It invites us to move beyond our self-centered activities and act in more ethical, loving and compassionate ways."[17]

> Nothing contributes so much to soothing the mind as a steady purpose—a point at which the soul may fix its intellectual eye.
>
> **—Mary Wollstonecraft Shelley,** British novelist

> Begin with the possible;
> begin with one step.
>
> —P. D. Ouspensky,
> G. I. Gurdjieff,
> Russian philosophers

> When you are inspired by some great purpose, some extraordinary project, all of your thoughts break their bonds: Your mind transcends limitations, your consciousness expands in every direction, and you find yourself in a new, great and wonderful world. Dormant forces, faculties, and talents become alive, and you discover yourself to be a greater person by far than you ever dreamed yourself to be.
>
> —Patanjali,
> Indian philosopher

A meaningful life, says Irving Singer, Ph.D., professor of philosophy at the Massachusetts Institute of Technology in Cambridge and author of *Meaning in Life*, "is a continuous process that includes purposive goals as well as consummations related to them. A person's behavior becomes meaningful by virtue of the ends that matter to him, whatever they may be. . . . The concepts of meaning and happiness are thus interwoven."[18]

One technique to help you get in closer touch with what you value and how to make that the basis of your long-term goals is the "Ten Loves" exercise developed by Sidney B. Simon, Ph.D., a pioneer in the field of values clarification.[19] This exercise asks you, "Am I getting what I really want out of life?" To begin, list the ten things you love to do the most. To the right of each item, answer these questions.

1. *Date*: The date you last did this.
2. *Alone*? Do you prefer doing this alone (a) or with other people (b)?
3. *Approve*? Would the person closest to you approve of this?
4. *Past*? Did you enjoy doing this five to ten years ago?
5. *Future*? Do you plan to do this five or ten years from now or after you retire?
6. *Risk*? Does it involve either physical or emotional risk?
7. *Health/Energy*: Is your present level of health or energy interfering with doing this?
8. Put a star by the five you love most.

Once you have completed this exercise, take a few minutes to reflect on what pursuits would bring you the greatest feelings of fulfillment or balance, notice the inconsistencies between your ideal values and your actual living habits and identify what things you could begin doing now to deepen the values in your everyday life.

Lift Your Sights with 5-Second Images: "Qualities of the Heart"

In a relaxed yet highly focused manner, begin a short list of what you consider admirable "qualities of the heart." Add to it from time to time. Ask yourself, What are some deeper *qualities* of living that I would like to experience more frequently in the weeks ahead, such as:[20]

Appreciation	Goodwill	Reality
Beauty	Goodness	Renewal
Brotherhood	Gratitude	Resonance
Bliss	Harmony	Service
Balance	Humor	Simplicity
Calm	Humanitarianism	Serenity
Communion	Inclusiveness	Silence
Compassion	Joy	Synthesis
Creativity	Kindness	Trust
Detachment	Love	Tranquility
Energy	Light	Truth
Enthusiasm	Liberation	Understanding
Excellence	Order	Vitality
Freedom	Patience	Wisdom
Faith	Positiveness	Wholeness
Friendship	Power	Wonder
Generosity	Quiet	

On a practical level, you might bring more of these meaningful qualities into focus by committing a few daily minutes to "Activities from the Heart," which might include:
• Pausing each hour to be certain you're taking the best care of yourself and supporting the people around you.
• Reducing television viewing—and, in its place, spending more minutes each week reading, reflecting and enjoying great conversations and fun-filled activities with loved ones and friends.
• Making it a pleasurable weekend habit to help others (see chapter 26) or to initiate or support a cause you deeply believe in.
• Pursuing a craft or hobby that has long interested you.
• Stopping to notice nature—smell a flower, marvel at birds in flight, gaze up at the stars, admire the clouds and watch the sun rise and set.
• Writing a note or postcard to a loved one or friend, a politician or school board member, the person in charge of a cause you believe in or someone who has done something worthwhile in your community.

Practice 5-Minute Power Visioning

Plato used the expression *techne tou bious*, which means "the craft of life," to inspire us to sensitively shape and guide our awareness toward creating more of what is possible. According to research by psychologist Robert Masters, Ph.D., director of the Foundation for Mind Research in Pomona, New York, and author of *Neurospeak,*[21] by merely *describing* sensory experiences or visions, there are subtle, instantaneous responses in the motor cortex of the brain, and in turn, the body's muscles and neural networks—dramatic evidence "that suggestion leads to image leads to immediate physical change."[22]

However, no matter how qualified or deserving we are, we will never reach a better life until we can imagine it for ourselves and allow ourselves to have it. Carefully consider what you want to create. It might be some immediate need, or perhaps it's something of such significance or value that it will outlast your lifetime.

1. Envision a complete outcome image. It might be more vitality, for example, or a closer love relationship, a greater sense of joy in your family, hope for inner-city children, a safer neighborhood and so on.

2. Create a richly detailed mental picture of one specific, highly desirable aspect of this outcome image. It might be something like feeling greater mental alertness and physical energy from mid to late afternoon (a time when perhaps you typically feel tired), or a different way of handling anger or arguments with your spouse or children, or experiencing more laughter and camaraderie during family mealtimes each evening, or creating new successes in your work, or preparing to launch yourself in a brand new career. It's vital, however, not to take something that matters to you and translate it into a sense of obligation—where you end up trying to manipulate yourself using self-admonishments or guilt—into doing it.

3. Follow Robert Fritz's advice: Describe what you currently have in relationship to the exact result you want.[23] Be honest. Acknowledge gaps in your knowledge, skills or resources. What current pressures and needs are holding you back?

4. Contrast "current reality" with your specific outcome image. The image should be *precisely* what you want to create "out there," up ahead. As uncomfortable as this contrast may be, it can effectively create a healthy "structural tension" inside your mind that draws you naturally—with the least resistance—toward the precise outcome you're seeking.

> This is the true joy in life, the being used for a purpose recognized by yourself as a mighty one; the being thoroughly worn out before you are thrown on the scrap heap; of being a force of Nature instead of a feverish selfish little clod of ailments and grievances complaining that the world will not devote itself to making you happy.
>
> —**George Bernard Shaw,** in the dedication to *Man and Superman*

> When there is no vision, people perish.
>
> —*Proverbs* 29:18

Follow through with 5-Second Focused Actions

This is the place to examine your resources, make specific plans and start implementing them. Once you've taken the first step, you'll gain some direct knowledge about what is working and what isn't. And then you can modify your plans. As your experience—and wisdom—increase from each creative effort, so will your ability to more quickly and accurately evaluate the merits and weaknesses of each action you take. One of the keys, says Fritz, is *building momentum*—gradually adding energy and force to each new result you want to create. Once you've arrived at a creative goal, clearly acknowledge it. Then look ahead for your next creation.

> Your vision will become clear only when you can look into your own heart. Who looks outside, only dreams; who looks inside, also awakens.
>
> **—Carl Jung, M.D.,**
> Swiss psychologist

Resources

The Courage of Conviction edited by Phillip L. Berman (Ballantine, 1986). Thirty-three prominent men and women reveal their beliefs—and how they put those beliefs into practice.

The Creative Spirit by Daniel Goleman, Ph.D., Paul Kaufman, and Michael L. Ray, Ph.D. (Dutton, 1991). Companion guidebook to the PBS Television series.

The Examined Life by Robert Novick (Touchstone, 1989). A brilliant, reflective journey to uncover what makes a life worth living.

The Gift of a Letter by Alexandra Stoddard (Doubleday, 1990). Letters are one of the most meaningful human expressions—yet few of us seem to write them anymore. Here's a warm, inviting guide on putting pen to paper to touch those you love and make your presence felt in more of the ways that matter most.

The Path of Least Resistance (Fawcett, 1989) and *Creating* (Fawcett, 1991), both by Robert Fritz. Two of the best books on creating more of whatever matters most to you.

Overcoming Regret: Lessons from the Roads Not Taken by Carole Klein and Richard Gotti, Ph.D. (Bantam, 1992). Converting the negative energy of regret into a positive force for making peace with your past and wiser choices for your future.

PERSONAL POWER NOTES
A Quick-List of This Chapter's Power-Action Options

Enrich yourself with a 5-minute reflection: "How I want to be remembered at the end of my life."

Gain the benefits of 5-minute Power Valuing.

Lift your sights with 5-second images: "qualities of the heart."

Practice 5-minute Power Visioning.
- *Envision a complete outcome image.*
- *Create a richly detailed mental picture of one specific, highly desirable aspect of this outcome image.*
- *Describe what you have right now in relationship to the exact result you want.*
- *Contrast "current reality" with your specific outcome image.*

Follow through with 5-second Focused Actions.

PERSONAL NOTES

_____

_____

_____

_____

_____

_____

_____

_____

_____

_____

_____

_____

_____

EVERYDAY SPIRITUALITY

Bringing Authentic Presence
and Higher Power to Your Daily Path

We are not human beings having a spiritual experience. We are spiritual beings having a human experience.
—**Pierre Teilhard de Chardin**, French philosopher

Someone once remarked that, "If the stars came out only once in a
lifetime, all of us would be out to see them and would be left speechless
by the grandeur of that sight . . . but when they shine every night we go
for months without ever looking up."[1]

None of us is going to live forever. *The Power of 5* has focused on a
wide range of practical, sensible ways to *stay younger longer*—to live with
uncommon vigor, enthusiasm, compassion, wit and wisdom. None of us
should be caught unaware as we enter the final years of our life. Still, why
do so many of us sit up with a start one day and blurt out something like,
"How did I get here so fast?" How tragic to witness the frustration and
fear that hits those older men and women who suddenly feel the "enormous sense of emptiness" of which University of Chicago professor Allan
Bloom, Ph.D., spoke in *The Closing of the American Mind*.[2]

Throughout human history, some individuals from all walks of life
have cultivated the ability to live in a spiritual way, perceiving needs to
which others were blind and expressing compassion in genuine, selfless
ways that few of us ever do.

Have you ever wondered how much your spirituality—your philos-

The wind blows over the lake and stirs the surface of the water. The visible effects of the invisible manifest themselves.

—"Inner Truth,"
The *I Ching*

ophy of life, religion or faith—influences your lifelong well-being? Perhaps considerably more than most of us may have thought, say scientists. Although most commonly nurtured through organized religions, spiritual health can certainly thrive independent of them. And as a source of deep reassurance in turbulent times and of many hidden truths we take for granted but seldom speak, "a spiritual life of some kind is absolutely necessary for psychological health," theologian and psychotherapist Thomas Moore, Ph.D., explains in *Care of the Soul.*[3]

Spirituality encompasses faith, which in its truest sense goes far beyond platitudes. Faith is what your heart tells you is true when your mind can't prove it. It's one of the final extensions of your powers of perception, your higher self. "Optimal spiritual health may be considered as the ability to develop our spiritual nature to its fullest potential," writes health educator Larry S. Chapman. "This would include our ability to discover and articulate our own basic purpose in life, learn how to experience love, joy, peace and fulfillment and how to help ourselves and others achieve their full potential."[4]

Albert Einstein said that we often suffer from a kind of optical delusion. We act as if we're not connected to everything and everyone on earth, in the universe. We think we have nothing in common with people who look or speak or believe or live differently than we do. We act as if we're not connected to life in all of its forms. In his estimation, this is the most painful delusion on earth.

Studies confirm that an important ingredient of lifelong well-being is the sense of meaning and purpose that many people find in their spiritual beliefs or faith.[5] In a statistical research review, Morris A. Okun, Ph.D., and William A. Stock, Ph.D., at Arizona State University in Tempe, found that the two best predictors of well-being among older persons were *health* and *spirituality* (religiousness). Elderly people are generally happier and more satisfied with life if they are spiritually committed and active.[6]

According to Frederic Flach, M.D., adjunct professor of psychiatry at Cornell University Medical College in New York, "From prisoner of war camps to divorce courts, from the hospital bed of someone you love who is dying to the playing fields where you reach out breathlessly for the will to win, I believe the most vital ingredient of resilience is *faith*. For some, faith will exist within the framework of formal religion; for others, it lies in the deepest level of our unconscious minds in touch with eternal truths."[7]

POWER ACTION: FIRST OPTION
Take 5 Minutes to Appreciate the Gift of Stories

According to some researchers, *richness of experience* is one of the key generators of greater spirituality and wisdom.[16] "I don't want to get to the end of my life and find that I just lived the length of it," says Dianne Ackerman in *Meditations for Women Who Do Too Much*. "I want to have lived the width of it as well."[17] Doing this requires opening your senses—and daily lifestyle—to more of the richness of experience all around you, and bringing a larger sense of adventure and purpose to each hour. But perhaps even more, it requires weaving spiritual experiences, past and future, into *stories*: both in answer to the seemingly intrinsic desire to hear and tell great stories—to uncover guiding tales that can carry us through life's highs and lows—and for the growth of your soul and spirit, your Higher Power.

"Our interest in telling and hearing stories is strongly related to the nature of intelligence," explains Roger C. Schank, Ph.D., director of the Institute for the Learning Sciences at Northwestern University in Evanston, Illinois. "Children love to hear stories. Adults love to read or watch reproductions of long stories and love to tell and listen to shorter stories. People need to talk, to tell about what has happened to them, and they need to hear about what has happened to others, especially when the others are people they care about or who might have had experiences relevant to the hearer's own life."[18]

Emerging research indicates that *human memory is story-based*.[19] That's not to say all memories are stories but rather that we learn best by stories. "Memory, in order to be effective, must contain both specific experience (memories) and labels (memory traces)," says Dr. Schank. "The more information we are provided with about a situation, the more places we can attach it to in memory and the more ways it can be compared with other cases in memory. Thus, a story becomes useful because it is interesting and comes with many indices. These may be locations, attitudes, quandaries, decisions, conclusions or whatever. The more indices we have for a story that is being told, the more places it can reside in memory, and the greater the learning."[20]

In many spiritual traditions, whenever tales and legends are remem-

> However many words you read, however many you speak, what good will they do you if you do not act upon them?
>
> **—The Dhammapada,** "The Path of Wisdom," c. 200 B.C.

bered and retold—and new stories created as life moves forward—the re-counting itself serves as a focus point to share and spread the forces of love, suffering, mercy, generosity, considerateness and strength.[21] Collections of cultural and personal stories—especially family stories—offer potent balm, even remedies, for present and future ills. Even the ancient tales of tragedies averted, crises overcome, help arriving at the last moment, the inevitability of death, foolish adventures and hilarity unbounded have this effect, as Jungian-trained psychoanalyst Clarissa Pinkola Estes, Ph.D., observes:

> At any moment I could start being more of the person I dream to be— but which moment should I choose?
>
> **—Ashleigh Brilliant,**
> author of the
> *Brilliant Thoughts* series

The tales people tell can warm the coldest emotional or spiritual nights. . . . Whether you are an old family, a new family or a family in the making, whether you be lover or friend, it is the experiences you share with others and the stories that you tell about those experiences afterward, and the tales you bring from the past and future that create the ultimate bond.

There is no right or wrong way to tell a story. Perhaps you will forget the beginning, or the middle, or the end. But a little piece of sunrise through a small window can lift the heart regardless. So cajole the old grumpy ones to tell their best memories. Ask the little ones their happiest moments. Ask the teenagers the scariest times of their lives. Give the old ones the floor. Go all around the circle. Coax out the introverts. Ask each person. You will see. Everyone will be warmed, sustained by the circle of stories you create together.

Though none of us will live forever, the stories can. As long as one soul remains who can tell the story, and that by the recounting of the tale, the greater forces of love, mercy, generosity and strength are continuously called into being in the world, I promise you . . . it will be enough.[22]

In this age of television, there seems to be less time than ever for couples or families to sit together and share stories. Yet this is a tradition we cannot afford to lose. You might begin by making a small diary listing of your favorite personal and family tales. One of our many favorite stories is "The Day We Flew the Kites," by Frances Fowler (see page 490). It first appeared in a 1949 *Reader's Digest.*

POWER ACTION: MORE OPTIONS
Choose Your Best 5-Second Metaphors— and Gain the Positive Effects of "Word Pictures"

As a followup to the idea of recalling and retelling meaningful stories, you can assemble your own collection of favorite metaphors to draw upon—5 seconds at a time, anywhere you are—to uplift your attitude, add a dose of simple humor, or shift your focus. In more ways that most of us imagine, *we are what we say.* How you see yourself, others and the world is shaped significantly by the metaphors you use, often unconsciously.[23] You'll remember from your English classes that a metaphor is a figure of speech, the "application of a word or phrase to something that it does not apply to literally, as *a mighty fortress is our God* or *the evening of one's life.*" As James A. Autry, president of the magazine group of the Meredith Corporation, explains in his book *Love and Profit*, that definition ignores the potency of a metaphor—"the power that can change the way we think about our world, our work, our lives."[24]

As Autry points out, there's no such thing as friendly skies, the wings of man, reaching out to touch someone over the telephone, hitting the bull's-eye, or getting rid of deadwood. And we don't really mean it when we say it's a jungle out there, this place is the pits or we're stuck on life's treadmill. All these things are only metaphors. They aren't really true. Or are they? Could it be that they are true but just not literally accurate? Could it be that by saying these things, we *make* them true? The answer, says Autry, is "Yes to all of the above."

"We do make things true by what we say. . . . Things *and* people are what we call them, because in the simplest terms, we are what we say, and others are what we say about them. Words, after all, are powerful symbols of ideas. For those of us who do not paint or sculpt or compose music or dance or excel at athletics, words are the most powerful symbols we have."[25] Some noted physicists agree, stating that "new thoughts generally arise with a play of the mind. . . . Metaphoric perception is fundamental to all creativity and involves bringing together previously incompatible ideas in radically new ways."[26]

For these reasons, write down the metaphors you notice yourself using. Examine them. Replace the tiresome old word images that don't seem to serve you well (or that your children are tired of hearing!). Choose or create new ones as an inspiration to make things in life what they should be or could be—not merely what they are. Here are a few examples of metaphors that were identified as "worn out" in one re-

> The great malady of the 20th century . . . is loss of soul. When the soul is neglected, it doesn't just go away; it appears in obsessions, addictions, violence, and loss of meaning. If the soul's capacity for creativity is not honored it will wreak havoc. . . . No age has been exempt from the loss of soul, but this century's loss is compounded further by our ignorance of what the soul is. The soul has been waxed and polished by theologians into oblivion. It is impossible to define but I think of it as a kind of spiritual force that grazes where it will, always striving to connect more firmly to life.
>
> —**Thomas Moore, Ph.D.,**
> *Care of the Soul*

POWER KNOWLEDGE: EVERYDAY SPIRITUALITY

MYTH #1: Prayer is merely one of many spiritual traditions. It may lift the mind and soothe the soul, but praying has no medically proven healing power or health benefits.

POWER KNOWLEDGE: The compelling results from a double-blind study at San Francisco General Hospital involving nearly 400 patients in the coronary care unit suggest that when we pray for someone who is ill, this may—at least in some limited ways—aid the healing process.[8] There are numerous recent studies indicating that prayers may enhance health and promote healing.[9] Sociologist Christopher Ellison, Ph.D., has found that the spiritual disciplines of prayer and meditation enhance many people's sense of acceptance and intimate relationship.[10] In their book, *The Varieties of Prayer*, sociologist Margaret Poloma, Ph.D., and pollster George Gallup report that nine of ten Americans pray from time to time and that 88 percent of these people say they sometimes experience a deep sense of peace and well-being while doing so.[11]

MYTH #2: I'm afraid of death. If I try to face it I'll just get stressed out. There's no point.

POWER KNOWLEDGE: Yes, there *is* a point. Psychologists

---

cent group discussion. Do you agree? Begin your own list.

• Winning isn't everything; it's the only thing.
• Winners never quit; quitters never win.
• Back when *I* was a child, things were *so* hard that . . .
• Clean your plate—there are starving people in the world.
• Boys will be boys.

Perform 5-Second to 5-Minute Acts of Love and Compassion

Scientists call it unconditional positive regard. But, plain and simple, it means "compassion" or "love." Love is a dazzling, intriguing mixture of caring, inner joy, expansiveness and concern. While good health

Sheldon Solomon, Ph.D., Jeff Greenberg, Ph.D., and Tom Pyszczyn-ski, Ph.D., report from their research that all worldviews are, in essence, efforts to cope with "the terror resulting from our awareness of vulnerability and death."[12] Cultural views define how to live good and meaningful lives, and different spiritual philosophies or faiths offer different ways of doing this, but each offers the hope for meaning or life beyond death.

"The fear of death—its inevitability and finality, its grotesque mysteriousness—is perhaps the source of more misery for more people than anything else," says Larry Dossey, M.D., author of *Meaning and Medicine*. "There is ample evidence that hopelessness, loss of meaning and an impending sense of doom are toxic to the body in many ways. These emotions often accompany our attitudes toward death. Today we know they exert a depressant effect on the body's immune function and can set in motion irreversible, sometimes fatal processes in the heart and circulatory system as well. Thus it is no exaggeration to say that our attitude toward death literally can be a matter of life and death."[13]

There is general agreement among major world religions that a meaningful life is possible only after death is accepted as a basic condition of living.[14] And there is strong evidence that by recognizing the finiteness of your own existence, you are permeated by a healthy urgency to dispense with superficiality, reduce materialism and to live a more meaningful life each day.[15]

habits are important to staying healthy, being loved and giving love are just as important. The edict "Love your neighbor as you love yourself" is more than just a moral mandate, it's a physiological and psychological mandate. We *need* to live with compassion, we need to care,[27] we need to strengthen our ability, in Santayana's words, "to love the love in [everything]."[28]

Once you've given some increased attention to your primary relationships (see chapter 27), consider exploring the values of extending this powerful emotion—as universal love or compassion, rather than roman-

True religion, in spirit, is a sense of the heart.
—**Jonathan Edwards,** American theologian

(*continued on page 492*)

THE DAY WE FLEW THE KITES

"STRING!" shouted Brother, bursting into the kitchen, "We need lots more string."

It was Saturday. As always, it was a busy one, for "Six days shalt thou labor and do all thy work" was taken seriously then.

Outside, Father and Mr. Patrick next door were doing chores. Inside the two houses, Mother and Mrs. Patrick were engaged in spring-cleaning. Such a windy March day was ideal for "turning out" clothes closets. Already woolens flapped on back-yard clotheslines.

Somehow the boys had slipped away to the back lot with their kites. Now, even at the risk of having Brother impounded to beat carpets, they had sent him for more string. Apparently there was no limit to the heights to which kites would soar today.

My mother looked out the window. The sky was piercingly blue, the breeze fresh and exciting. Up in all that blueness sailed great puffy billows of clouds. It had been a long, hard winter, but today was spring. Mother looked at the sitting room, its furniture disordered for a Spartan sweeping. Again her eyes wavered toward the window. "Come on, girls! Let's take string to the boys and watch them fly kites a minute." On the way we met Mrs. Patrick, laughing guiltily, escorted by her girls.

There never was such a day for flying kites! God doesn't make two such days in a century. We played all our fresh twine into the boys' kites and still they soared. We could hardly distinguish the tiny, orange-colored specks. Now and then we slowly reeled one in, finally bringing it dipping and tugging to earth, for the sheer joy of sending it up again. What a thrill to run with them, to the right, to the left, and see our poor, earth-bound movements reflected minutes later in their majestic sky dance! We wrote wishes on pieces of paper and slipped them over the string. Slowly, irresistibly, they climbed until they reached the kites. Surely all such wishes would be granted!

Even our fathers dropped hoe and hammer and joined us. Our mothers took their turns, laughing like schoolgirls. Their hair blew out of their pompadours and curled loose about their cheeks; their gingham aprons whipped about their legs. Mingled with our fun was something akin to awe. The grownups were really playing with us! Once I looked at Mother and thought she was actually pretty. And her over 40!

We never knew where the hours went on that day. There were no hours, just a golden, breezy Now. I think we were all a little beyond ourselves. Parents forgot their duty and their dignity; children forgot their combativeness and small spites. "Perhaps it's like this in the

Kingdom of Heaven," I thought confusedly.

It was growing dark before, drunk with sun and air, we all stumbled sleepily back to the houses. I suppose we had some sort of supper. I suppose there must have been a surface tidying up, for the house on Sunday looked decorous enough.

The strange thing was, we didn't mention that day afterward. I felt a little embarrassed. Surely none of the others had thrilled to it as deeply as I had. I locked up the memory in that deepest part of me where we keep the "things that cannot be and yet are."

The years went on; then one day I was scurrying about my own kitchen in a city apartment, trying to get some work out of the way while my 3-year-old insistently cried her desire to "go park and see ducks."

"I *can't* go!" I said. "I have this and this to do, and when I'm through I'll be too tired to walk that far."

My mother, who was visiting us, looked up from the peas she was shelling. "It's a wonderful day," she offered, "really warm, yet there's a fine, fresh breeze. It reminds me of that day we flew the kites."

I stopped in my dash between stove and sink. The locked door flew open, and with it a gush of memories. I pulled off my apron. "Come on," I told my little girl. "It's too good a day to miss."

Another decade passed. We were in the aftermath of a great war. All evening we had been asking our returned soldier, the youngest Patrick boy, about his experiences as a prisoner of war. He had talked freely, but now for a long time it had been silent. What was he thinking of— what dark and dreadful things?

"Say!" A smiled twitched his lips. "Do you remember . . . no, of course you wouldn't. It probably didn't make the impression on you it made on me."

I hardly dared to speak. "Remember what?"

"I used to think of that day a lot in PW camp, when things weren't too good. Do you remember the day we flew the kites?"

Winter came, and the sad duty of a call of condolence on Mrs. Patrick, recently widowed. I dreaded the call. I couldn't imagine how Mrs. Patrick would face life alone.

We talked a little of my family and her grandchildren and the changes in the town. Then she was silent, looking down at her lap. I cleared my throat. Now I must say something about her loss, and she would begin to cry. When Mrs. Patrick looked up, she was smiling. "I was just sitting here thinking," she said. "Henry had such fun that day. Frances, do you remember the day we flew the kites?"

> It is only with the heart that one can see rightly. What is essential is invisible to the eye.
>
> —**Antoine de Saint-Exupéry,**
> *The Little Prince*

tic love—to other areas of your life. "Love is not primarily a relationship to a specific person; it is an *attitude*, an *orientation of character* which determines the relatedness of a person to the world as a whole, not toward one 'object' of love," writes Erich Fromm, M.D. "If I truly love one person I love all persons, I love the world, I love life. If I can say to somebody else, 'I love you,' I must be able to say, 'I love in you everybody, I love through you the world, I love in you also myself.' " Reflect for a moment: In what specific ways can you become more compassionate, more loving to yourself and others?

As you reach out to others and are touched by their struggles and sufferings, remember that while life is filled with heartaches, it is also filled with many mysteries and marvels. In the *Metaphysics*, Aristotle wrote that wonder is the origin of philosophy, and Einstein stated that a person who has no wonder about the universe is "as good as dead: his eyes are closed."[29] The ability to gaze upon life and the world with wonder is both a technique and a skill that are indispensable to creative thinking and late-life wisdom. The imperative advice seems to be this: Keep your sense of wonder alive and well at every point in your life through reading, stimulating conversations, travel, star-gazing, nature-watching and vivid imaginings that can keep sparking your curiosity and extending your thoughts in new and varied directions.

Express Your Own Everyday Spirituality

We each express our spirituality in many ways: through the values we demonstrate to our children and grandchildren; through how we deal with conflict and loss; by how we greet times of success and good fortune; by selflessly praying for others in need; by volunteering our time in specific, useful ways to help others; by embracing and valuing the plain and simple acts of daily living; and by increasing our sense of "home." "No matter how little money we have," writes Dr. Moore, "we can be mindful of the importance of beauty in our homes. No matter where we live, we live in a neighborhood, and we can cultivate this wider piece of earth, too, as our home, as a place that is integrally bound to the condition of our hearts . . .

"Care of the soul requires that we have an eye and an ear for the world's suffering. . . . Living artfully, therefore, might require something as simple as *pausing*. Some people are incapable of being arrested by things because they are always on the move. A common symptom of modern life is that there is no time for thought, or even for letting impressions of a day sink in. Yet it is only when the world enters the heart that it can be made into soul. . . . Akin to pausing, and just as important in the care of the soul, is *taking time*. I realize these are extremely simple suggestions, but taken to heart they could transform a life."[30]

Many of the ordinary daily arts practiced at home can be used to deepen and extend our spirituality because they foster contemplation and demand a degree of artfulness—such as cooking, cleaning, doing dishes, arranging flowers, raking leaves, driving the children or grandchildren to various activities, washing the car, commuting, sewing or knitting and making household repairs. These ordinary activities can be used to help bring the sacred to light and are of much greater importance to our health and spiritual well-being than their simplicity suggests.

In short, there are many spiritual paths. Whichever is yours, follow it, exemplify it and keep climbing up your own tree of life to glimpse at the world with a sense of perspective altogether missing from those who, in the words of the poet Charles Wright, have learned to preach but not to pray. Set aside time—even just a minute or two each morning and evening—for spiritual renewal, for your own personal choice of prayer, meditation, contemplation or reflection.

Make Peace with Dying

No matter *how* young we stay, or for how long, dying is inevitable—and acknowledging it can help make us whole. As Montaigne wrote: "Facing death teaches us to live."[32] Sages and scholars of various traditions have long said that we must incorporate the inevitability of death into the fabric of life in order to fully experience life's true meaning, beauty and power. And—as scientific evidence now indicates—only by confronting our own mortality can we live each day with eagerness, meaning and richness. "Being aware and open to the reality of death appears to be linked to all that we value in human experience, including love and creativity," say Anees A. Sheikh, Ph.D., chairman of the Department of Psychology at Marquette University in Milwaukee, and Katharina S. Sheikh, president of Milwaukee's Institute for Human Enhancement.[33]

But there's little chance for this to happen unless we first stop running away from ourselves. "Human beings have always employed an enormous amount of clever devices for running away from themselves . . ." writes John Gardner, the noted educator and author. "We

> We look at it and do not see it;
>
> Its name is The Invisible.
>
> We listen to it and do not hear it;
>
> Its name is The Inaudible.
>
> We touch it and do not find it;
>
> Its name is The Formless.
>
> **—Lao Tzu,**
> Chinese philosopher

"WHEN YOU SMILE AT THAT CHILD IN YOURSELF, YOU SMILE WITH COMPASSION"

Many people were abused or beaten by their parents, and many more were severely criticized or rejected by them. Now in their store consciousness, these people have so many seeds of unhappiness they don't even want to hear their father's or their mother's name. When I meet someone like this, I always offer the meditation on the five-year-old child, which is a mindfulness message. "Breathing in, I see myself as a five-year-old child. Breathing out, I smile to the five-year-old child in me." During the meditation, you try to see yourself as a five-year-old child. If you can look deeply at that child, you can see that you are vulnerable and can be easily hurt. A stern look or a shout can cause internal formations in your store consciousness. When your parents fight and scream at each other, your five-year-old receives many seeds of suffering. I have heard young people say, "the most precious gift my parents can give is their own happiness." By living unhappily, your father made you suffer a lot. Now you are visualizing yourself as a five-year-old child. When you smile at that child in yourself, you smile with compassion. "I was so young and tender, and I received so much pain."

> All which we behold is full of blessings.
>
> —**William Wordsworth,**
> British poet

can keep ourselves so busy, fill our lives with so many diversions, stuff our heads with so much knowledge, involve ourselves with so many people and cover so much ground that we never have time to probe the fearful and wonderful world within. . . . By middle life, most of us are accomplished fugitives from ourselves."[34]

Here are several final suggestions for enriching your life by confronting your own mortality. By doing these exercises you'll likely help awaken a deeper, more authentic commitment to *living*. Peter Koestenbaum, Ph.D., professor emeritus of philosophy at San Jose State University, describes death and immortality mental-imagery experiences which he feels can prove very insightful and effective.[35] Here are two suggestions.

Take 5 minutes every month to write your own obituary. This is a variation on the exercise discussed in the previous chapter on "How I Want to Be Remembered at the End of My Life." This act leads you to face a crucial question: What does it mean to be a human being, what is

The next day, I would advise you to practice, "Breathing in, I see my father as a five-year-old child. Breathing out, I smile to that child with compassion." We are not used to seeing our father as a five-year-old child. We think of him as always having been an adult—stern and with great authority. We have not taken the time to see our father as a tender, young boy who can also be easily wounded by others. So the practice is to visualize your father as a five-year-old boy: fragile, vulnerable, and easily hurt. If it helps, you can look in the family photo album to study the image of your father as a boy. When you are able to visualize him as vulnerable, you will realize that he may have been the victim of his father. If he received too many seeds of suffering from his father, of course he will not know how to treat his son or daughter well. So he made you suffer, and the circle . . . continues. If you don't practice mindfulness, you will do exactly the same to your children. The moment you see your father—or mother—as a victim, compassion will be born in your heart. When you smile at him with compassion, you will begin to bring mindfulness and insight into your pain. If you practice like that, you will soon smile to your father in person and hug him, saying, "I understand you, Dad . . ."

involved with passing your life well, and most important, what does it mean to be *you*?

Take 5 minutes a month to imagine your own death and funeral. Imagine that you're suddenly, unexpectedly about to die. This imagery exercise was drawn from our experiences in counseling and with our own families and communities. We've seen that the survivor(s) of tragedies view life very differently from that moment on. They're forced to confront deeper questions about existence and suffering and the meaning of life. What would you want to say to each of your friends and loved ones before you die? Use mental imagery also to visualize your funeral services. What do family and friends say about the role you played, or failed to play, in their lives? How do you *feel* about what they say? What would you change about how you relate to them?

As you finish any of these or similar exercises, pause

There is an old story that Plato, on his deathbed, was asked by a friend if he would summarize his great life's work, *The Dialogues*, in one statement. Plato, coming out of a reverie, looked at his friend and said, "Practice dying."[31]

To laugh often and love much; to win the respect of intelligent persons and the affection of children; to earn the approbation of honest critics; to appreciate beauty; to give of one's self; to leave the world a bit better, whether by a healthy child, a garden patch, or a redeemed social condition; to have played and laughed with enthusiasm and sung with exultation; to know even one life has breathed easier because you have lived—that is to have succeeded.

—Ralph Waldo Emerson, American essayist and poet

to consider the ways you might use what you've learned from *The Power of 5* to make small, well-focused changes in your habits and priorities today, this week and this year. As we said at the outset of this book, these are the kind of *leverage points* that we've been seeking: simple, ultra-specific, highly practical choices—drawn from a full range of new options—providing benefits that can far outweigh the time and energy invested.

In their book, *The Lessons of History*, Will and Ariel Durant write, "The future never just happened, it was created." Through the choices you make today, you're creating the future. But here's the key question: Will that future fulfill your goals and dreams—or will they be lost in the rush and roar of life? With *The Power of 5, there is time for accomplishing more of whatever truly matters to you:* health, joy, adventure, success, service.

Resources

Beyond the traditional resources that can be found in your own religious or spiritual tradition, consider broadening your horizons:

The Ageless Spirit: Reflections on Living Life to the Fullest In Our Later Years edited by Phillip L. Berman and Connie Goldman (Ballantine, 1992). A treasury of humor and profundity, gentle wit and hard-earned wisdom from some of America's best-known—and least-known—creative men and women over seventy.

Being Peace by Thich Nhat Hanh (Parallax Press, 1987). A small treasure about being the change you wish to see in the world.

Care of the Soul: A Guide to Cultivating Depth and Sacredness in Everyday Life by Thomas Moore, Ph.D. (HarperCollins, 1992). A profound and moving original work.

The Courage to Grow Old edited by Phillip L. Berman (Ballantine, 1989). Forty-one prominent men and women reflect on growing older, with the wisdom and experience that comes from a rich and varied life.

Death Imagery: Confronting Death Brings Us to the Threshold of Life edited by Anees A. Sheikh, Ph.D., and Katharina S. Sheikh (American Imagery Institute, P.O. Box 13453, Milwaukee, WI 53213; 414-781-4045; 1991). A scholarly book on this underacknowledged aspect of a healthy life.

Final Passages: Positive Choices for the Dying and Their Loved Ones by

Judith Ahronheim, M.D. and Doron Weber (Simon & Schuster, 1992). A caring, responsible work that deals with the dilemmas faced by the dying and their families.

A Gift of Story by Clarissa Pinkola Estes, Ph.D. (Ballantine, 1993). A small, delightfully important book on the keeping and sharing of stories.

Healing Words: The Power of Prayer and the Practice of Medicine by Larry Dossey, M.D. (HarperCollins, 1993). Revealing one of the best-kept secrets in medical science: prayer heals.

Inevitable Grace: Breakthroughs in the Lives of Great Men and Women—Guides to Your Self-Realization by Piero Ferruci, Ph.D. (J.P.Tarcher, 1990). An inspiring book that explores the higher reaches of the human spirit.

The Oxford Book of Death edited by D. J. Enright (Oxford University Press, 1990). A collection of thoughts about death from pages ancient and modern. Reading this engenders a sense of the fleeting wonder of life.

The Perennial Philosophy by Aldous Huxley (Harper & Row, 1945). Ranks among the modern classics of spiritual literature.

PERSONAL POWER NOTES
A Quick-List of This Chapter's Power-Action Options

Take 5 minutes to appreciate the gift of stories.

Choose your best 5-second metaphors—and gain the positive effect of "word pictures."

Perform 5-second to 5-minute acts of love and compassion.

Express your own everyday spirituality.

Make peace with dying.
- *Take 5 minutes every month to write your own obituary.*
- *Take 5 minutes a month to imagine your own death and funeral.*

PERSONAL NOTES

_____

_____

_____

_____

_____

_____

_____

_____

_____

_____

_____

_____

_____

_____

_____

_____

References

CHAPTER 29

1. Peterson, C., and Bossio, L. M. *Health and Optimism* (New York: Free Press, 1991): 8.

2. Seligman, M. E. P. *Learned Optimism* (New York: Knopf, 1991): 292.

3. Ibid.; Peterson and Bossio. *Health and Optimism*.

4. McGinnis, A. L. *The Power of Optimism* (New York: HarperCollins, 1990): 18–19.

5. Dakof, G. A., and Taylor, S. E. "Victims' Perceptions of Social Support: What Is Helpful from Whom?" *Journal of Personality and Social Psychology* 58 (1990): 80–89.

6. Hales, D., and Hales, R. E. "Killing with Kindness." *American Health* (Nov. 1987): 61–65.

7. A. M. Isen et al. "Affect, Accessibility of Material in Memory and Behavior: A Cognitive Loop?" *Journal of Personality and Social Psychology* 36 (1978): 1–12.

8. Peterson and Bossio. *Health and Optimism*; Ornstein, R., and Sobel, D. *The Healing Brain* (New York: Touchstone, 1985); Ornstein, R., and Sobel, D. *Healthy Pleasures* (Reading, Mass.: Addison-Wesley, 1989); Justice, B. *Who Gets Sick? How Beliefs, Moods and Thoughts Affect Your Health* (Los Angeles: J. P. Tarcher, 1988).

9. Peterson, C., and Barrett, L. C. "Explanatory Style and Academic Performance." *Journal of Personality and Social Psychology* 53 (1987): 603–607.

10. E. A. Locke et al. "Goal Setting and Task Performance." *Psychological Bulletin* 90 (1981): 125–152.

11. Peterson, P., and Seligman, M. E. P. "Causal Explanations as a Risk Factor for Depression: Theory and Evidence." *Psychological Review* 91 (3)(1984): 347–374; Seligman, M. E. P. "Helplessness and Explanatory Style: Risk Factor for Depression and Disease." Paper presented at the annual meeting of the Society for Behavioral Medicine (San Francisco, Mar. 1986).

12. Seligman. *Learned Optimism*; Peterson and Bossio. *Health and Optimism*.

13. Peterson and Bossio. *Health and Optimism*: 16.

14. Peterson, C., Schulman, P., Castellon, C., and Seligman, M. E. P. "The Explanatory Style Scoring Manual," in *Handbook of Thematic Analysis*, ed. Smith, C. P. (New York: Cambridge University Press, 1992).

15. Horney, K. *Neurosis and Human Growth* (New York: Norton, 1950).

16. Wegner, D. M. *White Bears and Other Unwanted Thoughts* (New York: Viking, 1989): 174; Reed, G. F. *Obsessional Experience and Compulsive Behavior* (Orlando, Fla.: Academic Press, 1985).

17. Wegner. *White Bears*: 175.

18. Williams, R., and Williams, V. *Anger Kills* (New York: Times Books, 1993): 147.

19. Ibid.: 151.

20. P. H. Knapp et al. "Short-Term Immunological Effects of Induced Emotions." *Psychosomatic Medicine* 54 (1992): 133–148; Berk, L. S., Tan, S. A., and Fry, W. F. "Eustress of Humor and Associated Laughter Modulates Specific Immune System Components." Proceedings of the Society of Behavioral Medicine's 14th Annual Scientific Sessions (Abstract D41; Mar. 10–13, 1993): S111.

21. Peterson and Bossio. *Health and Optimism*: 153.

22. Williams and Williams. *Anger Kills*: 175.

23. Peterson and Bossio. *Health and Optimism*: 175.

24. Rothbaum, F., Weisz, J. R., and Snyder, S. S. "Changing the World versus Changing the

Self: A Two-Process Model of Perceived Control." *Journal of Personality and Social Psychology* 42 (1982): 5–37.

25. Antonovsky, A. *Unraveling the Mystery of Health: How People Manage Stress and Stay Well* (San Francisco: Josey-Bass, 1987).

26. Podell, R. M. *Contagious Emotions* (New York: Simon & Schuster, 1992).

27. "Exercise and Mental Health." *University of Texas Health Science Center Lifetime Health Letter* 5 (3)(Mar. 1993): 7; "Mild Depression: Self-Help Methods May Banish the Blues." *University of Texas Health Science Center Lifetime Health Letter* 5 (7)(July 1993): 4–5.

28. Meichenbaum, D. *Cognitive Behavior Modification: An Integrative Approach* (New York: Plenum, 1977).

29. Myers, D. G. *In Pursuit of Happiness* (New York: Morrow, 1991): 125; Peterson and Bossio. *Health and Optimism*: 154.

30. Pelletier, K. R. Introduction to Rossman, M. L. *Healing Yourself* (New York: Walker, 1988): ix.

31. Sheikh, A. A., and Kunzendorf, R. G. "Imagery, Physiology and Psychosomatic Illness." *International Review of Mental Imagery* 1 (1984).

32. Kiecolt-Glaser, J. K., and Glaser, R. "Psychological Influences on Immunity." *Psychosomatics* 9 (1986): 621–624; Justice, B. *Who Gets Sick? Thinking and Health* (Los Angeles: J. P. Tarcher, 1988). More than 1200 references cited; Solomon, G. *Journal of Neuroscience Research* 18 (1988): 1–9; Hornig-Rohan, M., and Locke, S. E., eds. *Psychological and Behavioral Treatments for Disorders of the Heart and Blood Vessels* (New York: Institute for the Advancement of Health, 1985). Annotated bibliography of 916 scientific studies; Locke, S. E., ed. *Psychological and Behavioral Treatments for Disorders Associated with the Immune System* (New York: Institute for the Advancement of Health, 1986). Annotated bibliography of 1,479 scientific studies; Locke, S. E., and Hornig-Rohan, M., eds. *Mind and Immunity: Behavioral Immunology* (New York: Institute for the Advancement of Health, 1983). Annotated bibliography of 1,453 scientific studies.

33. *Lancet* (July 20, 1985): 134.

34. Rossman. *Healing Yourself*: 14.

35. Engler, J., and Goleman, D. *The Consumer's Guide to Psychotherapy* (New York: Fireside, 1993): 461.

36. Hirschfield, R., quoted in "Beating Depression." *U. S. News & World Report* (Mar. 5, 1990): 49.

37. "Depression: Lifting the Cloud." *Johns Hopkins Medical Letter: Health after 50* 2 (9)(Nov. 1990): 4–5.

CHAPTER 30

1. Bloom, A. *The Closing of the American Mind* (New York: Simon & Schuster, 1987); Bloom, A., quoted in "The Closing of the American Mind." *Publishers Weekly* (July 3, 1987): 25–28.

2. Fulghum, R. *All I Need to Know I Learned in Kindergarten* (New York: Villard, 1988): 161.

3. Goleman, D., Kaufman, P., and Ray, M. L. *The Creative Spirit* (New York: Dutton, 1991): 34.

4. Fritz, R. *Creating* (New York: Fawcett, 1991): 305.

5. Smith, M. *A Practical Guide to Values Clarification* (La Jolla, Calif.: University Associates, 1977); Ornstein, P. *The Search for the Self: Selected Writings of Heinz Kohut: 1950–1978* (New York: International University Press, 1978).

6. Carkhuff, R. and Berenson, B. *Sources of Gain in Counseling and Therapy* (New York: Holt, 1967).

7. Pacheo, C. C. *Breaking Patterns: Redesigning Your Later Years* (Kansas City: Andrews and McMeel, 1989): 179.

8. Chopra, D. *Ageless Body, Timeless Mind* (New York: Crown, 1993); Kabat-Zinn, J. *Wherever You Go, There You Are* (New York: Hyperion, 1994); Pelletier, K. R. *Longevity—Fulfilling Our Biological Potential* (New York: Delacorte, 1981); S. Wolf et al. *Occupational Health as Human Ecology* (Springfield, Ill.: Thomas, 1978).

9. Frankl, V. E. *Man's Search for Meaning* (New York: Pocket, 1939, 1963); Frankl, V. E. *The Unheard Cry for Meaning* (New York: Simon & Schuster, 1978).

10. Einstein, A., quoted in Schilpp, P. A. "At 92," in Berman, P. L. *The Courage to Grow Old* (New York: Ballantine, 1989): 314.

11. Friedman, H. S. *The Self-Healing Personality* (New York: Plume, 1991): 120-121.

12. Sugden, R. "Recrimination and Rationality." *Theory and Decision* 19 (1985).

13. Klein, C., and Gotti, R. *Overcoming Regret* (New York: Bantam, 1992): 10.

14. Fritz, R. *The Path of Least Resistance* (New York: Fawcett, 1989).

15. Emery, G. "Beyond Problem Solving." *Emery News: A Psychological Newsletter* 8 (1991).

16. Casteneda, C. *The Teachings of Don Juan: A Yaqui Way of Knowledge* (New York: Simon & Schuster, 1973): 122.

17. James, M., and James, J. *Passion for Life* (New York: Dutton, 1991): 10–11.

18. Singer, I. *Meaning in Life* (New York: Free Press, 1992): 104–105.

19. Simon, S. B. *Meeting Yourself Halfway: 31 Value Clarification Strategies for Daily Living* (Niles, Ill.: Argus, 1974).

20. List of qualities adapted from an uncopyrighted listing put out by the Psychosynthesis Institute of San Francisco in the 1970s.

21. Masters, R. *Neurospeak* (Wheating, Ill.: Quest Books, 1994).

22. Masters, R. Article in *Brain/Mind Bulletin* 18 (12)(Sept. 1993): 5.

23. Fritz. *Creating*: 27–28.

CHAPTER 31

1. Adams, R. S., Otto, H. A., and Cowley, A. S. *Letting Go: Uncomplicating Your Life* (New York: Science and Behavior Books, 1984): 131.

2. Bloom, A. *The Closing of the American Mind* (New York: Simon & Schuster, 1987); Bloom, A., quoted in "The Closing of the American Mind." *Publishers Weekly* (July 3, 1987): 25–28.

3. Moore, T. *Care of the Soul* (New York: HarperCollins, 1992): xii.

4. Chapman. "Spiritual Health": 41.

5. Myers, D. G. *The Pursuit of Happiness* (New York: Morrow, 1991): 189; Zika, S., and Chamberlain, K. "Relation of Hassles and Personality to Subjective Well-Being." *Journal of Personality and Social Psychology* 53 (1987): 155–162; Seligman, M. E. P. "Boomer Blues." *Psychology Today* (Oct. 1988): 50–55.

6. Okun, M. A., and Stock, W. A. "Correlatives and Components of Subjective Well-Being among the Elderly." *Journal of Applied Gerontology* 6 (1987): 95–112. See also: H. G. Koenig et al. "Religion and Well-Being in Later Life." *The Gerontologist* 28 (1988): 18–28; K. S. Markides et al. "Religion, Aging and Life Satisfaction: An 8-Year, 3–Wave Longitudinal Study." *The Gerontologist* 27 (1987): 660–665.

7. Flach, F. *Resilience* (New York: Fawcett, 1988): 259.

8. Byrd, R. C. "Positive Therapeutic Effects of Intercessory Prayer in a Coronary Care

Unit Population." *Southern Medical Journal* 81 (7)(1988): 826–829.

9. Dossey, L. *Healing Words: The Power of Prayer and the Practice of Medicine* (New York: HarperCollins, 1993). More than 100 studies cited.

10. Ellison, C. G. "Religious Involvement and Subjective Well-Being." *Journal of Health and Social Behavior* 32 (1991): 80–99.

11. Poloma, M. A., and Gallup, G., Jr. *The Varieties of Prayer* (Philadelphia: Trinity Press, 1991), summarized by Bezilla, R. "Review Essay: The Varieties of Prayer." *Emerging Trends* 13 (5)(May 1991): 4.

12. Solomon, S., Greenberg, J., and Pyszczynski. "A Terror Management Theory of Social Behavior: The Psychological Functions of Self-Esteem and Cultural Worldviews." *Advances in Experimental Social Psychology* 24 (1991): 93–159.

13. Dossey, L. Foreword to Sheikh, A. A., and Sheikh, K. S., eds. *Death Imagery: Confronting Death Brings Us to the Threshold of Life* (Milwaukee, Wisc.: American Imagery Institute, 1991): 1–3.

14. Long, J. B. "The Death That Ends Death in Hinduism and Buddhism," in Kubler-Ross, E. *Death: The Final State of Growth* (Englewood Cliffs, N.J.: Prentice-Hall, 1975).

15. Levitan, A. A. "Hypnotic Death Rehearsal." *American Journal of Clinical Hypnosis* 27 (4)(1985): 211–215; Sheikh, A. A., Twente, G. E., and Turner, D. "Death Imagery: Therapeutic Uses," in *The Potential of Fantasy and Imagination*, eds. Sheikh, A. A., and Shaffer, J. T. (New York: Brandon House, 1979).

16. Erikson, J. M. *Wisdom and the Senses* (New York: Norton, 1988): 177.

17. Schaef, A. W. *Meditations for Women Who Do Too Much* (San Francisco: Harper San Francisco, 1990).

18. Schank, R. S. *Tell Me a Story* (New York: Scribner's, 1990): xi-xii.

19. Ibid.: 12; *Brain-Mind Bulletin* (Jan. 1993): 3; "Go to the Head of the Class." *Fortune* (Mar. 22, 1993): 64; Armstrong, D. *Managing by Storying Around* (New York: Doubleday, 1992).

20. Schank. *Tell Me a Story*: 11.

21. Estes, C. P. *The Gift of Story* (New York: Ballantine, 1993).

22. Ibid.: 29–30.

23. Sacks, S., ed. *On Metaphor* (Chicago: University of Chicago Press, 1979).

24. Autry, J. A. *Love and Profit* (New York: Morrow, 1991): 72.

25. Ibid.: 72–73.

26. Bohm, D., and Peat, F. D. *Science, Order and Creativity* (New York: Bantam, 1987): 35, 49.

27. Lynch, J. J. *The Broken Heart: The Medical Consequences of Loneliness* (New York: Basic Books, 1977).

28. Santayana, G. "Ultimate Religion," in *The Philosophy of Santayana*, ed. Edman, I. (New York: Modern Library, 1936): 581.

29. Einstein, A., in *Living Philosophies* (New York: Simon & Schuster, 1931): 6.

30. Moore. *Care of the Soul*: 271, 273, 286–287.

31. Keleman, S. *Living Your Dying* (New York: Random House, 1974): 1.

32. Montaigne, M. E., quoted in Enright, D. H., ed. *The Oxford Book of Death* (New York: Oxford University Press, 1992).

33. Sheikh and Sheikh. *Death Imagery*: 19.

34. Gardner, J. W. *Self-Renewal: The Individual and the Innovative Society* (New York: Norton, 1963).

35. Koestenbaum, P. *Is There an Answer to Death?* (Englewood Cliffs, N.J.: Prentice-Hall, 1976); Koestenbaum, P. *Vitality of Death: Essays in Existential Psychology and Philosophy* (Contributions in Philosophy, No. 5, Greenwood Publishing, 1971).

ABOUT THE AUTHORS

HAROLD H. BLOOMFIELD, M.D.

Harold H. Bloomfield is one of the leading psychological educators of our time. An eminent Yale-trained psychiatrist, Dr. Bloomfield introduced meditation, holistic health and family peacemaking to millions of people. He is an adjunct professor of psychology at the Union Institute Graduate School in Cincinnati.

His first book, *TM*, was on the *New York Times* best-seller list for over six months. Dr. Bloomfield is the author or coauthor of other major best-sellers, including *How to Survive the Loss of a Love*, *How to Heal Depression*, *Making Peace with Your Parents*, *Making Peace with Yourself*, *Making Peace in Your Stepfamily*, *Inner Joy*, *The Holistic Way to Health and Happiness*, *Love Secrets for a Lasting Relationship* and *Lifemates*. His books have sold more than six million copies and are translated into 24 languages.

Dr. Bloomfield is a frequent guest on *Oprah Winfrey*, *Donahue*, *Sally Jessy Raphael*, *Larry King*, *Good Morning America*, CNN and ABC News Specials. In addition to being widely published in professional journals, his work and popular articles appear in *USA Today*, *Newsweek*, *U.S. News & World Report*, *Washington Post*, *Los Angeles Times*, *San Francisco Examiner*, *Cosmopolitan*, *Ladies Home Journal*, *Good Housekeeping*, *New Woman* and *American Health*.

In addition to his writing and research work, Dr. Bloomfield maintains a private practice in psychiatry, psychotherapy and executive counseling in Del Mar, California. He is a member of the American Psychiatric Association and the San Diego Psychiatric Society.

Dr. Bloomfield is a much-admired keynote speaker for public programs, corporate meetings and professional conferences. For futher information regarding lectures, seminars and personal consultations, please contact:

Harold H. Bloomfield, M.D.
1337 Camino Del Mar, Suite E
Del Mar, CA 92014
(619) 481-9950 (office)
(619) 792-1333 (fax)

ROBERT K. COOPER, Ph.D.

Robert K. Cooper is an independent scholar who has spent more than 20 years researching health sciences, psychology and personal effectiveness. He earned his Ph.D. in health education and psychology at the Union Institute Graduate School in Cincinnati, has taken graduate work at the University of Michigan and University of Iowa, and is certified as a Health and Fitness Instructor by the American College of Sports Medicine. He is a professional member of the Association for the Advancement of Health Education and the American College of Sports Medicine.

Dr. Cooper has appeared on national television and radio programs and is the author of numerous articles and several books, including *The Performance Edge* and *Health and Fitness Excellence*: *The Scientific Action Plan* ("one of the best researched and most helpful books published during the past decade"—*The Detroit News*; "A 'wellness bible' for the 1990s"—*Library Journal*). He is a member of the advisory board for *Vitality*, a corporate wellness and fitness publication with more than two million readers, and his work and writings have been featured in *Prevention*, *Longevity*, *Self* and *American Health*.

Dr. Cooper also serves as chairman of Advanced Excellence Systems (AES), a corporate consulting firm, and he designs and presents leadership training and professional educational programs for prominent organizations in the United States and abroad—including 3M, Arthur Andersen and Company and AT&T.

He lives with his wife, Leslie, and three children on Lake LaSalle, Minnesota.

INDEX

Note: Underscored page references indicate boxed text.

A

Abdominal fat
  alcohol and, 98
  exercises for
    effective, 132–35
    ineffective, 130
  health risks of, 128
  from high-fat foods, 102
  muscle and, 129
  stress and, 135–36
  waist-to-hip ratio, 129, 132, 132
Abdominal roll-ups, 133–34
A.C.E. skills, 342–43
Adenosine triphosphate (ATP), 30–31
Adrenaline, 17–18, 45, 125, 406
Aerobic exercise. *See also* Exercise
  for fat burning, 130–31
  free radicals and antioxidants and, 244–45
  guidelines, 124–26
  weight loss and, 87
Age-related macular degeneration, 296–97
Agility and flexibility, 252–65
  balan-sation exercises, 253–57
  benefits, 252–53
  dance for, 257
  definitions, 255
  dynamic flexibility stretches, 257

exercises for specific body areas
  ankles and feet, 264–65
  arms, 262
  chest and upper back, 261
  hips and knees, 264
  neck, 258
  shoulders, 259–60
  waist and lower back, 262–64
  wrists and hands, 262
myths and power knowledge, 254–55
Aging
  foods slowing, 217, 220–30
  mental abilities and (*see* Mental abilities, aging and)
  posture and, 266, 271
  sex and, 413, 414–16
  values and, 474
Agreement frame, for improving communication, 387
Air, alertness and, 37
Air conditioner filters, 308
Air pollution in home, 307, 308–9
Alarm clock, insomnia and, 52
Alcohol
  beer bellies from, 98
  sleep and, 56
Alertness, biological "switches" for, 35–41
Altruism, 377, 394–96
  spiritual aspects, 488–89, 492